ADVANCE PRAISE FOR *ACADEMIC REPRESSION*

"This courageous and chilling book reminds us that the Academy is always a site for intellectual exchange and political struggle. Don't miss it!"—**Cornel West**, Princeton University

"This book takes us into the Corporate University, and it's not a pretty sight. From firing critical thinkers to putting students in debt, the system is failing America. Time to take it back by fighting for free higher education."—**Jim Hightower**, populist speaker and editor of the "Hightower Lowdown"

"To the litany of claims by academics that the university is a safe haven for intellectual and political dissent, this book offers a convincing counter-argument. *Academic Repression* is a long overdue collective study of the long and sorry history of violations of academic freedom, iconoclastic thought and political dissent in US institutions of higher education. The editors have assembled an impressive group of scholars who, often through personal experience as much as analytic acuity, have supplied us with commentary as much as documentation of the central thesis of the book. This book should be required reading in all of the social sciences, humanities and education courses."—**Stanley Aronowitz**, author of *The Knowledge Factory: Dismantling the Corporate University and Creating True Higher Learning*

"For over half a century, matters of knowledge and education have been central to the political struggles shaping our world, and the university has been a primary battleground. This collection is a chilling and powerful survey of contemporary battles, their stakes and possibilities. We should all be scared, and we should all concerned enough to take a stand."—**Dr. Lawrence Grossberg**, University of North Carolina at Chapel Hill

"Using the tired canards of anti-semitism, terrorism and radicalism, rightwing zealots are carrying out a merciless campaign of ideological cleansing on American campuses, often with the shameful complicity of university administrators. *Academic Repression* takes you to the frontlines of this fierce battle for the mind, telling stories of purges, institutional cowardice and resistance. Here at last is a strategic plan for how to fight back against the New McCarthyites. Read it twice and then throw the book at them."—**Jeffrey St. Clair**, author *Born Under a Bad Sky*, co-editor of *CounterPunch*

"The editors have drawn together a diverse and competent group of scholars to assess critically the climate of academic repression. This is an essential book for anyone with a deep concern for the future of the academy. It will help raise awareness of crucial issues that face the universities. We ignore this challenge at our peril."—**Dr. Andrew Fitz-Gibbon**, Director, Center for Ethics, Peace and Social Justice, SUNY Cortland

"As the editors and contributors of this valuable collection make clear, American academia has long been a combat zone, and never more than today. Eternal vigilance, and constant struggle, remain the watchwords if the free expression of thought upon which a good society depends is to be realized."—**Joel Kovel**, author of "Overcoming Zionism: Creating a Single Democratic State in Israel/Palestine"

"Nocella, Best, and McLaren's impressive book is an important window into the masculinist culture of control which has laid siege to academic institutions throughout the world. Reading the words of so many courageous and intelligent dissenters in one volume is not only a pleasure for the critical senses, but also a powerful act of counter-resistance."—**Marti Kheel**, Visiting Scholar, University of California, Berkeley and author of *Nature Ethics: An Ecofeminist Perspective*

"*Academic Repression* is an important book, not because it defends academics, but because it successfully connects the fight for academic freedom with the struggle to create a free society. I recommend this book to anybody interested in the convoluted history of ideological repression and it's contemporary manifestations." —**Luis A. Fernandez**, author of *Policing Dissent*

"Universities were once viewed as laboratories for free inquiry and debate. Today they are under siege from privatizers, ideologues and anxious college administrators. This book is an intellectual tour de force in which brave scholars share their struggles and strategies to once again, in Paulo Freire's words, make education the practice of freedom."—**Dr. Brian McKenna**, Anthropologist, University of Michigan-Dearborn

"In tracing the variety of ways ruling elites and bureaucratic machines have employed academic and intellectual repression as a tool for reconstituting status quo values in society and culture, this utterly unique collection of essays will both inspire and challenge educators, activists, scholars, and citizens alike."—**Dr. Clayton Pierce**, University of Utah

"*Academic Repression* is a wonderful book for teachers at all levels to expose their students to the concept of 'Unacademic Freedom.' Every article allows students from high school to graduate school to become critical thinkers in a world running head long towards fascism."—**Paulette d'auteuil**, EBC-East New York High School for Public Safety & Law & New York City Jericho Movement

"This book is the first shot fired in what I hope will be a revolt by those in academia who need to be heard." —**Dr. Carol Gigliotti**, Emily Carr University, Vancouver, BC, Canada

"A brave and timely book...essential reading for anyone concerned about the stifling of dissent and free expression in the academia and beyond."—**Dr. Uri Gordon**, Arava Institute of Environmental Studies, author of *Anarchy Alive!*

"This important collection documents the growing pressures on academic research in the arts and humanities and the institutionalised conservatism of the academy. It also rightly acknowledges that the university is a contested space, supporting a range of viewpoints, and that it consequently offers possibilities for challenge and change as well as conformity."—**Dr. Ruth Kinna**, Loughborough University, UK

Academic Repression

Academic Repression

Reflections from the Academic-Industrial Complex

Edited by

Anthony J. Nocella II, Steven Best, and Peter McLaren

AK PRESS
EDINBURGH · OAKLAND · BALTIMORE

Academic Repression: Reflections from the Academic-Industrial Complex

Ed. by Anthony J. Nocella II, Steven Best, and Peter McLaren © 2010
This edition © 2010 AK Press (Oakland, Edinburgh, Baltimore)

ISBN-13: 978-1-904859-98-7

Library of Congress Control Number: 2009922425

AK Press   AK Press
674-A 23rd Street   PO Box 12766
Oakland, CA 94612   Edinburgh, EH8 9YE
USA   Scotland
www.akpress.org   www.akuk.com
akpress@akpress.org   ak@akedin.demon.co.uk

The above addresses would be delighted to provide you with the latest AK Press distribution catalog, which features the several thousand books, pamphlets, zines, audio and video products, and stylish apparel published and/or distributed by AK Press. Alternatively, visit our web site for the complete catalog, latest news, and secure ordering.

Visit us at www.akpress.org *and* www.revolutionbythebook.akpress.org.

Printed in Canada on acid free, recycled paper with union labor.

Special thanks to Brian Awehali for his contribution to the interior design of this book.

The royalties from this book will go to the following worthy organizations:

www.transformativestudies.org—a social justice policy based think-tank and future free graduate school.
www.criticalanimalstudies.org—the first interdisciplinary scholarly center dedicated to promoting critical dialogue and research on the principles and practices of animal advocacy, animal protection, and animal-related policies in the fields of social sciences and humanities in higher education.
www.saccoandvanzettifoundation.org—provides annual scholarships on issues of political repression, civil liberties, citizenship, immigration, anarchism, and dissent.
www.politicalmediareview.org—an independent reviewing clearinghouse for social justice media. As a not-for-profit and fully-volunteer organization, PMR fills the gap of promotion and publicity of social justice media by acting as a reviewing database for social justice media.
www.afsc.org—carries out service, development, social justice, and peace programs throughout the world.
www.syracusesavethekids.org—a full-volunteer organization to support youth leadership, group building, and alternatives to violence.
www.peaceconsortium.org—the Central New York Peace Studies Consortium providing resources to regional peace and conflict studies programs.
www.greentheoryandpraxis.org—an ecopedagogical journal for scholars and activists.
www.outdoorempowement.org—an environmental youth based program to promote group-building.

Table of Contents

IV

Dispatches from the Margins: Gender, Race, Sex, and Abilities

V

Fast Times at Corporate Higher Ed.

VI

Twilight of Academia: Critical Pedagogy, Engaged Intellectuals, and Political Resistance

The Company We Keep

Michael Bérubé

I N THE COURSE OF MY CAREER, I've written any number of forewords and after-words to books; usually it's a routine kind of thing, just part of the job description of a working academic. I especially like bringing a collection of essays with me when I travel, poring over the manuscript on the plane or in my hotel room, making notations and dog-earing pages, and then parking myself in a local coffeeshop for a few hours to gather my thoughts. That's pretty much what I've done with this collection, a fascinating, timely, and truly necessary volume compiled by Steven Best, Anthony Nocella, and Peter McLaren. And yet this one is quite different. This volume is the first book I've ever introduced that managed to generate hostile commentary well before it was published—indeed, *even before I read the manuscript.*

I'm not kidding: about a month before I gathered my thoughts and sat down to write the words you're reading now, Marc Bousquet mentioned the forthcoming publication of this book on "Brainstorm: Lives of the Mind," *The Chronicle of Higher Education* blog, and the next morning, the very first commenter ("Fred" by name) responded by complaining about the American Association of University Professors (AAUP): "The AAUP's defense of [Ward] Churchill also prevents me from renewing my membership. What a waste of resources!" In response, Bousquet patiently pointed out that, to his knowledge, there was to date no AAUP "defense" of Churchill. Later that day, I posted a comment addressed to Marc (whom I had warned about the difficulties of "troll management" of obnoxious and hostile readers when he first asked me about starting a blog), asking whether commenters like Fred ever acknowledged that they were wrong about a factual point, or whether they simply moved on to the next post. An hour or so later, "Fred" reappeared to say:

> Here I am, Prof. Berube, and I am not wrong. The CU chapter of AAUP most certainly did advocate on Churchill's behalf, and the president of AAUP replicated Churchill's talking points in a public interview.

Whether the case went before Committee A or not is a mere technicality for the unwashed majority who are not privy to the organizations' inner workings.

While I have your attention, I am saddened that you have stooped to publishing with AK Press alongside Churchill (and Jensen, and Cloud, and the other lout-shouting [sic] extremists). The company you keep in this collection diminishes my respect for you and your work.[1]

Well, dear readers, as you might imagine, I was deeply saddened that this random person's respect for me had been diminished by the fact that I would be keeping such company as this. Churchill and Jensen and Cloud! Oh, my! How could I manage to write a Foreword to this book, and yet maintain the respect of angry anonymous people claiming to be my colleagues who were mouthing off on blogs and using Ward Churchill as an excuse not to renew their alleged AAUP membership?

Almost at once the obvious answer came to me: I would make it clear that I disagreed with Churchill and Jensen and Cloud, whatever their essays might say, because they are (shudder) *radical*, but that I will defend without qualification their right to say things I disagree with. That way, I could maintain an acceptable arm's distance from whatever disturbing or offensive "radical" things they might have to say, while craftily congratulating myself for my defense of academic freedom and my liberal tolerance of the company I keep in this collection.

Now, there's every good reason for me to disagree with some of the arguments in this book; I especially disagree with the suggestion that Ward Churchill is some kind of representative figure for the academic left. I would argue, instead, that Ward Churchill's case is entirely *sui generis*, insofar as it involved a mass-media frenzy over statements he made more than three years earlier, and which resulted in an internal review of his scholarship that faulted him on different grounds altogether. His firing by the University of Colorado thus raises exceptionally complex questions about investigations into alleged research fraud and the procedures of peer review—issues about which (remarkable as it may seem) reasonable people might in fact disagree. So when the right-wing noise machine shifts into high gear, insinuating (as have David Horowitz and Anne Neal) that there are thousands of Ward Churchills proliferating throughout American campuses, and when the left-wing defensive secondary falls into formation, insisting that an attack on Ward Churchill is an attack on all (a) Native American scholars, (b) Ethnic Studies programs, or (c) dissenters from the American imperium, I like to counter-argue that Ward Churchill is in fact one person, and that his case is exceptionally complex.

But I think there's a good reason not to do the arm's-distance thing here, regardless of how much or how little I agree with any specific essay in this volume. (For the record, though, I can't recall agreeing completely with *any* book for which I've written a Foreword or an Afterword, and I've never considered it a criterion for my participation in a project.) And that is because Robert Jensen's essay has it exactly right: we are not living through a new McCarthyism. There have been, for instance, no mass firings and no imposed loyalty oaths. To the dismay of conservative activists, tenure still exists, even if somewhat weakened and battered.

But we *are* seeing a sustained attempt to harass and intimidate scholars working in politically sensitive areas of study—ranging from the Middle East (most obviously) to gender and sexuality (as when the American Council of Trustees and Alumni pamphlet "How Many Ward Churchills?" indicted a young scholar for teaching a course titled "American Masculinities").[2] And in response to those campaigns of harassment and intimidation, all too often, the *best* one can hope for is that a tenured faculty member (like Jensen) will get the arm's-length response from a university official, defending his or her right to be wrong (and taking pains to make clear just how wrong he or she is). It does not help people in those areas of study, then, when university administrators or elected officials defend academic freedom but pointedly take their distance from, say, passionately pro-Palestinian or openly queer scholars. What is needed, rather, is an account of academic freedom that emphatically and explicitly defends a scholar's *right to be controversial*. This much should be axiomatic: academic freedom is essential to a free society, and a free society should not merely tolerate but actually *support* controversial scholars.

But just as I'm not going to distance myself from radicals, I'm not going to complain too much about tepid liberals, either. Liberalism too often gets a raw deal from the academic left—as if it is merely neoliberalism with chinos and Birkenstocks, chattering obliviously about how the law—as Anatole France once put it—should forbid both rich and poor from sleeping under bridges. For what's at stake in this volume is precisely the *liberal* principle that universities (and many other institutions in civil society) should enjoy relative autonomy from the state; and whenever a putatively "left" theorist tries to tell us that the distinction between liberal and totalitarian societies is simply part of the West's formidable propaganda apparatus, it's worth remembering Stuart Hall's wonderfully acerbic remark about "how often the fundamentalist left is scornful of civil liberties until they find themselves badly in need of some."[3]

So I'll close instead by underscoring a point this volume makes repeatedly and eloquently: Intimidation and harassment campaigns against individual scholars and/ or entire fields of study are only part of the story in American higher education. Underneath the radar, the academic labor force has been casualized over the course of decades; yes, tenure still exists—but only for the lucky few. Roughly three-quarters of the people teaching in American universities are now working without the protection—or even the hope of the protection—of tenure. They are at-will employees, often teaching on one-year contracts, and when they are fired—even when they are terminated for explicitly political reasons—they have no legal recourse and no one notices except for their friends and immediate families.

So whenever a controversial scholar or an emerging area of study is attacked, the chilling message goes out to thousands of instructors, adjuncts, and graduate students: *Watch what you say. Don't offend your students—or their parents. And above all, be careful about the kind of company you keep.* This is the challenge for the AAUP and for everyone concerned about the future of academic freedom in the United States: how to ensure that the most vulnerable people in the teaching profession, the teachers and scholars who have no more job security than the worker at Wal-Mart or Burger King, have the academic freedom they need to do their jobs well and responsibly. As one of academe's lucky few, then, I believe I have an obligation to keep good company: the company of people who dare to call attention to the plight of my untenured colleagues—and who dare to defend their right to be controversial.

Preface

Scholars Under Siege

Rik Scarce

PERHAPS THE GREATEST DANGER IN CONTRIBUTING TO A BOOK LIKE THIS is that authors can come across as whining, self-serving, or both. The scholars herein—or those who are written about—are victims of repression. Yet, in politically charged arenas like those of the "culture wars" that encompass many instances of academic oppression in the US, victims often are portrayed as perpetrators—as somehow the cause of their own downfall.

Maybe we are so easily labeled as instigators and trouble makers because the public is anxious and confused about what scholars do. Many of us take risks, teaching and writing about things that are controversial, important, and poorly understood. In the course of faithfully pursuing that work, we may say and do things that anger people. We give voice to minority opinions. We explore sensitive topics. We posit "radical" hypotheses. We speak truth to power. Fundamentally, by doing our jobs we unavoidably make many people—both those who embrace authority in any of its many forms and the authorities themselves—feel uneasy.

Of course, labeling the victims of academic repression as responsible in some way for their position as the oppressed dodges the question. That question boils down to whether scholarship is ever "free." And this, in turn, begs other questions: Can we tolerate freedom anywhere in society? Has academic freedom lost its importance, and is the opposite side of the coin—the repression of critical scholarship—a reasonable alternative?

If the answer to the latter question is "yes," it's an ironic response at this time in history. We live at a moment when societies are more closely interconnected than ever before, whether through trade, the homogenization of culture, or digital communication technologies. Whatever qualms one may have regarding globalization, surely the full range of Enlightenment values ideally ought to be part of that project if democracy (ostensibly the greatest potential benefit of globalization) is to flourish worldwide.

Yet those values so essential to democracy—which boil down to liberty in all its forms—do not travel hand-in-hand with that hallmark of globalization, the spread of capitalism, any more than do worker safety protections, human rights, or environmental regulations and sustainability.

Instead, in the US and abroad we find that the more scholars raise questions about the vexing issues of our day, the more roadblocks they find in the way of their career advancement and even, quite possibly, their very existence as non-persecuted or free citizens. Even as we witness the flowering of a global society, we observe the wilting of any number of freedoms.

The sources of that desertification of liberty on campuses are a bewildering array of the understandable, the confounding, and the hypocritical. These range from corporate-funded right-wing think tanks to sundry anti-intellectuals who comb universities from coast-to-coast, ever on the prowl for "objectionable," "irrelevant," "leftist," and "un-American" thoughts and values. Fearful of the independence tenure brings, and seeking greater control over campus affairs, college and university trustees increasingly question the value of tenure—long the core guarantor of scholarly freedom—and move to end what they see as "job security for life."

Often, conservative "campus watch" groups, and sometimes scholars' own colleagues, send obliging students into classrooms, not to explore intellectual alternatives but to monitor and report back any "left-wing" or "radical" deviation from conservative values and the dominant social ideologies. And quite often, directly or indirectly, academic oppression is connected in some way with the law.

My own experience is a case in point in multiple ways. As a graduate student in the early 1990s, I was researching the radical environmental movement (a topic on which I had already published a book). Believing that I had interviewed those responsible for a break-in at an animal experimentation facility on my campus, the FBI subpoenaed me to appear before a federal grand jury. When I resisted and refused to answer some of the questions posed to me by prosecutors on the grounds that the First Amendment protected all of society's fact finders (not only journalists, but also scholars and researchers), I was jailed indefinitely on a contempt of court citation. After more than five months behind bars, I was released from jail, having never answered the prosecutor's questions.

As my case wound its way through the courts, I was struck by the importance of the word "balance" in discussions surrounding the tension between academic freedom and the state's interest in solving "crime": a tension between freedom and order not unlike that which Michel Foucault analyzed so persuasively in books such as *Madness and Civilization* and *Discipline and Punish*.

Implied in the balance concept, as I witnessed it from my jail cell, is the idea that "absolute freedom" of any kind is a practical impossibility. The theoretical point is a simple one: eventually, someone's or some group's assertion of freedom will collide with another person's or group's understanding and exercise of their own rights. So, to avoid frequent clashes, lawmakers and the courts must strike a balance between what is fair for all parties and find impartial ways to mediate competing "rights claims."

Those who argue on behalf of the balance view must reject a couple of key tenets along the way. First, they assert the impossibility of a society where empathy for alternative viewpoints and tolerance of dissent and free inquiry are desirable human traits. Rather, they claim, the social order can be maintained only by trimming the especially noxious loose threads from the social fabric so that most of the cultural fiber remains unharmed. Government, fair and balanced, decides which of those jagged threads need to be snipped—in other words, whose rights are sacrificed.

The balancers also deny that there can be any place in society respected as especially open and liberal, such as civil spaces where "uncivil" ideas, debates, images, and inventions can thrive. Intellectually safe places—in particular, colleges and universities—must not be allowed to exist, the story goes, since they will inevitably generate social conflict.

So there appear to be numerous social and legal forces constraining what is taught and learned in college classrooms and the topics that scholars investigate. The academic oppressors so eager to restrict what we say and do enjoy disproportionate economic, social, and political power. Like all victims, oppressed scholars have at their disposal few resources with which to fight back.

Yet fight back we must. Our struggle centers on rights and freedoms that are threatened or that have been lost already and need to be regained, both on college campuses and in the broader society. Ironically, given right-wing rhetoric, it is we "radicals" and "subversives" who are "strict constructionists," who insist that it is the balance model that contradicts the original intent of the US Constitution and, far more importantly, that vitiates the liberties necessary for modern society to thrive.

What is so needed at this moment is that we challenge the limitations of the balancers, and engage in the corollary act of exploring the dangers of limited rights of freedoms. Oppression—whether it occurs in governmental torture chambers or in our everyday lives through reasonable-sounding legalese like "balanced rights"—has no place in the contemporary world, and a few scholars are among the vanguard of those countering the balance perspective by demanding the freedoms the Constitution guarantees us and by which we as individuals and society as a whole flourish.

Those teachers and researchers who have the courage to consider where things stand, and who grasp that our society is "liberal" only in (*laissez-faire*) economic terms, and who understand that the core values that emerged from the Enlightenment are under attack like never before. The equality of all persons, the freedom to inquire, the freedom to write and speak, the duty to resist authority: some academicians not only embrace those hallmark characteristics of Western thought, but struggle for them on a daily basis.

It surprises many that it is scholars who often are at the barricades of struggle, who are among the first to resist the attacks on rights that so many take for granted. Regrettably, however, far too few teachers, researchers, and scholars take up the call for resistance. Rather than conduct research into controversial social movements, organize ourselves to resist the diverse attacks on our peers, and demand the full measure of the freedoms available to all members of society, too many within the academy accept the desiccation of academic freedom. Too many cower and duck for cover. Too many nod in agreement with the balancers rather than dare to dissent. Too many look out only for themselves, assuming the roles of narcissistic careerists rather than concerned citizens.

Standing up and stepping forward for what is not only right but also essential is not to be taken lightly. Precisely because they so often challenge the powerful, those who would create and convey critical knowledge have never had it easy. Whether it was a pope, prince, college president, prosecutor, or legislature, some powerful person or organization has always been anxious about what we teach and research and eager to make us pay for doing so. Resistance is a painful process. But acquiescence is far more painful, not only individually but communally and socially, and not only in the short term, but also in the long run.

Yet, even in times like ours, in the grim and challenging garrison state of the post-9/11 era when it can be difficult to discern between ostensible democracy and outright authoritarianism, my colleagues in this volume refuse to back down, as the extraordinarily varied and uniformly disturbing chapters in *Academic Repression: Reflections from the Academic-Industrial Complex* make clear. If a tolerant society is not in the immediate offing, these model critical intellectuals fight to carve out a civil space on our uncivil campuses. Their experiences and analyses, so thoughtfully compiled by Anthony J. Nocella II, Steven Best, and Peter McLaren demonstrate that the mythical city on a hill is a place full of victims chafing in their oppression, a site replete with risk takers and resisters who work in the service of that most powerful of ideologies: intellectual freedom.

Acknowledgements

In our personal and political philosophy, we could not do anything without the support of everyone and everything on this planet, as we are not isolated or separate from the ecosystems, biodiversity, and other individuals in society. We believe that all are interdependent and for this reason we stress that acknowledgements are important, and not merely a place to drop names and flatter. More than a mere list, moreover, acknowledgements are a true philosophical critique of individualism, of fragmented learning, of monoperspectival and single-disciplinary theorizing, and of the elitist systems and institutions that promote the antithesis of what critical pedagogy strives to achieve.

To play off the *double entendre* that entitles this section, this entire book is an acknowledgement in another sense: not as a giving of thanks, but rather a recognition of the many things that are occluded but need to be dragged into the light: of systemic repression of students, staff, and faculty in higher education; of the diversity of stories, experiences, and identities that exist but are rarely heard and respected; of the institution of higher education that is in a crisis, having been hijacked by a myriad of interests that aim to transform and deform it into a mockery of its highest ideals; of a social world and planetary ecology in crisis due to economic and political domination, deficits in democracy, and insufficient resistance.

First and foremost we would love to thank our families—without their support and love we would not be here! We also wish to thank all members of the Institute for Critical Animal Studies (ICAS) for helping to fulfill our unique academic mission and to spur exciting growth and progress. We appreciate Richard White for stepping up in grand fashion as the new Chief Editor of *The Journal of Critical Animal Studies*, as we also thank the dedicated volunteers helping him, including Veda Stram, Sarat Colling, and Richard Twine. We especially appreciate Lisa Kemmerer, Nik Taylor, and Carol Gigliotti for their friendship and collaboration over the last decade almost, as we have struggled to put our organization on the map. We give a special nod to one particular member of our collaborative family, Richard Kahn—our brother from another mother—who has fought in the fray with us from the beginning. For all the people on the Executive, Advisory, and Editorial Review Boards, your amazing work is advancing the cause of critical animal studies as an exciting and qualitative leap over the staid, dry, abstract, esoteric, apolitical, and often speciesist doublespeak of mainstream animal studies.

Merci to Le Moyne College Criminology Department, SUNY, Cortland Criminology Department, Campus Ministry at Le Moyne College, the staff and residences of Hillbrook Youth Detention Facility, Syracuse Quaker Meeting, Caroline Kalterfleiter, Mecke Nagal, and Andrew Fitz-Gibbons (Director of the Center for Peace, Ethics, Social Justice), Barron Boyd (Director of the Program on Peace and Global Studies), and Robert Rubinstein.

We give a shout-out to our colleagues at The Institute for Transformative Studies, the International Network for Inclusive Democracy, *Green Theory and Praxis* journal, the Central New York Peace Studies Consortium, and the *Journal for Critical Education Policy Studies*. And to Carl Boggs and Doug Kellner: your critical acumen, tireless commitments, and prolific output of ground-breaking work never cease to inspire us.

We also would like to thank our many friends and colleagues who offer support and encouragement. In no particular order, they are: Cornel West, Jim Hightower, Cindy Sheehan, Stanley Aronowitz, Dave Zirin, Lawrence Grossberg, Jeffrey St. Clair, Joshua Frank, David Rovics, Joel Kovel, Greta Gaard, Mike Cole, Marc Bousquet, Brian McKenna, William T. Armaline, Marti Kheel, Clayton Pierce, Cesar A. Rossatto, Peter Mayo, Deric Shannon, Norm Phelps, John McCumber, Michele Pickover, "Crazy" Hazel Cohn, Zelma Opland, Bob "Ralph" Antonio, Steve "Great One" Bronner, John Sargis, Takis Fotopoulos, Susana, Jay, Brian, Jeremy, xJx, Owen of New Ethic Café, Bister, Kevin of Outdoor Empowerment in Syracuse, NY, Sarat Colling, Shawn, Shane, Andrew, Heather, Eden, Ben G., Kevin, Jimmy, Brandon Becker, Deric Shannon, Michele Pickover, Jason Miller, Jennifer, Brandy Humes, Laura Corman, Jacquelyn Arsenuk, Jason Bayless, Anastasia Yarbough, Allie Holaday, Syd Marcus, Carrie Smith, Richard Twine, Kevin Collen, Lindgren Johnson, Veda Stram, Nicole Pallota, Piers Beirs, Michael Becker, Ann Berlin, Camille Hankins, Pam and Jerry, Haralambie "Bobo" Athes, Abraham DeLeon, Luis Fernadez, Kostas, Camille Marino, Randal Amster, Anthony Rayson, Dave Hill, Eric Buck, Rich Van Heertum, Adriana Martin and Alison, Ruth Kinna, Uri Gordon, pattrice jones, Uri Gorden, Dave Hill, Nick Cooney, Dave with Hugs for Puppies, Justin Hand, Danae Kelly, Maxwell Schnurer, Richard Van Heertum, Bill Templer, Liat Ben-Moshe, Deana, Dene, Jitka, Lisa, and everyone from BCCC, Justin Goodman, Gary Yourofsky, Rik Scarce, Matthew Liebman, Will Potter, Paulette D'auteuil, elana levy, Tim Luke, William Harris, John Feldman, Ramsey Kanaan, Caroline Tauxe, John Asimakopoulos, John C. Alessio, Julie Andrzejewski, Toby Miller, everyone with the Alternatives to Violence Program, the astounding American Friends Service Committee specifically at the Syracuse office, Jason, Meg, Sandra, Micah, Egle, Betsy, Marco, Priya, Heather, Matt, Briarwood School, John Taylor, John Burke, and the Syracuse Bicycle crew—Dan, Paul, Brian, Bobcat Brian, Brad aka "Turbo," Chris, Christian, Tyler, Scott, and everyone else, *Political Media Review*, and the Sacco and

Vanzetti Foundation. We send support and gratitude to the SHAC 7, the Austrian 10, the AETA 4, and all other political prisoners locked away for fighting the real criminals, terrorists, and menaces to society: you galvanize us and are not forgotten.

This book would never have been possible if not for the courage of so many willing to speak frankly and truthfully about academic repression in a garrison-like environment that punishes dissent, criticism, non-conformity, engaged intellectuals, and deviations from the regnant theory-for-theory's sake research paradigm. Although for their personal and political reasons we could not include two recent infamous cases of academic repression involving David Graeber and Norman Finkelstein, we stand in solidarity with them and every other talented scholar and dedicated teacher who, for their dissenting views, are chewed up and spit out by corporate crooks, byzantine bureaucrats, and meddling mercenaries. This book is certainly not the last word on these important topics, and there are many voices that have not been featured but that should and must be heard. But it is a vital initial assessment of the US academic landscape in the post-9/11 world and this type of analysis is increasingly important as corporatization processes and the far right continue to imperil academic freedom. We hope that this book gives other people the courage to speak out against academic repression.

Anthony J. Nocella, II would also like to thank Lisa Mignacca, Nancy Piscitell, Peter Castro, Richard Loder, Thomas Boudreau, Micere Githae Mugo, Barbara Applebaum, Dalia Rodriguez, Don Mitchell, and Steve Taylor, and to everyone at the Program on the Analysis and Resolution of Conflicts and the PARC Crew of 2003–2004.

Steven Best extends his deepest appreciation to his beloved quadrupedal family—Koko, Shag, Willis, Chairman Meow, Kala, Gigi, and Slim Shady. Although these felicitous felines cannot read these words, they already well know the sentiments.

Peter McLaren wishes to thank his students at UCLA, and his *camaradas* worldwide who put so much on the line in their struggle for a better future for humanity and the entire Earth.

We cannot fail to thank the AK Press collective especially—Lorna, Zach, Jose, Kate, and Charles—who have been wonderful, supportive, and patient throughout the production of this book, as well as during the publication of Best and Nocella's *Igniting a Revolution* (AK Press, 2006), and helped us promote our first co-edited volume, *Terrorists or Freedom Fighters?: Reflections on the Liberation of Animals* (Lantern Book, 2004). We recognize that no university press would have touched this manuscript, but an anarchist collective like AK could welcome it without reservation. They truly are a fine press and we encourage fellow academics and activists to support and publish with them.

Finally, we must thank all of the contributors for their superb essays and stoic patience amidst the long editing and revision process; you made our jobs easier and now let your voices be heard.

Dedication

This book is dedicated to all those who have been silenced, harassed, demoted, fired, or imprisoned because of their uncompromising opposition to academic and political repression. We applaud your valiant efforts to carry the torch of enlightenment forward in these dark and desperate times, and to fight the neocons and elitists who aim to turn society's noblest institution—the university—from a space of wonder, critical thinking, ethical awareness, and citizenship skills into a bureaucratically administered information factory that produces research and student products for the functions of the military, the political and media machines, and global capitalism. The continuing decline, debasement, and corruption of education must not happen; the flames of your resistance show us the way.

Introduction:

The Rise of the Academic-
Industrial Complex and the Crisis in Free Speech

Steven Best, Anthony J. Nocella, II, and Peter McLaren

> *"[People] fear thought as they fear nothing else on earth—more than ruin—more even than death…. Thought is subversive and revolutionary, destructive and terrible, thought is merciless to privilege, established institutions, and comfortable habit. Thought looks into the pit of hell and is not afraid. Thought is great and swift and free, the light of the world, and the chief glory of [humanity]"*
>
> —Bertrand Russell

> *"There follows one corollary which itself deserves to be inscribed upon every wall of the city of philosophy: Do not block the path of inquiry."*
>
> —Charles S. Peirce

Given that the academy is a microcosm of social life in the US, and this nation—as a hierarchical, exploitative capitalist society—has never been free or democratic in any meaningful way, we should not be surprised to find higher education to be a place of hierarchical domination, bureaucratic control, hostility to radical research and teaching, and anathema to free thinking. Since Socrates and the earliest inceptions of the university system in the teachings of Plato and Aristotle, Western states and universities have attacked critical minds and kicked controversial and subversive figures out of the hallowed halls of learning, betraying the very mission of education and critical thinking that demands freedom of inquiry and speech.

Perhaps the largest myths to expose in our culture today still are freedom and democracy—institutional and personal conditions that are not only in steep decline in the current post-9/11 era, but in fact never existed in any significant form. The revolutionary experiment in democracy and equality launched in 1776 never had a chance, taking place as it did amidst the backdrop of the slavery of African people, the repression and impending genocide of the Native American peoples, the disenfranchisement of women, the institutionalization of people with disabilities, and the exploitation of working classes. The Founding Fathers never intended "democracy," "freedom," and "equality" to benefit anything but their own elite propertied interests, and history stayed faithful to their design. Despite the subversion of monarchy and aristocracy with the brash and impertinent notion of equality, the concept mainly functioned as an ideological smokescreen to mask a new form of hierarchy based on class domination, coupled with patriarchy, racism, and every other repulsive form of discrimination, subjugation, and violence. Notions such as "freedom" and "equality" hid the fact that the inherently hierarchical and exploitative corporate-state complex of capitalism was a system run by and for capitalists, corporations, and wealthy property owners. Big business and monopoly corporations commandeered the state—the oxymoronic institution of "representative democracy"—to advance and protect their own minority interests, to suppress majority opposition, and to quell dissent by any means necessary.

Political Repression and Control in the US

> *"The state is the most flagrant negation, the most cynical and complete negation of humanity."*
>
> —Michael Bakunin

From the signing of the Constitution in 1787 (whereby propertied white elites legitimated a new class system) to Bush's anti-Constitutional "signing statements" (which granted him unauthorized power) and beyond, the US has a long history of suppressing rights and liberties.[1] The alleged quintessential American right to free expression was not mandated with conformism and banality in mind, but rather to protect controversial words, dissenting opinions, and subversive ideas. While this right often has been interpreted as ending not at the point of defending and advocating violence against others, but rather speaking in a way that potentially precipitates it, citizens nonetheless enjoy (theoretically) a wide range of expression and behavior under the Constitution.[2]

Yet any US citizen who has attempted to exercise their First Amendment rights in a way that expresses dissent, challenges the government or institutional power, or somehow threatens the profits and power of the ruling elites knows that the corporate-state system responds malevolently to any provocation or disturbance with surveillance, intimidation, arrest, imprisonment, and even murder. Whether the affront is striking workers, anarchists protesting state power, Black Panthers organizing their communities, peace activists denouncing war, environmentalists protecting forests, or animal liberationists exposing the barbarities of vivisection and industrialized "farming," the power brokers respond to dissent and agitation as a body mobilizes to neutralize a viral invader. The system does not just routinely shut down free speech and dissent through political repression and control; it nullifies the conditions of citizenship through economic exploitation that enforces taxes, poverty, low-paying wages or chronic unemployment, and debt slavery, while capitalizing on the millions of people shuttled into the cages of the US prison-industrial complex, which has the highest rate of incarceration of any industrialized nation, locking up 1 of every 100 citizens.[3]

Key moments in the history of US repression include: the *Alien and Sedition Acts of 1798* (ostensibly to protect the country from enemy citizens, but used to suppress criticism of the government and to detain foreign nationals indefinitely); the *Espionage Act of 1917* (which made acts helping enemies of the state a crime); the *1918 Sedition Act* (that forbade "disloyal, profane, scurrilous, or abusive language" toward the government, flag, Constitution, or armed forces during times of war, as it also criminalized advocacy of the violent overthrow of the state, desertion from the armed forces, resistance to the draft, or membership in anarchist and Leftist organizations); the *1918 Anarchist Exclusion Act* (used to deport hordes of "radical immigrants" opposed to the government or involved in violent actions); the "First Red Scare" of 1917–1920 (enacted in response to the 1917 Bolshevik revolution and the violent resistance it inspired against the state); the 1919–1920 Palmer Raids (a series of mass arrests of thousands of suspected radicals that led to deporting over five hundred foreign nationals); the *1940 Smith Act* (which made it a criminal offense to "advocate, abet, advise or teach the duty, necessity, desirability or propriety of overthrowing the Government of the United States by force or violence"); Loyalty Oaths (enforced during the 1940s–1960s, which made repudiation of radicalism and allegiance to the government a precondition of employment for many teachers, state employees, and other workers);[4] and the *Enemy Aliens Act* (applied against foreigners from the late 1940s to the late 1950s as a means of deporting dissenters); and the "Second Red Scare" of 1947–1957 (erupting over fears relating to communist espionage, Russian expansionism, the Soviet testing of a nuclear weapon in 1949, the fall of China to communism after the Civil War of 1949, and the Korean War from 1950–1953). All these measures and more prefigured the frontal assault on free speech and the entire range of Constitutional rights by the USA PATRIOT Act of 2001 (see below), and are part of a seamless history of US political repression of foreigners and citizens alike.[5]

In the nineteenth century, during the Age of Reform, the positions of university professors were imperiled if they spoke against the religious principles of a college, but increasingly the main academic sin became voicing criticism of influential corporations, defending the interests of labor, or appearing sympathetic to communism (all three certainly interrelated issues). Already, major donors to universities often controlled hiring and firing procedures in clear cognizance of professors' research and politics.[6] An early academic casualty of the vengeful witchhunts unleashed in the name of anti-communism was Edward Bemis, Associate Professor of Political Science at the University of Chicago. Bemis studied corporate corruption, advocated municipal ownership of utilities, and supported labor during the massive 1894 Pullman railroad strike. Bemis also championed academic free speech and, ironically, was fired in 1895 for involvement in the Pullman strike, despite his insistence that he encouraged workers to end rather than to continue the strike.[7]

Richard Ely nearly met the same fate. Ely was an economist and noted figure in the Progressive movement, which pressed the state to ameliorate injustices such as brutal factory conditions and the exploitation of child labor, but he did not consider himself a socialist. Professor of Economics at Johns Hopkins University from 1881 to 1892, Ely thereafter took the Chair position in the School of Economics, Political Science and History at the University of Wisconsin-Madison, where he was popular for his unconventional theories and passion to improve the lives of the poor. It didn't take long for Oliver E. Wells, a conservative member of the Board of Regents, to move for Ely's dismissal. In a classic, pre-McCarthyesque series of invidious moves, Wells leveled false, slanderous, and unsubstantiated charges against Ely, published a scurrilous letter in *The New York Times* and *New York Post*; and generated enough outside pressure on the university to force a vote of termination. Amidst the deliberation process, however, the Board of Regents concluded that Ely's right to academic freedom trumped alleged ideological crimes, and in a Zen-like philosophy of non-interference the Board ruled, in eloquent and famous words, that, "In all lines of investigation the investigator should be absolutely free to follow the paths of truth, wherever they may lead. Whatever may be the limitations which trammel inquiry elsewhere, we believe that the great state of Wisconsin should ever encourage that continual and fearless *winnowing and sifting* by which alone the truth can be found."[8]

Ely's case was an important early victory in the struggle for academic freedom and showed that on at least some occasions, professors could prevail over demagogues, capitalists, bureaucrats, and the whirl of public controversy. But the enlightened outlook of Wisconsin's Board of Regent's was an exception to the benighted approach of most US universities, especially where greed, graft, and venality prevailed over dignity, duty, and honor. This invariably transpired, not coincidentally, when corporate executives sat on university boards or university executives operated with a serious conflict of interest between profits and principles.

In 1900, noted Stanford economics professor Edward Ross was fired because his critique of immigrant labor abuse by exploitative industries threatened the economic interests of Mrs. Leland Stanford, a railroad tycoon whose family's fortune relied heavily on importing cheap Chinese labor in defiance of federal law.[9] In 1913, an outspoken liberal professor at Lafayette, John Mecklin, was forced to resign for the crime of being a philosophical relativist and teaching evolution.[10] Scott Nearing, a socialist professor of economics, was fired from the University of Pennsylvania in 1915, at the beginning of World War I. Nearing wrote critical pamphlets such as "Great Madness" and "The Menace of Militarism," noting how the war commercialized and turned mass slaughter into a profitable investment. Nearing also publicly opposed the use of child labor in coal mines, which led to his academic demise when a mine owner on the University of Pennsylvania board of trustees pressured the institution's president to fire him.[11]

At the University of Chicago, where John Dewey taught, numerous intellectuals after Bemis ran afoul of the administration for their political commitments. Dewey believed that President William Rainey Harper was "afraid of hurting the feelings of the capitalists...and is relatively purblind to the real advances of life."[12] Dewey concluded from the Bemis case that "Chicago Univ. is a capitalist institution—that is, it too belongs to the higher classes," and he advised his colleagues in the social sciences to use caution when criticizing the established order and to speak in dispassionate tones about controversial issues such as class conflict.[13] Whether or not he realized the radical implications of his own critique, Dewey had touched on the serious question of whether academic freedom is *ever* possible under capitalism, under *any* conditions, given that corporations and rich businessmen command the entire political and legal machinery of "representative democracy." If ownership and money turned the state into an adjunct of private interest, certainly it commandeers administrative influence or control over universities, in a promiscuous exchange of money and labor and capital and knowledge.

Unlike many workers and labor unions steeled in battle against the Goliath of capital and state violence, academics were a largely placid and privileged bunch that lacked the practical savvy to organize to protect their interests. In the late-nineteenth and early-twentieth centuries, professors William Tierney and Vicente Lechuga write,

> administrative control was paramount and faculty input was nil. Tenure did not exist. Faculty meetings, if they did occur, concerned the grading and evaluation of students. If individuals had contracts, the terms were dictated by the president of the institution, and professors were dismissed at will. Faculty had no input on budgets, buildings, or what their work should be. Academic structures such as faculty senates, grievance committees, or promotion and tenure committees were nonexistent.[14]

This was clearly a dismal situation for academic freedom and job security, but thanks to a few visionaries the dynamics began to change favorably for professors.

Galvanized by cases such as Bemis and Ross, John Dewey and Arthur O. Lovejoy (who quit Stanford in protest over Ross' treatment) founded the American Association of University Professors (AAUP) in 1915. Lovejoy organized dozens of scholars from numerous states to attend the first organizational meeting to discuss the rights of scholars in higher education. Dewey was the Association's first president (1915–1916) and in his inaugural address he emphasized that its mission was to promote scholarship, not to defend violations of academic freedom. But when over thirty cases of repression of free speech were reported in the first two years, Dewey realized the defense of free speech had to become a priority, and he appointed a committee of fifteen members to report on issues of academic repression and tenure.

Dewey and Lovejoy set the AAUP on the long and crucial path of institutionalizing academic freedom in a formal tenure system. The new system of tenure rewarded those who passed a six or seven year probationary period, granting them permanent job security (barring grave academic misconduct or incompetence). Protection from unfair, arbitrary, and politically-driven attacks enabled professors to research, teach, and advocate as they saw fit, without fear or threat of reprisal from corporate board members, trustees, politicians, or administration.[15] In 1915, the AAUP prepared its first document on the "Declaration of Principles on Academic Freedom and Academic Tenure," which evolved into the "1940 Statement of Principles on Academic Freedom and Tenure" (revised in 1970). This document argues that the advance of knowledge, the instruction of students, the contributions to public service, and the overall quality of a university education is directly and inseparably dependent upon the strength of academic freedom.[16] In 1918, the AAUP began to address the problem of gender discrimination against women in higher education, and had already broadened its focus to include not only the political conditions of academic repression, but also the economic causes stemming from an exploited and vulnerable work force. Thus, very early in its history, the AAUP took up due process, shared governance, collective bargaining, and the labor aspect of academia, and, beginning in the 1990s, the organization placed great emphasis on the exploitation of part-time instructors and graduate students.[17]

Dewey advanced the concept of academic freedom in response to overweening corporate influence in society and the corrupt control of industry and private interest over the pursuit of knowledge and the social good. Dewey warned that the "business mind-set" itself is toxic for free thinking and progress in knowledge, and that the corrosive influence of capital was a threat to democracy everywhere. But Dewey saw not only corporate interests as seducing, corrupting, and perverting academia in nefarious ways; in the 1940s he warned that the corporatization of higher learning had begun. This involved a process whereby universities happily embraced the market paradigm such that they ran the campus like a business, on a top-down management model, with goals of efficiency and profit. For Dewey, corporatization does not just spread industry, markets, and money around in a slipshod way, but rather in a systemic process that seeks to commandeer social institutions like the university, and completely redefines their values, goals, and modus operandi. Indeed, universities were not just working for corporations, they had themselves *become* corporations, such that their primary concern was no longer to produce beautiful works of art, inspiring books of philosophy, or rigorous sociological studies; rather, the corporate university must compete in a cutthroat environment that transmogrifies knowledge from an individual and socially useful good into a commodity produced for profit.[18]

These dynamics are causes and consequences of a hyper-capitalism that continues to reshape the academic landscape, imperiling the integrity of academic freedom and degrading knowledge into a base utilitarian function. Given Dewey's belief that education is vital to producing intelligent and well-rounded citizens, we could not only say, with him, that "education is the midwife of democracy," but also that *democracy is the midwife of education*. Capitalist cultures rooted in the dynamics of profit, competition, commodification, and growth destroy both democracy and education, and transform a positive dialectic into a negative feedback loop in which society produces poorly educated individuals incapable of autonomy and citizenship who consequently become the pacified, exploited labor power for totalitarian, corporate-dominated societies.[19]

The Menace of McCarthyism

"Congress shall make no law...abridging the freedom of speech, or of the press, or of the people peaceably to assemble, and to petition the Government for a redress of grievances."
—First Amendment of the US Constitution

No sooner had Dewey written his seminal tracts about education as the precondition of autonomy, citizenship, and democracy, than the US was entering one of the most repressive and terrifying periods in its history (so much so that it inspired a veritable genre of science fiction films based on aliens and fear). For a new and much larger wave of anti-communism rolled through society until the late 1950s, causing devastating damage to civil liberties.[20] This new inquisition era began in 1934, as the Special Committee on Un-American Activities began to interrogate thousands of witnesses about how fascist propaganda entered the US and was spread by organizations opposed to the government. The focus on fascism, however, soon shifted once military and political bureaucrats sensed a greater threat of communism emerging in Eastern Europe.

From 1938 to the late 1940s, the House Un-American Activities Committee (HUAC), directed by J. Edgar Hoover and assisted by the FBI, began investigating the Federal Theatre Project. They compiled a list of "subversive" individuals they would subpoena to testify in relation to their own alleged communist sympathies and about others whom they thought might be real or potential communists. In 1947, and again in 1951, HUAC targeted the Hollywood film industry, believing that the entertainment culture was a major base of operations for communist politics and propaganda. In reality, there were many *liberals* but few, if any, *communists*—a conflation still used to great advantage by the right today—and the industry in fact went so far as to excise any potential leftist messages that they were producing films glorifying US imperialism.

HUAC called forty-one people to testify about their own possible involvement with the Communist Party, with each pressured to name any friends, colleagues, and/or acquaintances who may have had known- or suspected-involvement with communism. Witnesses who refused to testify—such as the famous "Hollywood Ten"—were cited for contempt of Congress, sentenced to six to twelve months in prison, and blacklisted. On the basis of testimony that was true or false, direct or indirect, actual or imagined, 320 people were banned from further work in the industry; most were unemployable for years to follow, and many became instant pariahs to acquaintances and friends who recoiled from the stigma of guilt-by-association.[21]

While the HUAC witchhunts were underway in the arts and entertainment center on the west coast, the same inquisition tactics were unfolding on the east coast in higher education. The Rapp-Coudert Committee, officially known as the "Joint Legislative Committee to Investigate the Educational System of the State of New York," was established in 1940 to investigate "subversive activities" at public and private colleges in New York. The City College of New York (CCNY) was a logical place to initiate draconian attacks, for throughout the 1930s CCNY faculty and students led vigorous protests against both fascism and capitalism. Many untenured teachers, concerned about being terminated for their political views, joined or formed unions and associations. CCNY students were organized as well, with many part of a national student movement affiliated with the Community Party. Remarkably, progressive student associations conducted mass protests and campus sit-ins that anticipated the pivotal free speech and democracy struggles at Berkeley and Columbia (see below) by three decades, and already, amidst the Great Depression, students were asserting themselves as a significant and progressive force of change and a distinct social movement with radical potential by virtue of their marginalized place in society.[22]

Moreover, in 1939, CCNY bolstered its reputation as a radical institution by offering a position to British mathematician and philosopher Bertrand Russell, a figure renowned for his analytical skills but also infamous for championing pacifism, atheism, and liberal sexuality. As news of the impeding hire spread, a gaggle of reactionaries—including members of the Catholic Church, the Hearst press, and local politicians—denounced Russell as an immoral, Godless, lascivious, corrupter of youth. During this early culture war and ensuing media spectacle, a woman named Jean Kay filed suit with the New York Supreme Court against the university, on the grounds that Russell was morally unfit to teach, and his views condoning sex before marriage would harm her daughter's virtue, even though her daughter was not a CCNY student. When Kay prevailed in court, CCNY withdrew the offer and an incensed Russell correctly observed that he was the victim of "a typical American witch-hunt," such as dated back to Salem, Massachusetts in the late-seventeenth century.[23] Within a year of the Russell hiring fiasco, the Rapp-Coudert committee subpoenaed and interrogated more than

100 CCNY staff, faculty, and students on activities allegedly related to the Communist Party. The committee denounced over 800 area public school teachers and college faculty members, it pressured the board of higher education to adopt new rules forcing employees to testify and "name names" of suspected communists or be terminated, and it fired over 60 CCNY professors.[24]

But the repression in New York, as elsewhere, continued uninterrupted into the 1950s, as evident by the 1949 New York State Feinberg Law, which barred members of the Communist Party from teaching in the public schools and colleges, and stayed on the books until 1967 when the US Supreme Court declared such legislation unconstitutional. Indeed, initiated by FBI director J. Edgar Hoover, HUAC, Congressmen Martin Dies, Senator Joseph McCarthy, and others, a so-called second Red Scare emerged full-blown by the early 1950s, building on the repressive laws, institutions, and mindset of the first Red Scare and Rapp-Coudert, while initiating a new and more malevolent wave of deportation of foreigners and surveillance and persecution of citizen dissent. With the fascist momentum building inexorably, no Bill of Rights could stand in the way of flagrant violations of the Constitution. "McCarthyism" became the term for a host of persecuting actions—embodied by Senator McCarthy, but utilizing a range of operations that preceded him and unfortunately lived through the century and into our own post-9/11 era. "McCarthyism," in other words, was a systemic, institutional attack on civil liberties by big business, the state, and sundry reactionary forces; it was a structural form of repression, not a persecution campaign of a sole deranged, authoritarian, power-hungry politician.

The tyranny of McCarthyism spread everywhere in academia, from large state schools and small private colleges to Ivy League universities.[25] The historical gains made in the struggle for academic freedom from 1915 to 1940 were effaced with surveillance, persecution, and the imposition of loyalty oaths. Neither the Constitution nor tenure status protected academics from being fired and blacklisted. As David Cole notes, the mere charge of disloyalty to the nation sufficed for the state to suspend constitutional protections—as would later happen after 9/11 with foreigners (and some US citizens) branded as "enemy combatants." Many academics chose not to cooperate, and roughly seventy tenured or tenure-track professors were fired during the McCarthy era for non-cooperation or alleged communist affiliations. Nearly all found it impossible to secure another teaching job in the US until the furies of anti-communist repression abated somewhat in the 1960s.

Meanwhile, the government continued to exclude droves of suspected communists from the country, including Nobel Prize winners such as Gabriel Garcia Marquez, Pablo Neruda, and Doris Lessing. Apparently these law-abiding artists were dangerous to national security not because of any weapons they might carry in or secrets they could smuggle out, but rather because of the freedom, creativity, and intelligence they exhibited. All this was menacing enough, indeed, to a paranoiac, security-obsessed, control-oriented, xenophobic nation-state. In preparation for the multitudes of communists, subversives, home-grown terrorists, foreign operatives, and enemies of the state who they projected would riot in the streets, Congress built huge detention centers in five states. These barbed-wired Gulags were erected in 1952, only a decade after the state constructed internment camps for 110,000 Japanese Nationals and Japanese-Americans, but this time the government was planning to lock up its own citizens, as evident by a 1954 FBI list of 26,174 "subversives" identified for rapid relocation if necessary.[26] Congress repealed the authorizations for these political prisons in 1971, but the fascist project of incarcerating citizens for even potentially disagreeing with their government has lived on through the decades and most recently inspired the Bush administration as a winsome way of dispatching domestic terrorists, to be rounded up by the armed forces amidst declaration of martial law.

In a seamless transition, just as McCarthyism proper was dying in the late 1950s due to McCarthy's own excesses and fatal tactical error of hunting commies in the ranks of the US army, yet another wave of anti-leftist political persecution, arguably the most menacing to date, was emerging. From 1956 to 1971, as a fierce backlash to democratization and the rise of the "new social movements," FBI, federal, and state police joined forces to roll back historical strides toward democracy. Government response to millions of Blacks, Browns, students, women, peace activists, and others demanding rights, equality, and democracy was not to belatedly and apologetically grant them long delayed justice, respect, and full inclusion in society, but rather to restore hierarchical harmony. Challenged to beat back not only militant leaders or small groups, but huge social movements, the state and law enforcement unleashed a sophisticated and sweeping search-and-destroy tactic based on the Counter Intelligence Program (COINTELPRO).[27] The victims of FBI and US state terrorism ranged from Dr. Martin Luther King Jr. and mainstream civil rights groups to the Black Panther Party and the Students for a Democratic Society (SDS), from sundry leftist factions to the National Lawyers Guild, from the women's liberation movement to anti-war and anti-nuclear committees. Even peacenik hippies baking bread in their communes were surveilled and listed for potential detainment inside capitalist concentration camps. The state ran roughshod over the Constitution in the name of patriotism; it provoked chaos in society in order to restore order; it used illegal methods to accost suspected lawbreakers; it psychologically and physically injured potentially "dangerous" or "harmful" activists; and the FBI agents and Chicago police, entrusted to preserve the peace, murdered Black Panther leader Fred Hampton in his sleep.

And while the state gassed, beat, clubbed, jailed, and murdered the harbingers of change in the streets, reactionary dragnets swept into the universities. As ever more professors supported the anti-war movement's call for US soldiers to leave Vietnam, over twenty state legislatures passed resolutions to dismiss faculty critics of US policy and to remove free speech protections from the tenure contract. But to their credit university administrators opposed and defeated these assaults on tenure and civil liberties, a backbone rarely evident in the spineless response to more serious threats to academic freedom after 9/11. While women and minorities were beginning to break into the white male enclave of academia, it was business as usual for political radicals. In 1971, for instance, Marxist theorist Bertell Ollman's bid for the position of Chair of the Department of Political Science at the University of Maryland was unanimously approved by broad faculty review, but President John Toll, buckling to external pressure, overrode their vote of confidence, defied the principle of diversity, and rejected Ollman as a politically safe appointee.[28]

Toll's cowardly hatchet job came two years after one of the most famous cases of academic repression in US history: when UCLA philosophy professor Angela Davis, a former Black Panther and protégé of Herbert Marcuse, was fired for her communist politics. Ronald Reagan, Governor of California and head of the Board of Regents, vowed that Davis would never work for the state education system, and he dredged up a 1940 resolution (already rescinded by both California and US Supreme Courts) that barred members of the Communist Party from teaching at a state university. On June 19, 1970, acting without legal authority, Reagan wrote this chilling note to all UC faculty:

> This memorandum is to inform everyone that, through extensive court cases and rebuttals, Angela Davis, Professor of Philosophy, will no longer be a part of the UCLA staff. As head of the Board of Regents, I, nor the board will not tolerate any Communist activities at any state institution. Communists are an endangerment to this wonderful system of government that we all share and are proud of. Please keep in mind that in 1949 it was reaffirmed that any member of the Communist Party is barred from teaching at this institution.
>
> Cordially[!],
> Ronald Reagan, Governor[29]

UCLA faculty condemned the decision as an illegal assault on academic freedom. Amidst a heated campus dispute, Davis was framed and placed on the FBI's most wanted list on charges of kidnapping three San Quentin prisoners and supplying the gun that killed four people during the incident, thereby driving her underground until her later arrest. Her sensationalist trial captured international attention until her acquittal in 1972, and Davis subsequently became an honored tenured professor and

Chair of the History of Consciousness Department at the University of California, Santa Cruz.

Despite the Church Committee reports of the mid-1970s that documented stunning abuses of power by US intelligence agencies in COINTELPRO and clandestine operations in decades prior, and despite the abolition of HUAC in 1975, *nothing changed in the tactics and goals of state repression* except that the FBI sought new technological means and legal loopholes to continue carrying out their *raison d'être*. Just as the CIA's task it to destroy democracies abroad, so the FBI is entrusted to decimate social movements at home.[30] Officially terminated in April 1971, COINTELPRO—and all other variations on McCarthyism and repression and control of dissent—merely continued under a different name. During the next two decades, the FBI targeted groups such as the Committee in Solidarity with the People of El Salvador (CISPES), the American Indian Movement, anti-globalization struggles, Earth First!, the Animal Liberation Front (ALF), the Earth Liberation Front (ELF), and Stop Huntingdon Animal Cruelty (SHAC), a militant direct action anti-vivisectionist group.[31] Although the FBI has always been a rogue force virtually unregulated by Congress and the courts, with the events of September 11, 2001 they were granted carte blanche authority for "homeland security," and the gloves came off in an aggressive bare-knuckled attack on virtually every form of protest and dissent (see below).

On Academic Freedom

"By academic freedom I understand the right to search for the truth and to publish and teach what one holds to be true. This right also implies a duty; one must not conceal any part of what one has recognized to be true. It is evident that any restriction of academic freedom serves to restrain the dissemination of knowledge, thereby impeding rational judgment and action."
—Albert Einstein

"I entered the classroom with the conviction that it was crucial for me and every other student to be an active participant, not a passive consumer...education as the practice of freedom.... education that connects the will to know with the will to become. Learning is a place where paradise can be created."
—bell hooks

The concept of academic freedom has roots in the High Middle Ages when medieval scholastics developed critical pedagogical methods to liberate students from authorities in order to freely pursue the truth. It was bolstered by the development of science and the rise of economic and political liberalism in the eighteenth and nineteenth centuries, and, in the late-nineteenth century, German universities advanced the notion of *Lehrfreiheit*, or the right of a professor to research, teach, and report findings freely in a tolerant environment.[32]

But "academic freedom" was not carefully elaborated or institutionalized to any significant degree until 1915, as Dewey, Lovejoy, and others became aware of the fast-growing influence of corporations on universities, targeting anyone unfriendly to business, sympathetic to labor, or simply too liberal overall.[33] The concept of academic freedom was developed not only for the negative purpose of warding off insidious threats from outside interests and from within the university itself, but also for the positive purpose of protecting the right to free speech and recognizing the direct relationships between academic freedom, the quality of higher education, and a democratic society. Although not an explicit constitutional right, Supreme Court judges have reasonably interpreted academic freedom as implicit within the First Amendment, and so by extension professors have legally-protected rights.[34] Academic freedom is important in any democratic institutional setting, but especially so in higher education. In colleges and universities, freedom to research, think, teach, speak, and act as a political being and citizen is not a dispensable luxury, a bonus, or a principle that applies only on occasion, it is, rather, the key precondition for knowledge and learning to take place at all. It is the oxygen of intellectual life and the legitimating concept of the university system.[35]

Knowledge cannot advance within conditions of intimidation, self-censorship, constraint, and penalties. In this stifling environment, knowledge dies. In an atmosphere of freedom, respect, diversity, tolerance, and open dialogue and debate, in contrast, knowledge grows and thrives. *Both* faculty and students must be able to experiment with ideas, test them in concrete interaction with others, unperturbed by artificially imposed ideological and political constraints. If able to proceed without pressure, threats, or coercion, thinking can be as it must be: bold, not timid; imaginative, not blinkered; fearless, not fearful; iconoclastic, not conformist; courageous, not obeisant. The guarantees of the tenure system are crucial, for real insight and questioning often burrows through arcane or unknown paths, such as the inquiry that led Einstein (as a high school student no less) to ask the surreal and seemingly unthinkable question, "What is the speed of light?"—a question that led him ultimately toward his general theory of relativity. Decades later, in an equally bizarre (to common sense) reply to Einstein's macro-theory, Niels Bohr proved Einstein wrong on key counts by boldly insisting the counter-intuitive, seemingly impossible proposition (contradicting Aristotelian identity theory that A=A, not something other than itself), that light can be both particle and wave.

Thought must be free to upset not only intellectual orthodoxy, but social and political dogmas as well, and thus to be critical, controversial, radical, and shocking if need be (as Nietzsche's atheism and Darwin's theory of natural selection were in the nineteenth century, and Russell's liberal sexuality was in the mid-twentieth century). Finally, as thinking is organically linked to doing, freedom of speech must allow one the right to *act* on one's beliefs and convictions, and so professors have every right to be citizens—not just functionaries—with particular values and political views that inform their politics, practices, and commitments.

Academic freedom is freedom *from* politically motivated intimidation tactics and punitive actions, and freedom *to* speak, write, teach, and act as one chooses. Academic freedom of speech is a subset of First Amendment protected speech, yet is unique by being exercised in an institutional setting where freedom is bound up with professional codes of duty. Thus—a crucial point that right-wing critics of liberal/left professors consistently fail to grasp and acknowledge—just as freedom in general is never absolute, so academic freedom is not unlimited and, as emphasized by the AAUP from the start, it cannot be uncoupled from *academic responsibility*.[36] Academic freedom is a right so long as attached to duties to respect: (1) relevant standards and ethical practices in research and teaching, such as to teach material relevant to the topic of the course, and (2) students as individuals with their own ideas. Regarding the first point, a professor may certainly express his or her own moral values or political views in the classroom, but these must apply to the topic at hand and in some cases—say, an anatomy or statistics course, rather than a philosophy class—these views may not be pertinent at all. As to the second point, a professor should not enforce his or her views as the truth, reject student ideas out of hand, nor, certainly, belittle students for thinking in different terms.

But none of these specific duties mean that a professor cannot argue his or her own point of view, and challenge and disagree with the student, no less than the fact that students have a right to disagree with and challenge their professors. Indeed, this critical dialogue between professor and students is a vital component of the educational experience, mutually beneficial to all, and no good teacher or student would try to close this down in favor of some rigid ideology or dogma. Moreover, a professor best respects a student's mind and autonomy by arguing, challenging, and encouraging them to clarify their positions and to think in new ways. Another point conveniently overlooked in right-wing attacks on the "academic left" is that, while professors do indeed have duties to treat students respectfully, so too do students have duties to treat their professors respectfully, to speak to the topic at hand, and to advance class discussion. Too often, however, conservative students—egged on and/or even paid by far right "watch" groups—simply target liberal professors, rudely attack them, bring up issues irrelevant to the class, and completely disrupt the dialogue and classroom learning environment.

Thus, academic freedom is a concept crucial for professors and students alike, and, as Paulo Freire emphasized, just as the professor's knowledge is vital for the student's education, so too the student's knowledge and critical questioning—the ability and freedom to question, challenge, and push the professor past unexamined assumptions)—is crucial for the learning of the professor. Despite the falsehoods and stereotypes of demagogues like David Horowitz (see below), the vast majority of professors do not require students to toe some ideological line, but rather raise controversial and topical issues to initiate the free and experimental expression of ideas in a classroom that respects different points of view. And where professors fail in these duties, faculty review boards exist to enforce academic responsibilities as well as to protect academic freedom.[37] Whereas the attention of the culture wars has focused on professors allegedly harassing students, it is more often the case that conservative students are harassing their professors.[38]

There is no academic freedom in the abstract; it is an ideal realized (or thwarted) in varying degrees by different universities at specific times. If *academic freedom* involves the right of professors (and students) to research, publish, teach, speak, and lead political lives as they choose, then *academic repression* is the manifold denial and negation of this right, such that professors are hassled, penalized, and often fired for holding unorthodox, nonconformist, critical, controversial, and dissenting views relating to topics ranging from US imperialism and Israeli state terrorism to animal liberation, anarchism, and radical pedagogy. If, since its inception, the Bill of Rights has been systematically violated, if lawmakers invariably are the lawbreakers, if freedom of speech and association is a myth in society as a whole, why should one think there is any freedom in the hallowed halls of academia? If corporations have dominated every sector and institution of this society, and the influence of the military and armed forces has spread into the fabric of the economy, social life, and foreign policy, why expect academia to be a protected site or sacred space whose ancient and noble ideals are uncorrupted by the vulgar affairs of commerce, militarism, and corporate power?

The idea of enlightened minds pursuing knowledge and wisdom in truth-seeking, non-distorted, earnest, and open forms of inquiry (Habermas' utopian paradigm of "communicative rationality") is consoling and pleasurable to entertain, but it is a hoary old myth and a dangerously naïve piece of fiction. The serene "internal" model of academia as its own self-referential universe occludes the truth of the "external" model that exposes the intimate relationship between knowledge and power; the ubiquity of hierarchical relations stretching up and down the bureaucratic chain of command; corporatization and the corrupting scent of money; the petty Machiavellian power games that play out in all departments; the primate behaviors of ambitious administrators and *Homo academicus*; the narcissistic egomania of anemic academics convinced of their own brilliance, relevance, and absolute right to detach themselves from a world in unprecedented social and ecological crisis.

To be sure, as human animals are not ethereal beings without bodies, interests, and deep roots in social life and natural evolution, the university is more like a battlezone than a grazing pasture, a prisonhouse than a polis. And while the prevailing corporate values and political ideologies favor conformity and acquiescence, the threat of the *Id* of subversion, counter-hegemony, and anti-hierarchy, as well as the pulse of resistance, rebellion, and revolution, always threaten to break through. Try as they do, the corporate and administrative overlords of "higher education" cannot completely contain the contradiction that threatens to do them in—the will to truth (as taught in many disciplines) turned against itself, such that trained critical minds become shrewd enough to recognize that the academic and social Emperors have no clothes. Thus, since institutions of "higher learning" train students to think, discriminate, reason, and judge, there is an inherent danger of producing critiques of capitalist society as a system antithetical to a social life that is happy, free, and sane, as well as to a sustainable planetary ecology. The possibility that critical thinking, resistance, or boredom might break out—such as it did in US universities in the 1960s, in Paris 1968, or the December 2008 riots sweeping through Athens, Greece—requires the threat of disorder to be contained and controlled by the bureaucratic cryptkeepers and functionaries of the state, lest academia produce its own gravediggers or breed a generation of malcontents and radical *philosophes*, in the French Enlightenment tradition.

Despite trumpeting the ideal of competition, in practice capitalism evolved into a closed system of control, centralization, and monopolization; just as the economy is dominated by a few corporate giants, so ideology is homogenized as a limited range of ideas. If the practice of capitalism stayed true to the theory, a thousand ideologies would bloom in university classrooms, and students could freely chose among the "marketplace" of ideas that vie for their attention. Radicals would not only be tolerated, but in fact would be hired specifically for the purpose of enhancing faculty diversity and ideological competitiveness. But of course capitalism is a power system that must reproduce itself, and so its assorted potentates seek to gag subversive discourse. Elites fear thinking minds because they understand, at some level, the weakness and vulnerability of their repressive system to radical critique.

One tactic of suppression draws upon the university and the school system at all levels, as "education" institutions are a core part of what Marxist theorist Louis Althusser called the "state ideological apparatus."[39] In this conservative and normalizing role of social reproduction, academia perpetuates and legitimates capitalist ideologies; rather than shaping the "critical reason" that spawns dissent and drives social change, it moulds the "instrumental reason" and skills relevant for global capitalist markets (see below).[40] A paradoxical logic binds academic freedom/repression into capitalist ideology. As Marx noted that the universal discourses of rights, democracy, and freedom were mystifying ideologies that disguised particular interests in the form of general interests and served the purposes of an elite minority not the social majority, so too the concept of academic freedom is often merely an alibi for the machinery of academic repression and control. Thus, as Ollman writes, "The conditions of modern capitalist society have turned the practice of academic freedom into academic repression and used the ideal to cover its tracks."[41] The concept of "academic freedom," in other words, is batted about as if it were real and substantive, but serves to obfuscate the realities of contemporary university life, such as rooted in the suppression of critical thought, the hyper-exploitation of part-time instructors and graduate students, and the absorption of higher education into the larger constellation of corporate-military power. The notion of academic freedom, moreover, assumes an illusory equality of conditions in which people exercise their freedom, but this equality is fictitious.

Two qualifications are in order here. First, academic freedom is not *only* a fiction and myth, it does exist in varying forms and degrees according to time, place, and situation. Our claim is not that there is no academic freedom, but that academic freedom—and our rights and liberties in general—is rapidly disappearing as the US under Obama continues its perilous decline into a militarist, soulless tyranny of a surveillance society and post-Constitutional garrison state. Second, Ollman correctly highlights the economic conditioning and class politics operating in the university today, but his analysis can be expanded. In academia, it is not only *economic* constraints that operate, but also *political* restraints policing and suppressing unorthodox views, as well as prejudicial ideologies that suppress racial, gender, sexual, and other forms of diversity and difference (see below).

Should the university become a carnivalesque (in the Mikhail Bakhtin sense) political scene and a volatile site of critique and dissent, the corporate-state-university complex deploys a *second* tactic of control, which is not the preferred means of domination through consensus but rather the more overt forms of power manifested in *political repression*. It is important to distinguish among state repression, political repression, and academic repression, given that they are all different, although often interrelated and overlapping, forces of control. State repression, for instance, may take the form of attacking labor unions that strike for higher wages, which involves both economic and political coercion by protecting capitalist industries through suppressing political activity. State repression and political repression, therefore, are closely linked dynamics and concepts. Similarly, while political repression typically entails state repression, as when the FBI and police are involved, universities have a relative autonomy from the state and readily take it upon themselves to monitor and attack radical ideology and oppositional politics in the faculty and student bodies. To be sure, except for "private" schools such as Princeton or Harvard, universities literally are state institutions—state funded and answerable to state government—but political repression is a broader concept than state repression.

The Logic of Academic Repression

"The essentiality of freedom in the community of American universities is almost self evident. No one should underestimate the vital role in a democracy that is played by those who guide and train our youth. To impose any strait jacket upon the intellectual leaders in our colleges and universities would imperil the future of our Nation."
—Supreme Court Chief Justice Earl Warren,
Sweezy v. New Hampshire (1957)

"All citizens, but particularly teachers and scholars, are called upon to challenge orthodoxy, dogma, and mindless complacency, to be skeptical of authoritative claims, to interrogate and trouble the given and the taken-for-granted. Without critical dialogue and dissent we would likely be burning witches and enslaving our fellow human beings to this day. The growth of knowledge, insight, and understanding—the possibility of change—depends on that kind of effort, and the inevitable clash of ideas that follows should be celebrated and nourished rather than crushed. Teachers have a heavy responsibility, a moral obligation, to organize classrooms as sites of open discussion, free of coercion or intimidation."
—Support Bill Ayers website

Academic repression—not a reified and implacable thing in itself but a controlling force exercised by individuals in institutional relations and able to be resisted—manifests in an endless variety of forms, and may sometimes be hard to detect. It affects both job candidates seeking entry into the professoriate and those working within the system at any level. It can hit part-time and full-time instructors; the non-tenured and tenured; contingent and emeritus staff; and assistant, associate, and full professors, although of course non-tenured and part-time instructors are most vulnerable. Academic repression targets critical and radical scholarship and activism in manifold ways, including discriminating against job candidates, denial of tenure or promotion, demotion (e.g., from department chair back to the ranks of faculty), and firing tenured professors, like the case of Ward Churchill. Conservatives can be victimized by liberals or radicals, just as liberals and radicals can be wronged by conservatives. The political orientations are polar opposites but the mechanism of repression are the same—targeting someone for their political views and identities rather than academic shortcomings, while fabricating deficiencies in the latter to mask the animus against the former. Whether the injustice moves from left to right or from right to left, it is equally wrong—although, right-wing belly-aching and hypocrisy aside, it is undeniably the case that critical liberal and left scholars are repressed far more often and severely than conservatives who harmonize with the capitalist/jingoist/patriarchal/homophobic/Christian status quo.

Academic freedom, in other words, is not a right/left or conservative/liberal/ radical issue, it is rather a vital concern for all scholars, whatever their race, ethnicity, gender, or ideological-political orientation. However else they may disagree, academics of any persuasion ought to support those with different or contrary approaches, not join the attack, for academic repression anywhere is a threat to academic freedom everywhere.

Academic repression knows no disciplinary boundaries; it can certainly draw a bead on controversial discourse in philosophy, history, and literary studies, but it can also affect the more "objective" and "factual-oriented" areas in the "hard sciences" when the "facts" become controversial and politically charged. Such a case occurred, for example, when Bush's Lysenkoesque henchmen censored the important work of James Hansen and other NASA scientists documenting accelerating human-caused global warming processes.[42] Repression, moreover, does not just silence unorthodox, controversial, and radical ideas. It can also attack unconventional methods, research paradigms, and theoretical perspectives (as Anglo-American and positivist philosophy faculty may unfairly deny tenure to Continental or postmodern theorists in contempt of their methods alone).

As cases such as Assistant Professor Norman Finkelstein and Full Professor Ward Churchill show, university presidents can fire faculty at all levels, but these hit jobs are brutal and messy, often sordid public spectacles, and are particularly difficult to execute against a tenured professor, leaving a damning trail of political DNA. In such a case, the dirty work can be dispatched by department colleagues who, in cooperation with a compliant administration, justify their putsch in terms of alleged *professional inadequacies* rather than naked *political differences*.

Academic repression can be blatant and heavy-handed in this manner, but it can also be subtle or invisible, taking the shape of normalizing influences that pressure professors to conform to apolitical conventions or to widespread prejudices that "true" scholarship is always objective, detached, and impartial, and never partisan, political, and linked to society and practice. Indeed, the long tenure process is *inherently repressive* as every assistant professor seeking promotion knows to play it safe and avoid controversy. Once tenure is secured, theoretically, professors have job security and greater protection for free speech. But they are already conditioned to be apolitical and set to worry about the next promotion, award, or grant, such that the institutional biases against controversial research, teaching, and politics *never end*.

Thus, academic repression occurs when the state, political groups, or the university administration attempt to muzzle the outspoken through punitive actions, but it also occurs—all too effectively—when fearful, self-concerned professors censor themselves for purposes of career advancement. Furthermore, one need not be demoted, non-promoted, or fired for academic repression to manifest, it is enough to be marginalized or treated with disdain. It does not require the actual exercise of power, it operates on the mere hint, suggestion, or threat of slapdown, and it thrives in the chilling afterglow of its prior victims whom the state, university administrations, and political assassins uphold to say: "Be careful, or the head on this stake could be yours."

Academic/political repression certainly stems from forces inside higher education (boards, regents and trustees, administration, colleagues), but in the current neo-McCarthyite era (see below) it increasingly flows from despotic meddlers outside the institution (such as politicians, right-wing interest groups, conservative media, lobbyists, donors, alumni, and individual crusaders like Alan Dershowitz or David Horowitz). Once again, academic repression has a profound economic nature and context, as evident when corporations with a vested interest in university research pressure the administration to fire a critic of their policies. Such was the case in 2003 when Novartis strong-armed the University of California at Berkeley to silence Assistant Professor Ignacio Chapela for exposing flaws in biotech crops and the corrupt relationship between Novartis and UCB.

Beyond such specific instances of corporate power, however, there is a *systemic structure* of economic/academic repression, which involves the breathless rush of universities to replace tenured professors with adjuncts, contract, part-time instructors, and graduate students, thereby considerably boosting the profits they make off each person enrolled in a class, which can add up to sizeable numbers.[43] Academic repression, in fact, is a *given* within capitalist social relations, as profit imperatives instrumentalize knowledge and corporatization dynamics proletarianize the workforce—and thus academic freedom is an ideal only realizable in a post-capitalist, fully democratically-managed economic and social system.

But academic repression transcends, and cannot be reduced to, economic issues such as capitalism, class, exploitation, profit, and competition, for there are independent causes, dynamics, and operations of different regimes of power, such as involve patriarchy, racism, homophobia, ablism, and speciesism. These are specific logics and systems of hierarchy which certainly operate with capitalism and class domination as part of a Hydra-headed monster of power. But the domination of men over women, whites over people of color, heterosexual over LGBT, and able-bodied people over "disabled" originate and operate in a way that no "class consciousness" theory or "class struggle" politics can adequately address on their own.

Just as well, the task of understanding different forms of academic repression cannot be reduced to political oppression, for typically when "minority" groups are denied promotions, rejected in the hiring process, or barred from consideration as qualified students or staff, this does not always stem from economic or political repression. It is often, rather, strategic and blatant discrimination based on gender, race, sexual orientation, age, nationality, religion, culture, ethnicity, and physical/mental abilities. Therefore, it is not only economic exploitation or political hegemony operating, it is also the dynamics of sexism, racism, ageism, nationalism, homophobia, and ablism.

Such prejudicial repression (which may or may not be conscious and intentional) involves *discrimination* and is bound up with so-called "identity politics,"

whereby individuals victimized by oppression articulate and boldly assert their identity, history, culture, or "subject position" against dominant or mainstream identities
(e.g., white, male, heterosexual). For when minorities are brushed aside, turned down,
denied interviews or glibly dismissed during or after them, hired on unequal terms in
relation to peers, fired or not promoted without just cause, politics may not even enter
into the mind of the academic repressor. He or she may be far less concerned whether
the applicant is conservative or liberal, Christian or atheist, free-market champion or
socialist, than whether the person is male or female, white or of color, straight or gay,
"normal" or "abnormal," speciesist or vegan and animal rights in orientation. Indeed,
despite the cloying lip service paid to "diversity," all too often administrators and faculty
do not respect or seek a plurality of ideas, politics, or racial/gender/sexual backgrounds.
Instead, the entrenched gatekeepers block entrance or promotion to those deemed too
"controversial," "radical," or "different," while they weed out non-conformist modes of
thinking through standardized testing and measuring procedures, evaluating individuals according to the degree they "fit" pre-determined norms and standards.

Like the larger society, the academy perennially works to police the irregular,
to co-opt the critical, and to disarm the threatening. Whereas its power can be gross
and overt, it also flows as a subtle force exercised through the techniques that Foucault
identified as "discipline" and "normalization," which target both the body and mind to
produce homogenous populations of docile and useful subjects.[44] And while we disagree that power doesn't also stop, block, restrain, prohibit, and repress, Foucault correctly identified the operation of power in its positive, productive, and enabling role.
Power, in other words, doesn't just negate and thwart, resulting in pain and frustration
and denial; it actively produces knowledge, desire, and subjects themselves, with affects
experienced as pleasure, helping to disguise the overall coercive functions and consequences of institutionalized systems of power/knowledge.

From Purple Haze to Days of Rage: Student Power and the 1960s

*"A spectre is haunting our universities—the spectre of a radical and militant nationally
co-ordinated movement for student power."*

—Carl Davidson, SDS

"College isn't the place to go for ideas."

—Helen Keller

Just as the commodification of society spread to its outer bounds in the 1960s, and a
post-war consumer culture exploded and co-opted the anti-materialist counter-culture, something utterly new happened after World War II, stemming from the rise of

the military to an increasingly prominent role in US society.[45] In his startling and prescient 1961 "Farewell Address to the Nation," President Eisenhower warned that "we must guard against the military industrial complex," and the threat that militarization, violence, chronic war, and a profit-making "defense" or "security" apparatus poses to civil liberties, democracy, safety, peace, and the integrity of higher learning.

Clearly, the emerging super-industry of weapons production and armaments evolved only through a growing interlocking relation between the military and corporate sectors, making war, weaponry, and killing a highly profitable enterprise. Universities merged with the corporate-military system in a mutually beneficial partnership: just as academia profited handsomely from research and development contracts—e.g., to build computers, develop napalm and space-based weapons, or formulate methods for pacifying populations—so the corporate-military sector mined universities for advanced research and cheap labor. Although, as Giroux notes, Eisenhower excised from his speech the phrase "military-industrial-*academic*-complex," the reference to universities is implicit, as the post-war, post-industrial world shifted focus from the manufacture of goods to the production of knowledge for the development of science, technology, and permanent warfare.[46]

As state funding precipitously declined, universities became increasingly reliant on and addicted to corporate funding and military research; they began to lose more autonomy, to further dilute and betray their higher missions, and to become swallowed ever deeper into the bellicose bowels of capitalism.[47] While corporations certainly wielded strong influence in universities at least since the late-nineteenth century, their post-war power spread viral-like so radically throughout the host body that universities did not just adopt corporate ideologies and serve corporate needs and agendas, rather they themselves *became* corporations. Increasingly, colleges and universities abandoned their mission to shape broad-minded citizens and enhance the public good in order to enter into mutually advantageous relationships with the most violent and exploitative forces on the planet.

But a significant counterforce was emerging parallel to these changes in the structure of capitalist society. Across the nation, in the midst of a corporate-military nihilism that valued the machinations of power and profit, the "silent generation" of 1950s students were becoming vociferously politicized in organized acts of rebellion against racism, capitalism, imperialism, patriarchy, war, authoritarianism, hierarchy, and other social evils. Just as universities were being taken over by the military-industrial complex, students were emerging as an increasingly powerful social force and began taking over universities. As in the mid-nineteenth century the abolitionist movement was the catalyst for other political movements such as the suffragettes, so the civil rights movement of the mid-twentieth century provided the impetus and matrix spawning other social struggles, including the New Left and the "new social movements" (e.g., student, feminist, and civil rights groups) that rattled the foundations of a complacent corporate society.

Founded in 1960 by Southern college students, the Student Nonviolent Coordinating Committee (SNCC) organized sit-ins against segregated businesses, launched voter-registration drives, and created the Freedom Riders—an integrated group of courageous students who risked their lives to challenge laws or customs enforcing apartheid-like segregation in nearly every aspect of social life. Youth involved in SNCC and organizations such as CORE (Congress of Racial Equality) were pivotal forces in the civil rights struggle and social change generally. The battle against segregation in employment, housing, restaurants, hospitals, and countless other areas of life unavoidably spilled over into the education sector, where poverty and racism thwarted Blacks from getting through high school, let alone obtaining a quality university training.[48] A landmark victory on the path to end legalized segregation in schooling emerged with *Brown v. Board of Education*, the 1954 Supreme Court decision that unanimously overruled the 1986 decision, *Plessy v. Ferguson*—which embedded the contemptible "Jim Crow" notion of "separate but equal" into American law and institutions—and found it to be in violation of the Equal Protection Clause of the Fourteenth Amendment. Another key legislative change was the Civil Rights Act of 1964, which outlawed racial segregation in schools, public areas, and places of employment, and also created the Equal Employment Opportunity Commission to adjudicate workplace issues such as fair treatment and sexual harassment. The Voting Rights Act of 1965 was significant as well, for it dispensed with poll taxes, literacy tests, and other blatant obstacles to minorities exercising their right to vote.

Following the rousing lead of Black youth in SNCC and CORE (and often volunteering in these groups), privileged white students were also rebelling—not because they were poor and *exploited*, but rather because they were affluent and *alienated*. Uninspired by soulless consumerism, dreary schooling, and hollow expectations, growing numbers of white youth contested racial discrimination, economic inequality, oppressive authoritarianism, and the menacing threat of nuclear annihilation, which they blamed on the US. Across the nation, thousands of placid, soporific, and dreary campuses morphed into sites of intense energy and struggle, as idealistic, altruistic, and visionary youth organized political groups such as the Students for a Democratic Society (SDS), which had roots in early-twentieth century socialist education organizations. The SDS mushroomed into a huge national organization and became the leading anti-war group on many campuses. They held their first annual meeting in 1960, in Ann Arbor, Michigan, and at their debut 1962 convention adopted their famous Port Huron statement, a passionate and visionary tract that calls for remarking the world through nonviolent civil disobedience and participatory democracy.

Cognizant of the dramatic changes wrought by the rising military-industrial complex, the SDS noted that "modern universities are little more than the training and research branches of the capitalist imperialist system." These dull-grey "knowledge factories" insidiously "absorb young people and prepare them for obedience and bureaucratic tasks through objective, value-free, technique-oriented courses... Proof of the fact that US universities have shifted their purpose from helping young people become independent, creative, sensitive intellectuals to turning out cogs in the system is manifold." Where "the day-to-day practice of our schools is authoritarian, conformist, and almost entirely status-oriented...higher education produces boredom, a feeling of alienation, and a sense of irrelevance." In these conditions, students "feel powerless, manipulated. Students are like the exploited factory-hands of the 19th century sweatshops." The corporatization of higher education was antithetical to the cultivation of critical thinking, value formation, ethical philosophy, and the fostering of autonomy and citizenship skills necessary for a functioning democracy. Instead, the university—more so than ever—became a site of social production and reproduction of laborers for the global capitalist market. Universities had become part of the "one dimensional society" (Marcuse) devoid of critical reason and autonomous actors. Building on the Marxist insight that "education" is a euphemistic mask for indoctrination, SDS member Carl Davidson noted that "the core of the university, with its frills removed, has become the crucible for the production, formation, and socialization of the new working class."[49]

But clearly there was another aspect to campus life, for it was at universities that students organized, protested, led teach-ins, became politicized, and transformed a repressive institution into a Deweyan "laboratory" of critical thinking and citizenship. And yet, true academic freedom requires genuine social freedom, and given that capitalist society is by its very nature a hierarchical system dominated by military, corporate, political, and media elites, there is no possibility of "academic freedom" or a "free university" in capitalist society, just as the concept of "socialism in one country" was absurd. Thus, Davidson wrote, "'We should always remember that we cannot liberate the university without radically changing the rest of society."[50]

Another crucial expression of student radicalism with great consequence for academic freedom and society generally erupted in the fall of 1964 at the University of California-Berkeley. A number of students, including Jack Weinberg and Mario Savio, had contested the campus ban on political activity and fundraising, but the "Berkeley free speech movement" began on the evening of October 1, when security arrested Weinberg at a CORE table for failure to show identification. Before police could drive him away, Savio jumped onto the car and led an impromptu protest, as 3,000 students blocked the vehicle for 32 hours during which they voiced their discontent. For the next two months, students occupied the administration building and when police moved in on December 3, the resulting protests nearly shut down the campus. In January 1965, Chancellor Martin Meyerson, forced into concessions, designated restricted places and times for discussions and literature tables, thereby opening a space for student activism that grew ever wider.

Elected to state Governor in the fall of 1966, Ronald Reagan vowed to "clean up the mess at Berkeley," but it was already too late as the Berkeley free speech movement helped to spawn the anti-war and civil liberties struggles and shaped the 60s milieu for the US and other Western nations. In 1969, however, Reagan got a chance to battle Berkeley radicals in the struggle over People's Park, a field the university built for the baseball team, but students and community members found more suitable as a park. After weeks of fractious conflicts, the university moved to bulldoze the area, prompting outrage and even more militant protests. Reagan ordered in the National Guard, touching off a melee in which over a dozen people were hospitalized, a policeman was stabbed, a bystander blinded, and a student killed. The university allowed the park to stand but retained ownership of the space.

Before the tragic battle over People's Park, however, another major free speech and student protest event erupted in 1967 at Columbia University; a turbulent struggle began when SDS activist Bob Feldman discovered library documents detailing the school's lucrative role in weapons research with the Institute for Defense Analyses (IDA), a think-tank for the Department of Defense. This perverse partnership provided a vivid example of the academic-military-industrial complex at work and enraged the student body.[51] From April 1967 to April 1968, students waged a vocal anti-war campaign and demanded that the university end all weapons-related research, while the SDS sought to advance a larger struggle for participatory democracy and to establish the university "as a base for movements to educate, radicalize, and mobilize the community as a whole for change."[52]

In 1968, students opened up a new front in their battle with Columbia in order to stop plans to build a gymnasium on the grounds of Morningside Park. On April 23, 1968, after a second clash with police, SDS leader Mark Rudd led an occupation of Hamilton Hall, which housed the administration office. Students commenced a prolonged sit-in which spread to other buildings including Lowe Library.[53] With key parts of the campus held down, students issued demands for Columbia to break ties with IDA, to end construction at Morningside Park, and to provide amnesty for everyone involved in the sit-ins. On April 30, the university's response came in the form of the NYPD storming in and aggressively dragging students out of occupied buildings. The toll came to this: 700 students arrested, 150 injured, and 30 suspended. But the protests and arrests continued throughout May, until the university agreed to sever ties with IDA and cancelled plans to pave Morningside Park.

As the Columbia protests were winding down, the far more turbulent "May '68" events in Paris were gaining momentum with escalating protests, riots, strikes, and clashes with students and workers against universities, industries, and police. Like many US cities, Paris was convulsed by student demonstrations and general social unrest, but French students went far beyond their American counterparts who inspired them by forming alliances with workers. The dynamics of May '68 began when a group of revolutionary students, to be known as the Enragés, occupied buildings at the University of Nanterre to protest the unbearable conditions of university life and their subservience to institutional authority in general, including the family and the state.[54] Like many intellectuals and artists, the Enragés were strongly influenced by Guy Debord and the Situationist International (SI)—cultural radicals who updated Marx's critique of industrial capitalism and alienated labor for the conditions of post-war consumer society and the alienation rife throughout everyday life, such as described in the scathing tract entitled *The Poverty of Student Life* (1966). Similar to disaffected American students, French students objected to a curriculum they found stale, boring, and irrelevant to personal growth and social change. Like the SDS, French students challenged the bureaucratic, domineering, and crudely utilitarian nature of a university system that was a microcosm of a dehumanized society in the service of capitalism.

From the outskirts of Paris in Nanterre, the Enragés settled into the Latin Quarter where, joined by sundry high school and university students, radicals, and SI members, they occupied the prestigious Sorbonne University. Police efforts to take back the building were repelled by vociferous chants, a hail of bottles and rocks, and makeshift barricades. The struggle advanced greatly in numbers and political significance once students joined labor in taking over workplaces and conducting a General Strike that paralyzed the country and prompted a stunned President De Gaulle to flee to Germany. But the formidable power of the student-worker alliance soon dissipated as the French Communist Party supported its bureaucratic compliment in the state, as the government and police reclaimed occupied schools and factories, and as Gaullists and their allies won big in the June elections.

The revolutionary struggles "failed," but students and workers made history, and their gutsy battles continue to inspire oppositional movements. Whatever the shortcomings of May 68, French students showed the world it was possible to rebel against alienation and exploitation, to reclaim subjectivity in the pacifying society of the spectacle, and to change history according to a moral and political vision far superior to the brutality and greed driving the capitalist rulers. In 1967–1968, students were demonstrating for free speech and other rights in countries such as Germany, Poland, Yugoslavia, Prague, Mexico City, Brazil, Chile, and Pakistan. In the short but exhilarating span of a decade, student radicals had changed the world, and academic life would never be the same.

It is important to stress that the groundwork for advancing and protecting academic freedom was laid down by students, not by professors—by the youth, the counterculture, and the New Left, none of whom had titles, positions, reputations, retirement packages, sponsors, bosses, or any such ballast. Independent of any system, and bereft of material possessions and social status, students escaped the gravitational pull of egoism and conformity to boldly pursue their desires and dreams. With nothing to lose but their library privileges, students didn't just *speak* truth to power, they *used power* to overturn established "truth." They fought for free speech and against academic repression, and yet were repressed in a far more fundamental and brutal way—not by politicians, administrators, and bureaucrats legislating their discourse, but rather by cops attacking, beating, gassing, and jailing them.

For the material and institutional reasons just described, it is problematic to look for professors to lead a social movement or group, given that for the most part they are politically vulnerable, economically insecure, and psychologically preoccupied with status and careerism. One should rather expect change to come from idealist and unencumbered students—and not all students, sadly, but specifically undergraduates, because graduate students are all-too-often as obsessed with jobs and careers as are their professors (although of course some have led efforts, for example, to unionize their teaching and form alliances with university staff and workers). It was students who organized the takeovers of campuses in the 1960s and 70s and stirred progressive change in society. It was students as young as Ruby Bridges who, at age six, put her life on the line to end segregation. It was students, not faculty, who sat in trees in UC Berkeley to protect the environment. It was students at Evergreen College who played a key role in organizing the "Battle in Seattle" in 1999. And it is students and youth in the animal and Earth liberation movements who, today, keep resistance alive. So, as Paulo Freire stressed to his fellow colleagues, the best teachers often are the students.

But let us not forget the times when students paid the biggest price for political activism, losing their lives not their jobs. Arguably, *the most momentous case of academic repression* occurred on May 4, 1970 at Kent State University, Ohio, during a protest against the American invasion of Cambodia, an event state Governor James Rhodes tried to preempt by declaring a state of emergency and ordering 1,000 National Guardsmen for "crowd control" on campus. After a series of skirmishes with protestors, and unsuccessful in their attempts to disperse them, a squadron of seventy-seven guards turned and fired wildly into groups of students, wounding nine and killing four, two of the dead being non-protestors walking to class.

Culture Wars, Round I: 1960–2001

"Who is in your face here? Who started this? Who is on the offensive? Who is pushing the envelope? The answer is obvious. A radical Left aided by a cultural elite that detests Christianity and finds Christian moral tenets reactionary and repressive is hell-bent on pushing its amoral values and imposing its ideology on our nation. The unwisdom of what the Hollywood and the Left are about should be transparent to all."

—Pat Buchanan

Amidst the 1960s and its aftermath, a brief yet unprecedented burst of mass political energy focused on resisting authority, challenging hierarchical society, defying the US imperialist war machine, exposing the bankruptcy of academia, ripping apart the hypocrisy of American capitalism as the pinnacle of "civilization," and generating a counterculture subversive in everything from its hairstyle, fashion, rock beats, drug use, and search for alternative modes of thinking and consciousness. Conservative hegemony was threatened for the first time from a phalanx of anti-establishment forces and through a large-scale social upheaval directed against the old order. The onslaught of new lifestyles, cultures, theories, critical methods, and pioneering radical analysis of US capitalism, imperialism, racism, sexism, authority, and hierarchy of virtually any kind stunned (and appalled) the political right. The White Male Christian Elite and sundry traditionalists were galvanized when they realized that these ideas flowed from emerging *social movements* trying to realize, radicalize, and institutionalize the norms of democracy, equality, rights, inherent worth, and diversity. The political forces that etched such a deep imprint on American life from the 60s onward pitted these progressive ideals—the product of eighteenth century enlightenment, revolution, and armed struggle—against the odious ideologies and systems of prejudice, discrimination, bigotry, homogeneity, and domination.

Despite widespread dissatisfaction with higher learning institutions as a microcosm of an oppressive, violent, utilitarian, market-dominated society, many students viewed careers in higher education as a desirable alternative to the frenzied conformist life in corporate America; to the mindless authoritarianism and naked violence of military genocide in Vietnam; to the impoverished, debt-strapped, and exploited existence of blue-collar workers; and to any number of abysmal options for young adults infused with hope for a better world. And whereas, after the exhaustion of the 60s, many retreated to building communes and "getting back to the land," others looked to academia to realize career aspirations as scholars and teachers. Certainly, higher education was a way to keep the dream of social change alive, and if there was an institution where non-conformists could survive it was in America's colleges and universities.

Reflecting changing trends in society, such as represented and bolstered by affirmative action programs mandated in 1965 by President Lyndon's Executive Order, higher education became increasingly inclusive, diverse, multi-ethnic, and multicultural, no longer a bland landscape of privileged white males.[55] And so Marxists, feminists, Black liberationists, gays and lesbians, Native Americans, Chicano/as, and other minorities assumed roles as teachers and professors, as student and staff make-up diversified as well. A more liberal, radical, and diverse faculty led to new programs, courses, and syllabi that incorporated the histories, voices, and interests of those marginalized from the narratives written by and for the staid, mainstream, patriarchal, Eurocentric, and racist elites who dominated academia like any other social sector. In place of the Great White Dead Men of Western History, professors began to introduce race, class, gender, and colonialism issues into the classroom at all levels. They rejected naïve views of scholarly objectivity—whereby the mask of neutrality hides distinct interests, biases, agendas, and perspectives—to openly politicize their topics and engage students in stimulating debates over weighty social issues. With the institutionalization of programs such as Women's Studies, African American Studies, Chicano Studies, and Native American Studies, a new generation of scholars prompted a shift from the traditional Eurocentric monoculturalism to a multiculturalism that validated a host of voices and perspectives traditionally devalued, caricatured, or ignored, as they initiated analysis of philosophical, social, historical, and political issues from fruitful new standpoints.

Critiques of capitalism and imperialism; social justice movements opposing racism, sexism, and homophobia; and multiculturalism and democratization threatened the ideological and institutional hegemony of the right and triggered a *culture war* that rages to this day. The phrase "culture war," harkening back to *Kulturkampf*—the 1871–1878 battle between the German government of Otto von Bismarck and the Catholic Church—indicates that the economic and political conflicts pitting one group against another is more than a clash over production, property, profit, and power; these struggles are also a contest over ideas, values, religion, and ideology—in a word, *culture*. As Marx well understood, capitalists advanced their power over working classes and the disenfranchised, not only through monopolizing the realms of *production* (and the system of parliaments and "representative democracy" inseparably bound up with capitalist control), but also the forms of *communication* in which capitalism produces and reproduces itself through the material, institutional, and ideological-cultural realms. Culture very much includes education as a crucial means of socializing people into a materialist, competitive, individualist, work-oriented, and hierarchical worldview in which the prevailing systems of oppression are deemed to be good, just, natural, inevitable, and inalterable.

As mass culture became ever more important, a determinant of consciousness in the late-nineteenth and early-twentieth centuries, Italian Marxist Antonio Gramsci, continuing a trend in Western Marxism to surpass forms of Marxist economic reductionism, focused on ideology and culture to spark revolutionary change. Gramsci emphasized the need to combat capitalist *hegemony*—ideological dominance (e.g., in media, education, religion, and popular culture) that legitimates class hierarchy and achieves control through consensus (as opposed to force)—with a *counter-hegemony*, a struggle to ignite critical consciousness, education, and new forms of thought and culture necessary to construct a revolutionary alternative to capitalism. Class struggle, in other words, cannot be separated from—and is not possible without—an ideological struggle to win the hearts and minds of the oppressed through new ideas and values.[56]

To invoke classical Marxian terminology, culture is no mere political and ideological "superstructure" derivative to the "primacy" of the economic "base" of society, but rather is itself a key terrain of social production and reproduction. Culture shapes economic and political dynamics as do commerce and the state. Gramsci's hegemony/counter-hegemony couplet applies not only to class issues but also to identity politics such as involves race and gender, for racism and patriarchy are themselves hegemonic constructions—related but not reducible to class power—that need to be contested on the ideological as well as the economic, political, and institutional fronts.[57] Contemporary culture wars are battles over concepts, not things; values, not social strata; and hot-button issues such as religion, prayer, secularism, patriotism, family, marriage, homosexuality, pornography, gun ownership, the portrayal of sex and violence in mass media, the "Hollywood elite," and the ethics of life and death (abortion, euthanasia, stem cell research). Although identifiable patterns emerge, there is no mechanical correlation between class and values, such that by knowing a person's class position one could read off their morals and values. The territorial lines of culture clash, therefore, are not between rich and poor but rather between conservative/traditionalist and liberal/progressive orientations.

Consequently, although many political possibilities exist, a perennial but increasingly intense characteristic of the American political scene has been the bifurcation between conservative and liberal and the bitter battles fought across the party lines of Republican vs. Democratic.[58] Radicals who oppose the capitalist system at its core, however, know that these seemingly monumental clashes are mere scuffles and sibling rivalries between opponents whose similarities—e.g., jingoistic, militaristic, and imperialistic braggadocio that capitalism is the best system ever devised and the US is the greatest country in the world—are more significant than their differences. In the current form of postindustrial consumer capitalism, class politics obviously persist—such as play out, for instance, in tax breaks for the rich, attacks on workers' wages and benefits, and massive bailouts for Wall Street with nothing doled out to Main Street—but they are often hidden and subdued. Culture wars, therefore, can serve as a distraction from class domination and provide an illusory condition of unity between the New York CEO and the rural Kansas farmer. Thus, as we have learned indelibly in recent election periods, the "one nation" of the United States, in fact, is deeply divided along lines such as class (with all its attendant problems ranging from elite control to poverty, homelessness, and unemployment). Mass media representations, however, gloss over the prodigious ethical and political issues of social and economic inequality to focus on ideological divisions—a country cleaved apart at the seams of Red and Blue states, Republicans and Democrats, and conservatives and liberals.[59]

These debates, in turn, are decisively framed and influenced by over a century of rabid anti-communism *entrenched* in US society, whereby anything short of a messianic embrace of God, Guns, Profit, and Flag is easily reviled as subversive, anti-American, and communist. Core liberal values—such as openness, tolerance, equality, justice, respect for diversity, and separation of Church and State—which formed the institutional and philosophical setting of the nation are vilified by arch-conservatives and the Christian Right as antithetical to the greatness, glory, and security of America. At least since the McCarthy era, conservatives have demonized liberalism and insidiously erased the substantive differences between liberals and leftists—fundamentally, the former seek to reform capitalism while the latter see systemic problems resolvable only through revolutionary social transformation. Consequently, in this crude conflating mindset, liberalism shades into socialism or communism and thus into anti-Americanism or even support of terrorism.[60] The hostility is especially intense in times of war or social crisis, and especially after the 9/11 attacks, and conservatives expect everyone to be "patriotic." This means to fall in line unquestioningly with government policy, and those who do not are traitors who "hate" their country and either intentionally or unintentionally aid the enemy, be it the Kremlin or Al Qaeda. The right is especially concerned when dissent comes from the quarters of academia, for they believe that, since the 1960s, academia "has been the major American institution most alienated from the rest of the country."[61]

Trying to hold back the rising tides of democracy, contemporary conservatives cling to their Eurocentric, Christian, white, patriarchal, racist, heterosexist power base amidst dynamic transformations involving science, secularism, immigration, civil rights, feminism, gay and lesbian rights, multiculturalism, popular culture, mass media, and so on. Like their seventeenth- and eighteenth-century predecessors in the Church and the monarchy, struggling to survive in the transition from a theocratic medievalism to a secular capitalist modernity, and with Friedrich Nietzsche's own *ressentiment* against nineteenth-century democratization, the contemporary right tends to equate change with corruption and decay of an eternal, natural, and superior cosmological and social order.[62]

Although conservative/liberal culture wars can be traced back at least to 1953, when the conservative Intercollegiate Studies Institute was founded to counter teachings allegedly promoting hostility to free markets and Western civilization as a whole (see Giroux in this volume), and we can certainly see conservative reaction driving academic repression even earlier in the 1939 debacle involving Bertrand Russell, the boundary line between "conservative" and "liberal" was not sharply drawn until the mid-1980s. For it was then that the Manichean battle between Good and Evil (that is, between conservatives and liberals, as the aggressor right-wing camp framed it) that dynamic social and political changes and conflicts had been transcoded in academia as well, leading to an ideological *battle royale* being fought on campuses from coast-to-coast. The composition of the professoriate had shifted, such that women, people of color, and progressives were better (certainly not adequately) represented. Entire new programs advancing the critical perspectives of women, Blacks, Chicano/as, and others were emerging. The canon and syllabi were changing dramatically as new voices and critical perspectives challenged entrenched biases. And progressive students began to fight discrimination on their campuses, such as through the controversial process of drafting "speech codes" that banned any speech or action deemed to be hostile, hateful, bigoted, or that used "fighting words."

Progressives' efforts to revitalize and democratize the Western canon and to rethink the stagnant positivism of science and philosophy ignited outrage among conservatives who saw barbarians at the gate. Conservatives deeply resented the battering ram smashing the doors of their decrepit ideological fortress, and they mobilized a massive counterstrike that revived the sleaziest tactics of the McCarthy school of political repression, while pioneering a number of new and more insidious strategies as well. The right vilified all academic trends since the 1960s, such as included various critical theories; the development of programs studying gender, race, sexuality, and multicultural difference; and engagements of mass, popular, and electronic media culture. Attached to religion-inspired notions of "objectivity" and "truth," conservatives bemoaned the alleged decline of academic standards, the so-called subversion of academic canons and disciplines, and the politicizing of education—as if it were not already politicized and framed by their own political ideologies. Hostile reactionaries clinging to putrescent Platonic metaphysics argued that foundational courses (such as Introduction to Composition) were being turned into "Marxism 101"; reactive, vindictive, hostile, and paranoiac, they saw genuine concerns for diversity, inclusiveness, and social justice as "nothing more than a justification for Marxist and radical-left designs."[63] Clearly, the anti-communist hysteria of Red Scares and McCarthyism continued to motivate and inform contemporary conservative critiques of radical scholarship as, indeed, they persist to this day.

Perhaps the first clear opening shot from the right came with the publication of Allan Bloom's book, *The Closing of the American Mind* (1987), a stuffy, uptight, high-brow, supercilious rant against the "insidious" influences of the 1960s counterculture, rock and roll and MTV, and the alleged relativist outlook of multiculturalism. For Bloom, the rise of leftism, multiculturalism, and mass culture contributed to the

decline of academic rigor, student thinking capacities, moral standards, family structure, and spiritual life as a whole—a paradigm shift which, for Bloom and the right, involved the destruction of everything good and golden in traditional culture. The crisis
in education, Bloom thought, reflected a larger calamity in civilization involving the
erosion of social and intellectual standards and conventional authority. The damage
can only be undone, he argued, through a return to pre-1960s religious and social life,
and the eradication of viruses of multiculturalism and postmodernism so that universities could return to the revered teachings of Socrates, Plato, Augustine, Descartes,
and other luminaries in the "Great Books" programs.

Liberals denounced Bloom's book as elitist, intolerant, and dogmatic, but it
breathed life into the moribund body of the right who championed it as a vindication of
conservative values. On its heels came a slew of increasingly hysterical diatribes against
sweeping social changes and the liberal/left sector in academia. The writings reflecting
and driving the culture war in the 80s and 90s included William Bennett's homage to
ancient virtues (mostly pitched to children), the jingoistic odes to patriotism, and the
revenge-driven, emotionally overheated, simplistic screeds against leftism, feminism,
multiculturalism, and postmodernism by David Horowitz and Dinesh D'Souza. Roger
Kimball's book, *Tenured Radicals: How Politics Has Corrupted Our Higher Education*
(1990), aimed "to expose these recent developments in the academic study of humanities for what they are: ideologically motivated assaults on the intellectual and moral
substance of our culture."[64] Kimball believes that an insidious postmodernism—in the
hands of an "elitist academic Left"—has hijacked the humanities, waged war against the
Enlightenment, diluted the Western canon with "diversity," politicized timeless truths,
and replaced classical rigor with alleged shoddy scholarship.

As scientists fought the external battle against a vacuous fundamentalism (re-
packaged as "intelligent design" theory) that persisted a century and a half after the
publication of Darwin's *On the Origin of Species* (1859), mainstream science fought an
internal battle within the quarters of academia itself. By the 1990s, the culture wars had
erupted into a "*science wars*" as a new breed of theorists began to criticize capitalist and
Western notions and uses of science and technology. According to classic conceptions
that have prevailed from the Greeks to the present, Western reason transcends the
vicissitudes of strife, contingency, illusion, and change in its pursuit of Truth, Beauty,
and the Good. This God-like Reason, champions of modern science argue, is able to
accurately grasp the Real through cognitive representations that "correspond" to the
objective world, and this project comes to a stunning climax with the achievements of
modern mathematics, science, and technology, which with free markets are the prime
drivers of Progress and thus the quantitative and qualitative enhancement of life.

Every element of these claims has been subjected to rigorous scrutiny and
critique in the last two decades by Marxists, feminists, multiculturalists, deconstruc-

tionists, postmodernists, postcolonialists, and others. From various perspectives, these critics rejected the positivist argument that knowledge was objective by situating it in its full historical and social context. They worked out the implications of Foucault's theory of knowledge/power—the dialectic of knowledge as power and power as knowledge— that revealed the interests behind "disinterested" knowledge, which pursued control over the social and natural worlds, in a way that fused objectives of power, profit, and privatization.[65] From various angles, radical academics argued that scientific knowledge is a social construction tainted with racist, sexist, and classist biases, and that science and technology are hardly unambiguous harbingers of progress to the world's peoples.

The questioning of scientific epistemology took on a far broader and more consequential term with critical scrutiny of the university institution itself, by charting the transformations of the mission and function of universities in the post-war era. Radicals threw down the gauntlet, and there was no shortage of positivists and Eurocentrists to pick it up. Two apologists in particular tried to meet the challenge in the form of a screed replete with ad hominems, misrepresentations, and straw arguments against opponents they were ill-equipped to understand. Paul Gross and Norman Levitt's *Higher Superstition: The Academic Left and Its Quarrels with Science* (1994) uncritically reproduced Kimball's mythology of a ubiquitous and omnipotent "academic Left" and portrayed contemporary critics as a hodge-podge of disaffected, atavistic, scientific illiterates out to subvert rationality and undermine the foundations of Western civilization (see Best and Kellner in this volume).[66]

The repressive nature of liberal/left ideology, conservatives argued, was evident in the strict "hate-speech" codes many universities began adopting in the 1980s, such as banned "harmful" or "offensive" language (e.g., racial, sexist, or homophobic epithets). Conservatives vilified PC norms as fascist, and valorized the "politically incorrect"—including repugnant discriminatory views—as good, free, and liberating from liberal/left moralizing. On the basis of flimsy and false anecdotes and outrageous over generalizations, they argued that leftist professors abused their power by dogmatically enforcing their views as absolute truth and chastising students who voiced contrary opinions. Allegedly, the academic left and their student progeny shouted down, silenced, and shamed anyone who dared to question their dicta, firing off epithets such as "Racist!," "Sexist!," "Homophobe!," "Eurocentrist!," and "Elitist!"

Throughout the 1990s, the culture wars moved from the confines of academia to the white hot glare of mainstream media spectacle. Reactionary demagogues like Rush Limbaugh, Bill O'Reilly, Pat Buchanan, Sean Hannity, Michael Savage, Laura Ingram, and Ann Coulter gave full play to venomous streams of anti-communism, anti-liberalism, and anti-intellectualism, while spewing bilious hate-speech against decadent liberalism. With potent propaganda platforms like nationally-syndicated radio shows and Fox News, they excoriated secularism and multiculturalism and tarred and feathered liberals as enemies of America who must be purged.[67]

Once, the enemy of the right was communism, a European foe out to destroy our economy, infiltrate our schools, capture the entertainment industry, and steal our nuclear secrets and annihilate us. But as the communist menace crumbled, broken up under its own bureaucratic weight, new enemies were needed to justify militarism, imperialism, and a despotic state. In the 1990s, the external threat shifted to Muslim extremists and jihadists, but a new internal threat emerged as well: no longer the communist left, but rather the "liberal left." Bloom, Kimball, Horowitz, D'Souza, O'Reilly, and Coulter tirelessly chant the same refrain that liberals control the media, dominate the schools, spread Godlessness and secular poison, and undermine sacred institutions such as marriage. Indeed, in works such as *The Enemy At Home: The Cultural Left and Its Responsibility for 9/11* (2007), D'Souza ignores US imperialism, military bases in Saudi Arabia, hard-line support of Israel, torture of Muslim prisoners, slaughter of Iraqi civilians, and global economic policies that impoverish nations and produce armies of desperate people eager to attack "Satan," in order to scapegoat the "cultural left" as the prime cause of a social decadence, depravity, and licentiousness so blatant it inflames terrorist hatred and inspires jihadist attacks!

The realities of post-60s academic life are completely unrecognizable in the fusillade of right-wing distortions, caricatures, stereotypes, false generalizations, and outright lies and ignorance. Their truth claims implode under the weight of ironies, contradictions, falsehoods, and hypocrisies. The demonization of liberals and all varieties of academic progressives as "left," the hatred of anything left of fascism, the scapegoating of the "enemy within" as the cause of all problems—rather than corporate capitalism, globalization, imperialism, and neoliberalism—shows that well into the twenty-first century *anti-communism and McCarthyism are alive and well*. In fact, anti-communism, anti-liberalism, and anti-terrorism/Islam have fused into something even more menacing, that is, *neo-McCarthyism*, which is poised to complete the destruction of every meaningful right and liberty yet to be destroyed by McCarthyism, the FBI, the National Security Agency (NSA), corporate domination of the political process. And even though Obama himself was targeted as a socialist and communist by the official hate machines of the Republican Party (which cannot tell the difference between John Maynard Kaynes and Karl Marx), he and many fellow democrats are themselves part of the neo-McCarthyite attack on civil liberties that stems from their post-9/11 mentalities and embrace of Bush's "war on terrorism," in principle if not in name.

While the problems in the conservative critique of the liberal/left viewpoints are legion, we will limit ourselves here to identifying four key misrepresentations.

These are: (1) the "academic left" as a whole, (2) "political correctness," (3) "multicultural relativism," and (4) critical pedagogy.

The fallacies begin with the very term "academic left," a totalizing generalization that, in McCarthyesque fashion, elides the substantive difference between liberals and radicals, who have less in common with one another than liberals have with conservatives. In fact, the coinage "academic left" conflates a myriad of disparate and often conflicting standpoints in one handy multipurpose phrase that serves less as a clarifying construct than as an obfuscation and homonym smear. Moreover, the hoary notion of an "academic left" in control of higher education and prevailing over conservatives like a Mafioso is as absurd as leftists controlling the US military-industrial complex.

In the 1960s, the left coined the phrase "politically correct" as an ironic and self-critical reference against potential dogmatism. In the 1980s, however, the right landed on a brilliant strategy and effective propaganda tool by appropriating the term, changing it to a pejorative meaning (often expressed as "PC"), and turning it against liberals and the left to characterize—or rather, caricature—them as smug, self-righteous, dogmatic, humorless, over-sensitive authoritarians hell-bent on policing thought, language, and behavior.[68] For, whereas liberal/left critiques proceeded on the grounds that conservative-dominated university structures were authoritarian and repressive, the right now could (disingenuously) argue that a hegemonic left had stormed the citadels, subverted words and knowledge to their political goals, and imposed a despotic culture of intolerance antithetical to free speech, education, and the First Amendment. The critique of "left-McCarthyism" allowed conservatives to play the role of victim, pariah, and minority outcast, and to uphold themselves as the real champions of free speech and diversity, as well as the guardians of morality and markets, of piety and prosperity, of all that marks Western culture as the superior "civilization" it is in their imagination.

In decades of academic experience among us we have not witnessed the kind of hostile teaching, political vendettas, or holier-than-thou sanctimony attributed to progressives, and know even that seasoned conservatives with an ounce of intellectual honesty reject these accusations as politically motivated and factually wrong. In *The Myth of Political Correctness: The Conservative Attack on Higher Education*, John Wilson refutes the right-wing charge that liberal/left progressives programmatically impose rigid free speech codes onto the campus body and tendentiously impose their own moral-political standards onto others. Through detailed case studies, Wilson concludes that left-wing "PC fascism is a *myth*, a falsehood, a chimera fabricated by the right to present themselves as the party of liberty and free speech."[69]

To be sure, while some schools found a reasonable balance between freedom and censorship, others drafted vague speech codes that clearly overreached legitimate boundaries.[70] In the early 1990s, for example, students at Antioch College, a small liberal arts school in Ohio, proposed enforcing a "sexual charter" that mandated explicit verbal consent and consensual agreement between partners before each step in the progression of sexual activity. This policy turned a valid concern (protecting women from sexual assault) into an invalid lunacy (demonizing men, infantilizing women, and mediating intimacy through bureaucratic protocol).[71] Moreover, since the 1960s, progressive students and faculty in colleges and universities throughout the country have often shouted down, assailed, pelted, and blocked conservatives from speaking on their campuses, thereby denying others the right to free speech they demand for themselves.[72]And in the infamous Duke Lacrosse case in March 2006, progressives passed instant judgment on student athletes falsely accused of rape. Such actions lend credence to the conservative argument that the left is intolerant and the right are the true champions of freedom.

But while there are instances of "PC" ideals being taken too far, these are exceptions to the rule that are hardly representative of most cases. The PC fascism charge could not more crudely distort the genuine moral intention of non-bigoted people trying to sensitize other people to language and behaviors (whether this involves blatantly insensitive and ignorant actions like a fraternity "slave auctions" or use of ablist metaphors such as "blind" and "lame" that are prejudiced, discriminatory, or hurtful). What the right unilaterally derides as "PC" involves education, dialogue, and practical changes to make society more democratic, inclusive, and respectful of all.

The right countered progressive attacks on discrimination, inequality, and social oppression by lifting an ironic in-joke among leftists, but they dodged the critique of hierarchy and oppression to manufacture an alleged left-wing fascism and intolerance. While they waged a holy war against the alleged relativism inherent in multiculturalism and postmodernism, the right failed to see that attacks on racism, sexism, homophobia, and the like come from a valid moral point of view that is grounded in the quintessential American discourse and tradition of rights, equality, and justice. To reject these critiques as "fascist" shreds the rational criteria needed to attack a moral wrong, and it is precisely the right-wing position, not the so-called politically correct view, which is relativistic. An additional irony is that conservatives have their own brand of morally, politically, and theologically "correct" thinking and behavior. Wilson captures part of the problem in his book, *Patriotic Correctness: Academic Freedom and its Enemies*, which exposes how the right imposes dogmatic jingoism as the litmus test for legitimate thought and acceptable discourse.[73]

Conservatives lean heavily on God, State, Markets, Order, Natural Law, and other Platonic verities as planks to stabilize their crumbling values and hierarchies; but these flimsy conceptual grounds are supported only through a question-begging appeal to tradition as something whose value and legitimacy has to be demonstrated not only asserted (over and over again). Conservatives in effect have no conceptual moorings, and thus their moral systems crumble into the very moral nihilism they smugly think plague the secular left. In truth, liberals and radicals often attempt to ground social criticism in a normative and logical framework established through rational justification and argumentation—hardly symptomatic of relativism. Yet, by denying that charges of racism, sexism, and homophobia could have any non-arbitrary meaning, normative force, and factual truth, and insisting instead that they are just emotive expressions of the "academic left" will to power, conservatives are the true relativists and nihilists.

If by "left" one means a viewpoint predicated on open-mindedness, tolerance, respect of difference, and earnest dialogue, regardless of the political or ideological content, this approach is simply the instantiation of the ideals of the modern liberal tradition. For over two centuries, liberals (who originated capitalism and *laissez-faire* philosophy, after all) have espoused the professorial standards appropriate to higher learning and democracy itself, whereas, in contrast, the conservative view abhors change and responds to any criticism of tradition as a hostile threat to be vanquished. Since the eighteenth century, to be "liberal" has consistently meant to be open-minded, respectful of difference, and tolerant of dissent; indeed, these are sound pedagogical values, such as radicals like Giroux and McLaren passionately defend in their writing and in practice in their classroom. But to be open and tolerant does not mean to be uncritical, to be disarmed from advancing normative positions, or to be trapped in a relativism where all views have equal logical validity and moral weight.

The flip-side of the strategy to demonize professors is to *infantilize students*. If progressive professors are derisive dogmatists who turn the podium into a bully pulpit, who transubstantiate words into scripture, who force-feed students ideological pabulum, who ridicule and humiliate anyone who dares to question their omniscience, and who completely abdicate their pedagogical responsibilities, then students are protoplasmic ooze devoid of brains, spines, or wills, nothing but helpless victims and empty vessels for left-wing Goebbels to fill with ideological cement. Conservatives encourage students to complain about "being forced" to read leftist literature in a class, as if positions opposed to their own are automatically and in all senses invalid, as if students should not encounter as many perspectives as possible, as if their job is not to cut and run but to stay and fight—to grow in critical thinking through debate, dialogue, and encounter with positions that test the mettle of one's own. Thus, conservatives actually undercut the role of the higher education, and the reality behind the appearance of paternal concern for students is that conservative demagogues cynically exploit them as means to their own political ends.

The Evolution of Student Activism

"Education either functions as an instrument which is used to facilitate integration of the younger generation into the logic of the present system and bring about conformity or it becomes the practice of freedom, the means by which men and women deal critically and creatively with reality and discover how to participate in the transformation of their world."

—Paulo Freire

Despite the right-wing betrayal of the very function and meaning of a university—which is to think, grow, and learn, and to assume responsibility for one's development—the myth of the apathetic and narcissistic "Generation X" student was exploded with the politicization of students in conjunction with the effects of corporate globalization and the rise of anti/alter-globalization struggles that sought democracy, justice, rights, ecology, and autonomy against the juggernaut of Western capitalists, bankers, lenders, and "developers." To be sure, there never was a death of student activism and idealism once the 60s went out with a whimper by the mid-70s; these political energies were channeled into sustaining fragments of the civil rights and feminist cause and redirected into advancing young or new politics relating to the environment, nuclear arms and energy, gay and lesbian (and later transgendered and transsexual issues), ablism, and animal rights. In the 1980s, students on campuses throughout the nation were passionately involved in the fight against US imperialism in Central America and the global effort to take down apartheid in South Africa, which involved pressuring university boards to fully divest as part of a very effective strategy of economic boycott. At the same time, different minority and oppressed groups were focusing on their own cultures and histories, developing a new form of "identity politics" that pursued each group's differences and unique history and culture apart from shared bonds, common interests, and related forms of oppression. Nevertheless, the heightened political awareness that flowed from identity politics helped to spark a critique of the canon and traditional forms of knowledge such as erupted in the first major round of culture wars described above.

The novel character of student activism during the 1990s, therefore, had nothing to do with a shift from passivity and despair to a rediscovery of meaning and politics; rather, the shift was from single-issue struggles and the fragmented identity politics of the 1980s to alliance politics and organizing against global capitalism in the recognition that it was the cause of systemically related problems involving human rights, labor standards, quality of living, biodiversity, and the environment. Solidarity across racial and gender lines on the same campus was rare enough, never mind privileged students building bridges with labor and championing the cause of the global underclass.

Moving from the local to the global, student activists supported the janitorial and service workers of their own universities in their demands for better wages and working conditions. Students also have, for decades, mobilized around issues such as tuition hikes and book costs, feeling that corporate greed endangers their ability to acquire a good education. Grasping the bigger picture, however, students at schools throughout the country, from Oregon and Madison to the University of Pennsylvania, Harvard, and Yale were taking on corporations like Nike for producing clothing made in sweatshops that intensely exploited workers, women and children above all. Student activists insisted that their universities replace industry-backed monitoring (through the "Fair Labor Association") with a student-founded organization (the "Worker Rights Consortium") in alliance with scholars, activists, and workers in the Southern hemisphere.

By demanding the removal of sweatshop labor products in favor of other manufacturers, students were able to put enormous moral and economic pressure on powerful global corporations, and thereby played an instrumental role in the anti/alter-globalization movement.[74] Their struggle unfolded on three levels simultaneously: they were challenging the privileges and uncritical consumption practices of their own classes and generation, they fought for human rights and social justice as universal moral requirements, and through concrete practice, they contested the corporatization processes transforming universities.

As some student activists during the 1990s were expanding humanist politics to a global level and formulating a rich alliance politics that reached across race, class, gender, and national boundaries toward a concept and practice of global citizenship, other students were surpassing humanist boundaries altogether to criticize speciesism—the arrogant conceit that humans are superior to all other animals by virtue of their allegedly unique ability to think and reason—in ways analogous to how students during previous decades condemned racism and sexism as prejudiced and discriminatory ideologies as vacuous in logic as violent in implication. These students, intent on helping to break the formidable chains of oppression binding nonhuman animals, were part of a global movement (if less consciously structured as such) and paradigm shift. But rather than try to bridge different human groups throughout the world, their goal was to close the ontological and ethical boundaries separating "us" from "them," by recognizing that human animals belong in a rich, variegated evolutionary community with fellow sentient beings possessing equal capacities for pain and pleasure, suffering and joy, such that the interests of all sentient beings were equally deserving of respect and protection.

Student activists advanced their critique of animal exploitation throughout the university: from the dissection and research laboratories of biology and psychology; to the athletics departments exploiting animals such as bears for mascots and "entertainment"; to the school of agriculture and "animal science" promoting agribusiness, factory farming, and flesh, dairy, and egg consumption; to the cafeteria serving up the same destructive menu—causing disease in humans, suffering and slaughter of animals, resource waste, and ecological devastation—without providing healthy vegan eating options. From the animal rights standpoint, the millions of animals confined, stabbed, jabbed, poisoned, maimed, dissected, and killed, are ultimately the greatest victims of repression emanating from universities and capitalism. This is true not in the sense that nonhuman animals have been stripped of the right to free speech, which obviously is meaningless to them, but rather in the sense of being deprived of the right to their own bodies, to live free from malicious human harm and free to express their natural behaviors and lifeways. Instead, billions of animals are enslaved, exploited, tortured, and slaughtered for gain and profit, such that still in the twenty-first century, within the bastions of the most intellectual and "enlightened" communities in the world, fellow sentient beings are still regarded as no more than a mere means to crude human ends.

Thus, as anti-globalization student activists challenged corporate greed from far-flung sweatshops to their own university bookstores, animal rights activists were also challenging global pharmaceutical, biotechnology, and agriculture corporations as they sought to shed light on the closed world of vivisection and pernicious role of "animal science" on university campuses, underscoring yet another way academia is integrally wedded to the military-industrial complex. However cognizant of the larger political and economic implications of their anti-speciesism and anti-vivisection activism, student animal rights groups, like their pro-labor peers, were mounting strong challenges against global capitalism and the corporatization of the university. Indeed, whereas by the 1990s growing numbers of professors were criticizing corporation globalization in theory, students were resisting and transforming it through action.

Akin to tactics of bullying and termination that administrators apply to professors, so university brass often intimidate radical students and threaten them with expulsion (see Starr in this volume). Even at posh and affluent ivy-league universities like Harvard and Yale, graduate students trying to organize unions (often in alliance with university staff, service, and maintenance workers), and the professors bold enough to openly support them, were met with hostile defiance. Students were often threatened with expulsion, just as professors bold enough to support campus union and labor issues were sometimes fired (as happened to David Graeber at Yale).[75]

The point must be emphasized, however, that while controversial thinkers have been repressed in education circles since Socrates and the founding of university institutions, the academy would not have been possible without the repression of all social institutions of nonhuman animals and the Earth's ecology. From Aristotle to the present day, academic disciplines such as biology, physics, and philosophy have analyzed, theorized, compartmentalized, reified, manipulated, and killed living processes in brutal ways that impede the understanding and the advancement of science, and of course centers of higher learning have been decisively important for developing the domineering, hierarchical, and dysfunctional worldview of Western civilization. From the labs of medical colleges to the research areas of environmental science, nonhuman animals and the natural world have been—in some general and profound sense—the target of academic repression, and throughout the last few centuries great minds trained in the academy have identified the process of genocide, species holocaust, and ecological collapse as "progress," and thereby spawned and perpetuated the most dangerous myth of our time.

Indeed, as their towers have grown ever higher and our fences and gates splayed wider and wider, universities have divided themselves—spatially, physically, intellectually, ethically, and emotionally—from the surrounding communities (e.g., Columbia and the University of Chicago), from humanity and society at large, from obligations as citizens, and from deep attachments to the sentient, biotic, and physical world that is our source, our origin, and our home. Scholars believed that to truly research one needed to be completely objective. It is for this reason we paint our walls white, build fences, have security on campuses, give titles to researchers, and surround ourselves with needless technology that only separates us farther and father from life, which we say we are so very intellectually interested in. We have only begun to see our self-dividing actions in the name of so-called objective scholarship based in a socially constructed positivist modernist notion through marginalized and resistance politics on campuses from departments such as women's studies, ethnic and cultural studies, gender studies, queer studies, critical animal studies, disability studies, and environmental studies to name a few of the marginalized camps that challenge dominate false, socially constructed notions of scholarship. But to truly fight for a complete and ultimately inclusive place of learning, we must develop a new ethics of respect and inclusiveness for all animals and the planet as a whole.

But with the rounding of the corner into the next millennium, the entire political scene in all dimensions was about to stop in freeze-frame, as panic, fear, insecurity, and uncertainty seized hold of the country. With the culture wars already blazing into the new millennium, a tanker of fuel was about to be poured on the fire in the aftermath of 9/11. In time, it became increasingly clear: their real source of attack was not the liberal-radical professoriate, but the tenure system itself; not the takedown of the left, but the subversion of the university.

9/11, Right-wing Resurgence, and Post-Constitutional America

"If you're against the president and his policies, you're unpatriotic and rooting against America."
—Dick Cheney

"This generalized, state-generated fear has been accomplished without a shot being fired, without even an acknowledgement of the decimation of civil liberties that has occurred. The silence and

*complicity of elites is akin to what must have occurred during the Nazi consolidation of power,
and during the anti-Semitic repression, when millions of right-thinking Germans simply failed to
raise a finger against the enormity of injustice that was being institutionalized."*

—Anis Shivani

*"We lose liberty bit by bit by bit, so you have to fight even the small erosions
of fundamental rights."*

—Chris Hansen, ACLU lawyer

During the 1960s, students rallied around free speech and had a profound influence on university and social life, as professors began the work of transforming the canon into a more inclusive, diverse, and critical body of literature. But a truculent right-wing reaction, the increasing absorption of universities into the military-industrial complex, the long and menacing reign of the Bush-Cheney regime, and the phony "war on terror" that manufactured fear to justify a Presidential putsch and the criminalization of dissent—started under Bush and continued with Obama—buried this political tradition. If tyrants, demagogues, and right-wing extremists ever had an ideal opening to seize institutional control, the thunderous collapse of the Twin Towers on the clear morning of September 11, 2001 signaled the time for an aggressive offensive to take back the universities from the liberal/left and to reverse or efface progressive social gains made in academia and society since the 1960s.

9/11 instantaneously transformed the political landscape. Though a tragedy for the nation, it was a blessing for the Bush-Cheney team, the military and security corporations, and the far right, for the "new Pearl Harbor" provided the ideal justification to impose tyranny at home and to pursue Empire abroad.[76] Neoconservatives were ecstatic, as they could finally put into play pet theories such as pre-emptive strikes against a real enemy instead of a computer simulation. A motley crew of cold-war hawks, oil barons, evangelical Christians, and zealous neocons, Bush-Cheney seized advantage of the new climate of fear, intensified it in every way possible (through lies, hyperbole, false threats, ubiquitous color-scale terrorist "danger" signs, and manufactured incidents), and declared a phony, ineffectual, and misconceived "war on terrorism."

Eager to seize the occasion to advance their global agendas and to quell dissent and protest, the right declared that liberties were a luxury and security a necessity. As announced to the world in August 2006 by Bush's erstwhile UK ally, Prime Minister Tony Blair, "Global terrorism means traditional civil liberty arguments are not so much wrong as just made for another age."[77] Indeed, 9/11 marked a *sea-change* in political thought and practice, whereby republicans and democrats formed a consensus on the need to expand surveillance and intelligence, strengthen security and police, bolster the military, torture terrorist suspects, and curb civil liberties. Since taking office in

January 2009, President Barack Obama has pursued militarist, imperialist and surveillance policies that promise not "change to believe in," but rather more of the same.

After 9/11, the gloves came off and no one escaped the juggernaut of state power.[78] In actions reminiscent of the Red Scare, the Palmer Raids, and the internment of Japanese, thousands of foreigners were rounded up, jailed, and/or deported without evidence of wrongdoing, and citizens also came under attack.[79] The air thickened with fear, conformity, and jingoism, as the nation rushed into war and goose-stepped deeper into a fascist police state that matched unlimited powers with zero degrees of accountability. Signaling the tyranny to come, Bush warned the world that, "If you're not with us, you're against us," but he was speaking also to any American who dared to challenge his (and Cheney's) bold usurping of power. Recycling the old bumper sticker bromide, "America: Love it or Leave it!," Bush, the far right, and Democrat collaborationists viewed constructive criticism of government policies in Afghanistan and Iraq as a betrayal of the country rather than a manifestation of citizen duty.

Press secretary Ari Fleischer warned people in academia and society overall "to watch what they say, watch what they do"—the implication being that if they didn't police their own actions, the government would do it for them. The Bush team and much of the corporate media framed critics of the Iraq war as traitors who give "aid and comfort" to the enemy. In September 2003, Secretary of Defense Donald Rumsfeld intoned that "critics of the Bush Administration's Iraq policy are encouraging terrorists and complicating the ongoing US war on terrorism," and three years later compared war critics to Nazi "appeasers." Dissent, and the right to free speech upon which it is based, was transmogrified into a value that is alien rather than integral to the US, and those who practiced it were widely denounced by the government and far right as allies of Nazis and terrorists rather than citizens and patriots. The FBI arrested people for wearing the wrong political T-shirts, hanging anti-Bush posters in their dorm room, or reading a provocative book.

On October 26th, less than two months after the 9/11 attacks, the government dusted off documents written for just such an occasion to debut the twenty-first century Security State. The 342-page tome, perversely called the USA PATRIOT Act was designed to supersede the Constitution by centralizing authority in the Executive branch of government, blatantly invading privacy rights, and criminalizing dissent. The document was rammed through Congress literally overnight; few read it and fewer still dared to challenge it, fearful of being labeled as weak, unpatriotic, or "soft on terrorism" in dire times.[80] Democrats caved in, the media championed ill-conceived and illicit wars, the public reveled in a jingoistic and xenophobic frenzy, and citizens were neither secure nor free.

The USA PATRIOT Act dissolves the system of checks and balances that support the Constitution, as the Executive Branch of government seizes control of legislation and the courts. Power became increasingly concentrated in the Bush's Leviathan state of fear and despotism. Under authority of this Act, with virtually no oversight, the government can access citizens' reading and purchasing records at libraries and bookstores; seize school, medical, banking, and travel records; monitor phone and email communications; undertake clandestine sneak and peek operations in homes and workplaces; and label any organization opposed to government policies as a terrorist threat. The USA PATRIOT Act thereby violates core constitutional rights, such as the First Amendment (the right to free speech and freedom of assembly), the Fourth (the right to security from unreasonable search and seizures), the Fifth and Sixth (rights to basic protections during criminal proceedings), and the Fourteenth (the right to equal protection for both citizens and non-citizens). The USA PATRIOT Act also created the new legal category of "domestic terrorism" that occurs when a person's action "appears to be intended to intimidate or coerce a civilian population [or] to influence the policy of government by intimidation or coercion." Purposely vague and amorphous, this definition of terrorism can expand to fit civil disobedience and virtually any anti-state remonstration, such that "protest" and "coercion," "citizen" and "terrorist," are cunningly conflated in a semantic chicanery and legal despotism that cast a chilling effect on free expression of all kinds.

In a nightmare replay of the 1950s, domestic activists of all kinds were surveilled, hassled, threatened, arrested, roughed up, subpoenaed to grand juries, and stripped of basic rights. With Big Business answering to Big Brother, telecommunication companies aided the government in conducting secret domestic spying programs; blatantly violating the First Amendment right to free speech and the Fourth Amendment right to security from unreasonable search and seizures. Bush used illegal wiretaps with impunity, and Congress granted immunity to his partners in crime, including AT&T, Sprint, Nextel, and Verizon.[81] The Defense Department, the FBI Joint Terrorism Task Force, the Department of Homeland Security, and local police forces everywhere surveilled "suspects" and combined data on citizen activities into a massive "terrorist" information bank, using systems such as FACTS (Factual Analysis Criminal Threat Solution).[82] The state surveilled *all* communications of *all* citizens, using sophisticated data mining systems such as Carnivore, Total Information Awareness, and MATRIX (Multistate Anti-Terrorism Information Exchange). With Bin Laden running loose, Al Qaeda plotting additional strikes, and the airlines, trains, ports, and nuclear power plants completely vulnerable to attack, the FBI was heavily involved in monitoring and disrupting the entire spectrum of citizen activism. The FBI and law enforcement were in hot pursuit not only of the top two "domestic terrorist" groups—the Animal Liberation Front and the Earth Liberation Front—but also above ground and legal groups including PETA, Greenpeace, anti-war protestors, university student organizations, Food Not Bombs (which provides free food for the homeless), and even vegetarian societies.

The entire spectrum of citizens' political activities were surveilled and documented as "domestic terrorist" suspects.

With the events of 9/11, the US entered a neo-McCarthyist period rooted in witchhunts, political persecution, and criminalization of dissent. The evil Other of Communism has been superseded by the new threat of Terrorism, both foreign and domestic. Now as then, the government declares the nation to be in a permanent state of danger, such that security, not freedom, must become the overriding concern. The alleged dangers posed by foreign terrorists are used to justify the attack on "domestic terrorists" within, and in a hysterical climate the domestic terrorist is any and every citizen expressing dissent. The Red Scare of communism morphed into the "Green Scare" of "ecoterrorism," and militant animal rights activists and environmentalists became prime targets given their bold attacks on corporate, state, and university "property" and the flames of resistance they kept alive.[83] To give the most recent vivid example of political repression and prosecution of (what once was) legal protest activities, four animal rights activists—the "AETA 4"—were arrested in February 2009 and charged with violating the Animal Enterprise Terrorism Act, and are facing up to five years in prison for picketing on the sidewalks in front of vivisectors' homes.

The USA PATRIOT Act authorizes the government to deny federal funding to colleges that ban the CIA from recruiting on their campuses. It grants the state complete access to student records and initiated increased scrutiny of faculty who teach controversial areas like Middle Eastern Studies. Researchers who do not toe the neocon line are considered security risks. The USA PATRIOT Act also revived the "ideological exclusion" of leftists, scholars, artists, and others for crimes such as voicing criticism of the Iraq war or opposing Israeli assaults on Palestine, dissenting viewpoints contorted and twisted into support for "terrorist activities." In clear violation of the First Amendment, the State Department blocked many artists, scholars, and activists from coming to the US (thereby also barring citizens from hearing their viewpoints) and even from taking academic positions offered to them (see Habib and Castro in this volume).[84]

As stunning as this shock-and-awe assault on civil liberties was, the USA PATRIOT Act was only the opening volley in the post-9/11 blitzkrieg on democracy. The "Domestic Security Enhancement Act of 2003," blocked when leaked to the public, aimed to criminalize nonviolent activities and to authorize secret arrests for anyone involved with or who donates to a "terrorist" organization. In October 2006, Congress passed the Military Commissions Act which granted the government unlimited powers to detain, interrogate, torture, and prosecute "enemy combatants" (which so far has included three US citizens) without a fair trial and habeas corpus rights, within military tribunal conditions that the word "Kafka-esque" barely begins to describe. The 2007 Defense Authorization Bill nullified the Insurrection Act of 1807 and the Posse Comitatus Act of 1878, two laws that limit federal government power to deploy armed forces for domestic law enforcement. The bill authorized the military to disperse not only "insurgents," but also "those obstructing the enforcement of the laws," granting presidents the power to declare martial law to restore public order—which smacks loudly of fascism.[85]

Moreover, Congress initiated another menacing move against academic freedom, one that reflects the neoconservative doctrine of pre-emptive strikes and would likely pit conservative professors against radical faculty in a legal and political forum, rather than just caustic exchanges in cyberspace. In October 2007, the House overwhelmingly passed by a vote of 404:6 "The Violent Radicalization and Homegrown Terrorism Prevention Act" (H.R. 1955).[86] The "thought crime prevention bill," as opponents called it, would coordinate academics, policy-makers, and members of law enforcement for the purpose of analyzing conditions that allegedly steer people toward criminal activity. Forebodingly, it calls for heightened scrutiny of those who do or may adhere to a violent ideology, and thus immediately imperils professors, critical thinkers, and controversial figures. Just as the Bush administration's invasion of Iraq enacted the neocon imperative of pre-emptive strikes against potential enemies, H.R. 1955 seeks to identify and muzzle potential critical thinkers. As with the USA PATRIOT Act, the Animal Enterprise Terrorism Act, and Bush's surveillance probes, the target is not those engaged in criminal activity (although this becomes defined in ever-broader ways), but rather citizens exercising their constitutional rights of free speech and dissent. There is clearly no logical end in sight for the enemies of free speech and the fearful haters of critical thinking, especially the critique coming from the quarters of academia.

Culture Wars, Round II: 9/11 and the Weapons of Class Destruction

"Ward Churchill is everywhere."
—American Council of Trustees and Alumni

"Education is under assault because it provides access to the historical truths, critical thinking, and alternative perspectives that lay the groundwork for structural change."
—Uncut Conscience website

Within a toxic post-9/11 atmosphere of fear, paranoia, jingoism, and the trumping of security over liberty, there was little tolerance for criticism of the Iraq war, siding with Palestine over Israel, defending animal liberationists, demonstrating against the World Trade Organization, or supporting anything that could be perceived as "terrorism," despite the fact that the biggest terrorist state in history—the US—was once again involved in the massacre of civilian populations in Afghanistan and Iraq.

Clearly, the fascist measures unfolding throughout the US carceral society could not but affect life in the academy.[87] If questioning an illegal war in Iraq was considered treasonous by the Bush-Cheney administration, the corporate media, and the far right, certainly conservative donors to universities and administrative overlords would not look favorably upon denunciations of US imperialism, speaking out at antiwar rallies, or conducting sit-ins at military recruiting centers. Given the perpetual state of surveillance and the choking fog of paranoia, professors began to dilute or mute the political content of their research and teaching, fearful of conservative student complaints or administrative penalties. The state and university bureaucracy do not have to police professors when they censor themselves.[88]

Rather than defend the core principles of academic speech more vigorously than ever amidst the most serious assault on the Constitution in the nation's history, most of academia cowered in fear and joined Democratic Party invertebrates as silent accomplices to torture and a criminal war abroad, and high crimes and treason at home. And as academics retreated, the far right surged forward. Eager to seize the moment, conservatives capitalized on widespread anxiety for "national security" and found their scapegoat in the grave "threat" of liberal values and left-wing politics. Emboldened by conservative hegemony in government, a Justice Department perpetuating injustice, and a fundamentalist President for whom God's laws (and his own) override the articles of the Constitution, the right stormed through every social sector and pursued the temples of education as spoils of war. Following Bush in exploiting 9/11 to maximal effect, the right stepped up its game, praised God and Flag, and wealthy donors generously funded books, think tanks, organizations, conferences, websites, and conservative student groups and newspapers in preparation for ideological warfare and a counter-counter-hegemony.

With academia in their crosshairs, conservatives targeted one of the last bastions (imperfect and rapidly deteriorating) of free speech and critical thinking. They came gunning for the "liberal elite" and the "academic left" who—in the paranoid delusions of their Machiavellian mindsets—prevailed from positions of power in faculty posts and administrative offices. Heavily-financed and well-organized, conservatives swarmed on campuses across the country, promoting a reactionary agenda powered by lies, distortions, and doublespeak. These flag-waving freedom-fighters claimed to be riding their cavalry into town to liberate "oppressed" students and "marginalized" conservative faculty alike from left-wing tyranny, but their real objective was to reclaim the heart of America and the Western Christian heritage under attack from both foreign and domestic enemies.

In fact, the goal of conservative groups and right-wing warriors was not to promote academic diversity, balance, and freedom, but rather to subvert these goals by vanquishing progressive faculty by any means necessary—including slander, distortion, and lies. They wanted, moreover, to promote radical structural changes in academia, including undermining faculty governance and weakening or destroying the tenure system and its protections for free speech. Ultimately, the right wants to drive a stake through the heart of academic life *in order to protect capitalism and to defend conservative hegemony from the threat of critical thinking and an educated middle class.*

While husband Dick was busy invading countries abroad and dismantling the Constitution at home, Lynn Cheney, former chair of the National Endowment for the Humanities, was engaged in battle against academic freedom. In 1995, with Democratic Senator Joseph Lieberman, former University of Colorado-Boulder president and US Senator Hank Brown, sociologist David Reisman, and Nobel Laureate novelist Saul Bellow, Cheney co-founded the American Council of Trustees and Alumni (ACTA). Their stated objective being to "promote academic freedom and diversity, academic excellence, and accountability in higher education." Lofty rhetoric that masked a lowly motive to squash the "liberal bias" in education, to attack diversity-oriented programs, to regulate classroom discourse, and to extirpate critical intellectuals and radicals.[89] ACTA seeks to accomplish its goals "by empowering students, alumni, donors and trustees," which means that they exhort conservative students to complain about liberal/left professors and they pressure alumni, donors, and trustees, along with governors and legislators, to exert political and financial pressure on universities harboring dissidents and derelicts in patriotic fervor.[90]

The tendentious nature of ACTA is evident in its financial backing by right-wing foundations such as Castle Rock (Coors), Sarah Scaife, and John Olin, and Lynde and Harry Bradley, and its association with powerful neoconservative groups such as the Federalist Society, American Enterprise Institute, Cato Institute, and the National Association of Scholars.[91] Considering ACTA's strong Colorado connections—which, in addition to Brown, include former Governor Bill Owens and University of Colorado-Boulder Regents Tom Lucero and Ward Connerly—a clear example of their commitment to "academic freedom and diversity" is evident in its team effort to fire Ward Churchill, a tenured professor and Chair of Ethnic Studies at the University of Colorado, Boulder. ACTA, in fact, became so politicized and inconsistent with its stated mission of promoting academic freedom, that even Joseph Lieberman, an opportunist if ever there were one, quit the organization in protest over a publication which he considered "unfair and inconsistent for an organization devoted to promoting academic freedom."[92]

ACTA's ominous debut report, "Defending Civilization: How Our Universities Are Failing America," is described by Joel Benin as the "first post-September 11 expression of the link between the neo-conservative political agenda and the attack on critical thinking about the Middle East."[93] The report portrayed America's universities as a fifth column, teeming with ingrate unpatriotic malcontents who formed the "weak link in America's response to the [9/11] attack."[94] "When a nation's intellectuals are unwilling to defend its civilization," the report asserts, "they give comfort to its adversaries," and thus assumes that the nation is always correct and, if not, intellectuals should defend it regardless. The definition of "intellectual," however, is a learned person who thinks, and thinking people do not defend unethical or untenable policies, although academics on this definition, despite the portrait ACTA painted, are in short supply.

The original version of the ACTA report documents 117 instances of alleged enemy-comforting anti-Americanism on college campuses, and yet, true to conservative form, nearly every citation is distorted, taken out of context, or is factually wrong. The first draft of "Defending Civilization" was a political hit list that posted online the names and affiliations of professors ACTA deemed insufficiently patriotic as they failed to teach the "truth" that civilization itself "is best exemplified in the West and indeed in America." "Many of those blacklisted" in the "Defending Civilization" document, Carolyn Baker notes, "are top scholars in their fields, and it appears that the report represents a kind of academic terrorism designed to strike fear into other academics by making examples of respected professors."[95] Baker draws uncanny parallels between the goals of ACTA, and the far right in general, and the tactics German Nazis deployed in the 1940s to ensure a compliant faculty whose teaching conformed to National Socialist doctrine. In fact, most of the dicta were from students and journalists, not professors, and sentiments as tame as calling for peace are condemned as anti-American/civilization.[96]

ACTA's paranoid fantasies of "an oppressive anti-American ideology [which] has taken over on campuses"[97] reached ludicrous heights in their May 2006 Annual Report, "How Many Ward Churchills?"[98] Stirring up dystopian visions of human cloning in Huxley's novel *Brave New World* or the film *Boys from Brazil* (1978), ACTA warned that Churchill was not merely a stray menace, but rather only one in a faceless mob of leftist lunatics tearing at the fabric of Western culture with hate speech and a hodgepodge of multiculturalism. To ACTA's horror, academic misfits abandoned reverent homilies of eternal verities (the Good, the True, and the Beautiful) for the politicized propaganda of matters such as race, gender, class, sexuality, capitalism, and oppression. As a neo-McCarthyite organization, ACTA surpasses Senator McCarthy himself by elevating the danger level and upping the ante of the culture wars in sounding the alarm to protect not only America, but ultimately (Western) "civilization" itself.

The paranoid, persecuting, and power-oriented atmosphere of post-9/11 set the stage for a dangerous reactionary and master of doublespeak. From the shadows of obscurity, David Horowitz—a self-proclaimed conservative "battering ram"—emerged to become point guard in the frontal assault on the progressive professoriate in order to silence opposition to the radical right.[99] Red diaper baby, political aide to Bertrand Russell, Black Panther insider, and New Left radical turned neocon extremist, Horowitz—in a tortured and protracted Oedipal struggle—renounced his 60's roots and the social advances his generation brought about.[100] Ambitious and tireless, richly diversified, a veritable conglomerate of disinformation outlets, Horowitz is president of the David Horowitz Freedom Center, the founder of the conservative online watchlist *FrontPageMagazine.com* and a liberal/left resource site, *DiscovertheNetworks.org*, and the creator of a Republican youth network (Students for Academic Freedom [SAF]) that monitors and reports on faculty teaching on some 200 campuses. He is also the prolific author of pugilistic polemics, including: *Hating Whitey and Other Progressive Causes* (1999), *The Politics of Bad Faith: The Radical Assault on America's Future* (2000), *Unholy Alliance: Radical Islam and the American Left* (2004), *The Professors: The 101 Most Dangerous Professors in America* (2006), and *Indoctrination U: The Left's War Against Academic Freedom* (2007). Horowitz is also the author of, and driving force behind, the Academic Bill of Rights (along with a similar version, the "Student Bill of Rights" developed for student governments), one of the most dangerous pieces of legislation against academic freedom ever to be introduced. Naturally, Horowitz does not run this machinery on a shoe-string budget, but rather takes money from many of the same corporations and foundations that fund Bennett, D'Souza, ACTA, and other mouthpieces of right-wing reaction.[101]

Horowitz attempts to validate the Bloom-Kimball postulate of a hegemonic left dominating university affairs by drawing false inferences from shoddy studies. Never one to let logic and facts stand in his way, Horowitz constructs a phantasmagoric picture of a Stalinist cadre of ultra-left professors hijacking colleges and universities from California to New York to indoctrinate impressionable minds with anti-American propaganda and to fulfill their hate-filled, terrorist sympathizing agenda. According to Horowitz, "a shocking and perverse culture of academics…are poisoning the minds of today's college students with…hatred of America…and support for America's terrorist enemies." Along with ACTA and other mercenary "scholars" like D'Souza, Horowitz shifted the debate from old-style McCarthyesque defamations of progressives as subversive communists to the new and improved neo-McCarthyesque discourse that vilifies them as neo-Communist sympathizers of Osama bin Laden and enablers of "Islamo-fascism."[102]

In a series of unsubstantiated ad hominem profiles, Horowitz reduces scholars and teachers to cartoonish caricatures of "ex-terrorists, racists, murderers, sexual deviants, anti-Semites, and al-Qaeda supporters." One cannot but feel reverberations of McCarthyist surveillance tactics, the chilling drone of "naming names," the sordid spectacle of accusations and defamations, and the tyranny of holding citizens accountable to the dogmatic standards of patriotism and morality established by a self-righteous fanatic. The Stalinism of "political correctness" clearly comes not from the "academic left" but rather from the far right and the codes of patriotic correctness. The entire Horowitz industry oozes with the slime of blacklisting, sloshed once again upon

educators, as the ultimate goal of the new Reich is to eradicate dissent and to exile critical thinkers and political subversives.

Like many conniving ideologues with totalitarian aspirations, Horowitz has
enlisted an army of followers who do his bidding and toe the party line. On some 200
campuses, he has organized a network of Republican youth groups (SAF) who join
him as foot soldiers in the culture war. Exploited for his own purposes under the cover
of paternalistic care, these true blue American students often amount to little more
than McCarthyite spy squads, shock troops, and mercenaries. The blacklisting tactics
work something like this: the big money networks fund Horowitz, Horowitz organizes
conservative students, and the students document liberal/left professors' pedagogical
sins. These are then posted online and peddled as lurid smut for newspaper articles
and Internet columns and blogs. Ideally, the lies are taken up by national radio and
television stations, lead to a manufactured scandal, cause a professor to be fired, and
discredit progressive views.

Disseminating falsehoods, ad hominems, and baseless claims to generate
public pressure against the accused is quintessential McCarthyism, and the tactic
grows more sinister once the mad villagers of the right begin to name names. The
Bruin Standard, the newspaper published by the UCLA chapter of the SAF, targets
progressive faculty and enjoins students to identify left-wing demagogues by name.
The SAF Handbook included a section ("Focusing on Specific Professors and Departments") on how to spy on progressive professors. In 2005, at the University of California, Los Angeles, the Bruin Alumni Association, headed by Andrew Jones, a former
campus Republican leader and one-time epigone of David Horowitz, offered students
up to $100 per class to surveil professors who opposed Bush and the Iraq War, and
who allegedly politicized the classroom.[103] By encouraging students to tape teachers'
classroom lecture, the Bruin Alumni Association employs tactics reminiscent of the
anti-Communist witchhunt of the 1950s. Preposterously, the site claims: "Very simply,
we're facing an exploding crisis of political radicalism on campus. It's endangering the
very core of UCLA—the undergraduate experience. One aspect of this radicalization
is an unholy alliance [!] between anti-war professors, radical Muslim students, and a
pliant administration. Working together, they have made UCLA a major organizing
center for opposition to the War on Terror."[104]

In 2006, the Bruin Alumni Association built the UCLAprofs.com website
which exposes the "left biases," Marxist rant, ideological coercion, and totalitarian
teaching methods that allegedly characterize a slew of UCLA professors. They followed
this up with a "Dirty Thirty" list that ranked "the worst of the worst" at UCLA, all of
whom allegedly used the classroom as a political laboratory to indoctrinate students
in subversive ideologies.[105] This diverse group of professors included scholars in labor
studies; women's studies; gay and lesbian studies; Chicano/a, Asian, Latin American,

and Middle Eastern studies; and a contributor to (Douglas Kellner) and co-editor (Peter McLaren) of this book. McLaren was placed at the top of this list, as UCLA's most dangerous professor.

Horowitz believes that, "Politics is about winning. If you don't win, you don't get to put your principles into practice. Therefore, find a way to win, or sit the battle out."[106] We agree that is exactly what politics is for those on the right whose siren song is not democracy, equality, and freedom, but Social Darwinism and the "survival of the fittest." True politics on and off campus is not about winning, but about collaboration, transformation, and an inclusive dialogue and society in which all participate. But the right has a rich panoply of discourses and mechanisms to exclude, subordinate, enslave, and imprison, and repression and control is the name of the political game. There is a fundamental difference here between the left and right, such that the left is about uplifting everyone, even Horowitz, while the right is about destroying and standing on top of people while they jump for joy in the name of victory.

Horowitz is not merely a writer but also an activist, and he has taken his fight not only to the campuses, conferences, and book tour circuits, but also to state legislatures throughout the nation in order to pass a chilling piece of legislation. Like McCarthy and countless fascists before and after him, Horowitz's passion, project, and *raison d'être* is to effect enduring political change that limits freedom of speech and ensures a rigid social order with an ideological barometer that moves between right and far right. According to Horowitz, however, his task is not to suppress free speech but rather to end the hegemony of leftist discourse and restore "balance" to teaching and discussion. In response to the alleged swing of the ideological pendulum toward the left over the last few decades, Horowitz began an aggressive campaign in 2003 to pass an "Academic Bill of Rights" (ABOR) a draft of legislation aimed at requiring liberal/left professors to teach—with an appropriate nod to Fox News—in a "fair and balanced" way.[107] Horowitz claims that appropriate discourse for a classroom is not a free speech issue but a matter of "professional standards," and while he would permit views representing the full political spectrum into the classroom, they must be expressed in the "appropriate" manner.

The protection of both professor and student rights; the vigilant enforcement of foundational academic principles such as freedom, equality, and pluralism; prohibiting faculty from being hired or fired on the basis of political or religious beliefs; requiring instructors to expose students to diverse perspectives—all this sounds commendable and reasonable on the surface. So why has Horowitz and his bill drawn such fierce opposition from academics and groups such as the AAUP, the American Federation of Teachers, the National Coalition Against Censorship, the National Association of Scholars, the American Historical Association, the American Library Association, and the AFL-CIO? Perhaps because Horowitz's arguments are as theoretically flawed as they are factually bankrupt and politically perilous.

The research in which he anchors his claim for a hegemonic "academic left" was backed by right-wing funding and is methodologically marred on numerous grounds (including narrow and biased samples weighted more heavily toward the humanities than the sciences and other conservative-capitalist-oriented disciplines such as business administration), and thereby fails to establish the main conclusion that liberals and leftists dominate the professoriate.[108] Horowitz relies on anecdotes and false generalizations that leap from a few isolated cases (many of which are misrepresented or flat-out wrong) to an absurd generalization regarding the entire faculty body. His characterizations of professors typically are grotesquely unfair, uninformed, incorrect, and riddled with ad hominems, as his claim that progressive professors victimize and conservative students are victims is wildly exaggerated on both sides.[109] Indeed, when states such as Florida, Montana, New York, and Pennsylvania have looked into conservative complaints, they found no serious problems and suggested no course of action not already implemented by colleges and universities. The main sources of "indoctrination" of contemporary youth, certainly, are not universities and professors of any ideological persuasion, but rather the capitalist and consumerist ideologies saturating advertising, mass media, corporate news, and popular culture.

The key to understanding Horowitz, D'Souza, and other neo-McCarthyites is to recognize that their approach is disingenuous, that their ecumenical moral rhetoric masks a narrow political agenda, and that their main discursive strategy is doublespeak, deploying a dissembling semantic of inverted signifiers. Just as Bush's "Healthy Forests Initiative" allowed clearcutting of protected forests and his "Clear Skies Initiative" weakened the Clean Air Act, so the Academic Bill of Rights is a Trojan horse meant to destroy academic freedom. As with the appropriation of the term "political correctness," here again, the right's clever tactic is to use liberal/left discourse against itself, to advance a far right agenda that strips progressive professors of the right to publish, teach, and act as citizens as they wish. The bill does not protect free speech, it molests free speech, and it does so by forcing professors to interject right-wing theories into the classroom, by legislating what can and cannot be said before one's students, by overriding faculty self-governance through the authority of the state, and by subjecting course content and teaching to bureaucratic review and rebuke.

The Academic Bill of Rights attempts to give the already advantaged and over-privileged political right more power than the surplus stock it holds. The demand for "diversity" and the call for "balance" are really ploys for conservative hegemony and ideological *imbalance*, for a pre-60s sterile groupthink, a conformist environment dominated by Fox News discourse without any true diversity among faculty, programs, courses, students, and campus and community intellectual life (if there would be one at all).[110] The common understanding of neutrality and non-indoctrination is altered by Horowitz in such a way that it actually functions as a form of indoctrination of right-wing views. This is because views that contradict those on the right are considered biased, whereas right-wing positions are considered neutral and form the universal backdrop against which the definition of bias is constructed. Unable to think outside of the corporate box and utilitarian model of education, they have no idea what real education is, a mission that includes encountering and engaging differing viewpoints; students would be denied this opportunity. It is healthy and vital for conservative students to hear radical perspectives, as it is for progressive students to hear conservative perspectives.[111]

While Horowitz and his crybaby students allergic to intellectual challenges proclaim they seek fairness and equal time for their views, including hiring conservative faculty, they oppose affirmative action for exploited minority groups. They take no notice of the contradiction and hypocrisy of opposing the self-governance and autonomy of professors while also fighting for a type of affirmative action for the right. For consistency's sake, Horowitz ought to shift from attacking the left and multiculturalism to launching a campaign to increase progressives' presence on campus. A true concern for balance would demand *more* hiring of Blacks, women, Native Americans, Hispanics, and radicals for they and their perspectives are devalued and excluded, unable to survive in the oxygen-free atmosphere of white, male, straight, patriotic, anthropocentric, speciesist orthodoxy. It would entail that Horowitz support progressives' efforts to introduce critical perspectives and issues such as race, gender, and class. In an administratively conservative and capitalist academic environment, where critical viewpoints are scattered, rare, and marginalized, hiring left professors and introducing radical viewpoints into the classroom *is* precisely the needed correction to achieve any meaningful pluralism and "balance."

Horowitz ignores the overwhelming corporate and right-wing *institutional* biases of the entire university, its budget operations, and research goals. Universities are corporate institutions dominated by narrow economic interests and conservative values. In sad fact, university power is a right/conservative/corporate power not a left/progressive/faculty power. Despite a strong cadre of progressives and radicals at campuses such as UCLA, probably nowhere are leftists—radicals, not liberals—a majority or significant political force. Most certainly, they do not work high up in administrative channels, they do not control budgets, they do not monopolize the power to hire and fire, and they do not impose radical agendas in classrooms, departments, and programs. The truth is, as this book documents, that left, critical, radical, progressive thinking, writing, speaking, teaching, and activism is discouraged, held in contempt, and, at best, tolerated.

Abstractions such as "academic left," "liberal-left," and "Dirty Thirty" vaporize salient distinctions and differences in totalizing clouds of rhetoric. The conflation of liberal into left obscures the key point that liberal views are far more palatable to administrators, regents, and right-wing interests, and that liberals have far more in common with conservatives than radicals when it comes to challenging the institutional logic of capitalism. The real power lies high up in the chain of centralized command, with Deans, Provosts, Presidents, Chancellors, Regents, and CEOs, all of whom, if not conservative in their politics, promote a capitalist agenda and the corporate model of education implemented in a state of mutual tension and antipathy to the political worldview and pedagogical philosophy of radical professors and many liberal ones as well. Moreover, it is increasingly the case, as we discuss below, that a host of individuals, institutions, and organizations exert powerful pressure and influence on universities to push capitalist and right-wing agendas and purge higher education of progressive thinkers teaching multiculturalism and programs such as Women's Studies. Thus, far from a hegemonic or monolithic bloc, academic leftists are an endangered species, and attacks on the tenure system threaten to render them extinct.

The ABOR is ludicrous for a number of reasons. First, it is redundant and ignores (or distorts) the fact that universities already have a conceptually sound code of freedom and responsibilities for both professors and students, such as have been clarified and promoted by the AAUP's "1940 Statement on Academic Freedom and Tenure," which specifies how teachers should conduct themselves in research, teaching, public forums, and with students. Predictably, however, instead of being viewed as articulated and enforced moral principles, such doctrines are rejected out of hand as left-wing propaganda. Second, the concept of "balance" automatically imposes mandates and constraints on professors, such as come from ideologues like Horowitz and outside political and legal institutions that strip autonomy and self-governance from faculty. Not only is the concept of "balance" vague, it is an impossible ideal to achieve; it revives discredited positive ideologies that professors can adopt a neutral (rather than always-already biased) stance and always give equal time and consideration to opposing viewpoints. The concept of "balance" and "equal" time are absurd if one is required to teach the KKK along with Martin Luther King Jr., flat-earth approaches in addition to contemporary astronomy, creationism in conjunction with Christianity. Apologists argue that, "the Academic Bill of Rights does not require the teaching of all views on every topic or any topic, nor does it mandate the teaching of any particular viewpoint…The only spectrum of opinion that it proposes that professors should explore is 'the spectrum of significant scholarly viewpoints on the subjects examined in their courses.'"[112] What is this spectrum? How many sides or perspectives does a professor have to teach to satisfy the proposed diversity requirements? And who determines the answers to these questions? Horowitz and his student foot-soldiers are chasing a Platonic archetype of a perfectly balanced debate, and heavy-handed efforts to realize pedagogical balance are more likely to stultify than to realize it.

As argued by Craig Smith of the American Federation of Teachers, the ABOR, like the ACTA "intellectual diversity" bill, "is nothing more than an ideological attack on institutions of higher education and the faculty who work in these institutions. It breeds distrust in one of our country's most valued enterprises and defames the work of dedicated professionals."[113] The real purpose of the bill is not to secure student "rights," Saree Makdisi argues, but rather "to institute state monitoring of universities, to impose specific points of view on instructors—in many cases, points of view that have been intellectually discredited—and ultimately to silence dissenting voices by punishing universities that protect them." [114] The bill threatens to strip faculty authority and to nullify strong collegial disciplinary norms by making decisions about pedagogy dependent upon the views of extra-departmental committees, university administrations, Congress, and the courts. In the rare cases where faculty behave inappropriately toward students, there are already regulations known by professors and enforced by their peers that act to protect students.

Far from improving these standards, ABOR would undermine them and cast a paralyzing chill over teacher-student relations by marching in political bureaucrats to act as pedagogical police. Imposed diversity and balance requirements, moreover, open the door to student complaints—especially right-wing students prodded by conservative organizations—of indoctrination, and can stop teaching before it can start. "Whatever the intentions of the drafters," the American Historical Association notes,

> the ABOR has already unleashed forces that seek to stifle free and open debate on campus. In Florida, for example, Representative Dennis Baxley says that his version of the ABOR would enable students to sue professors who do not teach Intelligent Design (ID)... The most serious danger posed by the ABOR, however, is that it could snuff out all controversial discussion in the classroom. A campus governed by the ABOR would present professors with an impossible dilemma: either play it safe or risk administrative censure by saying something that might offend an overly sensitive student.[115]

Horowitz appropriates the liberal language of balance and diversity as an ideological smokescreen to marginalize progressive views, fire radical teachers, and elevate right-wing doctrine and doctrinaires to a pre-60s level of ideological hegemony. He rails against politicizing the classroom, but he himself is pushing the most aggressive political agenda of all, peddling his program to congress, state legislatures, CEOs, reactionary televangelists, and the like. Quite transparently, the aim of Horowitz's ABOR is not to take politics out of the classroom but to politicize every facet of university research and teaching, to extirpate liberal and left professors from the university, and to restore the university to a one-dimensional ideological factory devoid of dissenting views, controversial ideas, and passionate political debate. His goal is to decimate progressive faculty and to force whatever people are left to pass an ideological litmus test before they can be hired and promoted. And all these fallacies, hypocrisies, errors, and posturing, to add insult to injury, are framed as benefiting students when in fact students are but pawns in a right-wing power play.

Philosophically vacuous and political laughable, Horowitz's fanatical positions and projects are ignored only at our peril and must be resolutely fought, along with every other recrudescence of academic fascism. We should note that among many radical academics, Horowitz's list of the "The 101 Most Dangerous Academics in America" is a joke and, rather than feeling intimidated, they are insulted that they didn't make the cut, and ponder strategies, somewhat tongue-in-cheek, to be put with such esteemed company.[116] Ultimately, the momentum gathered by the Academic Bill of Rights is no joke but rather a testament to the growing reactionary ideology of the far right in the post-9/11 era, which deploys tactics reminiscent of the anti-intellectual fascists of Nazi Germany.[117]

While the ABOR is not law in any state, it and related bills have been introduced by Republican politicians in over two dozen state legislatures such as Florida, Indiana, New York, Pennsylvania, Missouri, and California; although the legislation mostly died for inaction, versions of it have been passed in Ohio, Colorado, and Georgia; and Oklahoma used an academic freedom bill to smuggle in religious instruction in public science classrooms.[118] Most ominously, in 2007, Arizona passed a bill intended to ban any teaching that promoted the "denigration, disparagement or encouragement of dissent from values of American democracy and Western civilization" in any publicly-funded educational institutions, and would fire and/or fine teachers who violated state-imposed standards of right-wing patriotic correctness.[119]

While Horowitz himself said such measures went too far, his efforts inspire academic witchhunts and drive more stakes into the heart of academic freedom. Indeed, according to the Free Exchange Coalition, "Horowitz admits his proposal doesn't need to win in the legislature to have its desired impact. Provided that the media keeps reporting on it, and no one challenges Horowitz and ACTA along the way, they'll continue to hamper free speech."[120] To be very clear: there is a very serious intent behind the ABOR and Horowitz's political maneuvering. The intent is to discredit, marginalize, and eventually purge critical analysis from the precincts of the university, turning campuses into non-think tanks of the conservative and religious right and discursive factories for the reproduction of neoliberal capitalist consensus.[121] Funded by corporate organizations, plotting with ultra-conservative politicians, spreading his message to the vast wasteland of televangelism, Horowitz already has too much power and discretion on his side and is lusting for more.

Horowitz, D'Souza, and other neo-McCarthyite culture warriors surfaced at the same moment that neoliberal capitalism is transforming the universities and cutting back or eliminating whole departments and areas of study deemed not serviceable for producing research and grant money and luring corporate sponsors. As Horowitz aims to eliminate the "academic left," the military-industrial-state complex seeks to undercut the autonomy of the university, stripping decision-making and autonomy from faculty, and placing power in the hands of a legion of reactionary forces outside the university who are trying to influence and control the hiring, firing, and teaching processes that unfold within. Faculty must become aware, grow concerned, join forces, formulate a plan, organize unions, fight for radical social change, and thereby mount a counter-hegemony and resistance. Horowitz and the ABOR do not occur in isolation, but are part of a four decade long assault on public funding of higher education, just as the culture wars are a flank to an economic class war to de-fund colleges and universities and minimize the damaging effects of critical thinking on conservative hegemony.[122] Should there be any doubt whether the far-right prefers liberty over tyranny (to be precise, they seek "freedom" in markets and draconian control over moral, intellectual, and political life), at the 2007 Connecticut Forum, Ann Coulter professed her "hero" to be Joseph McCarthy, a fascist warrior that she and a frightening amount of others would welcome with open arms to help restore America to the decency, clarity, and chilling conformity of the 1950s era.[123]

The Tactics of Neo-McCarthyism

"War is too important to be left to the generals."
—Neo-conservative, Eliot Cohen

After 9/11, the far right, like their kingpin Bush and his neocon cabinet, saw at last an outstanding opportunity to advance their interests and they capitalized. By 2005, it was clear that the right had adopted a full-on, Al Qaeda-style, multiple-front commando raid on US colleges and universities, targeting academic freedom through dozens of networks, organizations, and ideologues, unleashed in order to cause maximal casualties to the their avowed enemy, the liberal-left, who are corrupting the youth, weakening America in a time of crisis, and undermining Western civilization itself.

The most infamous instance of academic repression in the post-9/11 era unquestionably is Ward Churchill, a full professor and Chair of the Department of Ethnic Studies at University of Colorado, Boulder (UCB). Given the protections afforded by promotion, it is rare for a tenured professor to be fired, unless through serious charges such as sexual harassment or criminal misconduct. But Churchill was fired for writing a critical essay against the US empire, arguing that 9/11 was legitimate payback and that the thousands of "little Eichmanns" in the World Trade Center were legitimate targets of war. However offensive his phrasings were to conservatives and the public at large, it was fully within Churchill's rights as an academic to publish a controversial critique in provocative words. Yet the right-wing outrage over his comments, and the ensuing media firestorm, put strong pressure on the University of Colorado to fire him, which the Board of Regents did on July 24, 2007, on absurd trumped up charges of sub-standard scholarship. Buckling to the demands of right-wing politicians, media windbags like Bill O'Reilly, and wealthy donors, UCB fired a tenured professor because of his political views, not for any academic malfeasance. Churchill became America's own Salman Rushdie, terrorized by the fatwa of the right, and the action taken against him was a blatant case of academic repression.[124]

Once the home of open thinking and political debate, classrooms are now pervaded by fear and paranoia. The firing of Churchill—a renowned scholar, superb teacher, and popular public intellectual—sounded a "warning to the academic community," the ACLU wrote to the UCB Board of Regents, "that politically unpopular dissenters speak out at their own peril."[125] Indeed, the Churchill affair was just one of many cases of attacks on academic freedom that eerily evokes the tyranny of the McCarthy era when artists were blacklisted and professors were fired, and we should never forget that for every high-profile case like Churchill's, there are a dozen more egregious instances of academic repression that receive little or no attention. To mention just a few salient cases, many of which are discussed in this book:[126]

- 1983, Boston University: President John Silber fired education professor Henry Giroux, following the mandate of meddling conservatives over unanimous tenure committee recommendations for promotion.

- 1992, Washington State University: Sociology professor Rik Scarce was brought before a Grand Jury to provide information on the sources he used to research his book on the radical environmental movement and was jailed for over five months for refusing to break his professional code of confidentiality with interview subjects.

- 2002–2009, Bard College: Following the publication of a controversial anti-Zionist essay, Joel Kovel was removed from the Alger Hiss Chair of Social Studies in 2002, ending a position he held since 1988. In 2007, strong political pressure by pro-Israel groups and a Zionist watchdog team (StandWithUs, an offshoot of Campus Watch, founded by David Pipes) prompted the University of Michigan Press to stop distribution of his book, *Overcoming Zionism: Creating a Single Democratic State in Israel/Palestine* (a decision the press later overturned due to heated criticism). In 2009, Bard terminated Kovel altogether.

- 2003, University of South Florida: An ill-fated 2001 appearance on *The O'Reilly Factor* whipped up renewed controversy that led to the firing, imprisonment, and deportation of an award-winning tenured computer engineering professor, Sami Al-Arian, on unsubstantiated charges that he belonged to a Palestinian Islamic "jihad" group.

- November 2003, University of California, Berkeley: Ignacio H. Chapela, Assistant Professor of ecology was denied tenure due to his public opposition to genetic modification of crops and his criticism of the ties between Berkeley and the Swiss-based biotechnology industry, Novartis (in May 2005, after Chapela's appeal and lawsuit, the university reversed course and granted him tenure).

- May 2004, Buffalo, New York: The FBI and the Joint Terrorism Task Force arrested and detained Steve Kurtz, an art professor at SUNY Buffalo on bogus charges of violating the US Biological Weapons Anti-Terrorism Act of 1989.

- 2004–2005, Columbia University: Acclaimed scholar and critic of Israel, Joseph Massad, after enduring many years of hostile non-students interrupting his classes, was subject to an inquisition-like investigation of his teaching methods after a student and a propaganda film by David Pipes falsely charged him with unfair treatment to students with pro-Israel views; the investigation was dropped despite demands from *The New York Times* (!) for a more aggressive inquiry.[127]

- February 2005, Columbia University: Rashid Khalidi, a respected Middle Eastern scholar and the director of the Middle East Institute, was dismissed from teaching professional development courses, as a result of his political views and a baseless story by the *New York Sun*, which said that he denounced Israel as a "racist" state with an "apartheid system."

- Spring 2005, Yale University: Assistant Professor David Graeber, an internationally acclaimed anthropology scholar, was fired amidst controversy over his anarchist politics and support of the Yale graduate student unionization movement.

- May 2005, University of Texas, El Paso: Steven Best, an outspoken supporter of the #1 US "domestic terrorist" group, the Animal Liberation Front, was banned from the UK, falsely accused of leading and recruiting students into the group, summoned to speak before the Senate Eco-Terrorism hearings, and precipitously removed from his position as Chair of the Philosophy department.

- January 2006, Southwestern Baptist Theological Seminary: Accomplished scholar Sheri Klouda was forced out of a tenure track position when the seminary reverted to the position that women were "unqualified by Scripture" and Biblically forbidden to instruct men in matters of theology and languages.

- June 2006, Brigham Young University: Just days after publishing a newspaper column in support of same-sex marriage, adjunct instructor Jeffrey Nielsen was fired by Daniel Graham, chair of the Philosophy department.

- November 2006, USA: Adam Habib, a noted South African scholar, was denied entry into the US and had his visa revoked indefinitely, because the State Department labeled him a "terrorist."

- 2005–2007, Barnard College: Palestinian-American scholar Nadia Abu El Haj's tenure promotion was imperiled due to the smear campaign of Campus Watch, FrontPage, alumnae at Barnard and Columbia University, and other pro-Israel ideologues.

- February 2007, Spring Arbor University, Michigan: Baptist minister and longtime professor, Rev. John Nemecek, is fired for failure to "model Christian character" after coming out as a transgendered person.

- June 2007, DePaul University: Professor Norman Finkelstein, the son of Holocaust survivors and an outspoken opponent of Zionism, was denied tenure, despite recommendations at both department and college levels, after the university President capitulated to a right-wing smear campaign led by Harvard law professor, Alan Dershowitz. Adding to the outrage, Professor Mehrene Larudee was fired at the same time, just nineteen days before becoming director of DePaul's program in International Studies, for no clear reason other than openly defending Finkelstein.

- August, 2007, University of California, Irvine: After offering the position of founding dean of a new law school to renowned lawyer and media pundit, Erwin Chermerinsky, chancellor Michael V. Drake withdrew—and subsequently restored—the offer on the grounds that he was "too politically controversial" and "polarizing" in his commentaries.

- April 2008, University of Nevada at Reno: After filing a complaint about laboratory animal abuse that resulted in a $377,000 loss in research money for his university, Hussein S. Hussein, Associate Professor of Animal Biotechnology, was fired and banned from the campus.

- Fall 2008: Noted education scholar and former member of the Weather Underground, Bill Ayers, was systematically attacked by the McCain-Palin ticket as an "unrepentant domestic terrorist," a charge pressed not only to urge the University of Illinois-Chicago to fire Ayers, but also to smear then Democratic presidential nominee Barack Obama. In 2009 Ayers was barred from speaking in Canada on two occasions and once at Boston College.

- Spring 2009, the University of California, Santa Barbara: For the audacity to speak out against the month-long Israeli invasion of Gaza that began in December 2008, and for the transgression of including images of this carnage in an email to his class for the sake of historical context and open debate, tenured sociology professor William I. Robinson was targeted by the Anti-Defamation League for the "defamation" of critical dialogue and examining both sides of an issue. Instead of dismissing the charges as nonsense, the compliant UCSB Academic Senate opened a formal investigation into "anti-Semitism" charges against Robinson.

- February 2009, San Francisco: With no substantiating evidence, in violation of faculty bargaining agreements, and in apparent retaliation for open disagreement with the administration, the San Francisco Art Institute declared the school to be "financially exigent" and commenced a mass firing ("layoffs") of nine of the thirty-seven tenured faculty members.

These and countless other cases cohere in a systemic pattern of repression. Of particular importance is the power of the Zionist industry and its attacks on anyone critical of Israel and supportive of Palestinian autonomy. The long arm and financial assets of the Zionist industry have reached out to hassle Massad and Khalidi at Columbia, to crush Finkelstein at De Paul, and silence Kovel at Bard College. The repressive power of Zionists is formidable in Canada as well, as evident in April 2009, when Denis G. Rancourt, professor in the Physics department for twenty-three years and a critic of Zionism, was continuously harassed and ultimately fired by President Allan Rock, a staunch supporter of Israeli policy.[128]

When faculty who are tenured, who have decades of experience, and who are internationally-renowned scholars can be hassled, threatened, defamed, imprisoned, and fired for holding critical views on controversial topics such as US and Israeli state terrorism, one can imagine the chilling effect this has on assistant or associate professors with far less experience and status, to say nothing of those toiling in part-time, adjunct, or rotating contract positions and whose fears and insecurities are exponentially magnified in depressed job markets and a recessionary global economy.

Right-wing attempts at an academic coup come straight out of the McCarthy-ite playbook, and utilize heavy doses of doublespeak for maximal obfuscation, coding an attack on free speech as a defense of the First Amendment and masking partisan interests as general concern. The surge in surveillance and repression has led to the term "neo-McCarthyism" becoming a genre in itself, signaling the recrudescence of the tactics used in that dark chapter of US history. Of course history never repeats itself in exactly the same way, yet current elements of repression not only reiterate McCarthyism but also revive earlier tactics of repression such as the Alien and Sedition Acts.

If central elements of McCarthyism included jingoism, anti-communism, surveillance, demonization of dissent, imposed conformity, witchhunts against domestic "enemies," overriding civil liberties by appeal to national security, guilt through association, subpoenaing, naming names, blacklisting, and paranoia of national security threats from abroad and within, then all of these tactics have been utilized heavily in the aftermath of 9/11 and the current neo-McCarthyist era that continues uninterrupted in the transition from Bush to Obama.[129]

First, like McCarthyism, neo-McCarthyism promotes fear and paranoia—over a terrorist attack on the nation and/or a communist-radical takeover of the university system—in order to create an atmosphere in which extreme control measures seem warranted and necessary, and where dissent is anti-American. Just as Bush falsely tried to link Saddam Hussein to Al Qaeda, so Horowitz, D' Souza, Bennett, Coulter, and other culture warriors attempt to connect the liberal/left professoriate to moral decay, social breakdown, and the enabling of jihadist strike forces. Indeed, neo-McCarthyites easily perpetuate paranoia because they *are* paranoid, that is to say, they nervously hallucinate malevolent forces or people out to get America. But no doubt in many cases the far right consciously distorts and wildly exaggerates its paranoia to justify their attacks on the liberal/left. The main delusions and errors, it should be clear, are that liberal-democrats are hostile and harmful to America (wrong), that leftists and radicals are overtaking US campuses (wrong), that the progressive faculty dogmatically indoctrinate America's youth (wrong), and that critical teachings are damaging to students or violate their rights (wrong).

Second, like McCarthyism, neo-McCarthyism is anchored in the demonization of its opponents (whether berated as liberals, leftists, radicals, or fascists) and stems from a fanatical and fundamentalist mindset that sees the world in dogmatic and Manichean terms of Good vs. Evil and Black vs. White. Then and now, the forces of fear warn not only of external threats (be it Russia or Islam) but also of the enemy within, including academics and radical animal rights and environmental activists ("domestic terrorists").

This dualistic logic draws on the either/or fallacy of reducing people to either Americans or traitors, patriots or defectors, conservatives or communists, pro-US or anti-civilization, but of course loyalty to one's country (should that liberal goal be a value) demands critical scrutiny of government to ensure it faithfully follows the Constitution and crafts sound strategies relating to domestic and foreign policy. One principle avenue this tactic takes is through unfounded insinuations and allegations against their left-wing opponents, denouncing them as anti-Semitic, un-American, or enablers of terrorism. One key point of congruence between McCarthyism and neo-McCarthyism is how ultra-conservatives cynically manipulate the patriotism of liberals, which conservatives insist orders closer on treason than on fealty. Just as McCarthyites endlessly pricked the staunchest anti-communists as "too soft on communism," so right-wing politicians like Dick Cheney invidiously belittle and impugn the patriotism of center and right-leaning democrats by accusing them of being "soft" on the "war on terror."

Third, neo-McCarthyites adhere to ideology, not facts. Their tar-and-feather tactics involve spewing lies, slander, and unsubstantiated charges, hoping something sticks. When not distorting their rivals' positions or taking quotes out of context, they resort to outright fabrication. We saw this, for instance, in a flurry of claims baselessly impugning Massad and other Middle East Studies professors as intolerant of dissenting student views. Perhaps more blatantly, David Martosko, from the Center for Consumer Freedom (a corporate PR and front group), blustered before top Congressional and law offices on live C-Span TV, accusing Steve Best of leading the Animal Liberation Front (of course, as an underground and decentralized network, it has no "leader") and populating his cells with cherry-picked students ready to strike a blow for justice—or at least extra credit.

Fourth, in the post-9/11 era, parallel to the 1950s, conservatives aggressively try to extirpate threats to tradition and social order through witchhunts, such as the relentless pummeling by Zionists of Finkelstein, Khalidi, and countless others, as well as Horowitz's aggressive assault on liberal and radical academics.

Fifth, enemies are identified through surveillance. Neo-McCarthyite forces do not leave it to the state to monitor and identify threats to education and society, they undertake this operation themselves. A novel and disturbing tactic of neo-McCarthyism is sending students (often for pay) into professors' classrooms, recording their words, and then posting their most controversial statements on sites such as Campus Watch, the David Project, and *Discoverthenetworks.org*. This tactic calls attention to professors who dare to question authority, vilifies them as a poor teachers (because a "poor" citizens), and pressures administrators to fire the heretic. Surveillance and enforcement of patriotically correct standards casts a chill and paranoia over the classroom, as professors frequently second-guess and self-censor course material and lectures.

Sixth, a key tactic of harnessing "subversives" is through applying the causal fallacy of guilt-by-association, such as when Bill O'Reilly demonized Sami Al-Arian as a terrorist through six degrees of separation to Islamic jihadists. This is a totalizing strategy that throws all suspects into the same conceptual cell, and one version of it is the conflation of liberals and radicals into the category of "leftist," "communist," or "terrorist," as the 2008 McCain-Palin campaign desperately tried to link Obama to Bill Ayers or Rashid Khalidi, and thus to terrorism.[130]

Seventh, naming names, blacklisting, and political hit lists are back with a vengeance. The ACTA report on forty "un-American" professors, Horowitz's compilation of the "101 Most Dangerous Professors," the Brown Alumni group's dossier on the UCLA "Dirty Thirty," and websites such as *Target of Opportunity* all name names as part of their black bag character and career assassination jobs.

Eighth, throughout the First Red Scare, the Second Red Scare, McCarthyism, neo-McCarthyism, and the recent Green Scare, the Constitution is violated routinely as the Bill of Rights and other laws are ignored or nullified with new laws and signings. But as later court decisions rescinded illegal state rulings and actions deployed throughout the twentieth century, so one can only hope future courts will repeal the most repressive measures of laws such as the USA PATRIOT Act and the Animal Enterprise Terrorism Act.

True, while we have not yet seen the firing of hundreds or thousands of teachers for political reasons, that time may come, and in the meantime, we are witnessing a virulent neo-McCarthyism that in many ways is worse than its prototype and other bleak eras in the history of US repression.[131] "There are parallels to McCarthy's days," Ward Churchill notes, "but the techniques have advanced. What that era didn't have is an articulated plan to convert the institutions of higher learning to the dominant ideology."[132] Similarly, Ellen Schrecker, author of numerous books on McCarthyism, notes the advancement in the techniques of repression: "What's different between now and the McCarthy Era is that, then, attacks were on individual professors for extracurricular activities with communist groups or whatever. At no time was anybody's teaching or research brought into question. What's different today, and I think more scary, are things directed against curriculum and classroom and attempts by outside political forces to dictate the syllabus."[133] Unlike the McCarthy era, most threats to academic freedom—real or perceived—do not yet involve the state. Nor are they buttressed by widespread popular support, as anticommunism was during the 50s. But in other ways, Ellen Schrecker argues, comparisons are apt: "In some respects it's more dangerous. McCarthyism dealt mainly with off-campus political activities. Now they focus on what is going on in the classroom. It's very dangerous because it's reaching into the core academic functions of the university, particularly in Middle-Eastern studies."[134]

Academic repression in the twenty-first century is far more organized and extensive than anything preceding it, and it is funded, not only by the finite budget of the state, but also from the virtually unlimited resources of the right. Today, in higher education, we do not see the hands of power coming from Congress and the FBI so much as we witness a proliferation of tentacles emerging from private interest groups, conservative foundations, mass media, right-wing student organizations, and professional mercenaries and hit-men like Dinesh D'Souza and David Horowitz, all of whom pressure university administrations to fire a targeted enemy or threaten to withhold donations and the like.

Moreover, academic repression in the post-9/11 era is far broader and deeper in reach, targeting courses, syllabi, and entire departments, extending surveillance mechanisms from individuals' homes or meeting halls directly into the classroom. And not only are the current embodiments of HUAC and Senator McCarthy trying to weed out dissent within universities, their ultimate goal is to irrevocably alter higher education by eradicating free speech and critical thinking and dismantling the tenure system. If, during the 1950s, the university was relatively autonomous from the corporate-military complex, today they are inseparably intertwined in the form of a military-industrial-academic complex. If, decades ago, academic freedom, the integrity of tenure and faculty autonomy, and the educational merit of the university as a whole had a cold, today higher education is reeling from a black plague, dengue fever, or Ebola virus that is spreading with lethal effect, and yet the professoriate by and large remains as complacent as the general populace struggling for life and laughter in the work camps and carnivals of advanced capitalism.

When looking for a pattern in the key forces decimating academic freedom over the last two decades, one is immediately struck by the ability of outside interests to shape hiring and firing decisions and academic policy in general, in matters that should be determined within university institutions in accord with faculty autonomy. While this pattern was set already by the late-nineteenth century, and was evident in cases such as Edward Bemis (discussed above) where major donors or corporate trustees could intervene in faculty affairs, the interference has escalated despite codified free speech rights and tenure protections. Right-wing ideologues appoint themselves as arbiters of truth. They adopt a zero-tolerance policy of criticism of the homeland, especially in the aftermath of 9/11 and during times of war. They identify the offending voices of dissent and organize a plethora of outside forces to coerce universities to silence or fire them.

Senators and congresspersons, sundry conservative foundations and interest groups, the powerful Israel lobby machine and pro-Israeli groups such as the David Project (which produced the propaganda film against Columbia University professor Joseph Massad), right-wing radio and talk show hosts, Internet sites such as Campus Watch, parents organized by the right, alumni associations, powerful corporations, wealthy donors and backers, influential meddlers such as Alan Dershowitz, and demagogues such as David Horowitz. These are the agents of repression. They bribe, threaten, and stigmatize. They target professors, attack "studies programs," and protect the "right" of students to not hear ideas that contradict their entrenched worldview. They pursue the common goal of eliminating critical thinking, restoring conservative hegemony, and attacking the foundation of academic free speech: the tenure system.[135] In a classic case of psychological projection, they aim to create exactly what they accuse the liberal/left of doing—namely, indoctrinating not educating.

It is important to emphasize that professors certainly are accountable to certain norms and standards and do not stand outside the purview of public criticism. Nonetheless, reactionary interests are imposing their partisan politics on universities in a blatantly political and intrusive way that slanders scholars, disrupts or destroys careers, and muzzles free speech by subjecting ideas to ideological litmus tests—all in the name of diversity, rights, and freedom.[136] The two generations of McCarthyites were right about one thing, there was an enemy within, only it wasn't the liberals, the democrats, or the animal and Earth liberationists; it was *them*—the Machiavellian mercenaries who had no fear or shame in acquiring and maintaining power. Politically motivated demagogues from outside should have no more right intervening in academic matters than academics should have to meddle in the affairs of doctors or policemen, matters better left to each organization's own internal review board. As the Ad Hoc Committee to Defend the University states,

> Academic freedom means not only the right to pursue a variety of interpretations, but the maintenance of standards of truth and acceptability by one's peers… It is university faculty, not outside political groups with partisan political agenda, who are best able to judge the quality of their peers' research and teaching. This is not just a question of academic autonomy, but of the future of a democratic society. This is a time in which we need more thoughtful reflection about the world, not less."[137]

Neoliberalism and Academia

"Education is not a preparation for life; education is life itself."
—John Dewey

"Education is our passport to the future, for tomorrow belongs to the people who prepare for it today."
—Malcolm X

"The function of education is to teach one to think intensively and to think critically… Intelligence plus character—that is the goal of true education."
—Dr. Martin Luther King, Jr.

It was not paranoia that led John Dewey in the 1940s to warn that a corporatization process had begun whereby universities learned to shape and pattern themselves on a business model driven by the need to compete and turn education into a profit-making enterprise. Nor was it delusional when, in 1961, President Eisenhower warned that the "military industrial complex" posed a threat to the balance of powers and to civil liberties. The fusion of warfare, capitalism, science, and technology cannot take place without knowledge, advanced technologies, and a low-cost labor base, such as one finds ready-made in universities and their graduate student labor pools. Where science, engineering, and technology are crucial to capitalist militarism and militarist capitalism, universities form the third leg in a triadic system of postmodern power. It is a telling fact that the US spends more in the military sector than the rest of the world combined.

Consequently, deconstructing fictitious humanist ideals, describing the real goals and imperatives of "higher learning," and delegitimizing the power systems that actually run universities, many theorists during the last two decades understood that the boundary lines between universities, corporations, and military/warfare/social policing systems were dissolving. They no longer saw three separate, unrelated entities, but rather one gigantic industrial complex. The term "academic-military-industrial complex" is shorthand for the intersection, overlapping, and implosion of universities, the corporate private sector, the Department of Defense and various armed forces services, and the security and regulatory apparatuses of the State—all knotted together in a vast, predatory bureaucratic system developed for social and geopolitical domination.[138/139] By the 1990s, certainly, the questioning of scientific epistemology took on a far broader and more consequential term with critical scrutiny of the university institution itself, by charting the transformations of the mission and function of universities in the post-war era. Building on attacks on the politics of knowledge driving university research, a number of radical theorists, such as Stanley Aronowitz, Henry Giroux, Peter McLaren, Sandra Harding, and numerous contributors to this book analyzed how the nobler purposes and missions of universities and institutions of "higher learning" became corrupted and degraded. Hence, a spate of important new critical works emerged deconstructing the mythology of higher education and the academy as an institution.

As capitalism changes, so must education, and the rise of science and technology to dominant "productive forces" in the postindustrial phase of capital transforms education increasingly from a focus on humanities to narrow functional knowledge. The noble functions of higher education such as inculcating critical thinking skills, identities as citizens and members of interdependent communities, and the ability to meaningfully participate in and shape a democratic form of government gave way to reconfiguring the university as a corporation, ideological state apparatus, and technical school for training laborers.

Universities had become part of the "one dimensional society" (Marcuse), they had the potential to devastatingly criticize and overturn in favor of richly educated, highly cultured, autonomous citizens. Increasingly, the humanities and liberal arts were eclipsed by science, chemistry, mathematics, agriculture, geology, engineering, marketing, business, accounting, advertising, and other fields including sports. The economic rationale to increase university profits and functional purpose of producing individuals trained for science, technology, and business had the ideological bonus of homogenizing thought and stifling critical thinking. And under conditions of economic recession such as began to devastate global markets in 2008, universities have to tighten budgets and reduce or eliminate "superfluous" knowledges. Simultaneously, students increasingly turn toward practical realities of careers and economic survival and forego the "luxury" of studying literature, philosophy, or art, fields that regardless are grossly underfunded as they occupy the bottom rung of budgetary priorities. As the 2008–2009 crisis worsened, plunging much of the globe into recession and depression, worried students fall in line with corporate academic policies that reduce or eliminate "superfluous" humanities requirements in order to peddle degrees in marketable careers.

Partly due to economic constraints and partly because of the growing hegemony of technoscience, it is hard to miss the implosion between universities and vocational schools that eliminate liberal arts requirements and do little more than job training and indoctrinating students with capitalist values of competition, individualism, materialism, greed, and so on. Vocational schools such as Phoenix University are themselves corporate behemoths with branches spread throughout the US like fast-food chains. Indeed, on the neoliberal-consumerist model of education, knowledge is nothing but information to be consumed as quickly as possible, a sugary pabulum as injurious to the health of the mind as Whoppers and Big Macs are to the life of the body. In a society organized around work, productivity, and maximal exploitation of labor, no one has time for a satisfying meal let alone a genuine education, and the "slow food" movement ought to be linked to a drive toward a "slow education" that allows students the time and leisure to think and mature as human beings in pursuit of autonomy rather than in the service of capital.

As corporations, universities were interested in buying materials, investing in research and projects, inventing and patenting new technologies or advances in science and medicine, and competing on the marketplace. In fact, by the 1980s and 1990s, universities and society as a whole were becoming increasingly corporatized, marketized, and globalized. Acting like capitalists committed to the tyranny of the bottom line, universities began the cut-and-slash tactics that Reagan took to social programs in the 1980s, for a profitable enterprise cannot have excess costs, and labor expenses must be minimized. The dynamic that led to the restructuring of universities along corporate lines stemmed from aggressive neoliberal policies. The *laissez-faire* spirit of early capitalism was revived as neoliberalism, in order to dismantle welfare states, trade barriers, environmental regulations, and anything that stood in the way of trade. Universities moved in consort with the social, political, economic, and military systems that were changing the nature of the world through an aggressive neo-imperialism policy that was part and parcel of neoliberal attempts to subjugate the entire world to corporate power and market logic, while hopefully reviving a moribund American Empire.

Following the dominant corporate model, universities initiated a "de-skilling" of labor, and replaced the skilled labor of faculty with technology.[140] Compliant with the needs of businesses and an overworked labor force, and updating higher learning for the age of the Internet, universities began to offer "long-distance learning" such that students could earn a degree at home through correspondence, with "teachers" reduced to functionaries who grade quantitative exams, raising the specter of a future university system that dispenses with teachers altogether in favor of computerized grading machines.[141] "Increasingly," Ollman writes, "university life has been organized on the basis of a complex system of tests, grades, and degrees, so that people know exactly where they fit, what they deserve, what has to be done to rise another notch on the scale, and so on. Discounting—as most educators do—their negative effects on scholarship, critical thinking, and collegiality, these practices have succeeded in instilling a new discipline and respect for hierarchy."[142]

As universities implemented the neoliberal model, and economic realities became more pressing, particularly in the global economic crisis of 2008, universities, like automobile industries and other businesses, continued a trend of downsizing that led to replacing tenured and full-time faculty with part-time, adjunct, and contingent instructors viewed contemptuously as an army of cheap surplus labor.[143] Increasingly inadequate state funding due to fiscal crises led many to advocate for the privatization of public education institutions, a shift perfectly consistent with the neoliberal trend toward gutting social services and privatizing public institutions. Serving the political-economic-ideological conditions of capitalism in one fell swoop, universities began their attack on the system of tenure in an effort to hire less-expensive, wage- rather than salary-earning part-time instructors with few benefits and even less influence, dropping tenure positions after professors retired, and moving toward renewable three year contract systems, such as those at Florida International University.[144] In fact, this is only one of over forty institutions around the country—including Florida Gulf Coast University, Evergreen State College, Bennington, Bradford, Hampshire, and the University of Texas of the Permian Basin—that hire teachers only on annual or multi-year contracts.

Downsizing and de-skilling not only saves universities salary costs and makes them more competitive (an economic benefit), it also creates a highly precarious faculty who, without job security, tend to be docile and afraid to speak out (an ideological benefit). Corporate apologists think that the tenure system is a relic from the industrial era that is outmoded in a postindustrial, neoliberal, post-Fordist, "flexible" labor economy. In this world of hyperflux, people typically have numerous careers; it is unreasonable, neoliberals argue, to expect security, stability, and permanence. By this thinking, academia ought to open itself up to this dynamic market and change its institutional patterns before the market changes it. Faculty, however, reject this argument as market fetishism and fatalism, and insist that while post-Fordism may be fine for the automobile industry, it is anathema for education, which demands the kind of system that can protect free speech, the heart of higher education. There is a direct connection between the quality of research, teaching, education, and the university system as a whole and the strength of academic freedom, tenure, and faculty governance. Academic freedom is a win-win for everyone but repressive corporations, controlling bureaucrats, and right-wing zealots.

Unfortunately, the fast capitalists are winning over academics who seek job security, and the statistics are alarming. For the last seventy years at least, there has been a clear pattern in the academic race to the bottom. As Roger Bowen notes in his mournful eulogy for the tenure institution, "Since 1940, and most particularly over the past 15 years or so, tenured positions have been on the decline, as more colleges have relied on less expensive part-time and non-tenure-track faculty members—even as those same institutions professed fidelity to the principles of academic freedom. The reason for the change is simple and brutal: To enhance their own economic security as institutions, colleges have enhanced the economic insecurity of professors by hiring more and more contingent faculty members—that is, cheap, part-time laborers who enjoy few prerogatives of the profession while suffering low pay, few (if any) benefits, and flimsy contractual rights."[145] By 2003, 43 percent of all faculty were part time teachers and a massive 65 percent of professors held non-tenure positions.[146] Thus, "Today two of every three new faculty members hired across the nation are not on the tenure track, up from about 50 percent in the early 1990s." The economic and ideological benefits are enormous to the capitalist system, and right-wing culture wars play a crucial part in drowning the embers of critical voices before they spread like a bonfire.

Crossroads and the Crisis in Academia

"The political function of progressive intellectuals is not to wage a solitary duel with the ruling power but to help enlighten, arouse, instruct the working people who have the power, by virtue of their numbers, organization and strategic social position, to change the course of history."

—George Novack

"Thinking is not the intellectual reproduction of what already exists anyway. As long as it doesn't break off, thinking has a secure hold on possibility. Its insatiable aspect, its aversion to being

quickly and easily satisfied, refuses the foolish wisdom of resignation. The utopian moment in thinking is stronger the less it...objectifies itself into a utopia and hence sabotages its realization. Open thinking points beyond itself."
                                        —Theodor W. Adorno

"Education is the most powerful weapon which you can use to change the world."
                                        —Nelson Mandela

In the post 9/11 era, a slew of dissenting voices have fallen to the ax of political repression, countless others have been intimidated into silence and conformity, some have been imprisoned, others have been deported, and still others denied visas and job offers. Pressured by a host of outside forces, college administrations across the US have put their campuses on intellectual lockdown in response to the fear-laden, jingoistic, and repressive social environment. Slowly but surely, over the last century, but especially in the last few decades, the university is being transformed from a space of free thinking, experimentation, value and ethics teaching, and development of citizenship skills into a narrow, restrictive, bureaucratically-administered, utilitarian institution that serves the technical and economic needs of corporations, government, and the military, while it fattens from the money trough it helps to produce, and exploits an increasingly tenuous and contingent teaching staff.

Intense cultural, political, and economic wars have been fought over the last few decades, and the clear aggressor has been conservatives reacting against what they perceive to be the ascendance of corrosive liberal and left politics. Conservatives draw on a long history of anti-radicalism and anti-intellectualism in the US, they ride the tides of McCarthyism and other modes of social repression, and they exploit their dominance, secured by the Bush administration and adjusted by Obama. While worrying about the marriage contract, the weakening of family ties, the erosion of tradition, the surge of multiculturalism and "relativism," and the overall "decline of Western civilization," they have set their sites on higher education. They believe that the academy is the last major hold-out for liberalism, dissenting views, and radical politics, such that conservativism could fully triumph by purging American universities of critical thinking and oppositional viewpoints.

Meanwhile, it appears that most academics don't know what is happening, are too involved in their own careers, remain passive in fear of losing their jobs, or are uncertain how to respond. Despite some notable critiques and defiance, the professoriate was largely silent through two terms of the worst and most repressive administration in US history and amidst the greatest extinction and environment crisis in the last 65-million years. Similarly, as Obama reveals his true elitist and hypocritical nature more clearly with each passing day, the progressive academic community has overwhelmingly failed to challenge his militarism, classism, his embrace of Bush's detainment policies, and compliance with political repression and criminalization of dissent as domestic terrorism. Academic repression and the corporatization of the university persist under Obama as they did under Bush, again underscoring the fact that 9/11 was a political earthquake that established a bi-partisan consensus for surveillance and prosecution of "domestic terrorism," and will shake the foundations of civil liberties for some time to come, whatever corporate party rules.

Cowardice, apathy, self-indulgence, and self-preservation among college and university teaching staff at all levels virtually guarantees that the Christian Right will impose the teaching of "intelligent design" in biology classes, that versions of the Academic Bill of Rights will subject professors to patriotic correctness tests, that the Violent Radicalization and Homegrown Terrorism Prevention Act will extirpate controversial viewpoints, that the tenure system will become increasingly anemic and moribund, and that "higher education" will degenerate still further into career training and capitalist socialization.

The first step to change is developing an awareness of the forces decisively shaping society and academia, and, to that end, this book offers a comprehensive account of academic repression in the post-9/11 era.[147] Our goals are to give a broad social, historical, and economic context to illuminate recent developments in academia, to provide numerous case studies of academic repression, to anchor understanding in theory as well as personal experience, and finally to suggest ways to take back the nation's colleges and universities, and to prevent education from becoming totally debased, commodified, and controlled, and thereby completely indifferent to professors, staff, and students alike.

This volume addresses not only overt attacks on critical or radical thinking, it also engages the *broad structural determinants* of academic culture, and the socioeconomic trends unfolding for decades since the emergence of neoliberalism. It is not just about *discursive* issues of free speech and repression, as if academia would become a utopia should universities actually adhere to their mission statements. This idealist illusion is only corrected through a materialist emphasis on the formidable economic and *institutional* barriers to academic freedom, critical pedagogy, enlightenment, and citizenship in the global and ecological communities. In many ways, the ultimate cause of academic repression is not the academy itself—as if it really were an ivory tower island severed from the outside world—but, instead, contemporary capitalist society as a whole, which strongly shapes the structure, function, and priorities of higher education, as well as who gets to teach, study, and work and under what conditions.

We hope this book can be a tool of education and struggle. *Academic Repression: Reflections from the Academic-Industrial Complex* brings together prominent scholars, many of whom have experienced academic repression first-hand. It is crucial that these voices be heard, for many are silenced, marginalized, discredited, and shut out of public discourse, yet they have important insights and stories to convey. Like the last two volumes co-edited by Best and Nocella—*Terrorists or Freedom Fighters?: Reflections on the Liberation of Animals* (2004) and *Igniting a Revolution: Voices in Defense of the Earth* (2007)—we seek, in this book as well, to showcase a diversity of voices, standpoints, backgrounds, histories, and politics to approach a problem (academic repression, in this instance) from a wealth of different perspectives. By reading the personal and political accounts of queers, people of color, feminists, people with disabilities, Arab-Americans, foreign nationals, animal and Earth liberationists, and students and teachers from various status positions (from tenured faculty to adjunct instructors), we not only gain a rich and varied understanding of higher education as it functions today, we also can recognize the systemic nature of academic repression.

It is crucial that academics are aware of the struggles of their colleagues, and stand in resolute solidarity with one another. Critical scholars are being picked off one-by-one because they are marginalized, vulnerable, and isolated from one another, whereas networks of solidarity, support, and resistance can deter many attacks and defend academic rights when they are threatened. One can engage controversial issues with greater safety if a large number of respected scholars are also willing to write and speak out. Where labor conditions are abysmal or precarious, full and part time professors need to organize together, whether in unions or another suitable form. Together, faculty can also understand the problem is not an individual one, but a structural one involving various forms of economic, social, and political domination and discrimination (see Tropea in this volume).

We must forge connections, build bridges, and find common ground amidst our differences, such that gays and lesbians, the transgendered, the disabled, feminists, anarchists, ethnic studies and Middle Eastern scholars, animal and Earth liberation advocates, and a host of others combine forces to decisively challenge oppression, injustice, discrimination, militarism, fundamentalism, imperialism, and the omnicidal destruction of nonhuman animals, ecological systems, and biodiversity. However any of the diverse voices may disagree over theory, values, or politics, all can potentially unite over the unifying principle of academic freedom that provides the space for their views, and a thousand others, to bloom.

Although the degraded reality hardly mirrors the noble ideals, academic freedom is not merely a myth—it has a basis in reality (e.g., in faculty governance, legal policies, and review courts). It is urgent that more scholars use the openings they have to challenge the hierarchical organization of society and the exploitative and unsustainable operations of the capitalist economy, and that they do so in organized and consorted ways. These spaces atrophy amidst apathy, and the political vacuum will quickly be filled by authoritarians, demagogues, politicians, bureaucrats, capitalists, and reactionaries who seek to stifle free expression and critical pedagogy and to dismantle the tenure system in favor of disenfranchised academic proletarians.

If professors are far from powerless, the university is hardly a closed system of total domination. While colleges and universities are crucial sites of socialization, they are not monolithic citadels or homogeneous systems of thought that grind out each and every student in assembly-line fashion as functioning pieces of the market and military machines. *For just as universities can train tomorrow's CEOs, generals, weapons makers, and CIA agents, so can they breed the next generation of visionaries, thinkers, activists, and agents of social change.* Indeed, the indeterminacy and unpredictability of what a university experience might be for a young student is precisely why conservatives want to control the hiring and firing, classrooms and syllabi. It is why they fear the power of critical discourse tearing apart the flimsy rationales for power and the transparently arbitrary justifications for authority, elite control, social hierarchy, and the division of labor.

In fact, because colleges and universities are some of the last relatively free spaces of personal expression and political activity left in a society of bureaucratic domination, the university can be a key ground on which to forge not only new educational institutions but also new social institutions as well. Building democracy in academia is a crucial model and platform from which we can shape new democratic communities and societies. The only viable path to progressive change is through stepping into the circle and quickening the dialectic between education and democratization, lest we hasten the negative dialectic perpetuating the "race toward catastrophe" (H.G. Wells). But when the open and free expression integral to university life is endangered, so is society as a whole, for academia—although often a conservative bastion—traditionally has been a key site of critical thinking, rich human development, knowledge innovation, and progressive political change. If we lose one of the most important spaces for fostering enlightenment, we risk well-rounded people, critical knowledge, and progressive change—the consequences for society will be grim, and they already are bleak enough.

And thus it is a promising sign that forms of resistance to the conservative fatwa against secularism, liberalism, radicalism, dissent, and critical pedagogy have begun to sprout, such as with groups like the Ad Hoc Committee to Defend the University, Scholars at Risk, the American Federation of Teachers, the Middle East Studies Association Committee on Academic Freedom, the Free Exchange on Campus Coalition, the Foundation for Individual Rights in Education, the AAUP, the Committee to Defend Academic Freedom at UCSB, and online petitions and websites in support for academics including Bill Ayers and Ward Churchill.[148]

We desperately need new voices, more perspectives, great inclusiveness, and processes that lead right from the classroom to the polis, or rather destroy their separation and merge one space into the other. We seek a liberatory pedagogy and counter-hegemony that links the classroom to social and ecological realities, that promotes critical awareness and thinking skills, that advances the goals of citizenship and radical democracy, and that builds institutions counter to existing systems of repression and control. We hope this book can contribute to these transformations that grow increasingly urgent by the day.

I
Contextualizing Academic Repression

Higher Education after September 11ᵗʰ

The Crisis of Academic Freedom and Democracy

Henry Giroux

The war against this enemy is more than a military conflict. It is the decisive ideological struggle of the twenty-first century and the calling of our generation.
—George W. Bush, 11 September 2006

IN THE AFTERMATH OF THE TRAGIC EVENTS OF 9/11, the United States has increasingly established itself as a punitive power, eager to dismantle all vestiges of the social state, militarize public space, and eliminate those institutional spheres and rights that enable dialogue, debate, and dissent.[1] In fact, an incessant assault on critical thinking itself and a rising bigotry have undercut the possibility for providing a language in which vital social institutions can be defended as a public good. Moreover, as visions of equity recede from public memory, unfettered brutal self-interest and greed combine with retrograde social policies to make security and safety a top domestic priority. As the spaces for producing engaged citizens are either commercialized or militarized, the crushing effects of domination spread out to all aspects of society and war increasingly becomes the primary organizing principle of politics.[2] While such anti-democratic forces have a long history in the United States, they have been intensified and supplemented by the contemporary emergence of a number of diverse fundamentalisms, including a market-based neoliberal rationality, a post-9/11 militarism, and an aggressive right-wing patriotic correctness, all of which exhibit a deep disdain, if not contempt, for both democracy and publicly engaged teaching and scholarship.

If Michel Foucault is right that war is now "the motor behind institutions and order" and "a battlefront runs through the whole of society, continuously and permanently," then we must try to understand what forces generate this permanent state of war and which side of the battle we want to be on, because, as Foucault insisted, "There is no such thing as a neutral subject." If we are to heed Foucault's warning that "We are all inevitably someone's adversary,"[3] then we must make our decisions carefully, based on an understanding of what kind of world we are currently living in and what kind of world we want to pass on to future generations of young people. Indeed, the war we are faced with today has gained a new intensity as a range of diverse fundamentalisms now threaten all of those public spheres that enable debate, dissent, dialogue, and justice. In a post-9/11 world, what Foucault viewed as a "coded war" has become an all-out attack on higher education as dissent is now answered not with the rule of law, however illegitimate, but with the threat or actuality of violence.[4] Viewed by many right-wingers as the weak link in the war on terror, higher education is increasingly becoming a site in which to instruct students in the dictates of "patriotic correctness," an ideology that privileges conformity over critical learning and that represents dissent as something akin to a terrorist act. This means that, while the American university still employs the rhetoric of a democratic public sphere, there is a growing gap between a stated belief in noble purposes and the reality of an academy that is under siege.

Just as democracy appears to be fading in the United States so is the legacy of higher education's faith in academic freedom and commitment to democracy. Higher education is increasingly abandoning its role as a democratic public sphere as it aligns itself with corporate power and military values, while at the same time succumbing to a range of right-wing religious and political attacks.[5] Instead of being a space of critical dialogue, analysis, and interpretation, higher learning is increasingly defined as a site of consumption, where ideas are validated in instrumental terms and valued for their success in attracting outside funding while developing increasingly "strong ties to corporate and warfare powers."[6] As the culture of research is oriented towards the needs of the military-industrial-academic complex, faculty and students find their work further removed from the language of democratic values and their respective roles modeled largely upon entrepreneurs and consumers.

With no irony intended, Philip Leopold argues that it is an "essential part of an academic career" that professors and administrators be viewed as business entrepreneurs, trained to "watch the bottom line." Like businessmen, academics too must be attentive to "principles of finance, management, and marketing" and the development of a "brand identity (academic reputation) that is built on marketing (publications and presentations) of a high-quality product (new knowledge)."[7] In another statement pregnant with irony, Robert Gates, the Secretary of Defense under George W. Bush, has recently proposed the creation of what he calls a new "Minerva consortium," ironically named after the goddess of wisdom, whose purpose is to fund various universities to "carry out social-sciences research relevant to national security."[8] Gates would like to turn universities into militarized knowledge factories more willing to produce knowledge, research, and personnel in the interest of the warfare and Homeland (In) Security State than deploy critical knowledges to tackle the problems of contemporary life while holding dominant institutions accountable, especially those that trade in force, violence, and militarism, by questioning how their core values and presence in the world shape democratic identities, values, and organizations. Unfortunately, Gates' view of the university as a militarized knowledge factory, Professor Leopold's instrumental understanding of faculty as a "brand name," and the university as a new marketplace of commerce are not lines drawn from a gag enacted by Jon Stewart on the Comedy Channel. Instead, such views have become highly influential in shaping the purpose and meaning of higher education. Hence, it no longer seems unreasonable to argue that, just as democracy is being emptied out, the university is also being stripped of its role as a democratic setting where, though in often historically fraught ways, a democratic ethos can be cultivated, practiced, and sustained over generations.

Higher education in the United States appears to be suffering from a crisis of politics and a crisis of legitimacy. Politically, higher education is increasingly being influenced by larger economic, military, and ideological forces that consistently attempt to narrow its purview as a democratic public. Public intellectuals are now replaced by privatized intellectuals often working in secrecy and engaged in research that serves either the warfare state or the corporate state. Intellectuals are no longer placed in a vibrant relationship to public life, but now labor under the influence of managerial modes of governance and market values that mimic the logic of Wall Street. Consequently, higher education appears to be increasingly decoupling itself from its historic legacy as a crucial public sphere, responsible for both educating students for the workplace and providing them with the modes of critical discourse, interpretation, judgment, imagination, and experiences that deepen and expand democracy. Unable to legitimate its purpose and meaning according to such important democratic practices and principles, higher education now narrates itself in terms that are more instrumental, commercial, and practical. As universities adopt the ideology of the transnational corporation and become subordinated to the needs of capital, the war industries, and the Pentagon, they are less concerned about how they might educate students in the ideology and civic practices of democratic governance and the necessity of using knowledge to address the challenges of public life.[9] Instead, as part of the post-9/11 military-industrial-academic complex, higher education increasingly conjoins military interests and market values, identities, and social relations, while John Dewey's once vaunted claim that "democracy needs to be reborn in each generation, and education is its midwife" is either willfully ignored, forgotten, or becomes an object of scorn.[10]

Prominent educators and theorists such as Hannah Arendt, John Dewey, Cornelius Castoriadis, and Maxine Greene have long believed and rightly argued that we should not allow education to be modeled after the business world, nor should we allow corporate power and influence to undermine the semi-autonomy of higher education by exercising control over its faculty, curricula, and students. Dewey, in particular, warned about the growing influence of the "corporate mentality" and the threat that the business model posed to public spaces, higher education, and democracy. He argued that:

> The business mind, having his own conversation and language, its own interests, its own intimate groupings in which men of this mind, in their collective capacity, determine the tone of society at large as well as the government of industrial society.... We now have, although without formal or legal status, a mental and moral corporateness for which history affords no parallel.[11]

All of these public intellectuals shared a common vision and project of rethinking what role education might play in providing students with the habits of mind and ways of acting that would enable them to "identify and probe the most serious threats and dangers that democracy faces in a global world dominated by instrumental and technological thinking."[12] All four theorists offered a notion of the university as a bastion of democratic learning and values that provides a crucial referent in exploring the more specific question regarding what form will be taken by the relationship between corporations and higher education in the twenty-first century. In the best of all worlds, corporations would view higher education as much more than merely a training center for future business employees, a franchise for generating profit, or a space in which corporate culture and education merge in order to produce literate consumers.

Higher education has a deeper responsibility not only to search for the truth regardless of where it may lead but also to educate students to make authority politically and morally accountable; it is obliged to expand both academic freedom and the possibility and promise of the university as a bastion of democratic inquiry, values, and politics, even as these are necessarily refashioned at the beginning of the new millennium. While questions regarding whether the university should serve public rather than private interests no longer carry the weight of forceful criticism they did when raised by Thorstein Veblen, Robert Lynd, and C. Wright Mills in the first part of the twentieth century, such questions are still crucial in addressing the reality of higher education and what it might mean to imagine the university's full participation in public life as the protector and promoter of democratic values. This is especially true at a time when the meaning and purpose of higher education is under attack by a phalanx of right-wing forces attempting to slander, even vilify, liberal and left-oriented professors, cut already meager federal funding for higher education, eliminate tenure, and place control of what is taught and said in classrooms under legislative oversight.[13] The American university faces a growing number of problems that include the increasing loss of federal and state funding, the incursion of corporate power, a galloping commercialization of knowledge, and the growing influence of the national security state. At the same time, the university is also targeted by conservative forces that have highjacked political power and waged a focused campaign against the principles of academic freedom, sacrificing critical pedagogical practice in the name of patriotic correctness and dismantling the university as a bastion of autonomy, independent thought, and uncorrupted inquiry.

Conservatives have a long history of viewing higher education as a cradle of left-wing thought and radicalism. Just as religious fundamentalists attempted to suppress academic freedom in the nineteenth century, they continue to do so today, only in its current expression the attack on the university has taken a strange turn in that liberal professors, specifically in the arts, humanities, and social sciences, are now being portrayed as the enemies of academic freedom. As the charge goes, they allegedly abuse their authority by dogmatically forcing their radical and traitorous ideas down the throats of helpless conservative students, while tolerating no dissenting views. To understand the current attack on academe, it is necessary to comprehend the power that conservatives attributed to the political nature of education and the significance this view had in shaping the long-term strategy they put into place as early as the 1920s to win an ideological war against liberal intellectuals, who argued both for changes in American domestic and foreign policy and for holding government and corporate power accountable as a precondition for extending and expanding the promise of an inclusive democracy.

During the McCarthy era, criticisms of the university and its dissenting intellectuals cast a dark cloud over the exercise of academic freedom, and many academics were either fired or harassed out of their jobs for holding alleged communist views and even for being involved in moderately left-wing political activities outside the classroom. In 1953, the Intercollegiate Studies Institute (ISI) was founded by Frank Chodorov in order to assert right-wing influence and control over universities. ISI was but a precursor to the present era of politicized and paranoid academic assaults. In fact, William F. Buckley, who catapulted to fame among conservatives in the early 1950s with the publication of *God and Man at Yale*, in which he railed against secularism at Yale University and called for the firing of socialist professors, was named as the first president of ISI. The current president of ISI, T. Kenneth Cribb Jr., delivered a speech to the Heritage Foundation in 1989 that captures the ideological spirit and project behind its view of higher education. According to Cribb Jr.:

> We must…provide resources and guidance to an elite which can take up
> anew the task of enculturation. Through its journals, lectures, seminars,
> books and fellowships, this is what ISI has done successfully for 36 years.
> The coming of age of such elites has provided the current leadership of

the conservative revival. But we should add a major new component to our strategy: the conservative movement is now mature enough to sustain a counteroffensive on that last Leftist redoubt, the college campus…We are now strong enough to establish a contemporary presence for conservatism on campus, and contest the Left on its own turf. We plan to do this greatly by expanding the ISI field effort, its network of campus-based programming.[14]

ISI was an early effort on the part of conservatives to "take back" the universities from scholars and academic programs regarded either too hostile to free markets or too critical of the values and history of Western civilization.[15] As part of an effort to influence future generations to adopt a conservative ideology and leadership roles in "battling the radicals and PC types on campus," the Institute now provides numerous scholarships, summer programs, and fellowships to right-wing students.[16] *The Chronicle of Higher Education* reported in 2007 that various conservative groups are spending over $40 million "on their college programs."[17]

Perhaps the most succinct statement for establishing a theoretical framework and political blueprint for the current paranoia surrounding the academy is the Powell Memo, released on August 23, 1971, and authored by Lewis F. Powell, who would later be appointed as a member of the Supreme Court of the United States. Powell identified the American college campus "as the single most dynamic source" for producing and housing intellectuals "who are unsympathetic to the [free] enterprise system."[18] He recognized that one crucial strategy in changing the political composition of higher education was to convince administrators and boards of trustees that the most fundamental problem facing universities was the lack of conservative educators, or what he labelled the "imbalance of many faculties."[19] The Powell Memo was designed to develop a broad-based strategy not only to counter dissent but also to build a material and ideological infrastructure with the capability to transform the American public consciousness through a conservative pedagogical commitment to reproduce the knowledge, values, ideology, and social relations of the corporate state.

The Powell Memo, while not the only influence, played an important role in generating, in the sardonic words of Lewis Lapham, a "cadre of ultraconservative and self-mythologising millionaires bent on rescuing the country from the hideous grasp of Satanic liberalism."[20] The most powerful members of this group were Joseph Coors in Denver, Richard Mellon Scaife in Pittsburgh, John Olin in New York City, David and Charles Koch in Wichita, the Smith Richardson family in North Carolina, and Harry Bradley in Milwaukee—all of whom agreed to finance a number of right-wing foundations to the tune of roughly $3 billion[21] over thirty years, building and strategically linking "almost 500 think tanks, centers, institutes and concerned citizens groups both within and outside of the academy... A small sampling of these entities includes the Cato Institute, the Heritage Foundation, the American Enterprise Institute, the Manhattan Institute, the Hoover Institution, the Claremont Institute, the American Council of Trustees and Alumni, [the] Middle East Forum, Accuracy in Media, and the National Association of Scholars."[22] For several decades, right-wing extremists have labored to put into place an ultra-conservative re-education machine—an apparatus for producing and disseminating a public pedagogy in which everything tainted with the stamp of liberal origin and the word "public" would be contested and destroyed.

Given the influence and resources of this long campaign against progressive institutions and critical thought in the United States, it is all the more important that, as educators, we sit up and take notice, especially since the university is one of the few places left where critical dialogue, debate, and dissent can take place. A number of reputable scholars believe that the pace of the militarization and neoliberal reconstruction of higher education has accelerated within the last twenty-five years and is now moving at a dizzying pace, subjecting academe to what many progressives identify as a new and more dangerous threat. One of the most noted historians of the McCarthy era, Schrecker, insists that "today's assault on the academy is more serious" because "[u]nlike that of the McCarthy era, it reaches directly into the classroom."[23] Moreover, it is not only conservative trusties and academics who are in the driving seat, but also a growing number of well-funded and powerful right-wing agencies and groups outside the contained borders of the academy.

Joseph Beinin argues that many of these right-wing foundations and institutions have to be understood not only as part of a backlash against the protest movements of the 1960s—which called into question the university as a "knowledge factory" and criticized its failure to take its critical functions seriously—but also as political movements unconstrained by the professional standards of the university. He writes:

> The substantial role of students and faculty members in the anti-Vietnam War movement; the defection of most university-based Latin America specialists from US policy in the Reagan years, if not earlier; similar, if less widespread, defections among Africa and Middle East specialists; and the "culture wars" of the 1980s and 1990s all contributed to the rise of think tanks funded by right-wing and corporate sources designed to constitute alternative sources of knowledge unconstrained by the standards of peer review, tolerance for dissent, and academic freedom.[24]

Moreover, the new assaults being waged against higher education are not simply against dissenting professors and academic freedom but are also deeply implicated in questions of power, specifically regarding who controls the hiring process, the organization of curricula, and the nature of pedagogy itself. Subject to both market mechanisms and right-wing ideological rhetoric about using the academy to defend the values of Western civilization, the promise of the university as a democratic public sphere appears to be dwindling to an alarming degree.

While it is crucial to recognize that the rise of the "new McCarthyism" cannot be attributed exclusively to the radical curtailment of civil liberties initiated by the George W. Bush administration after the cataclysmic events of September 11, 2001, it is nonetheless true that a growing culture of fear and jingoistic patriotism emboldened a post-9/11 patriotic correctness movement, most clearly exemplified by actions of the right-wing American Council of Trustees and Alumni (ACTA), which shortly after the attacks issued a report accusing a supposedly unpatriotic academy of being the "weak link in America's response to the attack."[25] Individuals and groups who opposed George W. Bush's foreign and domestic policies were put on the defensive—some overtly harassed—while right-wing pundits, groups, and foundations repeatedly labeled them "traitors" and "un-American." In some cases, conservative accusations that seemed disturbing, if not disturbed, before the events of 9/11 now appeared perfectly acceptable, especially to the dominant media. The nature of conservative acrimony may have been marked by a new language, but the goal was largely the same: to remove from the university all vestiges of dissent, and to reconstruct the public sphere as an increasingly privatized zone for reproducing the interests of corporations and the national security state as it maneuvered for a front-line position in the promotion of an imperialist military agenda. In short, universities were castigated as hotbeds of left-wing radicalism, and conservative students alleged that they were being mocked and discriminated against in classrooms throughout the country by zealous radical professors and hordes of menacing Marxists.

The language and tactics of warfare moved easily between a critique of so called rogue states such as Iraq and Iran and universities whose defense of academic freedom did not sit well with academic and political advocates of the new neoliberal security-surveillance state.[26] McCarthy-like blacklists were posted on the Internet by right-wing groups such as Campus Watch, ACTA, and Target of Opportunity,[27] attempting to both out and politically shame allegedly radical professors who were giving aid and comfort to the enemy because of their refusal to provide unqualified support for the Bush administration. Academic "balance" was now invoked as a way to promote a form of affirmative action for hiring conservative faculty, while academic freedom was redefined both through the prism of student rights and as a legitimating referent for dismantling professional academic standards and imposing outside political oversight of the classroom. If the strategy and project of conservative ideologues became more energetic and persistent after 9/11, it is also fair to say that right-wing efforts and demands to reform higher education took a dangerous turn that far exceeded the threat posed by the "culture wars" raging over the last few decades.

Under the Bush-Cheney administration, the war on terror and the neoliberal mantra of privatize or perish became a battle cry for a generation of right-wing activists attempting to dismantle public and higher education as democratic public spheres. A right-wing coalition of Christian evangelicals, militant nationalists, market fundamentalists, and neoconservatives that had gained steam under the Reagan administration acquired unprecedented power in shaping policy under the second Bush presidency. Academics as well as public school teachers who critically addressed the US presence in Iraq, the neo-conservative view of an imperial presidency, the unchecked market fundamentalism of the Bush administration, or the right-wing views driving energy policies, sex-education, or the use of university research "in pursuit of enhanced war-making abilities"[28] were either admonished, labeled un-American, or simply fired. Similarly, academic and scientific knowledge that challenged the worldviews of these anti-democratic forces were either erased from government policies or attacked by government talking heads as morally illegitimate, politically offensive, or in violation of patriotic correctness. Scientists who resisted the ban on stem cell research as well as the official government position on global warming, HIV transmission, and sex education were intimidated by congressional committees, which audited their work or threatened "to withdraw federal grant support for projects whose content they find substantively offensive."[29] Educators who argued for theoretical and policy alternatives to abstinence as a mode of sex education were attacked, fired, or denied funding programs for education. And as the forces of patriotic correctness joined the ranks of market fundamentalists, higher education was increasingly defined through the political lens of an audit culture that organized learning around measurable outcomes rather than modes of critical thinking and inquiry.

As the web of surveillance, security, mistrust, and ideological damnation spread from enemies within to enemies abroad, the Bush administration increasingly revoked or denied visas to foreign scholars wishing to enter the country. All of those denied entry or forced to leave allegedly posed a threat to the country—though the nature of that threat was rarely ever spelled out by the Department of Homeland Security. For example, in 2007, the up-and-coming musicologist, Nalini Ghuman, was stopped at a San Francisco airport while on her way to perform at music festival at Bard College and told that "she was no longer allowed to enter the United States."[30] Ms. Ghuman, a British citizen, had lived in the United States for the last ten years and was at the time an assistant professor of music at Mills College. Leon Bostein, the President of Bard College, argued that Ms. Ghuman's case was "an example of the xenophobia, incompetence, stupidity and … bureaucratic intransigence" that now characterize the National (In)Security State.[31] In a similar case, Riyadh Lafta, an Iraqi professor of medicine, was denied a visa to visit the University of Washington in order to present his research findings on the high rate of cancer among children in Southern Iraq. Scientists familiar with his case believe that the government took this action because he had published a 2006 study in the British medical journal, *The Lancet*, which had "controversially estimated that more than 650,000 Iraqis—far more than officially reported—had died as a result of the American-led invasion."[32]

Not only are such cases troubling and abusive, they are also part of a broader pattern of censorship and denial of academic freedom put into place by a government that neither tolerates dissent nor feels any responsibility to provide reasons to those it denies visas, interrogates, or puts into prison. One of the more outlandish government abuses concerned the internationally recognized scholar Tariq Ramadan, a Swiss citizen and Islamic scholar, who has published over twenty books. In 2003, he was offered the prestigious Henry B. Luce Professorship of Religion, Conflict and Peace at the University of Notre Dame. Ramadan accepted the job, resigned his position in Switzerland, and obtained a work visa early in 2004. Nine days before he was to fly to the United States, the Department of Homeland Security revoked his work visa, thus preventing him from assuming his teaching position at Notre Dame. While not offering a specific explanation for revoking his visa, the government suggested, without any substantial proof, that Professor Ramadan "endorsed or espoused" terrorist activities.

In fact, Professor Ramadan was an outspoken critic of terrorism in all of its forms, and he was also a strong advocate of reconciling the democratic principles of Islam and Western modernity. Professor Ramadan's advocacy in the name of peace and against global violence later earned him the distinction of being named by former Prime Minister Tony Blair "to serve on a British commission to combat terrorism."[33] But the US government continued to reject his visa application, even in defiance of a federal court order, offering up new and specious arguments, all of which suggested that the real reason Professor Ramadan was prevented from obtaining a visa was because he was critical of Bush's Middle East policies and took a moderate position that refused the violence of all fundamentalisms. In 2006, he wrote an article in *The Washington Post* on why he was banned from the United States. His words are as ominous as they are important. He writes:

> My experience reveals how US authorities seek to suppress dissenting voices and—by excluding people such as me from their country—manipulate political debate in America. Unfortunately, the US Government's paranoia has evolved far beyond a fear of particular individuals and taken on a much more insidious form: the fear of ideas... Will foreign scholars be permitted to enter the United States only if they promise to mute their criticisms of US policy? It saddens me to think of the effect

this will have on the free exchange of ideas, on political debate within America, and on our ability to bridge differences across cultures.[34]

Another instructive instance pertains to the barring of foreign academics who, when arriving in the United States to attend conferences, are detained, interrogated about their political views, and then put back on flights to their own countries. This procedure has become so commonplace that many scholarly associations now hold their annual meetings in Canada. The arbitrary way in which recognized international public intellectuals and committed scholars have been denied visas by the US government serves as a chilling reminder that international knowledge production is being policed in an unprecedented fashion, and that appeals to the principle of academic freedom are largely viewed by the (In)Security State as either irrelevant or as what Herbert Marcuse called "a disturbance created by criticism" that is ultimately met with state violence and open brutality.[35]

Sadly, the government is not the only political entity restricting open inquiry, critical knowledge, and dissent in the United States. The current harassment of critical intellectuals after 9/11 has also been aggressively promoted by private advocacy groups. Media watchdogs, campus groups, and various payroll pundits not only held favor with the Bush administration but also received millions of dollars from right-wing foundations and were powerfully positioned to monitor and quarantine any vestige of independent thought in the academy. Since the events of 9/11, academics who challenged the political orthodoxy of the Bush administration have been subjected to intimidation and harassment by conservative politicians, ultra-conservative commentators, right-wing talk-show hosts, Christian zealots, and conservative students.

Some of the most famous cases include professors such as Joseph Massad of Columbia University, Norman Finkelstein of DePaul University, Nadia Abu El-Haj of Barnard College and Columbia University, and Ward Churchill of the University of Colorado. Though these cases received wide attention in the mainstream media, they represent just some of the many academics who have been attacked by the right-wing through a highly organized campaign of intimidation and an all-out assault on academic freedom, critical scholarship, and the very idea of the university as a place to question and think.[36] Ward Churchill, in particular, provides an instance of the expanding web of attacks against leftist academics whose political views are represented by right-wing media as symptomatic of most professors in academia. Menacingly, Newt Gingrich, former Speaker of the House, threatened to take out Churchill and virtually everyone not a White Male Republican: "We are going to nail this guy and send the dominoes tumbling. And everybody who has an opinion out there and entire disciplines like ethnic studies and women's studies and cultural studies and queer studies that we don't like won't be there anymore."[37]

While Gingrich was honest enough to reveal that Churchill was just a pawn in a much larger war being waged by right-wing extremists in order to divest the university of its critical intellectuals, diversity, and critically oriented curricula and departments, ACTA subsequently produced a booklet titled *How Many Ward Churchills?* in which it insisted that the space that separated Churchill from most faculty was miniscule, and that colleges and universities now "risk losing their independence and the privilege they have traditionally enjoyed."[38] And how do we know that higher education has fallen into such dire straits? This apocalyptic change was revealed through an inane summary of course syllabi taken from various colleges, allegedly proving that "professors are using their classrooms to push political agendas in the name of teaching students to think critically."[39] Courses that included discussions of race, social justice, and whiteness as a tool of exclusion were dismissed as distorting American history, by which ACTA meant consensus history, a position made famous by Lynne Cheney, who repeatedly asserted that history should be celebratory even if it means overlooking "internal conflicts and the non-white population."[40]

Rather than discuss the moral principles or pedagogical values of courses organized around the need to address human suffering, violence, and social injustice, the ACTA report claimed that "anger and blame are central components of the pedagogy of social justice."[41] In the end, the listing of course descriptions was designed to alert administrators, governing boards, trustees, and tenure and hiring committees of the need to police instructors in the name of "impartiality." Presenting itself as a defender of academic freedom, ACTA actually wants to supervise and police the academy, just as in the name of national defense Homeland Security monitors the reading habits of library patrons and the National Security Agency spies on American citizens with warrantless wiretaps.

Despite its rhetoric, ACTA is not a friend of the principles of academic freedom or diversity, nor is it comfortable with John Dewey's insistence that education should be responsive to the deepest conflicts of our time. And while the tactics to undermine academic freedom and critical education have grown more sophisticated, right-wing representations of the academy have become increasingly shrill. For instance, James Pierson, in the conservative *Weekly Standard*, claimed that when 16-million students enter what he calls the "left-wing university," they will discover that its ideology is both "anti-American and anticapitalist."[42] And for Roger Kimball, editor of the conservative journal *The New Criterion*, the university has been "corrupted by the values of Woodstock...that permeate our lives like a corrosive fog." He asks, "Why should parents fund the moral de-civilization of their children at the hands of tenured antinomians?"[43] Another example of these distortions occurred when former Republican presidential candidate Reverend Pat Robertson proclaimed that there were at least "thirty to forty thousand" left-wing professors or, as he called them, "termites that have worked into the woodwork of our academic society."[44] Inflated rhetoric aside, the irony of this rallying cry for a conservative project designed to legislate more outside control over teacher authority, to enact laws to protect conservative students from pedagogical harassment, and to pass legislation that regulates the hiring process is that, while dressed up in the language of fairness and balance, it cleverly expropriates, as Jonathan Cole suggests, "key terms in the liberal lexicon, as if they [the right] were the only true champions of freedom and diversity on campuses."[45]

One of the most powerful and well-known spokespersons leading the effort for "academic balance" is David Horowitz, president of the Center for the Study of Popular Culture, and the ideological force behind the online magazine *FrontPageMag. com*. A self-identified former left-wing radical who transmogrified into a right-wing conservative, he is the author of over twenty books and the founder of Students for Academic Freedom, a national watchdog group that monitors what professors say in their classrooms. He is also the creator of *DiscovertheNetworks.org*, an online database whose purpose is to "catalogue all the organizations and individuals that make up" what he defines in sweeping monolithic terms as "the Left."[46]

As one of the most forceful voices in the assault on higher education, Horowitz appropriated liberal appeals to intellectual diversity and academic freedom with great success to promote his Academic Bill of Rights (ABOR).[47] The central purpose of this project according to Horowitz, is to "to enumerate the rights of students to not be indoctrinated or otherwise assaulted by political propagandists in the classroom or any educational setting."[48] Horowitz's case for the Academic Bill of Rights rests on a series of faulty empirical studies, many conducted by right-wing associations, which suggest left-wing views completely dominate the academy.[49] The studies look compelling until they are more closely engaged.[50] For example, they rarely look at colleges, departments, or programs outside of the social sciences and humanities, thus excluding a large portion of the campus. And yet, according to the *Princeton Review*, four of the top-ten most popular subjects are business administration and management, biology, nursing, and computer science, none of which is included in Horowitz's data.[51] While it is very difficult to provide adequate statistics regarding the proportion of liberals to conservatives in academe, a University of California at Los Angeles report surveyed over 55,000 full-time faculty and administrators in 2002–2003 and found that "48 percent identified themselves as either liberal or far left; 34 percent as middle of the road, and … 18 percent as conservative or far right."[52] All in all, 52.3 percent of college faculty either considered themselves centrist or conservative, suggesting that balance is far less elusive than Horowitz would have us believe.

Furthermore, a 2006 study by the journal *Public Opinion Quarterly* argues that "recent trends suggest increased movement to the center, toward a more moderate faculty."[53] But there is more at stake here than the reliability of statistical studies measuring the voting patterns, values, and political positions of faculty. There is also the issue of whether such studies tell us anything at all about what happens in college classrooms. What correlation is to be correctly assumed between a professor's voting patterns and how he or she teaches a class? None. How might such studies deal with people whose political positions are ambiguous, as when an individual is socially conservative but economically radical? And are we to assume that there is a correlation between "one's ideological orientation and the quality of one's academic work?"[54] Then, of course, there's the question that the right-wing commissars refuse to acknowledge: Who is going to monitor and determine what the politics of potential new hires, existing faculty members, and departments? How does such a crude notion of politics mediate disciplinary wars between, for instance, those whose work is empirically driven and those who adhere to qualitative methods? And if balance implies that all positions are equal and valid in order to avoid bias, should universities give equal time to Holocaust deniers, creationists, or pro-slavery advocates, to name but a few dubious perspectives? Moreover, as Russell Jacoby astutely asks, if political balance is so important, then why isn't it invoked in other commanding sectors of society such as the police force, Pentagon, FBI, and CIA?[55]

The right-wing demand for balance also deploys the idea that conservative students are relentlessly harassed, intimidated, or unfairly graded because of their political views, despite their growing presence on college campuses and the generous financial support they receive from over a dozen conservative institutions. One place where such examples of alleged discrimination can be found is on the website of Horowitz's Students for Academic Freedom (SAF), whose credo is "You can't get a good education if they're only telling you half the story."[56] SAF has chapters on 150 campuses and maintains a website where students can register complaints. Most complaints express dissatisfaction with teacher comments or assigned readings that have a left-liberal orientation. Students complain, for instance, about reading lists that include books by Howard Zinn, Cornel West, or Barbara Ehrenreich. Others protest classroom screenings of Michael Moore's *Fahrenheit 9/11*, *Super Size Me*, or *Wal-Mart: The High Cost of Low Living*.

What is disturbing about these instances is that aggrieved students and their sympathizers appear entirely indifferent to the degree to which they not only enact a political intrusion into the classroom but also undermine the concept of informed authority, teacher expertise, and professional academic standards at many levels. The complaints by conservative students often share the premise that because they are "consumers" of education, they have a right to demand what should be taught, as if knowledge is simply a commodity to be purchased according to one's taste and never to be subject to opposing viewpoints. Academic standards, norms of evidence, reasoning, and the assumption that professors earn a certain amount of authority because they are familiar with a research tradition and its methodologies, significant scholarship, and history are entirely removed from such complaints, leaving the presupposition that students have the right to listen only to ideas they agree with and to select their own classroom reading materials. Because students disagree with an unsettling idea does not mean that they should have the authority, expertise, education, or power to dictate for all their classmates what should be stated, discussed, or taught in a classroom. What is lost in these arguments is the central pedagogical assumption that teaching is about activating knowledge, providing students with the tools to critically engage what they know and to recognize the limits of their own knowledge. It is also about learning to think from the place of the other, to "raise one's self-reflexiveness to the highest maximum point of intensity." It also means critically engaging students to believe in the power of ideas while recognizing that ideas alone do not shape the larger world.

One important component of critical pedagogy is that although the search for knowledge has to be defended at all costs, neither academics nor students can ignore the conditions that make such knowledge available or possible. But critical pedagogy is also about teaching students how to hold authority and power accountable, supplying them with the tools to make judgments freed from "the hierarchies of [official] knowledge" that refuse critical engagement, and providing them with the resources to skilfully engage in what Jacques Rancière calls "dissensus."[57] A key goal of critical pedagogy is to enable students to be reflexive agents who connect the search for knowledge, truth, and justice to the ongoing tasks of democraticizing the university and society as a whole.

For many conservatives, the commitment to critical thinking and the notion of pedagogy as a normative, moral, and political practice, rather than a disinterested and value-free technical task, is simply a mode of indoctrination. For instance, Horowitz attempts in his book, *The Professors*, to depoliticize pedagogy, deskill faculty, and infantilize students through the charge that a number of reputable scholars who take critical thinking seriously simply indoctrinate their students with alien political views.[58] The book, as detailed by a report of Free Exchange on Campus organization, is an appalling mix of falsehoods, lies, misrepresentations, and unsubstantiated anecdotes.[59] Not only does Horowitz fail to include in his list of "dangerous" professors one conservative academic, but many professors are condemned simply for what they teach, as Horowitz actually has little or no ammunition against *how* they teach.

Professor Lewis Gordon, for example, is criticized for including "contributions from Africana and Eastern thought" in his course on existentialism.[60] The extremes to which Horowitz would travel in his ad hominem invective is perfectly captured in a comment he made on Dr. Laura's talk show in which he averred that "campus leftists hate America more than the terrorists."[61] How does one take seriously Horowitz's call for fairness when he smears the American Library Association as "a terrorist sanctuary,"[62] or vilifies Noam Chomsky—whom *The New Yorker* named "one of the greatest minds of the 20th century"[63]—as a "demonic and seditious" traitor whose work seeks to "incite believers to provide aid and comfort to the enemies of the US"?[64] Indeed, what is one to make of Horowitz's online "A Guide to the Political Left," in which the mild-mannered film critic Roger Ebert occupies the same ideological ground as Omar Abdel Rahman, the mastermind of the 1993 World Trade Center bombing? Can one really believe that Horowitz is a voice for open inquiry when he portrays the late Peter Jennings, Supreme Court Justice Ruth B. Ginsburg, Garrison Keillor, and Katie Couric as activists for "left-wing agendas and causes"?[65]

Apparently, politicians at all levels of government *do* take Horowitz seriously. In 2005, Florida legislators considered a bill inspired by the ABOR that would provide students with the right to sue their professors if they feel their views, such as a belief in Intelligent Design, are disrespected in class.[66] At the federal level, the ABOR legislation made its way through various House and Senate Committees with the firm backing of a number of politicians and was passed in the House of Representatives in March 2006, but went no further.[67] In 2007, a Senate committee in Arizona passed a bill in which faculty could be fined up to $500 for "advocating one side of a social, political, or cultural issue that is a matter of partisan controversy."[68]

As Stanley Fish has argued, "balance" is a flawed concept and should be understood as a political tactic rather than an academic value.[69] The appeal to balance is designed to do more than get conservatives teaching in English Departments, promote intellectual diversity, or protect conservative students from the horrors of left-wing indoctrination; its deeper purpose is to monitor pedagogical exchange through government intervention, thereby calling into question the viability of academic integrity and undermining the university as a public sphere that educates students as critically engaged and responsible citizens in the larger global context. The attack by Horowitz and his allies against liberal faculty and programs in the social sciences and humanities such as Middle Eastern studies, women's studies, and peace studies has opened the door to a whole new level of assault on academic freedom, teacher authority, and critical pedagogy.[70] These attacks, as I have pointed out, are much more widespread and, in my estimation, much more dangerous than the McCarthyite campaign several decades ago. And in response to this attack on academic freedom even the most spirited defenders of the university as a democratic public sphere too often overlook the ominous threat being posed to what takes place in the classroom, and, by extension, to the very nature of pedagogy as a political, moral, and critical practice.[71]

The concept of balance demeans teacher authority by suggesting that a political litmus test is the most appropriate consideration for teaching, and it devalues students by suggesting that they are happy robots, interested not in thinking but in merely acquiring skills for jobs. In this view, students are incapable of thinking critically or engaging knowledge that unsettles their worldviews, and too weak to resist ideas that challenge their commonsense understanding of the world. And teachers are rendered instruments of official power and apologists for the existing order. An instructor's authority can never be neutral, nor can it be assessed in terms that are narrowly ideological. It is always broadly political and interventionist in terms of the knowledge-effects it produces, the classroom experiences it organizes, and the future it presupposes in the countless ways it addresses the world. Teacher authority suggests that, as educators, we must make a sincere effort to be self-reflective about the value-laden nature of any orientation, while shouldering the task of educating students to take responsibility for the direction of society.

While liberals, progressives, and left-oriented educators have been increasingly opposed to the right-wing assault on higher education, they have not done enough either theoretically or politically. While there is a greater concern about the shameless state of non-tenured and part-time faculty in the United States, such concerns have not been connected to a full-spirited attack on the forces of neoliberalism, managerialism, conservative hegemony, and repressive administrative governance.[72] Neoliberalism makes possible not only the ongoing corporatization of the university and the increasing militarization of knowledge, but also the powerlessness of faculty who are increasingly treated as disposable populations. The three major academic unions in the United States have neither waged a vigorous defense of higher education as a democratic public sphere nor have they moved beyond a limited support of academic freedom toward a restoration of democratic decision making to benefit faculty and students.

Moreover, as students increasingly find themselves as an indentured generation, there is a need for educators and others to once again connect equity and excellence as inseparable values and freedoms. Why aren't the unions producing their own forms of public pedagogy, educating the larger public about the nature of the crisis of higher education, particularly as it translates into a crisis of opportunity, public life, and democracy itself? What responsibility do the unions have to connect the work of higher education to a broader public good, to defend the rights of academics as public intellectuals, and to take seriously academic freedom as a discourse and practice that not only engages in the search for truth but also affirms the importance of social responsibility and civic commitment? Perhaps they are quiet because they are under the illusion that tenure will protect them, or they believe that the assault on academic freedom has little to do with how they perform their labor. If so, they would be wrong on both counts, and unless the unions and progressives mobilize to protect the institutionalized relationships between democracy and pedagogy, teacher authority and classroom autonomy, higher education will remain at the mercy of a right-wing revolution that views democracy as an excess and academic freedom as a threat to social tradition and order.

Pedagogy must be understood not only as central to any discourse about academic freedom, but also as the most crucial referent we have for understanding politics and defending the university as one of the last remaining democratic public spheres in the United States today. As Ian Ingus rightly argues, "The justification for academic freedom lies in the activity of critical thinking" and the pedagogical and political conditions necessary to protect it.[73] I believe that too many notions of academic freedom are muddled through a privatized approach divorced from the issue of democratic governance, without which no academic freedom can exist. Right-wing notions of teaching and learning constitute a kind of anti-pedagogy, substituting conformity for dialogue and ideological inflexibility for critical engagement. Such attacks should be named for what they are—an affirmation of thoughtlessness, and an antidote to the difficult process of criticism and transformation of the self and society.[74] Its outcome is not a student who feels a responsibility to others, but one who feels the presence of difference as an unbearable burden to be contained or expelled.

But the current right-wing assault on liberal and left values is directed not only against the conditions that make critical pedagogy possible but also against the prospect of raising questions about the real problems facing higher education today, which include the increasing role of adjunct faculty, the instrumentalization of knowledge, the rise of an expanding national security state, the hijacking of the university by corporate and military interests, and the growing attempts by right-wing extremists to turn education into job training or an extended exercise in patriotic xenophobia. All of these conditions undermine the idea of the university as a place to think, to engage knowledge critically, to make informed judgments, to assume responsibility for one's thoughts and values, and to understand the consequences of such knowledge for the larger world.

Higher education has become part of a market-driven and militarized culture imposing upon academics and students new modes of discipline that close down the spaces to think critically, while undermining substantive dialogue and restricting students from thinking outside of established expectations. The conservative pedagogical project is less about promoting intellectual curiosity, understanding the world differently, or enabling students to raise fundamental questions about "what sort of world one is constructing."[75] On the contrary, its primary purpose is to produce dutiful subjects willing to sacrifice their sense of agency for a militaristic sense of order and unquestioning respect for authority. This is more than a blueprint for conformity; it is also a recipe for a type of thoughtlessness that, as Hannah Arendt reminds us, lies at the heart of totalitarian regimes.[76]

In light of this right-wing assault on critical thought, educators have a political and moral responsibility to critique the university as a major element in the military-industrial-academic complex. At the very least, this means being attentive to the ways in which conservative pedagogical practices "deny the democratic purposes of education and undermine the possibility of a critical citizenry. Yet, such a critique, while important, is not enough. Academics also have a responsibility to make clear that higher education harbors other memories, brought back to life in the 1960s, in which the academy was remembered for its public role in developing citizenship and social awareness—a role that shaped and overrode its economic function."[77] Such memories, however uncomfortable to the new corporate managers of higher education, must be nurtured and developed in defense of higher education as an important site of both critical thought and democratization. Instead of a narrative of decline, educators need a discourse of critique and resistance, possibility and hope. Such memories both recall and seek to reclaim how the public and democratic role of higher education, however imperfect, gives new meaning to its purpose and raises fundamental questions about how knowledge can be emancipatory and how and education for democracy can be both desirable and possible. Memories of educational resistance and hope suggest more than the usual academic talk about shattering the boundaries that separate academic disciplines or connecting to students' lives, however important these considerations might be.

There is also, as Stuart Hall points out, the urgent need for educators, to provide students with "Critical knowledge [that is] *ahead* of traditional knowledge... *better* than anything that traditional knowledge can produce, because only serious ideas are going to stand up." Moreover, there is the need to recognize "the social limits of academic knowledge. Critical intellectual work cannot be limited to the university but must constantly look for ways of making that knowledge available to wider social forces."[78] If Hall is right, and I think he is, educators have a pedagogical responsibility to make knowledge concrete and meaningful for it to be critical and transformative. But such knowledge should be more than a provocation that takes students beyond the world they already know; it should also expand the range of human possibilities by connecting what students know, and how they come to know, to instilling in them both "a disgust for all forms of socially produced injustice" and the desire to make the world different from what it is.[79]

The current right-wing assault on higher education is in reality an attack on the most rudimentary conditions of democratic politics. A caricature of principled conservatism, the new ideological fundamentalism, in its political, market, and religious versions, views democracy as a deficit and the university as both a weak link in the war on terrorism and an obstacle to banishing all remnants of enlightenment rationality— with its legacy of critique, dialogue, thoughtfulness, responsibility, and judgment—in favor of a no-holds-barred militarized National (In)Security State. All of these antidemocratic ideas and social movements contribute to what Hannah Arendt once called "dark times"—a period in which the public realm has lost "the power of illumination."[80]

Genuine politics begins to disappear as people methodically lose those freedoms and rights that enable them to speak, act, dissent, and exercise both their individual right to resistance and a shared sense of collective responsibility.

While higher education is only one site, it is one of the most crucial institutional and political spaces where democratic subjects can be shaped, democratic relations can be experienced, and anti-democratic forms of power can be identified and critically engaged. It is also one of the few spaces left where young people can think critically about the knowledge they gain, learn values that refuse to reduce the obligations of citizenship to either consumerism or the dictates of the national security state, and develop the language and skills necessary to defend those institutions and social relations that are vital to a substantive democracy. As Arendt insisted, a meaningful conception of politics appears only when concrete spaces exist for people to come together to talk, think critically, and act on their capacities for empathy, judgment, and social responsibility. Under such circumstances, the academy, faithful to its role as a crucial democratic public sphere, offers "a hope that makes all hoping possible" while also offering a space both to resist the "dark times" in which we now live and to embrace the possibility of a future forged in the civic struggles requisite for a viable democracy.[81]

Academic Repression

Past and Present

Michael Parenti

F OR SOME TIME, we have been asked to believe that the quality of higher education is being devalued by the "politically correct" ideological tyranny of feminists, African-American and Latino militants, homosexuals, and Marxists. The
truth may be elsewhere. The average university or college is a corporation, controlled
by self-selected, self-perpetuating boards of trustees, drawn mostly from the corporate
business world. Though endowed with little if any academic expertise, trustees have
legal control of the property and policies of the institution. They are answerable to no
one but themselves, exercising final authority over all matters of capital funding, budget, tuition, and the hiring, firing, and promotion of faculty and administrators. They
even wield ultimate dominion over curriculum, mandating course offerings they like
while canceling ones that might earn their disfavor. They also have final say regarding
course requirements, cross-disciplinary programs, and the existence of entire departments and schools within the university.

On the nation's campuses there also can be found faculty members who do
"risk analysis" to help private corporations make safe investments abroad. Other faculty work on consumer responses, marketing techniques, and labor unrest. Still others
devise methods for controlling rebellious peoples at home and abroad, be they Latin
American villagers, inner-city residents, or factory workers. Funded by corporations,
conservative foundations, the Pentagon, and other branches of government, the researchers develop new technologies of destruction, surveillance, control, and counter-
insurgency. (Napalm, for example, was invented at Harvard.) They develop new ways
of monopolizing agricultural production and natural resources. With their bright and
often ruthless ideas they help make the world safe for those who own it. In sum, the
average institution of higher learning owes more to Sparta than to Athens.

On these same campuses, one can find ROTC programs that train future
military officers, programs that are difficult to justify by any normal academic standard. The campuses are open to recruiters from various corporations, the CIA, and the

armed forces. In 1993, an advertisement appeared in student newspapers across the nation promoting "student programs and career opportunities" with the CIA. Students "could be eligible for a CIA internship and tuition assistance" and would "get hands-on experience" working with CIA "professionals." The advertisement did not explain how full-time students could get "hands-on experience" as undercover agents. Would it be by reporting on professors and fellow students who voiced iconoclastic views?

Without any apparent sense of irony, many of the faculty engaged in these worldly pursuits argue that a university should be a place apart from worldly and partisan interests, a temple of knowledge. In reality, many universities have direct investments in corporate America in the form of substantial stock portfolios. By purchase and persuasion, our institutions of higher learning are wedded to institutions of higher earning. In this respect, universities differ little from other social institutions such as the media, the arts, the church, schools, and various professions.[1]

Most universities and colleges hardly qualify as hotbeds of dissident thought. The more likely product is a mild but pervasive ideological orthodoxy. College is a place where fundamental criticisms of the structures and values of society are not totally unknown but are just in scarce supply. It is also a place where students, out of necessity or choice, mortgage their future to corporate America.[2]

Ideological repression in academia is as old as the nation itself. Through the eighteenth and nineteenth centuries, most colleges were governed by prominent churchmen and wealthy merchants and landowners who believed it their duty to ensure faculty acceptance of theological preachments. In the early 1800s, trustees at Northern colleges prohibited their faculties from engaging in critical discussions of slavery; abolitionism was a taboo subject. At Southern colleges, faculty devoted much of their intellectual energies to justifying slavery and injecting racial supremacist notions into various parts of the curriculum.[3] By the 1870s and 1880s, Darwinism was the great bugaboo in higher education. Presidents of nine prominent eastern colleges went on record as prohibiting the teaching of evolutionary theory.

By the 1880s, prominent businessmen came to dominate the boards of trustees of most institutions of higher learning (as they still do). Seldom hesitant to impose ideological controls, they fired faculty members who expressed heretical ideas on and off campus, who attended Populist Party conventions, championed anti-monopoly views, supported free silver, opposed US military interventions abroad, or defended the rights of labor leaders and socialists.[4] Among the hundreds dismissed over the years were notable scholars such as George Steele, Richard Ely, Edward Bemis, James Allen Smith, Henry Wade Rogers, Thorsten Veblen, E. A. Ross, Paul Baran, and Scott Nearing.

The first president of Cornell, Andrew White, observed that while he believed "in freedom from authoritarianism of every kind, this freedom did not, however, extend to Marxists, anarchists, and other radical disturbers of the social order." In 1908,

White's contemporary, Harvard president Charles William Elliot, expressed relief that higher education rested safely in the hands of the "public-spirited, business or professional man," away from the dangerous "class influences… exerted by farmers as a class, or trade unionists as a class." [5]

During World War I, university officials such as Nicholas Murray Butler, president of Columbia University, explicitly forbade faculty from criticizing the war, arguing that such heresy was intolerable, for in times of war wrongheadedness was sedition and folly was treason. Noted historian Charles Beard, who argued that the US Constitution was written to promote elite interests not universal rights, was grilled by the Columbia trustees, who were concerned that his views might "inculcate disrespect for American institutions." In disgust, Beard resigned from his teaching position, declaring that the trustees and Nicholas Murray Butler sought "to drive out or humiliate or terrorize every man who held progressive, liberal, or unconventional views on political matters."[6]

Academia has seldom been receptive to persons of anti-capitalist persuasion. Even during the radical days of the 1930s there were relatively few socialists or communists on college teaching staffs. Repression reached a heightened intensity during the McCarthyite witchhunts of the late 1940s and early 1950s. The rooting out of communists, Marxists, and other radicals was sometimes conducted by congressional and state legislative committees or by college administrators themselves.[7] Among the victims were those who had a past or present association with the Communist Party or one of its affiliated organizations.

One study during the McCarthy period found that, though never called before any investigative body, many faculty felt a need to prove their loyalty. Almost any criticism of the existing politico-economic order invited the suspicion that one might be harboring "communist tendencies." Those who refused to sign loyalty oaths were dismissed outright.[8] The relatively few academics who denounced the anticommunist witchhunts usually did so from an anticommunist premise, arguing that "innocent" (noncommunist) people were being silenced or hounded out of their professions. The implication was that the inquisition was not wrong, just clumsy and overdone, that it was all right to deny Americans their constitutional rights if they were "guilty," that is, really communists. The idea that Reds had as much right as anyone else to teach was openly entertained by only a few brave souls.

During the Vietnam era, things heated up. Faced with student demonstrations, sit-ins, and other disruptions, university authorities responded with a combination of liberalizing and repressive measures. They dropped course-distribution requirements in some instances and abolished parietal rules and other paternalistic restrictions on student dormitory life. Black studies and women's studies were established, as were a

number of experimental social science programs that offered more "relevant" commu-
nity-oriented courses and innovative teaching methods.

Along with the concessions, university authorities launched a repressive counteroffensive. Student activists were singled out for disciplinary actions. Campus police
forces were expanded and used to attack demonstrations, as were off-campus police
and, when necessary, the National Guard. Some students were arrested and expelled.
At places like Kent State and Jackson State, students were shot and killed. Radicalized
faculty lost their jobs and some, including myself, were badly assaulted by police during campus confrontations.[9]

The purging of faculty continued through the 1970s and 1980s. Angela Davis
was fired by UCLA because of her membership in the Communist Party (she was later
rehired after strong community protests). Marlene Dixon, a Marxist-feminist sociologist, was fired from the University of Chicago and then from McGill University for
her political activism. Bruce Franklin, a noted Melville scholar and tenured associate
professor at Stanford, was fired for "inciting" students to demonstrate. Franklin later
received an offer from the University of Colorado that was quashed by its board of
regents, who based their decision on a packet of information supplied by the FBI that
included false rumors, bogus letters, and unfavorable news articles.[10]

A graduate student at the University of California, Mario Savio, won national
prominence in the 1960s as an anti-war activist and leader of the "Free Speech Movement" on the Berkeley campus. Savio served four months in prison for one protest activity and subsequently was denied admission into various doctoral programs in physics despite having a master's degree in the subject and a sterling academic record. He
spent the rest of his life unable to gain a regular appointment in higher education. After
many difficult years, Savio died in 1996 at the age of 53. His last job was as a poorly paid
adjunct at Sonoma State University.[11]

At the University of Washington, Seattle, Kenneth Dolbeare's attempts to build
a truly pluralistic political science department with a mix of conservative, mainstream,
and radical faculty, including women and people of color, came under fire from the
administration. After a protracted struggle, Dolbeare departed. All the progressive untenured members of the department were let go, as were progressive-minded members
of other departments, including philosophy and economics.[12]

Similar purges occurred across the nation. Within a three-year period in the
early seventies, at Dartmouth College, all but one of a dozen progressive faculty were
dismissed. In 1987, four professors at the New England School of Law were fired, despite solid endorsements by their colleagues. All four were involved in the Critical Legal Studies movement, a group that studied how the law acted as an instrument of the
rich and powerful.

To a long list of the purged I can add my own name. In 1972, at the University of Vermont, I was denied renewal by the board of trustees despite my publications in leading scholarly journals, and despite the support of my students, my entire department, the faculty senate, the council of deans, the provost, and the president. Unable to fault my teaching or scholarship, the trustees decided in a 15:4 vote that my anti-war activities constituted "unprofessional conduct."

A dozen or so years later, I went to Brooklyn College as a one-year visiting professor with the understanding that a regular position would be given to the political science department for which I could later apply. My chairman's feeling was that given my qualifications, I would no doubt be the leading candidate. The administration however decided against it. A short time afterward, a City University chemistry professor, John Lombardi, happened to be talking to a Brooklyn College vice president at a faculty gathering. Lombardi, who was familiar with my work, asked him why I had been let go. "We found out about him," said the vice president, who went on to indicate that the administration had discovered things about my political activism that they did not like.[13]

One could add many more instances from just about every discipline including political science, economics, anthropology, literature, history, sociology, psychology and even physics, mathematics, chemistry, and musicology. Whole departments and even entire schools and colleges have been eradicated for taking the road less traveled. At University of California, Berkeley, the entire school of criminology was abolished because many of its faculty had developed a class analysis of crime and criminal enforcement. Those who taught a more orthodox criminology were given appointments in other departments. Only the radicals were dismissed.

Even more frequent than the firings are the nonhirings. Highly qualified social scientists, who were also known progressives, have been turned down for positions at institutions too numerous to mention. The pattern became so pronounced at the University of Texas, Austin, in the mid-1970s, that graduate students staged a protest and charged the university with politically discriminatory hiring practices.

In 1981, the political science department of Virginia Commonwealth University invited me to become chairperson, but the decision was overruled by the dean, who announced that it was unacceptable to have a "leftist" as head of a department. She did not explain why the same rule did not hold for a rightist or centrist or feminist (she claimed to be the latter). It is evident that academia speaks with two voices. One loudly proclaims professional performance as the reigning standard. The other whispers almost inaudibly that if you cross the parameters of permissible opinion, your scholarly and pedagogical performance are of no account.

Scholars of an anti-capitalist, anti-imperialist bent are regularly discriminated against in the distribution of research grants and scholarships. After writing *The Power*

Elite, C. Wright Mills was abruptly cut off from foundation funding. To this day, radical academics are regularly passed over for prestigious lecture invitations, grants, and appointments to editorial boards of the more influential professional journals. Faculty are still advised to think twice about voicing controversial politico-economic perspectives. One historian writes that, when a young instructor and a group of her colleagues decided to offer "Marxism" as part of a social history course, she was warned by an older faculty member, "an ordinarily calm and rational gentleman," that it would be "unwise for their department to list a course on Marxism in the catalogue."[14]

An instructor at Seton Hill College in Pennsylvania confided to a leftist student that he subscribed to a number of left publications and was well versed in Marxist theory, but the administration refused to let him teach it. On some campuses, administrative officials have monitored classes, questioned the political content of books and films, and screened the lists of guest speakers—all in the name of scholarly objectivity and balance. In some places, however, trustees and administrators readily pay out huge sums for guest lectures by committed, highly partisan, right-wing ideologues.

The guardians of academic orthodoxy never admit that some of their decisions about hiring and firing faculty might be politically motivated. Instead, they will say the candidate has not published enough articles. Or, if enough, that the articles are not in conventionally acceptable academic journals. Or, if in acceptable journals, that they are still wanting in quality and originality, or show too narrow or too diffuse a development. Seemingly objective criteria can be applied in endlessly elastic ways.

College administrators and department heads, whatever their scholarly output, are often recruited to serve as conservative enforcers. Over the objections of the political science department of the University of Maryland, Baltimore, the chancellor gave tenure to Walter Jones, not a particularly distinguished member of the profession. Jones was then made vice-chancellor, from which position he denied tenure to a radical political scientist, overruling a unanimous recommendation of the school's promotion and tenure committee.

Professional criteria proved especially elastic for those émigrés from communist countries brought to the United States under the hidden sponsorship of national security agencies and immediately accorded choice university positions without meeting minimal academic standards. Consider the case of Soviet émigré and concert pianist Vladimir Feltsman, who, after receiving a first-rate, free musical education in the Soviet Union, defected to the United States in 1986 with the help of the US embassy. In short time, Feltsman gave a White House concert, was hailed by President Reagan as a "moral hero," and was set up in a posh Manhattan apartment. He then was appointed to the State University of New York at New Paltz, where he taught one class a week for twice the salary of a top-ranking professor, and was awarded an endowed chair and a distinguished fellowship. SUNY, New Paltz, itself was a poorly funded school with low salaries, heavy teaching loads, and inadequate services for students.

Mainstream academics treat their politically safe brands of teaching and research as the only ones that qualify as genuine scholarship. Such was the notion used to deny Samuel Bowles tenure at Harvard. Since Marxist economics is not really scholarly, it was argued, Bowles was neither a real scholar nor an authentic economist. Thus, centrist ideologues have purged scholarly dissidents under the guise of protecting rather than violating academic standards. The decision seriously split the economics department and caused Nobel Prize winner Wassily Leontif to quit Harvard in disgust.

Radical academics have been rejected because their political commitments supposedly disallow them from objective scholarship. In fact, much of the best scholarship comes from politically committed scholars. One goal of any teacher should be to introduce students to bodies of information and analysis that have been systematically ignored or suppressed—a task that usually is better performed by iconoclasts than by those who accept existing institutional and class arrangements as the finished order of things. So it has been feminists and African-American researchers who, in their partisan urgency, have revealed the previously unexamined sexist and racist presumptions and gaps of conventional scholarship.[15] Likewise, it is leftist intellectuals (including some who are female or nonwhite) who have produced the challenging scholarship about popular struggle, political economy, and class power, subjects remaining largely untouched by centrists and conservatives.[16] In sum, a dissenting ideology can awaken us to things regularly overlooked by conventional scholarship.

Orthodox ideological strictures are applied also to a teacher's outside political activity. At the University of Wisconsin, Milwaukee, an instructor of political science, Ted Hayes, an anti-capitalist, was denied a contract renewal because he was judged to have "outside political commitments" that made it impossible for him to be objective. Two of the senior faculty who voted against him were state committee members of the Republican Party in Wisconsin.[17] There was no question as to whether *their* outside political commitments interfered with their objectivity as teachers or with the judgments they made about colleagues.

How neutral in their writings and teachings were such scholars as Zbigniew Brzezinski, Henry Kissinger, Daniel Patrick Moynihan, and Jeane Kirkpatrick? Despite being proponents of American industrial-military policies at home and abroad—or because of it—they enjoyed meteoric academic careers and subsequently were selected to occupy prominent policymaking positions within conservative administrations in Washington. Outspoken political advocacy, then, is not a hindrance to one's career as long as one advocates the right things.

It is a rare radical scholar who has not encountered difficulties when seeking employment or tenure, regardless of his or her qualifications. The relatively few progressive dissidents who manage to get tenure sometimes discover that their lot is one of isolation within their own departments. They endure numerous slights and are seldom consulted about policy matters. And they are not likely to be appointed to committees dealing with curriculum, hiring, and tenure, even when such assignments would be a normal part of their responsibilities.

After serving for many years as a tenured senior faculty member of the Queens College, CUNY, political science department, the noted author and political analyst John Gerassi was moved to voice his displeasure at the treatment he had been accorded, including the case of my own candidacy. In a letter to his department colleagues in 1994, he wrote:

> I have never been asked to participate in anything meaningful in this department... Now since my colleagues tell me they like me, and I assume that they are not saying that just to humor me, the reason must be political. Indeed, I remember years ago when I informed my colleagues that a friend of mine who was nationally known, in fact internationally respected, Michael Parenti, who would be a great draw because of his reputation, was available for a job (at a time when the department was actually trying to fill a position), I was quickly informed that he would not be considered no matter what, and I was told in effect to stay out of department business.[18]

The only radical to receive tenure in the department of philosophy in the 1970s at the University of Vermont was Willard Miller, a popular teacher, published author, and political activist. Though he prevailed in his battle for tenure, Miller was made to pay for it. He was denied promotion and remained an assistant professor for thirty-three years with a salary frozen for a long time at below the entry level of the lowest paid instructor. He was passed over for sabbatical for thirteen years and finally received a one-semester leave only after threatening court action. And he was perpetually passed over for a reduced teaching load, a consideration granted to his departmental colleagues on a rotation basis.[19] He died in 2005, still an assistant professor.

Campus activism did not pass away with the Vietnam era. Student protests arose against the university's corporate investments in an apartheid-ruled South Africa, US involvement in Central America, the US invasion of Panama, and the US bombing and invasion of Iraq. There have been demonstrations in support of affirmative action, women's studies, and multiculturalism, and protests against racism, sexism, and Eurocentric biases in the curriculum. But such actions are rarely inspired by anything taught in the classroom, and often emerge despite what is taught.

Facing a campus that is not nearly as reactionary as they would wish, ultra-conservatives rail about how academia is permeated with doctrinaire "politically correct" leftists. This is not surprising since they describe as "leftist" anyone to the left of themselves, including conventional mainstream centrists. Their diatribes usually are little more than attacks upon socio-political views they find intolerable and want eradicated from college curricula. Through all this, one seldom actually hears from the "politically correct" people who supposedly dominate the universe of discourse.

Networks of well-financed right-wing campus groups coordinate conservative activities at schools around the nation, and fund over one hundred conservative campus publications, reaching more than a million students. Such undertakings are well financed by the Scaife Foundation, the Olin Foundation, and other wealthy donors. The nearly complete lack of a similar largesse for progressive groups further belies the notion that political communication in academia is dominated by left-wingers.

In addition, we witness the growing corporate arrogation of institutional functions, and increasing dependence on private funding, all of which militates against anything resembling a radical predominance. The university's conservative board of trustees dishes out extravagant salaries to top administrators along with millions of dollars in luxury cars, luxury dwellings, and other hidden perks for themselves and university officers.[20] Meanwhile, student fees are being dramatically increased, services slashed, and the numbers of low-paid and heavily exploited adjunct teachers (as opposed to fulltime professors) has increased considerably. No university is under leftist rule.

Among faculty in the social sciences there are more mainstream Clinton Democrats than Bush Republicans. In the business and engineering schools, and maybe also law and medicine, there sometimes are more conservatives. Conservatives seize upon the relative shortage of conservative social science faculty as proof of deliberate discrimination. This is an odd argument coming from them, Steven Lubet points out, since conservatives usually dismiss the scarcity of women or minorities in a workforce or student body as simply the absence of qualified applicants. That is not discrimination, they insist, it is self-selection. "Conservatives abandon these arguments however when it comes to their own prospects in academe. Then the relative scarcity of Republican professors is widely asserted as proof of willful prejudice." Lubet continues:

> Beyond the ivy walls there are many professions that are dominated by
> Republicans. You will find very few Democrats (and still fewer outright
> liberals) among the ranks of high-level corporate executives, military officers or football coaches. Yet no one complains about these imbalances,
> and conservatives will no doubt explain that the seeming disparities are
> merely the result of market forces.

They are probably right. It is entirely rational for conservatives to flock to jobs that reward competition, aggression and victory at the expense of others. So it should not be surprising that liberals gravitate to professions—such as academics, journalism, social work and the arts—that emphasize inquiry, objectivity and the free exchange of ideas. After all, teachers at all levels—from nursery school to graduate school—tend to be Democrats. Surely there cannot be a conspiracy to deny conservatives employment on kindergarten playgrounds.[21]

For years, mainstream academics scorned anti-war radicals and Marxists of every stripe. Now, ironically, some of these same centrists find themselves attacked by the emboldened student ultra-conservatives who complain that exposure to liberal and "leftist" ideas deprives them of their right to academic freedom and ideological diversity. What they really are protesting is their first encounter with ideological diversity, their first exposure to a critical perspective other than the one they regularly embrace. Conservative students grumble about being denied their First Amendment rights by occasionally being required to read leftist scholars. "Where are the readings by Sean Hannity, Ann Coulter, and Bill O'Reilly?" complained one.[22] They register these complaints with college administrators, trustees, and outside conservative organizations. Accusations of partisanship hurled by the student reactionaries are themselves intensely partisan, being leveled against those who question, but never against those who reinforce, conservative orthodoxy. Thus the campus headhunters act as self-appointed censors while themselves claiming to be victims of censorship.

In recent years, the underpaid adjunct teaching staff and heavily indebted student body have found still fewer opportunities for exploratory studies and iconoclastic views. The world around us faces a growing economic inequality and a potentially catastrophic environmental crises. Yet the predominant intellectual product in academia remains largely bereft of critical engagements with society's compelling issues. Not everything written by mainstream scholars serves the powers-that-be, but very little of it challenges such powers. While orthodoxy no longer goes uncontested, it still rules. Scholarly inquiry may strive to be neutral, but it is never confected in a neutral universe of discourse. It is always subjected to institutional and material constraints that shape the way it is produced, funded, distributed, and acknowledged. Money speaks louder than footnotes.

The War Against the "Academic Left"

From Gross and Levitt to Gitlin

Steven Best & Douglas Kellner

THE CULTURE WARS THAT HAVE BEEN RAGING SINCE THE 1960S put in question everything from US foreign policy to curricula and governance of the university. In the 1960s and 1970s, social struggles such as the anti-war and peace movement, the counterculture, women's liberation, and the gay and lesbian liberation movements, followed by struggles for the environment, animal rights, and many other progressive causes, shook up US culture, society, and academia, and were subject to fierce debates.

The right counterattacked in the 1980s during the Reagan presidency, when cultural warriors like Lynne Cheney became head of the National Endowment for the Humanities (NEH) and went after forces on the left and progressives of all sorts, who used courses like writing or rhetoric to address issues of gender, race, and class in the United States. A bevy of right-wing ideologues, heavily funded by conservative foundations, attacked new programs in women's, African American, Chicano, gay and lesbian, and cultural studies in the university, all mounting serious challenges to academic orthodoxy. The right also accused progressives of "political correctness," a blanket term that condemned the left as totalitarian or fascist whenever they criticized racist, sexist, homophobic, or other hierarchical and discriminatory ideologies and practices.[1]

Stacks of articles, journals, and books took on the culture wars which, as this book indicates, are still raging as right-wing foundations and ideologues attempt to expel progressives from the university—the one domain that they did not control in the waning days of the Bush-Cheney regime. Right-wing ideologues have been aided in their culture wars by former leftists such as David Horowitz, who has swung to the far right, and Todd Gitlin who employs a centrist liberalism to attack what he calls "the academic left." Curiously, as this article will show, criticisms of the "academic Left" come from both the right and the left and are often quite similar in thrust and substance. There is a long history of former leftists moving toward the right and attacking "the god that failed" through broadside critiques of Marxism, long the favored target of the right, especially during the Cold War. But there have also been post-1970s critiques from the left and the right of feminism, multiculturalism, postmodern theory, and other alleged intellectual, pedagogical, and political sins lumped under the category of the "academic Left." In this article, we will illustrate this reactionary trend through critical analysis of parallel attacks on the "academic left" from the right, by Paul Gross and Norman Levitt, and from the left, by Todd Gitlin. We argue that they use the same terminology for the target of their critique, make similar substantive criticisms of the "academic left," and show a similar ignorance of the objects of their critique. Their criticisms from the right and left target critical scholars and can be seen as providing collaboration with academic repression and rationales for attacks on progressive scholars and activists within the university.

Gross and Levitt's Higher Arrogance

> *"The aroma of sour grapes is in the air."*
>
> —Gross and Levitt

Angered by postmodern assaults on classical notions of truth and objectivity, Paul R. Gross and Norman Levitt responded vitriolically in *Higher Superstition: The Academic Left and Its Quarrels with Science* (1994). Outraged that non-specialists in science—cultural and social theorists like Stanley Aronowitz, Katherine Hayles, and Andrew Ross—would dare challenge scientific practice and norms, indignant that such critical theorists would politicize the eternal verities of dispassionate truth, and bemused that they would make an alleged litany of technical errors in the process, Gross and Levitt set out to discredit the motley army of scientific critics as ignorant, misguided, irresponsible enemies of reason and progress, as uniformed ideologues of the "academic left." Previously, they claim, natural scientists were either too timid to challenge philosophical or political critiques of their discipline, they were too tolerant, or they were even perversely fascinated by the critical perspectives of outsiders. But Gross and Levitt see themselves as part of the new post-wimpy crowd, tired of having sand kicked in their faces by postmodern bullies, filled with "skepticism and revulsion" at these puffed-up critiques, and ready to fight back with bare knuckles. Like the ninety-eight-pound weakling on the beach, however, they find themselves ill-prepared to take on the task.

Following their lead, Alan Sokal, physicist at New York University, penned a parody of postmodern science purposely riddled with errors, indigestible jargon, and total jejune crap that was—in a monumental calamity—accepted for publication by the editors of *Social Text*, an event which generated an unparalleled media response.[2] Even more so than the verbose and bilious book of Gross and Levitt—which was featured at the 1995 New York Academy of Science conference on "The Flight From Reason" and which the conservative National Association of Scholars sent to science deans and department chairs across the country—Sokal's hoax was widely publicized and discussed. It was featured in the pages of *Lingua Franca, The New York Times, Fortune, The Chronicle of Higher Education*, and *The Nation*, while triggering a passionate debate on the Internet among academics and demonstrating the passion still generated by postmodern debates.[3]

As the militia movement of the 1990s was a reactive response to the decline of white male culture, the hysteric critiques and antics of Gross, Levitt, and Sokal—the Gang of Three—are a reaction to the decline of positivistic conceptions of scientific objectivity. The lines drawn in the science war debates are not in all cases between right and left (Sokal describes himself as a leftist and feminist who taught mathematics in Nicaragua during Sandinista rule, and claims that Levitt is a socialist and Gross a liberal). Rather, the science wars are being waged between positivists and post-positivists, between those defending scientific realism and the preeminent role of science in Western culture and those challenging the ahistorical and Eurocentric claims to truth, theoretical purity, and modern science as the only plausible form of knowledge humans have ever produced.

Gross and Levitt argue that contemporary critiques of science represent "Higher Superstition" as opposed to Higher Education or Knowledge. Superstition, of course, is an irrational belief, founded on fear and ignorance, without basis in fact. But, as we shall argue, these Holy Warriors against Superstition and for Higher Truth fail to distinguish between rational and irrational critiques of science and technology, they crudely caricature their opponents' views, and they themselves are irrational in both their attacks on their "enemies" and their uncritical defense of outmoded conceptions of science. Furthermore, they are profoundly ignorant of the positions they malign and their polemic is undermined by a series of contradictions between their stated goals and actual writing, such as when they denounce the politicization of academia at the same time they call for the scientific policing of the humanities (1994: 215ff.). This is a typical McCarthyesque tactic that resonates with the authoritarian and regressive political forces in the post-9/11 era. It seeks to ensure "falsehood" doesn't corrupt "truth" and to suppress any ideas, values, or politics that don't pass their arbitrary notions of science or their tendentious ideal of the humanities. In the height of arrogance, they deify themselves as Gods of Reason, as Law and Order, and they are all too willing for themselves and any positivist colleagues they can bring into their brown shirt clans as they inspect classrooms, interrogate teachers, and police discourse for scientific correctness to receive the Positivist Seal of Approval.

Gross and Levitt claim that they worry about "a certain intellectual debility afflicting the contemporary university: one that will ultimately threaten it" (45). But their own uninformed and emotive screed exhibits a high state of debility, and fosters divisions and animosities across the disciplines that can hardly be healthy for the university as an institution. They claim that an arrogantly obscurantist assault is being mounted in which "the proliferation of distortions and exaggerations about science, of tall tales and imprecations, threatens to poison the intellectual cohesion necessary for a university to work" (57).

But, in fact, it is Gross and Levitt themselves who are demonstrably arrogant, ignorant, sloppy, and irresponsible in their review of the positions and critics they assail. We will accordingly attempt to show that Gross and Levitt are themselves guilty of a large array of deadly theoretical sins that they charge to scientific critics, and that their "refutations" involve puerile *ad hominems*; straw critiques, misrepresentations, and caricatures; quoting out of context; dodging the central issues and arguments; blatant ignorance of the subject matter; failure to cite adequate primary and secondary literature; lack of alternative positions; and apparent failure even to read the texts and authors they discuss *ex cathedra* and *ex nihilo*. Moreover, while they claim to worry about threats to the integrity of the university and divisions fostered by postmodern critiques, their own vicious polemics threaten to further divide and weaken a university under siege by a variety of reactionary social forces.

To begin, Gross and Levitt's attack on the "academic left" is seriously misdirected because it is the right who has traditionally carried out totalizing critiques of science and technology (conservative anti-Enlightenment ideology, Martin Heidegger, Jacques Ellul, and so on). Moreover, it is right-wing forces today (i.e. fundamentalist religious groups, creationists, and anti-government and pro-market organizations) that are leading the real offensive against science—in addition to certain New Age philosophies and a pervasive anti-intellectualism in American culture. But instead of taking on the real forces undermining the status and health of science in contemporary society, Gross and Levitt carry out a tendentious and distorted critique of a wide range of academic critics of science whose views they systematically caricature and distort.

Blatantly misrepresenting the arguments and intentions of a diverse range of scientific critics, they lump a disparate range of positions together as "postmodernist," the "postmodern left," or the "academic Left." Despite their awkward qualifications, Gross and Levitt's central construct "academic Left" is vacuous and bereft of analytic value. They say the phrase does "*not* refer merely to academics with left-wing political views" (9), but rather tries "to designate those people whose doctrinal idiosyncrasies sustain the misreadings of science" (ibid.). This crowd includes postmodernists, "radical feminists" (which, in fact, is a technical term designating feminists who privilege gender over class, but which Gross and Levitt misrepresent to include feminists in general), multiculturalists, and "radical environmentalists." There are obviously significant differences among these groups, but Gross and Levitt lump them all under one amorphous, misleading, ideologically loaded label (e.g., "academic and activist critics of science" would be better than the term "academic Left").[4]

The inaccuracy of their term "academic left" is obvious if one considers the politics of many postmodernists, radical feminists, and environmentalists which often have nothing to do with or are hostile toward traditional "left" politics. For instance, from a biocentric and often misanthropic perspective, Dave Foreman and others of the "radical environmental movement" are contemptuous of humanist values in general, to say nothing about left-wing or Marxist-style humanism, as many postmodernists are liberals or post-Marxists trying to transcend what they view as outmoded leftist politics. But such subtleties escape Gross and Levitt in their hurried attempt to reduce complexities to simple categories so they have time for *ad hominem* target practice. Their arrogant and authoritarian mentality is betrayed in one of many contradictions in their book. Claiming not to take pleasure in their acrimonious polemics, they ask the reader to believe that their "chief hope" in writing "is to convert friends (whose asseverations are for the moment our subject), or at least to persuade them to reflect" (2). Some thirty pages later, however, they offer a lengthy section on the "academic left" entitled "The Face of the Enemy"—conveniently providing targets for academic repression.

Most devastatingly, for all their condescension toward cultural theorists they believe misinterpret science, Gross and Levitt themselves misread the texts of Derrida, Foucault, and every major target of their critique.[5] While they denigrate non-scientist critics for lack of solid knowledge of the scientific tradition, their assault on postmodern theory reveals that they themselves are totally ignorant of postmodern positions, which they distort and caricature. The main figures and concepts of postmodern theory are hardly discussed at all, even though this is a major focus of their critique. Derrida is disposed of in a page and a third (76–77), Foucault in two paragraphs (77), and Lyotard and Baudrillard in two sentences each (79–80)! Not surprisingly, in superficial readings largely derived from secondary references, they make blatant interpretive errors, claiming that both Derrida and Foucault do not believe in an external world, and reading Foucault as reducing knowledge to power (75–78). Gross and Levitt apparently are unaware that Derrida himself rejected the idealist interpretation of his *bon mot* that "there is nothing outside of the text." Nor do they have a clue that Foucault allowed room for scientific objectivity untainted by social interests and power and that he derided the attempt to *reduce* knowledge to power.[6] The hermeneutic and deconstructionist claim that Derrida and Foucault oppose is not that everything *is* language, but that all knowledge is *mediated through* language, through culturally constructed conceptual schemes; this unavoidably shapes the ways in which we perceive a world which remains independent of the knower.

Indeed, their goal is not to understand the postmodern critiques of science and society, but to attack the most blatant errors made by academic critics of science in order to discredit the entire academic and postmodern left. It is not surprising that they identify postmodern theory per se with the most extreme versions of it, obscuring its variety and diversity, and thus providing a strawman caricature which they proceed to demolish. Thus, as Gross and Levitt excoriate their friends/enemies for faulty and incomplete histories of modern science, as well as for derivative and erroneous understandings of esoteric scientific theory, they succumb to the very same problems in their interpretation of postmodern theory and postmodern critics, not the least of which is their display of a "remarkable arrogance" (106) toward their subject matter and colleagues. As they demonize the "left" for dogmatism, one would expect non-dogmatic arguments from them, producing evidence for everything they try to "falsify," but they make rigid, rhetorical, and *ad hominem* arguments against everything that is not mainstream science, including phenomena like alternative medicine ("an ancient amalgam of quackery and self-delusion" [251]) and animal rights (part of the "intellectual junk-food of the 'New Age' movement" [199]).

In addition, they reduce the complex origins and uses of postmodern theory to the psychological deficits of its advocates, describing Foucault as "deeply neurotic" with "a self-despising personal life" (71). Their polemics rival Rush Limbaugh for nastiness and snide dismissiveness; they can't just refer to "feminists," but have to say "fire-breathing feminist zealots" or "a gaggle of post-everything feminists" (37). Similar disdainful epithets are thrown around throughout the book against gays and lesbians, blacks, multiculturalists, and ecologists. In general, Gross and Levitt try to dismiss the "left" critiques of science by reducing logic to psychology, claiming that the "left," mourning the failure of the radical project in history, seek a scapegoat to vent their frustrations, finding the perfect target in science, which for Gross and Levitt represents the highest achievement of Western civilization (27, passim).

Of course, their "critique" is a blatant, but unacknowledged, reprise of Nietzsche's theory of *ressentiment* (1967). Nietzsche argued that *ressentiment* (a form of extreme resentment of the weak against the strong) drives the moral criticism not only of Christianity, but also of anarchists and socialists. He reviled radical social critics as spiteful "lower types" whose jeremiads against a brutally exploitative nineteenth century capitalism were symptomatic of their own personal inadequacies, jealousy, and pettiness, rather than legitimate problems of social injustice. By using the psychological category of resentment, Gross and Levitt thereby seek to discredit the social and political insights of radical criticism, but they only obscure the complex social, historical, intellectual, and political context of the emergence and development of postmodern discourse.

If such psychological categories must be dredged up, they clearly apply to Gross and Levitt's *own* envy-driven descriptions of the "academic left's" prestige, allegedly high salaries, and social influence (e.g.: 34, 103, 177, 237–238), as well as Levitt's bitter complaints about earning only a "marginal" living as a mathematician (115). They systematically project their *own* failings (e.g., overweening arrogance, sharp biases, lack of understanding of the ideas that they are criticizing, etc.) onto their opponents. One might read *Higher Superstition*, therefore, as an acerbic, biased account of contemporary academic life, that is so resentful of challenges to their outmoded Science-As-God worldview that it grossly (pun intended) distorts everything it examines as it revels in ad hominems/feminems, exuding the bad aroma of Higher Arrogance on every page.

Ironically, in their imperious response to cogent criticisms of the methodological assumptions and practices of science, Gross and Levitt display the very linkage between knowledge and power that they otherwise try to erase by constantly evoking the superiority of science over all other academic disciplines; indeed, they argue that, if the entire humanities faculty of MIT was eliminated, the science and engineering faculties could make do, whereas the humanities would be paralyzed without mathematics and science (1994: 243). In their higher arrogance, they obviously believe that scientists lumbering around with the baggage of an obsolete epistemology, naïve objectivism, and no sense whatsoever of history, social dynamics, and cultural matters have nothing to learn from those adept in contextualizing science and other forms of knowledge.

Their "critique"—when it is not offensive or uninformed—is always undialectical and purely negative, erupting with *Schadenfreude* whenever they detect something erroneous or uniformed in the texts of their "enemies." But they rarely attempt to grasp or explicate what might be salient or informed critiques of the sciences by those on the "academic left," thus their book is more of a vendetta and polemic than the serious "objective" scholarly enterprise they champion. Indeed, despite the demagoguery of Gross and Levitt, most contemporary critics are not blaming science and technology per se for social ills, they are not attacking rationality in itself, and they are not denying the existence of an objective world independent of any observer. The critiques of science coming from Marxists, feminists, postmodernists, and others are characteristically *dialectical* in nature, granting the important benefits of scientific and technological developments, but also critical of unethical forms of research (on both human and nonhuman animals) and the destructive consequences of technoscience in warfare, environmental disasters, genetic engineering, and other ills of our time. But these dissidents of modern faith assign blame where it belongs—on the people, policies, and institutions that abuse science and technology, as well as on forces like the profit motive and class interests—rather than on science and technology alone, considered apart from social relations and interests.

A distinction therefore must be made between the critique of science per se and the critique of modern scientific ideologies and practices. It is the right, accompanied by a few extremists on what Gross and Levitt call the "academic Left," that attack science per se, whereas most contemporary critics of science criticize the modern scientific worldview and its ideology of scientism and positivism, or specific abuses of science and technology. These abuses include imperial claims that modern Western science is the sole source of truth and objectivity, that its view of the world is the only correct one, and that other discourses (art, philosophy, social theory) are only, in their words, so much "unalloyed twaddle," "hermeneutic hootchy-koo," and "magical thinking."

Although Gross and Levitt attack their targets for not justifying their positions and providing misleading accounts of science, they themselves rarely bother to explain difficult scientific theories and seldom explicate or defend their own positions, preferring polemic over pedagogy. Occasionally, however, they lay their cards on the table and reveal what they actually stand for, as in the following embarrassing and puerile praise of positivism: "we are unabashed technocrats, unashamed of the instrumentalism behind such assertions...Let us raise a glass to Bacon!... The more Baconian science we get, the easier it will be to believe that we have a fighting chance, if no more than that, on this lovely planet that spins its way through an unimaginably violent— and indifferent—space" (178). Here, their unabashed and crude version of positivism is transparent, disclosing "how easily," to use their own words, "a redemptive vision [viz., science] can slip free of reason" (216). Indeed, what is "lovely" about smog, oil spills, tree stumps, sewage, waste dumps, smokestacks, litter, and clogged expressways, to say nothing about children with distended stomachs, factory farms, or cities smoldering in the rubble of war? And how does one rationally combine the terms "lovely" and "unimaginably violent" in the same breath? Or the terms "violent" and "indifferent" for that matter? Still worse, how can these intoxicated sops for Bacon praise instrumentalism while *also* admitting "the instrumentalism available to our worst impulses have grown unimaginably lethal" (218)? Obviously, logic and consistency are missing in these scientific ideologues who endlessly praise such ideals, but rarely follow them.

Thus, the would-be Emperors of the Higher Truth are shown to be naked in their dogma and ignorance. Defenders of an outmoded positivism, objectivism, and instrumentalism, they seem unaware of the weighty developments in contemporary philosophy of science toward a post-positivist understanding of science, mediated by the postmodern critique. Their views are also politically problematic. Although Gross and Levitt seek to disavow themselves from the political right, their use of the term "left" plays into the right-wing assault on all critical modes of thought that have emerged since the 1960s and that attack traditional paradigms, and they have largely been endorsed and promoted by rightists. As Ellen Schrecker pointed out in the second round of the *Lingua Franca* Sokal skirmishes (July/August 1996: 61), the attacks on university-based critics of science tends to undermine critical academic discourse during a time when the right "is fighting a broad-based campaign to demonize those sectors of the academic community that encourage critical thinking and offer an alternative perspective on the status quo."

Consequently, the Gang of Three's target is misplaced; they limit their critique to academics whereas the truly dangerous critics of science are those right-wing groups who oppose secularism, rationalism, and scientific theory *tout court*. Although Sokal claims his hoax is aimed at saving the Left from pretension, jargon, and isolation from the public (1996b), in fact his intervention is congruent with that of Gross and Levitt, and all three serve to discredit radical critiques of science, as well as critical theory, cultural studies, and other progressive forms of thought, thereby playing and stepping up the game of the right.[7]

Todd Gitlin vs. the "Academic Left"

Todd Gitlin distinguished himself in the 1980s with well-received books that dealt with the role of the media in the 1960s anti-war movement and his activism with SDS and progressive movements. In the 1990s, he moved from the left toward a more reformist liberalism and began criticizing multiculturalism and what he saw as a fragmented postmodern identity politics in his book *The Twilight of Common Dreams* (1995).[8] Since 9/11, he has focused his critical energies more intensely on the left and in particular on the "academic left," a term he uncritically borrows from the right and, like them, never adequately defines, but which seems to cover any post-60s academic tendency or theory that he does not himself agree with.

Gitlin's recent volume, *The Intellectuals and the Flag* (2006), collects essays of the last decade ranging from his response to the 9/11 terror attacks to polemics against the academic left and its roots in postmodernism and cultural studies. Here and elsewhere, Gitlin's critique articulates with the right-wing attack on the university and academic left, reproducing positions such as associated with Allan Bloom in *The Closing of the American Mind* (1987).[9] Like Bloom, Gitlin bemoans the influence of German romanticism, Big T Theory, cultural studies, and certain versions of multiculturalism, thus positioning Gitlin as the left-wing of the right's assault on radical academics.

Gitlin's Introduction to *The Intellectuals and the Flag*, "From Great Refusal to Political Retreat," opens with a snide dismissal of Herbert Marcuse who popularized the phrase "great refusal" and influenced sectors of the New Left that practiced it. For Gitlin, the great refusal's "absolute rejection of the social order" represents a "purity of will" and "more than a little futility" (3). The concept "is the triumph of German romanticism" and "a shout from an ivory tower" (Ibid.).

In fact, Marcuse always countered the refusal of specific modes of thought and behavior with alternative ones, as when he championed critical and dialectical thought against the conformist modes of one-dimensional society, or pointed to art as a utopian projection of ideals of a freer and happier world in contrast to existing modes of suffering and domination.[10] Gitlin calls for an "intellectual Renaissance" and, arguably, the sort of grand theoretical and utopian vistas of Marcusean thought could help produce a rebirth of the left and the development of alternative politics and pedagogy.[11] Marcusean vision contained an unblinkered view of forces of domination and oppression, countered by the "great refusal" and projections of an alternative vision of emancipation, freedom, and justice.

Curiously, Allan Bloom too singled out Marcuse for attack, claiming in his infamous diatribe, *The Closing of the American Mind*, that Marcuse was the most important philosopher of the 1960s counterculture, and that the spread of his theories led to "the betrayal of liberty on America's campuses." Moreover, Bloom argued that German thinkers like Nietzsche, Heidegger, and Marcuse spread a corrosive nihilism and seduced the youth, writing that the US imported "a clothing of German fabrication for our souls, which… cast doubt upon the Americanization of the world on which we had embarked" (152). In an era of aggressive militarism and neo-imperialism from the Reagan administration through two Bush-Cheney administrations, we might argue that any skepticism toward US imperial aspirations is a salutary contribution for which Marcuse should be thanked. Revealing his inability to grasp the philosophical dimension and challenges of Marcuse's thought, Bloom also wrote of Marcuse: "He ended up here writing trashy culture criticism with a heavy sex interest" (226), a simply ludicrous claim.

Marcuse was a steadfast defender of the need for utopian vision of a better world and having a positive alternative to existing society to guide radical social change. Although Gitlin claims to appeal to intellectuals, a social type he never defines, he does not present an emancipatory vision for the left, beyond patriotism and liberal reform. Gitlin does not lay out a clear agenda or lines of activism for intellectuals in the present age, and on the whole seems more interested in the promotion of liberal thought and politics, and trashing the academic left.

Indeed, Gitlin is better in attacking the left and progressives than developing viable theoretical and practical alternatives to existing academia. In *The Twilight of Common Dreams*, he deplores fragmentation and identity politics and calls for "building bridges," but his polemics tend to burn rather than build alliances, and he does not offer viable suggestions for how to mediate different political orientations. Gitlin's mode of thought tends toward polarization and dichotomies rather than mediation. Championing the enlightenment and modern forms of rationality, he does not see how postmodern views can articulate with classical modernist ones to develop more robust modes of critique, theory, and practice. Nor, as argued below, does he offer ideas for the reconstruction of education that combine traditional ideas with newer ones.

While calling for articulating common dreams and hopes, this imperative has remained largely empty, as Gitlin continues to polemicize and ostracize rather than to synthesize and offer constructive perspectives for a better future. It is symptomatic of his largely negative thought that he chose to dramatize the twilight of common dreams, rather than the dawn of new ones.

Gitlin's Academic Nightmares

In Part II of *The Intellectuals and the Flag*, "Two Traps and Three Values," Gitlin's agenda clearly comes to the fore in a polemic against Theory, postmodernism, cultural studies, and what he indistinctly calls, via Gross and Levitt, "the academic left." Gitlin is put off by what the "academic left in particular has nourished … [as] 'theory': a body of writing (one can scarcely say its content consists of propositions) that is, in the main, distracting, vague, self-referential, and wrong-headed" (68). He cites Foucault as an example of postmodern vacuity: "Michel Foucault became a rock star of theory in the United States precisely because he demoted knowledge to a reflex of power, merely the denominator of the couplet 'power/knowledge,' yet his preoccupation was with the knowledge side, not actual social structures. His famous illustration of the power of 'theory' was built on Jeremy Bentham's design of an ideal prison, the Panopticon—a model never built" (69).

In fact, in a dazzling array of texts with different methodologies and problematics, Foucault explored relations between power, knowledge, institutions, discourses, and practices, and cannot be reduced to linguistic idealism as Gitlin suggests. Also, Foucault's analysis of the Panopticon illustrates a shift from one regime of punishment to another and is not a metaphor for the power of theory as Gitlin claims, and in reality shows Foucault's strong emphasis on social institutions and analysis.[12] Hence, like Gross and Levitt, Gitlin knows almost nothing about the critical theorists against whom he polemicizes.

Gitlin's method is to take some academic trend like Big T Theory (comprehensive in scope) or cultural studies that he sets up as an ideal model and then attacks. But as with his failed attempt to dismiss Foucault and Theory, he often misrepresents his object of critique and exhibits a kind of pop sociology of the sort he himself criticizes, rather than offering rigorous and illuminating analysis. Indeed, his own critique of superficial pop sociology could easily be directed against his own work: "Pop sociology is sociological imagination lite, a fast-food version of nutriment, a sprinkling of holy water on the commercial trend of the moment, and a trivialization of insight" (41).

As an example of Gitlin's own pop sociology, take his comments on the complexity of the postmodern debates that roared from the 1980s into the 1990s. Gitlin
opens his chapter on "The postmodernist mood" with a pastiche of the famous analysis of Fredric Jameson and Jameson's stages of premodern, modern, and postmodern
culture, and then reduces Jameson and David Harvey to exemplars of a "bleak Marxist
account" of the phenomenon (78). Gitlin generally dismisses postmodern theory and
culture as "blank," indifferent, and nihilistic, with "a taste for sarcasm, snarkiness, and
cultural bricolage" (80). Yet he does allow at the conclusion of his polemic a "good"
postmodernism defined as a "politics of limits [that] would be at once radical and conservative—it would conserve. It would respect horizontal social relations—multiplicity
over hierarchy, coexistence over usurption, difference over deference: finally, disor-
derly life in its flux against orderly death in its finality. The democratic vital edge of the
postmodern—the love of difference and flux and the exuberantly unfinished—would
infuse the spirit of politics, as it deserves to" (85).

Gitlin acts like he invented this model of a positive postmodernism, but in
fact it characterizes burgeoning traditions of the postmodern turn which Gitlin ignores
in his polemic, allowing him to present a more attractive version of postmodernism as
his own invention at the conclusion of his polemic.[13] In fact, Gitlin has not read much
postmodern theory, as his failed presentation of Foucault indicates, and his pop sociology does not present much of an engagement with the complex tradition of the postmodern, exhibiting intellectual regression rather than a Renaissance of critical thought
or advancement in scholarship.

Gitlin is not much better at cultural studies, opening his polemic with the
admonition that anyone practicing cultural studies should know to situate their work
in the context in which it emerges, querying: "why should cultural studies refuse to see
itself through the same lens?" (87) In fact, most of the major figures in British, North
American, and global cultural studies discuss the origins of and debates within cultural
studies, and situate their work within this context. There are by now stacks of books
and journal articles on the development of different traditions of cultural studies, divisions and debates within the field, and differing models and methods, that exhibit,
contra Gitlin, a high degree of methodological reflection and contextualization, as well
as intense polemics within the field.[14]

It is, in fact, not clear why Gitlin is so negative and polemical against postmodern theory, cultural studies, or Theory. It seems Gitlin has encountered some an-
noying and superficial examples or exemplars, which so outraged him that he dismisses
entire fields because some within, say, cultural studies fall prey to jargon, an affirmative
populism, or do trivial work. To be sure, one can find examples of shoddy scholarship
in any field or tradition, but Gitlin identifies his targets of polemic *tout court* with their
lapses, while failing to engage stronger aspects of the academic fields he is attacking. By

generalizing from the worst tendencies, he provides caricatures and easy straw targets that he can mightily demolish.

More portentously and tendentiously, he sees the upsurge in cultural stud-ies as a sign of the defeat of the left (90), an equation of style and politics (93), and engagement with the pleasures of popular culture and the discovery of tendencies of resistance within cultural studies as consolation for political defeat (95). In fact, Gitlin does not appear to like media or popular culture, providing a totalizing broadside as-sault rather than discriminating analysis and critique. In a summary of his book *Media Unlimited* (2002), Gitlin rails against the sentimentality, vulgarity, crudeness, fragmen-tation, triviality, and violence in pop culture, in a rant suspiciously close to conserva-tives. He worries about the collapse of the canon, of critical standards, and decline of reason itself much like your run-of-the-mill conservative (103–112).

In fact, individuals within the field of cultural studies study everything from the ephemeral artifacts of pop television or advertising to art film and classical music, many deploy aesthetic and ethical norms of critique, and most ignore divisions be-tween high and low culture which many claim are eroding because of cultural implo-sion on both ends of the divide.[15] While Gitlin asserts that "the informal curriculum of popular culture absorbs much of our students' mental attention" (108), he does not acknowledge how the media constitute a pedagogy, nor does he discuss developing media literacy as a counter-pedagogy, in which individuals learn to read, dissect, in-terpret, critique, and evaluate the media, thus empowering themselves against media manipulation. Likewise, he does not show much enthusiasm for computer culture, nor in his brief discussion of education does he talk of the need for information, computer, and multiple media literacies.[16]

Gitlin on Education and the University

Gitlin has not written much on education or the university, but after his polemic against the media in *The Intellectuals and the Flag*, he has a short section on "Education and the Values of Citizenship" (112ff). As noted, Gitlin cites "the informal curriculum" of the media, but like, Allan Bloom, believes its "immediate gratification" obstructs seri-ous education, and that colleges and universities can only achieve their higher goals when they "combat the distraction induced by media saturation" (113). Gitlin fails to note that media education can provide tools to empower students and citizens against media manipulation, that artifacts of media culture can be put to useful pedagogical purposes, and can inspire students to engage in a broad range of academic and political inquiries and debates.

Critically analyzing media texts, using them to illuminate contemporary cul-tural, social, or political realities, and showing how they articulate with public discourses and debates, can provide sources of critical knowledge. But in a firmly conservative anti-media position, Gitlin wants to wash his hands of the media, keep himself clean, and not engage in unsavory interaction with low culture. As Henry Giroux notes, however, US democracy in the Bush/Cheney era was increasingly "dirty democracy," and the media were highly implicated in the general morass, but part of the problem could also be part of the solution.[17] That is, teaching students media and information literacy can help them critically distance themselves from mainstream corporate media, seek out alternative sources of culture and information, but also learn much about contemporary media and politics by critically studying media culture.

But, oddly, Gitlin polemicizes against the universities and higher education providing any sort of political education or activist tools, claiming "universities ought not to be entrusted with any political mobilization in particular" (113). This comment is stunningly reactionary and bizarre coming from Gitlin who was involved himself in civil rights, anti-war, and other political mobilizations of the 1960s. Our generation received some of our most lasting educational experiences in political debates, mobilizations, and movements, and we would bet that Gitlin himself accrued career-making academic and political capital through the well-documented and usually self-touted political activity of the 1960s and 1970s that he often cites in his writings, and academically exploits.

Gitlin wants "universities to embrace citizenship, not particular uses of citizenship" (113). But precisely engaging in citizenship involves debate on particular issues like war and peace, immigration, civil rights, animal and Earth liberation, and other burning issues of the day. Such critical engagement often provides important pedagogical experience in sorting out different positions, developing arguments for specific views, coming to respect competing positions, mediating between conflicting positions, and, when possible or desirable, reaching consensus.

Gitlin asserts that "universities serve bedrock purposes of higher education in a democracy when they spur reasoned participation in politics and the accumulation of knowledge to suit" (114), and one can agree with him on this. But we would think that precisely "reasoned participation" in politics as part of an education for citizenship can be developed, refined, and improved in actual political participation; that one can learn through doing; and that there should be no absolute dichotomy between the university and politics, as if they were separate universes. Clearly, knowledge comes from political experience as well as books and seminars. To gain the informed and tempered information needed for intelligent democratic participation and citizenship, one should be open to multiple sources of knowledge and test ideas through practice, allowing one to further refine and develop one's positions.

Further, Gitlin's notion of reasoned reflection is rather thin and his pedagogy is non-existent. While there is a vast literature on deliberative democracy, practical rea-

soning, argumentation, and consensus building, Gitlin does not discuss or contribute
to this literature. In fact, he glibly states that: "for years, while teaching at Berkeley, New
York University, and Columbia, I have noticed how frequently students have difficulty
understanding what an argument is. Many, asked to make an argument on a particular subject express an opinion—or even an emotion ('I feel that'). Many high school
graduates arrive at the university without learning what an argument is" (116).

Gitlin blames this deplorable situation on an "educational system … in default," anti-intellectualism in American life, and the ubiquitous media. This polemic,
however, devalues today's youth and students, about whom Gitlin does not seem to
have a particularly high opinion. But Gitlin does not address how to overcome the
challenges of contemporary education to produce engaged and informed citizens,
and has nothing on pedagogy or how to educate students for democracy. Although
there is one reference to Dewey and the link between education and the cultivation
of publics (p. 35), he does not engage Dewey's copious writings on citizenship for
democracy, practical pedagogy, or reforming and reconstructing the institutions of
public education. Nor does he engage critical pedagogues like Paulo Freire or reflect
on the complex, dialectical relation between the "teacher" and the "student." Not only
does he not engage critical pedagogy, but he seems oblivious to the fact that pedagogy exists as a challenge for teachers to engage in more reflective, responsible, and
competent teaching.

To a significant degree, Gitlin's polemic against theory disarms him from providing the skills necessary for reconstructing education for democracy. For it is theorists like Dewey, Marcuse, Habermas, or Freire who provide tools to empower students
in the arts of argumentation, reasoning, consensus, and societal participation. Theory
helps provide the Big Picture that can help produce context for students to situate facts,
make connections, see contradictions and conflicting positions, and, if possible or desirable, reach consensus. For Gitlin, by contrast, theory is mere jargon and academic
status badges, and while there is no question theoretical discourses can degenerate into
babble and rote recitation of fixed positions and vocabularies, the challenge is to make
theory work, to engage it in practical problems and contexts, and to use it as a communicative and practical tool of pedagogy and insight, not theory without any anchor
in or reference to social realities. Simply eschewing theory per se, as Gitlin tends to do,
is disarming and disingenuous, and reproduces the worst sort of anti-intellectualism
that Gitlin otherwise distances himself from.

While Gitlin genuflects toward the conservative position that higher education should focus on teaching the canon and a "common curriculum" (115), he does
not offer any practical examples of how to critically engage texts, to contextualize them
in broader currents, to promote critical literacy, or to relate texts to both cultural traditions and ongoing and contemporary intellectual debates. Oddly, Gitlin never re-

flects in his book with "intellectual" in its title on what constitutes an intellectual, how education and intellectuals articulate, the role of intellectuals in politics, or particular challenges of intellectuals today.[18] He also fails to perceive that there is *no contradiction* between teaching the classics and contemporary texts from women, people of color, gays and lesbians, or other voices usually excluded from the dialogue of contemporary education. Innocent of dialectics and theory, and hostile to multiculturalism and variegated discourses and practices of his *bete noire* the "academic left," Gitlin performs instead in his discussion of education the reproduction of conservative clichés without advancing any critical thinking about the university and higher education today, or public education, beyond conservative complaints and nostrums.

Gitlin, Politics, and the Culture Wars

Thus, Gitlin is part of the war against the left in higher education. Gitlin sees himself as an independent thinker and heretic who dares to dissent from common left wisdom. In fact, issues and positions on the left itself have been fiercely contested since the 60s, and the positions Gitlin himself ends up affirming are ever more frequently simply those of conservatives, such as his trashing of theory, cultural studies, postmodernism, the "academic left," and university-based activism.

Gitlin generally ignores work on the university and the cultural wars, such as that of Stanley Aronowitz, Henry Giroux, and Susan Searls Giroux, which might enable him to see the extent to which his positions on education and the university articulate with the right and can be seen as part of a broader assault on the university as a democratic public sphere.[19] Gitlin's work also shares with the right attacks on the academic left as a political and pedagogical force for democratizing education, bringing in new voices and perspectives, and advancing a progressive multiculturalism. In the culture wars that have raged since the 1960s, Gitlin thus finds himself increasingly on the right, attacking progressive movements and tendencies within the university and, more recently, within society and the polity at large.

Gitlin has obviously suffered pain and indignities at the hands of the academic left, postmodernists, cultural studies, and critical theorists, and much of *Intellectuals and the Flag* and other post-9/11 writings can be read as a record of his anger and wounds. In a revealing aside, Gitlin bemoans the passing of forceful modes of writing "just as the strong silent style was about to pass into the netherworld, thanks to Kate Millett and other feminists" (45). Such below-the-belt polemical thrusts reveal a sharp animus against feminism that obviously clouds his judgment. Hence, although Gitlin champions reason against allegedly irrational avatars of the academic left much of his rant falls short of the demands of critical reason and strong scholarship.

In the concluding section on "The Intellectuals and the Flag" Gitlin recounts his experience of the 9/11 terror attacks in New York which took place about a mile from his home, his solidarities with New Yorkers, his emerging patriotism and support of the Bush-Cheney administration's Afghanistan incursion, and his disillusionment with their subsequent response to terrorism and their invasion of Iraq. Gitlin delineates in *The Intellectuals and the Flag*, a sharply critical position against the Bush administration that we share. But, once again, he sets up negative ideal types of leftists who are against all sorts of military intervention, while failing to see the dangers of Islamic radicalism, and are allegedly unable to connect with a broad public so as to work for progressive social change. No doubt, there are leftists that fit this model, but once again Gitlin's brush-strokes are too broad, villainizing the left as such, and particularly his *bete noire*, the academic left.

Many of us within the "academic left" have indeed engaged in critical analyses of terrorism, the militarism and authoritarianism of the Bush-Cheney administration, and threats to democracy in the contemporary era without falling into the extremism, dogmatism, or sectarianism that Gitlin vilifies.[20] Once again, Gitlin ignores completely a vast literature by critical scholars of the "academic left" who address 9/11, terrorism, militarism, and the Bush administration, as if he were the only one presenting reasonable political positions and protecting academia and the polity from barbarians of the right and left.

Recently, a number of UCLA faculty, including Douglas Kellner, were attacked by a right-wing ideologue and stigmatized as members of a "Dirty Thirty" who allegedly used the classroom to indoctrinate students.[21] No evidence of the latter was found, and the controversy fizzled out after a week of intense coverage in the mainstream media. The so-called UCLA "Dirty Thirty," re-self-defined as "In Good Company," included professors involved in labor studies, women's studies, gay and lesbian studies, Chicano, Asian, and Latin American studies, and other academic disciplines associated with social movements. Most, however, were blacklisted because of publications on their web-sites and in some cases political activities rather than their actual teaching or academic scholarship.

The attack exemplified right-wing interventions within the cultural wars that have raged on campuses since the 1960s whereby radicals and activists have been stigmatized as subversives of proper academic decorum, a critique Gitlin shares with Bloom and the right. For the past decades, right-wing ideologues have attacked the universities as hot-beds of radicalism and blamed leftists for indoctrinating students and illicitly politicizing the university. In turn, they have attacked all of the academic trends since the 1960s that include waves of critical theories, development of programs organized around studies of gender, race, sexuality, and multicultural difference, and engagements with media culture such as cultural studies. Conservatives decry the decline of academic standards, subversions of academic canons and disciplines, and the politicizing of education—positions that Gitlin increasingly shares.

Gitlin's arguments against the academic left, thus, ultimately reproduce and benefit the politics of the right in university cultural wars. Gitlin is repeating the criticisms that right-wing ideologues have been making against left academics since the 1960s, although he attempts to position himself in the liberal center, without really providing a defense or analysis of liberalism, which surely has its limitations and blindspots, like any other political position.

Positioning himself more and more with right-wing positions in the academic cultural wars, Gitlin derides those on the left who dare to criticize his work as "witch hunters" who are after "heresies." In an article "The Self-Inflicted Wounds of the Academic Left" in *The Chronicle for Higher Education*, however, Gitlin intensifies his polemic against the academic left, writing that in today's conservative hegemony and prevailing ignorance and unreason:

> dissenting intellectuals might gain some traction by standing for reason…. They might investigate how it happened that the academic left retreated from off-campus politics. They might consider the possibility that they painted themselves into a corner apart from their countrymen and women. Among the topics they might explore: the academic left's ignorance of main currents of American life, their positive tropism for foreign saviors, their reliance on intricate jargon, their commitment to keeping up with post-everything hotshots of "theory" from more advanced continents. Instead, in a time-honored ritual of the left, a number of academic polemicists choose this moment to pump up rites of purification. At a time when liberals hold next to no sway in any leading institution of national government, when the prime liberal institution of the last century—organized labor—wobbles helplessly, when most national media tilt so far to the right as to parody themselves, the guardians of purity rise to a high pitch of sanctimoniousness aimed at … heretics. Liberals, that is.[22]

This reductive assault on the academic left is pretentious and absurd. To deplore "the academic left's ignorance of main currents of American life" is insulting and ludicrous, and we could easily cite fifty colleagues at UCLA who could be identified as members of the "academic left" who know as much if not more about American life as Gitlin. To speak of the "positive tropism for foreign saviors" is equally absurd, for while there were cults of Che globally in the 1960s, and respect among the American left for revolutionists like Castro, Ho Chi Minh, Mao, and others, we know of few, if any, on the academic left who are searching for or celebrating "foreign saviors"—most certainly not Al Qaeda which is the ludicrous charge of right-wing lunatics such as David Horowitz and Dinesh D'Souza. Nor are there many examples on the academic left (there are a few) who in the Age of the Bush-Cheney Gang targets liberals as the enemy.

Gitlin makes wild, unsupported, and arguably indefensible generalizations about the academic left without documentation or supporting evidence. He claims, however, that his broadside against the academic left is confirmed by two recent critiques of accommodations of liberals like himself to dominant currents of the US political system and ideology, with the conjunction of an attack on the supposedly subversive role of US university professors by Horowitz.[23] In fact, none of the three books confirms the alleged far-reaching sins of the academic left that Gitlin paints in the lurid quote cited above. His *Chronicle* review is a tortured attempt to sort out the positions in Eric Lott's critique of liberals like Gitlin and defense of positions that Gitlin abhors; Timothy Brennan's critique of university cultural politics of left and right, some of which mirrors certain of Gitlin's critique; and Horowitz's disgraceful screed which should not really be compared with the other books or dignified by attention. Gitlin's associating of the three in the review implies a rather snide guilt-by-association.

Gitlin confesses that he himself was the subject of critique in all three books and so much of his polemic seems to be payback against critics who have bruised his ego or aroused his ire. Such polemics, however, articulate within broader ongoing debates, and Gitlin is positioning himself within the right-wing critique of left academics and advancing their positions and politics.

The fiercest attack on Gitlin's recent work appeared in a review in *The Nation* by Daniel Lazare of his book *The Intellectuals and the Flag*, and he responded with unrestrained fury. Lazare for Gitlin is "a hatchet man… who's sputtered against my work for years… On his Long March to expose apostasy and dig up Fragments of the True Left, no scruple impedes Lazare" and his "thuggish mind."[24] Although one could agree with Gitlin against Lazare that Gitlin responds to the New York 9/11 attacks on multiple dimensions and not just as an American (patriot), and affirm that Gitlin's wavering on the Iraq war should not be assimilated to Thomas Friedman's position (a just cause but botched), Gitlin does not answer Lazare's probing of his position on nationalism and patriotism, which is often quite different in varying countries and contexts. In fact, Gitlin does not really develop a coherent position on patriotism beyond quoting Mark Twain that "Patriotism is supporting your country all the time, and your government when it deserves it." As usual, Gitlin does not bother to sort out different concepts of patriotism and nationalism, positive and negative types and effects, nor present a viable concept of patriotism for the US as it (hopefully) negotiates the end of the Bush/Cheney era and an especially noxious period of US militarism and interventionism.

Gitlin has little on how patriotism has functioned, often in problematic ways, during US history, where it has been mobilized to defend destructive military adventures and colonial expansion. He has nothing on how a nationalistic and often crusading patriotism is cultivated in the schools, shapes media culture, and plays out in domains of everyday life in the United States ranging from sports to holiday parades.[25]

Hence, Gitlin has neither defined citizenship, sorted through the literature and debates on the topic, indicated how education could advance citizenship a la Dewey, nor spelled out a coherent account of patriotism and how it differs from nationalism. Gitlin's is a lazy thought and discourse, not engaging scholarly literature and failing to develop concepts or arguments, to sort out counterarguments and to adequately defend his own position. Nor does he make connections between topics like citizenship, patriotism, and education. This would, of course, involve theory that Gitlin avoids like the plague, thus disarming himself of the tools to make responsible arguments, show weaknesses in opposing positions, and to himself develop coherent positions. Further, his anathema to theory makes him rely on conservative and liberal commonplaces and to make unsupported generalizations.

Obviously, Gitlin has suffered academic insults and assaults that have traumatized him deeply, as have the horrific events of September 11 and the Bush-Cheney-Rove era of unparalleled crime, corruption, and assaults on the very foundation of US democracy. Certainly, we need to rethink theory and politics for the challenges of the present age, but it is not clear that Gitlin provides much useful material for this enterprise, or that he will be the ally of progressive forces in the struggles ahead.

Beyond that, Gitlin's work is illuminating as a symptom of the culture wars. Against the right-wing conflation of liberal and left, however, Gitlin's work shows unacknowledged affinities between right-wing and liberal critiques of the so-called "academic Left." Through hostile diatribes against critical theory, postmodernism, cultural studies, and anti-capitalism, liberals like Gitlin seem to share more with the right than with the left. Radical critiques of patriotism, the education system, mass media, the war on terrorism, militarism, authoritarianism, ecological crisis, and the like are vital for moving beyond the conservative/liberal paradigm and pseudo-option that seeks at best superficial reforms in a crisis-ridden system whose pathologies can only be resolved through deep, systemic social transformation.

Gitlin thus emerges as part of the war against the "academic Left," joining conservatives like Gross and Levitt in attacking progressive movements of the 1960s that promote multiculturalism, feminism, gay and lesbian liberation, social movements from ecology to animal rights, and new critical forms of thought, all dismissed by Gitlin, Gross, and Levitt as intellectual mischief and politicization of academia. In light of this onslaught by the right and their liberal allies against progressive activist social movements and radical theory, we need to affirm multiple forms of new critical theory and progressive politics, constantly developed to meet the needs and challenges of the present moment.

Systemic Aspects of Academic Repression in the New World Order

Takis Fotopoulos

Today, every single individual freedom, including of course academic freedom, has been effectively undermined, both on account of the systemic limitations imposed by the form of the system of market economy developed in neoliberal globalization, and on account of the corresponding limitations imposed by the semi-totalitarian transformation of representative "democracy" in the aftermath of the 9/11 events. In fact, the present form of the market economy and representative "democracy" constitute integral parts of a new totality which can be defined as the New World Order. The meaning of New World Order, or NWO, used in this essay has, however, little relation to the usual meaning given to this term, which simplistically refers to the changes at the political and military level that resulted from the collapse of the Soviet bloc and the end of the Cold War. Instead, the NWO in this essay takes a much broader meaning extending to the economic level (as expressed by the emergence of the present neoliberal economic globalization in the form of the internationalized market economy, which secures the concentration of economic power in the hands of the transnational economic elites); the political-military level (as expressed by the emergence of a new informal political globalization securing the concentration of political power in the hands of an emergent transnational political elite); and the ideological level (as expressed by the development of a new transnational ideology of limited sovereignty— supposedly to protect human rights, to fight "terrorism," and so on). In this essay I will try to develop a theoretical framework for the analysis of the systemic aspects of academic repression in the context of this New World Order.

1. Academic Freedom, Autonomy and "Neutrality"
Academic Freedom and the Negative Conception of Freedom

The adoption of academic freedom, as part of an entire set of individual freedoms, constituted a basic element of the shift to modernity, which in turn represented a break with the past. The new economic and political institutions in the form of the market economy and representative "democracy," as well as the parallel rise of industrialism, marked a systemic change. This change was inescapably accompanied by a corresponding shift in the dominant social paradigm (defined as the system of beliefs, ideas, and corresponding values that prevail in a particular society at a particular moment of its history, as consistent with the existing institutional framework).[1] In pre-modern societies, the dominant social paradigms were characterized by mainly religious ideas and corresponding values about hierarchies. On the other hand, the social paradigm of modernity is dominated by market values and the idea of progress, growth, and rational secularism. In fact, the flourishing of science in modernity has played an important ideological role in "objectively" justifying the growth economy (defined as the system of economic organization which is geared, either "objectively" or deliberately, toward maximizing economic growth)[2]—a role that has been put under severe strain in neoliberal modernity by the credibility crisis of science.

However, the two main institutions that distinguish modern society from premodern society[3]—namely, the system of the market economy, which superseded the (socially controlled) local markets that had existed for thousands of years before, and its political complement, representative "democracy," which replaced the classical conception of democracy based on direct democracy—determine also the systemic limitations of all freedoms and therefore of academic freedom as well. Liberal individualism and laissez faire economics constitute the pillars on which the familiar individual freedoms and rights were based: freedom of thought and expression—on which academic freedom is also based—and the corresponding rights to life and liberty, the latter supposedly ensured by the rights to participate in government through free elections and the right to property. Furthermore, in consistency with the liberal conception of freedom (defined negatively as the absence of constraints in human activity), these freedoms and rights are defined as "freedom from"[4] (e.g.: freedom from discrimination and from arbitrary arrest and torture), since their explicit objective is to limit state power without any reference to positive freedom, or "freedom to" (i.e., self-determination).

Academic freedom is also founded on the same negative conception of freedom, which has historically defined its systemic limitations, as well as the content of academic repression today. In other words, the distinguishing characteristic of the liberal conception of individual freedoms is the complete abstraction of them from their socio-economic base. It was this characteristic that allowed generations of Marxists to dismiss such freedoms as "formal freedoms" on the grounds that few people in capitalist societies could exercise them effectively. Yet, despite the fact that it is now generally accepted that the liberal rights and liberties are not merely formal—since many important freedoms, such as freedom of assembly and association, freedom to strike, and academic freedom itself, had been institutionalised after long struggles in the last

150 years—Marx's dictum that "equal right is still a bourgeois right" (in the sense that it presupposes inequality) is still valid.[5]

Heteronomous vs. Autonomous Societies and Academic Freedom

In this context, we may see the limitations on academic freedom of teachers and students and on the related freedom of thought—as expressed in the education process and research—as imposed by the "system" itself, i.e. the system of market economy and its political complement, representative "democracy." But, leaving for the next section the relationship between the market economy and the education process, let us focus here on the relation between representative "democracy" and education, which brings us to the intrinsic link between politics and education.

The meaning of education is defined by the prevailing meaning of politics. If politics is understood in its current usage, which is related to the present institutional framework of representative "democracy," then it takes the form of statecraft, which involves the administration of the state by an elite (i.e., by professional politicians who set the laws, supposedly representing the will of the people). This is the case of a heteronomous society in which the public space has been usurped by various elites that concentrate political and economic power in their hands. In such a heteronomous society, education has a double aim: first, to help in the internalization of the existing institutions and the values consistent with them (socialization process) and, second, to produce "efficient" citizens in the sense of individuals who have accumulated enough "technical knowledge" so that they can function competently, in accordance with society's aims as laid down by the elites.

On the other hand, if politics is understood in its classical sense that is related to the institutional framework of a direct democracy, in which people not only question laws, but are also able to make their own laws, then we talk about an autonomous society, which is capable of bringing forth self-governed individuals. Therefore, whereas a heteronomous society is based on a negative definition of freedom ("freedom from"), an autonomous society is based on a positive one ("freedom to") in the sense of self-determination, ("we posit our own laws"). In an autonomous society, the public space encompasses the entire citizen body, which in an inclusive democracy[6] will take all operative political and economic decisions within an institutional framework of equal distribution of political and economic power among citizens.

In such an autonomous society, we do not talk anymore about "education" but about the much broader concept of *paideia*, which is defined as an all-round, life-long, process of character development, involving absorption of knowledge and skills and—more significantly—practicing an active citizenship in which political activity is seen not as a means to an end but as an end in itself.[7] A precondition for the development of balanced personalities, as I stress elsewhere, is the achievement of an equilibrium between science and the aesthetic sensibility, including an appreciation of philosophical thought. This implies that "students should be encouraged in all areas of study and particularly in the general knowledge area to appreciate all forms of art and to be actively involved in practising creative art so that a meaningful balance could be achieved between scientific/practical knowledge on the one hand and aesthetic sensibility/creativity on the other."[8] *Paideia* therefore has the overall aim of developing the capacity of students to participate in its reflective and deliberative activities.

In the liberal view, human rights are mostly rights against the state and, in fact, it is only in forms of social organization where political and economic power is concentrated in the hands of elites that "rights" are invested with any meaning. On the other hand, in a non-statist type of democracy, which by definition involves the equal sharing of power, such rights become meaningless. As Karl Hess rightly points out: "rights are power, the power of someone or some group over someone else…rights are derived from institutions of power."[9] In this framework, the very concept of academic freedom makes sense only within a heteronomous, hierarchical society in which the state is forced to grant certain freedoms necessary for the self-protection of society. On the other hand, in an autonomous society, the issue is not one of forcing the state to grant "freedoms," but of institutionalizing individual and social autonomy in every social realm.

"Neutrality" and Academic Freedom

A basic tenet of academic freedom, which clearly shows the systemic limitations of this concept in a heteronomous society, is that of "neutrality."[10] Strangely enough, the thesis of neutrality was adopted not only by liberals but also by supporters of socialist statism, who also adopted the neutrality of technoscience, in the sense that it is a "means" which can be used for the attainment of a capitalist or socialist development of productive forces. Within the Marxist movement, it was only the Frankfurt School (Theodor Adorno, Herbert Marcuse, et al.) that denied the neutrality of technology thesis, arguing that, while technology serves generic aims such as increasing the power of human over nature, its design and application also serves the domination of human over human, and, in this sense, the means (technology) are not truly "value free," but include within their very structure the end of furthering a particular organization of society.

In fact, just as religion played an important part in justifying feudal hierarchy, science, particularly social "science," was crucial in "objectively" justifying the modern hierarchical (or heteronomous) society and the growth economy. Furthermore, applied science, like technology, is not "neutral" to the logic and dynamic of the market economy. As I tried to show elsewhere,[11] modern technoscience is neither "neutral," in the sense that it is merely a "means" that can be used for the attainment of whatever end, nor autonomous, in the sense that it is the sole or the most important factor determining social structures, relations, and values. Instead, technoscience is conditioned by the power relations implied by the specific set of social, political, and economic institutions characterizing the growth economy and the dominant social paradigm. On the other hand, in an autonomous society, both science and technology are reconstituted in a way that puts at the center of every stage in the process, in every single technique, human personality and its needs rather than the interests of those controlling the market/growth economy.

Social science in particular shows even more clearly the systemic limitations of academic freedom, given its obviously non-neutral character in a heteronomous or class society. As I tried to show elsewhere,[12] the object of study plays a much more important role in social than in natural sciences, with respect to determining the choice of a paradigm by a practitioner, as it is not possible for social scientists living in a heteronomous society to really dissociate themselves from their object of study, i.e., society. Social scientists, more than natural scientists, have to make an explicit, or usually implicit, decision on whether or not to take the existing social system for granted in analysing social relations. In other words, given the inevitable social divisions characterizing a heteronomous society, there is a correspondingly inevitable division among social theorists arising out of their stand towards the existing social system. The fact that, much less frequently, a similar inevitable division arises among natural scientists (although this is changing in neoliberal modernity, as we shall see below), could go a long way toward explaining the much higher degree of intersubjectivity (i.e. the degree of consensus achieved among the theorists in a particular discipline) that natural sciences have traditionally enjoyed over social sciences in interpreting their object of study. No wonder natural sciences are characterized as more mature than social sciences, given the higher degree of intersubjectivity that can actually be achieved at a given time and place among natural scientists compared to the relatively lower degree of intersubjectivity that can potentially be achieved among social scientists.

Yet, science itself does belong to the autonomy tradition because of the methods it uses to derive its truths and, sometimes, even from the point of view of its content (e.g., the demystification of religious beliefs). Thus, it may be argued that the essence of science lies in the constant questioning of truths, that is, in the procedures it uses to derive its truths. Science, may therefore, from the point of view of its content (as well as its technological applications), enhance either autonomy or heteronomy (mainly the latter, given the usual heteronomous institutioning of society which conditions the development of science), although from the perspective of the procedures used, it has historically been an expression of autonomy. Scientific "truths," as well as the procedures used to derive them, unlike mystical, intuitional, and irrational "truths" and procedures in general, are subject to constant questioning and critical assessment. The very fact that the scientific truths have so drastically changed over time, unlike religious doctrines and dogmas and mystical "truths" which take the form of permanent truths, is a clear indication of the autonomous nature of the scientific method.

It is, therefore, exactly the semi-autonomous character of science, which results from the methods it uses to draw its "truths," that makes the protection of academic freedom crucial in a heteronomous society like the present one. In other words, the moment academic freedom securing science's autonomy in the scientific procedures used ceases to exist in practice, then science becomes a completely heteronomous activity not worth pursuing. Having said this, it is obvious that a fully autonomous science, regarding both its content and its method, is impossible in the context of the existing power relations and the social paradigm which is dominant in today's heteronomous society. Therefore, the non–neutral and overall heteronomous nature of today's science precludes a truly democratic science. Yet, this does not imply that what is needed today is to jettison science in the interpretation of social phenomena, let alone rationalism altogether, in favor of irrationalism. What is implied, instead, is the need to transcend both the "objective" rationalism (grounded on "objective laws" of natural or social evolution) that we inherited from the Enlightenment, as well as the generalized relativism of postmodernism, and develop instead, as I tried to show elsewhere,[13] a new kind of democratic rationalism.

2. Systemic Aspects of Academic Repression in Neoliberal Globalization
Academic Freedom in Liberal and Statist Modernity

Although the fundamental institutions that characterize modernity and the dominant social paradigm have remained essentially unchanged since the emergence of the modern era over two centuries ago (something that renders as a myth the idea of postmodernity, into which humanity has supposedly entered in the last three decades or so),[14] there have, nevertheless, been some significant structural changes within this period that could usefully be classified as the three main phases of modernity, following the establishment of the system of the market economy in the late-eighteenth century: liberal modernity (mid to end of nineteenth century) which, after World War I and the 1929 crash, led to statist modernity (mid-1930s to mid-1970s), and finally to today's neoliberal modernity (mid-1970s to the present).

The various forms of modernity have created their own dominant social paradigms which, in effect, constitute sub-paradigms of the main paradigm, as they all share a fundamental characteristic: the separation of society from the economy and polity, as expressed by the market economy and representative "democracy"—with the exception of Soviet statism in which this separation was effected through central planning and Soviet "democracy." On top of this main characteristic, all forms of modernity share, with some variations, the themes of instrumental reason, critical thought, and economic growth. As one could expect, the changes involved in the various forms of modernity, as a result of the structural changes in the form of the system of market economy in each period, as well as of the corresponding sub-paradigmatic changes, had significant repercussions on the nature, content, and form of education, teaching, and research and, therefore, on the limits of academic freedom, both as a teacher's and a student's right.

Thus, the flourishing of the system of the market/growth economy in the liberal period created the need to expand the number of pupils/students in all stages of education to meet the needs of the expanding factory system, specialized training and rapid technical progress. Massive schooling was introduced along with the idea that education ought to be the responsibility of the state. Countries such as France and Germany began to establish public educational systems early in the nineteenth century. However, this trend was in contradiction to the dominant social (sub)paradigm of liberal modernity. This paradigm was characterized by the belief in a mechanistic model of science, objective truth, and themes from economic liberalism such as laissez faire and minimization of social controls over markets for the protection of labor. This is why countries such as Great Britain and the United States, in which the dominant social paradigm has been almost thoroughly internalized, hesitated longer before allowing governments to intervene in educational affairs. No wonder the idea of academic freedom, as a student's right (on top of the conception of it as a teacher's right), originated in mainland Europe and was transplanted to the United States in the nineteenth century by scholars who had studied at German universities. However, it was not only the access to education that changed during liberal modernity. The nature of education itself changed as well, with schools and universities expected to help in the internalization of the existing institutions and the values consistent with them (i.e., the dominant social paradigm), apart from producing "efficient" citizens in the sense of citizens who have accumulated enough technical knowledge so that they could function competently in accordance with society's aims, as laid down by the elites.

The statist phase in the West took a social-democratic form and was backed by Keynesian economic policies, which involved active state control of the economy and extensive interference with the self-regulating mechanism of the market to secure full employment, a better distribution of income, and economic growth. This phase reached its peak in the period following World War II, when Keynesian policies were adopted by governing parties of all persuasions both in Europe and the US, and ended with the rise of Thatcherism in Britain and Reaganomics in the US in the late 1970s, when the growing internationalization of the market economy—the inevitable result of its grow-or-die dynamic—became incompatible with statism. The statist phase was characterized by the post-war economic boom that required a vast expansion of the labor base, with women and immigrants filling the gaps. On top of this, the incessant increase in the division of labor, changes in production methods and organization, as well as revolutionary transformations in information technology required a growing number of highly skilled personnel, scientists, high-level professionals, and the like. As a result of these trends, the number of universities in many countries doubled or trebled between 1950 and 1970, whereas technical colleges, as well as part-time and evening courses, spread rapidly, promoting adult education at all levels. The massive expansion of education, accompanied with the conditions of job security established by the welfare state, facilitated the radicalization of the student body and a significant part of the university teachers. It was these developments which had created the objective conditions for May 68[15]—an event which led to an unprecedented flourishing of academic freedom in most Western universities.

Academic Freedom in Neoliberal Modernity

The emergence of neoliberal globalization during the last quarter of the twentieth century was a monumental event that represented a structural change rather than simply a change in economic policy, as was mistaken by the reformist Left. No wonder that many in the same Left believe today that the current financial crisis signifies the end of neoliberal globalization, if not of capitalism itself![16] The market economy's grow-or-die dynamic and, in particular, the emergence and continuous expansion of transnational corporations (TNC) and the parallel development of the Euro-dollar market were the main economic developments that induced the elites to open and liberalize the markets—a crucial event which characterizes the neoliberal form of modernity. Thus, neoliberal globalization implies a major intensification of the marketization process (i.e. the phasing out of effective social controls on markets),[17] which began with the establishment of the system of market economy two centuries ago.

An important characteristic of the neoliberal form of modernity at the political level was the emergence of a new "transnational elite"[18] which draws its power (economic, political, or generally social power) from operating at the global level—a fact that implies that it does not express, solely or even primarily, the interests of a particular nation-state. This elite consists of the transnational economic elites (TNC executives and their local affiliates); the transnational political elites (the globalizing bureaucrats and politicians who may be based either in major international organizations or in the state machines of the main market economies); and, finally, the transnational professional elites, whose members play a dominant role in the various international foundations, think tanks, research departments of major international universities, the

mass media, and so on. The main aim of the transnational elite is the maximization of
the role of the market and the minimization of any effective social controls over it for
the protection of labor or the environment, so that maximum "efficiency" (defined in
narrow techno-economic terms) and profitability may be secured.

Finally, at the ideological level, neoliberal modernity is characterized by the
emergence of a new social (sub)paradigm which tends to become dominant, the so-
called "postmodern" paradigm. The main elements of this paradigm are, first, a critique
of progress (but not of growth itself), of mechanistic and deterministic science (but
usually not of science itself) and of objective truth and, second, the adoption of neoliberal themes such as the minimization of social controls over markets, the replacement
of the welfare state by safety nets, and the maximization of the role of the private sector
in the economy.

The intensification of marketization in neoliberal modernity implies the effec-
tual privatization of both scientific research and education. As regards, first, the effects
of privatization of scientific research—following the scaling down of the state sector
in general and state spending in particular[19]—the "neutrality" of science has become
more disputable than ever before. Thus, as Stephanie Pain, an associate editor of *New
Scientist* stresses, science and big business have developed ever closer links in the present neoliberal era:

> Where research was once mostly neutral, it now has an array of pay-
> masters to please. In place of impartiality, research results are being dis-
> creetly managed and massaged, or even locked away if they don't serve
> the right interests. Patronage rarely comes without strings attached.[20]

In fact, as Pain argues, even more pernicious is the scientists' slide into self–
censorship in an attempt to ensure that contracts keep coming—an effort which is vital
for their survival after the institutionalization of the (formerly informal) links between
business and science introduced by neoliberals. In Britain, for instance, a 1993 government's white paper on science stressed the need to concentrate on research that would
help "the economy," whereas industry was asked to pick out the areas of science that
were likely to create wealth in the future. If, therefore, in the past, it was mainly the
"neutrality" of social sciences that was untenable, as we saw above, then today, as a
result of the multitude of formal and informal links between business and science established in neoliberal modernity, the neutrality of science in general is also becoming
increasingly untenable.

The marketization of scientific research is particularly evident in areas such as
agro-industry and biotechnology, whereby entire university departments are research
outposts for Monsanto, Novartis, Cargill, etc., while research on the environmental

and social impact of industrial agriculture is neglected or eliminated.[21] An even more disturbing example of the cooptation of science by corporate giants refers to the highly lucrative industry of climate change skeptics. Despite overwhelming evidence and a strong international consensus that human activity has caused climate instability and planetary warming, fighting the consensus every step of the way has been a powerful group of industry lobbyists, funded by corporations such as Exxon-Mobil, who, aided by a handful of scientists, "argued that global warming is a confidence trick to frighten governments into awarding large research grants...[and] who have helped drag out the negotiations to win the fossil fuel lobby a reprieve of almost a decade."[22] Thus, transnational energy corporations, their lobbyists and ideologues, together with ve-nal academics, have dismissed global warming as a dangerous myth and have urged that the global economy must roll along, spreading enough doubt and dissimulation that people become inactive and confused, despite the abundantly clear and alarming facts of a planet out of balance. Thus, as reported by *The Observer*, "a web of financial links exists between US university research scientists, fossil fuel lobby groups (whose members include Shell, Exxon, Texaco, and Ford), and industry paymasters including British Coal and the Kuwaiti government."[23]

The US Educational System as a Pilot Scheme for the Transnational Elite

The transnational elite, in neoliberal modernity, works on a pilot scheme on educa-tion which is based on the US case, which becomes obvious if we consider the drastic changes attempted at present in the European educational space and their consequenc-es on the systemic limitations of academic freedom. Thus, as early as 2001, the EU's Declaration of Bologna prescribed the creation of a European Space of Higher Educa-tion that would ensure:

> The international competitiveness of European Higher Education and,
> The effective linking of higher education to the needs of society and
> those of the European labor market.

The latter represents a direct linking of education to market needs, in contrast to the corresponding indirect linking during the social-democratic era. In this sense, it summarizes the essence of neoliberal globalization as far as education and research are concerned and has defining implications with respect to their own content and, of course, financing. Thus, it is explicitly being declared now that the University is in the service of private enterprise, while at the same time the financing only of those courses and research projects which serve "society's needs" (as far as they are identified with "market needs"), is being introduced, through various direct and indirect methods. Knowledge, like everything else in a market society, is becoming instrumental in the main aim of serving the economy and the elites controlling it, irrespective of the real needs of society, the desires of educators and the educated, and, by implication, the "pure" cognitive needs of science.

It is not, therefore, surprising that in social-liberal Britain one can observe, as from the beginning of the last decade, a continuous shrinking in the number of "theoretical" courses being offered (History, Political Economy, Philosophy, Arts, etc.[24]), in order to make way for "practical" courses directly linked to the market (marketing, business studies, management, computing, and so on). Needless to add, non-mainstream economics, politics, and similar social sciences courses have been simply phased out in all universities—apart from some elite universities—as such courses are not related to the demands of the market and do not create research "output" which is publishable in mainstream journals. The result is that such courses do not enhance the research profile of the relevant departments, a fact negatively affecting their financing. No wonder that the British theoretical journal *Capital & Class* predicted, on the basis of a well-documented study,[25] that non-mainstream economics will be eliminated from British economic departments shortly. Furthermore, a similar process is in action in natural sciences as well, with Chemistry, Physics, and other departments closing down "in response to market demands" and being replaced by courses in forensic science and applied physics such as nanotechnology. Thus, according to the Royal Society of Chemistry, twenty-eight chemistry departments closed in recent years, including the famous Kings College London department where the double helix structure of DNA was investigated![26]

All this was not the result of a satanic plot by the elites, but the inevitable outcome of neoliberal economic policies, which involved drastic cuts in tax rates (corporation tax, personal income tax, etc.) for the benefit of the privileged social strata financed through corresponding cuts in public spending, including funds for education. This has inevitably led to the creation of an "internal market," in the education sector and to an indirect privatization of study and research "from below." Thus,

• on the demand side, university applicants, facing today's rising unemployment and underemployment, select objects of study which are "in demand" in the job market, indirectly helping the channeling of more public funds towards them. Also,

• on the supply side, such "practical" courses easily secure sponsorship and private financing in general, both of which complement the dwindling public financing of education.

No wonder that this process has already led to the mass production of pure technocrats, with superficial general knowledge and, of course, without any capability of autonomous thought beyond the narrow and specialized contours of their discipline. This is consistent with the fundamental aim of education in neoliberal modernity which is the "production" of similar narrow-minded "scientists," who are called upon to solve the technical problems faced by private enterprise in a way that will maximize economic efficiency. Inevitably, this kind of mass production of similar "scientists" by no means implies that scientific rationalism has finally prevailed in thought. In the US, for instance, where this system of education has always been dominant, well-known scientists within their own disciplines (even in the natural sciences!) are religious, or adopt various irrational systems of thought whose central ideas have been drawn not through rational methods (reason in the sense of coherence between hypotheses and their implications and/or empirical evidence) but through intuition, instinct, feelings, mystical experiences, revelation, etc. The outcome of this is a Jekyll-and-Hyde scientist who is compelled to use the rational methodology while wearing his/her scientific hat, yet who becomes an irrationalist of the worse kind once this hat is removed. This was a relatively rare phenomenon in Europe before neoliberal modernity, but the present direct or indirect privatization of European universities is making such schizophrenic identities increasingly frequent.

Academic Freedom and Control of Education

No real academic freedom, as both a teacher's and a student's right, is possible in either a private or a state-controlled education. A private university education is nothing more than a commodity-manufactured mindset produced according to the principles of economic "efficiency," which aim to herd the maximum flow of students through the utilitarian curriculum as quickly as possible. Education priorities, in other words, are set according to the utility of research and teaching to the needs of the market system and of those controlling it. No wonder that even the most prestigious private US universities offer highly prized places to the offspring of generous sponsors and alumni relatively easily—a practice apparently well utilized by the Bush family![27] Furthermore, the abolition of free education, which inevitably follows as a result of the establishment of private universities, effectively denies the right of many citizens to any kind of specialized knowledge, being obviously a classist move.

A clear example is Britain, where the indirect privatization of universities through the introduction of tuition fees has mainly affected students from lower income groups. Thus, the new system of student loans (similar to the US system), which was introduced by the social-liberals of the "New" Labor party to replace the old system of student grants adopted by the "Old" Labor party of the social-democratic era, is not only pushing students to work in bars, McDonald's restaurants, and strip joints to complement their income, but is also leaving them with serious debts at the end of their studies.[28] This has the important (for the system) indirect social effect of creating a docile class of citizens struggling to repay their student loans, their mortgages, their credit card debts, and so on—the perfect formula for a hyper-exploited, ultra-passive, and conformist citizen, who works hard to buy (usually unnecessary) goods and services and follows the rules of the elites—the American prescription for a "dream" society.

Similarly, a state-controlled university means a university directly controlled by the political elites and—through their links with the economic elites—indirectly by the economic elites. However, although a state-controlled university is obviously not ideal, it is certainly preferable to a private-controlled university in at least one sense. It is much easier for changes in the programs of study and research to be imposed "from below," (i.e. by students and staff) in state-controlled universities, as opposed to private universities. This was the case in several Western European universities in the aftermath of May '68, when, as mentioned above, academic freedom flourished—even though briefly, before being mostly reversed within the context of neoliberal globalization.

3. Systemic Aspects of Academic Repression in Present Representative "Democracy"

It is not accidental that, historically, both state repression and counter-violence have flourished in the last two centuries. This is because representative "democracy" and the market economy, which flourished during this period, not only institutionalized the concentration of political and economic power (systemic violence) but also made easier the flourishing of counter-violence, some forms of which were legally recognized. However, there is no doubt that counter-violence in all its forms has increased significantly since the rise of neoliberal globalization. This can only be interpreted in terms of a significant increase in systemic violence (or even state repression) and the associated increase in the concentration of power at the hands of the ruling elites.[29] One may therefore conclude that the ultimate cause of the September 11 attacks should be traced back to the NWO, which has established a huge inequality in the distribution of economic and political power within and between nations.

The "War on Terror" as a Means of Controlling Populations in the New World Order

The so-called "war against terrorism" launched by the transnational elite in the aftermath of 9/11—like previous "wars" against Iraq and Yugoslavia—aims at securing the stability of the New World Order by crushing any perceived threats against it. However, this is also a new type of war. Unlike the previous "wars," this is a global and permanent war.

It is a global war, not in the sense of a generalized war like the preceding two world wars, but in the sense that its targets are not only specific "rogue" regimes (e.g., those of Hussein and Milosevic) that are not fully integrated into the New World Order, but any kind of regime or even a social group or movement that resists the New World Order. Thus, any such movement, from the Palestinian to the antiglobalization and animal liberation movements, is a potential target in this "war." Furthermore, it is a permanent war, because it is bound to continue for as long as the New World Order spreads throughout the globe. No wonder the US Pentagon called the war on terror a "long war."[30]

In effect, this latest war was planned to involve the entire transnational elite and was envisaged to take the form of an ongoing conflict, unlimited by time and space, as it could be fought in dozens of countries and for decades to come. It is therefore clear that the transnational elite decided to launch this new type of global war—with 9/11 as the perfect pretext—in order to secure its unchallenged hegemony for many years to come. In other words, the "war against terrorism" is a particularly expedient means of controlling populations that threaten the NWO.

This was achieved, mainly, through the introduction of draconian "anti-terrorist" legislation in the North, supposedly to fight terrorism, but in reality as an effective means to suppress the collective counter-violence against the present intensification of systemic violence. Thus, in US and UK, the electronic policing of every citizen's words, emails, and conversations have reached unprecedented heights. As the US now incarcerates 1 out of every 100 people, the USA PATRIOT Act anti-terror legislation has effectively suspended parts of the US constitution, thereby creating—as a Columbia University law professor pointed out[31]—"one of the more dramatic Constitutional crises in United States history." This means eclipsing the Constitution as a quaint relic from a pre-9/11 world, and giving the federal government sweeping new powers to investigate electronic communications, personal and financial records, computer hard drives, and other areas of private life normally outside the government's right to surveil and subpoena.

Similar legislation in Britain suspended parts of the European convention for Human Rights so that, among other provisions, foreigners could be detained indefinitely without charge or trial, on the basis merely of suspicion of terrorist-related activities. This legislation is currently extended by the social-fascist "New" Labor Government, so that any suspect can be arbitrarily arrested and detained for a period that could extend to forty-two days. Meanwhile, the UK security services brandish their right to "shoot-to-kill" any suspected bomber (as they did to their first victim, a worker from the shanty towns of Brazil, shot dead with seven bullets to the head). No wonder that, in a Panopticon society full of trigger-happy cops and paranoid citizens stripped of free speech rights, even the ex-head of Scotland Yard's anti-terrorist squad during the anti-IRA campaign feels that Britain is "sinking into a police state."[32] Still, as if all this was not enough, the same "Labor" government has surpassed itself by introducing new arrangements that punish thought itself, by penalizing the "glorification" of terrorism—something that, today, includes the justification of peoples' resistance against occupying powers in Palestine, Iraq, and Afghanistan and, earlier, the resistance against the Nazi occupation or British and French colonialism.[33] Similarly, the European Union had drafted legislation to define terrorism in a way that would even allow the arrest as terrorists of students and workers occupying public buildings.[34]

At the same time, the ideologues of the NWO undertake the theoretical justification of the elite's "wars" and attempt to defame every intellectual that would dare to reveal the criminal character of its actions. In this effort, the most valuable assistance comes from the ideologues of the system, particularly those in the "Left"[35] who, having abandoned any antisystemic vision after the collapse of the socialist project, have opportunistically endorsed the NWO in all its aspects. The assimilation process has been gradual in Europe. Thus, the first war of the transnational elite (the Gulf War) was adopted only by the centre-Left intellectuals and analysts; the second war (Yugoslavia) was endorsed also by most of the Green and broadly "Left" intelligentsia; finally, the present "war" against terrorism has been adopted by most of the remaining "Left" including several Marxists, ex-communists, and others. No wonder that, in this climate of fear and suspicion, whipped up by G8 states and widely spread by the fog machines of the mass media controlled by the transnational elite, significant majorities living in capitalist metropoles are ready to sacrifice their civil liberties for the sake of "security." Neither is it surprising, of course, that the meaning of "enemy'" is gradually being extended to include everybody whom the elites classify as "terrorist."

Academic freedom was therefore bound to be one of the first—and most important—freedoms to suffer. The cases of Ward Churchill and Norman Finkelstein, among others in the US, are well documented in this volume. Less well known are instances of academic repression in Europe, such as targeted Dr. Andrej Holm and Dr. Matthias B., as well as of two other persons, all of them engaged "in that most suspicious pursuit—committing sociology."[36] As Richard Sennett and Saskia Sassen point out, Dr. B. is alleged to have used, in his academic publications, "phrases and key words"—such as "inequality" and "gentrification"—common to a particular militant group (and, indeed, much of the population!). In fact, Dr. B. was not actually accused of writing anything inflammatory, but seen rather to be capable of "authoring the sophisticated texts" a militant group might require. Further, this scholar, "as [an] employee in a research institute has access to libraries which he can use inconspicuously in order to do the research necessary to the drafting of texts" of militant groups, though he has not written a single one.

The Zionist Case of Academic Repression

Perhaps the most systematic repression of academic freedom in the period since the launching of the "war against terrorism," and the ensuing classification by the transnational elite of Palestinian resistance against the occupiers as an act of terrorism, is the case of the repression exercised by the international Zionist movement against academics who do not adopt the official line on the creation of Israel and the present reality in Palestine.

In fact, however, contrary to what is commonly thought, Zionists do not just aim at distorting recent history, since the establishment of an expansionist pure Jewish state in Palestine—despite condemnation by prominent Left Jews like Hannah Arendt and Isaac Deutscher and the Left Zionists who demanded a bi-nationalist, instead of a Jewish state—but even earlier History, going as far back as Biblical times. Thus, against a divisive mythology that denigrates Arabs and upholds Jews as God's chosen people, Antonio Arnaiz-Villena, a genetics Professor at Complutense University in Madrid, showed convincingly that Middle Eastern Jews and Palestinians are almost genetically identical. Villena published his research in *Human Immunology*, a leading US academic journal, and for his ground-breaking study he won no prizes, but rather was sacked from the journal's editorial board following intense pressure from the journal's pro-Zionist readers, while academics who had already received copies of the journal, were urged to rip out the offending pages and throw them away![37]

Interestingly enough, a similar view (though not based on genetics) is supported by Shlomo Sand, a "Young Historian" professor at Tel Aviv University who is highly critical of the exclusively ethnic base of Israel, which, as he argues, stems from the racism of Zionist ideologues. Sand, in a forthcoming book,[38] attacks what he calls the myth that the Jews are the descendants of the Hebrews, exiled from the kingdom of Judea, and he argues that the Jews are neither a race nor a nation, but ancient pagans— in the main Berbers from North Africa, Arabs from the south of Arabia, and Turks from the Khazar empire—who converted to Judaism between the fourth and eighth centuries. His conclusion that Israel shouldn't be a Jewish state, but rather a secular democracy that belongs to all its citizens is not far from the solution to the Palestinian problem proposed by the Inclusive Democracy project, which calls for a multicultural state as the first step towards a Confederated Inclusive Democracy.[39]

Another prominent member of the so-called "Young Historians" is Ilan Pappé, who, having access to documents from sixty years of Israeli archives and the testimony of survivors of ethnic cleansing, further contributed to the discrediting of

Zionist mythology that the creation of the Israeli state was the result of a national liberation struggle rather than of the deliberate ethnic cleansing of Palestinians.[40] Pappe's
recent book clearly shows that the Zionist ethnic cleansing of Palestine was planned
and executed in order to extend Israel's territory, in effect to Judaize it.[41] Needless to
say, as Eric Rouleau stresses, Pappe's book "provoked a furor in Israel that forced its
author—like so many others—to resign from the University of Haifa and go into exile
at a British university."[42]

But, the most prominent case of academic repression by Zionists is that of
Norman Finkelstein, author of the seminal book *The Holocaust Industry*, which docu-
ments how Zionists the world over hurl the charge of anti-Semitism to disarm criticism
of Israeli state terrorism against the Palestinians. He shows, moreover, how the US
Jewish establishment—well known for its fanatical Zionism, and which, according to
Aronowitz, "tragically, enjoys the support of the overwhelming majority of organized
US Jewry"[43]—shamelessly exploits the Nazi Holocaust for financial and political gain,
as well as to further the interests of Israel. The price Finkelstein paid for challenging
Zionist dogmas and taking on powerful Jewish and Israeli interest groups was to be
denied tenure at one of the US' top twenty private universities. Apparently, this was
not penalty enough: On May 23, 2008, Israel banned Finkelstein (a prominent Jew and
child of Holocaust survivors) from entering the country for ten years.

Another notable case is that of two prominent US academics Stephen
Walt, the academic dean of Harvard's Kennedy School of Government, and John
Mearsheimer, a political science professor at the University of Chicago, authors of *The
Israel Lobby*,[44] a book that was condemned as anti-Semitic. Their crime was to reveal
the mechanisms used by the Zionist elite (wrongly called by the authors the "Israel
Lobby") to pursue its objectives, with the American Israel Public Affairs Committee
(AIPAC) playing a leading role by repeatedly targeting members of Congress whom it
deemed insufficiently friendly to Israel to drive them from office, often by channeling
money to their opponents.

Of course, the charge of anti-Semitism that is thrown against the Left by Zionists and pro-Zionists is nothing less than "poisonous intellectual thuggery," as even
a British Labor Government adviser characterized the Zionist attack against the Left's
universalism.[45] In fact, the radical Left, including the anti-Zionist Jewish Left, as was
recently documented by Stanley Aronowitz,[46] consistently stood against Zionism, an
effectively racist ideology and practice, in favor of a secular democratic state for all the
peoples of Palestine, Arab and Jews alike. This stand, of course, is anathema to the Zionist elite, as well as to the transnational elite led by the US elite, as it could potentially
lead to the control of Palestine by the peoples themselves, rather than by the elites, for
their own interests.

Finally, the double standards on academic repression adopted by Zionists became all too obvious in the case of the British Lecturers' attempt to boycott Israeli universities. Thus, when at the 2007 annual conference of the British University and College Union (UCU), representing all university teachers in this country, a resolution was passed for a nationwide debate on a proposed academic boycott of Israeli universities in protest at the continued occupation of the Palestinian territories, a huge campaign, led by US Zionist academics, was launched to stop any debate on the matter. Almost immediately after the passing of this resolution, tens of thousands of emails flooded the inbox of leading members of the Union accusing them of violating academic freedom, despite the fact that as two investigating journalists, Tamara Traubman (a journalist for the Israeli daily *Ha'aretz*) and Benjamin Joffe-Walt, pointed out, after a painstaking research:

> we found the vast majority of the tens of thousands of emails originated not with groups fighting for academic freedom, but with lobby groups and think tanks that regularly work to delegitimise criticisms of Israel… Campaigners have used academic freedom as a tactic in a political campaign seeking to redirect public discussion away from the question of the complicity of the Israeli academy with the occupation and discrimination in Israeli universities (a debate they are likely to lose) towards academic freedom (a debate they are likely to win).[47]

This massive campaign was accompanied by intense pressure "from above" against the Union and threats of legal action against it that could lead to its bankruptcy. As a result, the British academics' union was forced, a few months after it has taken the resolution for a debate on a boycott, to drop any action related to it! Yet, the percentage of Arabs in university faculties is about one percent and, while individual Israeli academics have spoken up in defense of academic freedom in the occupied territories, not one institution has officially condemned injustices related to the occupation, which culminated with the internment of the entire population of Gaza (including Gaza students who lost their scholarships abroad after Israel refused visas to them)[48] in a huge ghetto for committing the crime of voting democratically for the "wrong" party! Clearly, some are more equal than others as regards academic freedom (as well as any other liberal kind of individual freedom in a representative "democracy"), and the protection of the academic freedom of one group of people should be protected at all costs, even when it is dependent on—and often aids in—the suppression of the overall freedoms of other groups, academic and otherwise.

4. Conclusion

Hopefully, the above analysis should have made clear that unless universities are directly controlled by society itself (which alone could express the general interest) and the academic community (i.e. teachers and students), no real academic freedom is possible. This applies not only to the cases of universities controlled by economic or political elites (i.e. the cases of private or state-controlled universities respectively), but also to "intermediate cases" where universities are controlled instead by elites and social groups within society that express special interests, whether cultural (e.g. religious organizations or the Church itself) or industrial-military complex (e.g. the US Pentagon), and so on. The issue, therefore, is whether teaching and research programs are defined directly by society in general and the academic community in particular rather than by specific social groups with vested special interests—the economic and political elites created by the market economy and representative "democracy" respectively.

A democratic paideia, therefore, presupposes a struggle for radical change not just in the educational structures but also in the socio-economic structures, so that students are not forced to choose only those programs of study meeting market needs, but instead are able to select those programs of study genuinely meeting human needs. This choice is fundamental if we take into account the fact that there is little (if any) relation between market needs and human needs in the market economy system, in which what determines "market needs" is crucially conditioned by privileged social groups, through the concentration of income, wealth, and economic power in their hands. It is, therefore, only within the context of an inclusive democracy, which institutionalizes an equal distribution of political and economic power among all citizens that one could meaningfully talk about academic freedom.

II
Academic Slapdown:
Case Studies in Repression

Academic Freedom on the Rock(s):

The Failures of Faculty in Tough Times

Robert Jensen

Threats to academic freedom—direct and indirect, subtle and not so subtle—come from a variety of sources: Politicians, the general public, news media, administrators, corporations, and students. In my academic career, I have been criticized from all quarters. Though these attacks have been relatively easy to fend off in my particular case, the threats are real and should trouble us; they require sharper analysis and a strategic plan to fend off attempts to constrain inquiry. But, even with that understanding of the seriousness of these external threats, I will argue that the most important aspect of the current controversies is how they mark the complacency and timidity of faculty members themselves.

I will focus on two specific incidents in my career—one involving administrators and the other students—that illustrate these threats. From there, I will examine the responses of faculty members on my campus to the events, and offer suggestions for analysis and action. Throughout, I will remain rooted in my own experience at the University of Texas at Austin. While Texas may in some ways be idiosyncratic, I do not believe my experience at that university is radically different from other universities throughout the United States.

My concern with this issue is not rooted in optimism for the short term. While I would like to see US academics, as a class, take a leading role in movements to assert radical humanistic values that have the possibility of transforming society, I don't believe such change is likely, or even possible, in the near future. In fact, I assume that in the short term precious few progressive developments are likely to emerge in the United States, with or without the assistance of university-based academics. Instead, I will argue we should work to hold onto what protections for academic freedom exist to provide some space for critical thinking in an otherwise paved-over intellectual culture, with an eye on the long term. Toward that goal, I will suggest ways to approach these threats to academic freedom and attempt to assess realistically the conditions under which such defenses go forward.

History and Context

Although threats to academic freedom, and freedom of expression more generally, can come rooted in many political projects, it is in times of war and national crisis (real or manufactured) that such threats intensify and have the potential to undermine democracy most severely. Such is the case in the post-9/11 world. In this sense, the "war on terrorism" serves a similar function to the "cold war" as a way both to obscure the fundamental motivations behind US foreign policy (to extend and deepen US domination over the strategically crucial areas of the world through a combination of diplomatic, military, and economic control mechanisms) and to focus public attention on threats that, while not completely illusory, are overdramatized. In each case, politicians also hype the threat of terrorism to make it easier to marginalize any domestic dissent to that project of control and domination. One can see echoes of the late 1940s/1950s in the post-9/11 United States. In such situations, dissident intellectuals and their academic freedom become easy targets.

Despite these similarities, it is crucial to recognize that the repression of the cold war dwarfs anything we've seen in recent years. The Supreme Court upheld the criminalization of political discourse in what became known as the Communist conspiracy cases prosecuted under the Smith Act of 1940.[1] The law made it a crime to discuss the "duty, necessity, desirability, or propriety of overthrowing or destroying the government," an odd statute in a country created by a revolution against the legal government of that day. It was not until 1957 that the Supreme Court reversed the trend in those cases, overturning convictions under the act.[2] In that repressive social climate, principles of academic freedom and administrative protections around tenure meant little, as universities routinely ignored both principles and rules, with no objection from the courts.[3]

Both the general public and academics live with far more expansive freedoms today, primarily as a result of the popular movements of the 1960s and 1970s, which pressured elites to expand free speech and association rights. We should recognize that since 9/11, for example, many people critical of US foreign and military policy have written and spoken in ways that would have without question landed us in jail in previous eras (and would land us in jail, or worse, in many other nations today). Of course, it is crucial to note that such protection is still incomplete and is most available to those who are from the dominant sectors of society. I am white and American-born, with a "normal" sounding American name (meaning, one that indicates northern European roots), and while I have been the target of much hostility, I have never felt that my safety or job were threatened in any serious way. The hostility toward some faculty members has not stayed within such civil boundaries, most notably toward Sami Al-Arian, the tenured Palestinian computer science professor at the University of South

Florida who was vilified in the mass media and fired in December 2001 for his political views, and then subject to federal prosecution.⁴ Being a white boy with tenure offers added protection.

So, much of the discussion about academic freedom these days is not about direct attempts to remove or punish faculty members for their ideas (with some notable exceptions, such as the cases of Ward Churchill at the University of Colorado-Boulder and Joseph Massad at Columbia University). Instead, we are struggling with issues about the climate, on campuses and in society more generally. These questions are no less important, but we should keep in mind the relative level of the threat as we strategize.

From Administrators: "An undiluted fountain of foolishness"

About mid-afternoon on September 11, 2001, I began writing an essay that argued the United States should not use the attacks to justify aggressive war, one of several similar pieces that quickly circulated in left/progressive circles. At the end of the evening, I sent it to Common Dreams and other such political websites under the headline "Stop the insanity here."⁵ Just as I was shutting down the computer for the evening, on a whim I decided also to send the piece to several Texas newspapers for which I had occasionally written, though I did not expect that any would publish it given the emotional/political realities right after the attacks. Surprisingly, the *Houston Chronicle* ran the piece at the end of the week, under the headline, "US Just as Guilty of Committing Own Violent Acts."⁶ By mid-morning, right-wing talk show hosts in Houston had read the piece on the air and encouraged people to call and write University of Texas officials to demand my firing. The deluge of mail, to me and my various bosses, continued for weeks. On September 18, UT President Larry Faulkner began circulating an official response, which was published the next day in the *Chronicle*:

> In his Sept. 14 Outlook article "US Just as Guilty of Committing Own Violent Acts," Robert Jensen was identified as holding a faculty appointment at the University of Texas at Austin. Jensen made his remarks entirely in his capacity as a free citizen of the United States, writing and speaking under the protection of the First Amendment of the US Constitution. No aspect of his remarks is supported, condoned or officially recognized by The University of Texas at Austin. He does not speak in the University's name and may not speak in its name. Using the same liberty, I convey my personal judgment that Jensen is not only misguided, but has become a fountain of undiluted foolishness on issues of public policy. Students must learn that there is a good deal of foolish

opinion in the popular media and they must become skilled at recognizing and discounting it. I, too, was disgusted by Jensen's article, but I also must defend his freedom to state his opinion. The First Amendment is the bedrock of American liberty.[7]

This was the first time in anyone's memory that a high-ranking university official had publicly condemned a faculty member by name for a political or intellectual position. In addition to this public rebuke, some other administrators circulated notes privately with similar views. For example, UT Provost Sheldon Ekland-Olson wrote, in a note he copied to me: "What came to my mind when reading his column was a statement, at the moment I do not recall who said it, that the price of freedom of speech and the press is that we must put up with a good deal of offensive rubbish. For me, Professor Jensen's comments fall deeply into this category."

I had previously crossed paths with Faulkner and the UT administration during campus organizing efforts around affirmative action and the wages/working conditions for non-teaching staff. I had met Faulkner once during the former campaign, and I was aware that I was not on his list of favorite faculty members. But at the time of this incident I assumed (and nothing since then has changed my assumption) that his letter denouncing me had little or nothing to do with me and was simply a reaction to pressure from various key constituencies: alumni, donors, legislators, and the general public. I didn't take Faulkner's rebuke personally, because it clearly wasn't about me.

For some weeks after that, I was asked how I felt about Faulkner's statement and what effect it had on my behavior. I stated repeatedly in public that I didn't feel anything in particular; administrators' opinions about my writing had never been of great importance to me. Nor was I affected by the denunciation; I continued my political work without interruption and taught my classes as I would have if there had been no controversy. When people asked me if I thought my academic freedom had been compromised, I was tempted to laugh. I am a tenured professor at a moment in history in which tenure is honored in all but a handful of extremely controversial cases. My academic freedom was, at that moment, not in jeopardy. But I did critique Faulkner for his comments, on two points.

First, Faulkner's statement modeled bad intellectual practice. He engaged in an ad hominem attack, condemning me personally without attempting to explain what substantive disagreements he had with my positions. As far as I know, he has never made such an explanation in a public forum, though I know of one case in which he turned down the chance to engage me directly (on an NPR radio show). While refusing such an engagement was strategically sensible given his objectives, it was intellectually and morally cowardly.

More important, of course, was the possible chilling effect of Faulkner's broadside on others, especially junior professors and students. Whatever Faulkner's strategy—whether he was simply trying to placate important constituencies or actually intended to create a climate on campus hostile to dissent—I heard directly from one untenured professor and several graduate students that they had modified or ended political activities when they read the statement. I assume many others made similar choices.

Was any of this an attack on academic freedom? Not in direct fashion; no one's rights were abridged. But it was not the kind of practice one would hope for from the leader of a major university.

From Students: "The guise of teaching potential journalists to 'think'"

In 2004, a conservative student group at the University of Texas published a "professor watch list" of instructors who "push an ideological viewpoint on their students through oftentimes subtle but sometimes abrasive methods of indoctrination."[8] After a lifetime of being second-tier, I was finally number one in something, albeit a list of allegedly deficient professors.

I have long held that one of the most serious problems on my campus—which is among the largest in the country, with 50,000 students—has been that the student body is largely depoliticized. Given that lack of political engagement, I was grateful for anything that gets students talking about politics, especially the role of politics in the university. So, when my name ended up on this list of the alleged indoctrinators (with no clear indication whether I am subtle or abrasive), I wasn't upset, even though the group's description of my "Critical Issues in Journalism" course didn't quite square with my experience in the classroom:

> In a survey course about Journalism, one might expect to learn about
> the industry, some basics about reporting and layout, the history of
> journalism, the values of a free press and what careers make the news
> machine function. Instead, Jensen introduces the unsuspecting student
> to a crash course in socialism, white privilege, the "truth" about the Per-
> sian Gulf War and the role of America as the world's prominent sponsor
> of terrorism. Jensen half-heartedly attempts to tie his rants to "critical
> issues" in journalism, insisting his lessons are valid under the guise of
> teaching potential journalists to "think" about the world around them.
> Jensen is also renowned for using class time when he teaches Media Law
> and Ethics to "come out" and analogize gay rights with the civil rights
> movement.[9] Ostensibly, this relates somehow to his course material.[10]

It's possible that this watch-list strategy sprang fresh from the minds of the Young Conservatives of Texas, but it's more likely they were influenced by the national group Students for Academic Freedom (SAF)[11] and leftist-turned-right-wing-activist David Horowitz.[12] The strategy is simple: Rather than attack specific professors for holding views critical of the dominant culture and its institutions, better to claim that the universities are dominated by these critical intellectuals who are crowding out other perspectives. Instead of outright militating for the firing of lefties, the group, far more insidiously, calls for promoting greater "balance," out of its dedication to "restoring academic freedom and educational values to America's institutions of higher learning" through pursuit of four key goals:

1. To promote intellectual diversity on campus
2. To defend the right of students to be treated with respect by faculty and administrators, regardless of their political or religious beliefs
3. To promote fairness, civility and inclusion in student affairs
4. To secure the adoption of the "Academic Bill of Rights" as official university policy

Especially brilliant is the cooptation of the concept of diversity to argue that conservative forces (forget, for a moment, that conservatives, and fairly reactionary conservatives at that, just happen to run most of the world these days) are barely surviving under the jackboot of Stalinist intellectuals.[13] The strategy of the right[14] seems fairly clear: To avoid looking fascistic, these groups cloak themselves in an odd combination of core Enlightenment values (the importance of the university as an open intellectual space) and a caricatured postmodern relativism (everybody's truth is valid, so the goal is simply balance because no definitive judgments are possible).

In such a world, it seems to me that one of the main tasks is to challenge a key assumption of the right-wing project: Professors can, and should, eliminate their own politics from the classroom. For example, the UT professor watch list valorizes one professor who "so well hides his own beliefs from the classroom that one is forced to wonder if he has any political leaning at all." These illusions of neutrality only confuse students about the nature of inquiry into human society and behavior.

All teaching—especially in the humanities and the social sciences—has a political dimension, and we shouldn't fear that. The question isn't whether professors should leave their politics at the door (they can't) but whether professors are responsible in the way they present their politics and can defend their pedagogical decisions. It's clear that every decision a professor makes—choice of topics, textbook selection, how material is presented—has an underlying politics. If the professor's views are safely within the conventional wisdom of the dominant sectors of society, it might appear the class is apolitical. Only when professors challenge that conventional wisdom do we hear talk about "politicized" classrooms.

But just because the classroom always is politicized in courses that deal with how we organize ourselves politically, economically, and socially, we should not suggest that it's all politics, ideology, and professorial bias. Because there's a politics to teaching doesn't mean teaching is nothing but politics; indeed, professors shouldn't proselytize for their positions in the classroom. Instead, when it's appropriate—and in the courses I teach, it often is—professors should highlight the inevitable political judgments that underlie teaching. Students—especially those who disagree with a professor's views—will come to see that the professor has opinions, which is a good thing. Professors should be modeling how to present and defend an argument with evidence and logic.

For example, in both my introductory and law-and-ethics classes, I offer a critique of corporations in capitalism. For most students, corporations and capitalism have been naturalized, accepted as the only possible way to organize an economy. I suggest to them a fairly obvious point: The modern corporation—a fairly recent invention—should be examined critically, not taken as a naturally occurring object. Given the phenomenal power of corporations, including media corporations, in contemporary America, how could one teach about journalism and law without a critical examination of not only the occasional high-profile corporate scandals, but the core nature of the institution?

The conservative group claimed its goal is "a fair and balanced delivery of information" in the classroom. If that really were their concern, of course, the first place they would train their attention is the business school. I've heard scandalous reports that some faculty members there teach courses in marketing, management, finance, and accounting that rarely, if ever, raise fundamental questions about capitalism. Highlighting the selective way in which accusations of politicized classrooms are identified and faculty are targeted for sanction is crucial.

Faculty Responses to the Watch List: Chicken Little

Rather than focus on the threats posed by administrator condemnations or student campaigns aimed at left/liberal biases, I want to focus on the responses I have seen and heard from faculty members on my campus. Again, I don't pretend that the University of Texas is representative. Rather than claim this is the way most faculty in the United States act, I want to highlight what I consider to be the problems in some faculty members' reactions where I work. I'll begin with the watch list.

In informal conversations as these political campaigns have gained prominence, I have heard far too many of what I believed to be overly dramatic responses, including references to these student efforts as McCarthyism or a suppression of academic freedom. Yes, these student initiatives are part of a broader goal of shutting down some of the remaining institutional spaces left for critical, independent inquiry. But it is inaccurate and counterproductive to compare a student-initiated endeavor (even if the inspiration for it comes from right-wing political operatives) to the use of state power to fire professors and destroy people's lives on a large scale. Could we someday return to the suppression of the two major Red Scares of the twentieth century? Of course it's possible, but it's not happening now. And to talk in those terms is to invite being labeled by the public as over-reactive, whiny, self-indulgent intellectuals who are cut off from the day-to-day reality of most people's struggles in the employment world, where job protection on the order of academic tenure is the stuff of dreams. The public is quick to label us that way, in part because it is so often an apt description of so many faculty members. Professorial rhetoric that bolsters the perception is not strategically helpful.

For example, one of my UT colleagues said in a television news story about the watch list: "I feel like they [students observing his class for potential inclusion on the list] were put there to watch me. And this watch list or my position on this watch list is a result of that. So, do I feel like I'm under surveillance? I am under surveillance."

First, is it accurate and/or strategic to describe the presence of a student in your class, even one there to keep tabs on any hint of professional failure, as being under surveillance, given that the term carries a connotation of being shadowed by law enforcement? Second, why is it a bad thing for students to be paying close attention to our teaching? In my large classes, where there is physical space available for visitors and their presence would not disrupt the flow of the class, I invite anyone to sit in. In fact, I would be happy to have a team of right-wing ideologues sit through my classes, for two simple reasons. One is that knowing they were present likely would make me strive to be more precise in my use of language; knowing someone from a dissenting position is in the audience tends to make me more conscious of what I'm saying, which is good. Another is that I am confident that I can defend the content of my course and my teaching methods, and I would invite a debate in which I could defend myself.

In short: The sky is not falling because of a student-generated professor watch list. Yes, we are in a period of backlash and reactionary right-wing domination of all the society's major institutions. Yes, we struggle to cope with how to handle students in a modern liberal university who are often resistant to considering any critique that goes against their preconceived notions of the political and moral order. There are more than enough serious issues to grapple with, and taken together these concerns suggest this society is on a dangerous course. But we should talk about the danger in that context, not episodically and overly dramatically. The sky is clouding but it is not falling.

Faculty Responses to Administration Condemnations: Little Chickens

After fifteen years in academic life, I have concluded that the vast majority of faculty members are like the vast majority of any comfortable professionals in a corporate capitalist empire: Morally lazy, usually cowardly, and unwilling and/or unable to engage with critics. I say that with no sense of superiority; I can look at my own life and see examples of such laziness and cowardice.

Let me offer an anecdote to illustrate. During fall semester 2005, I was leaving a meeting of the University of Texas' faculty Committee of Counsel on Academic Freedom and Responsibility. By some fluke, I had been elected to this university-wide committee, which is charged by the Faculty Council with the task of monitoring these issues on campus. (All of this is window-dressing; at the University of Texas, there is no faculty governance and all committees are merely consultative.)[15]

As a fellow committee member and I walked back to our offices, he asked what action this committee had taken in 2001, after Faulkner had condemned me. (That's an indication of the importance of the committee and its pronouncements; virtually no one remembers what it says, or even that it exists.) I told him that the committee had passed a weak resolution that reasserted the basics of academic freedom and asked people to be nice to each other, but made no reference to the controversy and rendered no judgment about the UT president's actions:

RESOLUTION FROM THE COMMITTEE OF COUNSEL ON ACADEMIC FREEDOM AND RESPONSIBILITY

Given current national and global events and the importance of members of the University community discussing these matters on campus and extramurally, the Committee of Counsel on Academic Freedom and Responsibility submits the following Resolution.

Resolved:

1) That all members of the University community—students, faculty, staff, and administrators—be reminded of the principles involving Academic Freedom and Responsibility as stated by the American Association of University Professors in the 1940 Statement of Principles on Academic Freedom and Tenure, including:

a) "The common good depends upon the free search for truth and its free exposition."

b) "College and university teachers are citizens, members of a learned profession, and officers of an educational institution. When they speak and write as citizens, they should be free from institutional censorship or discipline, but their special position in the community imposes special obligations. As scholars and educational officers, they should remember that the public may judge their profession and their institution by their utterances. Hence they should at all times be accurate, should exercise appropriate restraint, should show respect for the opinions of others, and should make every effort to indicate that they are not speaking for the institution."

2) That these principles of Academic Freedom and Responsibility be widely disseminated to the University community via e-mail and in the *Daily Texan* [campus student newspaper] so that all students, faculty, staff, and administrators have these statements as guiding principles for discourse on campus and extramurally.

3) That the members of the academic community treat one another with dignity in both their words and actions during the days ahead.[16]

Shortly after that resolution was passed, I asked the chair of that committee why something more forceful wasn't presented to the faculty council—something that at least raised the actual question instead of reproducing boilerplate. The chair explained that any resolution of that kind would not have received support from the committee. The implication was that there was no significant support for me, my political position, or the notion that a faculty member with such positions should be defended on principle.

I reported this to my faculty colleague on the current committee, and he expressed outrage. "How could the committee not have taken a more forceful position? Whatever the disagreements with my politics, didn't they see the issue about creating a supportive climate for free expression and scholarship?" he asked.

I offered no judgment of the committee, but instead asked this colleague what action he had taken at the time if he felt so strongly about the principle? He hesitated. I pressed: We are faculty members in the same department. Did anyone in our department circulate a letter of support? Did anyone on the faculty generate a petition critical of the president? He froze and didn't respond, but the answer is, no. I know of only one UT professor who, in a letter to the campus paper, publicly criticized the president's actions. On a progressive listserv there was discussion of a petition drive that never materialized. I was busy in those weeks and may have missed it, but to the best of my knowledge there was no public faculty action to rebuke a university president who had singled out a faculty member for ridicule in the largest newspaper in the state. Some professors told me later that they weighed in privately with the president, but such private interventions clearly were not going to result in any change in the president's public stance and, hence, were politically irrelevant. Beyond that, such private action did nothing to resist the narrowing of discussion in public.

So, on one of the largest university campus in the United States with about 2,500 faculty members, the committee charged with protecting academic freedom was silent on the most prominent attack on a faculty member for political reasons in recent memory. But, more striking, a faculty member who had done nothing to support academic freedom in that crucial moment seemed to have rewritten history in his own mind to forget that he, like virtually all the others, had remained silent in public.

It is one thing for members of a privileged class to decide they will avoid confrontations with power in order to protect there privilege. Depending on the context, we may deem that to be cowardly or expedient. But for such people to then twist reality to allow them to valorize themselves is, in any context, pathetic. It shows, I think, the degree to which some (perhaps a majority) of faculty are ill-equipped to assess threats to academic freedom or present an effective defense.

The Corporate Challenge to Academic Freedom

Meanwhile, as direct attacks on faculty members for their intellectual and/or political positions continue to pose a threat to academic freedom, other institutional rules and procedures can also compromise that freedom in ways that are quieter and slower. These concern the rules for tenure and promotion and the distribution of resources, and in my experience the majority of faculty members are far too timid in confronting these issues as well.

An example: A few years ago the dean of my college informed us during a faculty meeting that from that point forward, a record of securing grant funding would be expected for tenure and promotion cases. The ability to raise money, up to that point, had never been explicitly listed as a requirement, and many of us who had been tenured in past years had not been expected to raise money. But as public universities have been increasingly pushed to find more private funding, the pressure to raise money has filtered down to the faculty level. In some fields, especially the natural sciences, the expectation that faculty members would attract grant funding has long been in place, as have funding agencies for those disciplines, such as the National Science Foundation. And, although there are political forces that shape the funding in the sciences, there is money available for research that is not overtly tied to ideological positions.

In other fields, especially certain disciplines in the humanities and social sciences, funding is harder to come by and more overtly ideological in character. In my own area, journalism, the major funders are connected to the industry, either in the form of the media corporations themselves or the non-profit foundations they sometimes establish. These entities have never funded critical research that might lead to conclusions in conflict with their interests. In short, in a field such as journalism, grant funding flows to those researchers who do not challenge the fundamental structure of the commercial media system.

When the dean announced this shift, it was put forth as a neutral rule: Everyone who goes up for tenure or promotion faces the same expectations. One might dispute whether or not the change in policy was wise, but on the surface it appeared to be applied fairly across the board. But such an analysis at the surface is predictably superficial. I raised my hand to offer a different perspective.

Given that the sources of funding for scholars doing critical research are considerably fewer than for those doing research that accepts the existing system, isn't this demand on faculty, in fact, going to result in less critical research? I asked. I pointed out that I had pursued such critical work during my own tenure period and had never even applied for a grant. Luckily for me, I had been granted tenure based on my scholarly work, not my contribution to the university balance sheet. Did this new rule mean, in essence, that if I were going up for tenure today I would be denied? If that's the case, it seems likely that faculty members with similar interests can choose to either (1) pursue critical research interests and take the risk of being denied permanent employment, or (2) abandon such work and take up topics that are safely within the parameters acceptable to the industry. No matter what an individual chooses, the result is that there will be fewer professors pursuing critical ideas and, therefore, far less critical research. So, in fact, this allegedly neutral rule could have a dramatic effect on the intellectual content of our program, given that curriculum is largely faculty driven.

At that point, the dean gave me a look that seemed to contain equal amounts of amusement and exasperation, and said, "I'm just telling you about the policy from the Tower [central administration]." So, the lead administrator from the college, who is in charge of the academic programs of five departments, admitted she would not defend the principle of free and open inquiry and would do what she was told. Perhaps that's not surprising—deans are not known for bucking the system, which tends to slow career advancement. What was more disturbing was the reaction of my faculty colleagues, which was no reaction. Not a single faculty member supported my critique, nor offered any comment. I can certainly understand why the junior faculty, those still not secure in their positions, might have chosen to remain quiet in front of the administrator who would have considerable power in their tenure case. But even senior faculty—full professors, some with endowed chairs and professorships—chose to remain silent.

That's a well-disciplined intellectual class. The members of it who have risen to administrative positions and are charged with formulating and executing policy know which master they serve. The more secure members keep quiet to make sure their privilege is not disturbed. And the less secure members shut up in the hope that they will be allowed to move up a notch. In such a setting, elites cannot guarantee complete conformity from intellectuals, but the system works well enough to keep things running relatively smoothly these days. It is a system that is increasingly corporate in internal organization and character, and more corporate-friendly in its external relations.

What I Am not Saying, Politely:

I am not arguing that all faculty members must commit themselves to my politics or my style of public political engagement.

I am not bitter. Given the contemporary political landscape, I do not expect support from faculty members for my political activities.

I am not disappointed. As a class, faculty members act in ways that one would expect a privileged class to act.

I am not overly optimistic that these conditions—either in the political culture generally or in academia specifically—will change in the short term. The struggle is best understood as a long-term effort on all fronts.

I am not spending a lot of time worrying about this, given the myriad other ways I can spend my time and energy in political engagement in the world. Academic freedom matters, but not to the exclusion of other pressing issues.

And, I am not trying to paint with too broad a brush. I am aware that throughout the United States there are faculty members who take academic freedom seriously and are diligent in attempts to defend it.

What I Am saying, Bluntly:

The American Association of University Professor's (AAUP) 1915 Declaration of Principles—freedom of (1) inquiry and research, (2) teaching within the university, and (3) extramural utterance or action—is worth defending, but not because most faculty members can be expected to make serious use of these privileges to challenge power, and not because at this moment in history the university is a space where most faculty members pursue truly critical, independent inquiry. I find much of the university with which I am familiar (the humanities and the social sciences) to be populated with self-important and self-indulgent caricatures. Much of the intellectual work is trivial, irrelevant, and/or flabby. Most components of the contemporary US university system have been bought off, and acquired fairly cheaply. As a result, in the words of my friend Abe Osheroff, the institution is generally "a fucking dead rock."

Osheroff is a radical activist who, more than anyone I have ever met, exemplifies an organic intellectual. In a 2005 interview in which we discussed a wide range of contemporary intellectual and political issues, I asked Osheroff—then eighty-nine years old—about his experience with universities and faculty members:

> You can take this as a criticism, an indictment, of your profession, but most academics aren't worth shit as activists. You're overpaid, and you still all complain about the workload. I was lucky. I got out of the academic game early. What saved my ass was becoming a carpenter... The fact is that I have contempt for most of academia. Not just criticism, but contempt for it as an institution. I know there are some wonderful teachers here and there, but to me the universities are mostly fucking dead rocks. There are some diamonds and some gold that you can discover, but basically it's a fucking dead rock. I have a professor friend who tells me about his investment in his career. Yea, well while academics are doing their thing, some guys were down in a hole in the ground digging coal and making concrete and building your houses. Let's think about those people. Don't talk to me about your fucking investment. Academia was not too difficult a road. There are things worse than having to sit up at night and read books. Try 'em. Go out and dig a hole in the ground every fucking day, eight hours a day, and then you come back and we'll talk about it. I'm a little extreme, I must admit, but just the word academia makes me growl.[17]

Those of us who have the privilege of making a living as academics would do well to take Osheroff's words to heart. Osheroff is not anti-intellectual. He has taught in a university as an adjunct and is a serious student of history, recognizing the relevance of history and theory to political activism. Osheroff is not simplistically glorifying manual labor, but instead suggesting that an extremely privileged group of people should reflect on that privilege toward the goal of avoiding self-indulgence. His target is not the increasingly large number of low-paid apprentice and itinerant academics (graduate teaching assistants and permanent adjuncts, routinely exploited by universities to lower labor costs) but the tenured and tenure-track faculty members who make a comfortable living doing generally enjoyable work with more autonomy than most workers.

While Osheroff may be a bit harsh in his condemnation of professional academics, the spirit of his remarks seem fair to me. It is a reminder that we—even those of us who try to commit significant amounts of our time and energy to our obligations as citizens and human beings, and who attempt to leverage some of our institutional resources for progressive public activity—should always be asking a simple question: Are we doing enough? I know no one, including myself, for whom the answer is a definitive yes.

The impetus to protect academic freedom should be seen in this context, as part of a long-term strategy of protecting a saving remnant of intellectual integrity that at some point in the future may provide the core of a politically activated group that can be part of a meaningful shift in values in this society. There are no guarantees. But we can be reasonably sure that the common faculty reactions today—(1) duck-and-cover when things get edgy, or (2) whine when there really is little at stake—guarantee failure.

The Myth of Academic Freedom

Reflections on the Fraudulence of Liberal Principles in a Neoconservative Era

Ward Churchill

The University of Colorado was created and is maintained to afford men and women a liberal education in the several branches of literature, arts, sciences, and the professions. These aims can be achieved only in an atmosphere of free inquiry and discussion, which has become a tradition of universities and is called "academic freedom." For this purpose, "academic freedom" is defined as the freedom to inquire, discover, publish and teach truth as the faculty member sees it, subject to no control or authority save the control and authority of the rational methods by which truth is established. Within the bounds of this definition, academic freedom means that members of the faculty must have complete freedom to study, to learn, to do research, and to communicate the results of these pursuits to others. The students likewise must have freedom of study and discussion. The fullest exposure to conflicting opinions is the best insurance against error.... All members of the academic community have a responsibility to protect the university as a forum for the free expression of ideas.

—Laws of the Regents of the University of Colorado
Article 5, Part D: Principles of Academic Freedom[1]

AS A RULE, exploration of the gulf separating rhetoric from reality stands to shed considerable light upon the actualities—as opposed to the mythologies—of institutional character. This essay concerns mainly how officials at the University of Colorado at Boulder (UCB or CU), especially the Board of Regents whose "Laws" are quoted above, comported themselves the first time their willingness to defend the principle of academic freedom was subjected to a serious test. The situation at UCB fits into a broader pattern of intellectual/scholarly repression now prevalent in the United States and thus has implications for the academy as a whole.

The Liberal Dimension of the Liberal Arts

In July 2004, I was contacted by Nancy Rabinowitz, director of the Kirkland Project for the Study of Gender, Society and Culture at Hamilton College in upstate New York, and agreed to deliver a public lecture there in February 2005 in conjunction with Susan Rosenberg. Rosenberg, a former political prisoner whose sentence had been commuted by Bill Clinton,[2] had been contracted to teach for the Project during the spring semester. I was unaware, although it would not have altered my decision, that the Kirkland Project—a conspicuously left-leaning enterprise in an especially "conservative" area of upstate New York—had been targeted for elimination by a small circle of reactionary faculty members working in concert with off-campus organizations like David Horowitz's Scaife/Olin/Bradley-funded Center for the Study of Popular Culture (CSPC, which houses the conservative Students for Academic Freedom) and Lynne Cheney's American Council of Trustees and Alumni (ACTA).[3]

In October 2004, a well-coordinated campaign was launched against the Project's plan to employ Rosenberg, and by December publicity surrounding the attack had caused Rosenberg, on parole at the time, to withdraw.[4] Infuriated by what transpired, I decided not to cancel my appearance, at which point, *I* became the target of the same clique that orchestrated the anti-Rosenberg initiative. By late January, Hamilton professor Theodore Eismeier had found and circulated a three-year-old op-ed piece from the electronic journal *Dark Night Field Notes*, in which I described the investment bankers, stock brokers, and other finance technicians killed in the World Trade Center on September 11, 2001, as "little Eichmanns."[5]

The "story" first appeared in the Hamilton student newspaper and was picked up by the *Syracuse Post-Standard*.[6] The storm broke quickly as my "Eichmann" analogy was featured in a *Wall Street Journal* editorial[7] and on Fox News Network's *The O'Reilly Factor*.[8] New York governor George Pataki publicly demanded that Hamilton rescind its invitation.[9] Despite initially insisting the college would "never compromise" its commitment to academic freedom,[10] Hamilton president Joan Stewart ultimately caved in to the mounting political and financial pressure, citing public safety concerns to pull the plug on my lecture hours.[11] Rabinowitz, who had attempted to reschedule my appearance, was removed from the directorship of the Kirkland Project, which she'd co-founded, and the Project itself was subsequently placed in receivership.[12]

To all appearances, the small group of right-wing faculty who instigated the "controversy" prevailed. The expedients to which Hamilton's staunchly liberal president resorted will ensure that the college will "survive" and that she will remain at the helm for some "respectable" interval. The price paid, however, was the bedrock of academic freedom upon which any liberal arts college worthy of the name must stand. In its stead, she substituted a *realpolitik* wherein neocons waving checkbooks dictate what must—and what cannot—be said on campus.

"The Ward Churchill Factor"

Bill O'Reilly announced Stewart's capitulation as a personal triumph, trotting out David Horowitz to assert that funders were up in arms because Hamilton was functioning as a "bastion of radicalism."[13] By February 4, 2005, with commentators like Sean Hannity, Rush Limbaugh, and Joe Scarborough happily piling on, O'Reilly exulted that my talks were being "cancelled on campuses all across the country."[14] Actually, there were only three cancellations, one of which was overridden by faculty and student demands.[15]

On my own Boulder campus, an ad hoc coalition of student organizations arranged my first public address since the controversy began. Barely twenty-four hours before the event, interim chancellor Philip DiStefano, like Stewart a purported lifelong liberal, peremptorily "postponed" the event, expressing the standard "concern for public safety."[16] As would be the case at Eastern Washington University, the students and I—in this instance joined by community representatives—filed for injunctive relief in federal court[17] and DiStefano abruptly reversed himself. My talk was delivered on February 8 as originally scheduled and there was no hint of violence. The more than 1,500 people who attended were both orderly and overwhelmingly supportive.[18]

The same was true on a smaller scale at the University of Wisconsin's Whitewater (UWW) campus on March 1. Although O'Reilly mounted a concerted effort to cancel that talk as well, enlisting state legislator Steve Nass to denounce the "irresponsibility" of the university's "use of taxpayer dollars" to sponsor a lecture by "a guy who hates America,"[19] and calling on Wisconsin's former Republican governor to "explain" why his Democratic successor had not joined New York's Pataki and Colorado's Bill Owens in publicly demanding that I be fired.[20] UWW Chancellor Jack Miller, however, held firm, and the only actual disturbance at the event was caused by swarming media personnel.[21]

By early March, it was clear that O'Reilly's campaign had backfired, at least among people inclined to treat the principle of academic freedom as something more than a catch-phrase. The morning after O'Reilly triumphantly announced that my lectures were being cancelled—and partly in response to such gloating—I was invited to speak at the University of Hawai'i.[22] Other offers began to flow in, initiated by students and faculty of color, often with the support of white radicals. In no instance was the vaunted "threat of violence" realized in even a minor way. Hence, both the spurious nature of the "public safety issue," and the cynical manner in which liberal educators were trotting out this red herring to disguise a collective scuttling of their oft-professed "enlightenment ideals" in the face of anti-intellectual coercion, had become obvious by early May.

Equally apparent was that the constituencies of color and white radicals—somewhat paradoxically coalescing around the liberal value of academic freedom while the liberals themselves capitulated—were quite capable of realizing an agenda ensuring free speech on campus, irrespective of efforts by administrative accommodationists to prevent it. Hence, despite his devotion of, by my count, forty-one consecutive nightly segments to me[23]—making himself look so foolish that his program came to be laughingly referred to as *The Ward Churchill Factor*—O'Reilly had spectacularly failed to achieve the exemplary silencing he'd trumpeted as a *fait accompli* in early February. No longer able to crow about how *"The Factor* could influence the national discourse" in this respect[24] he was largely reduced to supporting the media's enhancement of the University of Colorado's "internal" drive to oust me from my tenured professorship.

On the Home Front

Attempts by the extreme right to purge selected faculty members from the University of Colorado are nothing new. In 1925, when the then-Klan-controlled state legislature threatened that the institution would no longer be "subsidized by the taxpayers" unless it rid itself of Jewish and Catholic professors, University President George Norlin flatly refused to comply. The Klan actually cut off public funding for a year, but the University weathered the confrontation, largely because of support garnered from the clarity of principle embodied in Norlin's stand.[25] Things were much fuzzier by the early 1950s, when the FBI, investigators from Joe McCarthy's Senate committee, and an ambitious Republican governor converged on CU. Beginning in 1951, University President Robert Stearns purged eleven junior faculty members accused by the FBI of having "subversive" links.[26] In 1954, however, with McCarthy neutralized, Stearns suddenly discovered his spine, rebuffing further pressure to fire more professors.[27]

Since then, UCB has gone to great lengths to distance itself from its 1951 "lapse." The glowing affirmation of Academic Freedom quoted above was incorporated into the Regents own "Laws" and Norlin's name bestowed upon the main campus library for preserving UCB as a repository of "diverse ideas" during the crisis of 1925. A yearly award by the alumni to the faculty or staff member who best reflects Stearns' 1954 defiance of McCarthyism has been established, as has an annual "Thomas Jefferson Award" given to faculty and staff members for exemplary contributions to the civic discourse. (Instructively, I've received both awards.) Most ostentatiously, a "free speech area" outside the student union has been named in honor of Dalton Trumbo, a one-time UCB student *cum* celebrated novelist/screenwriter who resisted blacklisting by McCarthy.[28]

As recently as 2002, a "lavish ceremony" was conducted in which then-university president Elizabeth Hoffman formally apologized to the late Morris Judd, one of the brightest stars among the young academics purged in 1951, "creating a scholarship in his name" to mark the transcendence of that "sad era in CU's history."[29] As executive vice chancellor Phil DiStefano solemnly intoned at the time, it was necessary both to "acknowledge the injustices of the past" and to "renew our commitment to the ideals of academic freedom without fear of retribution." This sentiment was seconded by regent Susan Kirk, who vowed "we shall never again allow such transgressions of academic freedom."[30] At the first real test of these "commitments," however, both the regents and UCB administrators scurried in the opposite direction.

Indeed, the administration's reflexive response was to join the right-wing media offensive launched in January 2005, with interim chancellor DiStefano immediately issuing a statement denouncing my analysis of 9/11—which he'd apparently not bothered to read—as "abhorrent," "repugnant," and "hurtful to everyone affected."[31] Within twenty-four hours, several members of the board of regents had also recorded their "ire" and at least one implied my tenure should be revoked.[32]

These positions were taken not in response to substantive pressure from the right, but purely in *anticipation* of it. DiStefano's statement, for example, was released before Colorado's arch-reactionary representative Bob Beauprez became the first member of Congress to demand my resignation.[33] It was issued three days before Governor Bill Owens and a "chorus" of state Republican legislators joined Beauprez in demanding that I resign.[34] It was made four days before Owens, seeking no doubt to restore his "moral" reputation, badly tarnished by a festering adultery scandal,[35] made the first of several demands that I be summarily fired;[36] and five days before both chambers of the Colorado legislature passed resolutions condemning me and threatening to withhold part of the university's annual budget unless I was "removed."[37]

Faced with such bluster, the regents convened an emergency session on February 3 to consider what might be done about a senior professor bold—or naïve—enough to have taken at face value their own guarantee of a strong institutional defense against precisely what was happening.[38] DiStefano asked the board to defer action for thirty days while he and an ad hoc investigating committee composed of acting dean of the UCB law school David Getches and Arts and Sciences dean Todd Gleeson determined whether I'd voiced other views that "crossed" some undefined "line," thereby bolstering the case for firing me on speech grounds.[39] The regents quickly accepted this proposal and passed yet another resolution apologizing to the nation for my analysis of 9/11.[40]

The thirty-day grace period afforded the administration time to attempt to "resolve" the issue without really addressing it. A typically liberal fix was undertaken through back-channel negotiations to buy out my tenure,[41] an option administrators apparently believed I might accept because I'd voluntarily relinquished my position as chair of UCB's Department of Ethnic Studies.[42] I was willing to consider early retirement in exchange for truly nominal compensation, but my *quid pro quo* was that the regents publicly affirm the validity of the standard peer review process by which the quality of my scholarship had been vetted at each stage of my career and openly *re*affirm their commitment to the principles of academic freedom articulated in their own laws.

Tellingly, the last point proved to be the deal-breaker, as the regents were unwilling to issue a public defense of academic freedom.[43] Instead, under strong pressure from Owens and Republican legislators, they announced their intent to comprehensively review the entire system of tenure.[44] Hence, although they claimed that a curiously-timed accusation of plagiarism caused them to break off negotiations with me, their actual motives were decidedly different.[45] The thirty days having almost expired with no resolution in hand, DiStefano asked for what became a thirty-day extension to see what sort(s) of pretext might be drummed up for proceeding against me.[46]

Meanwhile, on March 3, President Hoffman, addressing an emergency session of the Boulder Faculty Assembly, warned that "a new McCarthyism" was afoot.[47] Although Hoffman sought to "balance" her warning with a suddenly-discovered "institutional need" to investigate my academic record on grounds other than speech, few faculty members were convinced, locally or nationally. Already, nearly 200 tenured UCB faculty members had placed a full-page ad in Boulder's *Daily Camera* "demanding that school officials halt their investigation of Ward Churchill's work."[48] On March 1, UC Santa Cruz philosophy professor Angela Davis spoke on campus, expressing solidarity,[49] and, on March 22, a full-page open letter endorsed by hundreds of scholars across the country appeared in the *Camera* demanding that the regents' and administration's "gratuitous and inappropriate action[s]" be reversed.[50] Still another full-page ad appeared in the *Camera* on March 25, sponsored by an "Ad Hoc Coalition in Support of Ward Churchill."[51]

By then Hoffman, under heavy fire from the right for her observations on the resurgence of McCarthyism,[52] had resigned her presidency.[53] Although my controversies were by no means her only problem,[54] her demise was undoubtedly catalyzed by a veritable blitzkrieg of hostile coverage of my case in the local media.

All manner of academically-irrelevant information about me was being published as "news," including my driving record, credit history, and baby pictures.[55] For about a week, it was something of a fashion statement to dredge up a personal or political adversary to recount how at some point ten or twenty years ago, I'd supposedly "intimidated" him/her.[56] Another week or so was devoted to blaring headlines about how I'd supposedly relied on misinformation to obtain my faculty position.[57] There was no pause slanderous ad hominems: the moment the falsity of one allegation was exposed, reporters simply dropped it and move to the next.

Coupled to this Westbrook Pegler-style smear campaign, the sleaziest aspect of which came down to sheer race-baiting,[58] was a concerted effort by the press to discredit my scholarship, thereby "assisting" the UCB administration in bringing charges of academic misconduct. This charade began on February 8 when UCB law professor Paul Campos, who doubles as a *Rocky Mountain News* columnist, not only contested my ethnic identity, but aired disagreements posted by two obscure "scholars" at other universities. Campos observed—falsely—that one of them, University of New Mexico law professor John LaVelle, had accused me of plagiarism.[59] From there, the media's "critical scrutiny" of my scholarship quickly gathered momentum.

Although the allegations drummed up were ludicrous, and evidence that I was solidly-supported by both faculty and students at UCB was overwhelming, DiStefano convened a press conference on March 24 to announce that while his ad hoc committee had concluded that no action could be taken against me for my "speech activities," it had "discovered" possible academic misconduct. These allegations, he said, would be forwarded to the faculty's Standing Committee on Research Misconduct (SCRM) for further review and might result in my "termination for cause."[60]

Although quite predictable, this administrative ploy accomplished the desired result: Owens and his neoconservative cohorts were freed—at least temporarily—from having to defend their blatantly anti-constitutional posturing in court, while the self-styled civil libertarians could pretend that the First Amendment had been duly vindicated.

The Charges

In a classic example of "trial by media," only those matters that had been heavily-reported were referred as allegations to the committee.[61] In its original form, DiStefano accused me of having: (1) "fabricated an historical incident" by stating that in 1837 the US Army, having withheld vaccine, had deliberately infected Mandan Indians at Fort Clark (on the upper Missouri River) with smallpox, unleashing a pandemic that claimed the lives of more than 100,000 native people;[62] (2) falsely asserted that a half-blood quantum standard was applied to identify Indians during the government's compilation of tribal rolls under provision of the 1887 General Allotment Act;[63] (3) falsely asserted that, under provision of the 1990 American Indian Arts and Crafts Act a quarter-blood quantum is required of artists and artisans identifying themselves as being of native descent;[64] (4) engaged in three instances of plagiarism;[65] and (5) identified myself as being of American Indian descent as a means of enhancing my academic credibility.[66]

On June 15, just a few days after a university spokesperson had stated that institutional rules precluded news reports from being treated as misconduct complaints,[67] DiStefano forwarded as "supplemental allegations" some 59 downloaded pages from the *Rocky Mountain News*' weeklong series "The Churchill Files."[68] As a result, I was also charged with having: (6) fabricated another historical incident by stating that there is "strong circumstantial evidence" that Captain John Smith deliberately infected the Wampanoag Indians with smallpox;[69] (7) plagiarism by incorporating material from a 1972 pamphlet produced by Dam the Dams, a Canadian environmental group, into my own work;[70] and (8) violated the copyrights of three scholars.[71] Although he had earlier acknowledged that there was no basis for doing so,[72] in August DiStefano sought to add yet another set of charges by forwarding a complaint from my former sister-in-law that I'd committed "academic fraud" in an introduction to a posthumously-published collection of my late wife's writings.[73]

With fourteen allegations on the table—eighteen, counting subparts—there can be little question that the administration was using the time-honored prosecutor's tactic of "shotgunning" in hopes that something might "stick." DiStefano's attempt to palm off my sister-in-law's accusations as "research issues" proved a bit much even for the SCRM to swallow, and they rejected this set of charges on its face.[74] Several of the remaining charges, including the allegation of "ethnic fraud" and the supposed copyright violations, were dismissed as unsustainable shortly thereafter.[75] Despite serious questions as to why the rest of the charges were not similarly dropped, a seven-count "indictment" was returned by the SCRM's subcommittee of inquiry[76] and DiStefano solemnly announced to the press the necessity of a full investigation.[77]

About that "Panel of My Peers"

According to the CU system's rules, the investigation was to be non-adversarial; conducted by a small panel of impartial scholars, preferably senior in rank and experience, and with demonstrable competencies in the issues.[78] From the outset, however, the SCRM held that all 200 UCB faculty members who'd signed the academic freedom petition in February were ineligible because they'd expressed "bias" in my favor. I countered that in light of the unprecedented media involvement—to say nothing of official posturing—*no* University of Colorado faculty members should be included, and that the panel be composed entirely of "outside experts."[79]

This rather common expedient was quickly rejected, although it was agreed that "some" of the panelists might be drawn from the national pool.[80] I then moved that if UCB faculty members were to be appointed, none should be from the law faculty, given its relatively small size and the clearly negative roles played by two of its influential members, Getches and Campos.[81] Additionally, I named several individuals in the

College of Arts and Sciences who would be unacceptable, citing hostile statements in each instance. Tellingly, the SCRM did not reply.

Unbeknownst to me, SCRM chair, business professor Joseph Rosse was already arranging for UCB law professor Marianne Wesson to head the investigation. I was unaware that Wesson had made derogatory observations about me in personal correspondence as early as February 2005, when she had written:

> I confess to being somewhat mystified by the variety of people this unpleasant (to say the least) individual has been able to enlist to defend him…. [T]he rallying around Churchill reminds me unhappily of the rallying around OJ Simpson and Bill Clinton and now Michael Jackson and other charismatic male celebrity wrongdoers (well, okay, I don't really know that Jackson is a wrongdoer).[82]

When confronted with a copy of this e-mail during subsequent Privilege & Tenure Committee (P&T) hearings, Rosse claimed that he'd not seen the email, but admitted he'd been informed of two others of a similar nature.[83] These, he opined, were not reflective of bias, thus he had felt no obligation to notify me of their existence.[84] Moreover, despite the university's requirement that such proceedings be non-adversarial,[85] Rosse asserted that Wesson's background *as a former prosecutor* who could "make sure that the process [would] run smoothly" outweighed other considerations.[86]

The next selection was UCB Distinguished University Professor Emeritus Marjorie K. McIntosh, an archival researcher specializing in Medieval English women's history.[87] Then came Michael Radelet, chair of UCB's sociology department and a specialist in the death penalty.[88] To this mix were added two "outsiders": Bruce Johansen, a well-respected professor of journalism and American Indian Studies at the University of Nebraska, and Robert A. Williams, Jr., a professor at the University of Arizona and a leading expert on the evolution of Indian law.[89]

Although Williams was the only Indian—indeed, the sole person of color— on the panel, it was my sense that his involvement, together with Johansen's, would be sufficient to counteract the near-total ignorance displayed by the three UCB panelists with respect to both my discipline of American Indian Studies (AIS) and the matters addressed in my work. I was therefore prepared to accept the panel's composition. Wesson and Rosse apparently were not, however, and set about correcting the situation.[90] After Williams in particular stressed the need for the panel to adopt a clear set of standards by which my material would be assessed, panel members were placed under what amounted to a gag order.[91] Then, on November 1, 2005, the names of the panelists were released to the press.[92]

Within hours, the Clear Channel hacks had gone into overdrive with a continuous blare about the panel being a "fraud" because I once blurbed a book by Johansen—at the request of the publisher, not Johansen—and Williams had issued a statement asserting my right to academic freedom several months previously. Both men were also pronounced guilty of occasionally citing my work.[93] Such radio spew was augmented by editorialists at the *Rocky Mountain News* who announced there was "no choice" but to remove both Johansen and Williams from the panel in view of their "obvious lack of objectivity."[94]

Simultaneously, Jim Paine, a Colorado horse-breeder *cum* self-appointed authority on the integrity of scholarship and proper use of taxpayer monies, employed his "anti-Churchill" blog, PirateBallerina, to launch a smear campaign against Johansen, accusing him among other things of being in some sort of *quid pro quo* arrangement with me.[95] With the message thus writ largely on the outhouse wall, the university maintaining a silence in the face of the onslaught, and precluded from defending themselves by the university's gag order, both Johansen and Williams resigned.[96]

Several worthy replacement candidates were passed over on questionable grounds.[97] Selected instead were literature professor José Limón of the University of Texas[98] and Robert N. Clinton, an expert in federal Indian law at Arizona State University who also claimed expertise in American Indian Studies on no discernable basis.[99] I strongly protested the panel's new composition—it included no American Indians, only a single person of color, nobody grounded in the relevant areas/methods of history, and nobody with a demonstrated competency in American Indian or even Ethnic Studies—but Rosse informed me that the matter was "settled."[100]

Upholding Scholarly Standards?

When the panel finally convened what I understood to be the "initiation of the investigation" with a preliminary meeting on January 28, 2006, I was informed by Wesson that the panel intended to submit its final report "in early May."[101] I was given a deadline of April 3 to submit any written responses I wished to have considered,[102] a period closer to *sixty* days than the 120 provided by the rules.[103] Meanwhile, unbeknownst to me, Wesson had "started the clock ticking" on January 11, when she had a "confidential" meeting between the panel, Rosse, university counsel, and the university's public relations director.[104]

Things went rapidly downhill from there. My attorney David Lane repeatedly requested clarification of the standards to be applied by the panelists in assessing the allegations against me,[105] and was eventually told, in effect, that the panel had no idea. Given that in academia there are significant differences in the definitions and standards employed by various professional organizations, it was the responsibility of both the

SCRM and its investigative panel to inform me at the outset exactly *which* "research community"—or communities, given the interdisciplinary nature of my work—they would be considering "relevant."

The SCRM never *did* meet its obligation to cite the "clearly established standards" it claimed I violated. In its report, it says it used "the 'Statement on Standards of Professional Conduct' prepared by the American Historical Association as a general point of reference," but that it had "made no decisions based solely upon it."[106] What *else* the panelists might have relied upon was left unstated. Later, it became clear that they misrepresented even the university's own general formulation of standards. SCRM members also later claimed that I'd "concurred" in this nebulous approach,[107] a matter easily disproven during Privilege & Tenure committee hearings conducted in January 2007 to review the SCRM findings.[108]

The university retained a self-styled "specialist on academic ethics," Rutgers University professor of business management Donald McCabe,[109] to try to establish that the standards invoked by the investigative panel not only existed but were appropriately and equitably applied. Under cross-examination, however, McCabe was unable to point to *any* clear articulation of standards pertaining to authorial practices that Wesson's panel, citing nothing to support its assertion, claimed were condemned by "an overwhelming consensus" of academics.[110] Indeed, McCabe was unable to show that my practices did not meet the NSF standard of being "accepted [within] the relevant research community" or communities.[111]

The SCRM investigative panel submitted its final report on May 9 and a press conference was convened on May 16.[112] The report concluded that I'd engaged in research misconduct on several counts, and noted that two of the five panelists did not believe their findings warranted dismissal, two others believed dismissal was acceptable but not the most appropriate sanction, and only one recommended dismissal.[113] The entire 125-page screed was ostentatiously posted on the university's web site as a "scholarly work product."[114] It was then approved by the full SCRM, which voted 6-3 for dismissal,[115] and DiStefano topped off the institutional dog-and-pony show on June 26, 2006, by delivering unto the press corps his long-awaited recommendation that I be fired.[116]

Assessing the Verdict

Unlike the investigative process, in which I was not allowed to directly question even my own witnesses, the internal faculty review procedure enabled me to question anyone who gave testimony. These P&T proceedings were also less rushed than those of the SCRM.[117] While the sheer mass of information to be sifted and the number of issues involved still took their toll, the result was an appreciably different set of findings than those of the SCRM investigative panel. On the main points concerning my interpretations of law and historical events, the P&T reviewers concluded that the SCRM had failed to meet the burden of proof necessary to sustain its "verdict" that I'd engaged in either falsification or fabrication.[118] With respect to several secondary points concerning my analysis of the 1837 smallpox pandemic, however, they blinked clear evidence to arrive at the opposite conclusion. By and large, they also turned a blind eye to evidence that, to make its case, Wesson's panel had itself massively engaged in the very sorts of fraudulent scholarship of which I'd been accused.

While limitations on the length of this essay preclude detailed discussion of the merits and demerits of the P&T reviewers' findings—more detailed explanations are presented elsewhere[119]—it seems appropriate to offer brief summaries.

On Matters of Legal Interpretation

Regarding my contentions that both the 1887 General Allotment Act and the 1990 Indian Arts and Crafts Act define "Indians" in terms of blood quantum requirements, the P&T reviewers held that, at worst, I'd conflated the language of the Acts with the manner in which they were implemented, and that "failure to be precise about this distinction [does not fall] below minimum standards of professional integrity."[120] In fact, the reviewers implicitly questioned whether research misconduct charges on such points should have been pursued in the first place, observing that "academic debate seems a more appropriate method for deciding the question than disciplinary proceedings."[121]

On Matters of Historical Interpretation

With respect to the SCRM's findings that I was guilty of falsification or fabrication by contending that there is circumstantial evidence that John Smith may have deliberately infected the Wampanoags with smallpox before the landing of the Plymouth colonists in 1620, that US Army deliberately infected the Mandans and other peoples of the upper Missouri in 1837, and that vaccine was available but withheld from the Indians once the outbreak was underway, the P&T reviewers again concluded that there was no "clear and convincing evidence for the conduct alleged."[122] Indeed, the panelists found that in her zeal to *disprove* my contentions, McIntosh, who wrote both sections of the investigative report at issue here, had repeatedly "exceeded [her] charge."[123]

On the other hand, they concurred with McIntosh's findings that I was guilty of fabrication in stating that the infected items came from an infirmary in St. Louis,[124] and that "post surgeons" subsequently instructed Indians who'd been exposed to the pox to "scatter," thereby infecting healthy communities.[125] The reviewers also concurred that I'd misrepresented the work of UCLA anthropologist Russell Thornton by once observing that he'd suggested that the resulting death toll "might have" run as high as 400,000.[126] There are significant problems with each of these findings.

- On whether smallpox-infected items came from a military infirmary in St. Louis, I acknowledge that I probably erred—additional evidence has now convinced me that the items were more likely brought from Maryland[127]—but the proposition that I "fabricated" the St. Louis connection is rather strained. Even one of McIntosh's expert witnesses, Michael Timbrook, testified that he has always suspected the source of the infection to have been the army infirmary at the Jefferson Barracks, in St. Louis.[128]

- The issue of my using the term "post surgeon" was/is mainly semantic. Many others have used it to refer to medical personnel assigned to facilities designated "Forts."[129] The crux of McIntosh's argument was that she'd found "no evidence of...*anyone* with medical training...at Fort Union or Fort Clark [emphasis added]."[130] This is directly contradicted in at least two of the sources she claims to have consulted in preparing her 43-page rebuttal of my passing mentions of the "Fort Clark episode" (the longest of which was two paragraphs).[131]

- As to infected Indians being told to scatter, there are multiple accounts in the very literature referenced by McIntosh in the investigative report. One concerns another fur company employee who served as post surgeon[132] and who describes exposing a group of Assiniboins camped outside the fort to a child in the most highly-contagious stage of the disease and then telling them to flee to their home village(s).[133]

In another, the commander of Fort Clark[134] is recorded as having dispatched a trader and his infected Hidatsa wife to visit her relatives in a nearby village which had until then managed to avoid the epidemic by quarantining itself.[135] The Hidatsas were thereafter decimated by the pox, suffering a mortality rate second only to that of the Mandans (who were, by all accounts, virtually annihilated).[136]

- The claim that I misrepresented Thornton's material is simply false. While Thornton for the most part does not correlate numbers of fatalities to his list of peoples ravaged by the pandemic, he *does* provide a handy reference: "(Stearn and Stearn,1945: 94)."[137] Turning to page 94 of the Stearns' seminal study, as McIntosh claims she did,[138] one finds a chart offering very much the same list of peoples as Thornton, but also providing estimated death tolls. Adding up these numbers, the total exceeds 350,000. If one includes standard estimates for the peoples named by Thornton but not listed by the Stearns, one obtains a figure well within range of the 400,000 I said Thornton offered as a "maybe."[139]

Virtually all of the information presented here was in the record—in much greater detail—available to the P&T reviewers when they began their deliberations in January 2007 and was fully recapped in my "closing argument."[140] There is thus little excuse for the reviewers to have missed the obvious in these matters. Of course, it's always possible that, to borrow a phrase from their report, "something more than just sloppy research" was involved.[141] Unfortunately, their performance with regard to the issue of "accepted practices" in authorial attribution lends some credence to such suspicions.

On Plagiarism

From the start, several members of the P&T panel displayed a palpable hostility to even considering the question of applicable standards, with the panel's chair, Professor Philip Langer, ruling consistently that evidence on how things are done in various disciplines was irrelevant.[142] The panelists, he declared, were going to "stick to evidence about practices accepted in [Arts & Sciences]."[143] When questions concerning the prevalence of ghostwriting in political science became uncomfortable, however, Langer declared that irrelevant as well.[144] So, too, history,[145] and then communications—the discipline in which I was trained—when it was shown that ghostwriting is actually considered a professional competency.[146]

In the end, although somewhat more qualified in their assertions, the P&T reviewers joined their investigative predecessors in masking the realities of how authorship is *commonly* attributed in academia behind an unsupported assertion that ghostwriting and similar practices are condemned by "an overwhelming consensus" of scholars.[147] Thus, it is unsurprising that the SCRM's verdict that I'd "failed to comply with established standards on the use of author names on publications" was upheld on three counts (two on plagiarism, one on ghostwriting).[148]

The first plagiarism finding concerned the 1972 Dam the Dams pamphlet. All parties agreed I'd been asked by someone purporting to represent the organization to rework the pamphlet for publication in 1987.[149] Everyone also agreed that when I included the resulting essay in an edited volume a year later, I appropriately credited Dam the Dams,[150] and that when still another version was published by *Z Magazine* in 1991, an editorial decision was made to remove the group's co-authorial credit without my knowledge.[151] None of this, including the last fiasco, was deemed by either the investigative panelists or their P&T successors to constitute plagiarism.

My supposed plagiary comes in my incorporation of material from Dam the Dams into a pair of subsequent essays, and my subsequent citation of the 1988 book chapter rather than the original pamphlet.[152] Most conclusively, according to the P&T reviewers, was that while I claim to have disavowed the Z article because of its inaccurate attribution of authorship, I "continued to cite" it in the later essays.[153]

The problem with the last assertion—which the P&T reviewers appear simply to have parroted from the SCRM report—is that it is false.[154] I have *never* cited the *Z* article, *only* the 1988 book chapter. While I should perhaps have indicated in my annotation that the book chapter derived from the 1972 pamphlet, the relationship between the two is stated in the chapter itself, which names every member of Dam the Dams involved in producing the pamphlet.[155] In any case, citing the pamphlet *rather than* the book chapter, as both panels seem to suggest I should have done,[156] would have been absurd, since the pamphlet had long been inaccessible to readers by the time I might have cited it.

As was recently observed by Marc Cogan, chair of the AAUP Committee on Professional Ethics, "the whole point of plagiarism is to pretend that you wrote something somebody else wrote."[157] It follows that, "As a general rule, if the sources are given, and given clearly enough so they can be seen, so [that readers] can go back and spot it, then plagiarism doesn't come in…because clearly there was no intent to hide" the fact that use has been made of someone else's material.[158] Though my citational practices may have been imperfect, they comport with this "general rule" accepted—and routinely employed—by the academic community.

The second plagiarism finding upheld by the P&T reviewers concerned the incorporation of material written by Dalhousie University professor Fay Cohen into an essay attributed to the Institute for Natural Progress (INP), included in *The State of Native America*, a 1992 book edited by my ex-wife, M. Annette Jaimes, now a member of the Women Studies faculty at San Francisco State University. While I readily acknowledged having performed copyediting/rewrite functions on the INP piece at Jaimes' request,[159] and that I'd suggested crediting the essay to the INP to keep her name from "showing up too many times" in the book, no one contradicted the evidence that the manuscript I'd "tuned up" had actually been written by Jaimes and others.

The reviewers asserted that "Legal Counsel at Dalhousie University has provided a 'well-documented conclusion' that Professor Churchill plagiarized Professor Cohen."[160] This is a gross misrepresentation of the Dalhousie document; it concludes only that Cohen's material was plagiarized, *not* that I plagiarized it.[161] Furthermore, Cohen has never contended that I was responsible for the plagiarism, even declining an open invitation to do so during the investigative process.[162]

However, Cohen did state that her contact with UCB had been initiated by Dean David Getches through John LaVelle.[163] LaVelle is the University of New Mexico law professor falsely described by UCB law professor Paul Campos as having accused me of plagiarism.[164] LaVelle was also the supposed complainant—actually, he filed no complaint[165]—regarding my depictions of the 1887 and 1990 Acts discussed above. In the P&T hearings it was established that Getches, acting as a member of DiStefano's ad hoc committee, had in effect solicited LaVelle—who Getches conceded was plainly motivated by personal/political animus—to serve as a "complainant."[166] LaVelle then functioned as a go-between in soliciting additional "complaints."[167] The capstone to the whole charade was an e-mail exchange between Cohen and Getches in which she informed him that she was "planning to prepare her own submission in a timely manner," only to be told by Getches that "[t]his will be handled" by DiStefano's ad hoc committee.[168]

Notwithstanding the magnitude of such factual and procedural problems, the P&T reviewers plunged ahead, ultimately advancing the rather oxymoronic proposition that they'd found "clear and convincing evidence" of my being "somehow…involved" in plagiarizing Cohen and affirming the SCRM investigative panel's vacuous finding that I was "at least an accomplice."[169]

On Ghostwriting

The P&T reviewers followed the SCRM investigative panel in absolving me of allegations that I'd plagiarized portions of an essay attributed to former Arizona State University professor Rebecca Robbins—and, as a subtext, several essays attributed to Annette Jaimes—in accordance with the time-honored dictum that "one cannot plagiarize oneself."[170] In other words, they accepted that I'd ghostwritten *all* of the material at issue. However, the reviewers again echoed the SCRM investigative report by asserting that ghostwriting constituted another supposed failure to comply with established standards regarding author names on publications, thereby constituting "conduct fall[ing] below minimum standards of professional integrity."[171]

The basis for these conclusions is a bit mysterious since, to a far greater degree than the SCRM investigative panel, the P&T reviewers openly "acknowledge[d] the difficulty in finding specific guidelines related to ghostwriting" (which is to say, they could find none at all).[172] Further, unlike the investigative panelists, who claimed a clear violation,[173] the P&T reviewers observed only that the "practice may (or may not) violate an already stated University policy." Even this was a stretch, since they'd had already admitted that the "University 'Research Misconduct Rules'…are silent on this issue."[174] Moreover, three noted experts were on record in my case as describing the treatment of ghostwriting as a violation of ethical standards to be a "curveball" for which they were aware of no precedent.[175] Nor could the university's own expert witness provide an example in which ghostwriting—as opposed to taking credit for ghostwritten material—has been construed as research misconduct.[176]

One might suspect that the P&T reviewers meant "accepted practices" when they concluded I'd violated "established standards." In that case, it would be reasonable to expect the panel to have cited considerable evidence that the practice of ghostwriting is *not* accepted—that is, not commonly undertaken without censure or penalty—in the research communities relevant to an interdisciplinary scholar like myself. Indeed, to uphold a "guilty" verdict, they were ethically/legally obliged to do so. However, apart from a bald assertion that "no credible evidence [has been] provided that [ghostwriting] is an accepted practice for academic research in Communications and/or Ethnic Studies Departments"[177]—a claim which no doubt insulted several witnesses who testified to the contrary, and which shifted the evidentiary burden from the university to me (inverting the P&T's own rules)[178]—the reviewers made no effort to do so.

The SCRM investigative panel had claimed that my citation of "two *apparently independent third-party* sources [emphasis in the original]"—i.e., material I had ghostwritten—constitutes a "form of evidentiary fabrication" which was "part of a deliberate research stratagem to create the appearance of independent verifiable claims that could not be supported through existing primary and secondary sources."[179] A gross distortion is readily apparent in their assertion that no "independent third parties" were at issue.[180] Ghostwritten material is, by definition, written *for* a third party. And, unless s/he is somehow coerced into accepting attribution of authorship, the third party is *always* independent, i.e., inherently empowered to revise or specify revisions to anything in the text incompatible with her/his own thinking, or to simply reject the material.

Consequently, the investigative panel's assertion that my "self-citation" of material I'd ghostwritten "creat[ed] the false appearance that [my] claims are supported by other scholars" was itself false. So, too, was its pretense that I was ever "the only source for such claims." As was thoroughly demonstrated, a number of other scholars have arrived quite independently at conclusions virtually identical to mine.[181] Accordingly, the P&T reviewers overturned the SCRM panel's findings that I'd engaged in "falsification" with regard to both the 1887 Allotment Act and 1990 Arts and Crafts Act. This *should* have been the end of it. Nevertheless, the review panel found that I "contributed" to a supposed failure to comply with established standards regarding author names on publications by citing to the ghostwritten Robbins essay.[182]

Aftermath

On May 8, 2007, the P&T review panel submitted its final report to president Hank Brown, a former Republican senator and ACTA cofounder who had replaced Hoffman.[183] On May 25, Brown submitted a letter to the Board of Regents in which he overruled the reviewers and expert witnesses, reinstating the investigative panel's findings that I had misrepresented both the 1887 and 1990 Acts and recommending that the Regents revoke my tenure and fire me for cause.[184] This was done by an 8-1 vote on July 24.[185]

David Lane filed suit on my behalf the following morning,[186] but the counterattack had begun well before. By late March, Cornell professor and American Indian studies scholar Eric Cheyfitz and others had begun to go public about the myriad misrepresentations of fact littering the SCRM investigative report.[187] In early April, apparently unnerved by news that Cheyfitz would shortly be the featured speaker at a colloquium titled "Re-Examining the Academic Case Against Ward Churchill," co-sponsored by the UCB English Department and the campus AAUP chapter,[188] Wesson attempted a preemptive strike of sorts, publishing an open letter in the university's *Silver & Gold Record* admitting that the panel had "misunderstood" one of the sources I'd cited and consequently "erred" with regard to certain "facts" they'd presented on the John Smith/smallpox question.[189] Wesson claimed that the panel would "soon take steps to ensure that the error is corrected for the scholarly record." Eighteen months later, no such corrections have been made, i.e.: no revisions have been made to the *Investigative Report*, which remains posted on the university web site under the guise of a "scholarly work product," and neither Wesson nor any other panelist has made any public statement on the matter.

Similar misrepresentations of fact were being detected on virtually every page of the investigative report. On April 23, seven members of the UCB faculty, joined by Cheyfitz and University of Kansas Indigenous Nations Studies Professor Michael Yel-low Bird, published an open letter citing "a pattern of violations...of standard scholarly practice so serious that [they were] considering the additional step of filing charges of research misconduct" against the panelists, observing that the report was so deeply flawed that it "cannot be salvaged by individual corrections," and therefore demanding that the report be retracted.[190] When Michael Poliakoff—an ACTA veteran hired as Brown's assistant in early 2006—refused their demand, the group, joined by two addi-tional members of the Boulder faculty, filed a formal complaint with the SCRM.[191]

This was followed, on May 13, 2007, with a statement placed by the Boulder and Denver Faculty Ad Hoc Committee to Defend Academic Freedom in Boulder's *Dai-ly Camera*, denouncing ACTA's subversion of the investigative process by "enlist[ing] trustees (regents), alumni, governor and legislature to bring political and financial pres-sure" to bear on the university. On May 28, a second research misconduct complaint against the investigative panelists, this one signed by two attorneys and four professors at other universities, was filed with the SCRM.[192]

I followed up by filing a pair of complaints, the first naming Radelet as the primary offender and detailing the panel's falsification of evidence to support its find-ing on the John Smith/smallpox allegation, the second focusing on McIntosh and providing numerous side-by-side quotations illustrating her extensive plagiarism of both Lamar University assistant professor Thomas Brown and unpublished material provided by an independent researcher named Joseph Wenzel.[193] Wenzel himself sub-sequently filed yet another research misconduct complaint with the SCRM, citing not only McIntosh's appropriation of his material, but also what he described as systematic misrepresentations of "fact and law" in the sections of the investigative report dealing with the 1887 and 1990 Acts.[194]

Meanwhile, on July 10, a P&T panel considering a grievance I'd filed *nearly two years* previously[195] finally returned its verdict. It concluded that the UCB administration had clearly and repeatedly violated my right to confidentiality under the university rules pertaining to personnel matters, and that such violations had "a prejudicial or detrimental effect on [my] reputation."[196] The grievance panel also found that while the lengthy "delay to hear [my] grievance compounded the damage to [my] reputation given the continuous media coverage," the source of the delay was the P&T Committee itself rather than the administration.[197] Nonetheless, it recommended that there be "a public statement, i.e., press release and/or website posting acknowledging the breaches of the SCRM rules by the University against Professor Churchill."[198] Unsurprisingly, the recommendation was rejected by Chancellor G.P. "Bud" Peterson,[199] yet another ACTA notable "brought aboard" by Brown.[200]

Then, on July 18, I received a letter from SCRM chair Rosse, informing me that the SCRM would "not be reviewing [my] allegations regarding the report of the investigating committee, nor any future allegations regarding the report."[201] The reasons, as reported in the *Silver & Gold Record*, were that:

> To avoid a possible conflict of interest, the [complaints were] submitted to the Committee on Research Ethics (CRE) at the [University of Colorado] Health Sciences Center, according to the letter, a copy of which Churchill provided to S&GR. But Rosse wrote that the CRE chair notified him on July 18 that "complaints of scientific misconduct lodged against the committee which investigated Professor Churchill do not fall within the purview of the Standing Committee because the activities of [investigative panel] did not constitute research[;] rather, they were an administrative investigation and are therefore not scientific misconduct."[202]

No one, of course, had claimed that the SCRM panelists engaged in "scientific misconduct." More significantly, the claim that the investigation of my work was merely "administrative," not scholarly, completely reversed the university's many public representations of the investigative report as a scholarly document resulting from research undertaken by a select group of senior professors.[203] This was certainly claimed by the panelists themselves, both in direct statements in the report[204] and through the trappings of scholarship with which they'd larded it.[205] So, too, Wesson's earlier depiction of the report as forming part of the "scholarly record,"[206] and the panelists' insistence that their report would pass muster under the same standards they'd applied to me.[207]

While the SCRM's ploy was clearly intended to immunize the panelists against the consequences of their fraud, there were larger implications. As I explained at the time, "President Brown claims that I should be fired to preserve 'academic integrity.' Yet he relies on a report which the University refuses to investigate against credible and well-documented charges of falsifications, fabrications and plagiarism. The University cannot have it both ways. If the investigative [panel's] report is scholarship, it must be held to the same standards to which it claims to be holding me accountable. If not, President Brown's recommendation is based on no credible evidence at all" (or at least none that could withstand scholarly scrutiny).[208]

Most of this information had been provided to the regents prior to their meeting on July 24.[209] That the motive underlying their vote had little, if anything, to do with academic concerns is evidenced by the fact that Brown had already prepared a missive to donors and alumni—posted the moment the results were official—informing them of my firing and urging them to proceed with the financial contributions they'd been withholding.[210] Over the next week, he worked overtime, justifying of the university's actions—and effectively soliciting funds from ACTA-aligned donors—in venues ranging from the local press to *The Wall Street Journal*.[211] To all appearances, his efforts cemented a record-breaking influx of contributions to the university foundation.[212]

Mission accomplished, Brown announced his retirement, effective as soon as a "suitable replacement" could be hired. Here, the wages of liberal accommodation to the reactionary right were finally visited, full-force, on the CU faculty. Brown's choice, and the *only* name presented to the regents, was Bruce Benson, a man whose "qualifications" include a BA in geology, a career spent as an oil company executive, and considerable experience as a Republican activist.[213] Despite much hand-wringing by the "campus left,"[214] Benson was voted president of the University of Colorado by the regents on February 20, 2008.[215] His first major initiative was to establish an endowed professorship of "conservative political philosophy."[216]

In the interim, the university attempted unsuccessfully to have my lawsuit dismissed.[217] The case is currently scheduled for trial on March 9, 2009. While one can never predict the outcome of such proceedings, it can be said with certainty that the rules will be very different from those prevailing in the university's twisted version of "due process." I've been designated the "worst professor in America" by the *Weekly Standard*,[218] among the "most dangerous" by David Horowitz,[219] and the benchmark by which academic subversion should be measured by ACTA.[220] Perhaps the extent to which I've deserved such flattery will be clarified in the judicial arena.

At any rate, as David Lane has observed, it's surely "going to be fun." Be that as it may, having taken their best shot with my conscience still uncut by compromise, I will continue to do as I've always done, speaking the truth as I see it, not *to* power but in its very teeth. After all, as one who actually believes in freedom, academic and otherwise, it seems the very least I can do. [221]

Operation Get Fired

A Chronicle of the Academic Repression of
Radical Environmentalist and Animal Rights Advocate-Scholars

Richard Kahn

> To make reality opaque is not neutral. To make reality lucid, illumi-
> nated, is also not neutral. In order for us to do that, we have to occupy
> the space of the schools with liberating politics. Nevertheless we cannot
> deny something very obvious. Those who make reality opaque through
> the dominant ideology, through spreading, multiplying, reproducing the
> dominant ideology, are swimming with the current! Those who demys-
> tify the reproducing task are swimming against the current! Swimming
> against the current means risking and assuming risks. Also, it means ex-
> pecting constantly to be punished. I always say those who swim against
> the current are first being punished by the current and cannot expect the
> gift of weekends on tropical beaches!
>
> —Paulo Freire

THE MYTH OF CONTEMPORARY INSTITUTIONS OF HIGHER EDUCATION is that
they are scholarly places firmly grounded in the ideal and practice of intellectual freedom. University presidents, it seems, are especially fond of this ivory
tower tale and spend time every year promoting their institutional commitment to
advancing tolerance for diverse and marginal perspectives, which they see represented
in the larger academic discourse taking place across the disciplines. The imaginative
charm of such language is that it functions to evoke college campuses as representative cities upon a hill, places that are capable of modeling for civil society (and other
levels of schooling) how enlightened communities should be established and function
in their affairs. This romance of higher education tends to represent campus culture as
a meritocratic and fertile support for individual excellence and ambition, even as the
university is consecrated to the unbiased uplift of all it serves. The myth of academic
freedom, then, purposively connotes the spirit of inclusion, of frank and democratic

debate, and of administrative transparency and fairness—in short, of the open society (Popper 1971).

To be sure, higher education *does* allow for a level of debate and ideological inclusion that is certainly welcome, and depending upon where one lives, it may in fact serve as a veritable sanctuary for faculty, students, and citizens who are interested in pushing beyond expected social norms in their research agendas and lifestyles. Moreover, it is undeniable that the academy has historically been a friend, though one neither exclusive nor always discerning, to the political and cultural left; and it continues to offer spaces of collegial support where progressives can organize politically, fraternize with countercultures, and receive a paycheck for engaging the minds and hearts of others in potentially meaningful work.

I myself am an academic and, truth be told, have spent almost the entirety of the last twenty years as either a teacher or a student within the hallowed halls of higher education. But, as Noam Chomsky invariably remarks at every lecture in which he savages the American State for its brutal atrocities and Big Lies, so I am happy to identify as an academic (as well as an American), but this does not mean that I act as an apologist or with blinders on. In fact, the privileges that come with such status as I have been afforded by the academy perhaps place an ethical demand upon me as a scholar—that I undertake an ongoing critique of the limitations and contradictions of my place in society as a professional intellectual, that I attempt to reveal the manner in which the academic experience is neither a friendly nor emancipatory one, and that I interrogate the larger repressive society itself as ruthlessly as possible. My particular work in the academy responds to this demand: I am a critical theorist of education working within the philosophical tradition known as critical pedagogy, which was founded by Paulo Freire and is broadly carried on today by important figures such as Peter McLaren, Henry Giroux, bell hooks, Antonia Darder, Donaldo Macedo, Douglas Kellner, Joe Kincheloe, Bill Ayers, and others.

As the epigram by Freire at the beginning of this essay makes clear, critical pedagogues view educational institutions as contested terrains that afford the possibility of resistance, but which are necessarily related to and work on behalf of the larger society of which they are themselves a part. Thus, one of their dominant roles within the social structure is to serve as factories for the production-line formation of massified values and norms. This is done through the standardization of schooling's hidden and avoided curricula as much as it is through that which is overtly taught and sanctioned as knowledge. In all of its primary curricular modes, higher education, no less than elementary or secondary education (and possibly even more so), communicates intimately with the capitalist marketplace and the conservators of social power. Indeed, we are increasingly bearing witness to the rise of what Giroux (2007) terms a "military-industrial-academic complex" in which educational leaders commonly initiate strategic planning to forge deep alliances among the university, the corporate private sector, the Department of Defense and various armed forces services, as well as the security and regulatory apparatuses of the State. This has proven to be an ominous development for those who seek to define education as an avenue for moral progress in, as H. G. Wells once put, its race against catastrophe.

Those who are arguably now at the forefront of attempting to turn back society's trend toward the catastrophic are the activist-educators who are struggling for a new paradigm and a social movement of planetarity—a truly sustainable and ecological world comprised by a diverse range of earthlings existing (wherever possible and desirable) peacefully together in evolving orders of mutuality. Who are these educators? They are the environmentalists who oppose the globalization of technocapitalism in its many guises. They are the vegan abolitionists. They are the Earth and animal liberationists who take up direct action to put an end to violence, as well as all those who recognize that the pedagogy of the oppressed must now be conducted across species lines. They are the activists who recognize that the great emancipation of peoples must occur concurrently with the reconstruction of "personhood" as an ethical category, as well as "community" as an ecological category, lest social justice be a progressive ruse that fails to meet the challenge of an unprecedented mass extinction event and sustainability crisis now underway at a breathtaking pace. As such, these activist-educators swim headlong against the tide of the dominant ideology, not only of the capitalist establishment, but also of the "radical" Left opposition of one type or another, all of whom still all too often share the anthropocentric and speciesist values of capitalism and majoritarian Western society.

Against this truly fundamental critique of the ideologies and lifeways of capitalism and Western culture, the corporate State has reacted with a campaign of terror, a Green Scare, designed to severely punish leading contributors of this oppositional movement for social-ecological change, to generate paranoia and fear amongst its potential sympathizers, and to provide a *causus belli* for a new series of highly repressive laws designed to limit the free speech and civil liberties of the movement's adherents. A centerpiece of this State response has been Operation Backfire, an FBI-led, multi-agency criminal investigation and COINTELPRO-style infiltration of the revolutionary environmentalist and animal rights advocacy communities, whether they be found in the valleys of California, the mountains of Oregon, or the streets of the Twin Cities. Yet, in ideological lockstep conditioned by the chilling post-9/11 atmosphere, the academy as an institution of social reproduction has followed suit and become involved in this attack on radical environmentalists and animal rightists as well.

This essay, then, will attempt to briefly chronicle the wide range of academic repression that has resultantly taken place against scholars, students, campus activists, and university groups; these are uniquely intelligent and caring individuals who have dared to swim upstream against social hegemony in order to challenge some of the most greedy, corrupt, violent, nihilistic, corporate, and Statist forces and fight on the side of the Earth and all its oppressed inhabitants. By doing so, I believe readers will ultimately conclude that when those within higher education move beyond the campus proper to challenge the forces behind the Green Scare, the repressive aims of the State are likely to be brought to bear upon their academic freedom in an intrusive and overtly anti-democratic fashion. The academy has itself maintained an attitude of what Herbert Marcuse (1969) termed "repressive tolerance" towards the green and animal rights radicals who work within its midst—creating an institutional cult that mouths the value of tolerance to preserve the status-quo, while at the same time trying to block discourse and actions that work outside acceptable levels of controllable dissent. My underlying supposition is that this development is itself intolerable.

The Green Scare Rattles the Ivory Tower

Academics around the world cannot necessarily rely upon their scholarly position to prevent them from being jailed and even, in some cases, forced into exile when their work threatens those in power. Notably, this happened to Freire himself when he worked on behalf of the popular education movement in Brazil in the 1960's. By contrast, while the United States has witnessed periods of governmental attempts to forcibly limit academic voices from being gadflies for social transformation—such as the imposition of faculty loyalty oaths during the Cold War era and the COINTELPRO effort to monitor, undermine, and destroy the student/civil rights movements of the late 1960s—on the whole, American academics have apparently been granted greater latitude to act as dissident public intellectuals (Altbach, 2007). Of course, there are those, especially those whose stories are catalogued in this book, that might beg to differ. However, even if it is true that the American academic is provided with relatively greater intellectual freedom than others, this means that when academics within the United States begin to experience significant checks upon their ability to champion particular social and political positions, it is *more* worthy of attention than in places where scholars knowingly work under a demand for self-censorship such as China, Iran, or Singapore. In this context, then, it is important to assert that the recent growth of groups that espouse support for radical environmentalist and animal rights ideology in countries like the US and UK has been the occasion for groundswell of State repression against American academics whose work is thought to be encouraging or supporting these aims, or even just describing and analyzing them from a scholarly viewpoint.

One of the most famous and alarming cases of such repression is the case of Rik Scarce, which dates back to 1992, amidst the wave of attacks conducted by the Animal Liberation Front (ALF) against fur farms and animal vivisection labs known as

Operation Biteback. At the time, Scarce was engaged in ethnographic doctoral work at Washington State University and researching the radical environmental movement, a project which grew out of his acclaimed 1990 journalistic exposé, *Eco-Warriors*. When ALF members raided and smashed a federally-supported vivisection laboratory at his university, the FBI subsequently sought Scarce for information, believing that he had interviewed and knew of relevant conspirators—in particular ALF veteran Rod Coronado, who had served as his house-sitter. Ultimately, Scarce was brought by the federal government before a Grand Jury to name names (Scarce 2005). However, in Scarce's opinion, he was bound as an academic sociologist to comply with the American Sociological Association's "Code of Ethics," which mandated he abide by the confidentiality agreements he had made with his research subjects as a precondition to interview them for his dissertation. Thus, he declined to provide evidence to prosecutors, citing his First Amendment rights to guarantee a free press ("press" being interpreted broadly) in order to claim that he was shielded as scholar-journalist from being forced to divulge his sources. Yet, the court system proved hostile to this defense and, consequently, the State found him guilty for contempt of court. Following a failed appeal, Scarce was jailed in 1993. He then remained behind bars for over 5 months, the longest period of time any scholar has ever been imprisoned in the United States for protecting research sources, a practice he continues to this day.

Since his release, Scarce has publicly wondered why so-called "shield laws" can protect journalists from divulging sources, but not academics. Importantly, the latest and strongest shield legislation to date, the Free Flow of Information Act of 2007, harbors bloggers under its protective measures but still fails to provide scholars with the equal right in court to protect the identities of their informants. As faculty must often institutionally attest to uphold the confidentiality of the people that they study in order to be granted the right to conduct research on individuals or groups, the government's retaining of the right to demand such information for prosecutorial purposes obviously presents a major obstacle to doing above ground scholarship on underground groups, such as those involved in radical environmentalism and animal rights advocacy, and thus constitutes a clear case of a First Amendment right violation.

A more frightening example of State-induced academic repression (as related in the film *Strange Culture*) involves the case of Steve Kurtz, Professor of Art at SUNY Buffalo and a founding member of the Critical Art Ensemble (CAE), an internationally-acclaimed performance art group that uses BioArt to interrogate the dangers of biotechnology in the service of public awareness and debate. The collective has also issued books such as *Electronic Civil Disobedience* (1996) and *Digital Resistance* (2000), and thus urged radical critiques of contemporary science and technology in a way that the research communities and State might identify them as threatening subversives. In 2004, Kurtz and his wife (another Ensemble member) were preparing an exhibit about genetically modified agriculture to be shown at the Massachusetts Museum of Contemporary Art when his wife suddenly died of heart failure. In responding to the incident, the police became alarmed by the Kurtzs' installation, entitled Free Range Grain, which according to the CAE Defense Fund "consisted of several petri dishes containing three harmless bacteria cultures, and a mobile lab to test food labeled "organic" for the presence of genetically modified ingredients."[1] Deciding that Kurtz was acting suspiciously, they promptly informed federal officials of the professor's activities. What followed next is a post-9/11 story of how keystone cops stage the war on terror, while nonetheless menacing citizens and repressing free speech rights.

On his way to his wife's funeral, Kurtz was apprehended and detained by the FBI and the Joint Terrorism Task Force who brought serious bioterrorism charges against him, as hazmat agents swarmed his house, condemned it as a potential health risk, and removed its contents as evidence. Amongst the many items impounded by the FBI were a book manuscript Kurtz was at work on and various Critical Art Ensemble pieces dealing with the horrors of transgenic organisms, germ warfare, and seed biotechnology that were worth tens of thousands of dollars in materials alone. These have never been returned and the book manuscript had to be pieced back together from other notes.

While Kurtz was eventually cleared of all bioterrorism charges, what occurred next revealed that his story had moved beyond being just a tragically unfortunate misunderstanding. Instead, State repression continued to run amok and his nightmare endured, as a federal Grand Jury was convened that indicted him and Robert Ferrell, a Professor of Genetics at the University of Pittsburgh Graduate School of Public Health and CAE collaborator, on two counts each of mail and wire fraud. At stake, the government claimed, was how Ferrell allegedly used his professional position to acquire $256 worth of benign bacteria samples from the American Type Culture Collection (ATCC), which he then provided to Kurtz for his art, thereby defrauding the University of Pittsburgh and the ATCC. Under the penalty guidelines of the revamped USA PATRIOT Act, the charges brought against each scholar carried staggering five to twenty-year sentences! Though both Kurtz and Ferrell claimed their bacteria exchange was simply common academic practice, something perhaps born out by the fact that neither the University of Pittsburgh nor the ATCC ever sought to initiate their own lawsuits against them, both men were put through hell over a line item of a couple hundred bucks and daring to work outspokenly as academics against the leading corporate technoscience of the day. In April of 2008, Kurtz was finally cleared of all charges by a judge who ruled that even if they were true, his actions would not constitute a crime. Sadly, following his initial arrest, Ferrell (undoubtedly due to the tremendous stress of being prosecuted federally and having one's hard-earned reputation destroyed overnight) fell victim to a series of strokes. This led him to accept a plea deal in 2007, in which he accepted guilt for his actions as misdemeanor crimes. The dangerous conclusion of the Kurtz saga, I believe, is that it reveals how the government can selectively use criminal law to intimidate and damage academic researchers. This moral holds especially true for those radical scholars involved in critiquing policy avenues like biotechnology or agribusiness that the corporate State holds dear.

Other cases reveal the manner in which the government is not content to simply repress academics, but will trespass into the domain of higher education and exert direct pressure on the nature of campus life. Such is the ongoing situation of Steven Best, Associate Professor of Philosophy at the University of Texas, El Paso (UTEP). According to *The Chronicle of Higher Education*, the primary trade publication for US universities and colleges, Best is "one of the leading scholarly voices on animal rights" (Smallwood, 2005). In this capacity, he has not bothered to make his reputation through Cartesian fireside meditations or sterile and abstruse modes of philosophical writing that are alien and obtuse to activist communities and the public as a whole. Rather, in a manner resembling previous critical theorists such as Marcuse and Marx, Best has turned his attention to the engaged students, activists, civic intellectuals, and others who are confronting society over its indefensible speciesist ideologies that inform the brutal exploitation and slaughter of billions of animals. Besides penning numerous critical broadsides for grassroots publications that have explored the relationship between corporations, the government, and the ongoing animal Holocaust, Best has led animal rights groups, co-hosted his own animal rights radio show, served as the Vice-President of the Vegetarian Society of El Paso, co-founded the Institute of Critical Animal Studies (for which was the Chief Editor of *The Journal of Critical Animal Studies*) and the North American Animal Liberation Press Office. He has also co-edited (with Anthony J. Nocella II) the books which serve as veritable primers for today's animal and earth liberation movements: *Terrorists or Freedom Fighters: Reflections on the Liberation of Animals* (Lantern 2004) and *Igniting a Revolution: Voices in Defense of the Earth* (AK Press 2006). Best has also toured the world (including Russia and South Africa) speaking on behalf of direct-action politics, explaining the history, ethics, and philosophy of contemporary animal and Earth liberation movements, and deconstructing the corporate-State discourse of "terrorism." While quick to deny that he has in any way been involved with underground movements other than to theorize their motivations, philosophies, and tactics, the quality and quantity of Best's work on this matter undeniably serves to figure him as one of the major theorists of animal liberation and radical ecopolitics today.

In this context, Best was "strongly encouraged" in March of 2005 to "submit" to testifying before the United States Senate Committee on Environment and Public Works by its Chair, Sen. James Inhofe (R-OK) for a hearing on the topic of "ecoterrorism" in May. Not coincidentally, in a clear move to intimidate and jeopardize his position, Inhofe sent his detailed "invitation" letter to Best's Dean, university President, and the entire Texas Board of Regents. Inhofe, a rabid pro-industry political leader, is also arguably the country's most brazen anti-environmentalist (Best 2006) having called global warming "the greatest hoax ever committed on the American people" and having remarked that the U.N. Intergovernmental Panel on Climate Change (the world's foremost body on the science of global warming) and Al Gore's film *An Inconvenient Truth* have been "refuted scientifically".[2] No stranger to the "extremist" views he condemns, Inhofe has also asserted that Gore's documentary could be appropriately likened to Hitler's *Mein Kampf* (Connelly, 2008). It was obvious, then, that Best was not asked to Washington D.C. as an explanatory expert to lead an earnest and serious debate about animal liberation and ecological ethics, but rather to be publicly vilified and used as a pawn towards strengthening legislation like the Animal Enterprise Terrorism Act.

As Best was already scheduled to be out of the country, he felt no compunction in declining Inhofe's "invitation." However, Best's name was entered into the record of the "ecoterrorism" hearing regardless, with Inhofe openly questioning whether academics such as Best should be allowed to speak on university campuses in ways that defend or support criminal and "violent" elements in society. Additionally, David Martosko, research director of the lobby for the meat, fast food, liquor, and tobacco corporations otherwise known as the Center for Consumer Freedom, volunteered to speak to the Committee, and came well-prepared with an insidious and libelous agenda. On live C-Span television, Martosko displayed photos of Best posing with high-profile animal advocates and liberationists in a brazen McCarthyesque guilt-by-association smear tactic. He claimed that Best was a "leader" of the ALF (apparently ignorant of the obvious fact that decentralized movements do not have "leaders") who "recruits" his students to join him in an underground movement in order to undertake clandestine and criminal sabotage actions! Before powerful Senate members, the head of the FBI, and a roomful of high-ranking, head-busting, law enforcement types, Martosko intoned, "Dr. Best's academic position affords him a position of regrettable influence within the animal rights movement...I urge this Committee to fully investigate the connections between individuals who commit crimes in the name of the ALF, ELF, or similar phantom groups, and the above-ground individuals and organizations that give them aid and comfort."[3]

Meanwhile, Best began feeling heat from other sources—from as far away as the British Home Office in London. After the July 7, 2005 bombings in London, the Home Office created new laws against "the glorification of terrorism." Yet, they did not apply these first to the radical Muslim clerics shouting "Death to England and Western society!" choosing instead to reach across the Atlantic into the forlorn deserts of El Paso to pinch a US professor of philosophy who dared to condemn vivisection and the UK pharmaceutical industries. In pompous bureaucratese that would be the envy of Sen. Inhofe himself, Britain declared that anyone writing, speaking, teaching, or publishing a website to "foment, justify, or glorify violence in furtherance of particular beliefs" would be either jailed (if a British citizen) or banned (if a foreigner). And so, on official Home Office stationary emblazoned with the ironic letterhead slogan, "Building a Safe, Just, and Tolerant Society," the UK Police State cast Best into the select ranks of a few other US animal rights activists who the year before had received the same fascist punishment. Already branded a "domestic terrorist" by the US government, the UK thereby upgraded Best's status to that of "international terrorist." While Best argued that ALF actions were nonviolent, exposed the hypocrisy of the imperialist British State and empire, and warned of the slippery slope from censuring to outright fascism once philosophers without a criminal record are banned for controversial discourse, the Home Office insisted the exclusion was for life and was non-negotiable.

The pressure to speak before the ecoterrorism committee, the scurrilous and baseless charges of Martosko, and the lifetime ban from the UK were not isolated events in Best's life, but rather integrally related forms of blowback one can expect to receive by waging war on speciesism and defending the use of tough tactics against cold killers and brutal regimes of exploitation and killing. And so it is no surprise that one other payback from the corporate-State-academic complex was delivered in March 2005, when Best suddenly found himself removed as Chair of the Philosophy Department. According to his Dean, the controversy that ensued on an international level was misplaced, as it was really just a "normal rotation of the Chair position" (to which Best quips it was "about as normal as the rotation from John F. Kennedy to Lyndon Baines Johnson in the office of the President"). Best's colleagues, in contrast, averred that the department replaced him due to strong dissatisfaction with his job performance. Best, however, insists he was on the wrong side of a Machiavellian power play, one motivated by resentment of his politics, by selfish concerns that his notoriety might bring problems to the department, and by the irrepressible stirrings of a department cabal to seize control.

One could hardly blame Best's suspicion that the loss of his position was more likely a by-product of the Green Scare and linked to the political nature of his research and activism. For per "normal rotation" protocol, he was in fact due another year as the department head. In addition, the negative performance review that was cited as evidence for removing the Chair from him (a review in which he received a startling score of 0 on a 5-point scale after 4 previous years of consistent 5s) came quickly on the heels of all these events. Moreover, at this time there was also a burgeoning national scandal in the academy over the—ultimately successful—Rightist attack upon Ward Churchill (who had written the foreword to Best's *Terrorists or Freedom Fighters?*), and Best was himself told by UTEP students that prior to the decision against him they overhead professors saying, "If we don't get rid of Best, we're going to have another Ward Churchill on our hands" (Smallwood 2005).

But, again, this was also a period in which the government was increasingly going public with its concern about the domestic security threat of "ecoterrorism" as part of a campaign for new security and legislative measures (hence, Inhofe's hearing). Years after the fact, it is now known that governmental tip-offs alerting high-ranking university administrators of potentially troublesome and radical faculty in their midst (such as Inhofe's office did with Best) were strategically utilized by the FBI during the 1960s to inhibit the advancement and power of New Left faculty (Cunningham 2004). Is it really that unreasonable to suspect that during the era of George W. Bush's fascist administration that similar procedures became reinstated and that sectors within the government reserve the right to work behind the scenes and assert themselves in academic affairs as they feel necessary? To add fuel to the fire, Best—who boasted a prodigious publishing record, excellent teaching evaluations, and outstanding levels of community service—has since been denied promotion and continues to receive information from trusted insiders that university administrators are actively seeking routes to challenge his tenure and to sever the university's relationship with him completely. For sure, lacking a smoking gun, there is only rumor, mounting circumstantial evidence, and the grounds for paranoia in suspecting a repressive conspiracy at work against him. Notably, however, such rumor and paranoia were themselves a primary methodology and outcome of the COINTELPRO operations as well—a point that should not be taken lightly.

Obviously, what occurred to Best sets a chilling precedent of academic repression for others in at least two ways. On the one hand, repressive "anti-terrorist" legislation such as drafted by the UK Home Office handicaps engaged scholars who must frequently cross borders as citizens of the world if they are to understand and provide a check upon increasingly transnational flows of power and be a viable member of an increasingly global intellectual community. On the other hand, UK radical environmentalist and animal advocacy politics have often been ahead of the scene in the US, resulting in more stringent laws against such politics being advanced there first and then exported as a perverse form of repressive British invasion. Best's case, then, may serve as a harbinger of potential changes to American law in the future—a cause that should alarm *all* academics, not just those in support of direct-action politics on behalf of animals and the Earth.

Best also had the distinction of being in attendance at two conferences co-organized by his colleague, Anthony J. Nocella II (a scholar who the David Horowitz Freedom Center's *discoverthenetworks.org* lists under "Activists Posing as Professors"), in which the State aggressively intervened. The first conference took place at Fresno State University. It was entitled "Revolutionary Environmentalism: A Dialogue Between

Activists and Academics," and involved leading activists committed to militant direct action and economic sabotage on behalf of nature and animals. This group included Rod Coronado, Gary Yourofsky (former ALF prisoner and now vegan educator), Craig Rosebraugh (former ELF Press Officer), and Paul Watson (head of the Sea Shepherd Conservation Society), as well as affiliated scholars such as Best, Scarce, and Bron Taylor. Generating tremendous public scrutiny and right-wing outrage—the Center for Consumer Freedom flattered it with a report called *Legitimizing the Lunatics*—a decision was made to close the conference to non-university members and a heavy police presence was ushered in, ostensibly to guarantee the conference participants' safety (Best 2003). However, the real issue came after the fact, when US Rep. Richard Pombo (R-CA)—whose legacy includes attempting to repeal the Endangered Species Act— and several Republican California State senators began to publicly excoriate the event, with one opining, "They should all be behind bars, not feted at taxpayers' expense. If Fresno State has so much money as to throw it away on this kind of garbage, then they can obviously stand a cut to their funding."[4] This led to a governmental initiative to reduce Fresno State's funding by the amount it spent on the conference. While only a few thousand dollars, the message provided by government to university administrators spoke volumes: watch what you sponsor because we're watching you.

Another conference under the watchful eye of federal representatives, in this case the FBI, was the First International Animal Liberation Philosophy and Policy Conference held at Syracuse University in April of 2004. As a personal attendee, I can vouch that the conference was swarming with police and other security agents, unmarked cars following anyone and everyone, and menacing, dour federal agents taking copious notes on Steven Best's keynote speech, "Seven Arguments In Defense of the ALF." It was a truly spooky and intimidating atmosphere, which felt more like a penitentiary at times than a college campus. The repressive height of this event, however, came on April 23 when Sarahjane Blum, a spokesperson for the nonprofit animal welfare group, Compassion Over Cruelty, took the stage to preview a showing of her searing undercover documentary, *Delicacy of Despair: Behind the Closed Doors of the Foie Gras Industry*. The movie revealed an open rescue of ducks at one of the nation's major factory farms for foie gras production, showing "ducks blinded by disease and infection, ducks languishing in their own blood and vomit, and ducks confined side by side with rotting corpses."[5] Upon finishing, Blum was met immediately offstage by police, handcuffed, and rushed away from the conference to be indicted on felony burglary charges for the acts recorded in her movie. The question of open rescues' illegality aside, especially problematic here was the way in which an academic conference presentation was turned into criminal evidence and an act of self-incrimination. Blum's arrest serves as another precedent for State involvement in surveilling and delegitimating lines of research involved in eco-ethical and animal advocacy issues.

In closing this section, attention must be paid to the manner in which higher education has now treacherously allowed national security agencies to implode into its institutional makeup. While offices like the CIA have recruited for years from select programs across the country, more nefarious is the growing willingness on the part of university administrations to grant the FBI field offices on campus and to entertain briefings from Special Agents as part of the FBI's Academic Alliance College and University Security Effort program. More egregious still is another FBI outreach effort that resulted in the creation in 2005 of the National Security Higher Education Advisory Board. The FBI-led Board, which is chaired by Graham Spanier, President of Pennsylvania State University, involves presidents and chancellors of nineteen of the nation's top research universities, as well as the president of the Association of American Universities. According to the government, its mission is to serve the FBI with "a means to open the doors of understanding and cooperation with leaders in higher education on matters related to national security, terrorism, counterintelligence, cyber threats, and certain criminal matters".[6] More specifically, in his latest editorial Spanier (2008) listed "Threats to faculty members and university property by animal rights terrorists and eco-rights terrorists" as one of the key issues to be addressed of the Board. This is clear confirmation that American higher education is actively supporting and complying with forces attempting to generate repressive policies against the movement of radical environmentalists and animal rights advocates. As I have outlined in this section, such repression can easily become aimed at scholars who focus on these movements as well, which works in ways that serve to damage academia's intellectual and civic mission.

Cases of University Repression of Radical Environmentalist and Animal Rights Advocate-Scholars

As evident in the case of Steven Best, the bureaucratic nature of higher education often makes it difficult to prove where clear repression has occurred and who within a labyrinthine administrative system is calling the shots. Still, in the instance of radical environmentalist and animal rights advocate scholars, I think there are some contemporary examples of faculty, student, and organizational removal that warrant concern and are representative of the general tenure of what is taking place today within the academy.

As Ward Churchill's suspension and firing from the University of Colorado at Boulder grabbed headlines in 2005, the university's concurrent removal of Adrienne Anderson—an Environmental Studies faculty member since 1992, who was also known to be one of the nation's top environmental whistleblowers—took place much more quietly, but no less importantly. Anderson has been likened to Erin Brockovich and Karen Silkwood for her work in the university and as the Western Director of the National Toxics Campaign, in which she has assisted labor unions and poor communities in holding corporate polluters like Rockwell International, Martin-Marietta, and ASARCO Metals (as well as corrupt government officials) accountable for their toxic misdeeds against people. An activist professor who brought her struggle for environmental justice into the classroom, a major goal of her pedagogy was to teach students how to file FOIA and Open Records requests in pursuit of uncovering the social and environmental damage done by government and industry. Anderson's particular pet project was to have students investigate the Lowry Coalition, a collection of some 150 companies that spent years dumping unregulated waste into a Denver metro-area landfill and then worked to cover up the presence of radioactive materials found therein, as the landfill sludge was greenlighted for use as agricultural fertilizer. Anderson filed suit on this matter in 1997 and winningly argued that the Coalition's activities posed significant threats to the public health on numerous levels.

Strongly championed by her students and having received nothing short of exceptional job reviews over the course of her teaching career (despite constant friction by certain university forces), Anderson suddenly found that her department had closed her classes without warning in 2005. While she alone had developed and taught a mandatory course for the major, being untenured and without opportunities to teach, the university happily declared Anderson expendable. Those familiar with her story, though, quickly pointed out that many of the companies in the Lowry Coalition are significant university investors. One—Scripps-Howard, the media monopoly in the Denver-area—also funds a faculty member in her department, who the American Association of University Professors (AAUP) alleges worked to undermine Anderson's reputation with other faculty, as well as to dismantle her appeal for rehiring by leaking confidential and false information about her and her work.[7] As the AAUP statement makes clear, what occurred to Anderson has broad significance and should be properly seen as part and parcel of a current right-wing attempt to use the University of Colorado as a test case for imposing a corporatist model of education that weakens tenure, faculty governance, and due process, as well as academic freedom generally. But it also reveals how the academy can work to suppress crucial environmental research and willingly jeopardize sectors of society in order to protect powerful allied interests.

Such repression is aimed not only at professors. Students also are under unprecedented attack from university administrations, students like T. Hayden Barnes. Barnes was expelled in October of 2007 by Valdosta State University President Ronald M. Zaccari for publicly protesting Zaccari's decision to spend $30 million dollars of student fees on constructing an environmentally hazardous set of parking garages. Having learned of the decision from the school newspaper earlier in March, Barnes posted flyers around campus detailing sustainable alternatives and listed the contact information for Zaccari and the Georgia University system Board of Regents should anyone want to send opinions regarding the project (something he did himself). Four days later, members of Students Against Violating the Environment contacted Barnes to let him know that Zaccari was angry, and in response Barnes removed the flyers. However, he was hardly finished campaigning and, over the next month, he posted a collage lampooning the parking garage project to his Facebook page, wrote a letter to the editor of the student paper critiquing the proposed garages, and then wrote Zaccari himself to request an exemption from paying the mandatory student fee that was to be contributed toward the construction project. According to the Foundation for Individual Rights in Education (FIRE), which ultimately took up his case, on May 7, Barnes found a note from Zaccari slipped under his dormitory door which read "as a result of recent activities directed towards me by you, included [sic] but not limited to the attached threatening document [the Facebook collage], you are considered to present a clear and present danger to this campus."[8] While lawsuits filed by FIRE and Barnes resulted in Zaccari announcing his early retirement and the Board of Regents overturning Barnes' expulsion, Valdosta State remains notorious for officially quarantining expressed free speech on its 168-acre campus to a small stage area that must be reserved two days in advance and can only be used two hours each afternoon.[9] Alarmingly, the university is not unique in this practice.

Although the University of California system is not amongst those with designated public free speech zones for political expression, it has moved to enforce a ban on a wave of ongoing protests by both legal and extra-legal animal rights groups against primate vivisection practices taking place on some of its campuses. Though framed as a defense of faculty research and an attempt to preserve academic freedom from direct-action militants who targeted the property of specific vivisectors in recent years, flagship campuses like UCLA, UC Berkeley, and UC Santa Cruz are actually involved in deploying repressive tolerance. UCLA, in particular, is considered to play a leading role in developing national academic security strategies. As a member of the National Security Higher Education Advisory Board, working in concert with the FBI and other agencies after a supposed ALF hit on a researcher's home in 2006, UCLA has moved to check animal advocacy on campus by barring student activists from entering university buildings during demonstrations, by coordinating information about student groups with law enforcement, and by increasing its powers of surveillance generally. Moreover, it has sought and won court injunctions against the websites of legal organizations such as the UCLA Primate Freedom Project (founded by a UCLA student), and has suppressed the public speech rights of numerous individuals. Such anti-activist actions as the university are engaged in are now promoted as "Best Practices for Protecting Researchers and Research" by the Society for Neuroscience (Murr, 2008). The demented idea of standardizing protocols which serve to make animals as vulnerable as possible to the unnecessary needles and knives of vivisectors reveals the manner in which corporate science and the security State have come together to set higher education policy, with UCLA presently serving as the principal model for other academic institutions to redraft their policies in similar fashion.

While other academic institutions such as the University of Utah have similarly worked with government officials to legislate the criminalization of protests within 100 feet of faculty residences, recent legislation crafted by the UC system related to its lawsuit against animal rights activists has moved beyond the anti-democratic and into the realm of the unconstitutional. Specifically, the measure AB2296, submitted by Assemblyman Gene Mullin (D-San Mateo), was created to forbid political activities targeting corporate researchers on campus; with its initial aim being "to restrict public access to information about academics who do animal research and to make it illegal to post personal information about them online" (Krupnick, 2008), such as their names, addresses, and photographs. Although the bill's language was scaled back slightly when passed into law in October, 2008, it is revealing that, as originally drafted, it attempted to exempt requests about university research from public records requests, In other words, those in charge of the UC system unabashedly sought to create a non-transparent situation for university research in which it would be legally impossible to have civic oversight over the public university system's work. While the immediate aim may have been to block the names of laboratory vivisectors from animal advocates, this legislation would have also shielded all manner of military, biotech, and other forms of ethically dubious experimentation from public inquiry. The University of California's repression of animal rights activists and student groups is therefore an affront that should concern all people, and it is crucial that it be challenged appropriately as such repression serves not only to blunt moral progress but also the realization of a more democratic science of the people in the process.

Closing Remarks on Greening the Academy

I am an ethical vegan who has openly supported the animal and Earth liberation movements for a number of years, but never engaged in any illegal actions. Yet I have been the target of gossip and innuendo by faculty in my former doctoral program. During the height of Operation Backfire, unmarked cars sat outside my home and I recognized that I was under observation by the authorities. For my own good, friends in the academy have on more than one occasion advised me to strike the topic of animal advocacy, or anything of an overtly radical political nature, from my work and vita. As an untenured faculty member, it is entirely plausible that I could be jeopardizing my own future career opportunities in the academy by not following such advice, so that I can pursue my inherent interest to theorize and comment about these vital social, political, and environmental issues and the most dynamic struggles of the day, in as unencumbered, non-anxious, and free a manner as possible.

I hope *not* to be another casualty of what amounts to Operation Get Fired. I do not expect an all-expenses paid cruise to the Cayman islands, nor do I hold any revolutionary fantasies about being a victim of and martyr for State and university repression, so I that too can be crucified by the likes of Sean Hannity. Still, it is my belief that if we are to have a more peaceful, sustainable, and free world in the coming decades, it will not happen without the concerted effort of committed scholars in the present. The price paid by the academics whose accounts I have provided here, as well as by activists such as Judi Bari, Ken Saro-Wiwa, Chico Mendes, Tre Arrow, Kevin Jonas, Josh Harper, Rod Coronado, Barry Horne, Jill Phelps, Jerry Vlasak, and Pamelyn Ferdin means that the least I can do is to help spearhead efforts to develop the radical environmentalist and animal rights advocacy movement's cognitive praxis within higher education. The only way forward is to push and be pushed back, to take a risk with our work to aspire to the ethical transformation of the world. It will not be easy. Nothing worthwhile ever is.

Postmodern Fascism
and the Long Arm of Israel

Reflections on the Finkelstein Case

Bill Martin

THESE DAYS WE ARE IN UNCHARTED WATERS on the question of academic repression. There are elements in the current scene that echo earlier periods of
repression, mainly the McCarthy period of the 1950s. However, there are at
least three differences from that period. First, academia is different. Second, the place
of academia in the larger society and culture is different. Third, and most important,
the larger society itself is different. In this essay I will address these matters from the
standpoint of the case of Norman G. Finkelstein at DePaul University, a noted Jewish
scholar whose controversial work on *The Holocaust Industry* enraged Israel apologists
and right-wing extremists, who subsequently put land mines throughout what should
have been a smooth path to tenure. DePaul happens to be my own university, where I
am a professor of philosophy. I therefore had some personal involvement in the Finkelstein case and feel that I can speak to some of the issues from a certain "inside" perspective that I hope will shed light on the question of academic repression.

First, let's quickly review the facts of the case. Assistant Professor Norman
Finkelstein gained notoriety for his provocative analyses of the "holocaust industry" in
which he alleged unconscionable individuals exploited the murder of six million people for their own gain. This earned him the implacable wrath of Zionists and staunch
Israeli supporters who—despite the fact that Finkelstein is a Jewish scholar whose
parents survived the horrors of Nazi death camps—maligned him as a "Holocaust
denier" and an anti-Semite. In typical McCarthyist fashion, these critics besieged the
President of DePaul University, Dennis Holtschneider, with complaints and demands
that he fire Finkelstein for slanderous and shoddy scholarship. Most prominent and
vocal among this pack was Alan Dershowitz, a militant pro-Israel Harvard law professor. Despite his avowed commitments to free inquiry, Holtschneider buckled to
the pressure, discounted the unanimous vote for promotion by Finkelstein's department and a university committee, and fired him for alleged scholarly deficiencies and
sins. Against standard university practices, Finkelstein was not allowed to teach one

last year after the negative decision, and the university ushered him out the door as quickly as possible. Having successfully dispatched a scholar who dared to challenge Israel, Holtschneider unashamedly reassured everyone concerned about the state of academic freedom there that "All is alive and well at DePaul." From the perspective of appeased Israel apologists this was true, but for champions of civil liberties and watch-dogs of social repression, democracy and higher education ideals, Holtschneider had not only committed a gross injustice to a prominent scholar, he had more generally undermined academic free speech.

Although there were academic controversies prior to the 1920s in the United States, and there is much history here to be studied, there is also a sense in which the political scene in American colleges and universities was relatively settled and more "pre-censored" or self-censored than controlled by outside political and economic forces. In the post-WWI period, and into the early fifties, because of the influence of the Communist Party, USA and the global prestige of the Soviet Union as the power that had actually defeated the Nazis, there were a fair number of left-wing academics (CP and otherwise). The McCarthyite witch hunts aimed to purge the academy of Left-ists, and this largely successful effort was overtly politicized in terms of "Americanism" versus "the global spread of Communism" (however that concept was understood, be it in terms of actual radicalism or simply the power machinations of the Soviet state). The academic scene was similarly politicized in and through the Sixties, when it seems conservative elites made the decision to "confine" the radicals to the university—better to have them on the quad than on the streets. In fact the academy became one of the few politicized (if often ineffectually so) spaces in a society that was entering a new phase of depoliticization, a phase I associate with the idea of "postmodern capitalism." Here the three interrelated spheres of difference described above come together in a kind of "perfect storm," to give us the case of Prof. Finkelstein.

It has been said that the Bush regime itself represented a kind of perfect storm, one involving a confluence of numerous contingencies, but not predicated on mere coincidence. Instead, a fascistic domestic agenda, driven first of all not by (what right-wingers call) "values," but instead by a perceived need to bolster US global hegemony in the aftermath of the Soviet bloc and the rise of new global economic and military forces (China, India, the European Union, and now increasingly Russia again). This agenda unfolded, first through the initial "coup de Bush" in 2000, and then with the events and aftermath of September 11, 2001. What I am calling "the agenda" is itself a cobbled thing, and it plays out in the terms of postmodern capitalism, perhaps signified best by the idea that the average "citizen" (a term depoliticized into near meaninglessness) can show his or her patriotism by racking up credit card debt and shopping at the mall. It is not clear to me that even a postmodern capitalist society "on the march," in a "war on terror," and where the Constitution is in some sense held in abeyance by the USA

PATRIOT Act, needs outright fascism, as the latter would involve a kind of repoliticization process. There is something purposely vague and murky—involving, of course, elements of outright bullshit that are a large part of the capitalist system's stock-in-trade (whether in the right-wing or the "mainstream")—in the way the agenda unfolds, both in society generally and the institution of higher education specifically. Academic repression, consequently, reflects this new form of "postmodern" fascism.

The individualist, fragmentary, and consumerist logic of the capitalist system, for instance, registers in academia as expectations that professors need to stay within their supposed subject areas and fields of expertise. One irony here is that this insistence on the supposed sanctity and insularity of intellectual fields is predicated on the idea that the educator is primarily a dispenser of information, and that information has some inherently "neutral" character—we know this neutrality has been violated if there is anything that smacks of "advocacy," and advocacy generally is what runs contrary to the agenda. For the most part, the agenda itself does not want advocacy, because that might spark politicization and debate; as Donald Rumsfeld said only days after 9/11, this is not the time for debate or "understanding." This perspective fits just as well with a consumerist model of education as information transmission as it does with a larger authoritarian social agendas and murderous military campaigns in foreign lands.

Even so, and I say this partly tongue-in-cheek, why isn't it widely understood that the September 11 attacks represented something like "the chickens coming home to roost"? Why isn't it readily known that the State of Israel was not in fact established as a "land without a people for a people without a land"? That it is a garrison state for American power projection (and provocation) in the Middle East? That it is a brutal prisonhouse for the previous inhabitants of that land? And that some characters, in Israel and the United States, have in fact created a "Holocaust industry" that exploits tragedy for personal gain?

The Finkelstein case, which included the termination of his colleague and open supporter, Assistant Professor Mehrene Larudee, was traumatizing for many of us at DePaul. To be honest, because in many ways DePaul had been a politically progressive university, I did not think that the President would fire Finkelstein. However, it is quite likely that, because DePaul had the reputation it did, and after all because DePaul was the sort of place where Finkelstein would be hired to begin with, the forces of repression from outside of the university prosecuted their case so vigorously. Of course, we have every right to call out these scumbags for what they are—people such as David Horowitz, Dinesh D'Souza, Alan Dershowitz, and Lynne Cheney for their post-9/11 campaign against left-wing and radical academics, as well as the worthless blowhards from Fox News and other disinformation outlets. But we also have to attempt a bit of cold analysis and discern how this present form of academic repression works and where it is going.

In the summer of 2007, I wrote an article about the cases at DePaul (Finkelstein and Larudee), which was published at the online site *Dissident Voice* and then disseminated somewhat widely. The final paragraph of the article bears further discussion:

> For now, a great victory has been handed to people who are essentially fascists. Why is it a great victory? Because, as with Germany in 1933, a decisive role was played by people who are liberals and even progressives. Even more, because a university that should have been one of the last places where something like this could happen is instead one of the first.

In the following months, I wondered if I had overstated the case somewhat. How does the straight-up fascistic academic repression represented by repressive campaigners such as David Horowitz square with the generally depoliticized form of postmodern capitalism, even with post-9/11 fascistic tendencies? Stupidity and ignorance are always a major factor in the arsenals of fascist movements, but even here there is a postmodern twist. The "traditional" fascist movements could be said to represent certain "values," even if sick values, of natural hierarchies within humanity, reified in terms of ethnicity (or color, race, nationality, even language), gender, and sexual orientation. To be sure, there are those within the imperialist ruling class of the United States, and within fascistic movements such as the right-wing "Christian" groups, who do believe in such things. And yet much of the rhetoric of such hierarchies is no longer acceptable in what passes for a public sphere, and, furthermore, it is the ruling class that primarily makes use of the fascistic and authoritarian ideologues ("Christian," including in the present case the crazy apocalyptic "Christian Zionists," as well as Straussian neo-conservatives) and not the other way around. For the most part, the cynical power manipulations of this ruling class continues to depend on a consumerist, postmodern capitalist strategy where there can be no larger public debate of fundamental political (or ethical or philosophical) questions. Yes, there is jacked-up rhetoric, and yet even the jingoism is mixed with cynicism, and this is as true with the super-patriots and right-wing fundamentalists as with the initiators of this rhetoric.

Indeed, one lesson that absolutely has to be learned in the wake of the coup de Bush and 9/11 is that there is a ruling class, and this lesson needs to be taken to heart in the academic sphere as elsewhere. What we might wonder is why we academics are so resistant to learning this lesson and confronting the real workings of power, even as we also quite rightly demand that the academic sphere be a place of radical questioning. With the current fascistic tendencies of postmodern capitalism, we also have an obligation to do what we can to make it clear that the restoration of the critical role of intellectuals will require more than university reform, it will require larger social transformations. Otherwise, academia driven by corporatist and consumerist criteria (something beyond narrow pragmatism; rather, the truth is what sells and what shapes people into docile consumers), in other words the academic institutions of postmodern capitalism, will only have to "snip off" the remaining intellectuals who cross certain trip wires in order to continue with its evermore "fully administered society" (as Adorno put it).

Clearly, Ward Churchill and Norman Finkelstein did trip the wires of acceptable discourse. Two quick comparisons in the case of DePaul University will help us bring out the postmodern fascist character of the dismissal of Prof. Finkelstein. First, some readers may know that DePaul University was the first Catholic university or college to establish a Queer Studies program. Different sexualities and attendant cultural, political, and scientific questions and expressions seems like an obvious enough field for critical study—but then so does the real situation in Palestine and its history. I don't know what kinds of discussions went on behind the scenes with the establishment of the LGBT concentration—perhaps none, for all I know. On the other hand, surely there are those in the Roman Catholic world, in the Church hierarchy, in academia, and undoubtedly among "ordinary" Catholics, who are not happy that the largest Catholic university in the United States has such a program. But so what? From an intellectual standpoint, it's an open-and-shut case. And yet the same thing could be said for Norman Finkelstein's case for tenure, and it bears repeating what has been said many times already, just change the subject (Israel and the Israel lobby) and there is no question.

The second example, which I won't dwell upon, is that there are others of us who also have been engaged in radical intellectual activity and activism in our time at DePaul, and we have not been repressed or at least not denied tenure and promotion. In my own case, for instance, I went to Lima, Peru, in the fall of 1992, to help with the effort of preventing the government there from being able to summarily execute the captured leader of the Shining Path, Abimael Guzman. Six of us in my group were arrested, interrogated for about a day and a half, and deported. I was only in my third year at DePaul and did not have tenure. This episode was followed by about three years of hassles (some that affected me very deeply) with my department chair, but never with the rest of the department, and never from any administrator, and three years later I received tenure and promotion on schedule, as I also received promotion to full professor. Again, not to dwell on my own circumstances or work, but I think there are some interesting comparisons to be made with the Finkelstein case that might illuminate the present situation with academic repression.

First, very obviously, my episode in Lima (among other things, and I would like to think that my actual intellectual production figures into this as well) occurred before the Bush-Cheney clique took power.

Second, I am completely aware that things might not have gone so well for me at other universities, and there are many of them where I would have been ridden out of town on a rail. One of the difficulties for me personally in the Finkelstein case is that some of the same administrators (and senior faculty in the Political Science department) who supported me in the aftermath of the Lima episode were the ones leading the charge against Finkelstein. Does this speak to a difference between two radical intellectuals, or to something about DePaul, or even to something about these specific administrators and professors? All three areas could bear some fruit upon closer examination.

Third, there is the fact that Norman Finkelstein is a political scientist and I am a philosopher. There is more in this difference than can be spoken to here, but the essence of it can be summed up readily: speaking from the discipline of political science, if one does go outside of the mainstream of acceptable political discourse, one is much more likely to touch a nerve than if one is speaking from the discipline of philosophy. For one thing, most of political science is in fact a legitimizing ideological discourse (especially all of the "empirical" stuff on voting patterns, how legislatures function, etc.), so if one goes outside of that, it stands out all the more starkly.

Of course, Prof. Finkelstein went outside of the legitimizing discourse in a particular way, which will again turn out to make all the difference in the end. It also bears examination that one of the few outstanding counterexamples, Peter Singer's remarks on euthanasia, received widespread debate in western Europe (where figures such as Jurgen Habermas and Umberto Eco regularly write newspaper editorials), but not in the US. Or we might even consider Daniel Dennett's contributions to the so-called "new atheism." To attempt to refute him, right-wing fundamentalists would have to actually study some deep and complex thinking, and we surely don't want to encourage that! One final example, which I have always found especially irksome, was George W. Bush's use of the phrase "will to power" in the speech he made to Congress three days after the events of 9/11. One can be sure that use of this philosophically-loaded expression was pure rhetorical "deployment," indeed it is about as good an indicator as any that there is "no one home" in what counts as Bush's brain. Neither before nor after the use of that phrase did Bush have any sense of its meaning, and neither did he ever care, and neither should the average American citizen either—because the point is not to think about anything or to encourage critical discussion. So, while I would like to think that my actual written work is radical and crosses many boundaries of "legitimate" discourse, it could also be said that some things in the intellectual and academic worlds remain under and are dealt with well enough by the workings of postmodern capitalism, which renders much of philosophy simply ineffectual and irrelevant, at least outside of a relatively narrow sphere. In other words, repression in philosophy primarily works by rendering philosophy merely academic, a fact with which all too many philosophers are entirely comfortable.

Fourth, maybe there are some personal differences with Finkelstein. There are some who praise him for certain aspects of his personal style, for the eviscerating way in which he calls out those with whom he disagrees. For my part, although I have never met Prof. Finkelstein in person, I could imagine that we might not make the best of buddies, in part because of the invective he directed at someone I will always hold in high esteem, Jacques Derrida. It's completely unfair, but in the Finkelstein case it was not hard to see how these personal factors allowed some who were sitting on the fence in terms of their support for Prof. Finkelstein to back away. And yet of course this is complete bullshit, and we in academia know it: you can't vote against someone's tenure because you don't like them, or even because they may have been personally insulting to you, or because you take strong exception to their views on a particular subject. Many of us in academia have flaws, I daresay that the people who carried out the machinations to deny tenure to Prof. Finkelstein may have a flaw or two; the question is how these flaws are taken up as part of a repressive agenda. (For my own part, I have no flaw shortage, and it is also the case that, if I had a dollar for every ridiculous and cruel thing I have heard said about Jacques Derrida, then I could at least buy that Gibson bass guitar I've had my eye on.) Perhaps there is a larger lesson here about what we ought to do with the flaws of the mortal folk of academia—actually, I hope there is *not* a lesson, but I'll come back to this.

Fifth and finally, I think the Finkelstein case is about one of the two or three ultimate tripwire questions in our presently postmodern fascistic society, namely the State of Israel and associated issues, though perhaps even more the Israel lobby in the US. Let's just put it very directly and bluntly: unless you have an extremely solid foundation from which to do so, you just can't mess with that crew. Their goal is not to have a debate, it is to destroy all opposition, and they have shown very well that they will do so by whatever means they deem necessary. Actually, let me put it this way: I don't even know if there is a solid enough foundation from which to oppose the Israel lobby, not a foundation that one can expect to still be standing upon at the end of the encounter, and perhaps not a foundation that itself can stand.

Here, I want to make a key point, not only about the Finkelstein case, but about how at least some forms of academic repression work today (though here there are some significant echoes of past repressions). As I said before, the case was traumatizing for many of us at DePaul, and here we might emphasize the old Greek meaning of the term, "trauma," as a "cut" or "break," as in a break in the skin. Not only were we disturbed by what was happening to Norman Finkelstein and Mehrene Larudee, but those of us who had been proud of the politically progressive cast of DePaul had to wonder if either the university had fundamentally changed in a very bad way, or if we had been terribly naïve (and, again, idealistic in both senses, politically and philo-sophically, in the latter case taking the "world of ideas" for the whole world, and not recognizing larger social realities) to believe that DePaul was especially progressive in the first place. In either case, some of us felt that the university was being destroyed in the process of firing Prof. Finkelstein.

However, this is where the three "situations" I mentioned at the beginning of this essay all come together and interact—academia, academia in society, society more generally. Again, to put things in a very blunt way: DePaul University is not a solid enough foundation from which to go after the Israel lobby or the State of Israel. The forces that were arrayed against Norman Finkelstein would have destroyed the univer-sity itself, if they deemed it necessary, in order to prevent Dr. Finkelstein from receiving tenure. On the way to that, these forces would have caused the president of the uni-versity to be removed, and perhaps some other administrators as well. I still think it is right to say that the administration at DePaul, and its president, did the wrong thing, but I don't see how they could have done the right thing. The forces at work were simply too powerful, and to understand academic repression today, we need to take the full measure of this situation.

Of course, the lesson cannot be that, if you don't want to be repressed, then it's better to be in philosophy and to stay away from the Israel question! For what it is worth, there may be one or two tripwire questions in philosophy, too, and it might even be said that one renders oneself a docile ideologist of the existing order by simply avoiding them. I am going on the assumption that any deep investigation into the true, the good, and even the beautiful will bring one up against the falseness, the evil, and the ugliness of the social system at some point, and we might take our cue from the fact that the powers-that-be have *politically* gerrymandered issues such as biological evolu-tion which becomes a "controversial" question where creationists insist that "alterna-tive theories" should also receive attention in the academy.

On the other hand, and keeping with my "postmodern" thesis, we might study the particular tripwire questions in more detail to understand the strategies of the pres-ent repression, the way that it is circumscribed in a way that represents elements of fascism, but that is more within the orbit of postmodern capitalism. One direction this investigation might take is to ask the differences that cases such as those associated with Ward Churchill and Norman Finkelstein made to particular universities, to aca-demia in general, and even to society as a whole. As for the latter question, we see post-modern capitalism *and* postmodern fascism in the fact that the typical morons who take their cue from Bill O'Reilly and the Fox News Channel still wouldn't be able to tell you who either Ward Churchill or Norman Finkelstein is, though they might have been able to recall their names for some brief moment (which is not the same as telling us who they are) as vile academic extremists they regretfully help fund through their tax dollars. One would hope that it at least makes most of our administrators sick that they have in some cases been forced to kowtow to this sort of agenda, which ultimately has to do with reforging American power and nothing to do with critical questioning and investigation. Regarding the first question, there are differences between the University of Colorado and DePaul University that ought to be studied. DePaul, unfortunately, is not free of the corporatist influence that pervades public institutions these days. However, there is also a language at DePaul that can serve us well when questions of justice arise, and our Fox News idiots can't claim to be paying the salaries of our faculty. There is more to be said on these things, and yet, obviously, we won't find a solution to academic repression in pointing out these differences. Indeed, to repeat, an argument can be made that it was precisely because of these differences that it was important to the forces of repression to make a stand at DePaul.

Add to the previously-enumerated questions, another important query: What door has been opened by the Finkelstein case, the Churchill scandal, and other instances of academic repression, whether infamous or unreported? Putting this in the context of "the agenda" more generally, it is very difficult in the summer of 2008 to see where things might go. There appear to be three possibilities.

It may be that the postmodern fascists have done enough work for now to keep postmodern capitalism on track, and that the effect in academia will be chilling enough. Thus, the usual timidity and self-censorship will prevail, and even radical intellectuals will think too much about the strategies and tactics of tripwires and seemingly circumscribed repression, as opposed to principles that direct us to pursue truth, wherever it leads us. Certainly the postmodern fascists, having their own careers to pursue (that's part of what makes them postmodern: on some level this bullshit is just a job and a niche to the likes of David Horowitz and Bill O'Reilly), will try to keep the pressure on, but they may recede a little, either out of their own tactical considerations, or because they have been reined in by the ruling class, acting out of its own strategic necessities. Here biological evolution again stands out, as it is not clear how long a society that depends on advanced technology can sanction the undermining of scientific investigation itself, and it is to the latter that the attack on evolutionary science ultimately leads.

It may be that we will experience a period of respite from fascistic trends, though such a respite may not be so different from what I just described, unless the respite also includes vigorous efforts to push things in the opposite direction.

Or it may be that the fascistic agenda will redouble its efforts, spurred once again by some all-too-convenient "trigger," and academic repression will expand. Again, we need to better understand the strategic necessities of the imperialist ruling class, but we also have to understand the role that is played by certain "bold and visionary" elements within that class. And we have to understand the fact that, with all of the intellectual tools at our disposal, we are not very good at countering these fascistic and imperialistic visions; we are too locked up in academia, and the fascistic agenda is one where even that is not good enough for the reactionaries, they want to go after us even in the place that had previously been something of a refuge. But if things go in this direction, perhaps it will indicate that society in general is ripe for civil war, and perhaps this civil war ought to be unleashed in its own form in academia itself.

I hated what Alan Dershowitz did to Norman Finkelstein, I hate what he therefore did to all of us, even the non-radical intellectuals who will just go about their business of keeping their noses clean, I hate what he did to my university, and to the academic system in general. But, speaking in purely academic terms, why shouldn't I hate Harvard as well, isn't there a question here of Finkelstein's platform versus Dershowitz's platform? At the conference on academic freedom, held at the University of Chicago in November 2007 in the wake of the Finkelstein case, I was pained to hear from two different speakers that perhaps DePaul was too "small" to stand up to the Israel lobby, unlike their own elite schools, Columbia and the University of Chicago. But I don't see these schools rushing out to hire the Norman Finkelsteins of the world, either. DePaul is not "small" (it has more students than either of the aforementioned), but it is not rich and powerful. On the other hand, if Norman Finkelstein was up for tenure at either Columbia or the University of Chicago, it's not clear how that would have gone, either.

Unfortunately, we intellectuals are not good at meeting power with counter-power, and we are not adept at navigating a scene where this is the way things work. We'd like to think we could just go out in the world with proposals for the true, the good, and the beautiful and have a good discussion. Even those of us who know better on some level find it difficult to accept this reality, and the problem is that there is something to be said for "keeping it unreal," for not accepting that this reality could ever be legitimate. Meanwhile, postmodern capitalism circumvents lines of thought by placing the category of legitimacy—as a normative concept with some "objective" weight—in abeyance.

None of these alternatives is acceptable, and neither is hate enough. We also need systemic analysis, and we need a deep love of a different possibility for human-kind and even for the place of intellectual inquiry. And then we need some strategic thinking about what to do. My broad conclusion, though I realize that it is not very satisfying, is that in confronting academic repression we are up against the parameters of the imperialist and sometimes fascistic system of postmodern capitalism itself. Perhaps, however, even in the world of the Fox News Channel there might still be a word to be said for open inquiry; so that we might give a more powerful answer to that brilliantly-expressed question, "Is our children learning?"

But that means we have to recognize and go up against one of the main pillars of postmodern capitalism: the empowered campaign of stupidification that has especially unfolded in the wake of the Sixties. As we all know, this is extraordinarily difficult, it takes a lot more than just being "smart," articulate, and studied. This is not very satisfying, but we won't be able to do our work of speaking truth to power without understanding the way things work now. Even then, our work will be very difficult, as it is integral to postmodern capitalism (in a way different from "classical" capitalism) to make our work difficult, or even to find it at all.

Radical Is as Radical Does

Practical Engagement and the Politics of Campus Organizing

Amory Starr

THIS ESSAY DRAWS ON MY SERVICE AS AN ASSISTANT PROFESSOR during a very political time period from 1998–2007 at two universities, categorized by the Carnegie ratings as a Research 1 and a Private Masters 1. (When referring to the universities, I will call them R1 and PM1.) This time period included an intense period of student activism across the country regarding anti-globalization. Having filed my dissertation on the possible emergence of an international anti-corporate social movement a year prior to the Seattle WTO protests, I was thrilled to join my students in this movement, traveling with student-community groups to Seattle and eleven other global economy protests within four years from 1999–2003 and participating in related local and regional social justice campaigns and educational events. This time period also included 9/11 and a time of extraordinary ideological hegemony and censorship, as well as courageous exercise of first amendment activity by a broad array of citizens concerned about the future of our country and the world. Finally, this period included an unprecedented international anti-war mobilization of diverse tactics and participants.

As a scholar trained at a prestigious R1 school focused on publications and cutting edge intellectual battles, which were carried out at full force in faculty meetings and in the hallways, in an atmosphere in which faculty were regularly combating their own university over policies regarding race and gender, I was completely unprepared for the quite different cultural expectations at my first job, where I spent five years (I left for personal reasons unrelated to my career or the political climate). In both of my positions, I found myself perceived as responsible for every political action taken by students on campus.

I also found myself perplexed and paralyzed by the geography of campus dissent. Students reported my peers' quite partisan statements in the classroom, and I observed cynical and pointed political messages displayed in cartoons and newspaper articles on colleagues' doors across many different departments and colleges on campus. However, when I spoke out publicly or organized around these very same issues, I found myself vilified and alone.

This essay is an attempt to characterize forms of academic repression, drawing on my own experience. While my relationship to the alterglobalization movement is unique, my relationship to the events of 9/11 and its aftermath is certainly not unusual. Although this essay does not make claims to representative data, it may be that I occupy a useful position for reflecting on these matters during this time period.

The Geography of Campus Dissent

Radicalism v. Activism: There is a very clear distinction between what people write about and the actions they take in the world. It is not possible to identify allies on the basis of the political positions and claims they make in their scholarship. Many academics who take a "critical," indeed "radical" perspective in their scholarship do not participate in activism, do not support activism, and will not ally themselves with activists in any way regardless of the similarity between their own scholarship and the political issues and perspectives being acted upon.

Private v. Public Statements: Many faculty will have conversations on campus in which they strongly espouse an antiwar position. They may argue passionately for these issues in their classrooms, and even for or against electoral candidates. They may paste very clear political positions to their office doors. However, these persons may avoid associating themselves with any formal public statements, public appearances, or campus visibility about these issues.

What is most interesting about this is that the "private" space I am referring to is *not* the private space of home and off-duty time. There is a perception that classrooms, office doors, and chatting at the beginning of faculty meetings or in the hallway, are "private" safe places in which to express politics, but appearing at a campus event, associating oneself with a student group, or participating openly in a campus campaign, is a more official and vulnerable "public" stance.

I don't know why my perception of space was inverted. I treat my classrooms as spaces where I need to carefully maintain a scholarly stance. I communicate clearly about issues of "bias" and, although I find certain scholarship more convincing than other scholarship, I do not spend class time discussing my personal opinions on political matters. I assiduously avoid any possibility of association with electoral issues (since that is the legal definition of "political" activity that affects public funding for student groups and 501(c)(3) status). I also avoid partisan conversations that could polarize colleagues. My office door encourages critical and anti-oppression perspectives, but I would never put an anti-Bush message on my door, since I worry that could alienate students who I want to communicate with. I do assertively take political stances regarding militarism, economic globalization, and criminalization issues at rallies, on- and off-campus events, and in petitions and other public texts. I believe it is part of my responsibility as a public intellectual to participate fully, contributing my analyses and skills to such public fora.

Target Location: With the exception of the first few months following 9/11, faculty feel most comfortable taking a position on distant political events. Involvement in contentious civic issues is less common. Finally, taking a position on administrative polices is viewed as especially unwise or even "career suicide." For example, faculty may feel comfortable using the term "racism" to describe federal policy with regard to Hurricane Katrina. They would be reluctant to use that word with regard to a local event like a police shooting. They would be unlikely to use the word with regard to campus policies; doing so would be considered antagonistic.

To an outsider, this all makes little sense. People unfamiliar with the university might expect it either to be a normal organization, in which people work, leaving their politics at home, or a realm of unlimited free speech. The political containment zones are hard to understand.

Confrontational behavior regarding campus policies, while it cannot be directly censored at a university as insubordination, is seen as unwise from a career perspective, because it indicates conflict with administration. In his book, *Disciplined Minds*, Jeff Schmidt explains that the most important function of graduate training is to enforce ideological discipline not over the personal political viewpoints of professionals (which have little impact on the world), but over their willingness to conform to professional hierarchies (which has much more serious consequences). He begins the book by noting that "professionals are fundamentally conservative" (4) in the workplace even though most are liberals in their social views. He notes that "depression is most likely to hit the most devoted professionals" because they "entered their fields expecting to do work that would 'make a difference' in the world and add meaning to their lives… In fact, professional education and employment push people to accept a role in which they do not make a significant difference, a politically subordinate role" (2).

The professionals maintain the status quo through the work they define and permit. In the social sciences, the gold standard is publishing highly specialized articles in elite journals. In medicine, it is "patching people up…never to take a stand against the social inequities that generate so much stress and disease" (109). Aspiring professionals who are unable or unwilling to conform are weeded out, marginalized, or abused (always using the rhetoric of meritocracy). As junior professionals realize they will not be able to fulfill their vision of social transformation, they embrace ego and status (and, in fields that offer it, high pay) as the "compensation for intellectual interests and social goals abandoned… Deprived of political control over their own work, they become alienated from their subjects and measure their lives by success in the marketplace" (119, 146). Success is determined by conformity with institutional business. "The qualifying attitude, the way it is favored and the way it is measured are very much the same across the professions" (21). The attitude which must be demonstrated is "subordination."

Social Concepts

Collegiality: Although universities mete out little oversight or sanctioning of professors, an informal set of priorities serve to restrict political action. In my experience, "collegiality" is one of the most important. It is the secret, determining, ingredient in hiring and promotion decisions. It is an acceptable framework through which to communicate discomfort with or disinterest in queers, women, and people of color.

To me the biggest shocking difference between the R1 where I was trained and the R1 where I found myself working was the latter's top-priority emphasis on collegiality, over and above research quality and productivity. Now I certainly like people to be friendly, but several times I saw collegiality get in the way of attempts to assess quality, competence, and the department's diversity responsibilities. Indeed, I was punished for providing an expert assessment of a candidate; this was perceived as an uncollegial act although the task at hand was assessing competency. I thought I was doing my job as a faculty member, only to find out I had a new, overriding job which countermanded scholarly expertise.

While some political activity seems to be *part of* collegiality, such as standing in the halls discussing (loudly and with clear partisanship) presidential candidates and party strategy, other activity is interpreted as an affront to collegial norms, such as inviting colleagues to participate in campaigns consistent with their analyses and espoused politics. During the joke-filled announcement section of a faculty meeting, I announced that the local chapter of Jubilee 2000 was looking for good speakers to speak in churches about third world economics. Since many of my colleagues had published prolifically in this area, I wrongly assumed they might be interested. Another very serious violation of collegiality involved a poster produced and distributed by the organizing committee of a teach-in regarding 9/11, of which I was a member (along with other faculty, students, and university staff). The poster included the phrases "Faculty: Send your students!" and "Students: Walk out!" This poster was interpreted as *my* "disrespect" of fellow faculty members rather than as a contribution to the work and traditions of the university and the faculty.

"Brainwashing"/"ringleading": After some attempts to organize political action with fellow faculty and graduate students, I concluded that they were not a fertile field. Meanwhile, students were pouring into my office asking for my support and help with

their projects. I decided to "work with the people who are ready to move" (King 1981). Over the years I worked with several formal student organizations and also with many ad-hoc groups involving a few fellow faculty, along with students, staff, alumni, and community members.

1999–2002 was an upsurge in political activity regarding globalization all over the country and around the world. Students were in the leadership of this activity in the US. Amazingly, I was seen as orchestrating this activity on our campus. Despite my colleagues' manifest knowledge of the great difficulty of manipulating our students into reading, they believed that I had the capacity to manipulate students into endless meetings, complex planning, uncomfortable travel, and frightening situations involving police. Proud of my teaching as I am, my powers seem to have suffered a marked decline since 2003—along with the US alterglobalization movement. On the basis of my association with some student activities and activities, I received hysterical phone calls from facilities management blaming me for events about which I had no knowledge whatsoever. Due to phantasmic beliefs about my powers and goals, by 2001, any rumor about me was believable, no matter how unprofessional. My patient department chair would call me in "just to check" that I hadn't "actually offered your students extra credit for throwing bricks through the windows of Starbucks."

"*Your students*": While I may logistically or proudly refer to students as "my students", it is quite apparent that they do not do what I want or hope they will do. I know that all my colleagues know this to be the dynamic with even their favorite students. Since my days as a graduate student instructor, not one of the 200 students I have worked with each year for more than a dozen years has done what I would have had them do. Standing in the street with my students as they are approached by TV news cameras, they do not say what I would have them say. So if the meaning of "your students" has something to do with ideological or behavioral obedience, I have been a total failure—a common experience which I know to be a painful one for many faculty.

This is because our students are very much their own people, living in a highly individualistic society, and finding their own path. Any exposure to critical education such as what I and my colleagues offer in our fine sociology courses only expands the array of political and professional opportunities that our students consider. My colleagues know this to be true. Yet when students speak up in colleagues' classes, organize events, confront administrators, and write newspaper articles, they are seen as my puppets. Not only does this indicate a terrible disrespect for *our* students, but it indicates a desire to vilify my work in the basest way, as a cultist. "My" students have been disrespected in this way for conveying information from *The New York Times* of the prior week, for persisting in the use of the word "queer" despite a non-gay professor's discomfort with that word (and their having provided him with documentation of the use of the word in the academy and by the GLBT movement), and for their sophisticated choice of thesis topic (to which I contributed only one part of the methods section).

At PM1, students who had never actually taken a class with me engaged in spontaneous confrontation with an administrator. The event occurred during a picnic I had no knowledge of until afterwards. They spoke on behalf of an organization of which I was not a participant and which had ignored the advice they sought from me. Their actions were discredited (and I along with them) as "my students."

Fear & Safety

The next layer of understanding academic repression is how faculty deal with their fear and try to establish security. Worried about academic repression and its potential career percussions, faculty try to stay "safe." They do this by navigating the political geography carefully, by disassociating themselves from activities or persons they think might be "dangerous," and by trying hard not to say the wrong thing.

The most interesting case in this regard is Ward Churchill. When the press, the state of Colorado, and his university sought to punish Ward for a controversial piece of writing, his peers across the country, many of whom agreed with the substance of his points if not the rhetoric, did not jump to support his academic freedom and constitutional rights. Instead, to a shocking degree, they agreed that he had been unwise in his choice of words and kept their critical distance. They bulwarked their personal sense of safety by believing that the massive political assault geared against Churchill would only be used against people who actually *did* something.

As an activist, I know that state repression does not use this kind of fine grain policy and technical distinction. Instead, it releases illegal force indiscriminately to intimidate people from behavior it does not want. The assault on Ward Churchill successfully discouraged academics from speaking their minds, from asserting their rights to speak, and from advancing the university's historic role in safeguarding unpopular ideas in the interest of the future.

Scholarship Under
the Gun, Lawsuit, and Innuendo

Understanding and Navigating Academic Repression

Christian Davenport

Those engaged with questioning and/or explicitly challenging the status quo within modern nation-states frequently find themselves subject to political repression. These are attempts made by government authorities to restrict and/or eliminate the questioning and/or change-making efforts being made (Goldstein 1978). While a focused attention on these efforts over the last forty years has proven useful (e.g., Walter 1969; Wolfe 1976; Goldstein 1978; Tilly 1978; Donner 1990; Poe and Tate 1994; Davenport 1995; 1999; 2007a,b; Fein 1997; Harff 2003; Cunningham 2004; Davenport et al. 2004; Hafner-Burton 2005), providing information about when such actions will take place, who will be targeted, and what are the likely aftereffects, these approaches tend to neglect other forms of repression that exist within the same jurisdiction. For example, some have highlighted the "softer" methods of social repression (e.g., Ferree 2005), noting the importance of stigmatization, ridicule, and "silencing" employed by diverse authorities. Others highlight "channeling" methods of repression (e.g., Gamson 1975; Earl 2003), noting the importance of accommodating viewpoints in order to coopt them.

Unfortunately, these efforts are almost exclusively focused on targets that are engaged in directly challenging the status quo (i.e., social movements and dissidents). Citizens not directly engaged with explicit behavioral challenges, but who attempt to question and challenge the existing order in less direct ways, like some academics, are ignored by this approach. Such an omission is important because repression is clearly influential and there are likely very particular methods and processes of control exerted within different institutional contexts. Research on how religious institutions and private corporations attempt to shape the behavior and thoughts of their members has revealed this to be the case. Acknowledging this work, it seems clear that a more accurate characterization of the situation within modern nation states (especially in democracies which attempt to reduce overt government activity) would address the fact that there are a wide variety of nefarious people engaged in repression, varying by the particular actor who undertakes the activity and the degree of connection they have with political authorities and social-economic elites.

In this essay, I focus on repression as it operates in universities and colleges. I begin with outlining exactly how academic repressive behavior functions, then move to a discussion of how I have attempted to navigate this terrain, whereupon I note the few instances where my efforts were successful as well as a few that were not.

On Freedom and Repression

As noted by Gross and Simmons (2007), the concept of freedom within a university and college setting—in the West in general and the US in particular—is a rather recent phenomenon. In the seventeenth and eighteenth centuries, most of these institutions were religious in nature and those involved with them had to adhere to the particularities of the faith in question. If they did not, then they were sanctioned and there was little to no recourse for those deemed inappropriate. In the nineteenth century, an interest in science and knowledge began to outweigh strictly religious concerns and with this there were some criteria around which those involved with these institutions could find some space for expression. Discretionary power was still held by those governing the institutions but given the importance of conjecture and refutation as well as examination of bizarre hypotheses within the scientific method, there was wiggle-room. This was improved significantly in the twentieth century, although there were some major setbacks during the persecution of communists and socialists amidst the McCarthy era, and throughout much of the Cold War. Despite this period, however, there were some clear protections that were increasingly adopted and enforced, and were to some degree adhered to.

Crafted under the direction of the American Association of University Professors (AAUP) and the Association of American Colleges and Universities (AACU) during 1940, the basic tenets of academic freedom in the United States were articulated in the "Statement of Principles on Academic Freedom and Tenure." These are summarized below in the following three points:[1]

> Teachers are entitled to full freedom in research and in the publication
> of the results, subject to the adequate performance of their other aca-
> demic duties; but research for pecuniary return should be based upon
> an understanding with the authorities of the institution.

> Teachers are entitled to freedom in the classroom in discussing their
> subject, but they should be careful not to introduce into their teaching

controversial matter which has no relation to their subject. Limitations of academic freedom because of religious or other aims of the institution should be clearly stated in writing at the time of the appointment.

College and university teachers are citizens, members of a learned profession, and officers of an educational institution. When they speak or write as citizens, they should be free from institutional censorship or discipline, but their special position in the community imposes special obligations. As scholars and educational officers, they should remember that the public may judge their profession and their institution by their utterances. Hence they should at all times be accurate, should exercise appropriate restraint, should show respect for the opinions of others, and should make every effort to indicate that they are not speaking for the institution.

The logic of the document is simple: (1) teachers should publish without fear of negative sanction but only if their other business is handled, (2) teachers should teach without fear of negative sanction but only as long as they stay "on point" and (3) teachers should remember that even though they think they are off-duty many will view them as being on duty.

The document is important for it reveals a high degree of sensitivity to the different activities that teachers engage in as well as the different audiences that are addressed by them. The document also establishes for us a relatively clear indication of what "academic repression" would look like. For example, we would consider a teacher "repressed" if they were sanctioned for publishing something when their other responsibilities are adequately dealt with, when they were sanctioned for teaching something while on the relevant point, and when it was deemed that they spoke inappropriately as a private citizen but were believed to represent an institution.

Although suggestive about where one might actually see academic repression, however, the document does not really help us understand the true complexity of the matter. Indeed, it does not tell us what the other responsibilities are as well as how they are to be evaluated, exactly what "staying on point" is and exactly how/when teachers are "off-duty." These are crucial issues which are constantly being developed and revised. In addition to this, the document does not really tell us who/what should be monitored, how diverse actors can be involved at once and what factors could/should be mobilized on behalf of the academically repressed. Seeking some guidance for how to think about this process, I attempt to outline it below.

Figure 1. Basic Model of Academic Repression for Teachers/Professors

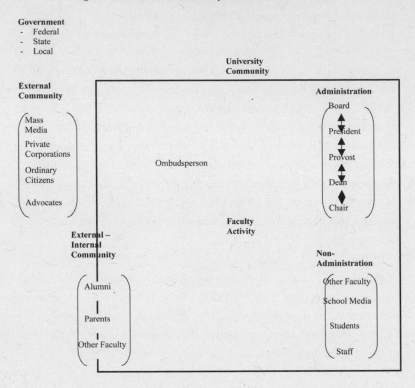

The key to understanding academic repression is to get an understanding of the different actors that could be involved. The most obvious starting point is the government, but only as they can indirectly influence other actors. If they directly sanction the teacher/professor or fail to protect them when they are supposed to, then this would be included under the rubric of state repression. If they influence other actors, however, by providing priorities, threats, laws, and the like, then this could fit under academic repression. Note that it is extremely important to divide these actors into their federal, state, and local components, for these might not be uniform in their approach to a particular issue. Of course, there are other actors directly outside of academic institutions that are relevant. For example, the mass media could be involved. The actual involvement varies, however, for they can either serve as a mechanism of repression—especially with regard to "softer" forms, or they can serve as a mechanism of resistance and clarification. One could also include private corporations here that might have a vested interest with a particular educational facility.[2] Ordinary citizens could be included, for they can directly engage/intimidate/threaten professors/teachers. Lastly, I include organizations like AAUP who serve as advocates on behalf of faculty by directly advising them, lobbying, presenting amicus briefs, monitoring and highlighting abuses, monitoring laws protecting these individuals, as well as attempting to sanction wrong-doing through naming/shaming.

There are a group of institutions and individuals that are partially connected with academic institutions, but that also maintain connections outside of them. Depending upon the relationship with the particular faculty member, the influence of these actors could either be repressive or facilitative/protective of civil liberties. For example, one actor concerns alumni who have a vested interest in what transpires on campus as well as how different aspects of the relevant institution function. Parents count in this category as well, given the fact that they have direct connections with members of the university/college but they have other interests outside of this community. Finally, faculty at other institutions are involved because they represent a particular class of which individual faculty are members.

The third and final group of concern to the basic model involves those directly housed at the institution of interest. This includes the administration: the chair, dean, provost for faculty affairs, president, and the board of regents. There are non-administrative actors who include the faculty, the school media, the students, and the staff. Again, similar to the last, these actors can either be the instruments of repression

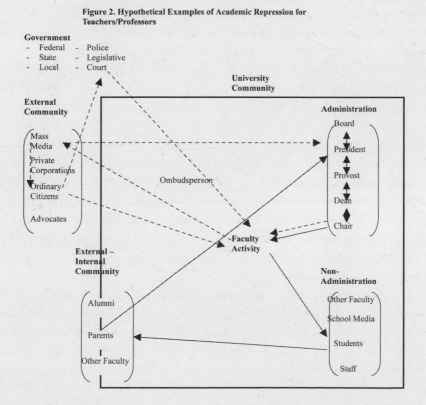

Figure 2. Hypothetical Examples of Academic Repression for Teachers/Professors

or freedom. Finally, there are frequently a group of actors whose job it is to serve as a liaison between faculty and other actors on campus—an ombudsperson.

Acknowledging the diverse actors is important for it is possible that different combinations are either for or against the faculty member in question—some serving as mechanisms of freedom, while others serve as mechanisms of repression. It is important to allow for the variation so that potential allies are not missed and enemies are appropriately grouped together. For instance, in example one (denoted by the solid line in Figure 2), a professor says something in a lecture which is deemed inappropriate by a student, who passes on this information to their parent. The parent then decides to contact someone in the administration who, positively responding to the request for censorship, passes down the censure through the chain of command. This results in the department chair telling the faculty member to stop engaging in the offensive speech. In example two (denoted by the dashed line), a professor writes something in a newspaper article, journal, or book that is deemed inappropriate by various individuals in the mass audience. Some directly contact the professor and tell them that they are inappropriate and suggest that they stop. Others decide to go to court and pursue legal action against the professor. Still others contact the administration. Positively responding to the request for censorship, these individuals pass down the censure through the chain of command. Again, this results in the department chair telling the faculty member to stop engaging in the offensive speech. Clearly, the second situation is far more complex than the first. In the latter, the professor has to deal with attempted repressive activities emerging from three different locales—emanating from both within as well as outside of the institution. In the former, the professor has to deal with attempted repressive activities emerging from only one locale within the institution.

The model is useful in certain respects for it assists in identifying potential threats to freedom as well as potential supporters against repression. At the same time, the model is problematic because it suggests that efforts at suppression are clearly understood as such by the professor involved as they are happening. This is not always the case. Sometimes those behind the repression are not revealed until much later and the evidence needed to prove an attempt at restricting speech/association/assembly is not available. Additionally, the alleged victim of academic repression is compelled to disprove other explanations for the attempted censure (e.g., personal malice and incompetence in the performance of one's duty).

Unfortunately, there are no manuals on how to navigate the model described above; hence the necessity for a book such as this. Many of us learn from the experience of others as we work our way through the academy. Rarely, however, do we talk about these issues outside of a bar or café and, even then, with hushed tones. Below I will discuss several incidents that influenced me as I was beginning to enter academia. I will then address numerous instances of attempted academic repression that I was forced to deal with.

Into and Around the Matrix: Some Personal Experiences

My awareness of the restrictiveness of university campuses was always rather high. I first became alert to academic repression as an undergraduate at Clark University in Worcester, Massachusetts under the instruction of Cynthia Enloe, Zenovia Sochor, and Knud Rassmussen. At this time, a group of students were engaged in the anti-Apartheid, divestment movement (Soule 1997). The activities at Clark had been moderately contentious, involving shantytowns, petitions, speeches, and public demonstrations. As students, we were all well aware of the fact that these activities were something of an embarrassment for the administration. Several faculty members in political science and sociology in particular supported the effort, but very few expressed this support openly. None of the students were aware of all of the activities being undertaken by the administration, but several student activists told me that many of them had been subject to some type of "review." Those with good grades were essentially left alone (there was nothing that could be done to them as students did have the right to say what they wanted), but those with poor grades, those on scholarships, and those on student visas were told by the administration to suspend their activities. The activists I knew complied and, as many of the students engaged in relevant activity fell into the three vulnerable categories, mobilization was somewhat curbed. Clark inevitably divested (or, rather money was moved from direct investment to indirect investment), but the lesson was clear: change-making was not going to be easily tolerated in educational institutions and to engage in political activities in this locale one had to be effectively immune from administration repression. Yet I was not an excellent student, I feared the consequences of a review, and thus my participation was limited.

My second experience was also at Clark, but it had less to do with the suppression of political beliefs than with how educational institutions functioned with reference to their faculty. During my junior year, I began taking classes with an extremely popular political science instructor—Kent Trachte. Professor Trachte was something of a cult figure. He was insightful about world politics, conversant on a wide variety of topics (especially radical political economy), charismatic and cool in a beatnik kind of way (cigarette in hand, dark and disheveled clothing, messed up longish black hair). During that year, Trachte had come up for tenure and was denied. His publication record was not deemed acceptable, but, as his teaching evaluations were stellar and he inspired many of us, students came together on his behalf, signing petitions, holding vigils, talking with senior faculty, and organizing a rally. Confronted with this activity, the administration did not budge and it was clear that, rhetoric aside, the only thing that mattered to the university was the publication record; as Trachte did not publish, he perished. I thought that this was somewhat unfair but again easily recognized the lesson: if one wanted to do anything controversial in the university setting as a faculty member, they had to be relatively bullet-proof.

My third and final experience relevant to the topic, before officially entering the academy, came in graduate school. During my second or third year at Binghamton University (1989/1990), a rather cantankerous senior professor, Richard Hofferbert, decided that he was going to defy the president's ruling that members of the Ku Klux Klan could not be brought on campus. He was going to bring them right into his class—the inner sanctum of the American academic institution. There was some controversy leading up the event. Faculty seemingly lined up either for or against Hofferbert as the day approached. Everyone seemed to be waiting for the president's response. What would he do? What would happen to Hofferbert? The campus was awash in speculation.

At the event, absolutely nothing happened and even the faculty initially against Hofferbert supported him in the end. No one wanted to challenge his right to do whatever he wanted in his classroom, because they did not want to have anyone telling them what they could do in theirs. The lessons from this event were twofold: (1) if Hofferbert could get everyone's support for bringing the Klan on campus, then I could get support for bringing black nationalists or European anarchists, and (2) certain aspects of academic institutions were held sacred by all who worked at the institution.

To these insights, I added the daily commentary of several progressive professors (e.g., James Petras, Immanuel Wallerstein, and Ali Mazrui) who attempted to understand as well as to challenge the world around them, while at the same time engaging in diplomacy with their institutions to prevent political fallout. These professors generally did what they wanted. As a consequence, while guarded, I came out of graduate school with an exaggerated sense of what was possible.

With these experiences, I went to take my first job in academia at the University of Houston before moving to the University of Colorado, then to the University of Maryland, and now the Kroc Institute for International Peace Studies at the University of Notre Dame. What follows are a few examples where I believe that I encountered some form of academic repression. For comparison sake, I also identify some cases where I was subject to racism and political repression. Truth be told, I think that I have navigated around most of these successfully—with little psychological, political, and/or economic damage (at least thus far). The reason for this is relatively simple. I have essentially taken up two careers: one dedicated to publishing mainstream, conventional social science and another dedicated to archiving as well as militating against state repression and human rights violations. Without the first, I would be vulnerable regarding my efforts to engage in the second.

The Problem of "Credible" Sources

At Houston, I had my first experience with academic repression. In my third year of teaching, I became interested in repressive action directed against the Black Panther party in Oakland, California. While on the Special Collection committee, I discovered a decent collection of Black Panther Party newspapers, and I wanted to content analyze them to figure out exactly who did what to whom. Toward this end, I submitted a grant proposal to the Harry and Frank Guggenheim Foundation. Although sympathetic to the topic, the reviewers did not like my selection of the Panther newspaper, perceiving this to be a "biased" source. As a result, I did not get funded. Somewhat jaded by the experience, but curious about the frequent comments made in the review regarding the appropriateness of using the Black Panthers as a source, I submitted the same exact proposal to the National Science Foundation, but switched the source; now I was going to use *The New York Times*. All other aspects of the proposal were kept the same. This time I was funded. The conclusion from this was clear: certain sources are deemed valid and others are not.

Now, was this academic repression? I believe that the validation and success of the project by the NSF revealed that it was the source that was the problem. The Guggenheim reviewers (members of the external community) did not wish to authorize and facilitate a professor's work employing an undesirable and allegedly unreliable source. In a sense, they were blocking the project's completion. For the record, once the funding for the project was received, I used not only *The New York Times*, but also the Panther newspaper, a white radical newspaper (the *Berkeley Barb*), a white mainstream local paper (the *Oakland Tribune*), and a black moderate paper (the *Sun Reporter*).

The Radical Information Project

Acknowledging that what radical organizations had been subject to required actually discovering the trace evidence of what they were doing as well as what was done to them, I began a data archiving project dedicated to the collection of such information. The compilation of this information was not easy, however. There were several reasons for this. First, the US government had not released most of this information and what was released could be reclassified once again, removing it from the public domain. Second, radical organizations did not generally have the space to hold or interest in holding this information. Even if they did have the information, they did not generally have the ability to archive or read it. They had lives to live, bills to pay, and a legacy of activism to deal with. Third, even if the information was available for sharing/distribution, given the experience of the activists, it is not likely that they would hand it over to just anybody. As a result, anyone conducting research in this area had to deal with the blowback of state repression. This has clearly been my experience.

To deal with the Black Panthers, I had to meet, engage with, and describe my interests in detail with relevant information to numerous Panthers (discussed in Dahlerus and Davenport 2000). This became difficult because too much time spent with any one individual had implications for you working with others, unless of course they were involved with the same faction. Now it made sense that individuals would maintain this position. Not only were the Panthers infiltrated by the state but, through scholarship, they were frequently misrepresented and/or delegitimized, thus reducing their trust not only in government but also in researchers. In a sense, state harassment closed the door on access to the Panthers, which represented an interesting intersection of political and academic repression.

Working with groups that had been victimized by the state was only part of the problem. Occasionally, universities became involved. After several years, I had negotiated an arrangement with members as well as affiliates of the Republic of New Africa (RNA) to gain access to their "Red Squad"—these are records that document in great detail exactly what diverse law enforcement agencies (i.e., the Detroit police department, Michigan State police, and the FBI) were doing to the RNA, and what was taking place within the RNA (who attended meetings, what activities were they engaged in, and where/when). At this time, I was at the University of Colorado. The records contained informant reports and police records following arrests and physical surveillance. Additionally, it contained information from the RNA itself: pamphlets, flyers, unpublished manuscripts, newspaper articles, and even a black nationalist coloring book. After I acquired the records, I put several of the documents on my webpage. Now, to this day, I do not know who informed whom, but I was contacted by someone in the legal department about the legality of the records, informing me that many were confidential and not to be circulated.

This was a moment when things could have gotten repressive but, to my surprise, after I discussed how I acquired the records, the nature of my project (the discovery and distribution of information about state repression and political dissent from around the world), how the Detroit police department had actually lost a law suit regarding the distribution of this material, and that the records were approximately thirty years old, they said that there was no problem. While I was able to pursue my research agenda, the lesson was not lost on me: there is always someone watching and one always needs to be prepared for an attempted restriction.

"Denying" Genocide and the Rwandan Backlash

In 1998 (after I had moved to the University of Maryland), I began working on a research project in Rwanda. Initially, I interacted with the National University of Rwanda in Butare and the Centre for Conflict Management, but later I worked with diverse human rights organizations throughout the country. Over time, I had compiled what amounts to the largest variety of documents on the political violence that took place during 1994. In 2004, at the tenth anniversary of the "genocide," those of us working on the project decided to present some of our preliminary results. We thought that the work provided some interesting insights and, given the potential amount of attention going to be given to the anniversary, it seemed like it was going to be a perfect opportunity.[3]

In order to publicize our work, I interacted with the University of Maryland's media liaison and developed a press release. While I attempted to include all of the nuances and complexities of the research, the liaison kept trying to push a more streamlined, simplistic version. I was told that it needed to be short and if anyone were interested in the story, then they would contact us.

Now, essentially the message from our research was this: a genocide took place where extremist Hutus in the government targeted Tutsis throughout the country. But, at the same time, the extremists also targeted Hutus, and the predominantly Tutsi rebel organization killed both Hutus and Tutsis upon their entry into the country, as Rwandans of both ethnicities turned on each other. Given this complexity, one could not simply call this ubiquitous violence a "genocide." Rather, what took place in Rwanda during 1994 was much worse as it involved multiple forms of killing at the same time.

On April 3 (three days before the anniversary), the press release was picked up and spun by Matthew Green at Reuters under the title "Rwandan Killings Not Genocide—US Study." Green leads off noting:

US researchers are challenging the conventional view that the 1994 massacre of some 800,000 Rwandans was a "genocide," drawing an angry response from the government who accused them of insulting survivors.

Green continued:

Davenport agrees that the killings began with an organised cadre of Hutu militiamen, but argues that they quickly cascaded into an ever-widening circle of violence, with both Hutus and Tutsis playing the role of victims and aggressors.
"Our research strongly suggests that a majority of the victims were Hutus—there weren't enough Tutsis in Rwanda at the time to account for all the reported deaths," said Davenport, who worked with an associate, Allan Stam, from Dartmouth College.
"Either the scale of the killing was much less than is widely believed, or more likely, a huge number of Hutus were caught up in the violence as

inadvertent victims. The evidence suggests the killers didn't try to figure out who everybody was. They erred on the side of comprehensiveness," Davenport said.

Many researchers and the government maintain that most of the victims were Tutsis, while Kagame, himself a Tutsi, has based much of his legitimacy on his role in leading the Rwandan Patriotic Front rebels who ended the genocide.

"It's an insult to survivors and to Rwandans in general," said Alfred Ndahiro, an adviser to Kagame. "I think we should treat it with contempt. It's incredible that such things can come up at this time," he told Reuters on Saturday.

He said the government had not yet seen the report, but insisted that any attempt to deny genocide took place would be to deny the truth.

Things just deteriorated from this point.

The Reuters piece was picked up by UPI and ABC news and distributed around the world. I was subject to a barrage of phone calls and emails from individuals throughout the globe who attacked me for getting things wrong because I was naïve or, alternatively, purposefully distorting the truth because I was an apologist for the US government or the "killers" in Rwanda. I cannot convey how horrific some of these interactions were. Indeed, in one instance, a Rwandan woman that I had known for some time called me and said that she could not believe that I had reported what I did. She argued that my "pseudo-research" was as bad as any propaganda put forth by the extremist government at the time of the genocide. This was academic repression as I defined it above, but the delivery was far more personal than I ever thought I would experience.

In response to the angry backlash, I stopped answering my office phone, I ignored hundreds of emails, I removed my home phone from publicly distributed lists, and I cancelled a few speaking engagements. I attempted to get something into an op-ed but the format was too short for what I needed. In addition to this, my media liaison had basically disappeared. When I finally did get a hold of him, he apologized for pushing us to simplify the message and said that he was trying to figure something out. Now, had I thought that his actions were intentional, I would say that he was also engaging in overt academic repression, but I believe that he was simply untrained in political conflict as well as unprepared for the emotions evoked by the findings of my work. Given the lack of protection that he was able to exert however, I would argue that this was still academic repression of a different sort.

Now, I was protected by the University of Maryland in a general sense. My chair was contacted as well as other members of the University. They were asked, "How could they allow such work to be done?" I was not told what they said in response, but at no point in time did anyone ask me to stop. Individuals contacted members of my family, my high school, and various listservs concerned with conflict studies in an attempt to discredit me, but again this was more a nuisance than a serious restriction on my academic freedom. The high school issue was actually quite funny because someone had contacted the staff in the Northfield Mt. Hermon alumni office (that had recently issued an article on me), asking them "if they knew what kind of person I really was."

Realizing that I had to address a correction in a different media that would allow more time to explain the research, I moved to some radio programs (first Tavis Smiley on NPR and then Kojo Nmamdi). These provided a little more room for explanation, but, as both shows involved other guests who had very little knowledge about Rwanda, the message was not as clearly communicated as I would have liked.

The next waves of articles were approached with even greater care. When asked to participate, I now asked what the story was going to be about, who else they were interviewing, and what their interest in the topic was. One of these pieces, published in the *Vancouver Sun* on April 8, was especially good at communicating the results of our work:

> "The current regime has a definite interest in classifying the slaughter as a genocide," says Christian Davenport, a political science professor at the University of Maryland and lead author of the study.
>
> "We are suggesting that there was much more to the tragedy. There was ethnic targeting, but there was also political and personal targeting, which doesn't have much of a platform for discussion when everyone is calling the killings a genocide."
>
> Simple math raises doubts about conventional accounts, says Davenport and the study's co-author, Allan Stam, professor of government at Dartmouth College in Hanover, N.H.
>
> In 1994, Rwanda had 650,000 Tutsis, or eight percent to 11 percent of the population. Most estimates say about 150,000 of them survived the three months of slaughter triggered by the assassination of the Hutu president, Juvenal Habyarimana (our research actually says about 300,000 survived).
>
> If the frequently used figure of 800,000 is taken as approximating the total number of dead, about 300,000 Hutus and the tiny minority Twa would have been among the victims, the US researchers say.

Because the government of Paul Kagame frequently says at least one million died, the number of Hutu and Twa deaths would have equaled or exceeded the number of Tutsi dead.

After communicating as much as I could and feeling the aftereffects, I was exhausted. In a span of a week and a half, I had been physically and verbally threatened, insulted, abused, questioned, slandered, and ridiculed at my home, my office, and at various other locales. Indeed, the distinction between academic repression and social repression was almost completely obliterated. In this context, I withdrew and did not speak about my Rwanda research for several years. Now, this was partly because the Minister of the Interior in Rwanda subtly threatened my project co-director and me during a trip right before the anniversary of the mass killings. It was also, in part, because I wanted to go back into the data yet again and make sure that we had the story right.

In the final analysis, I believe it will be revealed that we did report the story correctly, and we have just begun expanding it into a book. Regardless, the experience was a sobering one about exactly how vulnerable we are as scholars. I was insulated because I was a full professor with a decent record and reputation. At the same time, "out there" getting threatened left and right, I was only able to continue because, as a New Yorker, I was simply used to (and somewhat thrive off) hostility.

Academic Repression
and Academic Responsibility

Some Personal Reflections

A. Peter Castro

I AM A UNIVERSITY PROFESSOR WHO WAS HIRED SPECIFICALLY as an "applied" anthropologist, doing policy-oriented work. My academic department is part of the Maxwell School at Syracuse University, one of the leading public affair institutions in the United States. As a research specialist on issues of poverty, natural resource management, and, increasingly, conflict management, I have served many times as a consultant to the United Nations, the United States government, and other organizations. In addition, I have also participated in collaborative research projects sponsored by the American government. By its nature, my research sometimes involves travel to impoverished, conflict-prone areas. Over the years, I have worked in countries such as Somalia, Ethiopia, Kenya, and Bangladesh. Attendance at international conferences has taken me to other countries. International travel is vital to what I do in my university duties. Usually, arriving at a US airport from overseas signifies the end of a worthwhile journey. Recently, however, my arrival ultimately carried me to a new destination: detention.

In December 2006, while returning from an anthropology conference in South Africa, I was detained at JFK airport as a possible "person of interest" by the Department of Homeland Security. The customs official who informed me that I must follow him offered no reason for this action; indeed, if I recall correctly, he did not ask me any questions. He simply took my passport—an American one, as I was born in California—and led me away from the booth. I entered a room with uniformed Homeland Security officers working from a counter and desks. There was a central section with seats for those under investigation. It was almost empty, probably due to the early morning hour. Those people caught in the same predicament seemed to be from Middle East and Asia; we were joined later by Africans and other travelers whose planes had arrived. I was told to approach the main counter, where I was asked three questions by an official: What were my weight, height, and my social security number?

These struck my as odd questions and I recall thinking, in an effort to cheer myself up, that I better not lie about my weight. After having been on a twenty-plus-hour flight, I found it hard to recall the correct order of the last four digits in my social security number. I worried that my fumbling did not serve my cause. I tried to explain to the officer who I was and what I had been doing, but he politely dismissed me, sending me back to my seat. As the minutes passed, I grew increasingly worried about my wife Denise, who had accompanied me on the trip. When I was being lead away she asked the officer, "What should I do?" "Go collect your luggage," he responded coolly. She saw me disappear behind a closed door, wondering what was going on, and feeling embarrassed, as people waiting in line seemed to look on and ask, "What bad things did that man do?" The trip had been Denise's return to Africa after a twenty-three-year absence, and it had been a pleasant vacation as well as a business trip. But now was the real adventure about to begin?

What was going on? I felt a sense of dread. Part of my concern arose from confusion: what was I doing in that room? To be frank, I am not a very politically-active person. My involvement is largely limited to the serenity of the voting booth with my secret ballot. While my scholarship is hopefully progressive in nature—emphasizing the use of anthropological skills and knowledge for poverty alleviation, sustainable resource management, and participatory development—it can perhaps be viewed as mainstream and non-controversial. Ironically, my purpose for going to the Cape Town conference had been to present results from a research project on poverty in Ethiopia financed by the United States Agency for International Development (USAID) through an entity called the BASIS Collaborative Research Support Program.

Stewing in that room, I assumed that my occasional trips to Ethiopia, to Italy (on behalf of the Food and Agriculture Organization of the United Nations, whose headquarters are located in Rome), and now to South Africa triggered some profiling program. Perhaps the fact that I worked in the past in Bangladesh (for the United Nations), in Kenya (for USAID), and in Somalia (for CARE with USAID financing) prompted my fear of some damning information in my "file." I had gone to Turkey a decade before for a UN meeting on natural resource conflict management. They might have been thinking I have visited too many countries with Muslims and potential terrorists, but poverty researchers need to go where poor people live, and many Muslim nations have very impoverished populations. I also suspected that my name—which is listed on my passport as Alfonso Horacio Castro set off a racial or ethnic profile alarm. What mischief would a Latino be up to, traveling in Africa—trafficking in terror or narcotics? Was there doubt about my identity, or had I been confused with someone else? Since I had no information about my predicament, and no one wanted to talk with me, my detainment was a complete mystery. The possibilities seemed endless, as I watched, waited, and worried. Would I encounter similar delays and screenings in upcoming international travel that I had scheduled in the months ahead? Could I be detained at airports in other countries? "Sometimes I've believed as many as six impossible things before breakfast," the Queen told Alice. I thought I knew what she meant, sitting in the early morning waiting to see what happened. At that point I hoped the experience would be more reflective of Lewis Carroll's narrative of absurdities in *Alice in Wonderland*, rather than Franz Kafka's disturbing tale of Joseph K in *The Trial*.

I was stuck, and there seemed nothing that I could do about it. In the wake of the September 11, 2001 attacks, the Bush administration had systematically dismantled our constitutional rights under the cover of fighting a "war on terror"—a national mobilization and military campaign against an abstract noun!—that is supposed to last indefinitely. The USA PATRIOT Act enlarged the government's authority and capacity to intrude in our lives, while correspondingly diminishing the guarantees of freedom long held to be an essential part of "the American way of life." For most American citizens, including myself, these changes were troubling, yet they seemed abstract and distant from everyday life. Legal analyst Geoffrey Stone (2004) provides at least a partial explanation for this phenomenon. He contends that compared to previous wars and armed conflicts the federal government showed a greater degree of restraint in criminally prosecuting citizens for openly criticizing its new terror policies. In addition, Stone suggests that some of the measures instituted appeared "modest in scope and addressed serious deficiencies in the nation's intelligence apparatus" (552). However, Stone emphasizes that the Bush administration engaged in further measures that were less publicly visible yet more far-reaching in terms of our society and lives:

> The more questionable restrictions included indefinite detention, with no access to judicial review, of more than a thousand *noncitizens* who were lawfully in the United States and had not been charged with any crime; blanket secrecy concerning the identity of these detainees; refusal to permit many of these detainees to communicate with an attorney; an unprecedented assertion of authority to eavesdrop on constitutionally protected attorney-client communications; secret deportation proceedings; the incarceration for more than two years of an American citizen, arrested on American soil, incommunicado, with no access to a lawyer, solely on the basis of an executive determination that he was an "enemy combatant"; significant new limitations on the Freedom of Information Act; expanded authority to conduct undercover infiltration and surveillance of political and religious groups; increased power to wiretap, engage in electronic eavesdropping, and covertly review Internet and e-mail communications; new power secretly to review banking, broker-

age, and other financial records; and expanded authority to conduct clandestine physical searches (ibid.).

With much of this activity occurring secretly, and with little accountability to courts and Congress, it is little wonder that so many of us have been lulled into accepting things largely "as is." As E.L. Doctorow (2008: 31) warned, however, this "incremental fascism" combined with the Bush administration's extremist social policies to nurture a "culture of antidemocracy" in our country.

Airports offer spaces where increased scrutiny by the state is highly visible. There, I had grown accustomed to being singled out for the extra security search in the boarding lines. Although a nuisance, I accepted it as a petty and harmless bit of misguided profiling that one had to live with in post 9/11 America. I told my daughter about my frequent selection in airport security lines, and when we traveled as a family to an anthropology conference in New Orleans in 2002, she saw it happen twice. I remember her muttering to Denise, "This is racist what they're doing to dad." Denise and I motioned for her to be quiet. Protesting at that moment seemed likely to make things worse for all of us.

Now, sitting at JFK I worried whether Denise would be able to obtain from a lawyer a writ of *habeas corpus* to bring my case to a court if the need arose. More than forty minutes had gone by. As the room filled up with new arrivals from different parts of the earth, I went to the main counter and asked for a supervisor. One soon arrived and listened to my plea to be understood and released. He said he would do what he could. Kindly, he permitted me to go outside, with an armed escort, to tell Denise that I was okay. She had gathered our baggage long ago and waited in the luggage area for my return. The relief of seeing her was soon replaced by the sadness of again having to go back into the screening room.

Vulnerable Visitors: International Scholars Seeking to Travel to the US

Being detained by Homeland Security revealed to me in a direct and threatening manner that the USA PATRIOT Act and other security measures have gravely eroded the rights of American citizens. Yet citizens are not alone in this predicament. As noted by Stone (2004), foreign nationals and visitors to the US have suffered the greatest erosion of rights under the USA PATRIOT Act and related policies. Changes were to be expected in immigration procedures, given that the conspirators in the 9/11 attacks were not American citizens. I had served as chair in the Department of Anthropology of the Maxwell School at Syracuse University from 2000 to 2005, when the new rules for international students had been implemented. The revised procedures were more complicated, and penalties for non-compliance more drastic. University officials, our departmental graduate directors of that era, and the office staff did a great job of trying to keep up with the new requirements and taking care of our students. Nonetheless, I witnessed a dark side of the supposed enhanced security procedures for visiting scholars and students.

On a research project in Africa during the summer of 2001, I worked with an excellent local anthropologist who had recently completed his MA thesis at a national university, the highest degree granted in their program. I encouraged him to apply for doctoral training at Syracuse. The social science faculty members at the university identified a female student as another very promising scholar worthy of advanced training. I also asked her to apply. Both individuals were accepted to our program for the 2002–2003 academic year with support as teaching assistants. Unfortunately, their attempts to obtain visas were thwarted in the post-9/11 environment, which treated Africa generally as a potential terrorism trouble-spot. Why their visa applications had been turned down did not seem very clear. Neither student was a Muslim, and they were not politically active, at least as far as I could determine. From Syracuse I tried writing letters to ambassadors and other strategies to support their applications.

Meanwhile, another colleague, a faculty member at the national university who had been an integral part of the BASIS Collaborative Research Support Program, had the opportunity to work with American and Latin American colleagues in Central America on issues of household recovery from economic shocks. This possible tri-continental scholarly collaboration seemed very promising for all involved, though perhaps especially so for one of our invited African scholars. Few opportunities exist to support research by African researchers in Latin America. This faculty member already had visited the United States, including Syracuse, on a study tour financed by USAID through BASIS in the summer of 2001. Once again, the US government would be financing his travel and research. This time around, though, he encountered insurmountable problems trying to get required transit visas through the United States and Great Britain. We were told that the new demands for security in the wake of 9/11 compelled stricter controls over travel by foreigners, including ones in transit. Given that he was from a dangerous part of the world, the risks were supposedly amplified. After many tries, his opportunity vanished, as the project needed to move on.

I still held hope for the two prospective doctoral students from Africa. We kept their files active, and in 2003, while on a research trip, I visited the US embassy in their country to discuss their cases with a consular officer. It was one of the oddest conversations I had in my life, befitting more Lewis Carroll's Wonderland than the consular station at the embassy. The officer kept telling me again and again that the students would have "to sell themselves" when applying for their visa. "What does that mean exactly?" I asked in a puzzled and, as it turned out, very naïve manner. "Sell themselves" the person replied. "Is that a kind of personality approach?" I thought perhaps the students had been too timid for this American officer's liking. As it turned out, the person spoke in literal terms: a bribe was desired. It took months before the US government caught on to what was happening, and replaced the venal bureaucrat. On the one hand, this corruption reflected a singular, unusual event, a wayward official who tarnished the reputation of the rest of the embassy staff. On the other hand, circumstances of rushed security and heightened secrecy attached to immigration procedures opened the possibility for arbitrariness and lack of accountability to the population being served, which this particular officer pushed for pecuniary gain, ironically threatening US national security in the process. In the end, a unique research opportunity in Central America for an African scholar, to be funded by the US government, was quashed by the new security procedures. Happily, however, the students eventually secured visas and attended Syracuse University.

Back to JFK and Beyond

As I waited, the room filled up with more international travelers. An hour and half passed; what to do? "Castro!" I looked up to see the supervisor holding my passport. "You are no longer a person of interest." I recall feeling odd. What had this been about? Why had I been of interest, and now why was I…well…no longer interesting? Rather than seek further explanation, I rushed to be reunited with Denise, who had stayed marooned at the baggage carousel. We made it through the rest of the entry process, and managed to catch our flight to Syracuse. Both of us felt dazed. After a wonderful visit in South Africa, all we could focus on was the morning's event. I worried whether this treatment would be repeated on the overseas trips I had planned for my upcoming sabbatical. Had this been a unique occurrence or the herald of things to come?

In returning to Syracuse, I contacted officials at the university to let them know what had happened, and to seek their advice about what to do next. In one of the emails, I admitted to feeling "very confused and angry" about the incident. Our Chancellor Nancy Cantor and her staff were quick to respond with both sympathy and practical advice, putting me in contact with the office of Congressional Representative, James Walsh. He and his staff forwarded "my concerns" to the US Customs and Border Protection in Washington, D.C., for a response. In the meantime, I took, with some trepidation, a research trip to Africa, and then a brief visit to the Caribbean. Fortunately, the journeys were uneventful during travel and border crossings. In my check-in for the Africa trip, the airline agent asked whether I would be returning to the United States. I had a return ticket, and asked her why she asked such an awkward question. She apologized, saying she had been prompted (via her computer) to ask the question, but could offer no reason why it had to be asked. Her question, although trivial, made me fearful. Would I encounter trouble? Would I be detained in a transit airport? Thankfully, nothing else happened.

When my travels ended sometime in late February 2007, I received a letter from Congressman Walsh, forwarding the reply received from his query about my December incident. I was highly dissatisfied by its message: the government has the right to stop citizens and others at the border, and it does so for a variety of reasons, including random checks. Given national security concerns, the state is under no obligation to reveal what it does or why. Nothing specific was said about me. While it was reassuring to read that Professor Castro had not been identified as a possible "sleeper terrorist" or threat to the public, it was disheartening to know that the process could be repeated at any time. As I later discovered from a press release available online, the Department of Homeland Security provides "legitimate travelers" with a means "to redress and resolve possible watch list misidentification issues," such as if one is wrongly "delayed, denied boarding, identified for additional screening, or have otherwise experienced difficulties when seeking entry into the country" <http://www.dhs.gov/trip>. Allowing people to try to correct their official file, or to vent, can be a positive step in many ways, providing an avenue for individual problem-solving and organizational accountability. How efficient such measures are in solving travelers' problems and promoting accountability remains to be seen. Regardless, a complaint box is not the answer to the challenges that confront us regarding our threatened fundamental liberties.

Compared to the torture and dislocation inflicted directly on academics, such as experienced by my colleague Micere Mugo by the Kenyan government, my troubles have been minor. She experienced aggressive, open state repression in a way few American academics have imagined possible. Indeed, I do not claim that my "additional screening" was a deliberate act to repress my career as a scholar. On the contrary, I believe that my publications and teaching had nothing to do with it; nor was it an outcome of the content of my work as a policy-oriented applied anthropologist. But the event occurred within the context of my work as a researcher. Although my goals and activities related to the South African trip were essentially "technical" or "academic" in nature, I could not escape the political currents that flow around me, of which I am a part willingly or unwillingly. In seeking to cross international borders, I placed myself in a situation where agents of the American government exercise much tighter controls over personal freedom. Other means of surveillance and control, such as illegal wiretapping, are less visible, but nonetheless real and troublesome. I personally believe that the government needs sufficient authority and capacity to carry out *legitimate* national security tasks. This is the reality of the world we live in. Yet such authority and capacity needs to be exercised responsibly, within the legal and political context established in our constitution, with appropriate checks and balances. The Bush administration far exceeded its legal mandate, acting in a reckless and radical manner to dismantle our liberties. In the interest of expediency, in an atmosphere of manufactured fear, we have surrendered too many our rights as individuals and as a nation.

In entering the United States from overseas, citizens and especially non-citizens now have reduced constitutional guarantees and statutory rights to defend themselves against possible arbitrary arrest, detainment, and, for some, deportment. The possibility of being held incommunicado, indefinitely, with no habeas corpus rights, is no longer theoretical, but a reality. An old song tells us wisely, "You don't miss your water until your well runs dry." While the singer was concerned with lost love, I think the message is also true of our civil liberties. I am not suggesting that America had in the past a golden age when authorities always respected civil liberties and all people equally shared access to justice. The American past contains many "perilous times" regarding the repression of civil liberties (Stone 2004). Moreover, the ability to exercise freedom has always been socially mediated through class, gender, ethnicity, and other attributes of power. The current assault on our rights however is unprecedented, as the claim by officials that the curtailment of civil liberties must continue indefinitely is ominous.

Meanwhile, my ability, or willingness, to engage in overseas work now must confront new kinds of risks, including having my passport taken and my travel delayed as officials try to sort out who am I, whether I am a threat, and similar concerns. It is a chilling environment in which to work and live. The Traveler Redress Inquiry Program does offer limited possibility for redress, but it begs the question as to whether the massive apparatus of government surveillance, the harassment and intimidation of dissent, and the current reduction in civil liberties is necessary, effective, or appropriate. These are issues that Americans must increasingly reflect on and address.

Lessons from the Past

When I mentioned to a friend that I was writing this article, the person asked in all sincerity: "Do you think you will get in trouble with Homeland Security for doing it?" Sadly, it is a very astute question in these times: why make waves? Why draw attention to unpleasant experiences and concerns about civil liberties, especially when most people don't feel too affected by it anyway? The point is that as citizens, residents, or visitors to this country, we are already affected by the drastic changes in our rights and freedoms as brought about by the USA PATRIOT Act and other measures carried out legally and illegally by the Bush administration. Moreover, as David Price's (2004) important study of the impact of McCarthyism on the profession of anthropology reveals, adopting "silence, self-censorship, and the politics of fear" in the midst of political challenges may seem the safest way out, but it comes at a high cost. Besides damaged careers and reduced professional integrity, the field suffered a diminished capacity to explore and understand scientific and humanistic issues. It also experienced a reduced ability to contribute meaningfully and effectively to societal problems.

A great danger is the belief that the past is irrelevant for understanding our present predicaments. More than seventy years ago, Alexander Goldenweiser (1936) pointed out that a lot of human existence is "involutional" in nature—patterns of culture and behavior that consist essentially of "variations within monotony" when viewed over time. This is not to say that history repeats itself, or that social and political conditions today are identical, for example, with those prevailing during the McCarthy era of the late 1940s and 1950s. In human affairs, though, there tend to be limited possibilities, resulting in a convergence in people's patterns of adaptation. In seeking to deal with perceived "threats" identified by government and an uncritical media, by enlarging the police powers of the state, by diminishing civil liberties, and by opening universities to attacks by reactionaries we are traveling, as history has shown, down a very dangerous path. We need to reconsider the observations of scientist and educator Jacob Bronowski regarding the lessons to be learned from the Nazi death camps and similar political cultures that treat people as objects. Bronowski stated during his monumental television series *The Ascent of Man*:

> "There are two parts to the human dilemma:... One is the belief that the end justifies the means. That push-button philosophy, that deliberate deafness to suffering, has become the monster in the war machine. The other is the betrayal of the human spirit: the assertion of dogma that closes the mind, and turns a nation, and a civilisation, into a regiment of ghost—obedient ghosts, or tortured ghosts" (quoted in Malik 2001: 389).

Bronowski's powerful words still resonate, warning us about the dilemmas we face, and the possible consequences of our actions—individually and collectively. While the future is not mechanistically determined or fully predictable, it bears repeating that current approaches seem to be setting ourselves for further erosions of rights in the future and a precipitous slide toward authoritarianism. The ivory towers of academia will offer no haven.

"Reaction Waging War on Campus; Liberal Ideas, Books, Groups Suppressed"

This section title came from a newsletter headline. The accompanying article noted that, "reaction, extending its campaign against all liberal ideas, individuals and institutions, reaches into the school room to crush liberalism and progress." It documented violations of academic freedom at many campuses, including the University of California at Los Angeles, Hunter College, Cornell University, Michigan State, Syracuse University, University of Wisconsin, and the University of Southern California. The article sounds as if it could be written today, yet it dates back more than sixty years ago, published on May 19, 1947. The author, a crusading journalist named George Seldes, was writing in a small newsletter he operated, entitled, *In Fact*. Seldes entered my life when I was an undergraduate through a twenty-five-cent book my wife bought me at a thrift store. She thought the old book, which dealt with American politics and cited anthropologists, would be of interest. Her judgment was correct: I was stunned. Entitled *Facts and Fascism*, it presented a series of incredible, yet highly convincing, exposés of the threat to civil liberties and "the truth" posed by a wide assortment of entities: the tobacco industry, the National Association of Manufacturers, the Ford empire, *Reader's Digest*, the American Legion, Westbrook Pegler (the 1940s equivalent of our right-wing TV and talk-radio personalities), and so on.

Seldes discussed the connection between big business and fascism abroad, as well as with right-wing, racist interests here. The topics were fascinating, and the arguments were well documented. There was something else, too. As Nat Hentoff (1997: 69) put it: "Seldes' writing had a verve, an immediacy, a delight in risk-taking." In the public and university libraries in Santa Barbara, I found out more about Seldes, who had a long and distinguished career in journalism. Around 1940, he started *In Fact*, covering news ignored or censored by the mainstream media. Journalists, disgruntled government officials, and concerned academics often served as his sources. Much of what I learned about Seldes came from my own study of his books, as there was little written about him, at least until recently. Seldes (1997) claimed many times that his work had been largely ignored by the mainstream press for decades.

The university library had some copies of *In Fact* that I checked out. After more than thirty years, I still have photocopies of them. Sadly, the headlines often read as if written about today's news: "College Survey Shows Reaction Waging War on Campus: Liberal Ideas, Books, Groups Suppressed" (May 19, 1947); "US College Professors in the Service of Fascism" (October 29, 1945, about "endorsers of dictators" and "hired men or reactionary big business"); "The American School System Under Attack" (January 15, 1945, about "big business intrigue against free education"); "Corporations Which Sabotaged US Defense… Make Billions Out of War" (October 1, 1945); "A Free Press in the US Impossible Says Publisher Forced Out By Bank, Business & Advertising" (November 3, 1947); "Military Rule Creeps Up On the US As Army Takes Over State Dept" (March 18, 1948); and "Behind the Closed Door of a US Loyalty Hearing: Transcripts Show Incredible Breach of Civil Rights" (August 9, 1948). With its readership shrinking, intimidated by McCarthyism, the paper folded in 1950. I was delighted to discover that Seldes was still alive in the mid-1970s, and I wrote him a fan letter. The eighty-six-year-old author responded with a kind note, a recent article, and information on how to obtain his then latest book, *Never Tire of Protesting,* which had come out nearly a decade earlier. Fortunately, it was not his final publication. Seldes produced two more books, with the last becoming a national best seller in 1987 when he was ninety-seven years old. The success that he achieved with his final book, in which he continued to raise issues about freedom of the press, corporate control of the media, and other vital political topics, must have been sweet. Never tire of protesting indeed!

In the works of analysts such as Seldes and Carey McWilliams dating back to the 1940s and earlier, we can see many of the same features occurring on campuses today, particularly highly politicized attacks on academics for holding "liberal" or "radical" views, and the attempt by corporations and the government to influence university agendas and affairs. The danger then was no less than today: "business groups led by the National Association of Manufacturers and their kept Congressmen, newspapers and phony 'patriotic' societies are seeking to simplify the quest for knowledge by permitting only their point of view to be represented in the lecture halls, libraries and extra-curricular activities" (*In Fact,* May 19, 1947). This past is not simply dead history. These are recurring political and social processes that manifest in ideological intimidation, as well as the intensifying role of corporations, the military-industrial complex, and private foundations in influencing research and pedagogy (Wax 2008).

Academic Responsibility

I have pleaded for a greater understanding of the costs and consequences of reduced civil liberties in America, particularly in terms of the exercise of academic freedom. Even when politically restrictive measures are not aimed at directly repressing academics, there is still a negative impact on research, teaching, and learning. Academic freedom is a mirage in a land where constitutional guarantees and statutory rights are in steep decline. But the threats to academic freedom are often more direct, manifesting in political persecution of dissenting ideas and critical research, firing controversial tenured professors, as well as the exponentially growing influence of corporate, military, private foundations, and other sources of funding on university priorities and policies. These sponsors not only provide "resources," they also often seek to shape research and pedagogical agendas along conservative lines.

This issue is complex, with many ethical and professional dimensions. I know that in my own work as an applied anthropologist, I have sometimes taken an assignment with the hope that I can make a difference not only in shaping, for the better, the particular activity, but also the sponsoring institution. At the same time, there are some assignments that simply cannot be done because they violate the statement of ethics provided by professional organizations such as the American Anthropological Association and the Society for Applied Anthropology, of which I am a member. The current debate about the militarization of anthropology provides a good example. In my estimation, the Human Terrain Project, which places anthropologists into military teams in Afghanistan and Iraq, violates these ethical standards, particularly given the risks involved to local populations (see Sheehi in this volume). With a depressed job market, repeated official and media warnings regarding terrorist threats, and fervent appeals to patriotism, I can understand why some anthropologists might take up such posts. Such circumstances do not provide any justification, however, for engaging in an activity that is unethical and threatens to tarnish their entire discipline.

I believe that academics and applied researchers have a responsibility to uphold the standards of professional ethics in all activities. Let me emphasize that I am not calling on professors to retreat from politically or professionally controversial positions, to withdraw from using their expertise and experience in innovative if unorthodox ways, or to abandon social criticism in their actions as public intellectuals. On the contrary, such endeavors are vital for a free society and have an important place in any university. My concern is with individuals who would use the protection of academic or professional freedom as a cover for unethical behavior, such as engaging in the Human Terrain Project or in misrepresenting one's work for personal or other motives. These kinds of violations are actually very rare, and it is my impression, having been a professor for more than two decades, that academics do an excellent job on their own of detecting and dealing with such transgressions. Self-serving individuals and interest groups who feel that they must "monitor" academic activities threaten the integrity of higher education in America by their politically-charged attacks on academic freedom.

When it comes to academic freedom, my views are essentially libertarian: universities should be places for the free exchange and assessment of ideas, including contentious ones. This is not to say that anything goes. The exercise of free speech in the context of a university or college always carries with it personal and professional responsibilities. Furthermore, institutions of higher education are places of employment, where faculty members, students, staff, and, sometimes as rare as it may seem, administrators are evaluated according to performance standards. Evaluating people is never an easy task, and it is one that must have built-in checks and balances to ensure fairness and accountability. Although institutions seemed to have become better at making explicit their nominal standards, the process of evaluation always contains a subjective element, and thus will have a certain degree of tension and conflict inherent in it. To use these processes as a tool to punish people for their views or their identities is anathema to academic freedom. And yet it happens.

The violation of academic freedom is not a recent phenomenon, nor is it simply a recreation of the McCarthy era. As I have emphasized, institutions of higher education are not apart from society, but always enmeshed within it, including its relations of power. Given this situation, tensions and conflicts are inherent in terms of the exercise of academic freedom. Insights can be gained by looking to the past. In the early 1920s, for example, journalist and social critic H. L. Mencken wrote about the "conditioned" freedom of professors of economics. If they propounded economically progressive issues such as child labor or minimum wage standards, they invited trouble: "Political economy, so to speak," Mencken (1922: 282) observed, "hits the employers of the professors where they lived." He cited the case of Dr. Scott Nearing, who had been dismissed from the University of Pennsylvania:

> Nearing was not thrown out of the University of Pennsylvania, angrily and ignominiously, because he was honestly wrong, or because of errors that made him incompetent to prepare sophomores for their examinations; he was thrown out because his efforts to get at the truth disturbed the security and equanimity of the rich ignoranti who happen to control the university, and because the academic slaves and satellites of these shopmen were restive under his competition for the attention of the student-body (1922: 283).

Mencken's writing captures well the complex array of ideological and opportunistic motives that often occur—to this day—in such affairs. One is not only purging a heretic or troublemaker, but eliminating a competitor and opening up a line for new hiring. At a macro societal level, academic repression is a phenomenon almost always experienced by holders of liberal, leftist, and unconventional views. When dealing at the micro societal level, however, different allegiances to professional or local political factions, personal animosities, attempts at institutional empire building by academic entrepreneurs, and other complex motivations and circumstances make the situation murkier. Once again, the potential for abuse in academic evaluative processes, whatever the motivation, underscores the need for checks, balances, and accountability.

Times of Peril

Institutions of higher education, in addition to their formal duties, will always be potential societal hot spots and sources of controversy. This is their role: to provide an arena for the exchange and evaluation of ideas that are often critical and unpopular. These institutions, whether public or private, ultimately serve the wider public. To do their missions properly, however, universities cannot be subservient to the interests of powerful groups, whoever they may be. Academic freedom is vital. Ideas that today may seem outlandish, offensive, or obscure may have considerable value, whether measured in practical or intellectual terms. Yet academic freedom cannot thrive in societies where constitutional guarantees and statutory rights are being eroded. As Bronowski warned decades ago, ends can justify almost any means, and dominant dogmas can close the mind, undermining the greatest of nations and civilizations. In exercising their freedom, faculty also need to uphold professional standards of ethics in their teaching, research, service, and administrative endeavors. It may be trite, but it is also true, that freedom and responsibility are forever linked. Sadly, at this time it is crucial to highlight the threats to freedom, not only in the academy, but especially in the society at large.

III
Repression at Home and Abroad:
Middle East and African Perspectives

Teaching in a State of Fear

Middle East Studies in the Teeth of Power

Stephen Sheehi

A T FIVE A.M. ON FEBRUARY 20, 2003, heavily armed agents of the FBI and Homeland Security's Joint Terrorism Task Force raided the house of Professor Sami al-Arian, arresting him in front of his wife and three of his five children. Al-Arian was a tenured professor of computer science at the University of Southern Florida (USF). A prominent supporter for the Palestinian cause, he was a founding member of the World and Islam Studies Enterprise, the Islamic Society of America, the Tampa Bay Coalition for Justice and Peace, and the Hillsborough Organization of Progress and Equality. Only weeks after 9/11, Bill O'Reilly railroaded the professor, portraying him as a terrorist at a time when the American public was looking for scapegoats.

Al-Arian was a vocal critic of Israel's illegal occupation of Palestine, an advocate of the Palestinian rights, and a civil liberties activist. The professor met both Presidents Clinton and Bush and attended a White House briefing with Karl Rove. He assiduously worked with local and federal governments, and frequently, as Alexander Cockburn notes, he presented to "intelligence and military commanders at MacDill AFB's Central Command, inviting the FBI and other officials to attend meetings of his groups."[1] Ironically, al-Arian lobbied Congress to repeal legislation permitting the use of secret evidence (H.R. 2121). The impetus for this campaign was the illegal incarceration of Mazen al-Najjar, his brother-in-law and an instructor of Arabic at USF, who was held on secret evidence but never charged.

Under surveillance for ten years, the Justice Department accused al-Arian of being the chief of North American operations for the Palestinian Islamic Jihad (PIJ). While Janet Reno harassed him and al-Najjar throughout the 1990s, she yielded to constitutional law when the secret evidence legislation was repealed. John Ashcroft, on the other hand, personally made al-Arian a priority target after 9/11. He appeared on national television the day of the professor's arrest, announcing a fifty-count indictment, which included alleged plans for terrorist attacks in the United States and Israel. His six-month trial was preceded by a brutal two-year incarceration in solitary confinement, which cost the government 50 million dollars. Nauseating details of the trial include an obscenely pro-prosecution judge; the use of 200 out of 21,000 hours of 470, 000 wire-tapped conversations, which were initially withheld from the defense; admission of circumstantial "evidence" that implied guilt by association; and a battery of prejudicial witnesses including a score of Israeli intelligence agents. In the end, al-Arian, along with his two co-defendants, were acquitted on eight of the counts. The jury deadlocked 10-2 in favor of the defendants on the remaining nine counts. Despite the trial's obvious political motivations and the overwhelming consensus on the defendant's innocence, the US Attorney vowed to retry the professor.

The emotional and financial strain on his family compelled al-Arian to accept a plea. He pleaded to one count of conspiracy that he had contact with people "associated" with PIJ. Equally absurd, he admitted to hiring an attorney for his brother-in-law when detained on secret evidence. In other words, al-Arian secured counsel for a defendant who was never charged let alone convicted of any criminal wrongdoing. The plea recommended the minimum sentence including time served, at the end of which the defendant would be deported. During sentencing, however, Judge James Moody confirmed he presided over a kangaroo-court, by accusing al-Arian of having "blood on his hands," despite that the all evidence points to the contrary and, in turn, assigned him the maximum sentence.

Amnesty International has protested that the conditions of the professor's detention are "harsh and punitive," where prison guards and officials have subjected him to racist harassment, deprivations, and physical intimidation. In the meantime, Islamophobic federal prosecutor, Gordon Kromberg, subpoenaed al-Arian three times to testify in front of a Virginia Grand Jury investigating a Muslim philanthropic organization.[2] The professor refused each time because the request violated the government's "non-cooperation agreement." After a sixty-day hunger strike in 2007, al-Arian commenced another hunger-strike in March 2008 protesting Kromberg's reconstituting a third Grand Jury on the eve of his release in April. In the words of John Turley, the lead-counsel for al-Arian, "Having lost the case in Florida, the Justice Department has openly sought to extend his confinement by daisy-chaining grand juries."[3] The professor was granted bond three months after serving his sentence, but still was not released and kept in harsh conditions until he was returned to a prison in Virginia for his hearing regarding the grand jury subpoena.

On the academic front, Judy Genshaft, USF President and political aspirant, summarily revoked Prof. al-Arian's tenure, with utter disregard for any due process.[4] Genshaft took no precautions to defend al-Arian when death threats poured into the University after his dragooning by O'Reilly. Instead she summarily ignored procedure, wrongfully terminated al-Arian, and berated him despite the protestations of the American Association of University Professors. Likewise, Dick Beard, Chairman of USF's Board of Trustees, called al-Arian a "terrorist" and "cancer," thereby ceding his right to fair arbitration.[5] Jeb Bush appointed Beard and much of the Board and is suspected to have pushed the Department of Justice to move against al-Arian.

Throughout the whole ordeal, much of the local and national media, from the *Tampa Tribune* to *Newsweek* to *The O'Reilly Factor*, whipped Americans into a frenzy. Several hundred articles have appeared about al-Arian's case, confusing allegation with fact and demonizing al-Arian even after he was acquitted. In fact, some articles insinuated that his plea was an admission of guilt despite the overwhelming evidence to the contrary.[6] Prof. al-Arian's case exemplifies how the United States virtually institutionalized a pre-existing culture of intimidation towards vocal opponents of Israel and US Middle East policy. Persecution of pro-Palestinian activists and academics has existed for decades.[6] However, since 9/11, the state, sensationalist media, and Democrat and Republican apparatchiks have formed a nexus with pro-Israel and evangelical advocacy groups, student organizations, and right-wing think tanks and their failed and opportunistic academics in order to create a palatable environment of intimidation in the United States for pro-Palestinian activists and scholars. The harassment is not limited to Arab and Muslim academics, activists, and students, but the "culture of repression" is felt most strongly in Arab and Muslim American communities.

Sami al-Arian's story is emblematic of the pressure felt by both community members and academics. His persecution preceded 9/11, when the Justice Department hunted, accused, and then vindicated him of subversive activities in the 1990s. The exoneration only encouraged the US Attorney's Office and the FBI to continue tapping his family's phones and keeping them under constant surveillance. In fact, the more his public persona and political activism seemed genuine, the more the government, media, and advocacy groups portrayed him as a terrorist sleeper in masterful disguise. In the age of the "war on terror," the nexus between the highest echelons of the government, lobbyists, and advocacy groups, think tanks and their "experts," and the media is emblazoned in al-Arian's case. Previously, President Bush used the professor's credibility to court Muslim-Floridians in the 2000 elections. But after 9/11, he turned al-Arian into a boogieman in order to establish precedence for violating activists' and academics' civil rights.

Along with the McCarthyite tactics of Bill O'Reilly, the media rode roughshod over al-Arian's civil liberties by breaching the presumption of innocence, convicting him in the public eye, willfully ignoring his acquittal, and spinning the deadlocked jury and plea into a guilty-verdict. Neoconservative and Zionist advocacy groups, "experts," and websites (from David Horowitz's Freedom Center and Daniel Pipes' Middle East Forum to the *National Review*, Heritage Foundation, and *Militant Islam Monitor*) dedicated their energies and endless resources to making al-Arian a model. While all of these actors may act independently of one another, the sum total of these institutions, activists, and organizations established with the White House and legislators an atmosphere of implicit intimidation if not outright repression. This climate has been effective in the Arab, Muslim, and academic communities in dampening if not stemming vocal dissent regarding the US "war on terror," the occupation of Iraq and Afghanistan, and Israel's brutality to Palestinians.

A National Culture of Repression: Controlling Middle Eastern Studies

Arab-Americans and legal Arab immigrants have lived under siege in the United States for decades. In addition to planning a hijacking, the Jewish Defense League threatened, attacked, vandalized, and bombed Arab-American activists, politicians, and organizations throughout the seventies, eighties, and nineties.[8] They terrorized mosques, planted a bomb at the office of nominal Arab American congressman Darryl Issa, and murdered Arab American activist Alex Odeh in 1985. After 9/11, Human Rights Watch noted that anti-Arab hate crimes spiked 1700 percent, transpiring against the backdrop of a barrage of excoriating commentaries and opinion pieces that mushroomed throughout national and local media.[9] Few challenged statements like those by radio host Michael Savage who vilified Arabs as "non-human," "racist, fascist bigots" that deserve to be nuked.[10]

At the same time, 5,000 legally-documented Arab and Muslims were interned, most without charge. Many were held and tried in secret, deported, or subjected to the torture tactics employed in so-called "extraordinary rendition" operations. The Bush Administration also implemented a "special registration" regime for 80,000 Arabs and Muslims legally residing in the United States.[11] If this were not intimidating enough, government officials, US representatives, and mainstream media figures still justify racial profiling and mass internment as solutions to "Muslim terror." Peter Kirsanow of the US Commission on Civil Rights (USCCR) publicly threatened Arab-American leaders, saying no one "will be crying in their beer" about detaining Arab Americans *en masse* if further attacks occur on US soil.[12] Similarly, Michelle Milkan's frightening *In Defense of Internment* brashly advocates incarcerating Arab Americans.[13] The calls for internment seem credible when Halliburton announced on January 24, 2006 that Homeland Security contracted KBR to build new "detentions centers" in order "to support the rapid development of new programs."[14] If the threat of mass detention seems fantastic to mainstream America, only cursory attention uncovers the prevalent racist discourse that portrays Muslim and Arab Americans as a subversive fifth-column.[15]

As Professor Arian's case demonstrates, Arab and Muslim academics feel most acutely the national culture of repression. Many of the academics who experienced professional pressures, intimidation, death threats, tenure troubles, hiring-controversies, and denial of visas are a part of the Arab and Muslim American communities. Among these prominent academics are Nadia Abu el-Hajj, M. Shahid Alam, Kevin Barrett, Beshara Doumani, Hamid Dabashi, Rashid Khalidi, Saree Makdisi, Joseph Massad, Ali Mazrui, Aminah Beverley McCloud, and Wadie Said. Likewise, political interest groups, the media, and the government have publicly targeted scholars of Middle Eastern Studies.

This persecution had started some time ago, even before the American Council of Trustees and Alumni (ACTA) was founded in 1995 by Lynn Cheney, notorious hawk Joseph Lieberman, right-wing Zionist Saul Bellow, and neoconservative former-senator Hank Brown, the University of Colorado president who wrongfully terminated Ward Churchill. ACTA proclaims that "the threat to academic freedom comes from within. The barbarians are not at the gates; they are inside the walls."[16] This coded form of speech is intended to regulate, if not suppress, critical scholarship and inquiry within the Academy that might confront US foreign policy, if not the very assumptions of American white supremacist culture. After 9/11, pro-Israel politicians, pseudo-academics, lobbyists, and advocacy groups found fertile ground within this culture. An array of advocacy groups and politicians joined ACTA in hopes of controlling Middle Eastern Studies, and endorsed the International Studies in Higher Education Act, co-sponsored by Congressman Patrick Tiberi and thirteen other representatives from both parties.

H.R. 509 was the reconstituted version of H.R. 3077, authored in 2003 by right-wing vampire Peter Hoekstra, and introduced to the House on the second anniversary of 9/11. The legislation was intended as an "amendment" to Title VI of the Higher Education Act of 1965, which federally funds area studies programs. Title VI not only funds area studies research centers but also provides fellowships to hundreds of students who will become academics, professionals, and government functionaries. H.R. 3077 was promptly passed by the House and referred to the Senate. It withered on the vine after being forwarded to the Committee on Health, Education, Labor, and Pensions on Oct. 13, 2003. The legislation reappeared with Tiberi's H.R. 509, which was amended in June 16, 2006 in the Subcommittee on Select Education and forwarded to the House Committee Education and the Workforce, where it now is dormant.[17]

The legislation is really intended to recalibrate Middle Eastern Studies. In the words of Tiberi, the bill would "encourage institutions of higher education to be more responsive" to today's "global climate." Furthermore, "the bill also clarifies that programs under Title VI of the Higher Education Act are to support and coordinate with other federal programs in the areas of foreign language, area studies, and international business." In doing so, the legislation intends to produce the "next generation" of specialists "who can provide assistance to the government and the private sector."[18]

Apart from its utilitarian, corporatist, and political vision of Middle Eastern Studies, this legislation occupies new ground in the state's desire to control the academy, particularly scholarship and critical inquiry in the classroom among faculty and students who study the Middle East. Its authors do not hide a desire to micromanage area studies, including forming an Advisory Board that will advise the Secretary of Education and Congress "with respect to the needs for expertise in government, the private sector, and education in order to enhance America's understanding of, and engagement in, the world." The Board will "make recommendations...that will reflect diverse perspectives and the full ranges of views on world regions, foreign languages, and international affairs."[19] The Board is a political crucible consisting of three appointees by the Education Secretary, two by the House and two by the Senate. Two of seven must represent "federal agencies that have national security responsibilities."[20] Consequently, they are "authorized to study, monitor, apprise, and evaluate a sample of activities supported under this title in order to provide recommendations to the Secretary and the Congress for the improvement of programs under the title and to ensure programs meet the purposes of the title."[21]

While the Board is accountable to no one, the corporatist language of quality-control is the means by which Congress, the Secretary of Education, Homeland Security, political advocacy groups, and lobbyists gain leverage over academics' research, students, and classes. The Board can threaten to revoke an institution's Title VI status and funding if the center does not represent a "balanced" view, namely, give equal time to the American and Israeli official version of policy and history.

H.R. 509 also stipulates that the recipient program must give "recruiters of the United States Government and agencies access to students and student information... for the purpose of recruiting for graduate opportunities or prospective employment."[22] If the recipient university does not comply with the Advisory Board's interpretation of Title VI mission, its status will be revoked. Most major professional associations in the field, including the mammoth Modern Language Association, the American Association of University Professors (AAUP), and the Middle Eastern Studies Association (MESA) have criticized this legislation as "it conceals a political agenda behind a concern for efficiency."[23]

H.R. 509 and 3077 work in concert with other legislation to manage free speech, critical classroom inquiry, and objective research on the Middle East. The "Uniting and Strengthening America by Providing Appropriate Tools Required to Intercept and Obstruct Terrorism Act," or the "USA PATRIOT Act" targets Arab and Muslim scholars of the Middle East. Section 411 allows the government to deport foreign nationals with legal status (including permanent residents) in the United States, on the basis of "association" with organizations alleged to have ties with "terrorism." In its most high-profile use, the Bush administration used the provision to deny Tariq Ramadan a visa. The grandson of Hassan Banna, the founder of the Muslim Brotherhood, Ramadan is a Swiss-born scholar of Islamic Studies and public intellectual. While his most prominent work focuses on Muslims in Europe, he has written articles critical of Israel, the US occupation of Iraq, the use of torture, secret CIA prisons, and "other government actions that undermine fundamental civil liberties." He accepted a chaired position at the University of Notre Dame when the State Department revoked his visa on the basis that he had donated "$940 to two humanitarian organizations (a French group and its Swiss chapter) serving the Palestinian people."[24] The US Attorney's office also invoked Section 411 to prosecute a thirty-four-year-old Saudi doctoral candidate at the University of Idaho. Sami Omar al-Hussayen, a father of three, volunteered to be a webmaster for several Muslim websites, some of which praised suicide operations in Israel and Chechnya.[25] Federal prosecutors provided no evidence that Hussayen supported or even advocated violence abroad or in the United States. A jury in Idaho acquitted him. Like al-Najjar, he remained in prison and then was deported despite his legal immigration status.

Like the USA PATRIOT Act, the REAL ID Act of 2005 permits the federal government to deport or deny asylum to anyone who is a member of, provides "material support for," "endorses," or associates with any members or supporters of groups that are deemed by the United States to be linked to "terrorist-related activity."[26] Amnesty International notes that "Section 103 would make a person deportable unless he or she can show by clear and convincing evidence "that he or she did *not* know that the group they were supporting was involved in broadly defined terrorist activities." This sort of legislation reverses "innocent until proven guilty" by placing the onus of innocence on the accused, but also it puts scholars who study political groups in the Middle East at particular risk. More specifically directed at scholars, the "Violent Radicalization and Homegrown Terrorism Prevention Act," passing the House with only six-dissenting votes, proposes a campus-based "center for excellence" to root out "extremism." It promises to "bring the war on terrorism home" against "home grown terrorism" and "ideologically based violence." Rand Corporation employee and terror-baiter Brian Jenkins authored the bill, which *overtly* aspires to squelch civil disobedience and social justice activism on and off the campus, such as committed by Muslim student groups, alter-globalization organizations, environmentalists, and anarchists.[27]

National and state legislation has established an atmosphere whereby academics and activists, especially non-citizens, censor their speech and protestations, self-restrict their public actions, and take overly diligent caution with whom they associate. The government publicly demonstrates the will to hound academics who dare to make their criticism of US policy in the Middle East heard in the mainstream. The atmosphere has effectively muted those Arab and Muslim academics, most notably junior scholars and those who are who are legal immigrants, permanent residents, or naturalized citizens.

Coordinating an Atmosphere of Fear

The persecution of scholars started with the ascendance of Edward Said to a position of visibility within mainstream American media and politics in the 1980s. Said was called the "professor of terror" and various racial epitaphs in the 1980s and 1990s in the national and New York press. This seems benign compared to the firebombing of his Columbia University office in 1985 or JDL's plans to murder him and Rashid Khalidi in 1990.[28] The shock troops of this offensive portray scholars of the Middle East as unpatriotic, anti-Semitic radical leftists, and terrorist sympathizers virtually in league with al-Qa'idah. Rogue scholars like Martin Kramer, Fouad Ajami, and Bernard Lewis, as well as Islamophobic political hacks like David Horowitz, Daniel Pipes, and Robert Spencer have accused scholars of the Middle East of apologizing for "radical Islam," if not "enabling" extremism itself.[29] A substantial amount of commentaries and articles have already exposed these critics as the demagogues and racists they are. Several good taxonomies of the erosion of academic free speech as well as the "siege" of Middle Eastern Studies have been written. The studies by Beshara Doumani, Joel Beinin, and Zachary Lochman, president of MESA, are noteworthy because of their own prominence in the field.[30]

As the leading professional association on the Middle East in the world, MESA is the prime target of attacks. As such, it has strongly defended the academic freedom of its members and given visibility to the plight of many colleagues in Middle Eastern Studies.[31] Likewise, the AAUP has vocally denounced national legislation that clearly aims at regulating Middle Eastern studies if not spying on its faculty.[32] In this regard, the siege of Middle East studies and its faculty has been an overt concern within the academy. The forms of attacks on academics range from harassment, disrupting or sabotaging hiring and tenure processes, death-threats, and class-disruptions to surveillance, cancellation of talks and retraction of invitations to speak, and visa denials for academics outside the United States. Much of this harassment comes from outside the university, motivated by McCarthy-like campaigns conducted by advocacy groups and extremist activists.

The most vociferous of these perpetrators are the David Project, Middle East Forum's Campus Watch, *Frontpage Magazine*, the Bruin Alumni Association, Stand With Us, Israel on Campus Coalition, and Scholars for Peace in the Middle East. Among the tactics of these extra-mural organizations is to initiate hatchet jobs on their targets by cross-posting inflammatory articles on a network of websites, which eventually seep into mainstream media. These hacks impugn the scholarship of their mark, use incendiary language, misquote and take statements out of context, or just fabricate evidence. Upon this corpus of accusatory articles and lists such as "the Dirty Thirty" or "101 Most Dangerous Professors," the architects of these campaigns cajole and intimidate the respective universities to take disciplinary action against their mark. They lobby alumni and donors to use their leverage to intervene in university academic processes such as hiring or tenure procedures. Or, they threaten institutions with boycotts and legal action if invitations and hires are not retracted.

Many have commented on the most high-profile cases such the disciplinary actions brought against al-Arian, Ward Churchill, and Joseph Massad; the visa cancellation of Ramadan; the protestations against Columbia's recruiting al-Khalidi; the hiring sabotage against Wadie Said at Wayne State University and Juan Cole at Yale; and the anti-tenure campaigns against Norman Finkelstein at DePaul or Nadia Abu el-Haj at Barnard. Full scale assaults on academics critical of Israel include but are not limited to Hamid Dabashi and Gil Avijar at Columbia; DePaul's Aminah Beverley McCloud, SUNY Binghamton's Ali Mazrui; Shahid Alam at Northeastern; Berkeley's Snehal Shingavi; Mark Levine at UC Irvine; Juan Cole at Michigan; John Esposito at Georgetown; and Sari Makdisi, Sondra Hale, and Gabriel Piterberg at UCLA. The lesser prominent but equally egregious attacks on faculty throughout the United States are too numerous to recount but exemplified by campaigns against those like Kevin Barret at Wisconsin, Hatem Bazian at UC Berkeley, Brandeis' Natana Delong-Bas, and Douglas Giles at Roosevelt University.[33]

In addition to direct slander campaigns, Zionist and neoconservative advocacy groups and activists pressure universities to boycott academics, artists, activists, and politicians who publicly criticize Israeli policies. Both Desmond Tutu and Hanan Ashrawi were uninvited to speak at University of St. Thomas and the University of Colorado, respectively. John Meirshemer and Stephen Walt, authors of the well-publicized article criticizing the pro-Israel lobby, were uninvited to the Chicago Council on Global Affairs.[34] Similarly, talks by Tony Judt, Professor of European Studies at New York University, were cancelled at the Polish Consulate in New York City and Manhattan College because the Anti-Defamation League (ADL) and the American Jewish Committee protested. Judt, who served in the Israeli military, has since become a vocal critic of the state and, in a courageous article in the *New York Review of Books,* called for a bi-national state.[35]

One should not be tempted to blame the current witch hunts, kangaroo trials, and slander campaigns exclusively on fanatic ideologues, activists, lobbying organizations, and advocacy groups. The Departments of Justice, State, Homeland Security, and Education have been proactive in impeding the ability of scholars to speak, teach, and research on the Middle East. The most vulnerable scholars, as I have noted, are those of Arab and/or Muslim origin and who are foreign nationals. As in the case of Tariq Ramadan, the State Department has complicated or sabotaged the academic visits or appointments of several Muslim scholars. San Francisco State Arabic professor Muhammad Ramadan Hasan Salama was denied re-entry into the United States when he traveled to Toronto to renew and upgrade his initial visa. After three months and much protestation, he was allowed re-entry.[36] While Salama's plight is one clearly based on racism, other Arab and Muslim academics who have been banned include vocal critics such as South African scholar Adam Habib and Dr. Riyad Lutfa. Habib, was on his way to the National Institute of Health, the Center for Disease Control, and the World Bank. A vocal opponent of the United States war in Iraq, he was accused of having terrorist links, detained upon entry in New York and deported.[37] Similarly, Dr. Lutfa, a highly regarded epidemiologist, was denied a visa after publishing an article that asserted more than 650,000 Iraqis have been killed since the US "liberation" of their nation.[38]

The nexus between the advocacy groups, media, university administrations, and the government is most apparent in the cases of Massad and al-Arian. Massad was an easy target. A former student of Edward Said, he remains critical of the United States, Israel, and the Palestinian Authority. His class was kept under surveillance by the David Project, a right-wing Zionist organization committed to the suppression of any speech and scholarship critical of Israel. The David Project *squadristi* fabricated testimony asserting that Massad is an anti-Semitic opponent of Israel, who misrepresents historical fact and indoctrinates students. While Columbia initiated a highly publicized inquiry, Massad, along with others in his department, received tens of thousands of angry emails, menacing letters, and verbal threats. He was harassed by students and faculty. Dr. Moshe Rubin in Columbia's Medical Center, told Massad to "get the hell out of America you are a disgrace and a pathetic typical arab liar (sic)." Zionist extremists stole his identity and sent out terrorist threats in his name to the White House and Congress.[39] In the meantime, Congressman Anthony Weiner demanded Massad be fired and the New York City Council threatened to conduct its own investigation into the professor and his department. The campaign against those like Massad and al-Arian demonstrates the confluence of interests if not concerted efforts of pro-Israel advocacy groups, their zealot adherents, government officials, and the mainstream media from *The New York Times* to *The Village Voice*.

Manuals of Repression

The theory of a concerted effort to suppress critical views regarding Israel and the US Middle East policy is not conspiratorial but rather understands that government officials and agencies, the media, and political action groups share a common desire to suppress dissent to advance their own particular agendas. The explicit programs, projects, advice, and plans of pro-Israel advocacy groups demonstrate how universities are interwoven with these interest groups, state agencies, and media. These Zionist, largely but not exclusively Jewish, organizations deployed students as the foot soldiers in their campaigns of surveillance and control. They provide funds for the student activism and scholarships to attend workshops in Washington and Israel. More insidiously, they disseminate manuals, guides, and play books by which to propagate a "pro-Israel agenda" and monitor "anti-Israel" activism and speech on campus.[40]

Much has been made of David Horowitz's nakedly fascistic campaigns against Arab and Muslim faculty, students, and organizations. Yet Horowitz is little more than a petty-facilitator, creating events and pretexts around which Zionist and right-wing organizations like the brown-shirt Young America's Foundation can rally. Organizations like the American Israel Public Affairs Committee (AIPAC) run campus "training programs," workshops, and summer training camps, where "You can affect Israel's future and promote America's interests in the Middle East from your campus." These camps and workshops send students for "ten-day missions" to Israel, and network students with members of Congress in order to assist them to "define the debate" and "affect the opinion climate on campus."[41]

The relationship between student groups and these advocacy groups, PACS, "centers," and think tanks is no secret. The latter cultivate "boots on the ground" to overtly push a pro-Israel agenda within federal government and on colleges campuses. These boots are encouraged to monitor if not intimidate scholars and students that they deem "anti-Israel." The coordination between the Israeli government and these organizations, institutes, and student groups is immediately apparent at even a cursory look at these organizations websites. For example, the Israel on Campus Coalition is comprised of powerful organizations including Hillel, the Zionist Organization of America (ZOA), AIPAC, and the ADL, and funded by the deep pockets of the Charles and Lynn Schusterman Center. It draws right-wing extremists American-Israeli Cooperative Enterprise and Hamagshamim with liberal groups like Peace Now. The Coalition proudly advertises its relationship with the Israeli state and embassy in coordinating its activities. Among its campus pogroms, it published a thinly veiled threat, *Tenured or Tenuous: Defining the Role of Faculty in Supporting Israel on Campus*, which states: "This publication raises disturbing issues relating to the state of Israel studies, the prevalence of anti-Israel faculty, the relative dearth of pro-Israel scholars on campus, and the resulting impact on education about Israel and the campus environment." The booklet provides "tangible suggestions for how faculty can support pro-Israel students and proposals for proactive initiatives aimed at promoting pro-Israel scholarship on campus."[42]

The manual advises student groups, like-minded university faculty, and concerned citizens to "maintain control" of university hiring processes, thereby "vetoing" the hire of "hostile professors."[43] The booklet is a guide to manage the Zionist-Palestinian debate and to fortify pro-Israel elements and allies within the university, media, and electorate. This is achieved through cultivating the university administration, pressuring elected representatives to "reform" the Higher Education Act, insisting that "the Israeli perspective" is represented in every Middle East Studies course, and inundating the campus with Israeli cultural events and visiting scholars. Zionist students, faculty alumni, and donors are directed to "strengthen" the relationship between US universities and Israel by sending student, administrative, and faculty missions to Israel, increase study abroad programs, and encourage joint research programs and enterprises with Israeli universities and businesses. Within its long-term vision, the manual recommends compiling a database for potential donors and funding sources to create and control chaired positions of Israel Studies. The database will also provide information for funding sources to cultivate young Zionist students so as to create "attractive academic hires," while simultaneously funding to "train current scholars whose specialities [sic] may be in other fields, but who could be taught enough about Middle Eastern affairs to allow them to offer courses through their departments."[44]

Readily available manuals instruct students how ferret out faculty critical of Israel and associate their progressivism with radical Islam. Publications like John Tierney's histrionic *The Politics of Peace: What's Behind the Anti-War Movement* confirm Ellen Schrecker's assertion that Middle East scholars are the target of a new McCarthyism.[45] Tierney states, "peace is a tactical idea for movement organizers: it serves as political leverage against US policymakers, and it is an ideological response to the perceived failures of American society." The "peace movement" is "neo-communist," and its "struggle" against "oppression" and "imperialism" are code words in the lexicon of "revolutionary socialism."[46] In *A Profile of American College Faculty: Political Beliefs and Behavior,* Gary Tobin and Aryeh Weinberg warn that "faculty are ideologically critical of America and business...[They] hold a certain number of beliefs that are pervasive...[including] Criticism of many American foreign and domestic policies; Propensity to blame America for world problems:...A tendency to strongly support international institutions such as the United Nations; Strong opposition to American unilateralism; Criticism of big business; [and] Skepticism about capitalism's ability to help address poverty in developing nations."[47] The authors sound a clarion call that liberal humanist professors are, in fact, radical leftists in disguise who are waging an ideological battle on campus. "Anti-war, anti-Israel, anti-globalization, and anti-business [positions] are all part and parcel of the campus experience...Iraq is the new Vietnam, Israel is the new South Africa, and business is the new global colonizer."[48] When these "political ideologies" are "the norm," their danger is exacerbated because "less religious faculty are more likely to name United States policies as a primary cause for Islamic militancy."[49]

The cause of the misrepresentation is the prevalence of anti-Semitism propagated by progressive faculty and pro-Palestinian student groups, asserts Kenneth Stern, the American Jewish Committee (AJC) specialist on anti-Semitism and "extremism." His book, *Bigotry on Campus: A Planned Response*, relays anecdotal evidence about anti-Semitism incidents, associating criticism of Israel with anti-Jewish hate speech. Again, legitimate Jewish victimization is used to deflect anti-Zionist criticism, asking "how welcome can you feel, as a Jewish student, if the school newspaper claims Zionism is racism and compares present-day Israel to Nazi Germany?"[50] In *Why Campus Anti-Israel Activity Flunks Bigotry 101*, Stern "clarifies" propagandistic "inaccuracies" and "lies" that are perpetuated in the classroom and foster anti-Semitism. "Progressive, anti-Israel groups" ignore the "fact," for example, that the term "Palestinian" was a reference to Jewish presence, not Arab, in pre-1948 Palestine. Biased faculty signal out Israel for atrocities but fail to criticize Muslim governments. Worse, they support "thoroughly corrupt" terrorist organizations such as Islamic Jihad, Hamas, and Hezbollah.[51] Consequently "to be anti-Zionist is, by definition, to be anti-Semitic"; the term "Zionist" is a "code" word "to 'explain' away the defamation of a group," and "divestiture" is by definition a tool of bigotry."[52]

Stern's books are manuals that seek outside assistance to "defend" against anti-Semitic hate-mongers and terrorist faculty. The Committee for Accuracy in Middle East Reporting in America (CAMERA), founded to spin the Israeli invasion of Lebanon in 1982, is a "media-monitoring" organization that publishes a "student-focused magazine" called *CAMERA on Campus*. It instructs students on how to combat "literature," activism, and other "propagandistic assaults" on US campuses that "[create] harmful misperceptions of Israel." CAMERA's website directs students to "monitor" their campuses for "distorted and inaccurate articles" about Israel, to "document campus problems by collecting distorted or incendiary literature distributed on campus," and to counter with the "Israeli version."[53]

CAMERA recruits students and community members to become "activists," encouraging them to make lasting alliances with Christian student organizations and extra-mural political groups. The manual, like Stern's booklets, directs students to "combat anti-Israel action on campus" by drawing in administration and government on their behalf. "The simplest and often most effective way to deal with a persistent hostile environment at your school is to lodge a complaint with school administration officials and explore solutions with them."[54] Strategies range from networking with university officials, campus police, the campus newspaper, and other Jewish and non-Jewish groups. Student groups should be proactive in filing complaints with the US Department of Education, US Attorney General's office, local congressional representatives, and state officials. "Effective pro-Israel speakers and programs" should be brought "to campus, at least once each semester to counter anti-Israel messages."[55]

Fighting Back is menacing in its ability to orchestrate an atmosphere of intimidation by intentionally confusing acts of solidarity with the Palestinian cause with truly anti-Semitic acts (such as swastika graffiti on a sukkah).

The Mandible of Power

Slandering anti-Zionist groups, activists, and intellectuals as anti-Semitic is an effective publicity ploy to bait the federal government to intervene on behalf of pro-Israel groups. The tactic is explicit in the aforementioned manuals. The ADL's *Fighting Back: A Handbook for Responding to Anti-Israel Rallies on College and University Campuses* provides advice for how to engineer an Israel-Palestine "debate" that would draw US authorities to pursue "pro-Palestinian" faculty and student groups. The manual is sinister in its ability to speak without naming. While the First Amendment protects distasteful speech at public institutions, "speech that is criminal in nature—such as harassment, threats or intimidation—is not protected by the First Amendment, and is not permitted in society in any context, including on university campuses."

The lesson is clear: if anti-Israel speech is deemed "hateful" and incendiary, the Constitution does not protect it.[56] The manual reassures the reader that "*private* universities have greater leeway than their public counterparts to regulate and even prohibit speech on campus."[57] The manual implicitly guides the reader to understand the conditions under which invited guests to the university can be removed, how to use the university's "student code" as leverage, and how to control or target protests and rallies on campus. Likewise, students are encouraged to reach out to local and national media as well as place "anti-terrorism" ads in newspapers and to hold rallies "calling for the end to terrorism."[58] The optimal goal is more than to discredit, however. Like the ZOA's Center for Law and Justice, the real purpose is to push the federal government to prosecute those who speak against Israel on US campuses. They have been successful most notably in convincing the USCCR to investigate anti-Israel speech on campus.

On November 18, 2005, the government commission convened "a panel of experts" to testify regarding anti-Semitic activity on US college campuses, specifically discriminatory behavior covering activities regarding the Middle East.[59] The panel of "experts" consisted of Gray Tobin (President of the Institute for Jewish and Community Research), Susan Tuchman (Director of the ZOA's Center for Law and Justice), and Sarah Stern (AJC's Director of Governmental and Public Affairs).[60] These organizations, self-promoted as "Israel advocacy groups," are aligned with the most right-wing elements in Israeli political arena, and are dedicated, first and foremost, to the "safety and security of Israel.[61] Groups like the ZOA advocate the annexation of "Samaria and Judea," which they refuse to call the West Bank. They oppose even George Bush's pro-Israel "Road Map" and are suing the State Department for refusing to print "Jerusalem,

Israel" on the passports of US citizens born in (what is otherwise seen as) the indivisible and eternal capital of Palestine.[62]

Squadristi, Cops, and the FBI

In March 2006, Mohammed Reza Taheri-aza, an Iranian-American graduate of UNC-Chapel Hill, drove his SUV into a campus hang-out with the expressed intent to kill Americans because of their government's policies in the Muslim world. No sooner than UNC's Muslim Student Association (MSA) condemned Taheri-aza's deplorable act, anti-Muslim shrieks were insinuating collusion between the suspect and the MSA. MSAs have been targeted in North America for some time. The UNC chapter previously took a visible stance on several controversial issues. They defended the University assigning Michael Sell's book about Islam for its first year reading experience and vocally protested the Danish newspaper *Jyllands-Posten's* publishing of racist cartoons that characterized the Prophet Muhammad as a terrorist.[63] One Islamophobe sums up the hatchet job on the student group: "Whether providing support for terrorist organizations like Hamas, playing a prominent role in the antiwar protests, encouraging divestment from Israel, or defending convicted cop-killers like Imam Jamil al-Amin (formerly known as H. Rap Brown), the MSA promotes an anti-American agenda and a fundamentalist Islamic dogma that seems inappropriate to academic life."[64]

The USCCR launched several investigations of college campuses, targeting MSAs and Palestinian rights student groups. The accusation is that student groups have been infiltrated by "jihadis," who are indoctrinating the "philosophy of martyrdom" into the "heartland of America" and its youth.[65] The aforementioned advocacy groups, PACs, opportunistic politicians, and sensationalist media coalesce as twenty-first century *squadristi*. Like the fascist intellectuals and thugs of the thirties, these activists see a "link" between "foreign and 'home-grown' students and professors to terrorist and/ terror-related activities" in the United States.[66] Students are vulnerable and an easy mark, lacking resources and professional assistance when harassed. The most egregious student witch-hunts have taken place at University of North Carolina, UC Santa Cruz, San Francisco State University, and the University of California at Irvine (UCI). At the behest of the USCCR's report, the Department of Education's Office of Civil Rights (OCR) investigated students at UCI because they wore Palestinian-solidarity t-shirts during a week of protests and teach-ins on Palestine, where speakers allegedly spewed "hate-speech" against "Zionist Jews."

During this event, the FBI admitted to monitoring and harassing the Muslim Student Union (MSU). At the end of the week, Yasser Ahmed drove a pick up onto campus to help dismantle the MSU's mock "separation wall." An FBI agent tailed the student. Seeing he was followed, Ahmad got out of the truck and tried to see in the car's tinted windows. The agent rolled down his windows, announcing himself as a federal agent. Then, in full view of students and campus police, the agent started to push back Ahmed *with his car* before speeding away.[67] While the OCR investigated accusations of anti-Semitism, it did not investigate the FBI's intimidation of Ahmed. The OCR report found no evidence of anti-Semitism at UCI but the Task Force on Anti-Semitism at the UC Irvine reported that "hate-speech" against Jewish students is "unrelenting."[68] The "Task Force" misrepresents itself as "independent" and affiliated with UCI, while in fact it is established by the Orange County Hillel Foundation. Its report summarily convicts the students, faculty, and administration of anti-Semitism, repeating the stance adopted by the USCCR that the freedom to denounce Zionism is a "camouflage" for hate-speech.

Maintaining the threat of government intervention into the Academy is strategic. In California, the Academic Bill of Rights (SB 5) aimed to regulate professors, to "protect students" from "indoctrination," and to provide measures for students to air their "grievances." The bill was narrowly defeated but, compounded by a California AG's Anti-Terrorist Information Center, the atmosphere of governmental and legislative surveillance is established. The FBI and Army Intelligence have actively investigated students, professors, activists and professionals such as lawyers that participate in anti-war and Islam conferences.[69] At the University of Michigan, Rutgers, Ohio State, Georgetown, and Duke, pro-Israeli advocacy groups protested and even filed suits in state court to prevent the National Student Conference on the Palestinian Solidarity Movement. The student organizers of the fifth annual Awdah conference were forced to move the event off the UC Riverside campus because the administration obstructed its organization's from holding the conference at the university. Groups such as Stand with Us, Israel Solidarity Movement, and *Frontpage*'s Lee Kaplan boasted that the move successfully "marginalized" the movement.[70]

Within this environment, universities themselves have become more proactive in suppressing dissent and activism especially among anti-war and pro-Palestine students. When a small group of anti-war students at George Washington University posted a flier that parodied the racism of Horowitz's "Islamo-fascism Week," the campus police beat and arrested one of their members and investigated the seven, while the national media summarily convicted them as provocateurs without trial. Similar crackdowns by campus police on anti-war activities and speech have been seen at Clemson, Pace, Hampton, and Central Florida not to mention the famous "Don't taser me, bro" incident at the University of Florida.[71]

The Chill in the Air

What distinguishes recent academic repression is the degree to which the sustained campaign flows from all corners of the US polity: the government, both ruling parties, the media, the university, advocacy groups, funding sources, and so on. The powerful effect of 9/11 has enabled the ruling elite to further naturalize an Orwellian "newspeak" that equates "freedom" and "balance" with the repression of critical analysis, alternative thinking, and oppositional politics.

But the campaign is not intent on attacking every critical scholar of the Middle East or Arab thinker. This bold-faced crusade of terror would not sit well with the image of a liberal society in which Americans so readily wrap themselves so as to sleep comfortably at night. Rather, the confluent efforts of private interest groups, the media, and the State have established an atmosphere of fear, where only the *threat* of retribution has to exist for repression to be effective. This danger of losing one's job, of being portrayed as a pariah, an anti-Semite, or "terrorist," or even being incarcerated, are compelling motivators for self-censorship and self-surveillance in the academy. The same is true in the Arab and Muslim American communities where the mere possibility of prosecution, harassment, job loss, or deportation functions as a deterrent for public dissent.

Therefore, targeting the faculty of Columbia and UCLA by *squadristi* like the David Project and Campus Watch serves a very poignant function. The coordinated campaign against these two universities serves a complementary function. One university is private, elitist, and East coast, while the other is public, popular, and West coast. By targeting these two complementary universities, those intent on suppressing "anti-Israel" speech send a clear message to universities throughout the country, showing that neither elite Ivy League colleges nor marquee state schools are beyond their reach. The technique has successfully intimidated legions of scholars, especially untenured faculty who have as little job security as they have few resources to battle the relentless determination of pro-Zionist organizations.

Thus, with the disgraceful track record to back him up, Daniel Pipes bragged about the effectiveness of the national campaign to repress dissident speech, research, and activism, stating that the "intervention" of "concerned outsiders" into personnel, hiring, and tenure processes and decisions has begun "the process of redeeming the university." More damning, Pipes smugly boasts that "robust public criticism can keep [tenured faculty] in line by embarrassing them and hurting their credibility."[72] He then provides an inventory of successful espionage, including sabotaging the hiring of Cole and Said, complicating the promotions of Massad and Abu el-Hajj, and disparaging the research and teaching qualifications of Beinin and Barrett.

Success in terminating the contract of or actually charging faculty may be less the goal of the state or advocacy groups than naturalizing the voluntary surrendering of freedoms for "security" in the "war on terror." The cases of Sami al-Arian, Ward Churchill, and Norman Finkelstein only have to serve as high-profile *examples* of what *can* happen if faculty and students dare to speak "truth in the teeth of power."[73]]

This essay is dedicated to Sami al-Arian, Mumia Abu Jamal, Leonard Peltier, Jalil Abdul Muntaqim, David Gilbert, Herman Bell and their six comrades in San Francisco, and the many other political prisoners in US jail for daring to speak, organize, and act for true equality and freedom.

From Colgate to Costa Rica

Critical Reflections on US Academia

Victoria Fontan

More than four years ago, a political earthquake destroyed my professional life. My crime? Uncovering one of the most blatant public secrets of the Bush administration's disastrous occupation of Iraq. My punishment? Ostracism from US academia and, gradually, US territory as a whole.

I am now reputed to be "controversial" at best, or a journalist passing for an academic at worst. I will not be hired by any US institution whatever my effort and commitment, and I have not participated in a US-based international conference for five years. After obsessing about my disgrace for years in the manner of a Post-Traumatic Stress Disorder sufferer, I have come to realize that my marginalization from US academia was the best thing that ever happened to my life and career. For, currently, I no longer live in fear of any person or institution. I analyze what I find in the field without worrying about how my work will be received. I research, publish, and teach what I find valuable and interesting.

In retrospect, my research on the establishment of the Iraqi nationalist insurgency against the US from 2003 onwards has gained recognition, as many claims I made during the early years of the war have by now filtered into common knowledge and public consciousness. I was one of the few to see that Iraq was facing an occupation-based insurgency that was not going to recede through sheer violence and the use of force that the Bush administration's so-called "War on Terror" policies were advocating at the time. I did not know exactly why, but I knew that terrorism was much more, and less, than the US government made it out to be. It is only since I left the US that I have been able to make the necessary connections that debunk most of the government's foreign policy rhetoric on terrorism, such as it began under Bush and continues with the Obama administration (under a different name, but with the same basic militarist mentality).

A majority of Americans now believe that the Iraq war was a mistake, and are supporting the withdrawal procedures orchestrated by President Obama. The failure of the Bush administration in Iraq has been well-established at least since the beginning of Bush's second term in office, commencing in February 2005, and many columnists and pundits have commented on the impact that humiliation has on conflict escalation in that context. More importantly, yesterday's enemies—nationalist insurgent groups—are now US allies in fighting al-Qaeda in Sunni Muslim parts of the country. This strange alliance will likely endure for as long as the Obama administration keeps these newly-found allies on its very expensive payroll and honors its promises.[1]

All in all, my research on the impact of perceived humiliation in conflict escalation in Iraq now seems to be in very good company. My book, *Voices from Post-Saddam Iraq: Living with Terrorism, Insurgency and New Forms of Tyranny*, has even recently come out with a security studies publisher, and is getting good reviews. Yet, the same pundits that have moved with past and present currents of US public opinion on Iraq are now supporting a greater involvement by the US in Afghanistan, somehow disconnecting one conflict from the other, while suppressing any lessons learned from the Iraq debacle. I was vilified in the US for my research in Iraq, but would I also be vilified for my growing reservations about the US increased involvement in Afghanistan?

This essay will expose, to the best of my recollection, how my research, teaching, and writings were repressed by different sources both within and outside my academic institution during the 2003–2004 year, and how this repression led me to move from US academia into a forced exile. My own experience and analysis here concerns the dangers faced by any academics finding themselves at the crossroads between warmongering state politics, polarizing ideologies, and repressive education systems in relation to issues such as foreign policy. Of particular importance will be an illustration of the systemic mechanisms that allow young academics to be flushed out of US universities before being able to prove themselves as scholars and teachers, possible because of weak or non-existent solidarity and support networks. Consequently, I also reflect on structures that could be put in place to enable academic free speech, which might promote greater solidarity among critical or controversial scholars who face repression in their academic work.

Uncovering a Public Secret

I was raised in a conservative family in Brittany, in the northwest of France. Throughout my childhood, I saw television reports on terrorism as it affected Corsica and the French Basque Country. I also learned that France had a problem at some point in its history with Algeria, and that this was why bomb attacks shook Paris from time to time. All these recurring news stories made me ask what would lead human beings to injure or kill one another. I wanted to know who the individuals behind these attacks were, what motivated them, and how they saw us. If we considered them brutal, heartless, evil people, how did they regard the French? What made them kill innocents? Did they ever start the day, thinking: "Today, I am going to kill as many innocent people as possible?" I just could not bring myself to believe that my reality was necessarily the right one since it stemmed from my "civilized" way of being.

After studying politics at the University of Sussex in the UK, and being exposed to a version of the Algerian War that I would never have been encountered in France, I became interested in the politics of the Arab world. A course on Lebanese politics led me to embark on a doctoral study on peace-building in Lebanon. As soon as I arrived in Beirut in January 2001, I realized the strategic importance of the Hezbollah, known in Lebanon as the Party of God, and, there, considered a political party just like any other. My overall thesis was that, since none of the issues that had plunged the country into a seventeen-year civil war had been resolved, Lebanon—if it was to avoid succumbing to conflict again—would need the commitment of the Hezbollah as a powerful political broker.

My research, it seems, was not too far off the mark. Developments in Lebanon, since the 2006 war, point towards the same conclusion. Intrigued by the role played by the Hezbollah in Lebanese politics and social life, I set out to analyze their public diplomacy, ideas, social following, and so on. Since many colleagues at the American University of Beirut's Centre for Behavioral Research had already made contact with them, I did the same. After all, I was enrolled in an Irish university, and the European Union had not placed the Hezbollah on its terrorist list.[2] I therefore opened the Yellow Pages, looked to the "Political Parties Offices" section, and found the phone number of their press office. As they were used to meeting academic researchers from even the US, they received me. After a few preparatory meetings, they gave me *carte blanche* to contact any of their social institutions for the sake of my research. I therefore spent the next two years carrying out participant observation with many of their institutions, women's groups, girls' summer classes, agricultural development centers, and hospitals. Since Hezbollah's military affairs were not the focal point of my research, however, I never observed any military activities or trainings.

Upon successfully defending my doctoral thesis in Spring 2003, I saw, in the overthrow of Saddam Hussein, the potential for another Hezbollah-type organization to establish itself in a Middle Eastern country, this time in Iraq. As I knew nothing about that country, I asked the Hezbollah Press Office to help me arrange interviews with their Iraqi partners once I reached Baghdad. Both my contacts at Manar Television (the Hezbollah television channel) and the Press Office originally refused, invoking concerns for my security, since the consensus around the media at the time was that hell had broken loose in Baghdad. Upon my insistence, they finally agreed to contact the Beirut representative of their Iraqi partner organization, the Supreme Council for the Islamic Revolution in Iraq (SCIRI). The SCIRI representative in Beirut wrote a letter, in Farsi, for their Baghdad counterpart, saying that they should receive me once I reached Baghdad. I was also given a satellite phone number. Since there was no other type of communication available at the time—including email—this letter was my only hope for establishing contact.

I set off for Baghdad the next day, working as a journalist's researcher to pay for my passage, uncertain of where I would stay or who I would meet, and with this letter for unique direction. As I reached Baghdad fearful of what I was going to find, I ended up in a four-star hotel filled with "war correspondents" lazing around a busy swimming pool. I was surprised to see that Baghdad was not exactly the war zone that these same journalists were portraying in their reports. After a first disappointing meeting at the Baghdad SCIRI Headquarters, where my letter was confiscated and no one seemed to know what was happening, I realized that the SCIRI was not made of the educated, disciplined, rigorous crowd that I had observed in Beirut for the past two years. I knew after a few days that there would be no Iraqi Hezbollah, that the SCIRI was not interested in helping foreign researchers, and that I had to keep my eyes open for alternative research material.

A few days later, our news team arrived in Fallujah. As tensions mounted between US troops and residents because of a shoot-out on April 28, 2003, we witnessed a series of US raids in the following weeks.[3] From my first moment in Fallujah, I realized that what occurred here between occupiers and occupied would be an important part of the post-war equation. I saw burned-out US soldiers facing a crowd of residents, trying to uphold their perception of what constitutes security, while also concerned for their own safety and, more importantly, their individual and collective honor. In fact, both parties were afraid, unaware of one another's codes of conduct and perceptions. In a society where honor and vengeance are of utmost importance, violence was bound to escalate rapidly.

I met with ordinary people who had not been given reparations for the outrages they had suffered, and who decided to resort to violence to avenge their lost honor. In other Sunni Muslim parts of the country, I witnessed the same phenomenon— ordinary people taking up arms, asserting their rights, in the same way, it seemed, that US patriots once stood up against British rule. It was obvious, violent, tragic, and predictable. As I saw this catastrophe unfolding before my eyes, I realized that many journalists were reporting the stories that complied with their pre-set corporate editorial lines, as if the reality on the ground did not matter, as if they were captive to the ideologies they came to Iraq to validate. In their eyes, ordinary people became violent "terrorists," dangerous Islamists whose "fanatical" actions were fueled by their atavistic hatred of the West, freedom, and democracy. I soon realized that the media was not to be relied upon, and that primary research was the only valid course of action to understand what was really happening.

After witnessing many misunderstandings that turned violent, I decided to study the impact of perceived humiliation on conflict escalation in post-Saddam Iraq. I went to several Sunni Muslim parts of the country, interviewed various ordinary people, lived with some of them, and slowly began to come up with an Iraqi-based analysis of conflict escalation.[4] I have always believed that history is comprised of ordinary people, and should be understood as such, devoid of editorial lines, ideologies, state policies, or country alliances. It is people who die, whose lives are shattered and forever altered in times of conflict. I always tell my students that no flag is worth dying for, that compassion is key to the many issues we face as a world today. A compassionate reporting or academic research is not necessarily sympathetic to anyone; it only recognizes that people's lives are at stake, and that it often is their perception, their perceived humiliation in the case of post-Saddam Iraq, that will make them react the way they do.

I was not the only foreigner in Iraq to realize the importance of humiliation in conflict escalation: al-Qaeda also did. In the few months during which some ordinary people organized themselves into nationalist insurgency movements, others answered the calls of Islamic fundamentalism and al-Qaeda. This too was predictable and could have been avoided, had the US not unwittingly set conditions for Iraqis to rebel in the first place.

Throughout the initial months of the invasion of Iraq, the US realized that it was losing the peace, and initiated a propaganda war vilifying both nationalist and al-Qaeda-based movements. Under this framing of the conflict, any attempt—whether in print and media journalism or in academic departments such as political science—to separate the two movements or to understand the underlying factors that spurred violent resistance to US invasion and occupation was deemed "condoning terrorism." Once the US-led "coalition of the willing" decided to administer Iraq by imposing its own values and will apart from any understanding of the culture or conditions of insurgency, my research immediately became controversial and, indeed, was stigmatized as condoning terrorism.[5] As I would soon find out, what was happening to me was unfolding throughout US academia. Bush's "War on Terror," the USA PATRIOT Act, and the manufactured fear pervading society through the compliant and complicit corporate mass media had stifled dissent and labeled critics of Bush's policies as terrorists or traitors. As the isolation of "rogue" scholars intensified, the social pressure for conformity on the part of the rest of academia became a matter of survival for most.

Becoming "Subversive"

As I completed my first academic article on the escalation of violence in Fallujah, I was invited to the US to speak at various east coast universities in the Spring of 2004, among them the United States Military Academy at West Point and Colgate University. After a very successful intervention at West Point, I arrived at Colgate to make a presentation that turned into an interview for the position of Visiting Assistant Professor of Peace Studies for the following academic year. The overall findings that I presented during this lecture tour were very well received, both in Peace Studies and Military Studies contexts. At Westpoint, I showed a beheading video that I had purchased in Fallujah only a few months before, warning that this gruesome practice would be coming to Iraq if the US continued to humiliate its population. Less than a month later, American businessman Nicolas Berg was brutally murdered in the same manner.

At Wellesley, I emphasized how Iraqi women's rights were receding to a pre-Saddam Hussein era. A few months later, US pro-consul Paul Bremer traded away women's rights for Ayatollah Sistani's public support of the January 2005 elections.[6] Shortly thereafter, women were subjected to repressive *Sharia* law, which demands intense repression and subjugation of women to the rule of religion and men. A producer from the PBS show, *Frontline*, even enquired about making a documentary about the impact of humiliation on post-Saddam Iraq.[7]

Since no one objected to my findings, I was not initially alarmed about a political backlash. If anything, I looked forward to being a US-based academic engaging in a healthy dialogue with my peers on the Iraq war. Little did I know that I had only been preaching to the converted, and that, in the US, I would encounter fierce resistance to my theories, as well as bitter personal and political attacks. After a semester at Colgate University, I went to Iraq during the Christmas break to continue research and, early in the Spring semester, in January 2005, my life was turned upside down.

One morning, the Colgate University Press Office issued a statement that I had been "embedded" with the Iraqi insurgency during the semester break.[8] I had been talking with the Press Office for a while, and we had agreed that my time in Iraq would bring positive exposure to the university. Indeed, what an exposure it eventually was! The press release circulated at a time when the official Bush administration line was that all insurgent activities in post-Saddam Iraq were terrorist activities.

Had I been "embedded" with "terrorists"? Absolutely not. I had only met with local Iraqi people who either had engaged or were going to take part in insurgent activities as a result of a perceived individual or collective humiliation. In some parts of Iraq, this meant a lot of people. From where did the term "embedded" emanate? In my conversations with the Press Office, my contact and I informally discussed that my research and engagement in Iraq with families and citizens could be misconstrued as being "embedded with the enemy." "Embedded" is a loaded term, but, for reasons I still do not understand, the Colgate Press Office used it to describe my research. As soon as I read their statement, I made it very clear that I had never been "embedded" with groups planning or carrying out insurgent activity. I had only met with regular Iraqis, and never with al-Qaeda or any organization of this type. However, the damage was done, and my fate was sealed.

Barely a few days passed before angry e-mails flooded the Colgate Press Office. Then neo-conservative forums began to demonize my research. The California-based blog, *Little Green Footballs*, falsely reported that I was "negotiating to be embedded with the car-bombing, head-chopping *mujahideen* in Iraq." Reader comments ranged from calling me "Rachel Corrie's soul sister" to "useful idiot."[9] Once my office phone number was posted on the *Little Green Footballs* blog, I received a torrent of abusive messages. As readers became increasingly polarized against my research, their posts called for me to be beheaded in the same way that *The Wall Street Journal* correspondent Daniel Pearl had been, to die in a car bomb, to be abducted, and so on.[10] Other blogs raised the stakes by enjoining US soldiers to kill me when I returned to Iraq, urging that I be hanged for treason, or implying that I was a Nazi sympathizer.[11]

A few days later, a new blog appeared featuring a fake interview with me claiming that I had engaged in embedded research with KKK "freedom fighters" and that "if we would only listen, they wouldn't have to resort to lynching."[12] As grotesque as this assertion might seem, it did not look far off the mark to a colleague who asked if I had ever been in Chicago and spoken those words. By then, the Colgate Press Office was bombarded with angry e-mails from the public and from veteran alumni who threatened to cut off their donations to the university.[13] This prompted a panicked Press Office to publish a new release correcting the previous one that incorrectly described me as being "embedded" with the Iraqi insurgency.

At this stage, *Fox News* had taken interest in the controversy and wanted me to do an interview with Bill O'Reilly. I accepted at first, ready to defend my research and choices, but then received an e-mail from a Colgate administrator discouraging me from appearing on the program. Then it was another colleague's turn at a pep talk, as she expressed worry that O'Reilly would "humiliate" me. She informed me that the conservative e-magazine, *FrontPage*, had inquired about me, and confessed: "[David] Horowitz is after you, I am terrified."

A few colleagues comforted me in private, and I will always be grateful to them for this. In public, however, it was an earlier West Point colleague, Professor Scott Silverstone, who alone defended my research, by saying that it was extremely useful to the cadets and that I was "doing a valuable academic and, more broadly, policy service."[14] Without his support, I do not know what would have immediately happened to my visiting professor contract. Where was the healthy academic dialogue I had so naively looked forward to before my arrival in the US? A friend told me once that in the US, the land of opportunity, one's fortune could change from one day to the next, and I was indeed dizzy from the rapid turn of events.

Another blow came from a first-year student asking for help in becoming a journalist. His name was Mark Bello. As I wanted to mentor and help students in any way possible in my last few months at Colgate, I gave him two afternoons of my time during which I exposed him to the life of a journalist. I told him about how I had gotten to where I was academically, what I had witnessed in Iraq while shadowing Robert Fisk, and gave him some pointers on how to succeed as a journalist. I did not hear from him for a few weeks, until his interview "notes" appeared on a Colgate conservative student website.[15] The students running the site were engaged in a dispute with the university administration over its selling of chapter houses, and used me in their goal to discredit the university in any possible way.[16]

By the look of it, this student's shot at journalism makes him a prime candidate to work for a tabloid newspaper. The "notes," published under the title "Fontan in Iraq," were exaggerated, distorted, and often outright false. Sadly, they are still available online for anyone to read. While Bello states that I met with the wife of Abu Musab Zarqawi while in Jordan, I actually said that my newspaper's fixer in Jordan, Mayada al-Askari, had met her as CNN was looking to interview her.[17] Where he states that I "brag" about my Hezbollah ties, I simply said that I carried out participant observation with their social outlets in Beirut, an activity that many other PhD students were engaged in at the same time.[18]

A few weeks after this interview was posted, as I prepared to leave the US for Iraq, I received an e-mail from one of my academic referees, telling me that she no longer could act on my behalf since she could not write "unambiguous" letters about my scholarship. That is when I realized that the manufactured "hysteria" whipped up around Bush's "war on terror" and the demonization of dissent unfolding throughout society as a whole would cost me an academic career in the US. I pressed along with my "exile" from US academia and left the country, less than one year after my arrival, less than impressed with the celebrated "academic freedom" that US professors allegedly enjoy.

The Importance of Building Networks

Reflecting on those events and the reactions that I now get when asked about this painful period of my life and career, I realize that what I lacked was a strong network of advisers and supporters. While conservative blogs seized on the ambiguous Colgate press release and spread it like wildfire, I had no support or solidarity from any public organization, network, or group of individuals. No academic left-wing or liberal network was there to systematically pick up on every new case, as the conservative side did so well from their point of view. No one was organized for my defense. That is when I realized that the so-called "War on Terror" had thoroughly intimidated and decimated progressive academics and the US left.

The mistake I made when moving to the US was to expect an anti-Vietnam type of campaigning in academic institutions throughout the country, but the political energies of the 1960s were nowhere to be found during the Bush Administration years. There was no general interest, no accurate reporting on what was really occurring in Iraq. Something was missing from the Vietnam equation. Maybe the American youth was not as involved with massively denouncing the Iraq war because there was no more draft? In terms of faculty-based networks, no organization noticed anything related to my disgrace. Was it because my research was not high-profile enough? Because I was not tenured? Because I was a foreigner? After all, several US journalists had embedded themselves with the insurgency while the controversy was developing around my research, and nothing happened to them.[19] Some reasons can be put forward in connection to this at several levels.

First, as some of my colleagues' reactions at Colgate illustrate, many academics are terrified to be pilloried as I was, and hence seemed to keep a low profile. Very few were the colleagues who checked in with me on a daily basis to give me advice, express their support, or simply to see how I was holding up. Professor Jennifer Loewenstein, from the University of Wisconsin at Madison, who was exposed to far more vilification than I, called me almost every day, as did Robert Fisk, for whom I had worked as a researcher.

Second, the fact that I was not tenured did not raise many eyebrows. My e-lynching occurred at the same time as the Ward Churchill case. Had a critical mass of academics come together as a united front to defend Ward, me, and numerous others, it could have launched a debate on how common academic repression actually is. By approaching these injustices on a case-by-case basis, however, no sense of *collective and systemic* repression of scholars was allowed to emerge. This grave oversight, which thankfully is being corrected by this book, meant that many young scholars have been flushed out of US academia without a fair chance to prove the validity and importance of their research. After all, what I wrote and said shortly after the US invasion and occupation of Iraq is now official US policy in the Sunni parts of Iraq; it is called the "Sunni Awakening," whereby yesterday's insurgent groups are today's allies.[20] While I was shot down for differentiating between insurgent and terrorist groups a few years ago, this important distinction is now commonplace.

Sliding into "Exile"

After my first and last academic year in the US, I left for Iraq, where I had found a new position, feeling worthless and worried for my own safety, since a colleague, Marla

Ruszicka, had died in a car bomb a few weeks earlier. Penniless, I had no other choice than to press ahead. Before I left, I secured a link with Columbia University to develop a conflict resolution curriculum for them in Northern Iraqi Universities, in partnership with my new institution, Salaheddin University, based in Erbil.

A few weeks after my arrival in Erbil, however, I caught a mysterious disease (possibly cholera or salmonella) that almost killed me. I was saved by the Korean army, which kindly welcomed me in their military hospital in Erbil. I was treated in a room opposite from several Kurdish children who had been the victims of suicide attacks a few weeks before. A few days after my admission in that hospital, while I was still very weak and on an IV drip, a US army liaison officer with the Korean army told me I had to leave at once, since I was not a national of a coalition country. I told him that I was too weak, pleaded with him, protested, cried, but he wouldn't listen; my nationality had made me a pariah. While a Korean officer apologized to me later, telling me that we were all human beings and that I could stay as long as I wanted, I realized that the next time I fell sick I wouldn't be so lucky.

I immediately took an offer from the University for Peace, in Costa Rica, to join them as a Program Director in International Peace Studies. This formative experience made me realize the extent of the damage that the so-called "War on Terror" had done to American ideals and American people. The land of the civil rights movements, of Dr. Martin Luther King Jr., became for many non-nationals the land of racial profiling, the USA PATRIOT Act, false imprisonment, torture, and extraordinary renditions.

Overnight, my "academic exile" to Costa Rica turned into a golden retirement where I found a group of like-minded colleagues evolving in an institution displaying horizontal management practices and catering to exceptional students. In my four years at the University for Peace, I have never felt humiliated, disrespected, or sidelined as an academic. I often say that I died in the US and reached heaven at UPeace. My God-sent recruitment, however, almost never took place. After my search committee reached a consensus on pre-selected candidates, the then-Dean of the Faculty, Professor Amr Abdalla, "Googled" me and found all the sites mentioned above.[21] Yet, with insight and integrity rare among academics, he realized that my research had been repressed and chose not to volunteer his findings to the rest of the search committee as he felt that such "information" would, in turn, make the committee biased for or against me. I was therefore only to be recruited on my academic merit. Professor Abdalla gave me a chance that I try to honor every single day since I started to work for UPeace. I now work directly under him as leader of a project, which facilitates the establishment of MA Programs in Peace and Conflict Studies in sixteen universities worldwide.[22] I have also just been promoted to the rank of Associate Professor, an achievement I would never have thought possible only three years ago.

The Lived Impact of Academic Repression

In the year that followed my appointment to UPeace as Program Director, I have reflected on my short stay in the US, which was needlessly disputatious and dramatic.
What burdens do I still carry, personally and professionally?

Personally, due to a significant loss of academic self-esteem, it took me more
than four years to finish my book on the role of perceived humiliation in the escalation
of violence in post-Saddam Iraq.[23] While at UPeace, every time that I found a trace of
dissonance with the administration, I feared for my job security. The academic year of
2007–2008 was the first year that I had not been on the market due to my anxiety of
being sacked with nowhere to go.

Academic institutions are not alone in typing my name into a search engine:
someone at Homeland Security did the same and put me on a "terrorist watch list."
Consequently, since February 2007, every time that I step out of a US-bound plane I
am met by Homeland Security Officers who escort me for questioning. Every episode
supersedes the last, and on a recent trip to Washington DC, I was even questioned by
the FBI at Miami Airport. FBI Special Agent Catherine Windman and her Homeland
Security counterpart, Special Agent Christopher Riffenberg, questioned me about my
research, who I met in the field, what I thought about Bush's "War on Terror," and how
I perceived Iraq's future. In every one of these interviews, I meet dedicated and intelligent professionals interested in my research. Still, I would not dare enter the US from
any other airport in case I meet other Homeland Security officers and FBI agents not
so understanding.

As the US moves ever closer to a total surveillance system and a menacing
garrison state, I never know what will happen to me. Will I be branded an "enemy com-
batant," stripped of my constitutional rights, and sent to a camp like Guantanamo Bay?
Will I even be "taken out" when I am doing field work in a conflict zone, as some of
my detractors once wished? Although repressive state and academic apparatuses seek
to stifle thought, criticism, and dissent, I know that my research is my best advocate in
times like this.

Overall, I have recently come to realize that there is much more to academic
life than what passes as "higher education" within the repressive environs of US universities. As part of the project that I lead, I have the privilege to teach throughout
the world. I have learned that I am free from the scrutiny, political censorship, and
academic repression that vitiate and devastate the quality of research, teaching, and
learning in US institutions. Nor do I slave over a heavy course load for the sake of an
elusive tenure process. I do not wear the shackles of the US academic-industrial complex that turns professors into proletariat, knowledge into a commodity, and students
into consumers of information designed to secure jobs not enlightened minds. Far

away from the corporate bureaucracies of US universities, I can be the scholar that I am without fearing what the press will write or say. As I write these lines, I am teaching my insurgency class at Benhares Hindu University, in India. I have assigned a very controversial book about Kashmir to my class, and they energetically have risen to my challenge. We respect one another and engage in a healthy debate. Somewhere in the world, academics can still do their job.

In retrospect, would I do it again if I knew of the consequences? Hell, yes, although even more forcefully! Not only have I kept my academic soul, I have freed myself of the desire to become a functional clone of a rigid academic bureaucracy. With luck and pride, I tell the tale of my short US academic career.

Nonetheless, I am sad to see that the socio-political repression that crystallized during the tenure of Bush administration has continued under the Obama presidency. What safeguards can prevent this from occurring? As my experience demonstrates, a fearful and uncritical mode of reporting by the US news media not only allowed for my own public lynching to happen, it also prevented much of the American public from hearing or considering dissenting views on their government's foreign policy, which recent revelations have shown relied heavily on illegal acts of torture. As the US public was made to believe that the events on September 11, 2001 changed their nation and the world forever, a critical voice was simply too much to handle in relation to any foreign policy ensuing from this jingoistic paradigm. As mass media placed their fear of appearing unpatriotic above their duties as reporters, generally-liberal academics gradually allowed themselves to become subdued in the same manner, unlike the open and prolonged opposition US academics voiced against the Vietnam War during the 1960s. I hope that both journalists and academics will regain the courage to express dissent, and to protect the outspoken at every step of the way.

When Knowledge Kills

Repressive Tolerance and the Future of Academic Freedom

Mark LeVine

SINCE THE TERRORIST ATTACKS OF SEPTEMBER 11, the fields of Middle Eastern and Islamic studies have found themselves the target of fierce assaults by conservative commentators and politicians. Among the perceived sins of the majority of scholars in these fields is the supposed failure to give adequate attention to the threat posed by Islam-inspired terrorism, and an obsessive critical focus on the policies of Israel and the United States.

The high profile tenure wars surrounding scholars like Norman Finkelstein, Joseph Massad, and Nadia Abu el-Haj, and the attacks on "Islamofasicsm" and its supposed academic enablers, are only the most well-known examples of recent threats to academic freedom in the ominous post-9/11 era.[1] Below the media—and in some cases academic—radar screen are many more struggles in which younger and/or untenured, and often Arab and/or Muslim, scholars have been attacked because of, research, public speaking, and writing that the university, media, state, and policy-making establishments have deemed anti-American or anti-Jewish.

These and other assaults on academic freedom have been widely publicized, and have led professional associations such as the Middle East Studies Association (MESA) to call attention to what past MESA President Joel Beinin describes as the "policing of thought about the Middle East."[2] MESA's Committee on Academic Freedom, echoing the sentiments of the National Endowment of the Arts, argues that "The USA PATRIOT Act, censorship of certain topics, the withholding of federal funds, and outside intrusions have all threatened the ability of professors to seek truth."[3]

Attempts to censor academic and scientific discourses are certainly not new, and indeed began long before 1633, when Pope Urban VIII forced Galileo to recant his heliocentric theory of the solar system or be burned at the stake. The American Association of University Professor's (AAUP) 1940 Statement of Principles on Academic Freedom and Tenure, which is still the reference point for most discussions of this issue, was a landmark in the understanding by scholars of their rights and obligations, affirming that "teachers are entitled to freedom in the classroom in discussing their subject." Among the many important implications of this statement for the present discussion is that it facilitates true diversity of viewpoints and therefore threatens the power base and legitimacy of conservatives who seek at any cost to maintain their ideological stranglehold on university culture. Where their perspectives or theories (e.g., creationism) have been effectively challenged through secular, scientific, and progressive critiques, conservatives hypocritically call for "diversity" and "balance"—values they don't truly embrace—in the classroom to ensure that their hidebound views continue to be taught.[4]

In this article I explore a two-pronged attack on the fields of Middle Eastern and Islamic studies that is distinct from, and less well understood than, the assaults on individual professors and the broader campaigns against alleged scholarly sympathy for so-called radical Islam. I analyze, first, the marginalization of recognized academic experts from the mainstream public, media, and political spheres (e.g., print media; television commentary; and meetings with state officials who work on the Middle East and North Africa [MENA], Islam, security, and terrorism issues). Second, I examine the creation of a sophisticated, well-funded network of "experts" dealing with MENA and Islam affairs who are ideologues skilled in demagoguery rather than serious scholarship. More specifically, in the last two decades, the political and neoliberal Right (which includes a fair number of politicians, policy-makers, scholars, and commentators who are considered "moderates" or even socially "liberal," but in fact advance "pro"-Israel and pro-corporate globalization viewpoints) has developed a powerful, sophisticated, and politically engaged apparatus for the systematic production of practical political knowledge.[5]

Determining the "Present Danger"

Let's begin with a critical focus on what I term the "Conservative Middle East Studies Establishment" (CMESE). This is a loose collection of scholars, politicians, policy-makers, and commentators who have managed to position themselves as the "mainstream" consensus on core Middle East issues such as relate to Iraq, the "war on terror," and the Israeli-Palestinian conflict. In so doing, the CMESE has succeeded in defining the mainstream of scholarly consensus on these topics as naïve, dangerously left wing, anti-American, and biased against Israel.

Right wing figures such as Daniel Pipes and Robert Spencer, both recognized by the media and policy-making establishment as "experts" on Islamic terrorism, have sponsored well-known attacks on liberal or left-wing academics—the former through his (in)famous Campus Watch website that monitors the public writings, speeches, and interviews of professors; and the latter through his Jihad Watch website. Perhaps the most well-known recent example of this vilification process is the publication of David Horowitz's best-selling book, *The Professors: The 101 Most Dangerous Academics in America*. This book gathered international media attention and assured Horowitz innumerable television and radio appearances despite the often risible quality of his supposed exposés of traitors to the nation. In my own case, Horowitz admitted during an on-air debate that despite a chapter-long screed, he not only had not read my book but didn't even know the name of the intern who he admitted did the research (most all of which was inaccurate). My situation was not exemplary, for numerous other scholars attacked the book for its innumerable errors and shrill ad hominem approach.[6]

The Professors targets scholars whose research or public writings is critical of Israel or US foreign policy, or is merely based in disciplines (e.g., women's, queer, ethnic, or postcolonial studies) that challenge "Eurocentric" theories or methodologies. While Horowitz's book epitomizes the modus operandi of the CMESE, more dangerous still has been the well-organized and well-funded attacks on individual professors. Among the most well-known were the machinations to deny tenure promotion to Columbia University Professor Joseph Massad. The hit against Massad by leading CMESE scholar Martin Kramer, of Tel Aviv University, artfully combines different strategies. Kramer begins with ad hominem mudslings on Massad's character and scholarship. Kramer caricaturizes Massad as "one of Edward Said's less successful clones... So bad, in fact, that while Said achieved Columbia's highest rank, of University Professor, Massad strikes me as falling far below the minimal requirements for tenure."[7]

Kramer also utilizes a guilt-by-association tactic, trying to discredit anyone who supports Massad's work. As for the Middle East Studies Association, he argues, its bestowal of a dissertation award upon Massad demonstrates why "not a single MESA-acclaimed dissertation has made for a lasting and influential book." This is a demonstrably false accusation, as a large share of MESA winners of the award have gone on to become leading scholars of their fields—at least as recognized within the profession.[8] But if by "lasting and influential" Kramer means their impact on US policy-making, he is no doubt correct, as none have achieved anything close to the political influence of the writings of the CMESE. Indeed, Kramer hints at his narrow definition of valid scholarship when he explains that Massad's "tome, soaked in the impenetrable prose of postcolonial theory, isn't on anyone's must-read list." For Kramer, the very concept of postcolonial theory is "impenetrable," and the idea that European empire and colonialism and the struggles for independence across the Middle East and North Africa has heuristic value is incomprehensible.

Kramer suggests that the only way for Columbia University to "redeem itself [is] by spitting [Massad] out." The violence of the suggestion is illustrative of the language and imagery in which so much criticism of MENA scholarship—and of any political or social views that differ from those of the neo-liberal/neo-conservative Right—

is "soaked." Such attitudes, moreover, are an important component of the "larger social and cultural context in which academic institutions are embedded" today, and which frame the attempts to silence or sanction academics whose research or politics challenges dominant political and ideological paradigms.[9] Indeed, it helps account for attempts by the US Congress to pass legislation that would put university sponsored and government-funded research into MENA issues under explicit political control.[10]

The Scope and Power of the CMESE Networks

Let us here recall Edward Said's seminal definition of Orientalism as "a mode of discourse with supporting institutions, vocabulary, scholarship, imagery, doctrines, even colonial bureaucracies and colonial styles." At the same time, Orientalism is both an academic designation and a "style of thought based upon ontological and epistemological distinction made between 'the Orient' and (most of the time) 'the Occident.'"[11] While Said's definition has often been criticized for oversimplification, it is still relevant for analyzing the contemporary heirs to the Orientalist traditions he described almost two generations ago.

Specifically, the connection between private institutions, universities, government (military, intelligence, and diplomatic agencies), and media is dense and synergistic. We can see this by exploring institutions that comprise the CMESE network. Among the most important are the Washington Institute for Near East Policy ([WINEP] the research arm of the American-Israel Public Affairs Committee), the Heritage Foundation, the American Enterprise Institute, the Hudson Institute, the Hoover Institution at Stanford University, the Middle East Forum, and the more recently formed Committee for the Present Danger. All these groups are well-known for championing conservative agendas and uncritical support for Israel as the best defense against the "threat" that "radical Islam" (or "Islamofascism") poses to the security of the United States, Israel, and the core values of the "West" more broadly. Equally important today is the mainstream Brookings Institution, perhaps the most important mainstream foreign policy think tank in Washington. Previously headed by the former National Security Council official William Quandt, who is well known for his evenhanded scholarship, today Middle East-related issues are dealt with through the Saban Center for Middle East Policy, which is funded by a wealthy conservative Jewish donor and run by former AIPAC officer and Ambassador to Israel, Martin Indyk. Here I am not so much concerned with the content of the numerous reports, testimonies to the United States Congress, conferences, and opinion pieces, as I am interested in the how such discursive networks are produced, and how they are able to penetrate far more deeply into the mainstream media than most of the leading scholars in the field. A perusal of the list of fellows and/or experts at the above mentioned institutions reveals the strong connections among them and their larger impact. While upwards of 80–90 percent of the "experts" or "fellows" listed as being affiliated with them are non-Arabs or Muslims, there are just enough people from the Middle East and North Africa to counteract easy accusations of anti-Muslim or Arab bias, although many times the so-called experts are not in fact trained Middle Eastern scholars, but merely ideologues who share the conservative political views of the think tanks.[12] While the majority of the scholars associated with WINEP have training and language skills related to the Middle East and North Africa, the percentage drops significantly in other institutions, where journalists, ex-military or intelligence officers, and scholars without regional or relevant language training fill in a far higher number of spots.

The list for the Middle East Forum, run by Daniel Pipes, has among the largest catalogue of experts. These luminaries include several Jewish and Arab/Muslim businessmen, well known media personalities such as William Kristol, and experts from conservative think tanks and Israeli academia, such as Martin Kramer, Robert Satloff, Patrick Clawson (also with WINEP), Laurent Murawiec (a French security and terrorism expert), and Meyrav Wurmser of the Hudson Institute, who is a founder of the Middle East Media Research Institute (MEMRI), an Israeli group with close ties to that country's military establishment, which monitors and translates articles in the Arab press. The list also includes former high level government officials such as Ambassador Dennis Ross, who directed Middle East peace negotiations under the first Bush and Clinton administrations. The American Enterprise Institute and the Heritage Foundation follow a similar pattern, and also share affiliated experts, fellows, and researchers with other members of this informal network, while the Committee on the Present Danger (first formed in 1950 to confront Soviet Communism and reformed in 2004 for the third time to support Bush's "war on terror") features not just well known conservative figures and scholars from politically sympathetic think tanks, but also political luminaries such as former Czech President Vaclav Havel and even Egyptian professor and activist Saad Eddin Ibrahim.

Forging a New Middle East

In late 2007, the CMESE put all its various networks together under one institutional roof with the establishment of the Association for the Study of the Middle East and Africa (ASMEA). The principal founders, Bernard Lewis and Fouad Ajami, described ASMEA as "first and foremost, a community of scholars concerned to protect academic freedom and promote the search for truth to reach new heights in inquiry." They explain that the Association was formed as a response to the "absence of any single group addressing…[Middle East and Africa issues] in a comprehensive, multi-disciplinary fashion." Just as important, it seeks to "advance the discourse in these fields by offering

its members new opportunities to publish and present ideas to the academic community and beyond. ASMEA will offer its assistance to established and new scholars,
including untenured faculty, graduate students, and those in related fields to expand
the body of scholars and knowledge."[13]

Even more than with other institutions, ASMEA demonstrates the powerful
connection between the CMESE and the mainstream media and policy-making networks. To begin, both Lewis and Ajami were closely tied to the Bush Administration
and conservative policy-making and government advisory circles, while at the same
time each has a long history of writing on the opinion pages of the most important
newspapers in the United States, including *The New York Times* and *The Washington
Post*, as well as influential policy-making journals such as *Foreign Affairs*, where Ajami
serves as an Editorial Board member.

Lewis and Ajami are joined on the Association's "Academic Council" by foreign policy and media heavyweights such as Leslie Gelb, former Policy Planning Director at the Pentagon as well as Chairman Emeritus of the Council on Foreign Relations
and a former *New York Times* Opinion Page editor; Robert Lieber of Georgetown University; conservative military historian Victor Davis Hanson of the Hoover Institution; and Kenneth Stein of Emory University, who resigned from his post at the Carter
Center in criticism of former President Carter's controversial book *Palestine: Peace not
Apartheid*. While the list looks impressive, most of the board members do not have any
expertise or academic credentials in Middle East or African affairs.

Aside from the unsophisticated use of terminology such as "discourse" and
the pretentious claim to "reach new heights in inquiry," there is much to comment
about the vague description of the ASMEA's intentions. According to news reports
and interviews with the principals, it was formed to "challenge" MESA and "promote
high standards of teaching and scholarship on the Middle East." Its founding statement
accuses MESA of being "dominated by academics who have been critical of Israel and
of America's role in the Middle East" (that these same scholars have been equally critical of the numerous corrupt and authoritarian regimes in the Middle East and North
Africa is not deemed worthy of mention). According to Bernard Lewis, the organization and its members have fallen prey to "various political and financial pressures and
inducements," which have made "the study of the Middle East and of Africa… politicized to a degree without precedent" (the deep political connections of all the ASMEA's
board members doesn't seem to count to Lewis). Most importantly, Lewis continued,
his new organization is dedicated to strengthening the "acute need for objective and accurate scholarship and debate, unhampered by entrenched interests and allegiances."[14]

Having asserted a thoroughly discredited value-free knowledge theory,
AMESA partisans launch an explicitly ideological attack from their own ideological
fortress: "MESA is still fighting some of the old battles from the '60s and '70s," the

president of ASMEA, Mark Clark, explains. "They're dealing with nationalism in the territories, and anti-colonialism, which is far less important today." Such claims are advanced as if there are no occupations anywhere in the Muslim world; the Occupied Territories, Afghanistan, and Iraq don't figure into ASMEA's calculus. They attempt to legitimate their perspective by arranging a newspaper interview in which a seemingly mainstream voice—frequent *New Yorker* contributor, Jeffrey Goldberg—argues that the group's founding was "a great idea… Either you believe that the state of Israel was a justifiable response to 2,000 years of anti-Semitism, or you don't. Everything flows from this, which is why it's even hard to agree on sets of facts."[15]

The erasure of the diversity of views in fields such as Middle East Studies, and the focus on uncritically defending the history and policies of Israel as the litmus test of intellectual stature, is quite telling, particularly when offered off by a well-known journalist with no scholarly credentials, language skills, or other experience in the field, and whose articles have been criticized by other *New Yorker* writers for their uncritical acceptance of official Israeli positions and lack of analytical depth.[16] But Goldberg is correct in his focus on the importance of facts in the debate over Middle East Studies. Since facts, to quote Mark Twain, have always been "stubborn things," and Lewis and other members of the CMESE understand the difficulty of "properly" training a new generation of students through existing funding channels, they are establishing their own funding network to facilitate training graduate students who will have the appropriate knowledge base to build a more "pro"-American and Israel scholarly Middle East, North Africa, and Islamic studies establishment.

Indeed, when coupled with the new military and intelligence agency generated scholarships, and the proliferation of Middle East Studies programs in conservative universities and colleges, the new funding network could train a substantial number of specialists who, upon graduation, will be fast-tracked to work at conservative think tanks, newspapers, and universities (ASMEA is setting up its own "syllabi bank" where professors will be able to obtain, one imagines, more "accurate," or at least pro-American and Israeli government, syllabi). Graduates will also be diverted into the intelligence and military communities, particularly in the proliferation of "Human Terrain" systems that embed "scholars" (often civilians who took a few college level social science courses), but in which most mainstream scholars refuse to participate.

Repressive Tolerance and the "New Objectivity"

According to the Frankfurt School theorist, Herbert Marcuse, the production and dissemination of knowledge in advanced democracies is structured in such a manner as to militate against standard claims to "neutral" or "objective" outlooks. Even tolerance for dissenting views is never neutral, but rather powerfully circumscribed by a variety of forces that work together to constrain the wide dissemination of knowledge that could challenge official narratives and the policies they justify.[17]

Such a politicization of knowledge is, of course, not new. The evolution of the notion of "objectivity" in the human and social sciences—what Peter Novick has aptly described as the "myth" or "cult" of objectivity—was in fact a highly politicized affair, even more so with the social than the physical sciences. On the one hand, the evolution of the scientific method and the larger self-critical and reflexive approach to generating knowledge not governed by religious beliefs undoubtedly heralded a major development in human thinking. Yet modern theorizing was in no way a politically neutral enterprise, nor was it necessarily historically progressive.

As the notion of objectivity developed, scholars saw their function as avoiding "interpretation" in favor of mere "observation" of events, with the goal of merely "establishing facts" that awaited discovery. Such a methodology was supposed to insure that, by keeping descriptions as interpretation-free as possible, the inevitable bias of any individual observer would not cloud the representation of the events. But there was also a political component to this methodology, particularly as it pertained to the emerging human and social sciences, which was to insure continuity against threats of change in the wake of the French Revolution and capitalist industrialization.[18] The act of "observing" events stemmed from a perspective that reflected the political, social, and economic status quo. Such "disinterested neutrality" masked a profoundly conservative attempt to retain allegiance to a status quo that needed to be continuously reinforced by ensuring that the relevant "facts" "arrange[d] themselves" as demanded by the needs of the political elite, a task that was accomplished in good measure by similarly masking a will to power over all aspects of the natural and social worlds—people, animals, and nature together.[19]

Crucially for our discussion, it was around a century ago, in the wake of developing Marxist, socialist, and anarchist alternatives to unfettered capitalism, that humanistic scholars as well as social scientists began to develop a code of professional ethics and standards aiming to support independent research even if it challenged the political, economic, and social status quo. Consequently, scholars were warned by university administrators that "men who feel that their personal convictions require them to treat the mature opinion of the civilized world without respect or with contempt may well be given an opportunity to do so from private station and without the added influence and prestige of the university's name."[20] In other words, "mature opinion," by definition, supported the domestic and foreign policies of US and European elites. Anything that challenged these policies was automatically "immature" and "unreasonable"—labels that have a long history of use by Orientalist scholars and imperial policy-makers to characterize the mindsets of the peoples under their control.

This reaction led to the 1940 AAUP statement on Academic Freedom, which was written at the moment that American scholars were being called upon, as their colleagues in European empires before them had long functioned, to advise the US government, first throughout World War II and thereafter in the development of Cold War policies vis-à-vis the Eastern Bloc and the "Third World."[21] As I'll discuss below, this involvement became extremely intimate as the "best and the brightest" scholars of the post-War generation became the architects, enablers, and functionaries of the Vietnam War.

In the 1968 postscript to his classic essay, "Repressive Tolerance," Marcuse claims that,

> The progressive historical force of tolerance lies in its extension to those modes and forms of dissent which are not committed to the status quo of society, and not confined to the institutional framework of the established society. Consequently, the idea of tolerance implies the necessity, for the dissenting group or individuals, to become illegitimate if and when the established legitimacy prevents and counteracts the development of dissent. This would be the case not only in a totalitarian society, under a dictatorship, in one-party states, but also in a democracy (representative, parliamentary, or "direct") where the majority does not result from the development of independent thought and opinion, but rather from the monopolistic or oligopolistic administration of public opinion, without terror and (normally) without censorship.[22]

Marcuse was essentially arguing that in a liberal/bourgeois democracy, a "totalitarian" regulation of public thought becomes a central strategy for maintaining the hegemony of the governing ideology. As with any hegemony, this process involves both generating consent (or at least acquiescence) to state power by the majority of citizens, and, should this fail, deploying coercion and violent force against dissenting voices that in any way threaten ruling elites. If not suppressed or crushed by the state, subversives and rebels are marginalized by the political-media establishment. Thus, "tolerance" is tolerated only up to a point of challenge or disturbance; as Marcuse describes, "tolerance is not distributed evenly; some groups can dictate what is tolerated and what is not... The conditions of tolerance are 'loaded.'"[23]

Mapping Out New Terrain for Politicized Scholarship

"Repressive Tolerance" generated significant controversy because Marcuse called for progressives to exhibit "intolerance for intolerance," that is, to stop tolerating and start attacking the dominant political discourses that heretofore have acted to stifle or marginalize dissenting voices. Only through an aggressive and intolerant response, Marcuse argued, could we bring about a truly "universal tolerance" that allows the full expression and flowering of dissent. No longer a mere tool of pacification, Marcuse believed that "today tolerance appears again as what it was in its origins, at the beginning of the modern period—a partisan goal, a subversive liberating notion and practice."

Marcuse's argument, originally formulated in the midst of the Vietnam War build-up and the civil rights movement, raises the question of whether a similarly subversive understanding and politics is required today to deal with the repressive tolerance practiced by the corporate-state-media establishment. The contemporary struggle does not just involve winning greater space in public discourse for divergent and subversive viewpoints. Equally important is the struggle over the politicization—in fact, militarization—of knowledge by the government, particularly its various military arms.

The militarization of social science and humanistic knowledge is not new. During the Vietnam build-up the US Army established Project Camelot, whose goal, according to Montgomery McFate, was both to "predict and influence politically significant aspects of social change in developing nations."[24] The project was abandoned after it was discovered that a University of Pittsburgh anthropology lecturer doing research in Chile had concealed his employment by Camelot, leading to contentious congressional hearings about the project.

The most important controversy surrounding academic involvement with the military establishment since Vietnam has been generated by the "Human Terrain Systems" project, which embeds anthropologists with US military squadrons on the ground in Iraq and Afghanistan to help them negotiate the cultural obstacles that can often impede the successful completion of their missions (in fact, the people embedded have often had a fairly limited, undergraduate-level training in anthropology and related disciplines). As the initial phase of the program progressed, Defense Secretary Robert Gates (former President of Texas A&M University) approved a much wider program, called the "Minerva Consortia" project, which he envisioned as a consortia of universities that would promote research in specific areas, funded by the Defense Department, in order to produce knowledge useful to the Pentagon, such as concerns "the Iraqi and terrorist perspectives," "religious and ideological studies," and a "New Disciplines Project."

There are clear ethical and epistemological problems inherent in linking "Iraq" and "terrorist perspectives," and indeed doing so based on Iraqi sources "captured," in Gates' words, and taken to the US in contravention of international law. Yet, in a sign of just how powerful is the institutional muscle behind Minerva, in the summer of 2008, the National Science Foundation signed on to co-sponsor research programs with the Department of Defense through Minerva, even as most social science bodies and a clear majority of leading scholars were arguing for the NSF to subsidize such research in lieu of the military or security branches of the US government, *not* in cooperation with them.[25]

More troubling is having the military support studies of religion and ideology when many of its senior officials have very strong religious and ideological beliefs that are openly hostile to Islam, and when such analyses could be performed by scholars through funding agencies like the National Science Foundation and other non-partisan and non-military-related sources. Most important, perhaps, is the desire to create "new disciplines" whose funding would be controlled by the military, thereby creating a "court intelligentsia" that would help shape and promote the agenda of the US military and foreign policy elites, unconstrained by the need to traverse traditional peer review processes that would ensure such projects meet the highest scholarly standards.[26]

Already, however, the problems associated with military-sponsored knowledge production are clear. As Laurie King-Irani argues, "The military assumes, incorrectly, that it can use anthropology as a tool. But anthropology is intrinsically subversive and requires and demands an analysis of oneself, one's own assumptions, positioning, and interests."[27] It is this possibility for subversion of repressive political and economic orders by bringing in previously marginalized critical voices and analyses that makes anthropology and other human and social sciences threatening to the political establishment and its representatives in the CMESE.

The best contemporary example of the intersection (or perhaps collision) of subversive knowledge and knowledge production designed to serve the interests of the state is the controversy surrounding the military's development of "Human Terrain Systems" (HTS) programs. While the goal of this $40 million program—which has already cost the lives of two graduate students who were killed while embedded in combat situations with the US military in these two countries[28]—is to help reduce friction between occupying forces and local populations, and thereby reduce the use of deadly force by US armies, it has come under significant attack. Both the American Anthropological Association (AAA) and the American Psychological Association have had intense debates over the ethical implications of their members working in any capacity for the military, and particularly for the Human Terrain Systems project (the AAA came out against working for the HTS, but did not take a position on the broader issue).[29] An important consideration for those scholars advocating engagement was the need to ensure access to future sources of funding for themselves and graduate students in an environment where inexperienced "experts" can earn hundreds of thousands of dollars working "in theater," as funding for graduate studies at universities continues to suffer. Indeed, some anthropologists now argue that they and their colleagues "should be more, not less, engaged in interpreting, debating, and commenting on public policy, particularly, given the disaster of Iraq, foreign policy in the Middle East."[30]

One of the HTS program's chief advisers, Montgomery McFate, has a telling conceptualization of the relationship between the military, the larger government educational funding apparatus, and the academy. In a report for the US Institute of Peace (where she was a Senior Fellow in 2007), McFate argued that "the military spends very little on the social sciences," and she criticized the lack of "coordination of the social science research conducted by the various agencies of the federal government... As a result of the limited number of in-house government experts, the DOD relies heavily on external 'subject matter experts' (i.e. moonlighting academics, journalists, or foreign nationals) whose knowledge may be narrow, incomplete, or out-of-date."[31]

Such an evaluation is no doubt behind her desire to "anthropologize the military." In this regard, McFate argues that "the cultural knowledge gap's consequences for military personnel and for US national security are troubling. In the absence of any assistance or information from their headquarters, soldiers and marines are forced to conduct highly complex operations with almost no pertinent socio-cultural information. This means that military personnel often have a difficult time identifying the local leaders, thereby losing opportunities to gain intelligence, leverage support, and identify potential threats. As a result of the cultural knowledge gap, the military also has difficulty planning operations, and is forced to learn the same facts and lessons over and over again."

Here, it is clear that McFate is either unaware or unwilling to consider the implications of scholars being involved in the direct collection of "actionable intelligence," "leveraging support," and "identifying potential threats." Nor is she able to consider that in many cases—particularly in Iraq—the US military's presence poses the biggest security threat to local populations, thereby rendering any potential data and knowledge either militarily useless and politically damaging (since it would define US forces as the very threat that their presence is supposed to protect against), or scientifically and ethically compromised.

Equally troubling is the ideological role HTS pseudo-scholars play legitimizing Empire. As David Price explains,

> The military and intelligence community loves McFate and her programs not because her thinking is innovative—but because, beyond information on specific manners and customs of lands they are occupying, the simplistic views of culture she provides tell them what they already know. This has long been a problem faced by anthropologists working in such confined military settings... In this sense, Montgomery McFate's selective use of anthropology—which ignores anthropological critiques of colonialism, power, militarization, hegemony, warfare, cultural domination, and globalization—provides the military with just the sort of support, rather than illumination, that they seek.[32]

In fact, it does more, lending an "Ivy League cloak of legitimacy to counter-insurgency, which is inherently secret," and even helping the military to "formulate war-making doctrines and provide operational data that inevitably, in the words of one army commander, becomes 'part of the kill chain.'"[33]

Conclusion: Responses to the Challenges to Academic Freedom Posed by the Emerging CMESE

One of Marcuse's arguments in "Repressive Tolerance" is that "under the conditions prevailing in this country [the United States], tolerance does not, and cannot, fulfill the civilizing function attributed to it by the liberal protagonists of democracy, namely, pro-tection of dissent." Instead, he goes on to say, the majority of citizens become "'closed,' petrified... all but the opposite of Rousseau's 'general will.'" In conditions where citizens are effectively depoliticized, Marcuse describes tolerance as being "turned from ac-tive to passive, from practice to non-practice." Such attitudes will tolerate a growing intolerance for dissent, and the slow erosion of various rights. The United States since September 11, 2001 offers a seminal case study in how this process works.

Such a situation of "repressive tolerance" raises the seemingly "ironical ques-tion: who educates the educators (i.e. the political leaders)." The irony, and difficulty, is compounded when the political leaders have a vested interest in strengthening their influence over the production of knowledge that impacts their fundamental interests, policies, or hold on power. In this regard, it is perhaps not coincidental that 1965, the year Marcuse first penned his essay, was also the year in which the aborted Project Camelot was initiated. Camelot was also the "brief, shining moment" represented by the presidency of John F. Kennedy, when the "best and brightest" of the post-War gen-eration, heads flush with dreams of global modernization under the benign tutelage of the United States, proceeded to launch America's greatest military folly until the inva-sion of Iraq—Vietnam.

There is little doubt that the US government both fabricated "truths" to justify war (in Vietnam, the fabrication of the incidents that precipitated the Gulf of Tonkin Resolution; in Iraq, the accusation that the Hussein regime possessed weapons of mass destruction), while "continuous government lies [were] passed on by a compliant mass media" in the lead up to war and throughout its prosecution.[34] This situation continued until realities on the ground so contradicted the official narrative that the mainstream media could not cheerlead the war and maintain its credibility.

There are, however, many differences in the production and dissemination of knowledge in the two wars. First and foremost is that during Vietnam a large segment of the public was directly implicated in this knowledge because of the draft, which politicized university campuses across the country and gave legitimacy to the growing academic critiques of US foreign policy during this period. At the same time, the news media, and especially television, was not under direct control of large corporations whose economic interests meshed with those of the government in power. Finally, the civil rights and the counter-culture movements, whatever their flaws, offered a larger narrative of rights, justice, and suspicion of government intentions, and a network for mobilization, which the anti-war movement could capitalize on by the late 1960s to help change public opinion about the war.

But, even with all these factors, it took over a decade for the Vietnam saga to play out and the last US troops to leave Vietnam, while the militarization of US foreign policy, and with it the American economy, begin again in earnest only five years after the final American pull-out. Along with the remilitarization of the US political economy came a reshaping of public consciousness and knowledge about the Vietnam War that shifted the discourse about the war from one of a moral failing—it was wrong, and our incredibly destructive presence in the country was unjustifiable—to a perceived failure of political will to let the US military "get the job done." This new narrative was supported by Hollywood's myth-making apparatus and the veritable cottage industry of Vietnam rescue and revenge movies it produced.

Today, the intersection of a largely depoliticized and apathetic public, a "volunteer" rather than conscripted army, the psychological scars of September 11, the corporatization of the new media and the dominance of "infotainment" over substantive news coverage, the far more sophisticated management of news by the military, and the deeply rooted complex of institutions described in this paper for producing "legitimate" knowledge about the Middle East and the dynamics of US foreign policy more broadly, have so shaped public discourse on these issues that there is little substantive difference in the broad visions of the two major political parties over America's continued imperial presence around the globe. This fact holds despite the huge costs to the American economy, to US military personnel, and to the country's prestige around the world caused by the war.[35]

It is in this context that Beshara Doumani argues that that the notion of academic freedom is "at a crossroads," one that is forcing scholars to reconceptualize how to produce socially and politically relevant knowledge in an atmosphere of government-sponsored disinformation campaigns supported and encouraged by a powerful segment of the scholarly, policy-making, and media establishments.[36] While ever more scholars become alarmed over growing threats to academic freedom, there is no consensus on the proper response. Should academics, as Marcuse suggested, vociferously express their intolerance for the discourse of the CMESE and other groups attacking academic freedom—whether in the form of petitions, protests, or even violence (as some have argued Marcuse supported)? Or is it better to try to "educate the educators" at a moment when the political establishment is more tied to corporate and conservative interests than at any time in recent memory? Or, failing that, should the strategy seek to educate a depoliticized and largely ignorant public about the complex history and contemporary realities of Africa, the Middle East, and the Muslim world more broadly, hoping that the mere exposure to such knowledge would help citizens understand what's at stake and thus to assert more control over their government?[37]

Marcuse believed that against the repressive policies of a totalitarian democracy "there is little doubt that…the only authentic alternative would be a…universal tolerance" for diversity and dissent. Achieving such an evolution of political consciousness demands a far-reaching change in what Doumani describes as the "concept and praxis of academic freedom."[38] But such a development will be for naught unless it is accompanied by a wide-ranging transformation in American political culture and even identity—from a culture of passive, uncritical, and depoliticized consumption and towards a much more politically engaged, critical, and autonomous spirit.

Of course, this is precisely the intellectual and political maturity that over two centuries ago Kant determined to be the bedrock of enlightenment and the foundation of modernity when, evoking Horace, he called on humanity to "Dare to know!" (*Sapere aude*!). We must, Kant urged, leave our "self-imposed tutelage" and have the courage to use our intellect without guidance of others whose interests we too often wrongly assume match our own.[39] It seems that in terms of intellectual and political maturity little has changed since Kant's time. Until it does, the politics of fear and the national, cultural, and religious chauvinism that both motivate and support the attacks on academic freedom today will continue.[40]

The Role of African Intellectuals and Their Relevance to the US

Critical Reflections of a Female Scholar

Micere Githae Mugo

IN THE SPRING OF 1994, just one year into my new position in the Department of African American Studies at Syracuse University, I attended the New York African Studies Association conference. During one of the panel discussions, Joseph Okpaku, a longstanding publisher, launched a scathing critique of a colleague whose paper was so overburdened with the exposition of other scholars' theories that, according to Okpaku, there was little of his own reflections. Okpaku challenged him to compile a manuscript without a single footnote and he would publish it without conditions. The practice under challenge here is that elitist, academic culture regards a publication as unscholarly unless it is loaded with quotations and footnotes from established academic gurus. Okpaku's critique goes even further to identify this practice as a problem that could enslave and paralyze emerging scholarship, especially in Africana Studies.

Taking heed of Okpaku's intervention, this paper will be mainly based on my reflections. However, an attempt will be made to relate the recapitulated debates to theoretical formulations and ideological frameworks that help elucidate as well as contextualize them. The coverage will highlight the years 1973–82, the period I spent at the University of Nairobi, Kenya, East Africa, highlighting the plight of women intellectuals. The focus on women is pertinent because in spite of the milestones made by women's movements globally—especially during the United Nations' Women's Decade culminating with the Beijing conference and the years after—the woman's narrative still remains largely silenced under patriarchal domination.

But what is the connection between the 1973–82 Kenyan intellectual scene and a book on academic repression in the US over the last few decades? One key point is that, like Kenya, America's systemic injustices and repressive practices reproduce themselves within academia, directly or indirectly, and repression in academia inevitably leads to more repression through society as a whole. I will ground this proposition in the conclusion by showing the similarities between Kenyan and American encounters with academic repression. But we can see other parallels as well, such as the stigmatization of critical thinkers as "communists" and the vilification of intellectuals who engage in activism as "unscholarly," labeling that often affects their tenure and professional career.

The paper will be in two main parts. The first will deal with a definition of African intellectuals, placing them in three broad categories, followed by an analysis of the general characteristics typifying each. The second part will be a re-visitation of the Kenyan intellectual scene in 1973–82 with a focus on the plight of women intellectuals, highlighting some personal details. However, as intimated, the debates I describe within an African context are just as relevant in a US context, as non-elitist thinkers in all societies suffering from domination and repression share similar experiences.

The Historical Context

In defining intellectuals from the African world and their role in society, one cannot avoid making a historical connection between them and the colonial or neocolonial classrooms that intellectually fashioned them, as well as the economic-political systems to which molding spaces are answerable. This linkage is important because there is a growing tendency to view scholarship and intellectual endeavors as zones of "neutrality," "objectivity," and non-partisanship. The notion is propelled by the fact that intellectuals in Africa (and elsewhere) have always occupied a very privileged position in society, often being referred to as "the brains" of their societies, "the cream" of their nations, and the "think-tanks" of their worlds. Moreover, they are designated the prerogative of leadership—whether they have demonstrated leadership qualities or not. With years of hindsight, we realize that this may be a part of what is wrong with Africa's governments which are dominated by intellectuals from the colonial and neo-colonial eras.

In the case of Kenya, the majority of intellectuals would have received their education from legendary former colonial institutions that had the agenda of training an elite leadership reflecting the image and ideas of colonizing powers. The hidden agenda was that these elites would become collaborators aiding the domination of their own people. That some of them rebelled and became matriots/patriots and revolutionary leaders was, as far as the imperialist powers are concerned, tragic. Clearly, in Africa, what W.E.B. Dubois described as members of "the talented tenth" were groomed to become not just monopoly owners of intellectual production, but to act as deities and fixed points of reference in relating to *wananchi*.

Let us now examine Kenyan intellectuals within three major categories. This classification becomes extremely important as it leads to a clearer understanding of the various zones of demarcation and contestation that we shall encounter in revisiting selected academic debates.

Assimilated/Conservative Intellectuals

An examination of writing and theorizing from the so-called "Third World" unearths what can be identified as three broad categories of intellectuals: the assimilated or conservative, the liberal or co-opted, and the rebel or revolutionary. The first type is best dealt with by Frantz Fanon in his classic works, *The Wretched of the Earth*[1] and *Black Skin White Masks*.[2] In the preface to the former book, Fanon observes:

> They picked out promising adolescents; they branded them, as with a red-hot iron, with the principles of Western culture; they stuffed their mouths full with high-sounding phrases, grand glutinous words that stuck to the teeth. After a short stay in the mother country they were sent home, whitewashed. These walking lies had nothing left to say to their brothers; they only echoed.[3]

Okot p' Bitek has provided the most dramatic representation of this type through Ocol in *Song of Lawino*.[4] African Orature and the literatures of Anglophone, Francophone, and Lusophone Africa are teeming with these characters. Generally, they are seen as traitors, mimics, and extensions of the pertaining political regime, either willingly or through coercion. Often, they constitute the conservative intelligentsia that crafts the rationale and agenda used by the state to justify the repressive system. Some play the role of the "court poet," writing flattering books in praise of heads of state, including dictators.

Many of these intellectuals are so alienated from the people that the latter's suffering does not touch them. They live differently, dress differently, think differently, and speak differently. As indicated, they have mostly been reared in an academic environment patterned along foreign cultural paradigms. Some of them refer to themselves as cultural "high breeds," not so much in the sense of Mũgo wa Gatheru's *Child of Two Worlds*,[5] but in a spirit of distancing themselves from Africa. In their self-alienation, they sometimes imagine they have become the people whose ideas they imitate. They are perfect examples of "victims of invasion" described by Paulo Freire in *Pedagogy of the Oppressed*: "The more invasion is accentuated and those invaded are alienated from the spirit of their own culture and from themselves, the more the latter want to be like the invaders: to walk like them, to dress like them, talk like them."[6]

The largest section of the conservative camp of intellectuals consisted of an older group of scholars, pioneers of traditional colonial mission and government institutions. Many of them were the first to wear Makerere University gowns when this was *the* university in East Africa, perceived as an academic paradise or Mecca by any ambitious student on an intellectual pilgrimage. These were the men and women described earlier on as suffering from "the first one ever," "the only one," and "the one and only one" syndromes. Unlike the self-acclaimed "cultural high breeds," however, this group of academic veterans would invoke African traditions to legitimize behavior that benefited them whenever patriarchal structures accorded them privilege, power, and domination as "leaders," "elders," and "chiefs." This would happen whenever questions from the youth and other underprivileged groups, such as women and workers, challenged their positions.

In summary, conservative intellectuals in Kenya at the period under discussion more than fulfilled their role as defenders of mainstream ideas, however reactionary, including state terrorism, while justifying their function as "rational," "professional," and "intellectual." Many of them were patronizing, condescending, and even tyrannical towards students, treating them as irritating nuisances, especially when the students dared to criticize the government. They would scold the youth, accusing them of biting the hand that feeds them, while threatening them with serious reprisals, including grade "burial." They played the role of "Overseer" for the repressive regime very effectively. Similar types are to be found in the US academy where they operate as conservative agents for the preservation of the status quo.

Co-opted/Liberal Intellectuals

The main characteristic of the second group of intellectuals—the liberals—is that they view themselves and their ideas as ideology-free. They argue that academic and intellectual discourses should be "neutral" and "objective," neglecting to factor-in the role of class as well as various ideological interests. By and large, their elitist theorization and abstraction of ideas tend to limit and confine debates within the walls of the classroom. Some of their discourses are so enigmatic that trying to follow the arguments becomes an exercise in frustration, futility, and disempowerment.

The liberals have internalized the ethos of dominating education and are, at best, only prepared to criticize it from within its institutionalized structures and frameworks. They are fascinated with ideas and emphasize academic excellence in the liberal tradition, but they basically look upon knowledge as theory. The kind of practice and problem-solving approaches that would translate knowledge into transformative action are never urgent or high on their agenda. Using abstract notions of "academic freedom" and "freedom of expression," they argue that the role of the academy is to generate knowledge for its own sake, rather than for practical application to social problems. Many liberal intellectuals make good academic bureaucrats, often occupying departmental chairs, deanship positions, and other administrative positions in the university's hierarchy. A number of them get appointed in senior government positions within the civil service, becoming the political system's policy makers and enforcement agents. What Issa Shivji has called the ideology of "entrysm" is popular practice with this group, who have no serious quarrel with the status quo so long as the system leaves enough cracks for them to squeeze through. Their historic mission, as Fanon puts it, is "that of the intermediary."[7] Their posture in political debates is often accommodationist and at best reformist. It is no wonder their critics have depicted them as fence sitters on the boundaries of ideological discourse.

Most of the intellectuals at the University of Nairobi during the period I have chosen to investigate belonged to this group. A lot of them had benefited from education in Kenya's leading schools and had then proceeded to the universities of Makerere, Nairobi, Dar es Salaam, or other institutions abroad. They had been tutored in the best of the liberal academic tradition, demanding excellence and high competition but a moderate worldview, sometimes tempered with religious allegiance. Many of them espoused "academic freedom" and "freedom of expression," but when it came to confronting the system that repressed these rights, the majority would retreat. More importantly, when it came to linking struggles on the campuses to those being waged in the communities, they distanced themselves—especially where the working class and the peasantry were involved. Clearly, there was a dichotomy between their articulated theories and principles and their praxis. There was a lot of talk punctuated by ambiguity, yawning gaps, silences, retreats, and even abdication in the face of crises. These intellectuals were anxious not to be viewed as agitators, seeking to remain "reasonable" and "rational" people who stuck to their books and did not cause trouble to the system. Above all, even when they questioned aspects of human rights abuses, they were eager to explain that they were not "communists"—a phobia to which we shall return.

In *The West and the Rest of Us*, Chinweizu summarizes the role played by African liberal elite intellectuals in protecting and perpetuating the neocolonial status quo as follows:

> African liberals, as agents of an international liberal imperialism, have a special job: to spread the liberal ideology in Africa... Though they advertise themselves as serving Africa, they operate in an environment, with a mentality, and under conditioned attitudes and direct advice that all tend to yield policies that primarily serve the neocolonial powers, policies that often are in direct opposition to the genuine interests of the African peoples. Conditioned by a pro-Western miseducation, they see their class interests as tied to those of their imperialist masters, and they readily abandon the interest of their people to protect those of their class.[8]

Basically, this group believes in the system and will not endanger possibilities of self-advancement such as job promotion or nomination to executive positions. They dare not risk slowing down the race towards the acquisition of the good things of life, away from the poverty of academic existence: residential mansions, posh cars, gifts of land and national titles from the government in exchange for silence and/or co-operation, and so on. Only a select percentage has demonstrated enough principles and courage to withstand these coercive maneuvers from the powers that be. In the US, this type of intellectual is all too typical, consisting of careerists who mainly use knowledge for abstract projects and self-advancement.

Rebels/Revolutionary Intellectuals

The third category of intellectuals is constituted by rebels. Like their conservative and liberal counterparts, many radicals were educated in either mission schools, in colonial/neocolonial government schools, or in foreign countries. However, at some point they identified the classrooms that taught them the ABC's of dominating cultures as factories for churning out false consciousness. Africa is full of examples of this category of intellectuals, including state figures such as Kwameh Nkrumah, Amilcar Cabral, Agostino Neto, Eduardo Mondlane, Julius Nyerere, and Patrice Lumumba. In a classroom situation, those who belong to this category see themselves as positioned at the battle-front of contending ideas and clashing frontiers of knowledge. To them, scholarship, research, and learning are not neutral processes, but rather elements of a deliberate agenda specifically designed by the system in power to support its economic base and propagate its controlling ideas. They view themselves as advocates for the rights of ordinary people, but whether some of them live up to this self-appointed responsibility is another issue.

Many of them have been influenced by Marxism-Leninism as a political ideology and within this context see themselves as "the vanguard" for revolutionary change. Whether they will act differently once in positions of power remains a crucial test in the continuing struggles for genuine change. What has become clear over a period of time is that, generally, this group has also tended to be characterized by loud talking, exhibiting paralysis when it comes to action and effecting radical change. They have tended to treat revolutionary consciousness as an intellectual game. They will even go as far as cultivating personalities and lifestyles that define what they perceive to be "revolutionary." A number have been known to intimidate those around them with their arrogance and alienating elitism, while parading as the saviors of their worlds.

Moreover, in academic discourse some intellectuals from this camp have tended to theorize so much that the knowledge and experience articulated fails to touch real living individuals, remaining the abstract monopoly of the learned. This gap between theory and practice becomes very important when we examine the impact of this category of intellectuals on Kenya.

With time, it became clear that so long as the rebels just made noise among themselves on the campuses and other academic venues, the government remained unperturbed. The problem arose when the group started organizing around and outside the campus, crossing the academic fence in order to reach out to the community for dialogue and action. This turned into a threat against the status quo and harassment became the order of the day. The group was seen as crossing boundaries beyond which the government had not granted permits. They were undermining the controlling principle of "divide and rule" which was unacceptable because, as Paulo Freire has argued, the elites are taught to "think *without* the people," except when they need to woo them for purposes of control:

> ...they do not permit themselves the luxury of failing to think *about* the people in order to know them better and thus dominate them more efficiently. Consequently, any apparent dialogue or communication between the masses is really the depositing of "communiques," whose contents are intended to exercise a domesticating influence.[9]

Realizing the dangers inherent in this posture, waking up to the understanding that the people and the students they taught were their "constituent matrix, not mere objects thought of,"[10] the action-oriented dynamic of progressive intellectuals went all out to demystify their ivory tower status. They decoded their language so that there was communication and dialogue with the students and members of their constituent communities. They organized outreach symposia in schools and colleges. They initiated community projects and devised research methodologies that ensured the participation and the empowerment of the people. They became rebels. Important as these developments were, however, what these people often overlooked was the urgency of identifying tactics that would help them dodge the widening net of repression, denial of academic freedom, and abuse of human rights.

Progressive intellectuals needed to learn guerilla warfare tactics to avoid self-exposure. The heightened persecution of progressive academicians and gross violations of human rights eventually taught the rebels that they were dealing with a tyrannical system and needed new tactics. Under repressive neocolonial conditions, it is necessary for the class of progressive intelligentsia to become what Walter Rodney once described as the "guerilla intellectual." Although Rodney was advising the left on teaching in the capitalist classrooms of the United States of America, his advice is just as relevant when analyzing the Kenyan neocolonial university classroom:

I use the term "guerilla intellectual" to come to grips with the initial imbalance of power in the context of academic learning. Going beyond the symbolism of the building, I'm thinking also of the books, the references, the theoretical assumptions, the entire ideological underpinnings of what we have to learn in every single discipline. Once you understand the power that all this represents, then you have to recognize that your struggle must be based on an honest awareness of the initial disparity. And that's how the guerilla operates. The guerilla starts out by saying, the enemy has all and we have nothing in terms of weapons, but we have a lot of other things. We start to make and invent what we actually have, and use that strength to transform the actual logistical position over a period of time into one where we call the tune and ultimately carry the battle to the enemy. This is the symbolism, if you like, behind the use of the term "guerilla intellectual."[11]

In closing this section, it is important to acknowledge that over time Kenya has witnessed a significant presence of progressive intellectuals with true revolutionary consciousness. A number served terms in preventive detention and prisons on trumped-up charges, while others managed to escape the net and go into exile. Many lived for long periods under police terror and constant harassment. A number of those incarcerated returned home to join ranks of the unemployed, even though they possessed skills that the country was in dire need of. The government blocked their employment as a way of punishing them and coercing them to become collaborators. Their partners, children, and family members became targets of this harassment. The sheer will to survive became an act of heroism on their part.

It was partly to the credit of the rebel group that Kenya's neocolonial government came to be exposed to the international community as repressive. The sacrifices these intellectuals, their student counterparts, and the masses of Kenya made—especially during the seventies and eighties when rebellion was not fashionable—have greatly contributed to the minimal democratic space that Kenyan people have managed to negotiate during the last few decades. Similarly, US progressive intellectuals have historically played a vital role in the assertion of civil and academic rights, but ironically, the struggle grows tougher with the consolidation of American imperialism.

The University of Nairobi and the Kenyan Scene

Broadly speaking, the above three groups were the major contenders on the Kenyan intellectual scene in the seventies and one can safely argue that the categories apply to this day. However, during President Daniel arap Moi's dictatorship (1978–2002) the ranks of the progressives had shrunk while those of the liberals and the conservatives had grown. This was largely due to the dictatorship's tactics of coercion and bribery in an effort to isolate the progressives. During the 1992 national elections, many conservative university professors served as KANU "youth wingers," never mind that some of them were in their forties, fifties, and sixties! Even more ironic was the fact that some who once belonged to the revolutionary class had not only abandoned the ranks of progressives but joined the "Youth 92" movement. Undoubtedly, the notion of intellectuals as revolutionary leaders calls for serious interrogation given their opportunism, shifting loyalties and dubious alliances at critical moments in history. In this regard Frantz Fanon's analysis in "The Pitfalls of National Consciousness" remains prophetic.[12]

In the seventies and early eighties, the University of Nairobi campuses were beehives of academic activity all year round. Students, professors, and even the communities around the campuses seemed hungry for debate and intellectual exchange. A professor who went into the classroom ill-prepared regretted it. Students would go into the library, read on the latest debate and walk into the classroom armed with information, ready to test the professor's knowledge. Walking between the classroom and one's office made a long journey, for students would stop one every few yards to "disagree," or "partly agree," or "fully agree" with what one had said in the classroom. These extended debates outside the classrooms were the most exciting aspects of intellectual dialogue on the campus.

Then there were public lectures and seminars, featuring local, national and international speakers. On such occasions, the audience would sometimes arrive up to an hour ahead of time to secure seats. At times, lecture halls would be so full that students would sit on window sills, and debates often continued late into the night. All over the country, hunger for intellectual exchange was incredible. I recall speaking once at Chanzu Teacher Training College outside Mombassa in 1978. Although the public lecture was not compulsory, nearly the whole college turned out to hear me on a Saturday evening when they could have been out in the town's nightclubs. The sea of bodies in front of me inspired me. These were exciting times: historical moments for believers in the power of knowledge and its agency in creating true (as opposed to false) consciousness.

The years between 1973 and 1982 were bursting with critical issues, both on the campuses and around the nation. The biggest projects were: overhauling the up-to-then colonial secondary school curricula, promoting drama and theater in schools and colleges, expanding public lecture series for schools and colleges, increasing outreach to the communities outside the campus, applying individual and collective research to practical community needs, and so on. A lot of professors also served on national panels, boards, councils, organizations, and so forth. The Department of Literature (where I taught) sent out a free traveling theater around the country every long vacation. Other than the grading of public examinations, all these activities were voluntary. Undoubtedly, intellectuals on the campus were busier than they are given credit for in their service to the nation. It is important to make this point because politicians in Kenya have often dubbed university campuses idle places.

As intimated, in the mid-seventies critical national debates saturated the classrooms and corridors of academia as they did the entire country. They resulted from disillusionment with national independence and those who took over power on the eve of *uhuru*. More than a decade of independence had not registered serious efforts to address the concerns that Kenya's liberation had placed on the table. Instead, a capitalist, neocolonial economy had taken root; active promotion of foreign investment had become an official economic policy; the crisis of landlessness had remained unresolved; poverty had increased; rampant corruption and the amassing of wealth by the rich were the order of the day; continuing bans on workers' strikes were crippling the unions, and more. What Fanon had observed at the inception of African independence was true two decades after the words were uttered:

> There exists inside the new regime…an inequality in the acquisition of wealth and in monopolization. Some have a double source of income and demonstrate that they are specializing in opportunism. Privileges multiply and corruption triumphs, while the morality declines. Today the vultures are too numerous and too voracious in proportion to the lean spoils of the national wealth.[13]

Among the legislators who spoke up against these ills was the then-member of parliament for Nyandarua North and former Mau Mau detainee, Honorable J.M. Kariuki. Though a millionaire, Kariuki recognized the poor's grievances and advocated a systemic redistribution of wealth, including his own. He was extremely popular all over Kenya and was referred to as the poor peoples' advocate. Following a prolonged period of government harassment, including a trumped-up bankruptcy suit, Kariuki was assassinated in the most brutal manner. There was a national crisis with demonstrations bringing virtually everything to a standstill. For several weeks the people of Kenya claimed freedom of speech and set up *kamukunjis* following the lead of Nairobi university students.[14] For once, the majority of Kenya's population was with the progressive university community in their denunciation of and demonstrations against the assassination. A lot of liberals joined in and even a section of the conservative camp agreed that things had gone too far.

Following Kariuki's burial, the government mounted a vicious purge chiefly aimed at the campus. Progressive, outspoken student leaders were arrested, harassed, and ultimately expelled from the university. Many of their lecturer counterparts were similarly harassed and kept under fierce surveillance. During the following few years, every aspect of US-style McCarthyism informed the government's dealings with progressive academicians. KANU party hawks warned Kenyans against imagined "communists" on the university campuses who threatened the security of the nation. The police intensified their spy network on the campuses, including posting paid informers in the classrooms. Progressive faculty and students were rounded up for interrogation. The questions asked clearly pointed to the presence of spies in the classrooms where alleged "seditious" utterances were supposed to have been made. With the communist phobia there emerged sharp divisions among the various intellectual groupings described earlier. With time, some of the conservatives joined in the fray of McCarthyism and witch hunting. A few of these honorable academics were suspected to be paid police informers. Most of the liberals either observed silence or condemned what was happening in whispers behind closed doors. The hunt for the rebels was on.

The government was becoming even more repressive on the university campuses and all over the country.

More than three people having a gathering had to secure an official permit or the meeting could be deemed illegal. In the heat of these tensions, two calamities directly related to foreign ownership and the presence of US military bases rocked both the nation. At Thika, a town forty or so miles from Nairobi, a guard at a Del Monte pineapple plantation unleashed dogs on an adolescent school girl named Waithera as she was passing by on her way home from school. The animals mauled Waithera to death. The court set the offending guard free and imposed an insignificant fine on Del Monte company. There was a national outcry. Meanwhile, in Mombasa on the coast, an American sailor, Sandstrom, met a sex worker, Monica Njeri, and arranged to go to her apartment. When Sandstrom violated a verbal contractual agreement, a quarrel arose. He split Monica's stomach with a knife, ripped her guts out, and sprawled them on her apartment's the floor. A high court judge—English by origin, as were most judges at the time—fined Sandstrom 500 Kenya Shillings (approximately US $10 currently) and bonded him to be of good behavior for five years. The honorable judge described Sandstrom as a young man of good behavior, with a strong Christian background, who had been enticed by a "prostitute."

These events, coming as they did on top other grievances caused an outrage across Kenya. Progressive students and faculty organized public lectures, seminars, symposia and *kamukunjis* to denounce the atrocities. I was a part of this movement. There was country-wide solidarity with our efforts including some progressive religious groups. The liberals and even some conservatives participated in the public discourses. As expected the government stepped in. Forces of the paramilitary police, known as the GSU (the General Service Unit), and troops of the regular police force were unleashed on the campuses and, whenever they invaded these spaces, they came with a vengeance, violently attacking students and raping women. The offenders were never apprehended, let alone brought to justice and this remains a terrible stain on Kenya's historical canvas—a serious testimony to repression.

By the end of the seventies, it had become clear to the progressive wing of intellectuals that the most effective form of change would only come with the involvement of the Kenyan people. Correctively, intellectual activists began to structure their research projects to include participation from the people. The academic staff union made more deliberate linkages with workers unions and the Students' Union, with which a lot of informal networking was already in process. It engaged in an intensive recruitment campaign and emphasized networking among the various campuses, which created a sense of power whenever the union raised its voice. As campus activism heightened, the government announced more stringent measures to curb academic freedom, and President Moi banned the University of Nairobi's academic union.

The Fight Against Patriarchy

On the campus itself, it was becoming increasingly obvious that the state's efforts to co-opt administrators and academics in positions of power within the university structure were succeeding in enforcing repression. Most senior positions were occupied by men, and they tended to be just as autocratic as their government partners. They were generally ruthless with the students and condescending towards their colleagues, especially the "juniors." Some deans and department chairs were known to threaten outspoken colleagues, telling them that they would never get promotion unless they shut up. Students would be threatened with failure if they refused to be submissive. Some of these so-called male leaders were downright sexist towards their female counterparts. There were episodes of sexual harassment, but most victims would be threatened into silence. The campus was, undoubtedly, becoming a microcosm of the neo-colonial world. At the time, I was an active official of the Kenyan Writers' Union, an outspoken member of the University of Nairobi Academic Union, and an activist in several groups and organizations militating against repression and abuse of human rights underground.

Progressive intellectuals and activists were in agreement that Moi's repressive regime and its collaborators should be taken to task in spite of the inherent dangers. We constituted a strong caucus of faculty and featured prominently on intellectual fora around the campus. We decided to start with changing the academic leadership on campus. In the Faculty of Arts (comprised of the arts, humanities, and social sciences) deanship elections were due at the beginning of 1980 and we unanimously agreed to field a woman candidate. The choice of a female candidate was a deliberate statement in recognition of women intellectuals, who were a tiny minority in the faculty, most of them "juniors." I believe I was the only female senior lecturer in the

Faculty of Arts then. When I was nominated as the deanship candidate, all hell broke loose. I was plagued with all forms of intimidation, including stalking and life-threatening anonymous telephone calls. Still, I won the deanship with an overwhelming majority vote against a male candidate who was a conservative full professor and the administration's preference.

The CID (Criminal Investigation Department) police swung into action and threatened me with arrest if I did not step down. At times they would coax me to resign, advising me that my activism was not befitting of a respectable woman. When it became apparent that neither the activists nor I would give in, and that campus protests (referred to as "riots" by the government) were about to break out, the decision was reversed and I was "allowed" to assume the deanship.

At the gender level, that election campaign brought to the fore very important lessons, one of them being discrimination against women, especially if they happened to be progressive. As soon as the conservatives knew that a woman candidate was being fielded for the deanship, the patriarch in them emerged and they went on the offensive. Some of the attacks were general, maintaining that women were not capable of leading, while others were personal and vicious. At the personal level I was declared unfit for executive leadership because I was suing for divorce and, in their eyes, this was scandalous. The cowardly sent threatening, abusive, and sexually graphic messages anonymously via telephone. The point of reference had suddenly ceased to be my academic competence or tested leadership qualities, the sole criterion was now becoming gender.

Witnessing so much hysteria stirred by a woman's candidacy for the deanship was instructive of how viciously guarded the monopoly of male power and custodianship of knowledge had become in the academy. The conservatives regarded the protection of this monopoly as a matter of life and death. For them, allowing a woman to become dean was like standing by watching coup-makers overthrow them and their fiefdoms: niches of power they had inherited from colonialism, which was patriarchal itself, and that they regarded as god-given, hence the collaboration with agents of state coercion to stop my move. Concerned friends tried to persuade me to withdraw my candidacy. However, unwilling to abandon the activists' collective agenda, I became all the more adamant to face the challenge. Solidarity between progressive colleagues and student activists was so solid that there was no looking back.

Equally, the close connection between the university dons and government was clearly evident. Long before the elections, during an interrogation process, the police had leveled against me vile sexist insults. They had accused me of trying to be a man and failing to be a "proper woman" through my activism, advising me that politics were the prerogative of men. The interrogation session turned into a sexist harangue:

Remember this is not the university where you talk as you like. You are in front of men now. So, watch out… We can beat you senseless and so don't try your sharp tongue here… As for your husband: does he live with you in the same house?… Hey, God is strange indeed. How did he give you children?… Poor kids! They might as well not have a mother… You think you are a man, don't you?… If you play with us we will strip you and check you out!

These patriarchs were clearly offended by the idea of not just having to deal with a woman intellectual, but with one associated with struggles against neocolonial injustices. Manifestations of this resentment had been witnessed over time in the form of mass student rapes by the police and the GSU whenever the state unleashed them on the campus to stop demonstrations. This antagonism against women rebels is so socialized by patriarchal upbringing that the police came to use force and rape as tactics of crowd control. Another reason behind gendered violence is the need to create fear in order to silence women, for rebellion is the first step towards liberation. When women suffer silently and accept domestication, they are, in essence, assisting their captors to police their own oppression and enslavement. Those who exercise control love this docility because they do not even have to enforce subjugation; these women repress themselves. Conversely, police panic when they hear their victims articulate the source of their exploitation because, once the oppressed have named their oppression, the next sure step is likely to be a search for avenues of escape.

Clearly, it only requires a crisis to awaken the beast lying dormant in human beings. This is what happened when patriarchs and sexist bigots saw a woman stand for election to become a faculty dean. The same men, who will sentimentally proclaim how great their mothers are when it suits them, were hounding another woman for exercising her rights. One wonders whether beyond sentimental clap-trap these patriarchs truly perceive their own mothers, sisters, and wives as full human beings. My suspicion is that the only condition on which there can be tolerance of women is when they accept imposed servitude. Under patriarchal socialization to dare transcend or add onto the traditional women's roles as wives and mothers is a serious form of transgression.

Between struggling against state repression and patriarchal oppression, the academic environment at the University of Nairobi was no rose garden for women academicians. Even when opposition was not openly articulated, the atmosphere was often hostile and alienating. But I must emphasize that the patriarchal mindset and violent misogyny described above did not apply to all male colleagues. There were many exceptions, mostly among the progressives. For instance, progressive male colleagues were behind my nomination for the deanship, and not only campaigned vigorously for my election, but constituted the opposition that overturned the nullification. I was also fortunate enough to be in the Department of Literature where most men were advocates for gender equality, which is not to claim that they were altogether liberated from socialized and internalized sexism.

Conclusion

In concluding, I would like to go back to the question I asked at the beginning: what relevance does the foregoing have to the social-academic situation in the US? I would argue that there are direct and indirect applications. Direct applications involve the role of the state, especially after 9/11, to use "national security threats" as a pretext to violate people's freedoms and rights throughout all areas of society, very much including academia. Both Africans and the US have used "Red Scares" to demonize opponents as "communists," and now the very same tactics, more so in the US, are being used to vilify intellectuals and opponents of government as "terrorists," which then grants the state the presumed right to harass, repress, or imprison them.

Indirectly, it is critical to remind ourselves that repression does not have to necessarily use guns, weapons, torture, or terror to be effective in undermining academic freedom, for institutionalized racism, surveillance, profiling, policing of "proper" disciplinary and discursive boundaries, and other such practices can be just as repressive.

And whereas, unlike in Kenya, I personally have not experienced the police knocking at my door in Syracuse to take me away for security interrogation, I know fully well that many US citizens have been subjected to police brutality and state harassment, and many have been imprisoned for exercising their constitutional rights. What I have witnessed first-hand in the US, however, is institutionalized racism, gender inequities, disability marginalization, disciplinary discrimination, and many other practices that make a mockery of the claim that the US is the world's beacon of freedom and democracy. Similarly, although I have not been told what I can or cannot write and teach, nor am I punished for political involvement on campus or outside the university, I know that assaults on academic freedom take many forms, from the overt command to the subtle threat or reprisal or sudden termination. These abuses of free speech rights have become routine and systematic in US universities.

Thus, while we must be careful not to undermine or dismiss the impact of physical terror as it existed in Kenya during the seventies and eighties under a repressive state dictatorship, we must also recognize the seriousness of mental, intellectual, and psychological terror—so common in post-9/11 America. This is just as damaging since it affects the academy and the larger world. For, once critical thinking is chased out of the place where it flourishes most, there is no telling how severe an impact this could have in killing off what little intellectual culture remains in the US. Such censorship would not only greatly exacerbate an already existing crisis in education, whereby citizens are poorly equipped to challenge their oppressors, if they even recognize that oppression exists.

Banned!

Why a South African is Going to Court in the US

Adam Habib

S OMETIME IN NOVEMBER 2006, while my wife, Fatima, drove back from work in Pretoria to our home in Johannesburg, South Africa, she received a call from John Webster, an official at the American consulate in Johannesburg. John very apologetically notified Fatima that her visa had been revoked, as had the visas of my children, Irfan, eleven, and Zidaan, eight. Irfan had been invited to the US as part of the People to People Ambassador Program for young leaders established by President Dwight Eisenhower to promote understanding among peoples of the world. I had not made up my mind yet about whether to send Irfan. Scared that he might be harassed at US airports, I was conflicted. But now that decision was already made, and by somebody else. The "sins" of the father had been visited upon the sons.

Our saga began a month earlier when I arrived in New York on October 21, 2006. Having lived there before while earning my Ph.D. from the City University of New York, and having traveled there multiple times thereafter, I expected to be irritated, but nothing more. Even when I was sent to the Homeland Security waiting room in JFK airport, I was not overly concerned. But after five hours, I began to realize that this went beyond the normal harassment. By the time I called the South African Consulate and some US and South African officials, it was too late—the decision had already been made to revoke my visa and "deport" me. Soon I was escorted under armed guard to a plane bound for South Africa. But I never lost my cool. Partly, I think, because it was nearing the end of Ramadan, a period in which you are not only supposed to fast, but also to control your temper when daily challenges arise.

The US furnished no reason for the revocation of my visa. Despite repeated inquiries and protests by me, South African officials, and US organizations, to this day the US has never explained itself. There were, however, several guesses. Some suggested that it was racial profiling. But when my wife and children's visas were also revoked, this theory no longer seemed credible. Others, including some high-ranking public officials in South Africa, believe that it had to do with my involvement in anti-Iraq war demonstrations in 2003. Some suggested that photographs were taken of me addressing a rally in South Africa and downloaded into some kind of US database. But there was never any confirmation of this theory from any official or department in the US.

Am I critic of the US government? Absolutely. In addition to my active participation in anti-war demonstrations, I have been very critical both in my speeches and in my writing about American foreign policy in Africa and the Middle East. But I have also been equally critical of other governments—including my own. Is that a rationale for excluding me? I would hope not. Can you imagine if suddenly American academics and citizens were deported from South Africa because they criticized the government's policies on HIV/AIDS? If our governments get in the habit of excluding academics, intellectuals, journalists, and citizens of other countries for ideological reasons, then we are on a slippery slope to the abrogation of all kinds of freedoms. Having lived in apartheid South Africa, I know what this means.

While I remain excluded from the US without explanation, I continue to receive invitations to speak in the United States. Together with lawyers from the American Civil Liberties Union, I decided to re-apply for a visa. I was meant to speak at the American Sociological Association Conference in New York in August 2007, but was notified at the very last minute that my application would not be processed in time. To date, I still have not heard anything about my visa application. As a result, with the help of the ACLU, US organizations that have invited me to speak in the US—the American Sociological Association, the American Association of University Professors, the American-Arab Anti-Discrimination Committee, and the Boston Coalition for Palestinian Rights—filed a lawsuit today in federal district court to force the US government to act on my visa and end its effort to block a free exchange of ideas.

Why do I fight to get into a country where its government obviously does not want me? My answer has always been threefold. First, I have said my relationship with the US extends beyond its government. It is established through my relationships with American citizens. It is also constructed by my fond personal memories. My son, Irfan was conceived there. When I came to defend my dissertation at the City University of New York two years later, I remember feeding ducks in Central Park with him. I remember Irfan's love for riding the subway, which would lull him to sleep. I remember snow fights with Zidaan and Irfan in the middle of Manhattan a few years later. And all of us remember visiting Disney World in 2003. This is a country where we have memories and friends. It is part of our world and that should not be taken away by an arbitrary action of a public official.

Second, in my new job as the Deputy Vice-Chancellor of Research, Innovation and Advancement at the University of Johannesburg, it would obviously be inconvenient for me to be barred from the US. It is where we have relationships with scholars, institutions and donors. I routinely collaborate with US-based scholars on academic projects. While my exclusion from the US may not be debilitating, why should I be subjected to these inconveniences without any explanation from the US government?

Finally, and perhaps even more importantly, this case symbolizes a broader struggle in our world. I am concerned, as many others are, at the rise of what I would call "chauvinistic identities" across the globe. We see these identities in nations like the US and South Africa, where some define being American and South African in narrow racial and cultural terms. We see it in religious communities where some interpret being Muslim as having to hate Jew and Christian, where to be Hindu must involve hating Christian and Muslim. We see it in linguistic divides where to speak French means to oppress one who speaks Dutch, where to speak Arabic means to reject Farsi. This has also led to increasing conflict between peoples and nations. It leads to bombing, and counter-bombing, wars and counter-wars, each feeding off each other in an ever-vicious cycle. All of this has occurred at a time when structural developments like globalization require collaboration on an unprecedented scale.

And this is what this case represents for me. It was filed on my behalf, a South African, by the ACLU and other US organizations. The lawyers are American, the plaintiffs are Americans. The cause is the right of these Americans to hear and speak with a South African. We are not all of one ideological persuasion. Many of those who have stood up on my behalf, I don't even know. What unites us is that we stand for principle.

And this is the fight of the future. The coming struggles for freedom will be played on the global plane, and they will require progressives to build bridges and human solidarity across national, religious, and ideological boundaries. Assisting in this struggle is what we can bequeath to our children. Fatima and I can leave Irfan and Zidaan assets, but these can always disappear. Principles will always be with them. At least when they think back in years to come, they can say that their old man and old lady stood up instead of folding, built bridges instead of dividing, stuck to principle instead of capitulating. They can say we were on the right side of their struggle for freedom.

IV
Dispatches from the Margins:
Gender, Race, Sex, and Abilities

Women of Color, Tenure, and the Neoliberal University

Notes from the Field

Maria E. Cotera

I FOUND OUT ABOUT ANDREA SMITH'S TENURE CASE the very same day that I found out about my own. We both do research on women of color, and yet Andy, whose scholarship and activism had affected thousands of women, got a negative vote in the Women's Studies Department where we were both jointly appointed. My case got a pass. I knew her work of course, because it had so transformed my own, but more importantly I knew *her*; as a colleague, a friend, and a scholar/activist who had irrevocably shaped my idea of what could be achieved within the considerable constraints of the neoliberal university.

The truth is, I never imagined that Andrea Smith wouldn't get tenure. With two books out: *Conquest: Sexual Violence and American Indian Genocide* (by now nearly canonical in certain feminist classrooms) and *Native Americans and the Christian Right: The Gendered Politics of Unlikely Alliances* (Duke University Press), over a dozen peer reviewed journal articles, and three edited volumes, her productivity outstripped that of many of our tenured colleagues. I knew tenure was never a given, but I assumed that Andy's accomplishments coupled with her high visibility (she was nominated for a Nobel Peace Prize) would insulate her from the objections that frequently arise around cases like ours: lack of productivity, lack of balance between service, teaching and writing (we mentor too well, publish too little); and deficit of scholarly significance (our research is too specialized or arcane).

Making sense of this outcome seemed impossible, and for weeks after I got the news, I found myself in a fog of anger and relief, not knowing where to find my shelter. Compassionate senior colleagues warned me against "survivor guilt," and I struggled for the words and the courage to tell them that what I was feeling was not guilt, but a sense of outrage and disbelief. How could a *Women's Studies* department have come to this decision? How could feminist scholars not recognize Andy's impact on the lives of women around the globe, her tireless work on their behalf, and her galvanizing presence at countless national and international conferences? Most of all, how could they have so deeply underestimated her crucial significance to feminist thought ("Hetero-patriarchy and the Three Pillars of White Supremacy" is a must-read for *all* feminist thinkers)? Her theorizing had opened a path for women from disparate circumstances to come together and imagine new ways of being and acting. This lack of recognition seemed like an affront to the very intellectual and political impulses that animated my own work and being, both of which were putatively authorized by the positive decision in my tenure case.

This contradiction raises questions that strike at the heart of the university as a social and political institution: What is the purpose of tenure? Whom does it serve, and what structures, norms, and values does it preserve? In what ways does it shape the scholarly enterprise in an era that has witnessed the corporatization of academic institutions large and small, and a consequent shift in both the nature and the stakes of scholarship? These questions are more than rhetorical; they impact the lives, fortunes, and emotional well-being of multitudes of academic workers every year. *And they seem to affect women of color most negatively.*

Indeed our tenure cases were not the only ones swept into the contradictions of the neoliberal academic machine. A total of six women of color scholars came up for tenure at the University of Michigan's College of Literature, Science and the Arts program in 2007. The research and writing of five of these women of color scholars focused on the histories, social lives, and cultural production of people of color; and, perhaps not coincidentally, four were jointly appointed in multiple academic units. Those of us who were jointly appointed were effectively doing double-duty, and most of us were mentoring dozens of students outside our areas of scholarly expertise, largely because we were among a select few in the college who were exploring the intersections of race, class, sexuality, and gender. Our service to the institution was both instru-mental and invisible since we operated largely in the margins of multiple disciplines (and at the intersections of marginal fields like American Studies, Ethnic Studies, and Women's Studies). Regardless of these challenges we all produced numerous articles, books, and edited volumes, and enjoyed a high degree of visibility in our respective scholarly communities. Yet when tenure time rolled around, I was the only one of four jointly appointed women of color to receive a positive recommendation from both units in which I held an appointment.[1]

This is a depressingly familiar narrative for scholars of color. Trained in the rough and tumble academic world of elite institutions long before they become ju-nior faculty, scholars of color understand that the tenure process cannot exist outside of politics, and that a value free assessment of the "quality" and "excellence" of their scholarship is necessarily affected by the kind of work they do, and especially the kinds of communities it serves. Quite likely, as graduate students, they watched helplessly while the junior faculty of color with whom they worked fell one-by-one to the tenure axe, dramas that in the backward vista of their own career struggles take on new significance as ominous harbingers of things to come. Indeed, by the time I received my PhD from Stanford, I felt battle-ready, having witnessed the various ways, both overt and subtle, that the university machine relentlessly ground down junior faculty of color until they were either docile citizens of the academic-industrial complex or psychologically damaged, if not physically ill. My own mentor, a brilliant woman of color, was so unnerved by the insidious political maneuverings around her tenure case that the whole process likely contributed to her tragic suicide. My graduate experience, though extreme, is certainly not unique. We are all very familiar with the old "revolving door" concept of diversity enacted at elite institutions, in which token junior faculty of color are brought in to diversify the faculty pool, only to be let go at tenure time like so many downsized autoworkers.

Graduate students of color learn very quickly that the hiring process is a numbers game pure and simple, a bid to keep our universities looking "diverse" on paper while never really shifting the center. And they bring this knowledge to their professional lives, awaiting the moment six years hence when they, like their mentors before them, will face the scrutiny of a cadre of institutional intellectuals who are, in the worst cases, openly antagonistic to the methodological and conceptual challenges they pose through feminism, critical race theory, postmodernism, postcolonialism, and other non-mainstream approaches. So it was with no small sense of weary recognition (the relentless repetitiveness of this cycle does wear one down) that I watched as graduate students of color mobilized on behalf of the women of color who had been denied tenure at the University of Michigan. I recognized that their struggle constituted an education in the mechanics of power in the university, one that would serve them well if they chose to provisionally accept its logics and limitations and become academic professionals.

But much has changed since my graduate school days. In those days, the battles seemed to be about what kinds of knowledges could and should be produced in the ivory tower. We were fighting for a place at the table, believing, perhaps too naively, that scholarship itself was the primary site of our politics. What I did not fully understand then was the extent to which scholars of color must accept a *Faustian bargain* when they agree to act as agents of "diversity" the academy. Yes, we are allowed to bring new histories, cultural artifacts, political critiques, and methodologies to the table, but these things are only valuable to the extent that they can be circulated within the academic marketplace as commodities and chic objects of analysis, or, more cynically, as symbols of the diversification of knowledge. In this way, the logic of democratic inclusion (which stands at the very center of mainstream notions of multiculturalism) intersects with the increasing commodification of culture to shape both the core values and the institutional practices of the twenty-first century university. One might argue that this cultural cocktail has been the defining feature of diversity discourse in academia since the bitter culture wars that divided college campuses since the 1960s, but key shifts in the relations of production of research-one institutions (and increasingly, smaller colleges and universities) have radically transformed what "counts" as knowledge, and have consequently shaped the ways in which tenure is determined.

To be sure, universities have always served the interests of the power elite, producing scholarship and ways of knowing that largely conform to (and actively justify) the status quo. But they have also been historical spaces for the democratization of culture, especially in the post World War II era, when the GI Bill made it possible for returning soldiers (many of whom were working class) to access educational opportunities that were previously unattainable. Public universities in particular were affected by these demographic shifts, and with the rise of ethnic studies, women's studies, multiculturalism, and other critical and counter-cultural approaches to scholarship (such as postcolonial studies, working-class studies, and urban studies), many universities became key sites of political contestation. Most important was the emergent vision of the public university as a site of "public good," a place where the resources of the state (which are, after all, the treasures of the taxpayers) would be brought to bear on the most pressing issues of our time: urban blight, poverty, racism, sexism, and imperialism.[2]

Over the last thirty years, this vision of the public university as a "public good" has been radically altered by a new regime of culture, economics, and politics—neoliberalism. Often referred to as the "privatization of everything," neoliberalism promotes individualism as the primary locus of freedom, and deploys this ideological argument to transfer ownership of public goods from the community to the private sector with the ultimate aim, as David Harvey has argued, of shifting the balance of capital accumulation to economic elites and the ruling class. Public universities, which previously held promise as a site for the production of knowledge in the interests of the collective, have increasingly become another branch of corporate power, providing the ideological, philosophical, economic, and scientific underpinnings for a massive shift in capital accumulation that has widened the gap between the "haves" and the "have-nots." This situation has developed as a result of political maneuvering that simultaneously liberalized the laws governing corporate-state relations (patent law, technology transfer regulations, and the like) and erected barriers to free speech within the academy (recent attempts to establish state legislatures as the final arbiters of scholarly excellence are but one example). As an apparatus for the consolidation of wealth and power in the hands of a few at the expense of the collective, the neoliberal university largely reflects the values of the corporate sector, which envisions the utility of knowledge as tied to capital accumulation and promotes knowledge *itself* as a commodity.

Andrea Smith is a public intellectual in an era marked by the privatization of knowledge. As such, her work, which links theory-making to social justice, presents an

immediate challenge to the commodified vision of intellectual production that has become the norm at research-one institutions. This vision is reflected in the increasingly
entrepreneurial cast of new university initiatives (which tend to focus on income generating activities like patent development and technology transfer) as well as the rising
cost of tuition and changes in endowment investing strategies (Denning 2005, Ciafone
2005). More and more, the university is envisioned not as a space for the "democratization of knowledge" (insuring access to mass higher education, developing community/
university partnerships, and the like), but rather as a place where one might purchase
a valuable commodity—a university education—or, if one happens to be a pharmaceutical company, the research expertise and credibility of university-trained scientists
(Denning 2005). These shifts are a response to the ongoing neoliberal push to decrease
federal and state expenditures on public programs, a push that has transformed other
sites in the public commons (the privatization of the public school system, prisons, the
military, etc). And these forces inevitably shape what is considered good or valuable
scholarship within the university.

    For example, I recently agreed to serve on the advisory board of Arts of Citi-
zenship, a university-sponsored project to encourage "public scholarship" in the humanities. Convincing faculty that "public scholarship" is something worth doing has
been a difficult task, to say the least, primarily because the university offers very few incentives for this kind of work. According to Nancy Cantor and Stephen Lavine (2006),
public scholarship in the humanities, arts, and design, involves "research, scholarship,
or creative activity that connects directly to the work of specific public groups in specific contexts…[it] arises from a faculty member's field of knowledge; involves a cohesive series of activities contributing to the public welfare and results in 'public good'
products" (Arts of Citizenship Website). Public scholarship is neither top down, nor
bottom up, involving instead a coming together between stakeholders in the university
and the community in the interests of knowledge production for social change. Public
scholarship appeals to the kind of faculty who seek greater engagement with the worlds
they inhabit and who wish to make their work relevant in the broader community.
This is precisely the kind of work many left-leaning graduate students want to do once
they get an academic job. Indeed, most of the graduate students of color I have known
hope that their research might have some relevance for the communities that they care
about. And, yet, so many, once fed into the academic machine, defer these intentions
until after tenure, or abandon them all together in the interests of professional survival.
Too often, radical scholars of color retreat into the dusty archives, producing books
about marginalized histories and communities that, however illuminating, merely circulate in the market of scholarly goods while rarely engaging the communities they are
meant to serve.

What junior faculty quickly discover is that public scholarship contravenes the primary values of the neoliberal university as they are constituted in the promotion and tenure process. For example, public scholarship requires that scholars work collaboratively, primarily with community members, but also with other scholars and even students. The neoliberal university values intellectual individualism in humanistic pursuits (though not in scientific pursuits), seeing collaboration as a fatal diminishment of one's scholarly integrity, originality, and authority. Beyond collaboration, public scholarship demands that we envision our community partners as co-creators of knowledge, and as equal interlocutors, not as objects of analysis to be worked into our preconceived theories about what the community is. This co-equal relationship subverts the power relations at the heart of most scholarly inquiry in both the Humanities and the Social Sciences, which figures the academically trained investigator as the "producer of knowledge" and the community as the "object" that she analyses. Finally, and perhaps most importantly, the aim of public scholarship is to produce "public goods" not scholarly tomes. This means that the end result of public scholarship might be a program, or a political intervention, or a teaching guide, or a curriculum, whatever best serves the needs of the community not the university. While these public goods may have a tremendous impact on the community and even transform social policies, they are too ephemeral to "count" once tenure time rolls around. So, while my own university promotes its Arts of Citizenship project as yet another example of the "Michigan Difference" (in much the same way its promotes diversity), it actually undermines the goals of Arts of Citizenship through a reward system (or perhaps more accurately a system of disincentives) called tenure and promotion.

Which leads me back to the strange case of Andrea Smith. How did a world-renowned feminist scholar with so much important work under her belt *not* get tenure at the University of Michigan? I think it would be a mistake to hang our critique on assumptions about the University's antipathy to women of color, or even its resistance to some vague sense of "women of color scholarship." This is problematic not only for strategic reasons (the University did end up tenuring three women of color in 2007–2008, a fact that the institution will no doubt use in it's own defense), but also because focusing on numbers and bodies shifts our angle of vision away from the real question at hand. Andrea Smith's tenure case was really about the politics of knowledge production—who creates it, from what experiences it is created, and, most of all, who benefits from it?—and the diminishing role of the "public intellectual" and public scholarship in the twenty-first century neoliberal university.

Daniel Gilbert (2005) has argued that the corporatization of the public university has projected a "particular brand of academic engagement with society," one that centers on "capitalist production" and entrepreneurial relations between universities and the corporate sector. According to Gilbert, this shift constitutes "a grave threat to the future of the critical public intellectual, and the very survival of the public sphere itself. Indeed, as the university has become increasingly corporatized over the last quarter-century, the private intellectual has emerged in such force as to call into serious question the possibility of any kind of public intellectual" (5). Andrea Smith's case reveals the contradictions and disjunctures of a particular moment in the history of higher education in which two models of intellectual production uncomfortably cohabitate the same institutional space. As a critical public intellectual in the tradition of Edward Said (1994), Smith "speaks truth to power"; she strives to be "someone whose place it is to raise embarrassing questions, to confront orthodoxy and dogma (rather than to produce them), to be someone who cannot easily be co-opted by governments or corporations, and whose *raison d'être* is to represent all those peoples and issues that are routinely forgotten or swept under the rug" (11). But this definition of the intellectual does not concord with the highly privatized vision of scholarship at work in the neoliberal university. Indeed, if the corporatization of the university has resulted in a "sacking of the educational commons" that has transformed the "public good" into "private goods," then Smith's intellectual production, which mobilizes the resources of the university to bring about social change, enacts precisely the opposite objective, transforming "private goods" (her salary, her office, time off, and so on) into public good.

I suspect that Andrea Smith's bid for tenure was rejected not because she didn't produce enough important scholarship—this claim would have been ridiculous and indefensible—but rather because of the *kind* of scholarship she practiced, which has everything to do with the aim of her work: the kinds of spaces in which it circulated, and the kind of people to whom it was meaningful. She was punished for transgressing the enclosure, for working collaboratively (sometimes with non-academics) to produce better knowledge, and for transferring her insights to the social world. With its negative vote, the university said to her unequivocally (and to all of us implicitly): "We did not hire you for this purpose. We paid you to work for *us* not them, to produce books that *we* recognize as meaningful, to circulate scholarship that speaks in *our* idioms and for *our* interests. We paid you to make us look enlightened, charitable, democratic, and open. You were never supposed to change the world. That was not in your job description!"

Tenured faculty may have any number of reasons for voting negatively on a given candidate's case, ranging from personal antipathy and political disagreements with the candidate's work to serious concerns about the nature and quality of scholarship. I'm neither able nor interested in parsing the reasons behind the decisions that were made by the Women's Studies Department at the University of Michigan. Nevertheless, high-profile tenure decisions like Smith's case offer some key insights into the ways in which tenure itself—that "peculiar institution"—regulates and even produces good citizens through neoliberal forms of governance. The most obvious way in which this happens is that faculty who don't toe the line—those who don't produce enough, who don't have a "balanced" sense of priorities, who are too "political," or who can't get along with other colleagues—don't get tenure. In this instance, meeting tenure promotion requirements is a punitive process meant to punish faculty who disobey the rules, and to excise them as bad citizens of a given scholarly community. But the process itself is also an important object lesson in the norms and values of an institution, a lesson that insures conformity even as it claims to provide the ultimate guarantor of academic freedom: tenure.

The pedagogical function of tenure was made most apparent to me when junior faculty, lecturers, and graduate students came together to support the women of color who received negative recommendations in the Women's Studies Department. In the process of crafting a response strategy, we initiated a letter-writing campaign to the deans and met with tenured allies for advice on how best to argue our case. What became immediately clear in this process was the extent to which our rhetoric had to be shaped by the logic of the very institution that had denied the validity of the scholarship we were defending. For example, despite the fact that the Women's Studies Department claims to value work that integrates activism and scholarship, and regardless that Andrea Smith was recruited and hired as a scholar/activist, we were told that we shouldn't highlight the national recognition that she had received for her activism, because it might actually hurt her case with the college. We also wanted to emphasize the relevance of public scholarship to the historical development of Women's Studies, and how most of the canonical feminist theory texts that we teach in our core curriculum were written with *activist*, not academic, audiences in mind. We hoped to use this logic to contextualize Smith's "non-academic" writing (e.g., *Conquest*) as not only relevant, but *central* to the production of knowledge in Women's Studies. Again, we were told that our line of reasoning could actually undermine her case. As a result, our letter, like her tenure review, focused exclusively on her institutionally authorized scholarship and teaching, limiting the scope and the force of our intervention and her contributions.

What I am trying to convey in this recitation of the barriers we faced in challenging institutional biases, injustices, and the faults of the tenure review process is not that resistance is futile, but that the power of dominant ideological systems lies in the ability to *construct the very terms upon which we stake our resistance*. In order for our intervention to be intelligible to those who determine the fate of candidates for tenure promotion, it had to be made on their terms and within the narrow domain of the logic of neoliberal institutions which values individualism, private property, hierarchy, and profit above all else. What was most striking to me during this process was the way in which it translated our dissent into the idioms of the institution. Which is to say that tenure is in large part a hazing ritual, perhaps the *ultimate* hazing procedure, designed to keep us obeisant and submissive, to make us suffer through the indignities and illogic of dominance until we accept it as the *only* organizing logic, so that we emerge from the hazing process as compliant, apolitical intellectuals.

If our very gestures of dissent can be transformed into a pedagogical project that teaches us to submit to the logic of the norm, then is it possible to remain in the academic institution as resisting subjects, as critical public intellectuals whose work is transformative, challenging, and concretely engaged with the social world at large? I'm not sure, but to my mind this question is inextricably tied to the larger question of who benefits from our scholarship, a question that must always stand at the center of our work as radical scholars of color.

Teaching Theory, Talking Community[1]

Joy James

[P]eople of color have always theorized—but in forms quite different from the Western form of abstract logic…our theorizing (and I intentionally use the verb rather than the noun) is often in narrative forms, in the stories we create…[in] dynamic rather than fixed ideas… How else have we managed to survive with such spiritedness the assault on our bodies, social institutions, countries, our very humanity? And women, at least the women I grew up around, continuously speculated about the nature of life through pithy language that unmasked the power relations of their world… My folk, in other words, have always been a race for theory— though more in the form of the hieroglyph, a written figure which is both sensual and abstract, both beautiful and communicative.

—Barbara Christian, "The Race for Theory"[2]

Erasure in Academic Theory

CONTEMPORARY AFRICAN AMERICAN THEORISTS such as Barbara Christian, who writes that theory not rooted in practice is elitist, think within a community-centered tradition in which the creativity of a people in the race for theory sustains humanity. However, teaching theory as non-elitist, and intending the liberation and development of humanity, specifically Africana communities, contradicts much of academic theory, which is Eurocentric.[3]

All philosophy and theory, Eurocentric or Afrocentric, is political. Academic "disciplines," when sexualized and racialized, tend to reproduce themselves in hierarchically segregated forms. To confront segregation means recognizing that current academic or educational standards have never worked, and were never intended to work, for us as a people. Our paltry presence in (white) universities and colleges speaks to the fact that individuals, but not the community, may attain some success in an educational process centered on the marginalization of all but the "European" (socially constructed as white, male, propertied, and heterosexual).

In academia, many philosophy or theory courses may emphasize logic and memorizing the history of "Western" philosophy, rather than the activity of philosophizing or theorizing. When the logic of propositions is the primary object of study, how one argues becomes more important than for what one argues. The exercise of reason may take place within an illogical context. Catechizing academic canons obscures the absurdity of their claims to universal supremacy and the massive flaws in legacies; such as we find in Platonic and Aristotelian "universal" principles derived from the hierarchical splintering of humanity, or the European Enlightenment's deification of scientific rationalism as the only "valid" approach to "Truth."

Some thinkers have argued that theory and philosophy are open to the "everyday" person and intend the good of humanity. However, few identify Africana people as both equal partners in that humanity and important theorists in its behalf. Fewer still connect the 'life of the mind" to the understanding that "Black people have to a disproportionate extent supplied the labor which has made possible the cultivation of philosophical inquiry."[4] We have also disproportionately cultivated the philosophies that provide non-abstract meanings of freedom and justice. Surviving genocidal oppression allows insights into (in)humanity and (in)justice that transcend the abstractions of academic philosophy and theory. The root knowledge of African living thinkers, of democratic power and philosophy, is not often practiced inside ivory towers where provincial thinking, itself almost a universal in academia, reflects rather than critiques Eurocentrism.

Eurocentrism is not synonymous with European. Samir Amin defines Eurocentrism as:

> a culturalist phenomenon in the sense that it assumes the existence of irreducibly distinct cultural invariants that shape the historical paths of different peoples. Eurocentrism is therefore anti-universalist, since it is not interested in seeking possible general laws of human evolution. But it does present itself as universalist, for it claims that imitation of the Western model by all peoples is the only solution to the challenges of our time.[5]

In a society and culture where the white European represents both the ideal and universal manifestation of civilization, "black" as well as "white" people, unsurprisingly, adopt or adapt racist iconography in their worldviews. My own schooling in white-dominated institutions has painfully impressed on me the depth of indoctrination and the difficulty of deprogramming myself from "truths" formulated under the tutelage of institutional bigotry which relegated "blackness" and "femaleness" to savage superstition, invisibility, or exotica, and elevated "whiteness" and "maleness" to a paragon of virtue and to the sublime.

White supremacy rationalizes Eurocentrism's anti-universalist stance. It has shaped and misshapened European philosophy, with destructive effects on the material lives of the majority of the world's people, and the spiritual and intellectual lives of all. Cornel West's description of white supremacy applies to the Eurocentric academic mindset:

> the idea of white supremacy emerges partly because of the powers within the structure of modern discourse—powers to produce and prohibit, develop and delimit, forms of rationality, scientificity, and objectivity which set perimeters and draw boundaries for the intelligibility, availability, and legitimacy of certain ideas.[6]

Adhering to the tastes of white supremacy, "white solipsism" masquerades as philosophy within the myth of European "racial," therefore intellectual, superiority.[7] As legitimizing a world order of domination becomes an intellectual mandate, Eurocentrism, like the carnival house of mirrors, projects what it distorts. Its solipsistic reflections racialize (and sexualize) theory, "whitening" thinkers indispensable to its canons: the Egyptian philosophers, Aesop, Jesus of Nazareth, Augustine, and others. Historical African or Semitic figures are depicted in texts as physically "white," or taught paradoxically as if they had no ethnicity or race (in which case their racial identities are assumed to be "white"). With or without illustrations falsifying identities, students receive theory with the bias that theory and philosophy are the product of the minds of "great" white men, and in women's studies of "great" white women. (In Africana studies the prioritizing of men as theorists produces its own distortions.)

Resisting the Metaparadigm

With the European centered as "universal" or normative, all else, by default, becomes marginal. When Eurocentric bias is seen as incidental rather than endemic to academic thinking, "indiscretions" are thought to be containable if cauterized to allow the work to retain its status. Consequently critiques of (hetero)sexism, racism, and classism that fail to analyze individual writers as representatives of a collective consciousness reinforce Eurocentrism's hegemony as a master theory or metaparadigm, albeit a flawed one.

Philosophical traditions, such as those of service to ancestors and community, challenge the authoritarian, authoritative voice of this metaparadigm. Living thinkers operate outside the worldview of "scientific" materialism and "objective" rationalism, and within paradigms which hold the nonduality and interpenetration of reality—the sacred and secular, the political and spiritual, the individual and community. Presenting community as the foundation of reality and knowledge, these paradigms reject the elitism of academic thinking. They are consequently heresies; academia discredits indigenous cosmologies and their concepts of nonlinear time, nonduality and commitments to community, as exotic aberrations and primitive thought. Since academia largely fails to recognize the intellectual or moral authority of the (Africana) communities it dissects, and Africana communities do not determine how black people are to be "studied," misrepresentation seems the rule.

The designation of academia, with its biases, as the legitimate intellectual realm for philosophy and theory deflects attention from traditional cosmologies and living thinkers. Theorizing within a tradition for liberated communities presents a worldview centered in spirituality, community survival, and human development. The devaluation of community and Africana thinking overlooks the universal aspects of the philosophy and theorizing of Africana "traditionalists," particularly women. Academic thinking promotes not only obscurantism but also the erasure of Africana women from theory.

Playing by its house rules, academia can set standards that no Africana woman can meet as a black woman. If it is assumed that we only speak as "Black women"— not as women—or "black people"—not as human beings—our stories and theorizing are considered irrelevant or not applicable to women or People in general; they are reduced to descriptions of a part rather than analyses of a whole (humanity). When teaching about our lives as Africana women is viewed as a descent to the particular (everything Africana) in contradistinction from the "universal norm" (anything European), biology becomes destiny. European biology becomes manifest destiny. Receiving recognition as "theorists" or "intellectuals" because of the "Westernization" and masculinization of our thinking (and lives) still leaves us "unqualified" as Africana women. Acknowledging "theory" only from those in transmutation into Eurocentric form reduces theory to technique. If theory is only legitimized when presented in a particular form (that flowed into our lives from colonization), then we must be trained out of communal communication to do theory.

Technical jargon and writing that "explore" or "probe" the lives of "others" lend themselves, like all colonial interventions and invasions, to misrepresentation and falsification. Objectification through the "expert" voice of "trained" speakers, including the voices of Africana academics who attempt to "re-articulate" knowledge," is often a distorting interference.[8] Since "academese" is not designed to respectfully or adequately communicate experiences as expressed by nonelites, using it we may appropriate and disrespect our own voices and people.

Appropriation requires abstractions. When we are stripped, or strip our-selves, of our context in community, caricatures incompatible with theory or philoso-phy deepen our intellectual alienation. The categorization of black women in bipolar stereotypes—the "mammy-sapphire" swing of suffering or angry victims, without the *ashe* or power as ancestors and living thinkers—is the prerequisite for relocation to some ghetto in an academic mind.[9] Being ghettoized in our own minds, and those of others, prevents a serious encounter with Africana women and blocks meeting our-selves as theorists. By demanding recognition for a community that theorizes, we can turn our extreme location into an advantage. The vantage point to being out on a ledge of institutional alienation is the ken of the view. Out there, one can see the ways in which time, space, and people are strung up and strung out. Artificial timelines manip-ulate space and thought. In academic theory, time is European time; space is occupied by elites; great thinkers are the victors' mythologized ancestors.

Those who routinely accept that Europeans/whites competently critique and teach African (American) thought may find it incongruous (or racial heresy) to accept that Africans/blacks competently analyze and teach, and therefore contribute to, (Euro-pean [American]) thought. The complaints of white European American students who rebelliously argue, when assigned the writings of people of color, that they "thought this was supposed to be a course on 'theory' or 'women's studies'" are logical in this context. Their grievances are based on unmet expectations set by the false advertising of depart-ments and programs that reduce theory to Eurocentric thought and women's studies to white women's studies. Attempting to bring more realism to our program, I try to jettison dysfunctional paradigms and bias-ridden language. I look for meaning in the fact that generally white men do not title their works "White Masculinist Theory"; that white women do not qualify their writings as "White Feminist Theory"; and that Af-ricana men do not identify their publications as "Africana Masculinist Theory." What tends to accompany "de-centering" the European, as Barbara Christian notes in "The Race for Theory," is the claim that there is no center. That traditional African or Native American cosmology might contain a center is rarely raised in academic theory.

Attempts to recognize Africana contributions to understandings of philoso-phy and cosmology have focused on integration in spaces dominated by Europeans. Perhaps the most overworked decoy in academe's intellectual apartheid is curriculum "integration." Integration and "inclusivity," as new forms of segregation, can act as a subterfuge for racist, (hetero)sexist, and classist education. Curriculum integration, an easy home remedy to a racist canon, lends itself to the creation of more sophisticatedly segregated academic departments, programs, and courses. "Special interest" or "diver-sity" courses simultaneously integrate and segregate. They fail to transform disciplines that view racism as a problem of excess or indiscretion in the hegemony and not as the cornerstone of the hegemony itself. Disciplines seek to ameliorate exclusion through

integration rather than struggle for new meanings and philosophies; the panacea becomes paradigmatic reform rather than a revolution in paradigms. Not the African
community but academe determines the meaning, intent, and degree of "integration"
of historically white-dominated disciplines; under these conditions, the reproduction
of segregation (in new forms) is unsurprising.

In reform, the axis of the universe remains the same. Although academia
bestows degrees and grants tenure, it does not necessarily produce philosophers and
theorists. Eurocentric academic theory is hardly an honorable participant in the race
for theory. The purveyors of philosophy and theory courses retain their prerogatives to
introduce anonymous, interchangeable satellites as mirrors for their own reflections;
black women are viewed as cosmetic aides to those holding firmly to their place at
the center of the mirror. What does it mean that "academic theory" largely presents
black women thinkers as generic satellites in white star-studded galaxies? What would
it mean to revolutionize the teaching of theory in academe in order to present African
American women thinkers as builders of the shared universe, within a new understanding of cosmology?

Making Our Presence Known

Before I even teach theory, given its current social/biological construction in academia,
I am continuously challenged to "prove" that I am qualified. Comparing my work experiences with those of other African American women academics, I notice that despite
our having been hired through a highly competitive process, we seem to be asked more
routinely, almost reflexively, if we have a Ph.D. We could attribute this, and have, to our
"diminutive" height, youngish appearance, or casual attire. Yet I notice that white wom-
en and men about our height, unsuited, and under sixty, seem not to be interrogated as
frequently about their academic pedigree. Continuously asked my "qualifications" as a
"theorist" I refer to: my training—a degree in political philosophy; my research—a dissertation on a European theorist; or my employment—teaching theory courses in academe. These are prerequisites for institutional membership, but are not measurements
of competency. I accept that nothing will qualify me to students and faculty who do
not struggle with their racism, fear, and hostility towards African people, philosophy,
and theorizing centered on liberation. For me, teaching theory courses on the praxis
of African American women permits me to claim that I think. Connecting my teaching to community organizing allows me to say I theorize. Service in African liberation
qualifies me.

These qualifications make me a suspicious character, if not "unqualified" for
academe. A hydra for teachers and students who do not set them, criteria established
without our input are shrouds. The issue is not whether there should be standards and

qualifications; there always are. The issue is who sets and will set them, and ⎯
benefit they function. The reward of transgressing conventional academic sta⎯
reestablishing connections to community wisdom and practice. The specter o⎯
to meet institutional standards and "qualifications" inhibits the search for new models
of knowledge and teaching.

In teaching, I try to learn and share more about the history of social thought.
Teaching about the origins of the "academy," "philosophy," and "theory" as predating
the "Greek ancestors" of "Western civilization" broadens the scope of both the time
and space in which theory takes place; it expands academia's concept of who theorizes. Changing the concept of time or the timeline changes the context for philosophy and theory. Philosophy extends beyond the appearance of Europeans (and their
designated ancestors) in history; so theory extends beyond the spaces they occupy or
rule. To restrict our discussions of the contributions of cosmology and philosophy to
the "contemporary" period implies that we have no "ancient" or "modern" history in
philosophizing. Without a history, philosophy is not indigenous to us as a people; and
"contemporary" theorizing becomes disconnected from its tradition. That is why we
must reinsert ourselves in time and history on the continuum, and confront academic
disciplines attempting to erase us from that line.

Talking Theory: Activism in Pedagogy

My courses are informed by a pedagogy rooted in ethical concerns and an
epistemology based on a four-part process of experience, reflection, judgment, and
action.[10] Readings stimulate and challenge students to expand their experiential base.
They then enter their reflections in journals and essay papers, and compare their insights in small student work groups. Judging dominant norms, students design activities or projects to demystify and challenge economic and racial-sexual oppression, and
evaluate their own ideologies. Through organizing, they obtain a greater experimental base to reflect on philosophy and theorizing, cosmologies, freedom, and liberation
struggles. The last step in this epistemological framework is action. Ethical action expands experiences, stimulates self-reflections, and judging. Pedagogy should acknowledge personal experiences, make space for self-reflection, encourage judgment, and
connect action to insight. Guided by ethical concerns to organize to resist oppression,
we walk closer to the place where humanist activist political thinkers stand. There,
hopefully with a less distant and more substantial awareness of their theorizing, we
begin to comprehend and critique.

To respectfully teach about theorizing by African American women activists
requires a pedagogy based on ethics and active commitment to community liberation.
So, I reject the concept of education as value-neutral and use "extracurricular" activi-

ties as a lab component (for instance, the hands-on experience of "applied" knowledge to supplement "book" knowledge is indispensable in disciplines such as chemistry or architecture). These activities, encouraging students to take a active rather than passive role in their self-development advances critical analyses of child abuse, sexual violence, adultism, racism, (hetero)sexism, and classism.

I argue for activism as an indispensable component in learning. Action promotes consciousness of one's own political practice. Such self-consciousness is a prerequisite to literacy. "Interest" in democratic struggles is superficial and the "knowledge" acquired specious, if one remains illiterate in the language of community and commitment spoken by women activists. Activism promotes literacy. It is usually the greatest and most difficult learning experience, particularly if it is connected to communities and issues broader than the parameters of academic life.[11]

Theory and philosophy "born in struggle" carry extremely difficult lessons. Activism concretizing ethical ideals in action allows us to better comprehend a form of thinking unfamiliar in abstract academic thought—theorizing under fire or under conditions of confrontation or repression. Thinking to stay alive and be free is the heart of liberation praxis. For centuries, Indigenous and African peoples in the Americas and Africa have theorized for their individual lives and the life of the community. Theorizing as a life-and-death endeavor, rather than leisured, idle speculation, embodies revolutionary praxis. As faculty, we may find ourselves in positions where living by our beliefs and theory carries the hazards of not receiving grants, promotion, or tenure; students may lose scholarships and higher grades. We rarely, though, find ourselves in positions where living by our ideals carries the possibility that we may die for them. We generally never have to risk our lives to claim our ideals and freedom, as have radical thinkers and activists such as: Harriet Tubman, Anne Moody, Assata Shakur, Martin Luther King, Jr., Malcolm X, and, Fred Hampton.[12]

In the early 1990s, while a visiting scholar at a Midwestern university, I was able to learn more about how risk-taking and radical organizing test ideas, ideologies, and commitments. During my semester tenure, the Ku Klux Klan, based in its national headquarters in Indiana, decided to march and stage a rally in the local campus town. The general response against the rally centered on individual comments of fear and anger. There was little collective, organized response until one night, as part of a woman's film festival, a small number of students viewed William Greaves' documentary, *A Passion for Justice*, on the life of Ida B. Wells. An African American woman senior facilitated the discussion session that followed the video during which students shared how they were impressed by Wells' courageous and influential activism, which began at such a young age, their age. They were silent when asked about the relationship between their feelings of inspiration for the story of Miss Wells' resistance and their feelings of anger and fear about the upcoming Klan march. Exploring these issues later that night in their dorm rooms, students began strategy sessions: they decided to allow their admiration for Miss Wells to lead them to organize a counter-educational critiquing racism, homophobia, sexism, and anti-Semitism in response to the impending KKK march.

Africana women students led the organizing and formed a coalition with European Americans, European Jewish Americans, and gay and lesbian activists. Some of these African American women students had experienced the most violent racial/sexual assaults on campus. At an early organizing meeting, one African American senior spoke of being dragged off a catwalk into bushes as her white male assailant yelled "nigger bitch" while repeatedly punching her. As she struggled away she noticed white student spectators who made no effort to assist or intervene. The woman student stated that the university's investigation and handling of the attack were equally unresponsive.

Faculty criticisms and complaints about white dominated universities did not translate into support for the student-initiated organizing. Most African American faculty and administrators, like their white counterparts, were reluctant to publicly support a student "speak-out" against racist, sexist, and homophobic violence critical of the university. University employees mirrored the divisions among African American students in which more cautious or conservative students dismissed student organizers as "radical" and ridiculed them for "overreacting." Political differences among African American students, faculty and administration were exacerbated during the KKK organizing.

Fear of criticizing the administration or faculty, along with homophobia, sexism, and caste elitism allowed faculty and more conservative African American students to distance themselves from student activists. Yet students and youth face the greatest dangers from racial-sexual violence on campus and in society. Alongside community women and men, only two European American women and I actively organized as faculty with students educating against, in the wake of the Klan rally, increasing racist/anti-Semitic verbal abuse and physical violence on campus. The Klan rally highlighted faculty ambivalence and refusal to support student organizing and the university administration's unwillingness to publicly take an uncompromised stance against, and responsible action for diminishing, racist, anti-Semitic, homophobic, and sexual violence on campus.

It seemed that we faculty and administrators believed our class and caste status in academe granted us immunity from the violence assaulting many African American youth, women, and gay and lesbian students. My own inabilities, with others, to always speak and talk to community in the midst of organizing conflicts, were compounded by my impatience and frustration with the political rhetoric and passivity of nonactivists. The confusion and strains impressed on me the precarious balance of teaching and talking for justice and my own uncertainty and anger, with others, about the terrain of struggle and community.

Individual changes in classroom teaching to deconstruct racist-heterosexist curricula and build community are marginal if not supported by the department or program and other instructors. Often the struggles for more accuracy and accountability in education are labeled and depoliticized as personal (personnel) whims of faculty, rather than responsible action. I have found that personalizing my confrontations with Eurocentric thinkers or academic careerists is a form of depoliticization that contributes to my own isolation and ineffectualness. Supporting progressive curricula and pedagogies demands political change. Yet, my experiences show that few are willing to engage in the type of activism and restructuring necessary to supplant tokenism.

Still there is hope in remembering and being inspired by Toni Morrison's observations in "Rootedness: The Ancestor as Foundation," and applying her thoughts on writing to another art form:

> If anything I do in the way of writing…isn't about the village or the community or about you, then it is not about anything. I am not interested in indulging myself in some private, closed exercise of my imagination that fulfills only the obligation of my personal dreams, which is to say, yes, the work must be political. It must have that as its thrust. That's a pejorative term in critical circles now: if a work of art has any political influence in it, somehow it's tainted. My feeling is just the opposite: if it has none, it is tainted.[13]

"You are a Scary Woman"

The Personal Politics of the New McCarthyism

Dana L. Cloud

I was deluged with so much hate mail, but none of it was political. It wasn't,
"Dear Ms. Cho, I think you're being unfair to the administration"—
nothing like that. It was like,
"Gook, chink, cunt. Go back to your country, go back to your country
where you came from, you fat pig.
Go back to your country you fat pig, you fat dyke.
Go back to your country, fat dyke.
Fat dyke fat dyke fat dyke—
Jesus saves."

> —Margaret Cho, "Hate Mail From Bush Supporters" (2004)

My question to you. If you was [sic] a professor in Saudi Arabia, North
Korea, Palestinian university or even in Russia. etc. How long do you
think you would last as a living person regarding your anti government
rhetoric in those countries? We have a saying referring to people like you.
Only in America. My advice to you since I think you lack sex or engage in
lesbian sex, is to get laid with a good wholesome thick cock.

> —albert aaf1315@aol.com (March 7, 2007), example of Dana Cloud's
> hate mail

Introduction

THE REACTIONARY POLITICAL CLIMATE that followed September 11, 2001 affected many of my colleagues across the country. The resulting pressures influenced women intellectuals in a different and more intimate way than they did men. I do not mean to minimize the attacks against male colleagues, especially those Muslims and US minorities facing racist harassment. However, with few exceptions (in which emailers address male professors as "faggot" or otherwise feminize them), my male colleagues received little hate mail, or what they had received was of (at least superficially) political character. One colleague told me, "I get mail like that all the time. I don't give it a second thought."

Misogynistic hate mail is hard to ignore, however. Margaret Cho, Susan Sontag, and Madelyn Murray O'Hair, to name a few (see Carrol, 1979; AmericanPolitics. com 2004) have received hate mail so similar to mine that it is tempting to dismiss the genre as trivial. However, the fact that there is a near universally available repertoire— a formula—for woman-hating is cause for more, not less alarm. After commenting in a 2004 comedy sketch that Bush was not Hitler, but could be if he applied himself, comedian Margaret Cho received racist, sexist, and homophobic hate mail (American Politics.com 2004). A contributor to the *American Politics Journal* online wrote, "It is obvious to the most obtuse observer that the reservoir of misogyny which overflows here—in this type of hate mail directed at any woman who 'steps out of line'—is the self-same reservoir which fuels the stoning, mutilation, rape, and multifarious other abuses of women worldwide" (De C 2004).

In spite of the seriousness of these attacks, there is little scholarly literature on the subject of intimidating hate mail—what Friedman (2007) calls "cyberintimidation"— specific to women. What literature there is makes light of the phenomenon as something that has always characterized contentious politics (see Carroll 1979). Popular media have covered venomous correspondence targeting female editorial cartoonists (Wilkinson 2004), controversial bloggers (Carr 2005; Friedman 2007), military whistleblowers (Hanson 2002), nurses (Harrison 2008), corporate whistleblowers (Richardson and McGlynn 2007), as well as scholars (Valentine 1998). More study is needed, however, to understand the specific strategies and consequences of hate mail targeting women.

To that end, I wish to explain the situations in which I received hate mail, and analyze it thematically, distinguishing the more or less gender-neutral attacks (including charges of academic incompetence, charges of mental illness, comparisons to Hitler and other totalitarians, and employment-related threats) from the highly sexualized and misogynistic abuse and threats. My argument is that to be an outspoken radical woman is, in the perception of many conservatives, to be a double traitor—by ideology and by sex. After the survey and analysis of my mail, I describe how being targeted for private intimidation has implications for how we respond and seek support from others, and conclude by discussing the utility of "going public" against intimidation campaigns that rely on secrecy and non-accountability for their power.

Me and David Horowitz

I believe that I first came to the attention of conservatives in September and October of 2001, when I defended (Cloud 2001) my University of Texas colleague Robert Jensen, who published an anti-war editorial in the *Houston Chronicle* (2001). In response to Jensen's critique, then President of the University of Texas Larry Faulkner published a scathing response in the *Chronicle* (2001) calling Jensen as a "disgusting" "undiluted fountain of foolishness." In the summer after the attacks, I published an alternative pledge of allegiance—omitting reference to God and America in favor of a secular, international solidarity—in the University of Texas student newspaper (Cloud 2002). Those few lines drew hundreds of angry responses, mostly by email. This one is emblematic:

> You are a scary woman. A heads up to you, comrade, liberalism and communism died on 9/11. Your email was posted on a very popular website; expect major backlash over your manifesto of America hatred." (ptruax31r@msn.com, July 5, 2002).

These remarks suggest that some find me threatening not simply because I circulate unpopular ideas, but because I am *a woman* who circulates unpopular ideas. Gender, nation, and race are closely intertwined in public discourse (Yuval-Davis 1997; Cloud 2004). The responses to my pledge demonstrate a common gendered trope regarding colonialism in war, namely, the figuring of the imperial nation as a (white) female body vulnerable to penetration by evil. When a woman on the home front challenges the imperial project, she must be figured as something other than the real woman/nation.

My email traffic quieted down between 2002 and 2004, but in 2005 I raised the ire of conservative culture warrior David Horowitz when, among many others, I protested his appearance at the University of Texas. Then, in 2006, I found myself listed among the 101 "most dangerous" professors in Horowitz's book *The Professors* (2006; and in its 2007 rehash, *Indoctrination U*). During that same year, I signed onto a collective faculty letter against the Israeli invasion of Lebanon, which drew a brief torrent of generic hate mail collectively addressed. Most recently, the National Communication Association (my main scholarly organization) extended an invitation to Horowitz to debate liberal scholar Michael Berubé at our 2008 meeting. I argued forcefully against this invitation and subsequently was characterized as a censoring bully not only by Horowitz (who said he would need a bodyguard to defend himself against me should he appear), but also by a few of my scholarly peers (see Jaschik 2008).

Although many intellectuals and activists alike regard Horowitz as a crank or attention-seeker, Horowitz's theatrics and demagoguery mask a very serious agenda: to discredit, harass, and censor critical intellectuals. Horowitz has garnered publicity for his circulation of the Orwellian-named "Academic Bill of Rights" and has national influence as well. Alan Jones (2006) reported, "Horowitz, with assistance from Karl Rove and the former House Majority Whip Tom DeLay, has briefed Republican members of

Congress on his Academic Bill of Rights campaign, and DeLay has even distributed to all Republican members of Congress copies of Horowitz's 1999 political primer, *The Art of Political Warfare: How Republicans Can Fight to Win.* Rove has referred to Horowitz's pamphlet as "a perfect pocket guide to winning on the political battlefield."

Surprisingly (given declining public support for the war in Iraq), the past two years have seen an intensified and much more material effort on the part of conservative organizations to cleanse the academy of its most prominent leftists. The emblematic instances of this turn were the firings of Ward Churchill from his post as full professor and chair of his department at the University of Colorado, and Norman Finkelstein (a critic of the political misuse of the Holocaust by Zionists) at DePaul. In this context, it is not hyperbolic to label the efforts of conservative culture warriors as a "witch hunt." The exorcism takes public and private forms, from the ivory tower to the inbox.

Putting the Intellectuals in Their Place

In this analysis, I rely on my own archive of hate mail, containing approximately 300 messages, most of them from 2002 and 2007. I do not include all of my hostile mail in the category of "hate mail." In addition to the unfortunately representative examples I describe below, I have received long analyses of US history, compelling immigration stories, comparative political analysis, and many questions and invitations to dialogue. I have received a number of supportive letters from both Leftists and conservatives. One open-minded and thoughtful letter sent by a retired US Marine lamented violence, poverty, and desperation. "Life is unfair. I do not know why the innocent are battered, tortured, killed. I cannot comprehend why people are so horrid toward one another. It is an awful mystery" (William Curtis, date unknown). He explained that he felt called upon to intervene on behalf of others and asked me to try to understand the depth of his frustration and commitment.

Much of my mail, however, is characterized by insult, invective, belligerence, and threats, some in gender-neutral categories calling into question my intelligence, right to teach, and patriotism. I have been asked to leave the country and offered the funds to do it (and to please take Alec Baldwin with me). I have been called a Jew-hating anti-Semite, and a number of messages compare me to Hitler and/or Stalin, while yet others threaten to take action to fire me (see table 1).[1] Most of these messages could have been sent to either men or women, and nearly all of the letter writers are men.

One cluster of messages revolves around insults to intelligence and academic credentials, exploiting young professors' perpetual state of insecurity and self-doubt. For example, a correspondent in 2007 wrote, "You're an absurd, fucking fraud! You'd starve in the real world, which is why you've fled to the comfort of a college campus" (stellardrivepete@bellsouth.net). Often, Horowitz, Laura Ingraham, and other conservative voices on the air and on the Internet deride academics as unqualified, out of touch with reality, hypocritical, and opportunistic. Right-wing columnist Tammy Bruce (2002) charged me with hypocrisy, intellectual dishonesty, and incompetence, mocking my alleged membership in a latté-sipping "Academic Elite" out of touch with the honest, hardworking, patriotic, and grateful public at large.

Likewise, in a letter threatening to petition his church members against my continued employment, and sent to the University of Texas Chancellor and the Board of Regents, Gabriel Jones (michael_gabriel_jones@yahoo.com, March 6, 2007) wrote, "Laura made you sound stupid this morning. I would say you need to go back to school and get a bit more "edumicated" before tangling with a woman like her." In equally threatening manner, Retired Infantry Colonel Robert William Zerby, Ph.D. (doctorzerby@military.com) wrote to my Dean on March 7, 2007: "Just from a communications standpoint, Dr [sic] Cloud was crush [sic] by Laura. For someone who is in a Department of Communication, she was a failure in the debate... I have advised my nephews not to apply or attend UT and I will for the remainder of my years, advise any young people from attending UT... I would hope you will take the same approach to removing her as did the University of Colorado when they removed the tenured Prof Churchill. Just because Dr Cloud is tenured, does not mean that she cannot be removed. Do it!!!"

Columns like Bruce's and websites like FrontPageMag.com and FreeRepublic.com are sources for arguments and commonplaces that turn up consistently in my correspondence. Conservative pundit-turned-liberal David Brock (2004) recounts the rise of conservative talk radio as such a rhetorical resource. The Rush Limbaugh model, he argues, cultivates "ditto-heads" and calls them to action (435–459). "The radio broadcasts tell audience members what to say and teach them how to say it, politicizing every church social, every pool hall, and every workplace across the country" (459). Limbaugh and the radio hosts that grew up in his shadow employ the rhetorical strategy of "heresthetics," framing core values in negative terms, against those who challenge conservative opposing values (456). This strategy encourages animosity between his listeners and a demonized category of "liberals" and "feminazis"; not coincidentally, this discourse is openly misogynistic. When a noted environmentalist died, Limbaugh played the sound of a buzz saw and crowed that she had been cut down to size (Brock, 2004, 444).

Not surprisingly, my correspondents tell me that they saw or heard my words reproduced on conservative talk radio shows, right-wing web sites like FreeRepublic.com, and Fox News. The audience for conservative talk radio has traditionally been made up of older, white, working-class men, often suspicious of intellectuals. Right-wing talk radio shows often bait and belittle intellectual guests, and listeners do the same. Dan Hauck (danhauck@charter.net), in a March 29, 2007 letter to me, exulted,

"Let's just say it was quite surprising that someone who teaches courses on 'persuasion' was so unpersuasive in responses. Maybe you should add a course in 'how to dodge even the most straightforward questions.'" In the same vein, another 2007 letter (LS, fortuanecookie@gmail.com) began, "hey there Dana, heard you on the Laura Ingram [sic] program... Face it... Laura Ingram buried you! What were you thinking? It sounded like you were dodging all the questions she was asking you, which doesnt [sic] surprise me as all of 'you people' dodge questions." Interestingly, this letter and several others accused me of "dodging questions" suggesting that listeners take cues from conservative hosts regarding the best ways to ridicule Ph.Ds.

The strain of anti-intellectualism in my mail is prominent, but contradictory when correspondents go out of their way not only to impugn *my* intellect but also to demonstrate their own alleged erudition. Indeed, a number of the letters I have designated as "Ivory Tower critiques" are quite eloquent and witty. After the publication of my alternative pledge of allegiance, David Wrone (no email available, July 9, 2002) wrote,

> Your pledge only confirmed their opinion that the ivory tower is leaking
> anti-American venom at an alarming rate, and chewing lesions in the
> brains of our vaguely adultish children in the process.

I found this letter, replete with vivifying language, to be articulate, if unkind.

It may be demoralizing to be called a "condescending patronizing self-aggrandizing peacock" in a "stinkhole of slaver" (Donald Wissman, Dwismannjr@nc.rr.com, March 22, 2008) and "pugnaciously stupid" (Ben Gibbons, ben.gibbons@springmail.com, July 3, 2002), but one cannot deny the eloquence of the insults. By far, my favorite piece of conservative mail was that by Lawrence Fossi (lfossi@fossilaw.com, July 2, 2002), who had carefully read about my research on my website: "I was afraid that the fine art of parody had been lost, but this is magnificent! Of course, the 'Dana Cloud' creation is such an egregious jackass that no one possibly could believe any such person really exists... We have found a Jonathan Swift for our age—and her name is 'Dana Cloud!'" Writers comparing me to Hitler, Stalin, or other totalitarians also made use of the parodic style: "Dear Comrade in Arms, I admire and respect your use of intolerance in the name of tolerance... I could have used people like you. Sincerely, Adolf" (Don Newton, Don.Newton@brother.com, March 6, 2007). Apart from my being stupid or dictatorial, allegations of indoctrinating students comprised the most uniform message. Typical was that of N. Haynes (nhaynes@scarabimaging.com, July 3, 2002): "I hate that you and your like are indoctrinating young minds at OUR universities and getting subsidized with OUR tax dollars."

A second major approach of many letters is to accuse me of treason. "Face it dana, (sic) you are anti-american," wrote Lance (fortuanecookie@gmail.com, March 6, 2007). "My suggestion for you… Move to another country, maybe England… Or better yet the middle east where as a woman, you will be treated like a dog! Sound fun?" Another writer offered to by me an airline ticket and $500,000 if I would renounce my US citizenship "and promise never to come back to America. She doesn't need you anymore. You sleep with her enemy" (solarsail_5@juno.com, March 6, 2007).

Ironically, the phrase "sleeping with the enemy" resonates with the ideas of feminists of the late 1960s, some of whom found sleeping with men incongruous with the radical critique of the sex/gender system. Interestingly, solarsail's description of treason as "sleeping with *her* enemy" underscores how criticizing the nation violates the norms of womanhood. Why are female dissenters treated and represented differently both in public life and private correspondence than male dissenters, and how can we explain the character of this difference? The answer lies in the complex interconnections between gender ideology, national identity, labor, and justifications for war in the modern nation state. Grayzel et. al. (1999) explain that nationalist discourses figure national geography in terms of the virginal or maternal body, represent the ideal woman as one dedicated to national service and sacrifice, and render women's capacity to respond to war in almost exclusively emotional terms (see also Yuval Davis 1997; Kaplan, Alarcon, and Moallem 1999; Werbner and Yuval Davis 1999; RaNchod-Nisson 2000; Gould 2008; Hansen 2001; Stoler-Liss 2003).

Thus, it becomes somewhat paradoxical and dissonant (for committed conservatives) in this frame for actual women to mount a critique of nationalism and imperialism, or for any assertive and effective critic of nationalism and war to be, in fact, a woman.[2] A "good" woman defends the nation and reproduces and nurtures its warriors and workers. As a result, women who speak out against nationalism and war pose a dual threat to conventional gender roles and the sanctity of the nation state—and to the potent amalgam that works to secure allegiance to both regimes. Without this analysis, it is difficult to understand the intensity and the misogyny of my (and others') gender-specific hate mail.

Gender-Specific Hate Mail

These letters are fewer in number but more memorable and concentrated in their impact (see Table 2). They deployed fear, shame, and disgust in ways that resonate with my (and perhaps many women's) experiences of sexism and gender-related trauma. More than others, these letters were invasions of my private space and self, beginning with seemingly concerned attempts to "help."

ACADEMIC REPRESSION

"You need help."

"What is your major malfunction lady?" begins one of my letters (lschorle@ swbell.net, July 2, 2002). There is something essentially *private* and therefore aimed at the *feminine* about inquiries as to my mental health. To have spoken out against the war doesn't just make me wrong; it makes me broken and in need of repair. As Deirdre English and Barbara Ehrenreich (1978) have argued, advice-giving to women on the part of men (primarily) has always been a gendered form of social discipline from the fields of psychiatry to self-help literature. Foucault (1988) likewise describes madness as a social construct that imposes normalcy and controls disruptive subjects in manageable ways. In this sense, to say "I feel sorry for you" or "I will pray for you" is more of an insult than expression of actual puzzlement or concern. I received several letters in which writers have concluded that I am mentally ill or bereft without God. Such letters often mentioned my daughter, whose discomfort with pledging allegiance was mentioned in my column.

For example, Kathy Renn (kathyrenn@hotmail.com, July 1, 2002) told me that it was "very sad that you don't know God, but what's even sadder is that you aren't allowing your daughter to know God. My prayers are with you and your daughter." Another person wrote, "I pledge to pray for your poor daughter. How sad it must be to live with such an angry, confused person" (Robert Murphy, rjmurphyjr@hotmail.com, July 2, 2002). "Where does your bitterness come from?" asks Jon Geib (Jonathandgeib@yahoo.com, July 5, 2002). Chris Delmain (Chris_work@comcast.net, March 6, 2007) also believes that my problem is emotional, offering a mental health assessment based on an online photo:

> I have come to the conclusion (especially after looking at your picture on the U of T web site) that only someone who was deeply hurt or humiliated (probably early in life) could be bitter towards the country and society that gave you so much. The truth is I am sorry for you.

Conservatives may experience cognitive dissonance when an educated person makes arguments that are significantly contradictory to their beliefs (Festinger 1957). One way to discredit such a challenge is to frame criticism as the ranting of a "bitter," "hurt," "angry," or "confused" person, particularly if that person is a woman. Another way is to dehumanize the critic altogether.

"Hello, you disgusting pig."

US culture encourages women to discipline their hair, faces, and bodies in accordance with stringent norms, cultivating a sense of inadequacy and insecurity around these issues that men do not share (Wolf, 2007). Therefore, pronounced appearance-oriented insults hit a soft spot, and were combined in my email with other aggressive and dehumanizing insults. Interestingly, these messages resemble many of Margaret Cho's (right down to the "Jesus saves"). For example, Peter O'Brien wrote,

> Hello you disgusting pig… I feel bad for you that you are such an angry and hateful person, (sic) your ugly daughter will end up failing in life like you…. How vapid you are to even have a web page, do you really think anybody cares if you live or die outside of your ugly kids and dogs…. Lots of love you piece of garbage. God bless (peterobrien17@hotmail.com, July 8, 2002).

"A sexual deviant with a daughter?!!"

Mention of my family life makes Peter O'Brien's letter not just insulting but also invasive. Calling my daughter ugly extends the violation of the personal address into domestic space. The most hurtful and threatening emails make sustained accusations of child abuse—both sexual and ideological. The most pronounced example of this is from "solarsail" (solarsail_5@juno.com, March 6, 2007), who wrote, "You're a sexual deviant with a daughter?!! You should be arrested for child abuse!" Concerned about my capacity to indoctrinate young people, including my daughter, Tim Max (timmax@hotmail.com, July 8, 2002) wrote, "I ache for your daughter; what life she has in store after years of being spoon fed your distorted, relativist, socialist rhetoric."

Often, the criticism of my worldview runs parallel to contempt for my sexual orientation. For example, in a 2002 letter headed "Lesbo butch," "gm" (no email available) wrote, "Dear Butch, I feel sorry for you. What a warped view of things you have. But I'm sure you think you are 'enlightened.' If you hate America so much, hike up your skirts and head for the border." This example, remarkably, combines charges of America-hating with invitations to leave the country, denigration of women, lesbian-bashing, *and* an expression of pity. This letter's invocation of my sexuality is odd in its commanding a butch (who would not be wearing a skirt) to hike up her skirts. It could be that this instruction attributes sexual vulnerability to me in spite of my sexual orientation. The image of hiking up skirts and heading for the border also specifically points to gender as salient to my emigration (again, woman=nation; bad woman=alien). This exclusionary discourse symbolically expels bad women/critics from the national fold. There is another way that the bad woman may be disciplined. Albert (aaf1315@aol.com), quoted in my opening epigraph, suggests that raping a lesbian (advising her to "get laid with a good wholesome thick cock") will both restore her to her proper place in the arrangement between the sexes *and* cure her of her deviant beliefs.

"Where are your manners?"

The final category of messages is significant because it expresses a commonly held view across the mainstream political spectrum that non-violent confrontation and disruption are inappropriate violations of a speaker's right to freedom of expression. Ironically, antagonistic public expression is defined in these arguments as a form of censorship, even though every significant social change in the US involved disruptive confrontation. Many readers and contributors to this volume may accept the argument to decorum, even as Horowitz himself knows that this standard is a sham, albeit one very useful weapon in the current culture war. His appeals to diversity, tolerance, and decorum work to make his agenda—to win the culture war and to discredit the Left—as persuasive as it is cynical.

Furthermore, condemnation of indecorum is strongly gendered. The best example from my correspondence of this tendency came from a woman, Wendy LaMorte: "I think it is rude and crude to demonstrate when someone is trying to give 'another opinion' on campus. Shame on you…. Where are your manners?" (wenlamo@hotmail.com, March 6, 2007). It is difficult to imagine a letter asking an adult male, "Where are your manners?" Unfortunately, being outspoken has historically been, for women, tantamount to rudeness. In this way, the appeal to decorum is an attempt to make contests that are public, political, strategic, and antagonistic private and ostensibly resolvable through polite talk.

The Gender of Private Threats

Catherine MacKinnon reminds us that "social inequality is substantially created and enforced—that is, *done*—through words and images" (1993, 13). Physical threats and bodily aggression are sometimes entailed by misogynistic words. After asking, "Want to see how they treat women over in those countries?" "Lschorle" (lschorle@swbell.net) appended a URL for a news story about women being gang raped in Pakistan. (An irony of his letter is that his support for war is based on condemnation of the practices of Muslims, yet he would relish the sort of punishment such a regime might levy.) Kasyyyko (email withheld due to ongoing threats), whose March 18, 2008 letter is a long, obscene personal and political rant, wrote that he was glad that "it is dangerous for you to speak… you love immigrants fro (sic) the third worlds (sic) GO FUCKING LIVE WITH THEM, YOU DUMBASS CUNT DRINK THE WATER." Ominously, Abu Rankin warned me, "My own allegiance is to those who are brave enough to deal with the likes of you, in ways that you richly deserve. Fortunately, they are coming. Look into the camera and say after me: 'I am an academic. My mother was an academic… We are truly the daughters of hate" (Rankin103@aol.com, July 5, 2002). Strangely (especially given that my mother is a realtor), this writer invokes my maternal line as parallel to my academic hubris and my belief system. In cryptic form, his letter occupies several categories of messages: non-gendered threat, the ivory tower argument, and misogyny.

My analysis of my gendered hate mail has supported the conclusion that, in the psyches of activist conservatives, a female critic of the nation is a compound traitor. The line between sexual deviance and ideological treason is very blurry in the letters I have examined, so that the denigration of my gender, my sexuality, my body, my family, and my psyche become interchangeable with condemnation of my beliefs. Although my public political persona is tough, these messages affected me strongly because they addressed me not as a citizen in a public domain, but rather as a private person in an intimate setting. The privacy of the inbox shields these writers from public view and broader accountability. Although I would not equate symbolic violation with physical sexual assault, both rely on the shield of intimacy.

Conclusion: Private Intimidation, Public Accountability

When one strips the shield away, the power of private intimidation is lessened. Thus, like Margaret Cho, I have found publicizing my hate mail (mostly on my blog: txcommie.wordpress.com) to be a productive form of resistance that dispels the power of these insults. Cho describes what happened when she posted her hate mail on her website, including senders' email addresses and names: "I was getting apology emails flooding in so fast, I couldn't believe it."

Turning the tables on cyberintimidators and bringing their violations into the light of day has had some surprising consequences for me as well. First, it is surprising how many of my correspondents were shocked that I would actually post their words and offended that I would put them into a position of vulnerability similar to the one into which they had put me. However, many chagrined writers backpedaled on their original positions and/or apologized for the tone of their letters. With some, I engaged in productive, civil correspondence. One is Don (Don.Newton@brother.com) author of the Hitler "Dear Comrade" email discussed above). To his initial letter, I replied (in part):

> Turn that sarcasm around and see what Horowitz represents: exactly what you say—intolerance in the face of tolerance (March 6, 2007).

He responded:

Thank you for the lengthy response. I do appreciate it. What you say may
be true, but it still doesn't excuse your bad behavior and lack of tolerance
for opposing points of view. Horowitz may be despicable in your eyes,
but he does have a right to speak, as do you. Take care (March 7, 2007).

Undaunted, I replied again, attaching a long essay I have written called "In
Defense of Unruliness," to which Don replied:

I guess my real beef is that tolerance is either "tolerance or it is not", it
has to go both ways. I also feel that lack of civility is killing our sense of
decency and destroying our souls. What good is a kicking, screaming victory against a kicking, screaming opponent?...It has been a pleasure corresponding with you. I know you are busy, so good luck (March 8, 2007).

Over the course of three email exchanges, Don went from comparing me to
Hitler to appreciating my point of view, enjoying our dialogue, and wishing me luck. I
found this exchange to be a remarkable "teaching moment," an example of what I call
"the pedagogy of accountability." When people's words are dragged into the light of day,
the anonymity of email stripped away, those persons become accountable to a larger
community.

However simple and spiteful an initial piece of hate mail, it is possible to hold
a meaningful conversation about tolerance with someone who disagrees with me. Here
is another significant example:

I won't sugar coat it, I don't think any of you should doubt the seriousness of the "new McCarthyism". Many of us consider you traitors to this
nation... You have apparently overstepped your bounds (gregmc33@
gmail.com, March 29, 2007).

On my blog, I posted the complete text of this email under the title "Horowitz
minion admits to being a new McCarthyist." Outraged at the exposure, gregmc replied
that I had been "slaughtered" by Laura and charged me with operating in an "elitist
little bubble."

I doubted the utility of further discussion. But after one more exchange, gregmc wrote:

Admitting fault is a huge soul reliever. Trust me, I admit fault quite
frequently. I have several individuals who's [sic] views are not exactly
aligned with mine. Many of them are rabidly anti-capitalist and seem-

ingly anti-American but, I converse with them frequently and we admit fault to each other when such admission is due.

I won't postulate that you and I can ever see eye to eye but perhaps we can learn from each other. You are obviously an intelligent individual but in my humble opinion, your views are a bit skewed, a bit too far to the left. Down the middle is a healthy place to be. Let's keep these lines open. I will stay off of your site and just observe for a while. Maybe I will shoot you an essay or two of mine for your input and vice versa (March 27, 2007).

On March 30, in a comment on my blog, he wrote, "Indeed, I do seek further dialog with Ms. Cloud (apologies). Some learning on both of our parts will be productive. We are two people with different perspectives but one goal, to help this greatest nation on this most beautiful Earth." In these last notes, gregmc apologized, expressed willingness to engage people who disagree with him, and said he had respect for my intelligence. To me this transformation is profound. Even the limited publicity granted my blog provoked a shift in frame from the pseudo-intimate to the civic. These exchanges show that women assailed in private regarding public matters can reverse the vector of that relationship. However, that this transformation is not the product of reasoned dialogue alone. The pedagogy of public accountability is also the pedagogy of public shaming. My correspondents were deeply embarrassed to find words that they had assumed to be private on public display. By deploying their shame, I forced these writers to become accountable to an imagined community of civilized people.

Insults and threats are common in a contentious political arena, and those of us who spoke out against the wars after 9/11 got used to receiving them. However, I have argued that hate mail is a gendered phenomenon, and that hate mail targeting women constitutes an intimate violation rooted in misogyny. It is a longstanding feminist strategy to bring issues like rape, sexual exploitation, and pornography—long relegated to the private domain—into public visibility and political accountability. Secret violations eat away at women, but publicity may render them impotent. Thus, turning the hate-mail phenomenon inside out is a potentially empowering strategy for women who refuse to stay in their places.

Table 1: Major categories of gender-neutral hate mail with representative examples

Category	Description	Approx. number	Examples
Go away.	A defense of the ideals of the US and of the war, often referencing military service and the positive impact of US military and economic power and the free market; accompanied by invitation to me to leave the country; some long and relatively civil exchanges about the merits and demerits of US foreign policy; some defenses of Christianity; surprisingly few references to victims of 9/11, but some references to Taliban, Al Qaeda, and other "enemies" and my alleged support of them	46	"I'll buy an airline ticket for you to any country in the world that you think is better than the USA and give you $500,000 if you renounce your USA citizenship and promise never to come back to my America. She doesn't need you anymore. You sleep with her enemy." (Solarsail, solarsail_5@juno.com, March 6, 2007) "Face it Dana, you are anti-american. . . My suggestion for you . . . Move to another country, maybe England. . . . Or better yet the middle east where as a woman, you will be treated like a dog! Sound fun?' Lance, fortuanecookie@gmail.com, March 6, 2007) "You should fall to your knees and thank God that we have the brave men and women of the US military to protect our freedoms from those who would try to take it from us. . . You spit on the graves of these fine people by questioning the righteousness of the cause they died for." (Michael Champion, mschampion@butlermfg.com, July 8, 2002)
You are stupid.	Intellectual insults; expressions of fear that I might indoctrinate students; several long (and one or two eloquent) essays attempting to school me in the merits of capitalism, globalization, and US policy.	30	"It's hard to believe, listening to you, that you are any type of teacher. Every other thing you said was barely literate. . . . Amazing that you even graduated high school." (Chip Towne, March 7, 2007) "Let's just say it was quite surprising that someone who teachers courses on "persuasion" was so unpersuasive. . . . Maybe you should add a course in 'how to dodge even the most straightforward questions.'" (Dan Hauck, danhauck@charter.net, March 29, 2007 "I hate that you and your like are indoctrinating young minds at OUR universities and getting subsidized with OUR tax dollars." (N Haynes, nhaynes@scarabimaging.com, July 3, 2002) "You—whose IQ I am sure is very high—are precisely the sort of person I think of when I use the phrase 'pugnaciously stupid.' It's the aggressive nature of your idiocy, the in-your-faceness of your Jackassery, that so offends me." (Ben Gibbons, ben.gibbons@pringmail.com, July 3, 2002) "A lot of people are laughing at you today. You are ridiculous." (Joe Kozocas, email and date unavailable)
Ivory Tower	Anti-intellectual populist letters; often sarcastic, sometimes moving essays, pointing out alleged hypocrisy of left wing intellectuals; marked by attempts at eruditon on the part of letter writers; expressing contempt for academics who couldn't get a job in "the real world"; swipes at an assumed elite lifestyle; many observations that my column in	25	"I will not recite my cv to you. Suffice it includes graduate degrees and years teaching at the college level. . . . I think 'twit,' one who derides taunts or ridicules, is a pretty fair description of people such as you." (Patrick R. Glass, LTC [retired], prglass@qus.net, July 4, 2002) "I'm being oppressed by the Multi-Nationals!! Also, I'm depressed by the Multi-Nationals!. Will you Pledge, as it were, to help? I need you to do several things for me. Stop, immediately, driving a car, using a dishwasher, washing machine, dryer, T.V., telephone, computer, calculator, printer, hair-care products, feminine products, Levi-Strauss clothes, watching movies, and . . . paying all of your bills. Then . . . please send me all your money." (Danny Schroder, danny@staewidellc.com, July 2, 2002)

Category	Number	Description	Examples
		the paper was a brilliant self-parody This category informed and spurred by a column by Tammy Bruce, "A Scrap of Cloth," published on "FrontPageMag.com", part of which reads: "I think it's safe to say Cloud's mornings are consumed with making sure her daughter has the right soccer sneakers and whether or not to get a tall half-caf nonfat latté or cappuccino. This, before a day probably focused on getting published so she can achieve tenure, getting a manicure, and making more money so she can get that filler she needs for her Filofax, while struggling with whether to take the Pilates or yoga class. No, professor Cloud, you're not a radical; are you an ungrateful fraud."	"Your sad, silly, contrived politics are an affront to everything my family has worked and struggled for since the end of the 19th century. This 'corrupt nation' that you so snidely deride from your Ivory Tower is the same nation that liberated my family from the sewers of Europe! (Brad Torgerson, sub-odeon@attbi.com, July 2, 2002) "It would appear that a fiercely ideological, email-propelled tempest is roaring in Texas. Much of this energy is no doubt aggravated by your critics' frustration with their awareness that, contrary to your assertion that your own views represent but a slender reed of the overall university worldview, much of American academia is not merely 'progressive' or 'slightly left of center' but an entrenched, hard-core leftist animal. Your pledge only confirmed their opinion that the ivory tower is leaking anti-American venom at an alarming rate, and chewing lesions in the brains of our vaguely adultish children in the process." (David Wrone, July 2, 2002) "I was afraid that the fine art of parody had been lost, but this is magnificent! Of course, the 'Dana Cloud' creation is such an egregious jackass that no one possibly could believe any such person really exists. . . We have found a Jonathan Swift for our age—and her name is 'Dana Cloud!'" (Lawrence Fossi, lfossi@fossilaw.com, July 2, 2002) "With regard to that sinkhole of slaver that you offer as the new pledge: How dare you offer to speak for me? You condescending patronizing self-aggrandizing peacock!" (Donald Wismann, Jr., Dwismann@nc.rr.com, March 22, 2008)
Dear Comrade	12	Comparisons to Hitler, Stalin, Pol Pot, generally making the argument that socialism/communism is akin to Nazism, mistaking Stalinism for Marxism	"I pledge allegience (sic) to Karl Marx, whose philosophy brought the world more human misery than any other—nearly 100 million murdered, countless more imprisoned, failed economies, and otherwise miserably oppressed people." (HKDrcooks@aol.com, July 5, 2002) "Dear Comrade in Arms, I admire and respect your use of intolerance in the name of tolerance. I often employed it to great advantage. Your brilliant tactic of encouraging debate and free thinking and then organizing a protest against another's right to speak is brilliant. I love the hypocrisy of it. If only I had employed it myself, I may be alive today and leader of the 'Free' World. I could have used people like you. Sincerely, Adolf." Don Newton, Don.Newton@brother.com, March 6, 2007)
Fire her.	5	Threats to my employment in the form of letters to my Chair, Dean, Regents and public petitions	(Addressed to Chancellor, Regents) "How is it that a University like UT can employ a professor like Ms. Cloud? I have spoken with members of my church (Great Hills Baptist Church) about what Ms. Cloud teachers and her qualifications. We are starting a petition suggesting her removal from UT" (Gabriel Jones, Michael_gabriel_jones@yahoo.com, March 9 2007) (Addressed to Chair, Dean) "In my opinion, you've made a HUGE mistake in having her at UT and I would hope you will take the same approach to removing her as did the University of Colardo when they removed the tenured Prof. Churchill. Just because Dr. Cloud is tenured, does not mean she cannot be removed. Do it!!!" (Robert William Zerby, Ph.D., Colonel/Infantry [retired], March 7, 2007) (Addressed to Chair, Dean) "As a life long Texan I was appalled to read the filth spewed forth by Dana Cloud. Please terminate her immediately. There can be no excuse for employing such a malcontented and hideously twisted person to teach our children. Fire her." (Benjamin Dean, via "Stergil," fj40@hotmail.com July 8, 2002).

Table 2: Gender Specific Hate Mail With Representative Examples

Category	Description	Number	Examples
Disgust	Appearance-related and other abusive and dehumanizing personal insults, including challenges to my intellectual authority; close resemblance to Margaret Cho's. Of interest is the way in which invocations of God's authority warrant the aggressive reaction to my ideas and person.	5	"Hello you disgusting pig, put your money with (sic) mouth is and leave the country that you think is so terrible. . . . I feel bad for you that you are such an angry and hateful person, (sic) your ugly daughter will end up failing in life like you. . . . How vapid you are to even have a web page, (sic) do you really think anybody cares if you live or die outside of your ugly kids and dogs. . . . Lots of love you piece of garbage. God bless" (Peter O'Brien, peterobrien17@hotmail.com, July 8, 2002) "I just wanted to say that I think you are a disgusting hypocrite. . . . Just move away to a place that makes your pathetic soul happy. . . . You are an incomprehensible human being." (Frank, email and date unavailable)
Pity and Prayer	Offers—sarcastic or otherwise—of help and prayer for me and my daughter; paternalistic, but also emotional and conventionally feminine; this category includes the largest number of letters from women	8	"I pledge to pray for your poor daughter. How sad it must be to have to live with such an angry confused person. You should take her to Iraq where the possibilities for academic and political freedom are evidently so much greater." (Robert Murphy, rjmurphyjr@hotmail.com, July 2, 2002) "How very sad it is that you don't know God, but what's even sadder is that you aren't allowing your daughter to know God. My prayers are with you and your daughter." (Kathy Renn, kathyrenn@hotmail.com, July 1, 2002) "I have come to the conclusion (especially after looking at your picture on the UT web site) that only someone who was deeply hurt or humiliated (probably early in life) could be so biter towards the country and society that gave you so much. The truth is I am sorry for you, (sic) it must be difficult to get up each day knowing that there is nothing but hate, loathing and discontent to look forward too (sic). I will pray for you Dr. Cloud. I will pray that your eyes will be opened to the displaced anger or hurt that resides inside you. That you will see that holding on to such anger or hurt will and has turned you into a bitter proponent of some very destructive philosophical positions. I will also pray that you find some sort of personal happiness." (Chris Delmain, chris_work@comcast.net, March 6, 2007)
Child Abuse	Denial of my competence as a parent on the basis of my politics or sexual orientation; blurs with pity/prayer; some suggestion of challenges to my custody arrangement; strangely, most writers mention both sexual orientation and my socialist politics as basis for judgment.	7	"You're a sexual deviant with a daughter?!! You should be arrested for child abuse!" (solarsail, solarsail_5@juno.com, March 6, 2007) "I ache for your daughter; what a life she has in store after years of being spoon fed your distorted, relativist, socialist rhetoric." (Tim Max, timmax@hotmail.com, July 8, 2002) "It's hard to believe that an 11 year-old (sic) could be delighted by any court decision that didn't give her piles of candy or dates with the dreamest (sic) guy in the class. How uncomfortable can your 11 year old daughter really be? She only knows what she's learned from you. It's how sad to think she's going to hate this country and work to tear it down in stead of work for it. . . . Geez, teach your daughter something positive." (Dennus Unser, dennisunser@lycos.com, July 2, 2002) "Maybe she's not really thinking for herself yet and she's just reflecting what you think." (Michael Watkins, mikempw@hotmail.com, July 2, 2002)
Sexual Dimunition; Lesbian Bashing	Diminishes my status by using diminutive gendered language to name me; equation of lesbianism with treason	3	"Dear Butch, I feel sorry for you. What a warped view of things you have. But I'm sure you think you are "enlightened" If you hate America so much, hike up your skirts and head for the border." (gm, date and email unavailable) "My advice to you since I think you lack sex or engage in lesbian sex, is to get laid with a good wholesome thick cock. (Albert, AAF1315@aol.com, March 7, 2007)

| Threat | Implied physical threats, often with a gendered component | 6 | "My own allegiance is to those who are brave enough to deal with the likes of you, in ways that you richly deserve. Fortunately, they are coming. Look into the camera and say after me: 'I am an academic. My mother was an academic [she was not].... We are truly the daughters of hate.'" (Abu Rankin, Rankin103@aol.com, July 5, 2002)

"Want to see how they treat women over in those countries that you so jokingly pledge allegience (sic) to? http:story.news.yahoo.com/news?tmpl=story&uu=/ap/20020702/ap_on_re_as/Pakistan_gangrape 3 (a story about women being gang raped in Pakistan; (Lschorle, lschorle@swbell.net, July 2, 2002) (copied to the UT President) "You, dear doctor, are on the wrong side now. The PC police will not come to your aid. I firmly believe that your days are numbered as a member of the faculty at the University of Texas." Followed by dare to visit him in person, complete with address and cell phone (Phillip Lee Watts, president@po.utexas.edu, July 5, 2002) |

Decolonial Critics
for Academic Freedom

Emma Pérez

I N HIS RECENT PUBLICATION, *The Professors: The 101 Most Dangerous Academics in America*, David Horowitz notes: "the radical has colonized a significant part of the University system and transformed it to serve its political needs."[1] The controversial Horowitz has set out to malign the reputations of "leftist" and "liberal" academicians with whom he most disagrees. In his mind, the North American University is in chaos because the study of Western Civilization has been undermined by thinkers like myself, a self-proclaimed Chicana, lesbian, socialist feminist. Instead of focusing upon Aristotle and Socrates, for example, contemporary scholar-activists choose to analyze phenomena such as race, class, gender, and sexuality. My subject position, as a Chicana historian, a feminist and a lesbian, makes me an easy target for reactionaries who prefer to silence the histories finally being uncovered.

I mention myself because I was included in Horowitz's book as one of the "101 Most Dangerous Professors" who was demonized and berated alongside my former colleague, Ward Churchill. I was not particularly distressed when I heard I had been included; in fact I was honored to be among luminaries like Angela Davis and Noam Chomsky. And, when I read that I was dangerous because I claimed my identity as a Chicana historian, I was initially perplexed that such a moderate claim—that is, the study of Mexican Americans in the US and Mexico—could be considered so hazardous to our student population. Upon further reading the entry about me, I realized that Mr. Horowitz had no real understanding of historiography, much less the study of Chicanas and Chicanos or any racial/ethnic minorities whose histories are being recovered and probed. Furthermore, when Horowitz invoked colonialism in his introduction, he did so without any comprehension of colonization and its historical implications in a geographic terrain where only American Indians once lived in great numbers.

In my mind, we have all inherited a history of colonialism and that history is full of contradictory "truths." In fact, I would argue that precisely because we are people of the United States, we have been blinded by the nation's patriotic discourse, which functions as an alibi to justify colonization throughout US history. In my work as a Chicana feminist lesbian historian, I have focused on the *decolonial* as a method to help cut through the contradictions, myths, and lies that have often constructed the traditional, patriotic story of this nation.

To make sense of colonialist ideology, I decided that it was necessary to examine history from a decolonizing perspective, which I named the "decolonial imaginary." This new category of decolonial imaginary can help us rethink history in a way that recovers agency for those on the margins by bringing their lives and struggles to light. It is also important to convey that history without imposing a colonial way of seeing. "Colonial," for my purposes here, can be defined as a system of domination and violent coercion that conquering people use to govern those they have subjugated. We must also remember the irony that the colonized may also become like their invaders, by assimilating a colonial mindset. This colonial mentality accepts the dominant culture, gender, class, and sexuality as normal, natural, and good. The colonial imaginary is a way of thinking about national histories and identities that must be disputed if we are to grasp the lies, injustices, and naked power dynamics behind colonial narratives and values and construct new stories, identities, values, and, ultimately, societies.

The colonial mindset establishes the naming of things, which is already going to leave something out, leave something unsaid, and leave silences and gaps that must be uncovered. The history of the United States has been limited by an imagination imbued with unchallenged thinking about how things are named, such as "Progress" and the "American West." This means that even the most radical of histories are influenced in various ways by the very colonial imaginary against which they rebel. I have proposed a decolonial imaginary as a rupturing space, the alternative to a colonial history, but it is an alternative that must become a conscious decision to interrogate power relations in our society. It is a deconstructive tool to assist us as we contest the past to revise it in a manner that tells more of the unseen and unheard stories from the margins. Instead of falling prey to that which is easy—allowing white colonial rules and standards to (re)construct and interpret our past—I suggest we become decolonial critics to analyze and delegitimate interrogate colonial, racist ideologies.[2]

I interrogate colonialism to ask the question, what does it mean to be a decolonial critic in the twenty-first century? For me, decolonizing the mind, the spirit, the body, the geographic, cultural, and socioeconomic terrain we all live with and inside of, is our duty, our goal, and our challenge for this century. But what does it mean to decolonize the mind, the spirit, the land, and the socioeconomy? We're living in an age of rampant Empire building, an era of a new stage of global colonization, often named "neoliberalism," whereby transnational corporations like Halliburton and ExxonMobil seek to dominate resources, markets, and peoples throughout the world, often imposing aggressive privatization policies to gain "ownership" rights and economic and political control. Yet Horowitz and his supporters would not concede that their economic interests are inextricably linked to colonization. Instead, theirs is a fight for "freedom" and "democracy," ambiguous and tentative ideologies that have historically accompanied the colonizer's stance. But, it does not take much historical research to see that the invasion of Iraq is just one more colonial mission in a long line of many which began when American Indians were massacred and displaced in the sixteenth and seventeenth centuries, and when African slaves were imported like cattle to work the land from which the Indians had been exiled. And, when the US invaded Mexico to acquire the current Southwest in 1846–48, colonization was the means to their end— furthering the pursuit of Empire, property, wealth, and domination.

Today, we face a new level of ideological battles. A far more sophisticated backlash against the civil rights, fought for and won in the 1960s and 1970s is being waged against the rights of women, gays and lesbians, African Americans, Chicana/os, American Indians, Asian Americans, and animal and environmental advocates. Those with progressive politics have become the scapegoats of the post-9/11 era. In the last presidential election, eleven states banned gay marriage, but, more importantly, stripped away domestic partner benefits. When the far right demonized queers, most people were not surprised. Gays have always been easy targets. And when neoconservatives attacked First Amendment rights, I think that most people living in this country assumed that those rights are, for the most part, protected under the law.

But those of us who inhabit the margins of society and live with racist, sexist, homophobic, and class-based assaults on a daily basis were not shocked, when, shortly after the presidential inauguration of January 2005, an American Indian scholar from a Department of Ethnic Studies was held up for scathing scrutiny. Although the administrators at the University of Colorado publicly proclaimed that Ward Churchill's academic freedom should be protected, they did nothing to stop the allegations against him, charges that would not have existed if the administration of CU Boulder had stood up for his free speech rights in 2005. (To not admit mistakes amidst the debacle of the invasion of Iraq seems to have been a strategy in this country at this time) Instead, the University placated their right-wing investors and cowered before conservative attack dogs, and launched an investigation that initially wanted to challenge Ward for not really being "Indian"—that racist absurdity, however, was dropped. After months of rummaging through thousands of published pages of his writings, a committee at the administrative level concluded that a few footnotes had been erroneous, when in fact committee members blatantly upheld sources by scholars antagonistic to Churchill. Moreover, the committee found three separate publications they claimed Churchill plagiarized, charges that CU sociology professor Tom Mayor rebutted in detail.[3]

I would propose that the decision to attack an American Indian scholar's footnotes, based upon dubious arguments, is founded on a colonial understanding of our history. The colonial mindset has emerged from a history that conveniently omits and erases those on the margins, and has also massacred people who created problems by defending themselves on this geographic terrain. Once again, an Indian defended his stance and was punished by a hegemonic colonial ideology angry that he did not succumb to defeat. It is that kind of inherited history that can rationalize the investigation of the only formerly tenured American Indian professor on a campus where less than fifteen percent of all faculty and students are people of color. University of Colorado, as a state-run, public institution, does not represent its own population. Chicanos/as are over thirty percent of the state's growing population and less than ten percent of that population is represented on the Boulder campus. If, as scholar activists, we are committed to social change, and I believe we are, then what are we to do? I want to answer that question by turning to the importance of decolonization.

Land, like a body, is imprinted and policed by those traversing and claiming it as they would seize a body—both became property for the colonizers. In the seventeenth and eighteenth centuries, American Indians became as much the property of the Spanish as did the land that came to be known as the Spanish Borderlands—the present day western United States. In my own work, I have attempted to address colonial relations, of land and bodies, particularly Chicanas in the Southwest and Mexicanas in Yucatan. I argue that a colonial perspective is always present in the interpretation of history, and that we must move into the decolonial way of seeing to take apart all relations of power, whether gendered, sexual, racial, or classed-based.

What is also clear to many of us on the margins is that there is a relationship between the attack against Ward's scholarship and an assault on Ethnic Studies. Ward has published 10 books and over 100 articles. He continues to be one of the most cited scholars in his field of American Indian Studies. His contributions to Ethnic Studies are far-reaching and widespread. The many controversial essays he published throughout his career have helped to found Ethnic Studies and American Indian Studies at institutions of higher learning. In other words, his scholarship has consistently challenged the status quo and made it possible for Departments of Ethnic Studies to endure at the University. It is, therefore, ironic that someone who helped establish Ethnic Studies is now being investigated for the very thing he helped create—a department and program that would ensure diverse perspectives of historically under-represented communities. The vilification of Ward is only the beginning of many forthcoming attempts to discredit scholars of color who study the voices of those previously silenced through colonial means. To persecute Ward is to agree that all scholars of color are suspect.

Ethnic Studies on CU Boulder campus is, my opinion, both ghettoized and barrioized. It amazes me when I tell students or faculty outside of my department that there is such a program on campus. While visibility in many ways is up to us, I would like to point out that with so few professors in the department, we are stretched thin.

With such a small department, it is no wonder Ethnic Studies is not taken very seriously on this campus. In order for a campus the size of CU Boulder to be truly diverse in its faculty and student population, Ethnic Studies would have to be a much larger department with funded graduate programs. I often feel that, as scholars of color in our Department, we are only good enough to teach service courses to undergraduate students, and that our scholarship does not merit training graduate students. I wonder if CU will ever take scholars of color and students of color on campus seriously? Or is their concern only with profit and corporate service, while using ethnic studies as a front for a feeble commitment to diversity and liberal arts values?

Without a larger population of scholars and students of color on this campus, can we have the kinds of discussions necessary for our future? As the world gets smaller, as a variety of different people with different languages and cultures all come together in this country, as immigration from Mexico and Latin America, from Africa and Asia, continues to grow, Ethnic Studies will become more significant to the University. The study of a variety of cultures and ethnicities is the future. But, when I look around at the homogeneity on the CU Boulder campus, I am discouraged, and I wonder, how long before this campus catches up to the rest of the world? How long before this country realizes that it was founded on immigration and diversity? The prolonged, systematic machinations to censure, then fire, my colleague Ward Churchill, based on petty findings to support constructions of academic misconduct, is really an attempt to stop what I believe is already happening globally: people are recognizing the lies, the half-truths, the political agendas, the power plays, and the profiteering that benefit the privileged few in the name of democracy.

I arrived in Boulder in 2003. A year and a half later, Ward Churchill and Ethnic Studies were under attack. After predicting the oncoming assault, Ward decided to step down as Chair and asked me to fill in. He received hundreds of emails and phone calls harassing him in the first weekend after Hamilton College rescinded their invitation to him because the College became aware of a 2001 blog post about 9/11. The barrage of email, phone calls, and racial epithets hurled against Ward and our Department were violent, offensive and distressing. Here are a few examples:

Date: Wed, 02 Feb 2005 20:57:15 -0500
From: Kenan Walker <KBWalker@triad.rr.com>
To: Emma.Perez@Colorado.EDU
Subject: I am a veteran and a SOLDIER…… ….

May you come face to face with REAL Patriots (SOLDIERS, maybe US Army Rangers, Marines, SEALS, Green Berets), who will kick your sorry asses to Hell and back!!! May you rot in Hell, you sorry sons of bitches!!!

Go to a local VFW, or American Legion, and spew your bullshit, and see what happens, you punk.

Date: Wed, 2 Feb 2005 09:10:56 -0700
From: Dennis McDonald <DennisHMcDonald@worldnet.att.net>
To: emma.perez@colorado.edu
Cc: president@cu.edu
Subject: Churchill

After viewing your comments last night, it appears that American Indian "wannabe" Churchill and his wife are not the only assholes in the Ethnic Studies Dept. You are a disgrace to the teaching community and are probably just like Churchill—a person who never held a real job and spent years as a radical in college and eventually got some half ass degree from some crumby little school, eventually got a job at CU and hide behind tenure to push your radical views under the guise of education. You probably don't have a clue about the real world. There IS a limit to free speech and it is called racism! Last year voters came close to legislating against liberals on college staffs—well this will surely revive the legislation. I will be contacting the Board of Regents and recommend they clean out the entire Ethnic Studies Dept. The department served a need in the past, but has degenerated over the years to bunch of radicals who use tax dollars and aid money to advocate revolution. The whole issue of tenure needs reevaluating. I predict your days at CU are limited—you probably have no marketable skills—so let me give you a few phrases that may help in your next job; "Would you like fries with that?", "Sir, can I supersize that order?"
Dennis McDonald

Date: Wed, 2 Feb 2005 23:54:20 -0600
From: Paul Wickland <plwkd@wideopenwest.com>
To: Emma.Perez@Colorado.EDU
Subject: Press conference comments-Churchill

Professor:
I must say that I am utterly amazed at the sheer stupidity of the remarks you made on Tuesday. How can you possibly equate the trashy propaganda that Mr. Churchill has written as some form of scholarly work? Moreover, how can you bring yourself to defend this nutcase?

This parasite should be immediately terminated as should you for the absolute idiocy of your comments. I am not sure how in the world you achieved the level of associate professor, since it is obvious that you are not a deep thinker and painfully evident that you are a person of very limited intellect. Defending this lunatic clearly places you in the same category as your colleague from a mental acuity standpoint.

It scares me to think about the young minds you are likely poisoning by spewing this kind of garbage in the classroom. I would characterize it as coming straight from a cesspool. Moreover, the taxpayers of the state of Colorado are the poor losers in all of this. Heaven help those of us who live in other states if we are ever forced to spend our hard earned tax dollars for the blatant and obvious lack of quality that exists in Colorado's publicly supported institutions of higher learning, evidenced by your and Mr. Churchill's rhetoric.

Date: Wed, 9 Feb 2005 20:06:41 -0600
From: Paul Wickland <plwkd@wideopenwest.com>
To: Emma.Perez@Colorado.EDU
Subject: RE: Press conference comments-Churchill

How did I know that you would not have the intestinal fortitude to reply? You are obviously a spineless and poor excuse for a human being, not to mention a college professor. You can still reply, as I will be more than happy to listen to your story.

Are you familiar with the saying, "birds of a feather flock together?" Think about that as it relates to your relationship with another spineless loudmouth, namely Mr. Churchill.

Date: Sun, 6 Feb 2005 17:27:05 -0800 (PST)
From: Everett Lakoduk <lle7@sbcglobal.net>
To: Emma.Perez@Colorado.EDU
Subject: Churchill

You really need to rethink your position of defending a sick, fake joke like Ward Churchill. This piece of crap has been grandstanding and making a living by being "shocking" for a long time. Well, he got his wish. He shocked the entire nation of this great United States of America and he is finished. If you stand close to him you will also be "electrecuted" by the same outrage this nation has for him. Do you think it's time to rethink your moral values? We do.

Date: Wed, 9 Feb 2005 12:14:04 -0800 (PST)
From: Tay Weinstein <tayweinstein@yahoo.com>
To: emma.perez@colorado.edu
Subject: explain

PLEASE explain why you and others feel it necessary to defend Ward Churchill. Wrong is Wrong!!!!! Do you think that his views are correct? I understand (as an ex-CU student who has taken ETHN classes) that all your department is interested in is making white students feel bad, but c'mon. Anyone with a sense of right and wrong knows that Churchill's statements are fundamentally incorrect. Why defend speech in an academic setting if it is obviously false and hurtful? You are being irresponsible by allowing it to go on. The only people who support him are spoiled little trustfund babies and professors like you who probably fear his termination could lead to their own eventually. If you can defend the sneak-attack, cowardly assault on the WTC, please write back. I would love to hear your argument.

The following email was sent to President Elizabeth Hoffman, who resigned a few days after standing before Colorado's legislature to accuse Churchill's critics of "McCarthyism." Some would argue that, because of a too-tolerant stance toward Churchill, Colorado Governor Owen, forced her resignation.

From: Wild
To: president@cu.edu
Sent: Friday, February 04, 2005 11:38 PM

President Hoffman—
Why is Professor Churchill refusing to apologize to the 9/11 victims? He has already slandered their good name by calling them Nazis, as if they are to blame for what happened? That's psychotic, believing they deserved to die!!! Ward Churchill even looks like a psycho (and I'm not kidding). Well, perhaps Osama will be giving Ward a call on his cell real soon? He could use a crazy Indian to help out all the Muslim terrorists. If Churchill is on their side (Osama's), then get the hell out of this country and don't ever come back! Aiding and abetting terrorism will result

in a federal maximum security jail cell real quick. It seems certain that extremist writings sooner or later results in extremist behavior.

Please President Hoffman, return our universities to mainstream thinking, thought and action! Giving us scientists, researchers, businessmen, educators and leaders!

Leave the crackpots to UC Berkeley. Colorado is a conservative state, full of ranchers, farmers and outdoor pleasure seekers. Don't let a few, destroy our good name of "Colorado."

The key question President Hoffman, is why do you let this kind of thing go on? Why aren't you giving leadership and direction to all the Deans and Chairmans at every level? Resign, or start taking direct action. Every time I see you, you are hiding behind the Chancellor or some other administrator like Ron Stump. You can only delegate so much!!!
Jayhawkss

These emails are a small sample of thousands of electronic messages, letters, and phone calls that filled the boxes of Ward Churchill, the Department of Ethnic Studies, myself, and other colleagues in the Department. I have not even begun to assess the psychic and psychological damage inflicted upon our community by these colonizer mentalities that berate Ethnic Studies and Women's Studies programs that were brought to the University in struggle during the 1960 and 1970s. The interdisciplinary programs introduced the diverse perspectives of historically underrepresented communities into the curriculum. By definition these approaches must counter the standard canon of humanities and social sciences. Academic freedom is critical to this endeavor. The laws of the Colorado Regents (ART 5, part D) recognize that we have not only the right but the responsibility to engage in such critical analysis:

> [A]cademic freedom is defined as the freedom to inquire, discover, publish and teach as the faculty member sees it…faculty members should not be subjected to direct or indirect pressures or interference from within the university, and the university will resist to the utmost such pressures or interference when exerted from without.

Will Ethnic Studies disappear at CU Boulder? Will other professors be censured, persecuted, and fired? Are we censuring ourselves in our classrooms now? Given the politics of Ward's case, can we actively and in good conscience recruit students and faculty of color to this University? Unfortunately, what we are experiencing in Colorado is happening throughout the country and throughout college campuses; scholar-activists continue to assert the battle for social change instead of conforming to a status quo that often only serves to censure and silence inconvenient truths.

For me, Ward Churchill is a pioneering decolonial critic whose scholarship interrogates colonialism and challenges inconvenient truths about present-day colonialism. Churchill moves us through a decolonial path that seeks an understanding of history that is not common, that is unheard and often muzzled. By exposing the lies and motivations informing a demeaning and stereotyped history of American Indians, he contributes to a perspective that strips away racist perceptions like the ones exhibited in the emails above. And while I'm not sure about the future of Ethnic Studies here or anywhere else in the nation, I do know that the current political climate makes it difficult to conduct our academic work or to exist in programs like Ethnic Studies, when administrative support is dubious or tentative at best. As a Chicana, lesbian, socialist feminist who will continue to voice oppositional politics from the margins, I firmly believe that our ongoing struggles as decolonial critics will not permit academia or society as a whole to erase or silence us.

Regimes of Normalcy in the Academy

The Experiences of Disabled Faculty

Liat Ben-Moshe and Sumi E. Colligan

THE ACADEMY CAN BE CONSIDERED A FORM OF "IMAGINED COMMUNITY" in which bonds of "horizontal comradeship" trump distinctions of status and title (Anderson 1983 [1991]: 7). However, in reality, such communities generate suppressed hierarchies in order to maintain the illusion of sameness (of bodies, of mission, of pedagogical content and style). In this context, people with disabilities are only allowed to enter the gilded walls of the academy to the extent that they are able or willing, or are perceived as able or willing, to uphold the appearance of conforming to able-bodied assumptions and practices with regard to learning, teaching, and researching, as well as meeting additional requirements and standards of professionalism.

This expectation of "compulsory able-bodiness," to use Robert McRuer's (2006) term, often generates a dual process of "pushing down" and "holding back." On the one hand, those who wield power and influence within the academy may act as gatekeepers to those who embody or express challenges to the performance of "compulsory able-bodiness"; on the other hand, disabled students and professors may choose not to expose nor to pursue certain curricular or research interests concerning disability, to share their struggles as disabled persons, or to reveal normalizing structures, norms, and processes in an effort to maintain a toe-hold in a system that might otherwise exclude them entirely. Leaving able-bodied privileges unexamined and intact allows the academy to reproduce itself, concealing the harm done to all its participants.

The recent shift in the academy from a "for education" to a "for profit" institution has severe negative effects on all faculty and staff, but it seems that the already marginalized employees get even further repressed under current regimes of normalcy. Throughout this essay we disperse our own educational autobiographies as a way of setting the stage and framing our analysis of the mechanisms of repression, normalization, and exclusion that impact the lives of disabled students and professors. The irony of our collaborative endeavor is that joint projects in the academic world are considered less worthy of scholarly praise than those produced individually. Dismissing and disallowing collaboration is one more mechanism of repression, discouraging creativity and pushing disabled scholars, who might most benefit from such opportunities, to the margins. Throughout our essay, we intersperse numerous other personal narratives, allowing ourselves and others to "talk back" (hooks 1989) to these mechanisms. Perhaps most importantly, though, we want our readers to understand that denying certain disabled bodies/minds and ideas about disability a place in the academy robs all participants of different modes of knowing, instructing, and learning.

Sumi's Story:

> I grew up in a single family household with strong female role models. Education was a highly valued pursuit, although, initially, there was a certain assumption that my educational achievements would never match those of my able-bodied older sister and that I would need to seek education close to home. Luckily, I was raised in the San Francisco Bay Area and graduated from high school just as the disability rights movement and independent living movement were being launched, making my entry into UC Berkeley an easier one than it might otherwise have been.
>
> As an undergraduate, I developed a strong interest in anthropology. When I was preparing to graduate, a rehabilitation counselor suggested that I become a librarian rather than pursue a career in anthropology because I would have difficulty digging up bones! This advice amused me because of its ignorance of anthropology as a multifaceted field, and because I would have probably made a lousy librarian.
>
> Against this individual's advice, I sought admission to graduate school in anthropology anyway. However, I thought I'd hedge my bets by enrolling in an applied profession as well. After my experience with rehab counselors, I was convinced that this profession would benefit from employing disabled people who had a sense of life's possibilities. I was invited to an interview for this program and the rehab counseling professor who interviewed me turned out to be (not surprisingly) incredibly condescending. Rather than exploring my academic strengths and goals, he asked me to show him how I write! He also told me that I was "anti-therapeutic and self-contained" because I told him that I sought out the local rehab office for financial assistance, not counseling. His assumption was that physical disability is automatically accompanied by "psychological deficits" and character flaws. I wasn't accepted to that program. What a relief!
>
> To my initial delight, I was admitted to a graduate program in anthropology. I soon became discouraged, however, when I faced many

prejudicial attitudes. Apparently, one faculty person inquired to another, "How can a person with a disability become an anthropologist?" In a paternalistic fashion, I was told that departmental members were concerned about the dismissive treatment I might receive in the field. It seemed to me that they were simply displacing their own anxieties about disability into a global space. From their perspectives, it was the "Other" I needed to be worried about, not them. How was my situation any different from how they might be received as tall white guys or as women?

When I decided to do research in Israel, I was sent to the Near Eastern Studies Department to inquire about funds for language acquisition and travel. I was preparing to take a ten-week intensive language course in Hebrew that summer. The professor who met with me responded to my query by suggesting that I might not have the capability of learning Hebrew! (Would Turkish have been a better choice?) He also stated forthrightly that I appeared sufficiently well-dressed and that he was not running a welfare office! Disabled people, apparently, seek charity, while others seek support for laudable educational endeavors.

When I returned from the field, I felt more confident, accomplished, and worldly. Like many graduate students, I sought a teaching assistantship to begin to prepare myself for a teaching career. I was told by one faculty person that he wouldn't choose me because I couldn't carry his books; I was truly taken aback. I hadn't gone to graduate school to become someone's lackey.

The job market posed no fewer obstacles. After receiving invitations to on-campus interviews, I needed to inform faculty that I would require minor personal assistance during my stay. This disclosure immediately changed the dynamics. My vitae stated that I had conducted fieldwork in Israel but, in one instance, I was asked if I could fly. How do they think I got to Israel, via slow boat? After finishing the interview, I was told that I could have the job if I could use the key to open my office door. My normalization would be complete!

While I have generally felt supported in my current position, I think the pressures of normalization tend to encourage a masking of any difficulties one might face in accomplishing one's job, whether it be responding to emails or grading papers in a timely fashion. Colleagues are often surprised by how many hours I spend working; some assume I must be exaggerating claims in search of praise. I teach at a state college, one that is understaffed and under-funded. The faculty as a whole is expected to assume many different roles in order to maintain and expand the institu-

tion. Increased surveillance mechanisms are imposed with more complex post-tenure review processes. In this climate, it's hard to keep up and
hard to say "no"—to insist on quality of work rather than quantity of students taught, committees served, and conferences attended. We're kept
busy jockeying for position on the academic treadmill, a one-size-fits all
machine that is not molded to diverse bodies and life circumstances. This
discourages analysis of the way in which "fitness" becomes a measure of
academic citizenship, and serves to damage us all.

Disability and Employment in the Academy: A(n) (Anti) Legal Perspective

The academy is not accessible and welcoming to faculty with disabilities. According to
the US Department of Education statistics, as of 2004, teachers with disabilities made
up 3.6 percent of overall faculty, a significantly lower number then their percentage in
the population—about 19 percent currently (Anderson 2006). One possible explanation for these low rates is the costs that are often associated with hiring faculty with
disabilities. Although some disabilities require no substantive accommodations (such
as the case for people with mobility impairments on campuses which are already physically accessible), others require some modifications to the physical environment or
technological and communication aids (sign language interpreters, screen-reading
software on computers etc.). These costs are not offset by tuition, as opposed to accommodations made for students with disabilities. Disability in most universities is
not perceived as a form of diversity and an identity that will enhance the learning
environment as a whole, but it is seen instead as a financial burden to the university.
Most higher education institutions do not survey or track the numbers of faculty or
instructors with disabilities and do not include these figures in diversity initiatives or
reports (Ibid.).

Another reason for the low participation of disabled academics is related to
the low rates of students with disabilities, especially in obtaining higher degrees. Since
one can't become a faculty member without graduating with a higher education degree,
the discrimination and barriers that block disabled people from becoming students
also block them from becoming academic professionals. Moreover, because disability
is not included in most hiring initiatives as a priority of the university, most of the cost
of accommodation falls on individual departments that wish to hire disabled instructors and faculty. Some departments, such as the ones we are a part of (anthropology
and sociology), usually have miniscule budgets that are always cut when the schools
face a budgetary crisis. Under these conditions, many such departments would think
twice about hiring a person with a disability, which might increase their expenditure

with no university subsidy and commitment. Many schools and administrators do not even recognize this practice as a form of discrimination, but as the only choice possible to survive and "compete" in a neoliberal climate in which universities are encouraged to gather revenues and retool themselves as corporations with knowledge as their commodity, students and research as their product, profit-making their goal, and faculty and staff their laboring pool. Schools also do not perceive this exclusion as problematic because it is relatively easy to exclude disabled faculty in hiring, tenure, and recruitment within the bounds of existing law.

Within the legal terminology of the ADA (Americans with Disabilities Act of 1990), an institution does not have to modify its infrastructure or provide accommodations if these changes cause "undue hardship" to their operations or bottom line. It is not surprising that, under our conservative (in)justice system, the interpretation of this statute almost always leans towards the "hardship" and costs to the employer as opposed to the civil rights of the disabled plaintiffs. In fact, there is evidence proving that, since the passage of the ADA, the employment rates and hiring of people with disabilities have actually declined (Stapleton and Burkhauser 2003). Thus, universities, although legally mandated by civil rights law and the ADA, can discriminate against employees with disabilities by showing that they do not have sufficient funds or that the accommodation is "unreasonable." In an age of "reason" marked by neoliberal deregulation and gutting of social services, it is not surprising that inclusion and guarantees for full participation of all people in public and private settings are considered "unreasonable." If disability is considered at all in universities' hiring and firing policies, it is only as a legal and financial burden. Administrators in higher education institutions are more reactive then proactive when dealing with disability, and policies are usually driven by the minimum legal requirements required to comply with laws or with possible lawsuits or complaints (Anderson 2006). Within this mindset, it may not be surprising that the schools with the lowest rates of disabled faculty (less than half of the national average) seems to be law schools (Mikochik 1991).

Barriers to Inclusion of Disabled Faculty

A 2004 survey of SUNY schools offered a glimpse into disability discrimination of academics. It examined, for instance, certain access features (in policies such as evacuation procedures, in physical buildings, restrooms, etc.) and found that sixty percent were at a low level, if they existed at all. Faculty revealed to their interviewers that they were advised not to disclose their disability or to ask for accommodations. About a third of these faculty became disabled after they were already employed by the university (Anderson 2006).

Teachers who become disabled after their initial hire don't always have a choice about disclosure, and if they fail to disclose their new disability status they are subject to various forms of censure and stigmatization. For example, Virginia Hemby-Grubb (2007) was in a car accident that caused her traumatic brain injury soon after she submitted her file for tenure and promotion. She was out for a semester on medical leave, raising the issue of whether her tenure clock would be set back. She taught at a university with a four-course load, and upon returning to work she requested a single-course reduction as an accommodation. Administrators and colleagues blamed her fatigue and forgetfulness on age, totally dismissing the validity of her claims. After protracted litigation, she was offered a part-time position with part-time benefits, and decided to seek employment elsewhere. At her new university, she chose only to disclose her need for accommodations to the ADA director and was granted a three-course load, inviting negative comments from her colleagues concerning special "privileges" granted to her. In short, she was seen as pampered and lazy. In contrast, Mary Beth Slone (2007), a college professor who developed MS, talks about how disclosure deepened her relationship with her colleagues, allowing her to receive a reduced teaching schedule that maximized her classroom performance.

Unfortunately, this is not the common outcome to requesting accommodation. More typically, if a person minimizes the needs for accommodation, they are not viewed as disabled enough to receive it; and if one explains their needs in detail, they are construed as too disabled to hold the job (Abrams, 2003). The end result is a catch-22, in which the disabled employee faces potential ostracism and ridicule; can't meet tenure/promotion timetables; or endures course loads and schedules that undermine academic strengths and talents, possibly culminating in poor evaluations and ultimately dismissal. Part-time or adjunct teaching is not an option for disabled professionals who lack full-time medical benefits (largely denied under the current medical industrial complex), nor should such conditions be acceptable to any employee.

Teaching loads and teaching evaluations are not the only issues that interfere with tenure, promotion, or post-tenure review. Participation in conferences and other professional development opportunities, as well as publications and access to research grants, are crucial to meeting standards for retention and promotion. For a disabled person this may require conference hotels and sites to be fully accessible and, in some cases, scent free (if the person has chemical sensitivities). Unfortunately, many conference sites and forms of transportation are not fully accessible, thus denying participation of disabled academics from interacting with their peers. The costs of travel for some disabled professionals may include a personal assistant, interpreter, or a speech translator, all of which are services academic institutions typically don't provide for in their budgets. Moreover, access to research materials may be hampered if proper adaptive equipment or research assistance is not forthcoming within the framework of faculty or graduate student production timetables.

Liat's Story:

> One of the main gateways to becoming a professional academic is passing one's comprehensive exams and defending the dissertation. These rites of passage take various formats and differ by the specific department and institution. In my department, each potential candidate has to complete three different exams in the course of one week. Each exam is 8–10 hours long. In order to accomplish this task, given the current structure and the fact I experience back pain, I had to apply for individual accommodations, which would enable me to take each exam over a two-day period. My department was very gracious about my request and it seemed highly reasonable to them that someone with back pain would need longer breaks, especially when having to type over such an extended time.
>
> While studying for my exams I found out that my accommodations were not as individual as presumed by my department. In fact three more students taking the exam around the same time I did had also applied for similar accommodations, because of pain, fatigue, Carpal Tunnel Syndrome, and having a newborn. I am not trying to say they did not deserve it, but instead that we ALL deserve it. We deserve better. The current structure of exam taking has obvious benefits to young able-bodied men in particular, who are better positioned to receive full funding and do not usually act as full-time caregivers. But this practice also completely denies the realities that students have bodies and a need to care for themselves as well as others (such as infants, spouses, and other family members). Not everyone can afford to take a week out of their lives to write an exam, and if they manage, it is because they shift the load to others who may be already over-extended. The solution is not seeking out individual accommodations and exemptions, but to abolish the structure of exam-taking as it stands now, a structure that favors few and sets the rest up for failure.

Presuming Incompetence: Disability as a Master Category

Mary Lee Vance (2007) points out that when a disabled person is hired for a teaching or administrative position in the academy, rumors often circulate that the new person is simply an "affirmative action" hire. She states that such assumptions were made about her both as a Korean adoptee and as a disabled person. I (Sumi) remember similar accusations being leveled against me when I began my current position. These rumors have two effects: they undercut the accomplishments of people by labeling them "less competent" than able-bodied job candidates and colleagues; and they obfuscate the purpose of affirmative action policies in attempting to remedy long-standing inequalities and exclusions.

Within a campus context, students, faculty, and staff who are unfamiliar with a disabled instructor often conclude that he or she is not a faculty person at all since "professional" and "disabled" taken together is frequently considered to be an oxymoron. Consider Anne Finger's story. In the film, *Vital Signs* (1995), Anne shares a seemingly mundane story, but one which unfortunately happens frequently to visibly disabled faculty. Finger is an English professor, novelist, and wheelchair user who was looking for the Communication Department to return a key for a literary reading the prior evening. The person who offered to help directed her to the Communications Disorder Department instead. When her guide saw the wheelchair, all other information Anne provided about herself was ignored; she became a patient, instead of a college professor. Anne's story (and elements of Sumi's) reveals the internal prejudices faced by disabled students and faculty who simply attempt to do mundane things related to their profession or professional preparation. It seems that disability is a master identity, trumping other professional identities and qualifications so that the person is first presumed to be incompetent, instead of the other way around.

Ironically, the qualities that able-people see as a hindrance to professional achievement may actually enhance the relationship between faculty and student. Robert Murphy (1987) describes his connections to students as becoming more intimate after he became a wheelchair user. The rituals of distance and decorum were somewhat dispensed with, and students would spend hours hanging out in his office, conversing about a wide range of issues. This creation of an informal learning community can enhance student retention and the embodied professor can serve as a catalyst for new ways of knowing. Nonetheless, such intimacy may be perceived as a threat to other colleagues who strive hard to present themselves as disembodied entities, elevated in the "loftiness" of their detached selves.

Disability in the Classroom

Liat's story:
> A few years ago I was working as a teaching assistant for a course whose content was not of my choosing. The course itself was quite unconventional in its materials and delivery style, due to the instructor's commit-

ments as a feminist and postmodernist. Many of the course readings touched on oppression due to race, gender, and class. Although the material was quite progressive it did not include any mention of disability, unless one takes into account the ableist language in the texts themselves. As the TA who was a visibly disabled wheelchair user, I added my own angle, which sometimes included disability, but only minimally, as I was trying mostly to cover the material given by the instructor.

The only time disability issues were discussed in my three years as a TA was the day Christopher Reeve died. Christopher Reeve is best known as the actor who played Superman, and was injured in a horse riding accident which made him paralyzed from the neck down. After his injury the media described him as heroic and inspirational, and he became a spokesperson for stem cell research and other therapies aimed at preventing and curing disabilities. In the disability community, however, he was not a well-liked figure because they disdain the portrayal of disabled people as inspirational, and especially because disabled activists perceive disability as a positive identity and a form of diversity, not a curse to be removed. It was also clear that Reeve enjoyed class privilege and could have advocated for making buildings and health care accessible to all instead of raising money for expensive research and therapies with no guaranteed results.

Back to class. It was the day we discussed features of a postmodern society, and the teacher introduced the concept of the cyborg, which is an amalgamation of human and machine. Then a student inquired if Christopher Reeve would be an example of a cyborg, and another student asked if the class knew he died the preceding evening. The instructor replied by asking if anyone knew the cause of his death and added, "Did he kill himself because he found out he would never walk again?"

One might say that this is not a substantive example of academic repression, that maybe the instructor just forgot that I was in the class, and maybe she did not really mean to ask such a question. I think it is irrelevant what was meant or thought at that moment, but what matters is when and how disability enters into academic settings. It does not enter through the front door, as usually people with (especially visible) disabilities do not become academics (for reasons explained above). And when the topic surfaces, as in this instance, discussion of disability does not typically raise awareness or enrich the curriculum. Moreover, it entered class discussions only by way of its (literal) obliteration, as if it is taken for granted that people who cannot walk naturally want to kill themselves. But if we don't teach students otherwise, if we don't explain the richness, quality, and differences embedded in disabled life, why wouldn't it be taken for granted? This is more than academic repression, it is academic annihilation.

One of the factors that contributes to this repression/annihilation is the pervasive use of disability metaphors throughout the academy. Although disabled academics and disability as part of the curriculum are usually absent in higher education, disability is very present at least in one arena—that of language. In the English language, using disability as a metaphor, an analogy, and a derogatory term is common. Examples of such phrases and terms include: lame idea, blind justice, dumb luck, felt paralyzed, the argument fell on deaf ears, crippling, crazy, insane, idiotic, and retarded. One might argue that using these words without relating them to particular individuals is not offensive. However, using disability as an analogy not only offends certain individuals, but it also impedes clear communication, perpetuates false beliefs about disability, and creates an environment of unease and exclusion in the classroom.

Disability has negative connotations when used metaphorically, while the real experience of living with a disability can be quite enriching and empowering. In all the examples above disability is used in a value-laden way. "Lame idea" means bad idea or one that is not constructed in a sufficient and persuasive manner. When we describe someone as "blind" to a fact (as, for example, some men are "blind" to sexist practices), we mean that they are lacking knowledge or awareness of their patriarchal biases and actions. "Crazy" means excessive or without control. None of these phrases carries positive and empowering interpretations. Dominant notions of people who are blind, deaf, or labeled as mentally retarded come into play when we use disabling phrases, and these notions are usually taken from a certain position, of being non-disabled. These notions do not convey the complexity of living in a society that regards people with disabilities as the Other on the basis of perceived mentally or bodily difference. Students often say to me (Liat) that they felt "paralyzed" because of the magnitude of a particular assignment, for example. From the context I understand that they mean that they felt stuck and unable to move forward. But paralysis to me does not at all imply a lack of mobility, stagnancy, or dependence since there are augmentative instruments, such as wheelchairs and personal aids that secure independence and mobility. And I should know—I AM paralyzed, but also very active and mobile…

Countering Ableism in the Academy

As Marxists, feminists, and anti-racist activists and scholars have claimed for decades, the world is viewed mostly from the perspective of the rulers, and language is created in their image as well. Therefore, we should not be surprised that the use of disabling language not only persists, but is neither contested nor acknowledged. Disabling language accepts the assumption that disabilities are bad, unfortunate, or denote lack/deficiency; that they are invisible and insignificant to society as a whole; and that they belong to the Other and are distinct from what society calls "normal." One of the most transgressive acts we can engage in as instructors is to interrogate the use of ableist language by students and colleagues as an opportunity to expose and problematize their able-bodied privileges and prejudices that go unchallenged daily in the system of higher education. This has nothing to do with so-called "political correctness" or acting as a thought and language police; it has everything to do, however, with critical education, dismantling hierarchies, and teaching respect for difference and diversity. Ableism should not be accepted in higher education; rather, in the same breath as we call out racism, anti-Semitism, sexism, xenophobia, and homophobia, so we must confront and overcome ableism in our midst

Ableism in the academy does not just reside in the bodies of the people oppressed by it. It is an issue of concern for all of us who are dedicated to social change, inclusive communities, and education as a liberating tool. The fact that learning and teaching about disability issues has been relegated, at least until recently, to the fields of medicine, rehabilitation, and social work (Linton 1998) has contributed to pervasive negative disability imagery in the classroom and scholarship, as well as to a paucity of disabled professors. Simi Linton (2006) argues that the study of disability has been subjected to institutional segregation, thereby reinforcing the perceived lack of relevance of disability scholarship to the broader population. This inevitably perpetuates the assumption that disabled people are to be acted upon by "knowing" others, and thereby denies them agency, autonomy, and dignity, as it strips away their claims as knowledge producers over their own lives.

Disability Studies is a new academic field that springs in part from the disability rights movement. Like feminist and queer studies, Disability Studies provides a conceptual framework for a unique perspective on and critique of law, culture, and society. The basic approach that Disability Studies scholars share is that disability is not an inherent trait located in the disabled person's body and mind, but is rather a result of power and discursive dynamics that categorize some as "disabled" and devalue them for embodying these imputed labels.

Disability in the classroom not only enriches the curriculum but pedagogy as well. Rod Michalko is a sociology professor who, as a blind person, introduces the students not only to sociology, but to blindness. Michalko (2001) describes his students' wonderment when they encounter him on the first day of class. The disbelief that they have a blind professor could be due to the fact that they never encountered a blind professional before, or an instructor with a visible disability. However, Michalko claims that this is not the whole story behind the students' apprehension and surprise of encountering him as their teacher. It stems from cultural beliefs that privilege sight and connect this ability to knowledge acquisition. Being "blind" to something usually means not having knowledge of it. The privileging of sight in academe and everyday language and life is ubiquitous, yet we rarely "see" it. The practices of visual reading from printed materials, of writing on and reading the chalkboard, seeing who is absent and who is paying attention, grading papers are all tasks we think can only be done visually. But as Michalko teaches his students, the fact that sight is the dominant way of doing things does not make it the only possible way.

Like Michalko's exposition of sight as a hegemonic (and often oppressive) ideology within academic settings, it is important to interrogate able-bodiness as an identity and a source of unchecked privilege within academic settings as well as discussions of oppression. Similar reasoning has been made around the need to interrogate whiteness as "an invisible knapsack" of privilege (McIntosh, 2001) and a racial identity. Being white does not entail not being raced, and being male does not mean not being gendered. If one does not identify oneself as disabled, it does not mean one does not participate in the dis/ability signification system (Thomson, 2002).

What is important to understand about the regime of normalcy in the academy is that it affects all of us. It influences the growing workload related to the "publish or perish" demand and it shapes the requirement to obtain outside funding and grants for departments. Moreover, the triumph of neoliberalism and the management of the university as a flexible capitalist enterprise compelled to maximize profits and to minimize costs, conditions the increase in part-time instructors (who work for little pay, few benefits, and no job security) and the decrease in tenure-track positions. These are trends we are all left to reckon with as academics.

Nonetheless, succumbing to the pressures of increased workloads, reduced salaries, and zero benefits must be rejected as intolerable and unacceptable. The pace of work we currently must maintain in order to get tenure and promotion is unrealistic and harmful to our health and to our lives. It does not encourage us to have and raise children, to spend time with loved ones, to be creative and artistic individuals, to be involved in our communities, or to sleep and eat well. Instead of acquiescing to ever deeper cutbacks and more exploitative demands just to stay employed, we must fight against the proletarianization of our labor; the pressures toward normalization; and the ideology of ableism. Dismantling ableist systems, however, is not possible without recognizing and relinquishing able-bodied privilege. A more expansive and just perspective of society and academia will never be achieved without conscious and concerted efforts to bring about these transformations.

V
Fast Times at Corporate Higher Ed.

Adelphi Recovers:

"The Lengthening View"

Ali Shehzad Zaidi

Adelphi University is a rare instance in which state regulators intervened to halt egregious academic repression. The university is recovering thanks to its dedicated faculty and staff, and its capable president. Nonetheless, the story of Adelphi is a cautionary tale of what can happen when right-wing ideologues seize control of trustee boards. It also bears telling as a reminder of the need for better state and federal regulation of higher education. Hopefully, the story of Adelphi will spur a nationwide movement to empower university employees, students, and faculty to run the institutions in which they work, study, and teach.

In 1985, Peter Diamandopoulos became Adelphi's seventh president, ushering in an entire decade of "shock therapy" for the small commuter school on Long Island. Opposition to Diamandopoulos grew when it was disclosed that he was the second highest paid university president in the United States. Adelphi had purchased a $1.2 million Manhattan condominium for his use at a time when it was shedding employees and course offerings.

The Committee to Save Adelphi (CSA), an advocacy group of faculty, students, and alumni, held its first press conference in October 1995. Around that time, the faculty voted 131:14 for Diamandopoulos to resign. After a *New York Times* editorial called for an investigation into Adelphi's finances, the New York State Attorney General began to look into the perks of President Diamandopoulos and the process of awarding contracts at Adelphi.

The Adelphi administration filed suit to halt the investigation, claiming that New York's "business judgment rule" barred judicial inquiry into good-faith actions of corporate directors. The administration claimed that the attorney general had no jurisdiction over Adelphi, that his "witchhunt" threatened the independence of private educational institutions in New York, and that the attorney general's office had deliberately leaked to the media details of the purchase agreement of Diamandopoulos' apartment.[1]

Diamandopoulos' earnings would remain at the center of the Adelphi controversy. His first year salary of $95,000 in 1985–86 rose to $145,000 the following year,
well above the average for presidents at comparable universities. By the 1995–96 academic year, his total compensation, which included fringe benefits and deferred salary,
had soared to $837,000. Diamandopoulos had refused to disclose his income to the IRS
between 1988 and 1994, preferring to pay $11,850 in fines. He later explained that the
secrecy was meant to strengthen his hand with the faculty union.

Adelphi also provided Diamandopoulos with a severance contract worth $3
million; a country club membership; first class trips to France, England, Switzerland,
and Greece, and the use of an $82,000 Mercedes Benz. It reimbursed him for a $1,000
contribution to the 1992 presidential campaign of former Texas Republican senator
Phil Gramm; the premiums on his personal art collection; expensive dinners with fellow trustees John Silber and Hilton Kramer, which included $150 glasses of cognac;
and thousands of dollars in tips to his Manhattan apartment building staff. Adelphi
furnished Diamandopoulos' Manhattan apartment with wall-washer lighting, elec-
trified snow-melting grids on the terrace, and $1,800 in bathroom accessories, while
giving Diamandopoulos the option to buy the apartment for $300,000 less than its
purchase price.

The trustees also enjoyed the good life. In 1994, they took an expenses-paid
trip to Greece. Diamandopoulos claimed that the trip helped the trustees to "think
about the connection between democracy and education."[2] Diamandopoulos, himself an Adelphi trustee, brought business executives and right-wing ideologues to the
board. They, in turn, adhered to the corporate model of university governance that
Diamandopoulos admired. In an October 1992 letter to Donald Koster, Professor
Emeritus of English, Diamandopoulos wrote: "The University is neither a polity nor a
convenient umbrella for a collective of autonomous professionals. The University is a
corporation legally and a hierarchy in terms of leadership, educational responsibility,
and authority."

In a letter to the *New York Times*, anthropology professor Norman Ashcraft
expressed the disenchantment of the faculty with this model of university governance:

> Some people think of a university as a corporation with a strict hierar-
> chical structure. Power passes from a board of trustees through a chief
> executive officer and then assistants, provosts and deans, down to em-
> ployees (faculty), who serve solely to carry out the management's vi-
> sion. The more we favor this model, the more we release responsibility
> for education to managers. Teaching and scholarly pursuits are valued
> less than managing funds, people and curriculum… If other institutions
> pick up on these developments, education will be reduced to a pedes-

trian activity and the university will become a place where mandates are
issued from a self-ordained cadre of managers.[3]

The presence of former Secretary of the Treasury William Simon as honorary trustee underscored the extent of Adelphi's corporate reorientation. Simon had
personally amassed hundreds of millions of dollars by financing hostile takeovers with
junk bonds and then asset-stripping the companies. He also attracted negative publicity with his involvement in a pyramid scheme.[4] Simon, who died in 2000 at the age of
seventy-two, headed the John F. Olin Foundation, which was created by a munitions
manufacturer in 1953 to awaken "business and the public…to the creeping stranglehold that socialism has gained" in the United States.[5] The foundation undertook a new
mission when Simon became its president in 1977, as he declared in his bestseller, *A
Time for Truth*:

> Foundations imbued with the philosophy of freedom… must take pains
> to funnel desperately needed funds to scholars, social scientists, writers
> and journalists who understand the relationship between political and
> economic liberty… This philanthropy must not capitulate to soft-mind-
> ed pleas for the support of "dissent." Indeed, it is the economics and
> the philosophy of capitalism which represent "dissent"—dissent from a
> dominant socialist-statist-collectivist orthodoxy which prevails in much
> of the media, in most of our large universities, among many of our poli-
> ticians and, tragically, among not a few of our top business executives.[6]

In 1995, the year that the Adelphi controversy became public, Olin gave over
$16 million to university thinktanks, institutes, publications, and fellowships. The
foundation financed numerous programs at prestigious law schools, including those of
Columbia, Cornell, Harvard, Yale, Georgetown, George Mason, Stanford, Berkeley, Toronto, and the University of Chicago. Olin sought to transform public policy by diminishing the regulatory role of government, in effect leaving the environment, consumer
protection, and workplace safety to the mercy of "the magic of the market."

Olin gave out its last grants in 2005 and ceased to exist shortly thereafter, but
not before leaving its mark on academia. At Adelphi, Olin funded ten visiting professorships between 1992 and 1996, creating a class of privileged faculty. The Olin scholars, who earned about $100,000 a year, about twice the average Adelphi professor's
salary, included Carnes Lord, a former national security advisor to Vice President Dan
Quayle; Edith Kurzweil, editor of the *Partisan Review*; and Ronald Radosh, author of
a revisionist history of the Rosenbergs, the couple who were framed and executed for
espionage in 1953. Among the "scholars in residence" without teaching duties, were

two right-wing former editors, Brad Miner of the *National Review* and Bruce Bawer of the *New Criterion*. Olin also funded a lecture series, which brought Simon, William Buckley Jr., and Irving Kristol to Adelphi.

Diamandopoulos, in turn, gave Olin associates important positions at Adelphi. Newly appointed Adelphi trustees included James Piereson, Olin executive director, and Hilton Kramer, publisher of *New Criterion*, a journal which began with a $100,000 Olin grant and whose offices were initially housed within Olin's. Mark Blitz, from the Olin-backed Hudson Institute, was named Adelphi's acting provost.[7] In Spring 1996, however, with the Regents investigation approaching, Olin abruptly departed from Adelphi. Simon and Piereson resigned as trustees, thus avoiding the public embarrassment that would soon befall the other Adelphi trustees.

Under Diamandopoulos, Adelphi's students, like its faculty, were stratified into haves and have-nots. Diamandopoulos created an Honors College, an elite institution within the institution, in which students were given twenty-four hour access to state-of-the-art computers, and generous financial assistance that included full scholarships. Diamandopoulos simultaneously cut back financial aid and support services, a move that severely affected minority students. "I have heard that the President and his administration vow their commitment to intellect," noted David Smith, a business major. "One can't help but wonder whose intellect they are committed to. As a black student on this campus, I can assure you it is not mine... All the cuts in aid, the reduction of courses offered, and the president's outrageous salary have shown me that the president is only committed to his pocket."[8]

At the same time, the administration lavished funds on projects of scant educational value. When Adelphi hosted the Greek soccer team during the 1994 World Cup tournament, the administration spent $250,000 to construct a grandstand, press box, public address system, goal posts, and signs in Greek. Students, meanwhile, were complaining about cuts in athletic scholarships.

Under Diamandopoulos, undergraduate enrollment plummeted from 4,049 in 1987 to 1,895 in 1997. Course offerings were sharply reduced, and many students had to spend an extra semester or year to earn their degrees.[9] When asked about the class reductions, Diamandopoulos replied: "There is a silly and melancholy perception on the part of students, which is exploited by fighting faculty, that the more courses you have, the better education you get."[10]

During Diamandopoulos' presidency, tuition rose 140 percent, while the proportion of university expenditures devoted to instruction dropped nearly 15 percent. Between 1983 and 1993, there was a 19 percent decline in number of full-time faculty, from 329 to 267, while the size of Adelphi's administration nearly tripled.[11] In 1985, the year that Diamandopoulos became president, 958 freshmen enrolled at Adelphi. By 1996, only 311 freshmen enrolled, a 67 percent decline that threatened Adelphi's very existence.[12] Because of its minuscule endowment, Adelphi depended on student tuition and fees for virtually all its budget.

Students were upset over the phasing out of the New York State Higher Education Opportunity Program (HEOP) at Adelphi. HEOP provides counseling and financial aid to academically and financially disadvantaged students, those with SAT verbal scores below 600 and low family incomes; at the time, $18,650 was the eligibility limit for a family of three. Adelphi was supposed to guarantee university matching funds for state HEOP awards. Instead, the university demanded that HEOP students take out loans while Diamandopoulos attacked HEOP as "charity." In response, student newspaper editor Marie Alzi noted that HEOP support services simply gave students the means to complete college.[13] The HEOP cuts led many to conclude that Adelphi was simply casting off minority students.

On August 23, 1995, a terse notice appeared on the bulletin board outside Adelphi's student radio station: "WBAU-FM has ceased broadcasting." The night before, the administration had changed the locks to the entrance of WBAU, having sold the station to Nassau Community College for $30,000—a fraction of its actual value—without any bids. The student government association, which funded WBAU, had not been consulted. About half of the station's programming had been Black-oriented. WBAU, Dean Carl Rheins explained, was "at variance with the university's academic mission and philosophy."[14]

At a March 1996 forum, Diamandopoulos finally addressed student concerns, which included the phasing out of HEOP, the closing of WBAU, the lack of fundraising to augment the meager $9 million endowment, the elimination of academic programs (including Italian and the masters program in English), and the drop in library acquisitions to 20 percent of what they had been prior to Diamandopoulos' arrival. He dismissed the concerns, saying, "I have very strong views about what you need. I don't need to know what you think you need."[15] Diamandopoulos also refused to consider the inclusion of a student on Adelphi's trustee board. When students pointed out that other private institutions on Long Island had student trustees, Diamandopoulos simply said that he wished them luck.[16]

Nor did the Adelphi trustees inspire confidence. There was, for instance, Nicholas Samios, the director of the scandal-ridden Brookhaven National Laboratory, where workers were contaminated with radiation and where radioactive materials including tritium and cobalt-60 were allowed to leech into the groundwater.

And there was Leonard Riggio, the CEO of Barnes & Noble, which owns hundreds of university bookstores, including Adelphi's. At a forum on book publishing at which short story writer Cynthia Ozick was his copanelist, Riggio pointedly told the audience, in what New York Times columnist Kennedy Fraser called "a bullying moment of shattered privacy," that his chain had only sold a few hundred of Ozick's volume, *The Shawl*. As Fraser wrote of Riggio, "He is a true Horatio Alger, who has risen from work as a bookstore clerk to being the head of a giant corporation that has gobbled up its competitors like a killer shark. A stocky, feisty fellow in his 50s, he looks like a man who spent his youth prepared to knock down anyone who called him poor and in his maturity is prepared to knock down anyone who thinks he got too rich."[17]

John Silber, the chancellor of Boston University, was arguably Adelphi's most controversial trustee. During the 1994–95 academic year, he was the only university president to earn more than Diamandopoulos. Daniel Gross wrote in *Lingua Franca*:

> Setting himself as the ultimate expert on all matters relating to the university, and operating without meaningful oversight from the school's board of trustees, Silber has systematically shut the faculty out of every significant decision… Silber is in many ways a tangle of contradictions: a Kantian moral philosopher who has reaped immense personal gain from his stewardship of a nonprofit institution; a high-minded thinker capable of astonishing pettiness; a relentless promoter of standards, who has appointed cronies with questionable credentials.[18]

These words might have been written of Diamandopoulos who, taking his cue from his mentor Silber, sought to intimidate his opponents at every opportunity. Harassing phone messages were left on the answering machine of the American Association of University Professors union that represents Adelphi's faculty and librarians. Telephone service to the union office was cut, and the union's executive director, Cathy Cleaver, barred from campus. Adelphi petitioned the National Relations Labor Board to decertify the union. It sued five CSA members and threatened student editor Sara Hajduk with legal action. The intimidation backfired, as it demonstrated the breakdown of the principles of shared governance at Adelphi.

The Regents hearings, which began in July 1996, ended, in the words of Regent Saul Cohen, with a "positive wake-up call to all sectors of the academic community to observe with greater diligence their governance guidelines, as well as other areas of conduct."[19] The Regents chastised the trustees for their conflicts of interest and lack of oversight. A firm owned by a trustee, George Lois, had carried out Adelphi's advertising campaign, for which the university trustees had failed to seek competitive bidding. Diamandapoulos apparently concealed from other trustees the fact that Lois had received $155,000 in commissions for that advertising. The chair of the Adelphi trustee board, Ernesta Procope, had acted as the broker for Adelphi's insurance policies, awarding lucrative contracts to E.G. Bowman, a company which she owned and of which she was the director.

The Regents also criticized the trustees for failing to disclose pertinent information to those entrusted with overseeing Adelphi's finances. In 1990, William Borten, chair of the trustee finance committee, discovered that during the previous three years administrative salaries had increased 57 percent while faculty salaries increased by a mere 6 percent.[20] Borten decided to investigate the matter further, but when he sought specifics regarding administrative salaries he was rebuffed by both Diamandopoulos and James Byrne, who was then the chair of the trustee board.

At a trustee meeting in December 1990, Borten expressed his dismay about not getting the requested data. Byrne told Borten that he didn't need it. A week later, Byrne sent Borten a letter informing him that his resignation from the board of trustees had been accepted. Borten, in fact, had not resigned but found that he had been kicked off the trustee board.[21] During the Regents hearings, it was revealed that Byrne's wife, Carolyn, was earning $100,000 a year as Adelphi vice president of community relations and external affairs. What was at issue was not Carolyn Byrne's salary, but the fact that Borten had been unable to obtain that information as head of the finance committee.

Borten was not the only former trustee disenchanted with Diamandopoulos. William Nadel, who chaired the search committee that chose Diamandopoulos, described Adelphi's president as "a dangerous man who functions as a despot," adding that the decision to hire him was "the single worst example of poor judgment that a number of us exercised in our professional careers, one that I will always regret."[22]

Some Adelphi faculty surmised that the trustees had hired Diamandopoulos to take on Adelphi's faculty union, one of the very few at a private university.[23] Before coming to Adelphi, Diamondopoulos had served as president of Sonoma State University (SSU) from 1977 to 1983. In his study on Adelphi, *When Power Corrupts*, Lionel S. Lewis writes that "Diamandopoulos spent a good deal of time during his first few years at Sonoma State writing verbose and largely impenetrable memoranda… He continually referred to change, progress, and how much more he needed to accomplish, while what he actually did to promote teaching, education, or academic life was hardly discernible."[24]

As president of SSU, Diamandopoulos displayed the same contempt for shared governance that he would later show at Adelphi. SSU faculty were upset that Diamandopoulos had granted tenure to the Vice President for Academic Affairs and the Dean of Humanities despite the objections of their academic departments. Another concern was the fact that Diamandopoulos had failed to consult with the faculty before deciding to terminate twenty-four tenured professors due to financial exigency. As a result, the SSU faculty senate twice voted overwhelmingly to censure Diamandopoulos.[25]

The Regents hearings highlighted the extent of the corruption at Adelphi. Gerald Jodice, executive director of facilities and planning, who oversaw many bids at Adelphi, had already been imprisoned for embezzlement when Diamandopoulos hired him. Despite warnings from an internal auditor that Jodice had a criminal history and was defrauding Adelphi, Diamandopoulos promoted Jodice, giving him the opportunity to steal even more.

At the Regents hearings, the ever combative John Silber described the Adelphi faculty as "a rather large boil in a very sensitive spot that needs to be lanced," assuring the Regents that "once that boil is lanced there will be a very fine and effective operating University." He warned the Regents that should they dismiss the Adelphi trustees "there will be a rash of boils throughout higher education in New York State and around the country."[26] On February 10, 1997, the Regents removed eighteen of Adelphi's nineteen trustees, citing violations of the university's articles of governance and state laws governing non-profit organizations. By this action, the Regents fulfilled the prophecy on Adelphi's seal: "The Truth Shall Make Us Free."

The Adelphi controversy sparked a debate over the regulatory role of government in higher education, particularly that of the Board of Regents, which oversees New York's educational and cultural institutions. Robert Atwell, president emeritus of the American Council on Education, claimed that the creation of regulatory bodies would jeopardize the independence of private institutions. Instead, Atwell suggested, "the governing boards of private colleges should police themselves, by adopting policies to insure that they are operating in the public interest."[27] Adelphi, however, already had such policies in place. The problem lay with those charged with implementing them.

At issue during the Adelphi controversy was the university's century-long tradition of liberal education. In 1995, Adelphi commemorated its centennial as an institution of higher learning with an exhibit of giant photographs that traced Adelphi's history from its founding as a college in 1896 by Charles Levermore. The introductory text to the exhibit read: "As the quotations from Adelphi's founding and current presidents demonstrate, the University's history, despite all its twists, turns and returns, finally can be seen to represent the consistent pursuit of the liberal ideal in education."

The exhibit highlighted two quotes, one from Levermore at Adelphi's first convocation at the turn of the century, the other from Diamandopoulos in 1995. Levermore's advice to Adelphi's first graduating class expresses the ideal of liberal education:

> Hold fast to the lengthening view, to the widening interest in all the world. Cleave to the broad culture for which you have been so faithfully and wisely prepared in the Adelphi halls. The narrow, practical purpose, however necessary it may be, must yet never stifle your love for things of the spirit, human and divine... Such a thorough yet comprehensive culture has been the object of the Adelphi training for you—experiment

rather than recitation, discussion rather than memorizing, ideas rather
than repetition, the liberal before the special culture.

Compare this philosophy to the outlook of Diamandopoulos:

> The clue to becoming strong in the face of our overpowering and infi-
> nitely complex world is deliberately to fit select aspects of the world into
> your own educated world view; into your construct; into your own deter-
> mination of who you are and what the lasting pursuits of your lives will
> be. That is how human beings have dealt creatively over the millennia
> with their vulnerabilities and fragility, and that is how they have made,
> despite their limitations, lasting and powerfully significant civilizations.

In contrast to Levermore, Diamandopoulos conceives of education as a means
to power and wealth, "to becoming strong." His advice, to "fit select aspects of the
world… into your construct," evokes that "narrow, practical purpose" that Levermore
admonishes his students to forsake.

During Diamandopoulos' decade as president, Adelphi ran full page ads in
the *New York Times* proclaiming, "Good Is The Enemy of Great" (faculty would alter
the ones posted on campus to read "Greed is the Enemy of Great"). Other ads touted
Harvard as the "Adelphi of Massachusetts."

Harvard epitomizes the contradictions in our universities. The pride of clas-
sicists and humanists, Harvard was also the biggest recipient of Olin money among US
colleges and universities. The first university in this country to offer elective courses,
Harvard retains its reputation for innovation even as it represents the status quo. Richard Nixon and Joseph McCarthy may have castigated Harvard as the "Kremlin on the
Charles," but its degrees are credentials of privilege.[28]

At Adelphi, the Harvard analogy existed both as an image of excellence and
as an example of the fatuous distortions wrought by power. Diamandopoulos, who
studied philosophy at Harvard, appears to have been convinced that he was the em-
battled standard bearer of a meritocracy, the notion of which, writes John Trumpbour,
is "a convenient rationalization for entitlement to power, status, security and personal
gain."[29] Adelphi had never compared itself to Harvard until Diamandopoulos and his
friends came along. They betrayed Levermore's legacy by shortchanging the students
that Adelphi had traditionally served, and by turning Adelphi into a parody of a community of scholars.

The new trustees appointed by the regents promptly fired Diamandopoulos,
froze tuition, named faculty leaders as deans, and dropped the attempt to decertify the
union. Despite these long-overdue measures, Adelphi continued to face severe financial

problems after Diamondopoulos' removal. The old trustees had squandered millions of dollars of university funds on their legal expenses. The new Adelphi administration reached a financial settlement with Diamondopoulos, paying him $1.4 million to avoid protracted legal battles.

The faculty union agreed to accept pay cuts and to allow the administration to lay off tenured professors in case of financial need. Although the professors were willing to make sacrifices on behalf of their university, others simply could not afford to do so. In September 2000, clerical workers at Adelphi went on strike for fourteen weeks. Their average annual salary was just $23,400, a pittance given the cost of housing on Long Island. To make matters worse, the administration had decided to eliminate their free tuition benefits.

Adelphi faced a crisis of leadership for three years after the removal of Diamandopoulos in February 1997. Adelphi's provost, Igor Webb, became the acting president for the remaining three months of the academic year. Because Webb was tied to Diamandopoulos' corrupt administration, Adelphi's new trustees appointed an interim president, James A. Norton, for the 1997–98 academic year. Students were delighted to see on the president's office door, which had previously guarded Diamandopoulos' bunker, a sign that read, "Open, Please Come In."[30] Norton appointed history professor Armstrong Starkey as provost. He also named other dedicated faculty members as deans, including Biology professor Gayle Insler, who is now the acting provost at Adelphi. Soon, Adelphi began to recover. The size of the freshman class doubled within a year of Diamondopoulos' departure.

In fall 1998, Matthew Goldstein, the former president of Baruch College, was named the new permanent president. Many hoped that Goldstein, who had nearly doubled his salary by moving to Adelphi, would revive the university's fortunes. However, in August 1999, with four years still left in his contract, Goldstein left Adelphi to become the Chancellor of the City University of New York, which was already being savaged by the conservative trustees appointed by Governor George Pataki and Mayor Rudy Giuliani. The new CUNY trustees ended open admissions and privatized the university system.[31]

After Goldstein's departure, Steven L. Isenberg, a former publisher of *Newsday* and chair of the new Adelphi trustee board, served as interim president for a year. He helped stabilize Adelphi's precarious finances. Adelphi finally got the president it deserved in the person of Robert A. Scott, the former president of Ramapo College and a scholar on public policy and higher education. Scott joined Adelphi as president and as a professor of Anthropology and Sociology in July 2000. Facing a labor crisis, Adelphi did not celebrate Scott's inauguration until the following summer.

Since then, Adelphi has created new initiatives such as Levermore Global Scholars, which fosters civic awareness in students through community-based intern-

ships, study abroad programs, and two speaker series, "Human Rights in Global Perspective" and "Living with Conflict and Working for Peace." Student participants have
donated food to local charities, presented alternative plays, and performed volunteer
work abroad. Also noteworthy is Vital Signs, a partnership between Adelphi's School of
Social Work and the Long Island community, which seeks to identify and address local
health needs in order to inform public policy.

The liberal arts are on the mend. Adelphi has resurrected undergraduate majors in Spanish and French and has started new graduate programs in creative writing
and environmental studies. The English department, which had dwindled from twenty-seven to just five faculty members, is back on its feet, with fourteen faculty members
in 2008.[32] A new performing arts center, funded in part by a $5 million New York State
grant, opened in fall 2008.

Adelphi is greening its campus. The new sports and performing arts centers
will use geothermal heating and cooling systems to avoid burning fossil fuels. The university has eliminated the use of petroleum-based fertilizers and chemical pesticides
and herbicides on university grounds. It has reduced automobile use on campus by
creating a shuttle service and a storage area for bicycles.

Scott's articles and speeches on Adelphi's website reveal a thoughtful and
compassionate academic who honors Adelphi's legacy as an engaged university. In an
essay on the university as a moral force, Scott envisions the university as a "culture of
conscience" that is "dedicated to the search for truth, the transformation of meaning,
the examination of intended and unintended consequences, and the concern for equity, equality, fairness, and justice."[33]

Sometimes misperceived as an ordinary commuter school, Adelphi in fact
has a history of educational innovation. Adelphi created the first university program
in dance in 1938, and the first university program in clinical psychology in 1952. The
present Adelphi administration continues to honor that tradition. In his 2007 State
of the University address, Scott noted that Adelphi's legacy of public engagement is
hardly recent, describing how sociology professor Annie Marion MacLean, who taught
at Adelphi between 1907 and 1912, conducted her research posing as a factory worker,
department store clerk, and farmhand. Scott also celebrated the contradictions inherent in the university, central to society in its roles as creator of knowledge and as cura-
tor of its cultural heritage, yet on the margins as its critic. Scott appears to enjoy his job
immensely and he has even found the time to act in a student production of Thornton
Wilder's *Our Town*.

In 2005, Adelphi raised more than $9.5 million. To put that in perspective,
during his eleven years as president, Diamandopoulos raised less than $3 million in
private gifts and grants for Adelphi's endowment.[34] Adelphi's endowment is now over
$105 million and likely to grow at a hefty clip as students begin to give back to the in-

stitution that nurtured them. According to the latest information from Adelphi's Office of Research Assessment and Planning, between 2000 and 2006, undergraduate enrollment increased 52 percent and alumni giving by nearly 620 percent. The number of full-time faculty members rose from 201 in 2000 to 293 in 2007, a 46 percent increase that bodes well for Adelphi.

The memory of the Diamandopoulos years is fast fading. Adelphi has again become a participatory space that fosters ethical and imaginative dimensions of learning. Despite a decade of pillage, "the lengthening view" has triumphed over entitlement and privilege at Adelphi.[35]

The Carceral Society

From the Prison Tower to the Ivory Tower

Caroline K. Kaltefleiter & Mechthild E. Nagel

> *"Manipulation becomes a fundamental instrument for the preservation of domination. Prior to the emergence of people there is no manipulation (precisely speaking), but rather total suppression. In the antidialogical theory of action, manipulation is the response of the oppressor to the new concrete condition of the historical process. Through manipulation, dominant elites can lead people into an unauthentic type of organization and the can thus avoid the threatening alternative: the true organization of the emerged and emerging people."*
>
> —Paulo Freire

IN HIS SEMINAL TEXT, *Pedagogy of the Oppressed*, Paulo Freire (1990) outlines the necessary steps for individuals in their everyday lives to counter deceits and regimes (im)posed by the State. To oppose such manipulation and repression, citizens need to undertake a critical thought process that situates their lives in historic processes, power systems, and ideological frameworks. While the academy is often touted as a space that encourages the free and unfettered pursuit of research and inquiry, professors at US institutions who challenge dominant ideologies and paradigms and engage in political action realize that pursuit of their teaching, research, and causes may come at a high cost, such as manifest in denial of promotion, unfavorable working conditions, intrusive surveillance, and other forms of intellectual threat and containment.

Contemporary critiques of the academy are responses to the corporatization of the university, the commodification of knowledge, and the repression of free speech. Louis Althusser (1971) argues that schools—universities first and foremost—function as an "ideological state apparatus" by which the capitalist system perpetuates its norms and values in order to smoothly reproduce itself. Pierre Bourdieu (1970; 1990) notes that class domination is not only a result of economic warfare, but also a fight for cultural capital and symbolic power. Dominating classes use cultural capital, specifically that of knowledge, professional success, and institutional accomplishment to their benefit. Like Althusser, Bourdieu views the university system as integral to the (re)production of capitalist values, ideologies, and imperatives, such that "higher education" is designed not to cultivate knowledge and autonomy but rather to instruct students and professors how to labor in a market-dominated world.

Schools of journalism, for instance, often focus on the mechanics of writing and producing news without asking students to critically reflect on the social, cultural, political, or economic context and impact of their images, discourse, and narratives. Consequently, aspiring writers are taught to be workers (re)producing the stories and agendas of dominant elites. As Freire explains, "the dominant elites are so well aware of [the subversive nature of free inquiry] that they instinctively use all means, including physical violence to keep the people from thinking" (146). Freire's work is meaningful when reviewing the context of the virtual, mental, and, to a certain extent, physical imprisonment of contemporary academics living in the United States whose everyday work is challenged if it deviates from convention and accepted norms. Faculty may even be tormented by physical altercations and through virtual bullying. As such, some professors restrict their mobility and interactions to avoid confrontations/punishment. Subsequently they may choose to or migrate to spaces where their work is accepted, avoiding sites of resistances. Almost as if to reinforce anxiety and to colonize the last remaining spaces not under moral and professional control, academic repression enacted through subtle ideological and normalizing pressures is augmented with a technological regime of surveillance as interactions with students and colleagues are caught on videotape, wire taps, or written correspondence via electronic mail (see below).

Academics whose work transgresses traditional intellectual forums and enters political spaces beyond the walls of the university often find themselves—willingly or not—engaged in protests, public disruptions, demonstrations, and acts of civil disobedience against repressive institutions (e.g., through involvement in Earth First! actions, demonstrations against the World Trade Organization [WTO], or protests of the US invasion of Iraq). As Howard Zinn (2002) points out, educational practice is never neutral and the university is hardly benign in its various spheres of influence (e.g., the corporate, scientific, and military sectors of society) or its need to perpetuate business, governmental, and social practices, however corrupt or antidemocratic.

In this essay we address the social, political, and economic conditions that contribute to the current assault on academic freedom and the integrity of "higher education." First we contextualize intellectual labor within the academy and relate late capitalism to a politics of containment. Today's corporatization of the academy includes treating universities as businesses, complete with branding committees, marketing campaigns with taglines, bottom line economics, and pseudo-profit sharing schemes, as in the recent case of Kent State University where faculty gain commissions if they draw more students into their programs. Public institutions such our own university, the State University of New York, are increasingly dependent on private donations and elaborate fundraising campaigns. The imposition of the private and the public renders a discourse of treating students as clients and education as a commodity to be sold to them. As such, we examine today's realities of academic life at American universities, including situations at our own institution, through a lens of political repression. Finally we call for critical reflection that is grounded in radical pedagogy and social activism.

Learning to Labor in the Academy: The Myth of Meritocracy

In order to understand social conditions inside/outside the academy, we revisit the seminal work of cultural studies scholar, Paul Willis. In his ethnography on how working-class kids get working-class jobs, Willis (1977) discusses how post-war youth cultures were tracked and filtered into a menial labor market. Willis describes a politics of resistance that was cultivated in the everyday life of working class kids in the United Kingdom by rejecting "mental labor" and engaging in "cultural labor"—e.g., hanging out the streets, exploring creative art/communication, and looping in and out of trouble. The dilemma of Willis' UK lads represents the catch-22 of the working and popular classes in general: "challenging power requires (credentialed) knowledge, yet the acquisition of that knowledge is organized so that it reinforces credentialed system of power" (Abercrombie and Urry, 1983, 17).

Willis' work has been used to ground discussions that explore various types of schooling rituals, question the structure of learning, and analyze the emergence of a politics of resistance (e.g., see McLaren 1993; Catoriadis 1997; and Aronowitz 1998). We extend Willis' notion of "learning to labor" from a physical-based contest of menial work to a mental-based context of learning to do intellectual work according to prescribed dictates and boundaries. Academic labor relies on the "myth of meritocracy" to obscure the fact that rewards are not granted on the basis of work and merit. Andrea Smith (2007) notes, "In order to function as ideological state apparatus, the academy must disavow its complicity in capitalism by claiming itself a meritocratic system" (141). Translated, this suggests that only those who appear to work hard *and* whose efforts fall into legitimized research paradigms and standard disciplinary boundaries, *and* who disengage their "disinterested" knowledge from normative and political outlooks— only these "model citizens" of corporatized, militarized, and normalized academia are positively vetted through peer review processes. Conversely, however productive or praised a scholar's work might be, should it transgress entrenched norms and boundaries (such as, above all, through radical, controversial, or politicized research that links theory to practice and social change), this work will be disparaged or condemned on ideological grounds rather than being fairly evaluated on its merit.

Labor-process theorists point out that the intellectual division of knowledge along strict disciplinary lines is a casualty of an ever-expanding capitalist economy and the fragmentation of the social division of labor. The sheer scale of efficient production dictates that the work/thinking process be reorganized along factory-system and bureaucratic lines. The new social order is predicated on the distinction between productive and unproductive labor. This manual/intellectual labor continuum can be understood by using Marx's concept of the "socialization of unproductive labor" (Marx, 1976, 1024). Framed in this way, social activist organizing, seen as manual labor, takes a backseat to writing on social movements and action research, and scholars with the "dirty hands" of political involvement are viewed as second-rate and unprofessional, as "activists" but not genuine "scholars."

Educated labor professionalizes itself to develop knowledge as marketable capital, packaged in the form of intellectual credentials and practical skills that function as passports to the global capitalist job market. Educators organize themselves against other forms of work, capital, and the State to maintain control over forms of credentialed labor such as lawyers, legal specialists, business executives, accountants, and corporate scientists. As Andrea Smith (2007) points out, "The standardization of academic qualifications—a given amount of labor and time in academic apprenticeships is exchanged for a given amount of cultural capital [that]... enables a differentiation in power ascribed to permanent positions in society" (141).

The struggle for intellectual autonomy in the university system often relies on strategies that legitimate one mode of knowledge and delegitimate competing forms of (non-academic) knowledge purportedly lacking scientific status and rigor. For instance, one might only look to the divide between credentialed OB-GYN medical doctors and nurses and the work of mid-wives, doulas, and homeopathic health care. Here the formalized mainstream medical paradigm continues to wage hostile campaigns to discredit "unscientific," "alternative," or common-sense knowledge of women's health.

Capital and the Politics of Intellectual Containment

One fundamental way that late capitalist society accomplishes knowledge control in universities is to shift the gravity center of decision making from below to above, from faculty autonomy and free expression to the administrative hierarchy and bureaucratic management paradigm. Professors, students, classrooms, course content, and research are to be "managed" and patterned on a corporate model and culture imbued with honor codes, loyalty oaths, confidentiality agreements, trade patents, security measures, and profit imperatives

Capital has always had privileged access to academia. Economic elites fund academic research and establish civic partnerships that serve corporate interests and drive a wedge among competing disciplines (Strickland 2002; Smith 2007). For example, departments of business and hard sciences are often pitted against the arts and humanities whereby disciplines such as philosophy, literature, ethnic studies, and women's studies suffer the most financial cutbacks due to their unlikely role in bringing grant money to the university and to their purported failure to demonstrate "practical" skills useful to future laborers of a global capitalist economy. However, the "vocational skills" rhetoric masks the hidden agenda of the university system, which is to ensure that controversial topics, radical theories, and intellectual work requiring and cultivating critical thinking skills and political actions are contained. Antonio Gramsci noted such curriculum shifts and advocated a comprehensive form of education that would "take a child up to the threshold of his choice of job, forming during this time as person capable of thinking, studying and ruling—or controlling those who rule" (1971, 40).

Today radicalized curricula are limited and those who speak out are often silenced through punitive personnel decisions, above all by denial of tenure. The academic review process in US higher education that leads to tenure or dismissal has been described in popular jargon as a "hazing process." Due to its secret committee elaborations on the candidate by a "jury of peers," it is akin to a criminal trial process, where the candidate has to make a best case in order to win approval ("acquittal"). Yet the crucial difference to a trial is that the academic applicant is represented without counsel in the review process. At many institutions, it is marginalized individuals—e.g. political radicals, women, people of color (women of color especially), gay, lesbian, transgender people, and those with disabilities—who find themselves under the most intense scrutiny.

Consequently, throughout their review period, untenured faculty walk on egg shells, worry about saying the right things in department meetings, and try to cultivate alliances with the colleagues and administrators who could positively influence their tenure decision. It all amounts to an inhibiting, paranoid, dignity-stripping, hostile work environment, if not to the "minimum security" compound that Assata Shakur speaks about (see below). It is precisely the lack of minimal job protection that often creates a climate of fear and conformity among untenured professors as well as the vast majority of casual, seasonally employed adjuncts. (The case of Ward Churchill shows us that even tenured professors can be fired for radical views or indecorous remarks— hardly reassuring for anyone with dissenting political views.) Contingent or part-time instructors are joining the ranks of the academic lumpenproletariat across the US, and they make up 48 percent of faculty in all private and public universities and colleges (*Academe*, 2008).

What happens if one's political convictions come into conflict with an un-stated mission of an institution? Richard Jones, co-chair of the Radical Philosophy As-sociation (RPA), is a lecturer in the Philosophy department at Howard University. In 2002, he secured an invitation from his department chair to bring the organization's bi-annual conference to his campus. It would be the first time the group would meet at a historically Black university. Thereafter, the theme for the conference was agreed to be on "Philosophy against Empire," as the meeting would be held in the aftermath of the 2004 presidential elections. However, in Spring 2004 a new department chair refused to renew Jones' contract and so while preparing this international event, he was actually unemployed; yet Jones was still determined to hold the conference at Howard and pressured the chair to approve conference space on campus. However, as the phi-losophy department did not officially endorse the RPA, no university administrator participated in any capacity.

No doubt the theme of empire and the association with "radical philosophy" did not inspire confidence on the part of university officials. After all, Howard Univer-sity receives $250 million a year from the US Congress which they were not about to jeopardize. Jones shared his experience at Howard with a prominent member of RPA, who is named in David Horowitz's diatribe, *The Professors: The 101 Most Dangerous Academics in America*. Thereafter, RPA members submitted letters and emails in sup-port of Jones to Howard's administration, and Jones was reinstated as lecturer in 2005. Hearsay has it that his offer was first rescinded in 2004 on the grounds that "though Jones is one of our better teachers, he is far too radical for Howard—he belongs to Berkeley or Madison" (Jones, 2008, personal communication). Is this to suggest that some institutions known for their radicalism might become sanctuaries for radicals? In fact, such actions though signal another form of containment and self contain-ment and, indeed, these "islands" of respite increasingly are becoming prison yards of confinement.

Political Prisoners and Academic Fugitives

Few people holding a doctoral degree end up in prison. However, states the world over are threatened by radical thinkers who upset the "political order"; consequently, they must make examples of dissenters and discipline them accordingly, often meting out disproportionately long jail sentences, torture, or even death. We have much to learn from these imprisoned intellectuals, because they can speak truth to power in a way that academics often feel unable to do (being fearful of termination or perhaps suc-cessfully molded and normalized by the university system). Black political prisoners (Acoli, 1998) have charged that political repression tactics have first been tested on people of color. As Black Liberation Army member Assata Shakur, now a fugitive of the

American prison system and living in Cuba suggests, many people of color in the US live in "minimum security conditions" (e.g., on the streets or on Indian reservations), and far too many others languish in "maximum security conditions" (behind county jails, state prisons, and federal or military penitentiaries). In her autobiography (1987), Shakur describes her life in the underground, hounded by the State for her non-violent participation in the Black Liberation movement. "I don't have the slightest idea how to be free," Shakur writes after breaking out of prison in 1985 and living as a marooned slave in Cuba (1987, 60).

J. Edgar Hoover initiated a witch hunt against the Black Panther Party, with the intent of neutralizing its impact, even if it meant that individual leaders would have to be blackmailed or simply shot to death, as happened to Fred Hampton of Chicago in 1969. The question is whether the dragnet of repression has been extended to other segments of the population or institutions and, if so, to what degree. Perhaps if one considers the level of violence and assassinations leveled against the Black radical movements of the 1960s and 1970s, President G.W. Bush's endorsement of waterboarding, an internationally forbidden torture technique (in fact, dubbed *la tortura de agua* during the Spanish Inquisition), does not sound particularly distressing. However, it is ironic that in the post-9/11 era the CIA frequently engages in torture tactics such as waterboarding, even though in 1945, the US government sentenced several Japanese men to prison for using the "water cure" (as it was known then) on US prisoners of war (Wallach, 2007).

Like Shakur, Angela Y. Davis, hunted by CIA and FBI, became a political prisoner and academic fugitive. Her trial became an international media spectacle. She remained in the media spotlight until her acquittal in 1972 (Aptheker, 1999). Today Davis is a tenured professor at University of California at Santa Cruz (UCSC). For her to be granted tenure, the university administration had to defend itself against the UC board of trustees for the audacity of hiring Professor Davis. A veritable "enemy of the state" and on the FBI's 10 Most Wanted Fugitives list, she was captured and for a year, a remand prisoner in New York and California until, after a worldwide campaign, the presiding judge allowed her to post bail. Her saga seemed to have ended with an acquittal on all charges. Yet, with respect to political agitators, i.e. people who are seen as seditious, the government has a long and vengeful memory. Ronald Reagan, governor of California in the post-McCarthy era, vowed that never again a "communist" such as Professor Davis would be employed by the University of California system.

However, after twenty or so years of adjuncting in colleges in California and being active in the Communist Party USA, Davis was finally granted a tenured position in 1994 as Presidential Chair and Professor of History of Consciousness at UCSC. Her promotion was not secured without intense opposition by Ward Connolly, a University of California Regent and chair of the conservative Civil Rights Initiative. His group was a sponsor of California's anti-affirmative action legislation in 1996, which Davis opposed. Her activism against the initiative prompted Connolly to write a scathing letter, stating that "your record as a revolutionary is not merely disturbing but it may impair your effectiveness as a member of the faculty of one of this nation's most highly respected academic institutions" (cited in James, 1998, 22). However, this admonishment has not stopped Davis from continuing to agitate for the marginalized and the oppressed, in particular for prisoners in the California state system. She is one of the founders of Critical Resistance, a nationwide prison abolitionist organization.

For academics to bemoan the lack of academic freedom to pursue politically volatile research (e.g., for a Palestinian scholar to write books critical of Israel) is somewhat benign given the gravity of the situation faced by POWs housed in Guantánamo Bay, Cuba, declared as "enemy combatants" of the US. Yet, it is important to look at the erosion of the Bill of Rights, a steep decline in liberties dramatized in an ACLU advertisement that strikes some of the most important wording from the original document. It is crucial to consider the chilling political environment of post-9/11 USA. To what extent are intellectuals who do not consider themselves particularly radical or progressive now policing themselves? To what degree have they internalized social censorship and the academic superego, so that they no longer enjoy or even give thought to the erosion of academic "freedom" as they labor in a kind of "minimum security" complex?

These questions are of particular salience to scholars who study the "wrong" subject matter (e.g., the history of US imperialism and genocide or radical environmental movements); and it is deemed wrong precisely due to their politics of location. In the case of Abu El-Haj, for instance, a US academic of Arab descent, her "sin," Rabinowitz and Shamir write, was "to probe into a social scientific domain—the history, historiography, and anthropology of Israel—that is normally defined by Jewish Israeli scholars whose tendency has always been to position Palestinians as objects of inquiry. Abu El-Haj's work thus perpetrates the faux pas of inverting the 'proper' way of studying Israel-Palestine" (2008, 45). An unsuccessful email campaign was waged by irate alumni of Barnard College to deny Prof. Abu El-Haj tenure on the basis of her politically-suspect research. As we know from Norman Finkelstein's case (see Martin in this volume), others may not be so "lucky" to avail themselves of academic freedom without disciplinary prospects.

Surveillance and Silence in the Academy

Communication technologies, namely email, cell phones, and even social networking sites such as Facebook and MySpace have been used to not only wage attacks on faculty and their institutions, such as the Barnard alumni protest against Abu El-Haj, but also to amass relevant information needed to conduct surveillance, academic reconnaissance, if you will, on college campuses—all perfectly legal and routine in the Security State of post-9/11 America. In March 2008, during a closed session, the House of Representatives, the first since 1983, deliberated on updating electronic surveillance laws, focusing on a warrantless wiretapping program designed to monitor communications of US citizens (Miller 2008). On July 9, 2008, the United States Senate passed H.R. 6034, the Foreign Intelligence Surveillance Act [FISA] Amendments Act of 2008, and Bush signed it into law the following day. The revised measure expands the federal government's surveillance powers and immunizes telecommunication companies that cooperated with the Bush administration's systematic use of warrantless wiretapping (Ray and Sorscher 2008). In response, privacy advocates argued that the Act unduly and unaccountably expanded domestic spying powers. Meanwhile the new laws may soon be tested in a New York court, as the American Civil Liberties Union, Amnesty International, *The Nation*, the Global Fund for Women, and a host of other groups have filed a complaint seeking to have the law declared contrary to the First and Fourth Amendments (Ray and Sorscher, 2008).

Secrecy surrounding the wiretapping debate contributes to an ongoing "Big Chill" effect propagated by the USA PATRIOT Act, or the "Uniting and Strengthening America by Providing Appropriate Tools Required to Intercept and Obstruct Terrorism Act". As George Caffentzis notes, the USA PATRIOT Act defines "terrorist activity" so broadly that a police dragnet could easily entrap trade union picketers, raid the homes of animal rights or environmental activists, or arrest people who donate to humanitarian organizations whose outreach includes Palestinians or Iraqis. In May 2003, activists attending the BioDevastation Conference against Genetic Engineering in St. Louis, the seat of Monsanto, found themselves not only shadowed by police but also arrested en masse in "pre-emptive raids" on homes in the area (indymedia.org/ St. Louis, May 22, 2003). Such harassment of citizens, dissenters, scholars, and activists is as legal under the USA PATRIOT Act as it is now depressingly common.

Let's study two of the vague and ominous felonious acts described and proscribed in the USA PATRIOT Act:

1) "Terrorist activity": using a "weapon or dangerous device (other than for mere personal monetary gain)"; soliciting membership for, and providing material support to a "terrorist organization," even if this group is explicitly humanitarian.

2) "Terrorist organization": "two or more individuals, whether organized or not" who engage in terrorist activity. This vague umbrella term certainly outdoes the infamous RICO Act of the 1970s, ostensibly di-

rected against drug dealers and the US Mafia, but more specifically used to round up leftist revolutionary dissenters, such as the Ohio 7.

Anti-terrorism laws have a long tradition in the US. In particular, beginning with the jailing of Eugene Debs for his unpatriotic dissent over World War I under the US Sedition Act of 1918, which reads:

> Whoever, when the United States is at war, shall willfully make... false reports... utter, print, write, or publish any disloyal, profane, scurrilous, or abusive language about the form of government of the United States... *teach*, defend... favor the cause of any country with which the United States is at war... shall be punished by a fine of not more than $10,000 or imprisonment for not more than twenty years, or both. (emphasis added)

If we think of the USA PATRIOT Act as an extension of the US Sedition Act, then it makes perfect sense to prosecute teachers who defy the common logic of "good people" for acting in "seditious" rather than "patriotic" ways in times of war. The question is whether tenure committees represent nervous henchmen of the state in prosecuting academics who can't quite toe the line of quietist peers who champion rigorous quantitative research agendas. Such maybe the downfall of indigenous scholar Prof. Andrea Smith who was denied tenure by her colleagues in the Women's Studies Department at the University of Michigan in Spring 2008 (see Cotera in this volume). No stranger to radical politics, Smith published one of her scholarly books with South End Press, a noted leftist populist press. She also originated the term "the academic industrial complex" (Smith, 2007). It is not surprising that University of Michigan's faculty in Women's Studies serve as the enforcers of rigid standards (of the white conservative establishment), since the Supreme Court using Michigan's "flawed" admission's policy struck down Affirmative Action. Michigan has faced a noteworthy exodus of twelve women of color who were either denied tenure or left "voluntarily" in the academic year 2006–7 (Cox, 28, 1).

The USA PATRIOT Act granted law enforcement unprecedented powers of surveillance. Bolstered by new technologies, by the cooperation of the major communication companies, and by the manufactured fear of "terrorism," this Panopticon system spread throughout society. The Virginia Tech Tragedy in April 2007, followed in February 2008 by the shootings at Northern Illinois University, constituted a flashpoint where American colleges and universities began to witness subtle acts of repression through the implementation of revised emergency response procedures in the wake of "campus terrorism." Many schools use new technology as means to contact an entire campus population instantaneously through email accounts, automatic calls to campus phones, and postings on university homepages, to alert campus citizens of a genuine emergency. Such uses of these technologies have a positive and benign side, but they also have a negative and malign aspect to the extent that they promote a Panopticon-type surveillance environment.

At our own institution in upstate New York, university officials called for students, faculty, and staff to register their personal cell phone numbers with campus security as part of a comprehensive plan to execute an efficient crisis communication plan. The State University of New York (SUNY) entered into an agreement with the State Emergency Management Office (SEMO) in order to develop an emergency alert system. Students enter their numbers into the system for use in the case of emergency. Students are obligated to give their contact details (such as numbers or addresses for their home phone, cell phone, fax, email, and text) as part of the registration process. Meanwhile, faculty have the "option" of disclosing their personal contact details and cell phone number, but were "highly encouraged" to have that information on record to be accessed should an emergency occur. While some assurances have been made to students and faculty that their personal information will be used for emergency purposes only, the data collected, under the guise of protection, is another means by which the State is able to monitor its citizens.

Such databases could prove to be an invaluable tool to repress resistance with the ability to access and to activate cell phones as tracking devices, giving police information about the presence of those attending campus demonstrations, speak outs, and acts of civil disobedience with their precise accuracy. Faculty resistance to registering a cell phone is often met with a series of justifications, couched within a discourse of counter-terrorism, an attempt to ensure everyone's safety/loyalty within the university. Those who resist, referring to civil liberty issues, run the same risk as those who are deemed "unpatriotic" when calling for an end to US military interventions. Here a sense of "unconcern" for terror threats or emergency situations is coded as disloyalty, as safety, not liberty, becomes the preeminent concern of universities and police. Organizations such as SEMO prey on the public's/faculty's fear to create campus "safety," such as enforced through a 24/7 monitoring system at the disposal of the State.

While, to some, cell phone registration may be an innocuous mode of surveillance taking place on campus today, a more striking and obvious visual form of repression is the recent construction of closed circuit television systems and public address systems mounted on university buildings. These mammoth structures create electronic gates and digital watchtowers. Last fall at our institution, SUNY erected twenty-two public address speakers that resemble large megaphones, complete with a digital response signal that can be directed at five zones across our campus. The technology has the ability to create messages that can be targeted to a particular zone or all zones. Alert messages originate from the university police department. The presence of these speakers atop university buildings is akin to public address systems used to direct prisoners at correctional facilities. While campus residents go about their normal day, perhaps forgetting that their movements may be monitored continuously, students and faculty may subconsciously alter their behavior under the gaze of this contemporary Panopticon.[1]

The Loyalty Oath as a Sign of Academic Repression

At some universities, management of resistance begins with human resource departments requiring employees to sign loyalty oaths in accordance with state laws. According to US law there are two main categories of loyalty oaths. "Disclaimer oaths" are those reminiscent of the McCarthy era of the 1950s, in which citizens are told to certify that they are not present or past members of groups such as the Communist Party. "Non-binding affirmative" oaths constitute a second type of loyalty oath. Affirmative oaths ask people to pledge oaths to one's state of residence, its constitution and governing laws, to the United States Constitution, and to the United States republic. The conditioning of signing loyalty laws begins with children in elementary school where they are taught daily to say the Pledge of Allegiance, with hand on heart as they face the American flag. This oral recitation begins the indoctrination of nationalism in which the state and its actions are not to be questioned. Critical inquiry into words used in the Pledge of Allegiance is not incorporated into most elementary school curriculums. The words remain unchallenged and are recited as stated by children so as to avoid punishment for not conforming to the conditions of classroom.

Loyalty oaths are often referred to as a relic of the McCarthy era, yet they are alive and well—especially on university campuses. The United States Supreme Court has banned certain kinds of loyalty oaths, while affirming others. The Supreme Court barred "disclaimer" oaths in 1967 when faculty from our own university, the State University of New York, challenged an oath that stated that they had never been members of the Communist Party, and if they were they had to inform their university president (*Keyishaian v. Board of Regents*, 1967). Jaschik notes that, "The Supreme Court rejected the New York oath, citing values of academic freedom, and the dangers posed by creating any 'orthodoxy' requirement for teaching" (2008, 2).

While the courts have struck down "disclaimer loyalty oaths," affirmative oaths have been upheld in a series of court decisions. Needless to say, more academics find themselves in quandaries of signing loyalty oaths, despite their personal beliefs, or risk losing their jobs. This is especially true for adjunct and untenured faculty who function within the minimum-security complex.

Consider the case of Marianne Kearney-Brown, a graduate student at California State University, East Bay. Kearney-Brown, a practicing Quaker, lost her job as a mathematics instructor for refusing to sign the California loyalty oath for state employees because the oath conflicted with her religious beliefs. To find a compromise, Ms. Kearney-Brown tried to add a word to the state's Oath of Allegiance so it would conform to her Quaker beliefs. The change she tried to make was to insert the word "nonviolently" before "support and defend the Constitution of the United States." California's oath for state employees currently reads:

> I, _____, do solemnly swear (or affirm) that I will support and defend the Constitution of the United States and the Constitution of the State of California against all enemies, foreign and domestic; that I will bear true faith and allegiance to the Constitution of the United States and the Constitution of the State of California; that I take this obligation freely, without any mental reservation or purpose of evasion; and that I will well and faithfully discharge the duties upon which I am about to enter.

The university offered Kearney-Brown a chance to add a statement with her views to be attached to the loyalty oath, but insisted that she sign the oath unaltered, stating that they had to fire her if she refused. Such forced compliance demonstrates an untenable situation for a state employee who is living with minimal security. Here Kearney-Brown faced the forced dilemma of violating her own religious beliefs by signing something that she does not believe in or losing her employment at Cal State East Bay.

In response to her termination by the California State University System, the local chapter of the United Auto Workers (UAW) union filed a grievance on Kearney-Brown's behalf. Within two weeks of her firing, an attorney from the California State University chancellor's office presented her with a statement that read, "signing the oath does not carry with it any obligation or requirement that public employees bear arms or otherwise engage in violence" (Hendricks 2008). Kearney-Brown accepted the apology of California and was reinstated to her position with back pay.

Critical Reflection and Liberation

In an age of electronic surveillance, we see a need for critical reconnaissance in an attempt to expose actions taken inside/outside of the academy that constitute repression. We are drawn to the work of Marxist revolutionary and political prisoner Che Guevara, who spoke to the necessity of critical forums of education and cultural resistance until his death in 1967—a murderous act commissioned by the United States Central Intelligence Agency (CIA). According to Guevara, "study … and the place of study where you carry out your work is the patrimony of no one—It belongs to all the people… and it must be extended to the people or the people will seize it" (quoted in Retamar [1971], 71). Guevara's words reminds of us of the work of Antonio Gramsci, the Italian Marxist intellectual who was sentenced to more than twenty years in prison. At his sentencing, the Italian prosecutor urged the court to pronounce a sentence of civil death: "For twenty years, we must stop this brain from working" (Forgacs, 1971, 22). This imploration haunts the halls of the university today, silencing critical discourse through personnel management and citizen surveillance, with goals of stifling grassroots teaching, critical thinking, and cultural studies scholarship that critiques capitalist ideology and global imperialism.

As critical theorists, engaged intellectuals, and social activists, we argue for the necessity of critical pedagogy and political activism in the wake of recent assaults on academic freedom by exposing the myth of meritocracy and its role in the (re)production, distribution, and consumption of knowledge in a capitalist society. In a collective response (where possible, spearheaded by faculty unions or even faculty senates), scholars/activists must confront repression head-on by advancing competing global dialogues that emphasize justice, democracy, and liberation. To act collectively with one voice is ever important today, since individual faculty protesting repression out of their own conscience and bravery could easily be silenced, if not dismissed. That is why it was strategic, for example, to hold a conference on academic freedom and the "academic industrial complex" at University of Michigan in Spring 2008. Entitled "Campus Lockdown: Women of Color Negotiating the Academic Industrial Complex," colleagues organized the conference at the very time the administration was deciding Prof. Andrea Smith's tenure case. It was an important gesture of solidarity towards Smith, a radical indigenous woman, and it also put the national spotlight on the university's promotion review process of women of color who have been denied tenure at a high rate (see Cotera in this volume).

Collective actions opposing repression are carried out in the digital world as well. Consider the case of Karl James Buck, a journalism graduate student at the University of California at Berkley who was arrested by Egyptian police for photographing a demonstration. Egyptian police confiscated Buck's photo gear and notebooks. Unbeknownst to the police though, Buck had a secret weapon, the social networking microblog known as Twitter. As the UC student was being taken into custody, he typed a single word on his cellphone: ARRESTED. New Media journalist Matt Craven notes that, "The message went out on the cell phones and computers of a wide circle of friends in the United States and to the mostly leftist, anti-government bloggers in Egypt who are the subject of his graduate journalism project" (Craven 2008, 1). Bloggers, International lawyers, and journalists mobilized within minutes of Buck's arrest.

Within a day, Buck was released from jail and received assistance from Egyptian legal counsel and the US Embassy. Cyber-actions such as those on Twitter signal collective unity to stand up against repressive regimes within the academy and society as a whole. Physical and digital connections alike are crucial to creating a network of critical recognizance whereby the university is watched by those on the inside/outside and held accountable for punishments against those who speak out against the corporatization of the university and who take action against the academe's own complicity in perpetrating the political, cultural, social, and economic injustices of capitalist society in its oppressive totality.

A Working Class Student Is Something to Be

Anarchist Reflections on the Academy

Deric Shannon & William T. Armaline

CONTEMPORARY ACADEMIC REPRESSION IN HIGHER EDUCATION calls to mind cases like David Graeber, the anarchist anthropologist whose political commitments led Yale to deny him tenure, or Ward Churchill, a tenured full professor whose controversial remarks about the September 11th attacks on the World Trade Center and the Pentagon prompted a retaliatory investigation into his research, and ultimately his dismissal. These examples illustrate a common characteristic of higher education: scholars are systematically sanctioned when their work dares to challenge prevailing methodologies, ideologies, or social institutions.

In a repressive environment that marginalizes, sanctions, and silences radical critiques, how do those of us with commitments to social justice and political knowledges operate? How can we, as students, professors, administrators, activists, and community members (re)create and expand higher education as a space for free inquiry and democratic revolutionary praxis? Though we cannot address these questions in their entirety, we seek to participate in this larger conversation by presenting some of our own difficulties as radical scholar-activists with roots in the American working poor.

We are delighted that the editors of this volume have asked us to contribute a chapter on student concerns within our institutions of higher learning. We wish to broaden popular understandings of academic repression to include the ways that people from impoverished or working class backgrounds, particularly those with radical politics, experience higher education. Toward that end, we present personal illustrations as working class anarchists to discuss some contemporary forms of political and economic oppression in academia, along with possible strategies of resistance.[1] We do not seek to present ourselves as the horribly oppressed or completely silenced. As two males with graduate degrees in a world where over 50 percent of the global population lives or dies on less than $2.00 a day, this would be an inaccurate and insulting claim. At the same time, if any of our commitments to social justice and free inquiry drive us to question systems of domination and the very institutions (the state and the university) that employ us, it should not be at the cost of our livelihood, dignity, and careers.

To be sure, this essay is not simply about the lives and comfort of those of us in academe. Our entire system of education and intellectual production—from the training of public school teachers to whether or not we bother discussing sustainable living practices—is constrained by simple matters of what one can and cannot ask, discuss, consider, publish, or teach in the arena of higher education, let alone public policy. Further, while our practical suggestions for change are largely aimed at academics, they are easily extended into other areas of life, where "teaching" and "learning" are not static behaviors confined to the school or university. After all, a commitment to building a new society cannot be aimed solely at our educational institutions, but rather should seek to reconfigure the whole of social relations in a just and egalitarian way. But such experiments can and must begin within specific institutions such as the university.

Likewise, our experiences as anarchists can be extended to any political identification that has normative commitments to creating a new world free of structured inequality, domination, and control. Readers might also use this essay as a catalyst for investigating the ways that higher education structures the learning environment of women, people of color, the LGBTQ community, and the differently-abled in order to build reflective pedagogical practices that take these differences into account (Spring 2000; McLaren 1997; Weis and Fine 2000). It is our hope that by using personal experiences as a springboard, we can illuminate some of the structural and cultural factors that lead to academic repression in the context of student lives and provide our fellow educators with some suggestions for creating a more open environment for students from all walks of life and ideological perspectives. In the following sections, our individual first-person narratives appear in *italics*, where plain type indicates our collective voice.

Scholarship for Social Justice: Against the "Disinterested" Knowledge Factory

Activist scholars such as Feagin and Vera (2001) provide some historical context for the repression of scholarship and pedagogy that challenges dominant paradigms, institutions, and power relationships. Through a historical analysis of sociology and the social sciences in the US over the past century they demonstrate how the corporatization of higher education and the primacy of supposed "objective scientific inquiry" contributed to the contemporary academic condition.

Scholarship in the US is still largely driven by the pursuits of funding, mainstream publications, and job security (tenure)—all met most easily through academic work that presents itself as "non-biased," "scientific," often quantitative in method, and relatively unthreatening to dominant worldviews and systems of domination (Feagin and Vera 2001). To those of us in academe, this should not be a surprising revelation. The path to getting a job as a graduate student and to gaining tenure as a professor is a matter of pleasing gatekeepers: publishers, journal editors, committee members, evaluators of teaching and service, senior faculty, department chairs, administrators, and so forth. In the effort to gain or ensure employment there is a real risk in producing scholarship and pedagogy that challenges the authority or beliefs of gatekeepers, let alone the fundamental assumptions—such as the legitimacy of the representative "democratic" state and free market capitalism—that structure larger institutional (e.g., the university) and social hierarchies.

This is not to suggest that academe is totally absent of political or institutional dissent. To the contrary, many scholars—some are featured in this volume—have reached near-celebrity status for their work in direct opposition to capitalism, patriarchy, racism, heterosexism, and (less frequently) the state. At the same time, such work is typically done and published *despite* institutional and ideological constraints and should not be confused with the academic norm. Thus, we have created and sustained a situation in which scholarship that reproduces the status quo is rewarded and scholarship that runs in opposition to our relations of ruling is often sanctioned. What follows, then, are some suggestions for resisting this state of affairs and making education meaningful in a truly democratic sense.

Class(room) Struggle: The High Cost of Books and Materials

I began my undergraduate studies in earnest after dropping out in my second semester of undergraduate work, then having years of poverty, occasional unemployment, and intermittent periods of homelessness under my belt before I returned. Needless to say, I was not in a financial position to pursue my studies in the manner of my middle-class colleagues. Nevertheless, our rather meager programs for students with financial needs like Pell Grants and Stafford Loans allowed me to enroll in school and cover my rent.

Initially, there were few problems in obtaining texts and course materials as I enrolled, for the most part, in introductory courses that typically required only a single textbook. This changed as my academic career lengthened and I began taking upper level courses—the required book lists grew and sometimes my professors would assign additional course materials that were quite costly. This changed drastically when I started doing graduate work.

I still remember sitting in my chair when one of my first graduate professors handed over the required reading list to our class.

"Wow! That's a load of books!" one of my colleagues remarked.

"Don't worry," my professor countered, "I've put a copy of each book in the library on reserve for those of you who might have trouble purchasing them."

Of course, I knew what this meant for me. I didn't have time to sit in the library with the required texts every week; these were long and dense texts that would take me many hours to read. I'd have to figure out a way to get a hold of them for myself. Kicking around the internet did little good. The books were still way beyond a reasonable price range for me, even if I bought them used. In the end, I bought some, stole others (ahem! I prefer the term "liberate"), and awkwardly faked my way through a few weeks of discussions that were centered on texts I never managed to get.

As sociologists, we presumably study class dynamics. We know that one's class position affects one's opportunity structure significantly. So how had this happened? Did we really NEED this many texts to have good discussions, a productive exchange of ideas, or to meet the (rather ambitious) standards of the professor in charge? I managed to pull through that course, and many others, feeling alienated, often times left out of the discussion—not because I wasn't interested in the material, but because I couldn't afford the required texts and never got a chance to read them! (Deric Shannon)

Harris (2002, 377) writes that "class…is a problem in the academy. It is a problem that institutions of higher education for the most part ignore." That's certainly been our experience institutionally. Unfortunately, many professors do not take this into account when constructing their reading lists or requirements for course materials. So we would like for professors to keep in mind: When you just *have* to assign that ten page required book list for any given course, you are screwing working class and unemployed students over. Further, just because you have the power to assign readings doesn't mean anyone is going to read them, enjoy them, find them relevant, or internalize anything from engaging with the material. For those concerned with pedagogy, this is hugely problematic.

There are some pretty simple ways to avoid these problems. First and foremost, reading lists can be tailored down, and designed to reflect the desires and curiosities of professors *and* students. Not only does this make acquiring needed materials easier for poor and working class students, there are also important pedagogical reasons for structuring courses along these lines. Rather than designing readings around what students and instructors might find relevant to their lives and within their capacity to digest within a certain period of time, syllabi are often tainted by a thrust to "teach the canon." The uncritical commitment to teaching predetermined "canons" of literature points to a tendency toward "the banking concept of education," in graduate schools defined as "an act of depositing, in which the students are the depositories and the teacher is the depositor…knowledge is a gift by those who consider themselves knowledgeable upon those whom they consider to know nothing" (Freire 1970, 53). As Freire eloquently points out, such pedagogical practices are oppressive, hierarchical, alienating (to "students" *and* "teachers"), and often ineffective in fully engaging active learners.

Secondly, one could assign collections and edited volumes that touch on a variety of subjects relevant to the course material. Or, (the method we prefer when feasible) one can assign no books at all. For example, we have taught courses like "Revolutionary Social Movements around the World" at the University of Connecticut. The class was to be a course on ideas, rather than a litany of historical events complete with biographies of Leaders and Famous People. Students were to get a broad exposure to various types of Marxism, anarchism, revolutionary feminism, anti-racism, radical queer theory, and Earth and animal liberation. Lo and behold, there were a number of texts that fit that bill for free on the internet! The students left the course having read Karl Marx, Friedrich Engels, Mikhail Bakunin, Emma Goldman, selections from groups like Crimethinc, and class-struggle anarchist sites like Anarkismo.net. The department copier got put to use to make copies of smaller pieces of radical literature. All of this education and no book costs to students at all!

Radical activity needs to be connected with everyday life if we are going to transform society into a more humane place for all of us to live. We challenge each other to keep in mind the added hardships that students face when coming from poor or working class backgrounds. As scholars, we are well acquainted with how capitalism and its concomitant ranking of people by access to resources create vast inequalities, many of which structure our classrooms. As teachers, we might (re)consider whether we want to treat our students as objectified "depositories" or as human equals who, ultimately, decide for themselves whether particular materials or assignments are relevant, interesting, or worthy of engagement—whether "teachers" recognize it or not. We suggest, then, a reflective practice that keeps class and economic realities in the forefront of our minds as we construct our courses.

Let's Talk About Anarchism

When I began studying sociology as an undergraduate I was surprised that some professors would present radical worldviews in the classroom. After all, my high school teachers rarely mentioned radical politics except to demean them. The university seemed like an incredibly frank and open world for me. I was excited as my student colleagues and I were challenged to think about class from a Marxist perspective. Feminist theory was used to outline the ways that women's voices were routinely silenced and women were subordinated to men's demands. We studied critical race theory to demonstrate how white supremacy has been used as an ideological justification for the domination of people of color over the past five centuries. Queer theory gave us a glimpse into heteronormativity and how our available constructions of gender and sexuality assumed and enforced a monogamous, heterosexual subject. I was surprised, however, that none of these courses covering radical perspectives on inequality included anarchism in the curriculum.

Eventually, I started asking my professors why anarchism was absent in our course readings. The responses I got varied widely:

"Anarchism isn't really a theory."

"Anarchism, as a political movement, really doesn't exist anymore."

"Anarchy? Why would anyone advocate THAT?"

These replies, of course, did not jive at all with my personal experiences. I had read volumes of anarchist theory. Nearly every activist gathering, conference, or protest I attended included anarchists in the process. And, having experienced non-hierarchical methods of organization for myself, I had to wonder why anyone would NOT want to advocate for anarchism.

After I completed my undergraduate work and began the process of finding a graduate program I might want to join, I was flown to a campus interested in my application. After rounds of interviews with the professors in the department, the prospective graduate students were shuffled over to a faculty member's home for a party so we could all get to know each other better. I rode with one particular professor who asked about my research interests. I told her that, as an anarchist, I was interested in studying hierarchy and inequality. When we got to the party, she presented me to the rest of the faculty.

"Hello everyone. I'd like to introduce you to a prospective graduate student who actually takes anarchism seriously," she said contemptuously.

Needless to say, I was quite embarrassed by the prologue and I ended up choosing a different graduate program based on that exchange. I felt insulted, demeaned, and silenced before I even got the chance to talk about my ideas. (Deric Shannon)

These stories highlight some of the curious events that seem to surround anarchists who enter into the Academy. We are often subtly encouraged through social sanctions (like the off-hand remarks of the professor described above) to drop our political commitments. Further, anarchists in higher education often learn, as anarcha-feminist Peggy Kornegger (1996: 156) noted, that anarchists have "no existence at all." While students have typically encountered anarchist ideas in some form or another, most have never discussed it in their classrooms and a mention of anarchism in university text books is an extremely rare event—even rarer if it is discussed as a contemporary and living body of ideas rather than a historical aberration or Marxism's lesser known cousin.

Let us be clear in our suggestion here: we are NOT insisting that you, or anyone else, "agree" with us as anarchists. Rather, we simply want an existence in our classrooms. Anarchism, like any other political philosophy, should be critically taught and analyzed, not routinely ignored. And this argument for inclusion is not just for our own benefit. If "radical" academics are going to be relevant to everyday struggles, we should be talking about what's happening in the streets—and anarchist ideas have been steadily growing outside of the hallowed halls of the Academy.

Anarchist infoshops, for example, have become an international phenomenon, providing radical reading materials to the public and spaces for community organization. Decentralized networks such as Food Not Bombs, IndyMedia, and Critical Mass are likewise international in scope and growing every day—creating spaces for radical movement and critiques of the status quo from a distinctly anarchist perspective. Class-struggle anarchist federations are creating networks of activists across North America, Europe, parts of Africa, and Latin America.[2] Anarchists took organizational roles in the Battle of Seattle (when a coalition of groups shut down the World Trade Organization's 1999 conference in Seattle), in G8 Summits across the world, and they continue to do so in actions that oppose our corporate and political masters.

We are in the streets. More importantly, we are in your classrooms. While our radical professors and colleagues have prided themselves on breaking the barriers of dominant ideologies, there has been a wall of silence surrounding anarchist criticisms of the state and forms of domination that extend beyond the human world (e.g. our unsustainable and unethical meat-based diets and the ways in which humanity dominates and exploits our natural environment). Let's talk about domination in ALL of its forms. Let's talk about anarchism.

Hurdles and Gatekeepers: The Question of Legitimacy

Writing can be a terrifying experience in graduate school, above all if one presents theory or practice based in radical politics outside of the academic mainstream. For many students it is their first exposure to producing scholarship to undergo scrutiny, to be presented at conferences, and to be published for (presumably) the eyes of the public and Academy. There is a constant pressure in higher education to meet the expectations of academic and administrative authority figures—as in comprehensive exams, peer reviewed article submissions, final exams/papers, and thesis/dissertation defenses. As a result, especially in departments or university systems where resources are short and competition is high, this engenders students with a great deal of stress, anxiety, and self-doubt.

For working class and impoverished students, survival in academe is often conflated with survival—period. In our current economic recession, where unemployment and home foreclosures are rampant, the US dollar has lost great relative value, costs of living (fuel and food, for example) are skyrocketing, and education and social services are being gouged, the prospect of being forced out of school is dangerous indeed. Though assistantships are often limited, graduate school typically comes with the medical benefits and support structures necessary for day-to-day life, now absent for millions of US workers. Further, as we write these words, the entire California State University system faces nearly $400 million in immediate state budget cuts (California Faculty Association 2008). Where the CSU system is set up to serve California's working class and community college transfers, such economic conditions only add to the anxiety of students from impoverished and working class backgrounds in drastically shrinking their real and perceived opportunity structures.

Psychologically, these very real concerns can manifest as feelings of alienation, anxiety, and depression. Most academics know someone in graduate school or early university employment who has been diagnosed with "generalized anxiety disorder," "clinical depression," and the like—all, of course, treated to the delight of large pharmaceutical companies with any number of questionable medications. We have been no exception to this trend in academe and the "West" more generally.

> Even having entered the Academy with some amount of cultural capital
> (my father, who I reconnected with later in life, has been a professor for
> some time, albeit working for public, working class universities in the
> Midwest for modest wages), I entered from an incredibly impoverished
> and tumultuous background. Having worked since the age of fourteen
> (in seemingly every job imaginable), raised a younger sister since I was
> thirteen, and coming from the Midwestern rust belt, it has always been

difficult to relate to more affluent peers. Also facing the fears of not receiving funding for my schooling (or being able to live on that funding and outside employment), my feelings began to emerge as that of a "fraud." Until speaking with my advisor at the time, I thought I was alone in my fears and anxieties.

Frustrated enough with having to jump through the hoops of comprehensive exams and a dissertation proposal that, at the time, was simply an exercise in bureaucratic procedure (as with most ethnographers, I was forced to begin my research years in advance in order to finish "on time") I approached my advisor with the intention of leaving graduate school. I told her that I couldn't take the constant anxiety of evaluation and scrutiny that often defines the academic experience. I told her that I felt like a fraud. I felt as if, at any moment, people would "out" me as a cultural and intellectual nincompoop (even though I was one of the "top students" in the program at the time—whatever that is supposed to mean). It was an overwhelming feeling that I did not belong in the tight publishing, hiring, and social circles that ultimately determine one's fate in the Academy's mainstream.

Fortunately, my advisor had also come from a working class background, and through gendered and classed experiences, she had also battled the same self-doubt and anxiety. Older, male colleagues at her first places of employment would often second-guess her ability to take on challenging research and new teaching assignments. A mixture of patriarchal paternalism and resistance toward her radical (socialist) class politics became constant barriers for her success, and self-confidence. Though it was helpful to find I was not alone in my feelings or experiences, nothing actually changed (not that my advisor had the agency to single-handedly do so, but that is beside the point). That is, the academic processes and mechanisms that foster such feelings were not up for debate. (William Armaline)

In an earlier illustration on the cost of textbooks and course materials, we point out the contradiction of studying socio-economic oppression while simultaneously reproducing it. There is a similar contradiction in knowingly reproducing academic practices, such as seemingly pointless high-stakes exams (that, again, are based on a flawed "banking" concept of education), that potentially alienate and discourage students. Further, it is disingenuous to present the publication process (especially in "top tiered journals") as meritocratic, "objective," and so forth. In fact, it is arguably one's cultural capital (networks, presentation of "legitimate" perspectives, grasp of the publication process, etc.) that often determines whether or not work is published, and ultimately one's chances on the job market upon graduation. Often academics resist this characterization of the professional publication process, at times because it threatens the egos and identities of those already well established in academe as "legitimate scholars."

However, we must turn to a larger point here. The notion of "legitimacy" in academe is not only problematic in the sense that it is socially constructed by those who hold power in higher education and alienates those who do not. It is also problematic in the silencing of political and institutional dissent.

Especially in "prestigious" and/or "research intensive" universities and departments, there is a pressure for scholars to publish in order to keep their job—even at the cost of teaching and other professional responsibilities. This practice is so widespread and obvious it has given birth to the now trite phrase, "publish or perish." Under the "publish or perish" system, we are all coerced into meeting the expectations of ideological gatekeepers. For example, in order to gain employment as a professor and then, presumably, attain job security (tenure) or mobility (transfer), we are all typically expected to publish in peer-reviewed professional journals in our respective academic fields. The stated purpose here is to prove our legitimacy as scholars by allowing our "peers" to judge our anonymously submitted work by its "merits" (the suggested reason for anonymity), and thus choose to publish or reject our work. The process is presented on its face as meritocratic—an "objective" process by which scholars review, critique, and judge one another's work.

However, not unlike the false meritocracy presented in the broader US educational system, this process is deceiving. First, there is no such thing as objective "merit" here—the editorial review process, not unlike the act of teaching or writing, is ultimately partial and biased. Second, editors and editorial boards—especially of "top-tiered" journals are hardly the "peers" of graduate students and less established faculty; unless we are to completely ignore their relative *power* as editors and typically more established and "legitimate" professors. Third, journals don't simply publish articles through blind submission. Often articles and journal editions are published through far more transparent means, where editors will approach colleagues with solicitations, create journal editions from sections of a conference, or even dedicate editions to particular theoretical or methodological approaches. Thus publication becomes largely reduced to cultural capital and the strength of one's "reputation" and professional network.

In short, the journal publication process is presented as meritocratic and relatively "objective," when it is quite the opposite. Editors and editorial boards are in the powerful subjective positions as gatekeepers. They get to decide what work, through what means, gains entry to the journal. Editors and editorial boards are also given two key coercive tools here beyond the power to simply accept or reject submissions: (1)

they can insist that submitting authors make specific revisions before the piece is worthy of publication—thus giving them veiled substantive voice in the article, (2) they can hide behind anonymity such that no matter how ridiculous, empirically problematic, biased, careerist, or downright degrading their responses to one's work might be, they escape having to own up to their words in anything resembling an honest dialog with submitting authors.

Because there is such an institutional pressure for scholars to publish, and the publication process is hierarchical and inescapably biased and political, it is especially difficult to challenge dominant ideas while keeping one's job and professional "legitimacy." Further, since the journal publication process is central to academic credentialing and is presented as "objective," what functions as the creation of allowable discourse parades as the unbiased measure of one's virtues as a scholar. These institutional practices perpetuate a hierarchical status quo and discipline scholars into a detached and "impartial" scholarship that repeats, rather than challenges, our relations of ruling in form and substance. A source of frustration for us, as radical and anarchist scholars, has been the academic repression inherent in these processes—especially when it comes from our ostensibly "radical" colleagues. The careerism and deference to authority inherent in Academia has infected a number of scholars whose critiques of capitalism, imperialism, racism, patriarchy, speciesism, and so on are abstract, aloof, esoteric, and dauntingly distant to any relationship with concrete politics and "the street." Foucault (1980: 60) once noted that "power isn't localized in the State apparatus and that nothing in society will be changed if the mechanisms of power that function outside, below and alongside the State apparatuses, on a much more minute and everyday level, are not also changed." Indeed, if we are to bring about those changes in society that we as radicals regularly espouse, our practices in our daily lives should reflect those desires—working towards what the Situationists called a "revolution of everyday life" (Vaneigem 2003).

Some Humble Suggestions

In the sections above, we suggest that many academic mechanisms are innately alienating or employed in ways that foster alienation (e.g., professors and sometimes learning itself) and undue distress for working class and radical students. This alienation often creates fear, the feeling of being an outsider or fraud, anxiety, and depression. There is potential harm to affected students *and* the academic departments meant to serve them because such effects hurt the "productivity" of students in the program and their ability to secure employment.

Perhaps the larger point here is that we have the agency to investigate, recognize, and address practices and mechanisms that oppress students with working class backgrounds and/or radical politics. Perhaps it is time to reconsider and *tangibly resist* many practices in higher education that, through our scholarship and experience we know to be problematic, but through our own careerism, deference to dominant ideology, and acquiescence to institutional/bureaucratic inertia, we fail to address.

As an example of this questioning method, consider something as small as dress and presentation of the self. Should we seek to meet the standards of educational corporatization, and wear "formal" or "businesslike" attire in order to gain "respect" and a "professional" relationship with students? There is a certain expectation of meeting these norms in our classrooms, in our meetings (especially with administrators), in our hiring practices, in our professional conferences, and so forth. Although maintaining this dominant standard is helpful toward employment and tenure, what if we, as anarchists, find such (even implied) demands oppressive and elitist? What if we have a concern for *minimizing* the perceived difference between the false dichotomy of "teachers" who impart "knowledge" and "students" who dutifully receive it? Even classic works on critical pedagogical practice (Dewey 1938, 1944; Freire 1970) point to the importance of imploding this false dichotomy in the realization that knowledge and history are constantly being (re)constructed, and that "teachers" and "students" are participants in this intersubjective endeavor.

Both authors of this essay have clearly made a choice here: to present ourselves *as ourselves*. Both of us have sizable tattoos and do not fear showing them. Both of us wear what would be considered "casual" (i.e., comfortable, sensible, and sustainable) attire to our classrooms. Both of us employ slang and "colorful language" in the classroom. Where some mistake these choices (that might jeopardize careers) as "unprofessional," they are part of a pedagogical strategy reflexively constructed with the intention of disrupting hierarchical dynamics. They are deliberate strategies to resist the dominant expectations of academe in order to create less restrictive and less coercive learning environments for our students, colleagues, and professors/mentors. Further, they are means to employ our politics (in this case, anarchism as an opposition to all structured oppressive hierarchy) throughout our work and lives.

We have written this essay as a personal illustration of how we can begin to take tangible actions in our learning and working environments to address the alienation of poor and working class students in higher education. While it should go without saying, we wish to reiterate that changing the structure of education is not enough; rather, the whole of social relations must be reconfigured if we are to fully address the concerns of exploited, oppressed, and marginalized groups. Thus, while we express our politics in the ways that we teach, talk, and dress, for example, we also organize outside of the classroom. We leave our desks to involve ourselves in mass movements. We hope to see more educators doing these things.

When we talk about academic repression, it is important to identify that it is not only a concern of the educator—especially one who teaches controversial material. Rather, students also experience silencing, sometimes in subtle ways—although certainly at times it can be overt (consider, for example, how the Ohio National Guard used deadly force against non-violent student protesters at Kent State in 1970). If education is going to be an experience worth having for all of us, it is important that educators recognize this and take the silencing of students into account as we continue to refine our pedagogical theories and practice.

Finally, it is important to note that in order for "education" to be transformative and meaningful, it needs to take place within the context of egalitarian social relations. This essay examines a single institution embedded in a web of domination that is currently our institutional status quo. While working to create change within the halls of the Academy is certainly an important step toward social transformation, we must not lose sight of the fact that academic repression cannot be easily dislodged from the totality of oppressions that exist throughout the social world, and in our relation to the natural world, generally. Thus, a dedication to genuine education is, by extension, a commitment to building a new world—one free of structured domination, coercion, and control, a world in which we are the subjects of our own lives rather than passive spectators to an often brutal and violent reality, and where all living things are accorded dignity and respect, and the ethos of cruelty is replaced by a culture of compassion.

Academia and the Culture of Militarism

Mark Rupert

WELL-PUBLICIZED REVELATIONS HAVE MADE IT CLEAR how Donald Rumsfeld, Laurence Di Rita, Victoria Clarke, and the Pentagon pimped out a stable of retired generals to act as media military experts who recited Pentagon talking points in order to rouse public support for the Iraq War. They also colluded to influence press coverage so as to downplay public fears about Guantanamo Bay, and otherwise achieve what Ms. Clarke called "information dominance"—control over the US public, that is.[1]

What may be less well known or widely appreciated is the way in which a culture of militarism has permeated American society, and the ways in which the Pentagon has deliberately stoked and manipulated that culture in order to legitimate US military operations overseas and to create an environment of tacit or active consent for an imperial garrison state at home. This effort to reshape popular culture increasingly also impinges upon academia, generating political and ethical challenges for intellectuals, teachers, students, and administrators. This essay is a reflection on my own encounters as a professor with these processes of cultural militarization of the academy.

Militarism and Me: From Army Brat to Pussy Boy

Since early childhood, I have been aware that the US military establishment is actively engaged in major public relations efforts. The son of a career army officer, the first half of my childhood was spent on military bases. Among my more vivid childhood recollections from the mid-1960s are the annual rituals of Armed Forces Day, when the nation's military bases are opened to the public in a massive show-and-tell (and shoot) exhibition. Of course, military brats like me who lived on base could be first in line for the festivities. I remember my family waking to the sound of nearby artillery fire across the street from the base housing where we lived, in the parking lot of the elementary school I attended on weekdays; an artillery unit began firing blank rounds from a

105mm howitzer beginning at seven in the morning. If you could stand to be close to the noise of an artillery piece in action they would let you pull the firing lanyard, and even give you the spent brass shell casing (one such shell was a fixture in our house for years). After that auspicious beginning, the day was filled with rides on armored personnel carriers and battle tanks, opportunities to fire blank rounds from machine guns and toss dummy grenades, tour mobile field hospitals, and sit at the controls of army helicopters pretending to fly them.

By the end of the day I had a collection of certificates testifying that I had completed a (minutes-long) training course, for example, in the firing of an M-60 machine gun. On the nearby air force base, we would watch flyovers of military aircraft, including then state-of-the-art F-4 Phantom fighter-bombers: I still recall being briefly deafened by the indescribably loud roar as one of those awe-inspiring aircraft passed low and fast over the admiring crowd. Complete with shows, rides, and souvenirs, Armed Forces Day was Disneyland in olive drab. But even then I understood, if somewhat vaguely, that these events were not just being staged purely for the indulgence of my juvenile military fantasies.

Eventually I came to understand that the military was not just holding an open house for the public, but sending an implicit message which said, "Come and see your military machine, use their tools as your playthings, identify with and feel good about the awesome power represented here—your power!" Nobody mentioned Vietnam and what "our" military power was actually doing half a world away. That, of course, might have defeated the purpose of the exercise, which beneath the apolitical veneer was saturated with political meanings. In addition to demonstrating breathtaking (and deafening) power in a variety of forms, these military exhibitions forged an identification between the military and the public, suggesting that our military machine was as implicitly good and virtuous as we presumed ourselves to be, independent of the unacknowledged political purposes for which it was deployed and the actual human costs of exercising imperial power on a global scale.

All of these memories and my deep ambivalence about them were brought up for me recently when, in my capacity as Chair of a university political science department, I was invited to participate in another kind of military public relations exercise, a program the Pentagon calls: "Why We Serve." One day last fall I received an email from a Marine Corps major attached to the Pentagon's public affairs department. The Major asked me whether I would be willing to invite "recently returned warriors" from the "Global War on Terror (GWOT)" into my classroom or to a special event on campus that would offer "an avenue to meet the men and women who are making history in the GWOT."[2] The official Why We Serve web page depicts a smiling soldier with an Iraqi child enjoying a lollipop, and tells readers that:

By hosting uniformed service members to speak about their individual experiences in the Long War, audiences around the country are offered a personal view on military service. *The Why We Serve speakers do not address issues of Department of Defense policy*. Rather, each member relates his or her own experience in a manner that offers Americans a glimpse of military service as can only be seen through the eyes of our uniformed men and women.[3] [emphasis added]

I wrote back to the Major expressing skepticism about this program. It seemed to me that it was intended to substitute an allegedly "non-political" meet-and-greet the troops for a direct and explicitly political discussion of the issues. I think the effect of depoliticizing and personalizing the discussion in this way is to immunize US policy from criticism while fostering warm fuzzy feelings about the US military as represented by individually admirable service members. The Major responded assuring me that this was not a domestic propaganda campaign:

> Let me assure you that although we at the DoD view this program as a community outreach tool, we offer these returning vets to the general public without any stump-speech or overall communication agenda. All we ask of them is that they try their best to effectively communicate why they have decided to volunteer to wear the uniform of their country in a time of conflict. The reason I am reaching out to colleges/universities is directly related to what you mention—free thinking, open dialogue, learning, and shared experience. This is not a "pro-war" or "pro-administration" program intended to "win the hearts and minds," nor is it a recruiting campaign. I merely want to offer people another resource in order to make more informed opinions.[4]

This in fact did not reassure me, since my point was that this program appears to want to substitute one kind of discussion (personalized and non-political) for another (explicitly political and policy-oriented).

As I looked into this further I found an article from the American Forces Press Service (AFPS—the Pentagon's own in-house info factory), entitled, "Outreach Program Puts Human Face on Military Service," in which the Major with whom I was corresponding described the Why We Serve program in the following, more directly political, terms:

"What this program is doing is helping us win the 'war on narratives,' especially in the mainstream media," [the Major] noted. The program, he added, offers a different perspective about the war on terrorism, from the viewpoints of military members who've served in Afghanistan, Iraq or the Horn of Africa.[5]

In a similar vein, the article reported the remarks of an Army officer who is one of the program's hand-picked speakers:

Meeting one-on-one with the American public helps to combat misperceptions about the US effort in Iraq, he said. "It's a new fight. It's a very, very powerful information war."[6]

So it appeared that when the program is discussed within the Defense establishment (the AFPS article) they are more willing to link it clearly to the overall war effort, part of the "war on narratives" or "information war"; but when they contact university professors and ask to be invited to speak to students, they present the program as apolitical, as just one more source of information.

This was clearly a domestic propaganda operation, and as the statements above reveal, the military personnel in charge of the program viewed it as such ("war on narratives," "information war," etc.). But that's not what was decisive in my mind, since an open discussion in which a propaganda campaign engages with other perspectives could be productive and illuminating. The clincher for me was that the Pentagon wanted to present this in the guise of a personal interaction with "recently returned warriors" rather than as an honest and direct political dialogue about US military policy. This seemed to me to be disingenuous, expressly designed to create positive associations between college students and the military while displacing the political issues of US militarism and foreign policy in such a way that critical questions about the latter might be excluded from discussion. On those grounds I declined their offer to sponsor a Why We Serve event under the auspices of my department.[7]

As word of my decision got around, some conservative members of the university community contacted the media, attracting attention by framing the story in terms of the familiar right-wing narrative of predominantly leftist academics and elitist liberals heaping scorn on mainstream beliefs and attempting to exclude or silence conservative voices in order to impose a politically correct monologue on campus.[8] In terms of this story line, my decision represented the efforts of a left-leaning faculty member to censor the US military (as if any such thing was within my power) and a gesture of disrespect toward men and women in military service. Finding myself at the center of a public controversy, I had my fifteen minutes of (small-time) fame as a terror-symp, disloyal academic of dubious masculinity. For several days my email in-box was jam-packed with messages from people I did not know, all of it presuming bad faith on my part, and much of it hostile, abusive, or threatening. One correspondent addressed me as "Pussy Boy" before launching into a bloodthirsty tirade, while another simply suggested that I belonged at home with the women and children while real men fought for my freedom in Iraq.

My university employment was never jeopardized nor my academic freedom directly threatened, and my departmental colleagues were generally supportive of my decision and the reasoning behind it. I make no claims of political martyrdom here. Yet, the unpleasant experience of public vilification as an academic who was not play-ing my part for Team USA led me to wonder about the Pentagon's contemporary cul-tural significance and its relationship to the academy. I do not pretend to the expertise and experience of other writers in this volume, but I am learning some things about these topics which I think are worth sharing. In particular, Why We Serve is one piece of the Pentagon's astonishingly vigorous and comprehensive public relations cam-paign, which provides the Pentagon with public visibility and with a familiar, readily accepted presence across a wide array of popular cultural activities. I believe that *the academy is being deliberately targeted by Pentagon officials eager to breach what they see as one of the last sites where the culture of American militarism is not embraced as a matter of course.*

Support the Troops (Or Else...)

Why We Serve followed in the footsteps of a broader program designed to encourage Americans to support US troops, and to create among US military personnel an im-pression that their efforts and sacrifices are valued back home and that the American public stands behind them as they continue the occupation of Iraq and the endless "war on terror." This double-edged sword aimed at both a public and a military audience was called America Supports You (ASY).[9] Allison Barber, Deputy Assistant Secretary of Defense for Internal Communications and Public Liaison, has been in charge of the American Forces Information Service (parent organization of AFPS and the military magazine *Stars and Stripes*) as well as ASY. Explaining the mission of ASY in an envi-ronment when support for the occupation of Iraq was waning and Bush administration approval ratings were in free fall, Barber wrote in January 2007: "the American people are beginning to fatigue, even in their support for the troops... I don't think we have a minute to lose when it comes to maximizing support for our military, especially in the new political environment."[10]

According to AFPS, "The Defense Department launched [ASY] in Novem-ber 2004 to showcase support for the country's men and women in uniform from the

American public as well as the corporate sector."[11] With the aid of a multi-million dollar contract with a private public relations firm, a private foundation called the America Supports You Fund, major corporate partners such as Wal-Mart and Microsoft, and hundreds of local affiliate groups, ASY organized mass "Freedom Walks" in over fifty cities nationwide to commemorate 9/11 and encourage hyper-patriotic militarism. They sponsored pro-troop events at NASCAR and Indy 500 auto races, and induced professional wrestlers, golfers, baseball players, and rodeo cowboys to publicly express their support; developed a special "teaching supplement" inclusion in the *Weekly Reader* to encourage grade school kids to be grateful to and express support for US troops; and sponsored mass campaigns enjoining people to write appreciative text messages ostensibly sent to troops serving overseas at Thanksgiving. Also, ASY teamed up with Nashville's Grand Ole Opry to send holiday care packages to the troops and partnered with Wal-Mart to donate laptops, toys, food, and cash to military families at Christmas. They sponsored a special holiday "CD for the troops" in which thirteen recording artists contributed songs downloadable free of charge to service members; and distributed an ASY Calendar of Support highlighting occasions throughout the year when ASY wishes to prompt outpourings of public support. ASY strategically targeted a mix of old and new media: in addition to a radio show, ASY launched a blog, a My Space page, and uploaded videos to You Tube.[12]

On every important holiday throughout the year, and across a range of popular cultural activities and venues, ASY organizes mass expressions of popular support for the troops. Ostensibly apolitical, one of the underlying purposes of the ASY program is to combat the "Vietnam syndrome" in which popular opposition to US militarism was perceived as undermining the ability effectively to deploy military force overseas, as an AFPS report backhandedly suggests: "Barber, who heads the Defense Department's internal communications and public liaison programs, said servicemembers returning from war today are returning to heroes' welcomes, unlike their Vietnam-era counterparts. 'Vietnam has not happened yet because of you,' she said [to an audience of ASY activists]."[13] President Bush repeatedly encouraged public participation in ASY as a way to support the global "war on terror": "Our troops in Iraq, Afghanistan and other fronts in the war on terror are serving in a cause that is vital and just. And on this Fourth of July, I ask every American to find a way to thank the men and women who are defending our freedom and the families that support them."[14] Bush lauded ASY for sending the troops a message of unstinting support for "the vital work [they] do to achieve victory in Iraq."[15]

And ASY is just the proverbial tip of the iceberg. The *Military-Industrial-Cultural complex* is deeply entangled with movies and television, sports, video games and the Internet, schools, and colleges.[16] A strategy of global military supremacy presupposes the support or at least the tacit consent of the public for the maintenance of a massive military establishment and the routine waging of wars large and small. The popular disillusionment of the Vietnam era suggested that this support cannot be taken for granted and must be constructed and fostered through extensive cultural interventions of various kinds. Among the cultural constructions which have effectively redefined the Vietnam experience and made possible a resurgence of popular militarism are the factually baseless but deeply resonant mythologies of valiant and manly American soldiers "denied permission to win" in Vietnam (as Ronald Reagan put it), POWs betrayed and left behind by their country, and returning soldiers allegedly spit upon and vilified by antiwar protesters and hippies. All of these omnipresent popular mythologies speak of a virile, virtuous, and noble US military which could have "won" in Vietnam were it not for the dastardly back-stabbing liberals, leftists, feminists, gays, peace and anti-nuclear groups, and sundry other wimps, traitors, commies, enemies of "freedom," and elitists scornful of popular culture and the manly virtues of militarized American patriotism.[17] In terms of these popular cultural narratives, then, restoring American greatness requires silencing these disloyal social forces, remasculinizing America, and reestablishing the preeminence of a culture of militarism, which is to say that these mythologies embody a comprehensive conservative agenda for America and the world. Himself a former army officer and political conservative, the militarization of American culture has been highlighted, and lamented, by Andrew Bacevich:

> Americans in our own time have fallen prey to militarism, manifesting itself in a romanticized view of soldiers, a tendency to see military power as the truest measure of national greatness, and outsized expectations regarding the efficacy of force. To a degree without precedent in US history, Americans have come to define the nation's strength and well-being in terms of military preparedness, military action, and the fostering of…military ideals.[18]

To legitimate himself and his war in Iraq, President Bush (in)famously sought to play on these powerful cultural themes, triumphantly emerging from a navy jet in full fighter pilot regalia and striding manfully across the flight deck of the *USS Abraham Lincoln* to bask in militarized glory and celebrate "mission accomplished" in the wake of the initial US invasion.[19]

Storming the Ivory Tower

Despite the presence of numerous ties between academia and the military-industrial complex, the triumph of militarism is not yet complete on American campuses.[20] Writing in *Parameters*, the journal of the US Army War College, attorney and infantry platoon commander Marc Lindemann suggests that the military has felt itself unwelcome on many American campuses for decades, initially because of resistance to the Vietnam War and later because of hostility toward the official homophobia of military personnel policy. He notes with dismay the "exile" of ROTC programs from elite campuses such as Yale, Columbia, and Harvard, and the refusal of many other campuses to admit military recruiters to campus career fairs and placement events. According to Lindemann, the gates of the Ivory Tower were breached by a 2006 US Supreme Court decision upholding the federal government's authority to withdraw funds from universities which turn away military recruiters, effectively compelling campuses which receive federal monies to participate in military recruitment. A second important recent change involved the surge of patriotism and support for public (especially military) service following the 9/11 attacks. "The combination of campuses' changing attitudes to the military and Supreme Court-mandated access for recruiters presents a historic opportunity for the armed services. The military is now poised to avail itself of a group of talented young men and women from which it has largely been cut off for the past three decades."[21]

Among the tactics Lindemann suggests for "storming the ivory tower" are some which sound very much like the Why We Serve program: "Given the relative scarcity of recent veterans from universities such as Yale and Harvard, it is necessary to provide role models to whom students can relate. The military could continue to work with like-minded student organizations to bring charismatic service members to speak on campus."[22] In this way, the cultural imperative to "support the troops" can be used to open the nation's campuses to military role models who will simultaneously depoliticize and legitimize military service in the eyes of students, and open the way to creating a regular, familiar, and unquestioned presence of military culture on the nation's campuses.

But imperial militarism is not yet an unquestioned presence in the academy, even in disciplines such as mine (International Relations [IR]) where reasons of state and use of force are often taken for granted as "realities" of world politics. At the March 2003 meetings of the International Studies Association, just prior to the invasion of Iraq, I observed and participated in a respectably-sized antiwar protest staged by IR scholars themselves. I was told by a former ISA president that such a protest within the ISA itself was unprecedented in his experience. Further, surveys of International Relations scholars indicated overwhelming opposition to the war in Iraq, with 80 percent of respondents in a spring 2003 poll indicating that they were opposed or strongly opposed to the war. In another unusual expression of opposition, several hundred scholars of international relations signed a public statement condemning the war in Iraq and the larger policy of American empire.[23]

My academic discipline is not full of tenured radicals and peaceniks, but neither is it unable to formulate or express opposition to some of the more extreme manifestations of a US policy of global military supremacy. If International Relations—that most stubbornly Machiavellian of disciplines—continues to maintain space for informed dissent on questions of war and peace, it seems to me that the culture of imperial militarism has not yet conquered academia. This space of intellectual engagement, critical anaylsis, and public deliberation—limited and beleaguered as it may be—is worth defending. To my mind, this does not mean denying military personnel a place on campus or a voice in our deliberations, but it does mean resisting the imposition of a monologue of unreflective patriotism in the guise of support for the troops.

As other essays in this volume attest, there are numerous ways in which the militarization of American society impinges on academic life. Exposing and publicly criticizing domestic propaganda operations such as America Supports You and Why We Serve is necessary, but hardly sufficient, to preserve these crucial spaces of academic and intellectual freedom against aggressive encroachments from corporate fat cats and military top brass, both of whom want to snuff out academic freedom and critical thinking in order to transform higher education into a functional trade school that produces the bankers, brokers, and bombers of tomorrow.

Powerful Compassion

The Strike at Syracuse

Ali Shehzad Zaidi

It is worth the trip to Syracuse University (SU) just to see Ben Shahn's sixty-by-twelve-foot outdoor mural, *The Passion of Sacco and Vanzetti*. Unveiled in 1967, the mosaic tile mural tells the story of Nicola Sacco and Bartolomeo Vanzetti, executed in 1927 for a crime that they probably did not commit. Witnesses placed them miles from the crime scene when the murder of a paymaster occurred at a shoe factory in Braintree, Massachusetts.

After fleeing to Mexico in 1917 to avoid the draft, both Italian immigrants returned to the United States at the end of the First World War. At the time of their arrest in 1920, Sacco and Vanzetti were under surveillance for their involvement in strike activities, and their radical beliefs were used against them during their trial. Despite demonstrations and petition-signings in many countries, Alvin Fuller, the Governor of Massachusetts, sent Sacco and Vanzetti to the electric chair based on the findings of a commission that included the presidents of Harvard and MIT.[1]

Shahn's mural consists of three connected panels. In the first panel, a group of protesters symbolize the tumult that both led to and followed the arrest of Sacco and Vanzetti. In the second, Sacco and Vanzetti, handcuffed to one another, tower over the background in a symbolic representation of their moral stature. Their shadows slant accusingly towards a courthouse. Standing behind them, a diminutive governor Fuller, casting no shadow, reads his verdict. In the third, members of the commission, in top hats and academic garb, hold flowers over coffins containing the bodies of Sacco and Vanzetti.

Shahn wanted to create, as he put it, "works of art in which powerful compassion is innate, or which… will serve ultimately to dignify that society in which it exists."[2] On either side of Shahn's mural are famous words from a Vanzetti letter that conform more to the grammar of the heart than of the schoolmaster. "If it had not been for these thing, I might have live out my life talking at street corners to scorning men," wrote Vanzetti from prison to his son, "I might have die, unmarked, unknown, a failure. Now we are not a failure. Never in our full life could we hope to do such work for tolerance, for joostice, for man's onderstanding of man as now we do by accident. Our words—our lives!—our pains nothing! The take of our lives—lives of a good shoemaker and a poor fish peddler—all! That last moment belongs to us—that agony is our triumph."

The powerful compassion emanating from Shahn's mural could serve equally to define the SU experience in the aftermath of the unusual September 1998 strike. In the belief that current labor unrest and the erosion of the humanities at universities spring from a common cause, I visited SU for five days in September in order to research the strike and its origins.

In the summer prior to the strike, 750 unionized dining service workers, groundskeepers, janitors, and library employees at SU had found themselves without a contract. Negotiations between the SU administration and the union, Service Employees International Union (SEIU) Local 200A, had foundered over the abuse of temporary workers, pay equity for library workers, the use of unskilled labor, and above all, subcontracting.

Claiming that "modern institutions need flexibility," the administration had demanded the right to subcontract any department with less than twenty-five employees—in effect, virtually all SU dining halls and residences—in return for higher wage increases. It claimed, furthermore, that no union employees had lost their jobs as a result of subcontracting. The union disagreed, maintaining that a hundred union jobs had been lost to subcontracting within the last seven years.

Over the summer, SU Chancellor Kenneth Shaw told a group of concerned professors that while outsourcing was undesirable, SU did not want a contract that restricted it. As physics professor Rafael Sorkin later explained, the administration "wanted the flexibility to do the things they didn't want to do because they might want to do them at some point."[3]

Another concern was the abuse of temporary workers who were contractually permitted to work a maximum of twenty hours a week for eighty days at a single job. The workers were being shuttled between short-term jobs at different dining centers to get around the contractual limitation.

The union also wanted to halt the substitution of unskilled for skilled labor, which threatened the status and safety of workers. Union representative Coert Bonthius contended that an unskilled maintenance worker who tried to fix a boiler was almost killed when it blew up. The incident recalls the times of James Roscoe Day, SU chancellor from 1894 to 1922. Upton Sinclair in *The Goose-Step* (a 1923 romp through the nightmare of higher education) describes him this way: "The chancellor even carries his hatred of labor unions to the point of crippling the university. Workingmen have been changed two or three times in one week; the chancellor set the maximum price that a workingman is worth at twenty-eight cents an hour, and as a result, the boilers of the heating plant were ruined, and the cost was four thousand dollars."[4]

Additionally, the union proposed to increase the low pay of library workers in order to attain gender equity. SU ranked ninety-fifth out of 109 university libraries surveyed by the Association of Research Libraries in 1996–97 for average salary of professional library staff. Women held 70 percent of library jobs at SU, but received 20 to 25 percent less pay than men in comparable jobs.[5] One serials cataloguer, who had worked at SU for 23 years, was only making around $20,000 a year. In his June 1997 annual report, Head Librarian David Stam called for higher salaries for library workers, noting that "for some it is less than a living wage…and is a particularly demoralizing factor when combined with higher expectations of productivity, more work with fewer people, and often the requirement to attain new technological skills within the old classification framework."[6]

On July 28, against the wishes of a federal mediator, SU negotiators presented a final offer (which would have strengthened the administration's ability to outsource SU jobs) to the union. On August 16, union members voted, for the first time in twenty-four years, to strike. After the vote, Shaw refused to meet again with concerned faculty.

Sensing the distance between SU's rhetoric and reality, some professors urged Shaw to negotiate in good faith with the union. "As a teacher who ponders a great deal over the implicit social values I am responsible for communicating to my students," wrote English professor Gregg Lambert to Shaw, "I cannot take lightly the situation in which I am asked to convey the university's self-proclaimed values of mutual respect, fairness, and equity in a context where these basic principles are not honored by the university itself in its dealings with all its members."

Ironically, in late July, weeks after the expiration of the contract, SU completed its $4 million purchase of Marshall Square Mall, a commercial retail establishment near the university. A SU public relations official described the investment as "a real good opportunity to invest in the community and university." Students were concerned that the acquisition of the mall, which contains the only local competitor to SU's bookstore, might make them captive consumers.[7] Employees wondered why SU had money to acquire real estate but not to pay them a living wage.

Shortly before the strike, a memo which apparently originated in the office of the Director of Student Activities stated that union representatives were not allowed to distribute information on campus and that students could not do so as individuals, but could only through recognized student organizations that supported the union as a whole. The memo reminded graduate students that they held teaching assistantships and fellowships as university beneficiaries. Some wags noted that SU, which prided itself on being the "number one student-centered university," had become the "number one student-censored university." The SU administration later issued a clarification stating that the memo had been based on the second-hand report of a conversation. Free speech, however, remained at issue throughout the strike.

As classes began at SU, about 630 physical plant, food service, and library workers formed picket lines at 15 locations on campus. Only 10 to 15 percent of union employees reported for work. Some professors decided not to cross the picket lines and held classes instead at churches, a performing arts center, the Westcott cinema, or at home.

The administration brought in temporary workers to replace the strikers. Recruiters set up booths in student dormitories. "Need a job?," inquired an advertisement for dining services in the *Daily Orange*.[8] The administration maintained that students were being hired not as replacement workers, but for the College Work Study Program.[9]

On September 1, fifty faculty members organized a picket line and held a press conference in front of Bird Library. When SU security officers informed them that they could not hold strike signs on campus, the professors sat down for an hour and a half, courting arrest.[10] At a forum that evening, student dissatisfaction grew when Neil Strodel, SU's Associate Vice President for Human Resources, dodged questions about SU policy on free speech and about the purchase of Marshall Square Mall.[11]

The next day, 300 students, including members of the Cornell Organization for Labor Action, gathered for a teach-in on the quad where they heard poems, speeches, and live music. Later, 1,000 people marched in protest to the residence of Chancellor Shaw. Students demonstrated the following afternoon in front of the administration building, chanting for Shaw to be hired part-time, hoping that he too might someday have the opportunity to experience life without health benefits, job security, or a living wage. Approximately a dozen students broke from the main group to blockade the building's entrances by lying or sitting in front of them until closing time.

With momentum building, 96 percent of the employees voted to continue the strike. As news of the unrest spread, parents logged on to SU's "Q & A Strike Information For Parents" webpage, which reassured them that this union did "not have a propensity toward violence."

The administration's stance toward the union recalled Chancellor Day's iron hand. "The strike is a conspiracy and nothing less," thundered Day in his 1920 classic of oligarchic kitsch, *My Neighbor The Working Man*. "We deal promptly and effectively with conspiracies against property and persons in other matters. What delusion has closed our eyes to the true character of the labor strike which is one of the most glaring forms of conspiracy the world has known?" Day goes on to explain, in his hymn to big business, how disorder is inherent in strikes: "The character of a strike is seen in destruction of property, assaults and murders. The call for soldiers and an extra police guard tells the story. The strike stands for everything which America opposes. It is violence. It is riot. It opposes liberty. It is dangerous to life by exciting men to unrestrained and dangerous passions."[12] While passions were high during the 1998 SU strike, only one minor strike-related injury occurred, as a supervisor hit an employee while driving through a picket line at high speed.

The administration accused union officers of acting against the interests of SU employees. "It is important to note that none of the University's offers have been voted on by the union membership," wrote Shaw in an August 28 message to the SU community. "Paid agents of SEIU and designated union officers have consistently refused to allow the membership to ratify or reject the proposed contract." In response to Shaw, the parent of a SU student wrote: "I assume that by 'designated union officers' you mean 'elected union officers.' Why not say so and admit that the SEIU has a democratic structure? Unions are generally more democratic than universities. When was the last time that the workers, students and faculty got to elect you or the governing board?" Union members found Shaw's accusation ludicrous, since three of them had been elected to serve on the bargaining committee along with the union officers. Vanessa Dismuke, union steward for the library workers, said that the members had instructed the bargaining committee not to bring back an unacceptable offer.

After a week-long strike, union members overwhelmingly ratified a new contract granting significant wage increases for library workers and modest raises for other union workers. The contract also included protections against subcontracting, limiting temporary workers to 20 hours a week and 1,000 hours a year.

Both sides pledged not to take reprisals. The union agreed not to fine those who crossed the picket line while the administration agreed not to withhold tuition benefits from strikers. Some workers complained, nonetheless, that they were not being allowed to take breaks. Joan Hart, a picket captain, was written up three times within three days and demoted a pay grade for such infractions as wearing a union cap to work. SU's Office of Human Resources investigated the allegations of reprisals, and determined that supervisors had simply taken routine disciplinary actions.[13]

In his September 23, 1998 address to the faculty, Shaw asked professors who had refused to cross picket lines "to voluntarily inform their deans of the time missed so that their paychecks can be adjusted accordingly." Shaw reassured them that he was "motivated not by a desire to punish, but to ensure that the lesson of civil disobedience is not lost on our students." That lesson, intoned Shaw, was that "passionately held beliefs are worth sacrifice."

The strike was the first campus-wide challenge to Shaw since he took office in 1991. SU had welcomed its new chancellor with an extensive renovation of the chancellor's 9,000 square-foot, 20-room mansion. Simultaneously, SU instituted a salary freeze for its staff and prepared a restructuring plan that would cut 15 percent of SU's 4,300 employees and $38 million out of its $452 million annual budget by 1995.[14]

Nearly 20 percent of SU's tenured faculty—120 professors—opted for SU's "supported resignation program."

In February 1992, Shaw wrote in the Syracuse Herald American that "in order to ensure their survival, institutions of higher learning must now devote their energies to the enterprise of sausage making." Elaborating on this metaphor, Shaw observed: "Even with the most carefully chosen and healthful ingredients—turkey, organic cereals, natural spices—sausage making is an ugly process to witness. But after all the slicing, chopping, blood and gore, the end product can be delicious, nutritious and of remarkable quality. In short, America's colleges an universities must now pursue—and a number of them, indeed, have already been forced to begin—the kind of painful restructuring that is akin to sausage making and has been taken up in earnest by many U. S. corporations, from Chrysler and IBM to Time Inc. Ugly in the process, but, if done well, healthy in the outcome." 15

The day after the essay appeared, Shaw presented the restructuring plan to students and faculty in Hendricks Chapel. As he was speaking, a series of loud chopping noises suddenly rose from the central aisle. Joanna Spitzner, a performing arts major, and Michael Waddell, an illustration major, were kneeling on the chapel floor, slicing oranges on a cutting board.[16] University security quickly led the seniors away. "The chancellor is very good at talking around questions," said Waddell afterwards. "It's pretty pathetic to just let things happen."[17]

Soon afterwards, students and professors at the School of Music occupied a dean's office for a night to protest the cuts to their school; a dean, perhaps a relic from a bygone age, angrily took issue with Shaw's sausage-making metaphor.

Shaw took such reactions in stride. "Institutional restructuring, as I've stated, resembles sausage making in its ugliness," he wrote in his sausage-making essay. "And institutions undergoing major changes will experience a grief cycle just as individuals do, with phases of denial, anger, bargaining, depression and acceptance. In reporting on educational restructuring, the media will be able to report truthfully that faculty and staff morale is at an all-time low, people have never been more vicious to one another, and special interests have never been more in evidence. This should be understood as an honest part of the sausage-making process and of the grief cycle."[18]

It was to restore the smooth functioning of an educational organization, to help it cope with its grief cycle, that a corporate management strategy such as Syracuse University Improving Quality (SUIQ) entered the picture. "Our internal customers are first our students and also members of the faculty and staff," explained Shaw in his November 1991 convocation speech. "A total quality management approach leads to knowing whom we serve and how we can better serve them. It can lead to excellence in our processes and in the product."[19]

Thus, as employees lacked participation in the workplace and outsourcing deprived employees of even the fiction of institutional identity, total quality management (TQM), with its emphasis on communication, helped dissipate pent-up frustrations that might otherwise have turned nasty. By "listening" to the worker, TQM allowed authoritarian universities to appear caring, to create an illusion of participation and a semblance of satisfaction in the workplace.

Union organizer Larry Alcoff said of SUIQ that "allegedly it is to drive down decision-making to the point of production, to accept that the people who do the work have the knowledge, and that we should draw on that and flatten the bureaucracy." In practice, SUIQ rigorously quantifies the hours of training that employees undergo in a never-ending quest for "quality improvement." As Shaw explained to SU faculty, SUIQ "not only sought to change the processes by which we serve and support our students, but also to create a new mind-set."[20]

That new corporate mind-set was ultimately responsible for the strike at SU. Most corporations exist primarily to make a profit. In contrast, a SU faculty committee stated a decade ago that "the fundamental mission of Syracuse University is to advance knowledge and to preserve and transmit humanity's cultural heritage. It is through the continuing pursuit of this mission that the University makes its essential and unique contribution to society."

Faculty members typically oppose the importation of the corporate model into the university. "Our students are referred to officially as 'customers,'" said Sorkin in a tone of disbelief. "Can you imagine? Customers!" Sorkin believes that a university ought "to be a community of scholars dedicated to the search for truth, with a great concern for the well-being of everyone in society."

Philosophy professor Linda Martin Alcoff also deplores the supremacy of the market at SU. "The Philosophy Department had to prove, like every department, that we supported ourselves," she said. "They had this arcane system showing how many students were in your class and how much revenue they provided, and then matching that with the revenues of the budget, which is insane for a liberal arts institution, because you need some departments that don't support themselves."

Former SU professor Bill Readings describes the symbolic displacement of culture in *The University in Ruins*: "Interestingly, during my time at Syracuse, the University logo was changed. Instead of the academic seal with its Latin motto affixed to University letterhead and other documents, a new, explicitly "corporate" logo was developed, and the seal reserved solely for official academic documents such as degree certificates. This seems to me directly symptomatic of the reconception of the University as a corporation, one of whose functions (products?) is the granting of degrees with a cultural cachet, but whose overall nature is corporate rather than cultural."[21]

SU's corporate reorientation led to the recent suspension of graduate programs in German, foreign language teaching, and humanities. The Classics Department, reduced to only two professors, no longer offers graduate programs. Classics professor Donald Mills laughed when asked to explain the importance of classics to a liberal education. He inquired, "Have you got about three hours?" If the purpose of university education is to prepare one for the future, said Mills, then it helps to know where one has been. The classical world, Mills observed, is the source of such words as "republic" and "democracy," and for the very concepts that those words denote. I pressed Mills for a specific example of what the past might teach us. "The Roman Republic came to an end," said Mills, "when Roman politicians discovered ways of using the judicial process to embarrass and humiliate their opponents."

As Mills sees it, universities, trying to justify their ever-increasing tuition by convincing students that their degrees will lead to well-paying jobs, are becoming vocational schools. "I personally rebel at that. I think that's misguided," Mills said. "I tell my students, freshmen in particular, 'You're here for four years. Your job is to get an education. After that, you've got the rest of your life to find a job.'"

Mills recalled how the previous chancellor, Melvin Eggers, would often refer to "our product." In his 1988 address to the Greater Syracuse Chamber of Commerce, Eggers said, "The private nature of their business may have in the past made them wary of public government, but now the two are working in a partnership. Business and education are now partners. It's clear that those of us in higher education need you."[22] The Chamber of Commerce was appreciative of Eggers, and once named him "The Businessman of the Year." "It says so much," Mills sighed.

In 1991, Shaw replaced Eggers on the board of the Greater Syracuse Chamber of Commerce and became the vice president of the Metropolitan Development Association (MDA), which provides tax abatements and other incentives for corporations. At the time of the strike, MDA's president was none other than H. Douglas Barclay, the former Republican State Senator who stepped down as chair of the SU trustee board in May 1998.

In the material shift underway in higher education, skills training has replaced the education needed for critical thinking, citizenship, or understanding the human condition and our obligations to the natural world. SU's future is decidedly high-tech. The newly established Center for Really Neat Research recently won a $1.6 million contract from the Defense Advance Research Projects Agency to help build a mine-detection system.[23]

Another recent innovation at SU is the Center for Study of Popular Television. While the relationship of TV to corporate interests and the destruction of communal bonds merit scrutiny, it is difficult to comprehend the replacement of the classics with the study of popular television. The predicament is summed up in the title of a new book from Syracuse University Press: *Bonfire of the Humanities: Television, Subliteracy and Long-Term Memory Loss.*

In *The Moral Collapse of the University*, Bruce Wilshire ponders the implications of long-term memory loss:

> The numbness and stasis and disconnectedness so often seen in students are palpable and need to be explained and addressed. There seems to be no sense of being part of history, of sharing a common venture with those in power. The disintegration of a sense of historical community is amazing... Missing is any sense that anything is missing. Few students have...a clear awareness that there might be segments of human development which, when laid down, lead up to themselves and point beyond, and for which they have responsibility as the group of living human beings.[24]

Jamie McCallum, a sociology major and animal rights activist, was among the few SU students with such awareness. McCallum edited a zine called *Conformicide* and covered the strike as a photographer for the *Daily Orange*. The employees who clean floors and serve food represented for him the physical reality that makes academic life possible at SU.

While McCallum regretted the "dearth of knowledge of the importance of the labor movement and its relevance to students," he believed that the strike did much to create an awareness of labor history at SU. "The university did not consider for one second the possibility that we as students could learn more from the workers on strike than we could from the professors in class," said McCallum. "I can't tell you the number of kids that went out and saw the people on strike and talked to them, and learned in minutes the history of labor and how important it was to these people's lives." McCallum said that SU needs alternative means of educating students and collectivizing life on campus, including democracy teach-ins. While at SU, McCallum expressed his concern for others by collecting food for strikers in Watertown and handing out free vegetarian lunches with Food Not Bombs.

Ultimately, the strike was about the search for identity, which made the fight over outsourcing particularly bitter. Outsourcing deprives employees of institutional identity, making them transients in the workplace. As universities strip their employees of identity, they strive to create an illusion of community for students and alumni. At Syracuse, pride in the football and basketball teams goes well beyond the university. In a 1988 interview, then chancellor Eggers called SU's sports program "a vitality-generating activity, vitality-sharing activity" that "does provide a unifying theme, certainly more than anything I've seen in the community."

SU's mascot, Otto the Orange, an orange ball with a face, looks as though it might have escaped from an M&Ms commercial or a "Tom Tomorrow" cartoon strip. It is supposed to represent the school spirit that has powered SU sports to great heights. Sociology graduate student Katherine Gregory described the mascot's omnipresence on campus as a sort of "forced frivolity." "They're reproducing identity through their sports, their athletic teams, and…this orange man, whatever it is," said Gregory. "They want to instill it in their students so that they will eventually send their alumni checks." In a letter to Shaw in support of the strikers, Gregory wrote: "After years of temporary positions at numerous institutions of higher education, on the most personal level, I grasp the feeling of 'disposability' in the workplace. I spent over eight years without health insurance or benefits."

While Gregory appears to have few illusions about the university in general, or about SU in particular, she says that she came to SU in search of a "refuge." That search may well prove futile. At his convocation, Shaw quoted the University of Pennsylvania's Robert Zemsky who said: "We are coming to the end of sanctuary. The end of a time in which America's colleges and universities were sheltered from the cold winds that buffeted other institutions." Shaw then went on to say that SU was now "part of the larger action" and that "clearly, 'the end of sanctuary' includes Syracuse."[25]

One cannot help but be struck by the composition of the SU trustee board. Missing are the historians, poets, artists, scientists, heads of cultural institutions, and educators. SU trustees represent top investment firms, banks, and power companies. In 1998, honorary SU trustees included Roy Bernardi, the mayor of Syracuse whose budgets devastated local schools and Governor George Pataki, who enacted the largest cuts to higher education in the history of New York State.

Professor Sorkin views the conflicts at SU as systemic rather than local. "You think that some particular conjunction of events has happened at your university, that some particular administrator got in and followed this corporate model," he said. "But every place you go, you find the exact same phenomenon has occurred. The language is the same, the rationales are the same. It would be interesting to see the mechanism by which this is achieved." Sorkin believes that a long-term process is underway "for universities to be absorbed into the capitalist economy, into capitalist culture, and the capitalist way of organizing things," since "it's natural for capitalism to penetrate every institution and reorganize it along its own lines." Gregory sees events at SU in a similar light. "What's being said here is being said at a dozen universities throughout the northeast. The same story. The same dehumanization," she said.

Even so, faculty, employees and students spoke of a new feeling in the air, of exchanged looks of complicity in hallways, dining halls, and parking lots. "They [the administration] thought the strike would fracture this campus, but it has actually brought everyone together," said union representative Coert Bonthius.[26]

The union victory surpassed the guarantees in the new contract. The strike ended the invisibility of those who clean the floors, prepare the food, mow the lawns, and fix the heaters. It revived a sense of identity and community, bringing Shahn's powerful compassion to our remembrance, and his mural to life.[27]

VI
Twilight of Academia: Critical Pedagogy, Engaged Intellectuals, and Political Resistance

Intellectuals and Empire

Carl Boggs

FROM THE MOMENT I ENTERED ACADEMIC LIFE, as a political science graduate student at UC Berkeley in the 1960s, I held strongly to the belief that intellectual work and politics are—or should be—closely interwoven. I carried this stubborn precept into my teaching position at Washington University in St. Louis, and it eventually led to my banishment from mainstream academia when, in 1977, I was denied tenure following a lengthy, highly-politicized struggle against deeply-entrenched interests within both the political-science discipline and a hidebound university administration. For the next ten years I managed a series of one-year teaching jobs at UC Irvine, UCLA, University of Southern California, and Carleton University in Ottawa, mostly *outside* political science, before settling at National University in Los Angeles, a multi-campus institution catering to mostly working-class students in the age twenty-five to forty age group. Across the intervening years I have sustained a career as a teacher, writer, media worker, and political activist. My scholarly activity spanned not only political science but sociology, urban planning, and film studies. This background imparted to my work a far more "interdisciplinary" character than would otherwise have been the case.

I arrived at Washington University in a period of growing cultural and political turbulence, when new-left activism and the counterculture were at their peak, and a legacy of critical intellectual work in the sociology department had already left its mark. Political engagement was essentially a daily event. Most of the activity revolved around the Vietnam War and the movements opposed to it—movements that, in those days, organically linked campus and community, intellectual and political work. The university was alive with student and faculty participation that, to varying degrees, permeated and energized the classroom.

In my case, the courses I taught—modern political ideologies, social movements, and political theory—naturally lent themselves to critical discourses, and partly for that reason they were among the most popular offerings on campus. Students in those days readily made connections between the scholarly content of courses, larger events in the world, and social (especially antiwar) movement activity. My personal involvements helped embellish those connections: anti-ROTC struggles, McDonnell-Douglas anti-corporate organizing project, the local underground newspaper, anti-war protests, and the legal defense fund to assist those arrested during actions against the war. On campus, we had a perpetual round of meetings, lectures, teach-ins, conferences, film series, and mobilizations geared toward opposition and change. Radical questioning shaped the *Zeitgeist* of the period. Yet, as a non-tenured professor thoroughly immersed in antiwar protests, I was naturally vulnerable to conservative attacks from within the political science department, the university, and, to a lesser extent, the larger St. Louis community.

Washington University itself was controlled by three powerful local corporations—McDonnell-Douglas, Monsanto, and Ralston-Purina, all with headquarters in St. Louis. Sanford McDonnell was simultaneously chair of the university Board of Trustees and the corporation Board of Directors, and it was he who most vigorously called for my banishment in one of his 1975 speeches. The St. Louis *Globe-Democrat* (erstwhile home of Pat Buchanan) ran front-page "exposés" of Washington University radicals, replete with photos identifying me as a ringleader. As for the academic field of political science, while the local gatekeepers of disciplinary norms paid abundant lip-service to intellectual freedoms and never directly interfered with my teaching or writing, these same gatekeepers (though few in number) engineered my departure by blocking a tenured appointment, even though no one had ever indicated, in person or in writing, that my scholarly performance was anything but stellar. They succeeded, moreover, despite broad support I received across the university community, with hundreds of faculty and students joining my tenure defense committee.

What troubled the mainstream professors most was not so much my radical politics or even my critical pedagogy, but rather two more specific transgressions: connecting political activity with campus work and publishing in (mostly leftist) venues regarded as insufficiently "professional" or "respectable." That I wrote for such journals as *Socialist Review, Radical America, Telos, Liberation*, and the *Berkeley Journal of Sociology* turned out to be especially troublesome for the gatekeepers. Many professors who (privately) opposed the Vietnam War, strongly rejected the idea of bringing the war onto the campus or into classrooms. Disciplinary norms enforced a rigid, narrow intellectual approach that ultimately clashed with official pretenses of academic freedom. One professor who voted to deny me tenure stated publicly that he was offended by my disruptive antiwar actions, which he regarded as insulting to those faculty members needing peace and quiet for their abstract scholarly pursuits. A few other colleagues indicated that, while my book on the political thought of Antonio Gramsci was penetrating and well-written, it was not as much "political science" as it was "ideological" writing, and thus branded as an extreme departure from acceptable scholarship. Gramsci, after all, was a European Marxist and revolutionary far removed from the academic mainstream—a figure who, by definition, could have little if anything to say about the study of politics. (By the 1980s, of course, Gramsci had become a pervasive influence in the social sciences and beyond.)

Professors holding to these rigid views of legitimate scholarship were not hard-line right wingers but instead liberal social scientists who valued freedom and prided themselves on tolerance of diverse views and interests. In their work they often celebrated "pluralism" and "multiculturalism" and even championed "progressive" values like democracy and justice. During my seven years at Washington University no colleague or administrator so much as *questioned* me about my teaching, research, and writing, and no one ever visited my classrooms. No one raised questions about my politics or pedagogy. Established professional norms were simply *assumed,* and these included a rigid separation between the academy and change-based movements. No separation between the university and powerful external interests such as corporations or the military, conversely, was ever imagined or indeed considered possible. The gatekeepers felt that my work, indeed my very presence in the academy, had expressly violated disciplinary boundaries, although most if not all of these hypocrites had long been involved in a corporate world that straddled the university and community. What posed major problems for the mainstream academics was the audacity of bringing social-movement issues, agendas, and styles into the campus arena—a flagrant transgression as it involved mostly *anti-war* concerns that questioned basic corporate and imperial priorities. Here it is worth emphasizing that leftist scholarship was often tolerated, then as now, so long as it could be integrated into professional discourses and methodologies, stayed faithful to the academic religion of theory-for-theory's sake, and was detached from community activism. My own work self-consciously and systematically violated these ivory tower strictures.

More than any other problem of the day, the Vietnam War shaped the political landscape of the 1960s and 1970s, furnishing the backdrop of both social movement politics and academic repression. A supposedly open ideological terrain narrowed rapidly when faced with fundamental questioning of an imperialist war that was destroying an entire country. The war gave rise to intellectual ferment, ideological passion, and personal engagement of a sort that hardly seemed compatible with an orderly and aloof academic regimen. To participate in disruptive antiwar struggles lasting several years meant stepping over the boundaries of what was institutionally permissible. Yet these struggles were not only intellectually credible but also morally imperative to those of us who believed the Vietnam War was nothing short of criminal and barbaric. Leftist ideas were tolerable so long as they fit convoluted Marxist or post-Marxist theorizing around questions such as class relations and state formations; as abstract, esoteric, and depoliticized endeavors, they posed no real challenge to the academic status quo. For the political science mainstream, the pressing concerns of war, militarism, and imperialism were considered much too "ideological" and "extremist" to merit serious scholarly inquiry. Thus, throughout the nearly fifteen years of US intervention in Vietnam, the respected *American Political Science Review,* a beacon of disciplinary scholarship, published exactly *one* article on the Vietnam War—an embarrassing lacunae that would be repeated three decades later when the US waged another catastrophic war in Iraq.[1]

Like most other institutions of higher learning, Washington University was—and continues to be—fully immersed in a military-industrial apparatus that wields more power, domestically and globally, with each passing year. It was not surprising, therefore, to find even liberal professors (some with private misgivings about the war) choosing to keep silent, aware that antiwar sentiments or activism could jeopardize their jobs. By the early 1970s, the vast majority of Washington University students had come to actively oppose the war, but only a handful of faculty were involved—and these came mostly from disciplines *outside* the liberal arts, where political or intellectual linkage was less overtly an issue.

Although US militarism has obviously grown since the 1970s, with expansion of the war economy and security state along with renewed American designs on global hegemony in the Middle East, Africa, and elsewhere, campuses throughout the US have been strangely (or perhaps not so strangely) quiet. Student groups have proliferated around many issues—sweatshops, globalization, Tibet, Darfur, etc.—but the illegal and bloody US invasion and occupation of Iraq has drawn few protests, few demonstrations, and few teach-ins since the initial mobilizations in early 2003. Nor have other pressing issues related to US global behavior resulted in much outrage, criticism, or activism: the burgeoning growth of the war economy, worldwide US military deployments, clandestine CIA torture camps, denial of *habeas corpus* rights to prisoners in Guantanamo Bay, ongoing failed interventions, the resurfacing of the threat of nuclear warfare, obscenely expensive efforts to militarize space, and continued unconditional Washington support of Israeli aggression.

This ideological inertia and political quiescence reflects a profound rightward drift in the universities since the late 1970s. Despite its enlightened liberal values, its professed emphasis on diversity, and it reputed takeover by "tenured radicals," the academic public sphere has become increasingly closed, most pointedly on issues related to US foreign and military policy—at the very time when critical opposition and mass dissent is most needed. Liberals have smoothly morphed into technocratic professionals priding themselves on scholarly objectivity and detachment. Social scientists and historians working on the terrain of Marxism, cultural studies, postmodernism, or identity politics have been tolerated so long as they do not challenge disciplinary boundaries or invite disruptive activism. Their arcane rhetoric and theory-speak, indeed, is mobilized for maximal obfuscation among seminar room elites and hardly threatens to galvanize the masses. The reasons, as suggested above, are all too easy to locate: today, even more than during the Vietnam War, the academy is dominated by corporate, government, and military interests that deal harshly with subversives. And these interests are now thoroughly institutionalized, meaning that older forms of repression—disciplinary action, intimidation, firings, even tenure denial—are rarely necessary to ensure ideological conformity.

If intellectuals can be said to occupy a privileged niche in American society, with their educational credentials, relative affluence, access to information, and greater freedom of expression, the sad reality is that *academic* intellectuals have, for the most part, failed to meet the moral and political responsibility to speak out against barbarism. As US imperial power expands and the leading military force poses new threats to world peace, liberal and "progressive" academics have either adapted to this universe or suffered their protest in silence—exactly the type of marginalization process universities want to impose on different professors.

No US military intervention, no violation of international law, no infringement of global treaties, no illegitimate threat to other nations, no revelation of wartime atrocities has elicited much in the way of moral outrage, let alone political opposition. Worse yet, few academics have chosen to carry out scholarly research and writing that might challenge this outlawry and criminality. On the contrary, the bulk of academic political science, international relations, sociology, and history merely helps to perpetuate imperial hegemony. University-based papers, lectures, and panels routinely go along with the myth that US global behavior is dedicated to spreading democracy and human rights to lesser-developed souls around the globe, although occasional flaws, limits, and mistakes are duly recognized. These "liberal" disciplines are defined by norms of scientific objectivity, rational pragmatism, and political detachment grounded in a specialized, esoteric vocabulary that runs counter to oppositional discourses and common meaning. The deep critical analysis of US military power set forth by C. Wright Mills, in his classic *The Power Elite,* written a half-century ago, would today be dismissed as the work of an undisciplined ideologue writing outside his scholarly field of study.[2] That respected and resource-rich American universities have virtually nothing to say about Empire and the rapidly deteriorating ecological crisis has become perhaps the greatest tragedy of modern academia. Efforts to confront this behemoth, as in my case, can quickly turn out to be suicidal from a career standpoint.

Ironically, political science, ostensibly the study of politics and power, has precious little to say about either. What Noam Chomsky said about political science many years ago—that it is the "dismal branch of American scholarship"—holds even truer today.[3] The discipline features such subfields as comparative politics, international relations, and area studies (in which one can earn a study abroad degree), but in none of these subfields do we find any serious critique of US global power; American imperial ambitions are routinely embraced where they are not ignored altogether. In recent years, *The American Political Science Review* has published few articles on topics related to US involvement in the Middle East, none of them critical in substance. At the 2006 American Political Science Association convention, among roughly 1,500 presentations by scholars across the US only *three* dealt with Iraq—and none of those focused on any aspect of the war and occupation. The far-reaching consequences of the Iraq disaster would seem to be a topic of urgent *political* interest, but the discipline merrily goes about other agendas more compatible with their abstract rational-choice models, game theories, and so forth.

Meanwhile, the situation worsens. My own survey of thirty-six major texts used in political science and sociology reveals that twenty-seven of them contain *nothing* about US military power, the nine others incorporating only passing references that, for the most part, are bereft of critical insight. The Pentagon seems to remain a mysterious entity to the social-science enterprise, where studies of "the state" and "power relations" somehow manage to ignore the most powerful and far-reaching edifice of all. Books on social theory and contemporary sociology are just as woefully lacking in military focus so that, sadly, despite its many subdisciplines, we are left without a "sociology of the military." Even such influential "progressive" texts as G. William Domhoff's *Who Rules America Now?* contain absolutely nothing about *military* power in the US, as Domhoff appears to have forgotten the legacy of his intellectual mentor Mills.[4] Yet another well-received volume, Michael Hardt and Antonio Negri's *Empire*, does necessarily refer to the reality of US imperial domination, but, in adopting a postmodern view of power as dispersed and amorphous, it sees this as a positive force in a world that needs the blessings of American military power.[5] For Hardt and Negri, as for many "progressive" or even "Marxist" theorists, Empire is translated into just another abstract, impersonal expression of "globalization." Nowadays the leading academic disciplines, journals, think-tanks, and foundations operate mainly as cheerleaders of US imperialism, with opposition voices silenced or at least marginalized.

The unassailable truth is that nearly every trenchant critique of US imperialism has come from outside the university setting or, in a few cases, from its fringes. Radical critics of Empire like Noam Chomsky, Edward Herman, Michael Parenti, Tariq Ali, James Petras, Chalmers Johnson, and Norman Solomon produce work, much of it widely read, far removed from the professional milieu in which their prolific contributions are uniformly dismissed as ideological nonsense. A few critics, like Juan Cole, Norman Finkelstein, Ward Churchill, and Peter McLaren, have produced extensive work within the social sciences, but have been fiercely attacked as un-American, terrorist sympathizers, anti-Semitic, and more, with Finkelstein and Churchill having been driven from mainstream academia altogether. Throughout the postwar decades, rules of academic discourse have become firmly established, none more binding than the maxim (naturally unwritten) that any fundamental critique of American imperial and military power is taboo. Here, more than elsewhere, a reputedly "liberal" intellectual stratum has become embarrassingly subservient to the dominant interests. The question as to how such a large, privileged, and supposedly-enlightened population of academic scholars has ended up so complacent, self-serving, and bereft of critical spirit, so completely unable or unwilling to scrutinize American global power—a power so often used for criminal ends—requires far more space than is available here.

If we briefly turn our attention to other political contexts—for example, Nazi Germany, Mussolini's Italy, France during the German occupation and the Algerian struggle for independence, Eastern Europe under Soviet hegemony—we immediately see how a stratum of critical intellectuals might have functioned as a vital source of moral conscience and political opposition. In none of these instances would anyone (including, no doubt, the majority of American scholars) think that such an intelligentsia might routinely lend its support to the prevailing war machine—above all if that war machine were devoted to world domination and was prepared to carry out crimes of aggression. Nobody, moreover, would expect critical intellectuals to remain silent in the face of repeated violations of international law. The problem for American society today, however, is precisely the *absence* of a critical intellectual presence large enough to meet such moral imperatives. But one can hardly expect this to emerge without the current structure and ethos of the US university system—a conservative technocratic structure controlled by corporations, the government, and military exercise militates against this possibility at every turn. The result is an ideological conformity in the "liberal" academy that arises less from outright repression—although such repression always hovers in the background—than from deeper historical and structural trends leading to an elaborate system of institutional controls.

For a truly critical intelligentsia to flourish *within* American university life, therefore, the academic setting itself will require fundamental transformation. A broadening public sphere is the *sine qua non* of any such revitalization. The academy presently honors intellectual autonomy and diversity as a formal matter of "academic freedom" and "multiculturalism," but within fixed ideological parameters. If Herbert Marcuse was correct to argue that the critical spirit is pulverized by the workings of technocratic rationality, which in its instrumentalism and closed discourse tends to block oppositional thinking, then fundamental change means confronting professional norms that reproduce an insular, fragmented, depoliticized academic public sphere.[6] Broadened ideological space would likely empower a public intellectual stratum to address social and political issues of urgent concern—surely none more urgent that issues related to US global behavior, to war and peace, and to ecological crisis. In the end, however, such dramatic changes are imaginable only where popular movements can penetrate the academic fortress, bringing with them commitments, sensibilities, and discourses of genuinely open dialogue and prospects for radical change—precisely what occurred during the 1960s and most of the 1970s, when an explosion of new social movements helped spawn a dynamic critical intelligentsia within and outside the universities.

The Citizens Among Us

Science, The Public, and Social Change

Gabriel Matthew Schivone interviews Howard Zinn

AUTHOR AND ACTIVIST HOWARD ZINN was one of the speakers at a critical social forum held at the Massachusetts Institute of Technology in Cambridge, on March 3, 4, and 8, 1969, in which MIT students and scientists joined together to organize a research stoppage to protest the unexampled levels of US government violence in Southeast Asia. The event known as "March 4" included some of the world's most eminent and influential scientists coming together to make what they called a "practical and symbolic" gesture of halting their research activities to discuss the misuse of science in world affairs, particularly the relationship of American science—and the shared responsibility of American scientists—with the deaths of hundreds of thousands of people in Vietnam.

Together with a powerful invocation (known as the "March 4 Manifesto," signed by forty-eight MIT faculty) having been written for the event, addressed to the academic community and the public at large, the activities of March 4 (including several panels on engrossing subjects such as intellectual responsibility and the impending perils of weapons of mass destruction) were organized into recognizing the "dangers already unleashed"—those which presented "a major threat to the existence" of humanity—and providing possible solutions and raising serious alternatives to overcome them.

To the small group of determined organizers and concerned scientists, reason for their actions was self-evident: As a heavily bloody and calamitous war was being waged by the most powerful country on earth—while the majority of its academic community observed with relative silence—the very gesture of leading world intellectuals halting their professional, daily activities before the public and the world in order to consider the human consequences of their scientific work was to say, quite simply, that their role as human beings precedes their professional title of "scientists."

I sat down with Professor Zinn (who had participated in one of the March 4 panels entitled "The Academic Community and Governmental Power") in his office at Boston University on Wednesday, July 23, 2008, to discuss some of the issues.[1]

Science and War: A Macabre Dance

GMS: *Let's start with the second resolution of the "March 4 Manifesto": "To devise means for turning research applications away from their present emphasis on military technology toward the solution of pressing social and environmental problems." Would you explain the importance of this idea of scientific reconversion?*

HZ: It's been a long-standing problem of science being used for destruction or for construction. It goes back to Hiroshima and Nagasaki—it goes back to the atomic bomb. In fact, that probably was the first really dramatic instance of the use of the latest scientific knowledge to kill human beings. And the development of modern weapons technology—the atomic bomb and other weaponry—all that has become much, much more important in recent years as war has become more technological, and as the scientists have become more important in the making of war. So I would say that issue, which was put forward in the "March 4 Manifesto," is even more important today. At that time, it was important because the war in Vietnam was going on, and there was a direct connection between science used for military purposes and the deaths of people in Vietnam.

What has been, and is, the relationship of American science and scientists with the State throughout history until today?

Well, until World War II, I don't think the relationship between science and government was a particularly critical one. Now, sure, we had Alfred Nobel creating dynamite and therefore creating the possibility of weapons, bombs that used dynamite. In other words, there was always a scientific component to modern war. I mean, you can argue that as soon as guns became used, science became involved in their manufacture—rifles, machine guns, artillery. So, yes, there's always been this connection. But it wasn't until World War II, as I said before, with Hiroshima and Nagasaki that this relationship between science and government took an enormous leap forward. Or, you might say, backward. And then science became inextricably intertwined with governmental policy—and that's the way it's been ever since.

1 This interview was originally published on Znet, August 28, 2008, online at http://www.zcommunications.org/znet/viewArticle/18617.

What are some examples of scientists and intellectuals engaging their support of various war efforts?

In the First World War, intellectuals (who had first declared themselves against war) rushed to support the war, carried away by government propaganda against the Germans. John Dewey, Clarence Darrow, Upton Sinclair, Jack London, lent their names and their prestige to the war effort. Historians organized a committee to put out pamphlets in support of the war.

In the Second World War, virtually all intellectuals supported the war. (Dwight MacDonald and a small group of Trotskyists were exceptions, of course.)

The most dramatic example of scientists involved in World War II was the Manhattan Project in which the greatest scientists in the nation and scientist-refugees from other countries joined to produce the atomic bombs that obliterated Hiroshima and Nagasaki. There was only one of these mobilized scientists—Joseph Rotblat—who quit the project rather than work on the bomb. Other scientists developed radar and the Norden bombsight.

Prior to the Korean War, scientists worked on the creation of napalm, which was used in that war and again in Vietnam. In fact, the Dow Chemical Company became the target of anti-War protesters because of its role in producing napalm used in Vietnam.

A number of leading intellectuals rushed to support the invasion of Iraq in 2003, reflected in the pro-war editorials of the major newspapers—*The New York Times*, *The Washington Post*, *The Wall Street Journal*.

Objectivity and American Science: Image and Reality

Do you see any differences in the social sciences and the hard sciences concerning what some people call ideological control? Do you find one to be more or less prone to such constraints on themselves or their work than the other?

Let's put it this way: I think the difference between the hard sciences and the soft sciences is very much exaggerated. And there's a kind of traditional notion that scientists are less prone to subjectivity and ideology than social scientists—the historians and economists, and so on. But I think that's a delusion, and I think that, actually, the same problems apply to both of them.

In the case of scientists, there's more likely to be self-deception about objectivity. I think that social scientists are probably more ready to accept the fact that they're not objective, but with scientists—just the very nature of science with quantitative data and experiment, sort of creates the illusion of being objective and being free from political and ideological influences. But I would argue that it is an illusion and that, therefore, both hard and soft sciences are much closer together in that respect than most people think.

What do you think about using scientific method regarding human affairs? In other words, if one has such scientific training as we find in a university, does it make it easier to analyze certain catastrophic situations like the Iraq War? For example, do you find it helpful as a historian using such quantitative and qualitative methods?

I'm very suspicious of the use of so-called "scientific data" to come to moral conclusions. For instance, in the arena of political science: Political scientists in the last few decades prided themselves in becoming more scientific. In fact, what used to be called "departments of government" soon changed their names to "departments of political science." And the word "science" brought the so-called "political scientists" closer to the illusion that hard scientists have. And the fact that they were using quantitative data and statistical measurement made them think that they therefore were coming to more accurate conclusions about the world than they had before. I don't think that's true because I think the most important decisions are moral decisions, and no amount of quantitative data can really lead you to a correct decision on moral issues. In fact, they can deflect you from making moral decisions by sort of deceiving you about the scientific nature of what you are studying. So, I'm very dubious that using so-called scientific and quantitative methods brings you any closer to solving crucial moral issues.

The first point of the manifesto, "to initiate a critical and continuing examination of governmental policy in areas where science and technology are of actual or potential significance," stuck out to me differently than the others. It seems very basic to simply encourage critical thinking, especially among "educated" people who, it's generally assumed, have been taught critical inquiry from an early age. Is this always the case? It seems always assumed that scientists are always objective, critical thinkers.

Yeah, well, of course, that's one of the myths of science: that science is above and beyond ideology and politics. And, of course, science has always been tied into ideology and politics—certainly more and more in these sixty or so years since World War II. And I think it's very important for scientists to recognize that there's no such thing as neutrality in science; that your science has an effect on society in one direction or another. And if you hide that fact from yourself, well, you're deceiving yourself and deceiving others about the role of science in society.

Here's an interesting example from the University of Arizona (UA), in my home town of Tucson: There's a yearly memo proclaimed and circulated by the president of the univer-

sity (the one most recently appointed being Robert N. Shelton) addressed to the campus community, very strictly barring all "political activity" for university employees. It encourages UA faculty and staff not to engage at all in political activity while on "university time" or with "university resources," but rather to be political if they so wish—"on their own time." Now, although it is explicitly stated that the memorandum is enforced to protect state funding and the outcome of elections, one of the implications is that, in order to be effectively objective in their scientific professions, and to be good scholars, there must be a calling for disinterested scholarship in the face or shadow of political matters.

This is the president of the University of Arizona?

Yeah.

Well, this just shows how little wisdom you need to become the president of a university. Obviously this president has no understanding of the fact that neutrality is impossible, that objectivity is a myth. All intellectual work has a moral component and works either on behalf of the human race or against it. And, in fact, to claim neutrality and to dissociate yourself from participation in the world of ideas and the ideological and real conflicts in the world is really to permit the world to go on as it was. In other words, to refuse to intervene—to refuse to use your energy, your talent, your knowledge for the betterment of the human race. It means that you are allowing those people who have been in charge of policy to continue in their ways; it means that they can go on unimpeded. They can do whatever they want because, essentially, you have withdrawn an enormous number of people who have potential power—brain power, political power—you've withdrawn them from the political arena. And you've left the field to the so-called "experts"—who are not experts at all—and whose continued dominance is actually a danger to the human race.

It is ironic that the university, which prides itself on its intellectual superiority, should discourage faculty and students from using their knowledge and their analytical abilities, their moral judgment to participate in the social struggles outside the university. In other words, the university then becomes the servant of the dominant powers in society, who prefer that knowledge be used only to maintain the status quo, to train young people to take their obedient places in the existing society, rather than challenging the people in power.

The Citizens Among Us

Now, is it possible to drop out of this university system, as some have suggested, wanting nothing to do with it or its money because of the sheer amount of war collaboration? If so, is this necessarily the way to go, in your opinion?

Of course it's possible to drop out of the system. It's possible to say goodbye. But it's very, very difficult because people's livelihoods, people's economic security is very tied up with their jobs. And so giving up your job becomes a very serious personal hindrance to the security of yourself and your family. That makes it very difficult to drop out.

Now, there are scientists who have refused to work on projects. There were a few scientists who refused to work on the atomic bomb. Joseph Rotblat, as I said before, left the Manhattan Project—he didn't want to work on the bomb. And there've been other scientists who have refused to work on military-related technology but they do it at risk. They risk their jobs, their livelihoods. In other words, it's possible to do it, but it's difficult.

Point five of the manifesto reads: "To explore the feasibility of organizing scientists and engineers so that their desire for a more humane and civilized world can be translated into effective political action." How might an organized scholarship—scientists organizing themselves around such issues as dissent and non-participation—benefit society?

A very important factor in making it possible for scientists to move from military projects to civilian projects is having the support of your colleagues. That's why the growth of organizations like the Union of Concerned Scientists or the organization of the atomic scientists who put out the *Bulletin of the Atomic Scientists* are important supports for individuals who want to follow their consciences rather than their financial success and careers. So, it's still difficult, but it seems to me that when you get together with other people and you decide collectively that you are going to oppose the use of science for military purposes it becomes easier. And we have examples like that.

We have the International Physicians for the Prevention of Nuclear War (IPPNW). There are thousands of physicians of the IPPNW, and they certainly have sort of made it a principle for them to speak out publicly. And they've been successful—not successful enough, obviously, but successful—in educating the public of the dangers of nuclear warfare.

I remember when the IPPNW came out with its study—this was in the 1980s—of what the effects would be on the Boston area from a nuclear blast. Well, it went into great and horrifying detail and, you know, I think that was instructive and educational for a lot of people. So, there's great work that can be done by people in the sciences who are organized in that way.

Why do you think that the possibility of abolishing war is so difficult for people to understand?

One reason it is so difficult is that there's a tendency to believe that what has happened in the past must inevitably continue to happen in the present and future. In other words, since the history of humankind, there's been a history of repeated wars, almost continuous warfare. It's very hard for people to accept the fact that this might come to an end. Indeed, Tuberculosis was a scourge all through the history of humankind and it was hard for people to accept the fact that it actually might be done away with. The history of warfare likewise has made it difficult for people to accept the fact that there could be a break with history and war could be abolished. That's one reason.

Another reason is that there are certain wars that have been imbued with a grandeur and nobility. That makes people think that war can be useful, important, even necessary for valid human purposes. I'm speaking particularly about World War II.

After all the disillusionment that followed World War I, World War II made war acceptable again because it was a war against this great evil—fascism. And it is still today considered "the good war." It is still today presented as the example of "the just war." And while I seriously question this characterization of World War II, there is no doubt that its reputation has imbedded in people's minds the idea that it is possible to have a "good war," a "just war." I think that is a great obstacle to people accepting the idea of the abolition of war.

Going off your earlier comment on "experts," a word that's thrown around a lot in our society—I hear it a lot especially in university—is the word "professionalism." It's like a rule of propriety to people in various professions such as cooks, cleaners, retail and food service, artists, teachers, lawyers, doctors, etc., to "be professional," and to know their place and not involve themselves in matters that are deemed "political."

Yeah, well, this is a recipe for disaster. That is, to have everyone in society work only within their profession, within their job. Not to look outside the boundaries of their job means to withdraw as a citizen. It's actually the opposite of democracy. Democracy requires the full participation of all citizens, whatever their occupation, whatever they do, whether they're dishwashers, or college professors, or scientists. For them to not devote some part of their lives to examining the larger society in which they work is to really drop out of the social structure and allow a small number of powerful, political leaders to do what they want, uninhibited—uninhibited because there's no opposition, because everybody in society is paying attention only to their profession, essentially neutered, essentially helpless. So, as I said, this is the opposite of democracy, which requires the full participation of everybody in the political process of decision-making.

You've often mentioned an interesting quote from philosopher Jean-Jacques Rousseau about professionalism.

Rousseau wrote: "We have physicists, geometricians, chemists, astronomers, poets, musicians and painters in plenty, but we have no longer a citizen among us." He was pointing to the specialization in modern times, in which people were divided into professional groups who concentrated their attention on their narrow specialties, leaving the important decisions in society—war and peace, wealth and poverty—to be made by professional politicians. This was a surrender of moral responsibility by people who concentrated on becoming "successful" in their own field, and not risking their safety and economic security by entering the arena of social struggle and moral decisions.

Tying into our discussion: what do you think of the notion sometimes referred to as the "responsibility of the intellectual," that is, the more privilege you have in society, the more opportunity and choices you have and, therefore, the more responsible you are for the atrocities of your own government, since you are more able to speak out against them?

That is an interesting point. Intellectuals have a respected place in society, and have the ability to communicate, through writing and speaking, to the larger public. Therefore, they have a moral responsibility to use this special power on behalf of humane values, on behalf of peace and justice. Their failure to do so is therefore especially to be condemned.

Scientists pride themselves on the ability to make pure science and come to exact scientific conclusions, but it's also often assumed therefore that these sort of people—people with $100,000 educations, degrees, and technical specialties—are better equipped than others to act as experts or to reveal gospel and come to moral conclusions regarding human affairs. Do you agree? I mean, what do you think people need, then, to be able to make moral decisions, if not some kind of "special" credentials?

Sheer knowledge, whether of science, history, or any of the disciplines, does not make anyone more capable of making moral decisions, which only require common sense, common decency, compassion—all of which are traits possessed by all human beings, regardless of how much "education" they have had.

During the Vietnam War, for instance, all surveys showed that the people with the most education were most likely to support the government in that immoral war, and people with only a high school education were more likely to oppose the war.

Students and Social Struggle

During the Vietnam War it was students who originally envisioned and organized the

March 4 event. What importance do the issues we've been discussing today have on young people and students?

I would argue that there is nothing more important that an education can do than to turn the student away from the narrow confines of material success in the present society. That is, to turn the student away from merely becoming a cog in the machinery of current society and have the student think in broader terms of social justice and about creating a better world.

Unfortunately, our education system is geared to prepare young people to become successful within the confines of the present society. It doesn't prepare them to question this present society, to ask if fundamental change is needed. And so I believe the most important thing education can do is to take the students out of this narrow concern with learning what they need to be successful in their profession and make them aware that the most important thing they can do in their lives is to play a role in creating a better society, whether it's stopping war, or ending racial inequality, or ending economic inequality. This is the most important thing that education can do. And I think our most wise of educators—our philosophers of education, like John Dewey—have recognized this as the critical problem of education.

In your speech at March 4, you spoke of the young Harvard and MIT students, who, along with other classes of people, became enthralled by the fervor of the war effort during the First World War and eagerly joined the army under slogans like the one in the ironic mural in the Widener Library at Harvard that reads, "Happy is he who in one embrace clasps death and victory." However, you noted that things had changed for the young students of MIT and Harvard during the Vietnam War who were obstreperous and angry at the government. It's interesting to me that young people like Harvard and MIT kids possess often times debilitating privileges of race and affluence, yet there are examples of these kind of students placing themselves at the barricades, as it were, sacrificing as much as others who are more recognizably oppressed. What do you think accounts for this?

I think it's because young people have an inherent desire to do something important in society. And, therefore, if that desire becomes strong enough it overcomes whatever in their background might induce them to play a passive role. And so I'm not surprised that students at Harvard and MIT would become active.

But, of course, during the Vietnam War it's very hard to make a distinction between elite institutions and ordinary colleges in terms of student activism. Because, in the case of the Vietnam War, student activism took place all through the spectrum of universities from the most prestigious to the least prestigious. Sure, students at Harvard and MIT were active, but students at Kent State, just an ordinary state university, were very, very active. It's just that students at Harvard and MIT, when they became active, their activity was especially noticeable because of the prestige of their universities. But, in fact, there was no particular superiority of Harvard and MIT in terms of activism when you looked at activism around the country.

A Power Governments Cannot Suppress

Also in your speech at March 4, you suggested developing independent sources of power to counter the use of force and deception by governments. You stated that, "in a society held together by falsehood, knowledge is an especially important form of power." But how can knowledge overwhelm brute force when it comes down to it?

Well, knowledge can't, by itself, overwhelm brute force. It's only when that knowledge is translated into organization and mobilization, and that knowledge is reaching large numbers of people who then can resist the power of government, or corporations, or the military. I mean, if you are an ordinary worker, and you have the knowledge that you are being exploited as a worker, that obviously isn't enough. But if there are enough people in the workplace who have this knowledge and then transform what they know into organizing themselves, then they can act in unison and they can create a power which the most powerful corporation cannot overcome. Essentially, corporations and governments depend on an obedient population to maintain their power. If that population—that is, the people who work for the corporation, the citizens of the government, the soldiers in the military—withholds its support, stops cooperating, then the supposed all-powerful corporation, government, military become helpless. So it's a matter of transforming that knowledge into organized power.

The Three-Legged Stool

Shared Governance, Academic Freedom, and Tenure

Cary Nelson

THE AMERICAN ASSOCIATION OF UNIVERSITY PROFESSORS has long maintained that academic freedom is really only one leg of a three-legged stool. Academic freedom, tenure, and shared governance together support the higher education system we have had in place in the US for over half a century. As Robert Birnbaum puts it in an unpublished 1993 paper, "'Governance' is the term we give to the structures and processes that academic institutions invent to achieve an effective balance between the claims of two different, but equally valid, systems for organizational control and influence. One system, based on legal authority, is the basis for the role of trustees and administration; the other system, based on professional authority, justifies the role of the faculty."

Effective governance and job security are interdependent. You cannot really have either professional authority or academic freedom if you can easily be fired or nonrenewed, the latter being the fate of so many part-time faculty. But you do not have functioning academic freedom unless the faculty is in charge of the curriculum and the hiring process and can thus control who does the teaching and what they can teach. Shared governance agreements also shape and guarantee peer review, from grievance procedures to the tenure process. Academic freedom is an empty concept, or at least an effectively diminished one, if the faculty does not control its enforcement through shared governance.

The relationship between the three components that sustain the role faculty play in higher education is clearly under increasing threat from several forces: (1) the managerial model that now dominates the corporate university; (2) the massive reliance on contingent faculty, a trend that has doubled over the last thirty years, leaving most faculty with no structural role in shared governance; (3) the loss of faculty vigilance over and understanding of the relationship between shared governance and academic freedom, exacerbated by the presence of two generations of tenured faculty focused on their careers and disciplinary commitments to the exclusion of their community responsibilities; and (4) the renewed culture wars waged by the Right to deprive faculty of both academic freedom and the key elements of shared governance, most notable in the effort to restrict and surveil faculty speech in the classroom.

The public demand by politicians to dismiss Ward Churchill from his tenured position at the University of Colorado was simultaneously an assault on academic freedom and a transgression against shared governance. It triggered and compromised his subsequent evaluation by faculty committees. That remains the case whether or not one considers the later faculty reports to include serious violations of professional conduct. David Horowitz's efforts to legislate restrictions on classroom speech and to produce ideologically "balanced" faculties are similarly two-pronged projects; they threaten individual faculty freedoms and the shared governance processes by which faculty are appointed and curricula approved. Protests against aggressive campaigns Horowitz and other conservatives have fought may not be effective if they cite only the principle of academic freedom, while ignoring the shared governance structures that sustain it.

Just what it means for faculty to have no academic freedom, or to grasp how deficiencies in shared governance and academic freedom are mutually reinforcing, can be difficult to imagine for tenured faculty in relative comfort at major institutions. Consider this: at Antioch University McGregor in Yellow Springs, Ohio, where no one has tenure, faculty were asked to vote on a major administration project in 2006. The president gathered them in an auditorium, asked those who supported her proposal to stand, then wrote down the names of those still seated. The following year she informed the faculty that talking to the press about the university was grounds for dismissal. Proper shared governance would require a secret ballot for such a vote. Academic freedom would hold faculty harmless for such extramural speech. At Bacone College in Oklahoma, the president has no problem unilaterally eliminating from the curriculum all the courses taught by faculty he wants to fire, thereby circumventing both peer review and senate approval; the faculty member has no work to do and no place to exercise his or her academic freedom. At DePaul University, the president unilaterally denied Norman Finkelstein his appeal rights for his tenure case, a violation of governance agreements that certified the end of Finkelstein's job.

Fully functioning shared governance is also a protection against outside interference in university affairs. Those individuals outside DePaul who attempted to critically intervene in Finkelstein's tenure case, or in the cases of Middle East scholars at Barnard and Columbia, were essentially exercising their first amendment rights. Whether on not we endorse what they did, including misrepresent people's scholarship, is a separate issue. Good shared governance procedures make it considerably easier for both faculty committees and senior administrators to exclude all unsolicited communications from a tenure file and make certain that tenure cases are decided on the basis of the file alone.

A shared governance crisis often has a triggering event, but a review of American Association of University Professors (AAUP) reports about shared governance suggests there is typically also a history of problems at issue. A series of reports published in *Academe*—Elmira College in New York (1993), Lindenwood College in Missouri (1994), Francis Marion University in South Carolina (1997), and Miami-Dade Community College in Florida (2000)—give a convincing and troubling portrait of the pattern, meanwhile demonstrating that no part of the country is immune from repression of free speech rights. Reading accounts of pure violations of academic freedom can provoke a sense of near incredulity, as you realize how idiosyncratic some administrative behavior can be, or how diverse our colleges and universities are. Shared governance abuses, on the other hand, offer unsettling moments of recognition, as we remember similar incidents at our own institutions. The four reports cited above are each fairly long and quite detailed, but a few representative excerpts from two of them will illustrate what I mean.

At Elmira, the AAUP's investigating team noted, "aggrieved faculty members report having filed appeals with the Faculty Grievance Committee (FGC) which were sustained by that body only to have the FGC's positive findings and recommendations overridden by the dean and the president" (48). Faculty authority over appointments was compromised: "the administration refused to invite for an interview one of the candidates proposed by the search committee, allowed administrators who were not members of the search committee to review applicant files and rank the candidates, and ended up appointing someone whom the members of the search committee had expressly declined to recommend" (48). Meanwhile the Board chair suggested faculty members could face disciplinary sanctions if they made public "statements disparaging the college as a place for students to attend or for alumni or donors to support" (50).

At Lindenwood, 1989 began with a declaration of financial exigency. A new president, however, soon brought the school financial stability. Nonetheless, he announced a "freeze on tenure" the following year. He then notified faculty that their governance documents, the Faculty Constitution and Faculty Bylaws were voided. He unilaterally revised the Faculty Handbook to state that Lindenwood operated by annual contracts and did not grant tenure. Graduation requirements, plans for creating new majors and degree programs, and decisions to eliminate courses or add new ones were made without faculty input. Reappointments and promotions were approved or denied against faculty advice. Then the president began granting faculty status and professorial rank to full-time administrators. "Among the full-time administrators granted such status and rank are the president's daughter and son-in-law" (66). A comparable decision to ignore faculty authority took place at West Virginia University in 2007, when administrators awarded the state governor's daughter an unearned degree.

Would administrators at Elmira or Lindenwood be able to use shared governance to resist political pressures? The norms established by the AAUP are designed to put in place systems that will help prevent or resist such abuses if the norms are maintained. The AAUP issued a statement about shared governance in 1920 and revised it in 1938, but the organization's thinking on the subject continued to evolve and deepen until it published its "Statement on Government of Colleges and Universities" in 1966, later supplemented by other reports, among them, "The Role of the Faculty in Budgetary and Salary Matters."

While governance practices inevitably vary from campus to campus with different types of institutions, there is a clear need for generally-accepted norms. Too often shared governance now amounts to an opportunity for faculty to express their views, such that, as Greg Sholtz puts it, "once people have talked things over, those in charge make the final decision." But the AAUP's 1966 statement "does not conceive of the college or university in starkly hierarchical terms—as a power pyramid." Rather, Sholtz goes on to say, "it portrays the well-run institution as one in which board and president delegate decision-making power to the faculty." Indeed the AAUP's 1994 declaration, "On the Relationship of Faculty Governance to Academic Freedom," building on their original 1915 statement on academic freedom, makes it clear that faculty have fundamental autonomy in their areas of expertise.

Stanley Fish inaccurately suggests that some arguments on behalf of shared governance, including Larry Gerber's, are grounded in a mistaken belief that democracy is a supreme value in all institutions within a democratic country. But shared governance cannot install full democracy in a university. It is a negotiated strategy for sharing and adjudicating power and its application and effects. The negotiated campus standards for shared governance may lay out areas for collaborative decision making, for full autonomy, and for consultation followed by final decisions. All this, unfortunately, has become increasingly unclear to faculty over the last generation. Many faculty no longer have any idea what the norms for shared governance should be. As a 2003 survey report, "Challenges for Governance," shows, faculty disagree about how campuses are or should be governed. Few could readily offer a satisfactory definition of shared governance. Others are themselves skeptical about many shared governance procedures. Thus, it's clear that faculty are themselves partly responsible for the weakening of their rights and power.

As the new millennium began, it was clear the growing resistance to shared governance had become a point of pride for some university administrators. Increasing corporatization had repeatedly provided the local flashpoint. A chancellor or university president wanted to move quickly on a contract to provide services for a business partner. The prospect of significant income loomed. Then the damned faculty intervened. A bunch of cowards in the history department saw a "problem" with putting the university's logo on land mines manufactured by slave labor. Worse still: why would faculty object to having an arms manufacturer as a co-owner of all online courses on international relations? Could they come up with a more dogged distributor?

At a 2001 conference at UCLA, I heard former University of Michigan President James Duderstadt forcefully declare that faculty had to be taken out of the loop of university decision making. Higher education had to be restructured so administrators could make decisions and get the job done without interference by faculty. Derek Bok sought to counter that view two years later:

> The entrepreneurial university, it is said, must be able to move quickly. It cannot wait for windy faculty debates to run their course lest valuable opportunities be lost in the fast-moving corporate world in which we live. In fact, there is remarkably little evidence to support this view. Looking over the checkered history of commercial activity on campuses, one can much more easily point to examples of costly unilateral decisions by impatient administrators, such as ill-advised Internet ventures or grandiose athletic projects, than to valuable opportunities lost through inordinate faculty delays (B9).

Until Duderstadt talked, it had seemed that broad brush open contempt for faculty was limited to activists like University of California regent, Ward Connerly, who responded to a reporter's 1995 question about shared governance with the faculty by blustering: "We share too damn much with them now." Now it seemed lip service need no longer be given to the notions of dialogue, consultation, negotiation, and community. Even those with prestige university connections could freely express more than impatience with the time consuming character of democratic process. If we wanted to move forward we had to get the faculty out of the way.

It is worth noting, as Bob Kreiser of our national office pointed out to me, that the national AAUP does not get substantially more complaints about violations of governance expectations than it did a decade ago, though there is an area of significant increase. What we now get, as the case reports cited above may suggest, is larger numbers of academic freedom cases embedded with or overlaid with governance problems. In other words, academic freedom is now regularly curtailed or denied, or its erosion enhanced, by the failure to follow good governance practices or because the practices are absent. Shared governance, many of us now estimate, will be a focal point of higher education struggles over the next decade and more. Meanwhile, economic expediency makes many administrators resent the time and energy expended on governance processes.

An administrator who thinks he or she ought to be able to pursue or endorse commercial opportunities without subjecting such relationships and contracts to established channels for oversight may well come to feel he or she should be able to discipline faculty members with a free hand. Due process then becomes the next inconvenience to be set aside or circumvented. Appointing ad hoc, rather than elected, committees to handle these matters is one common strategy. On other campuses, administrators simply ignore decisions by faculty committees. That's one of the complaints I have received from University of Washington faculty.

It is a generally reliable rule that successful administrators avoid using all the power at their disposal, and that they consult with faculty more frequently than required by the charters that grant them their power. At my own campus, the University of Illinois at Champaign-Urbana, power is vested in line administrators in a fashion that imitates military chains of command. Beginning with department heads—who are not actually required to consult their colleagues about hiring, retention, curriculum, salaries, or tenure decisions—administrators typically have the authority to overrule the bodies that advise them. But an administrator who routinely dismisses such advice usually does not last long.

Used judiciously, that power can be a good thing. An inexperienced or poorly informed committee can make bad decisions that damage careers unfairly. Administrators should thus focus primarily on reversing ill-considered negative decisions. If a faculty committee acts to compromise academic freedom or deny recognition to a deserving faculty member, it should be asked to reconsider and, if necessary, be overruled.

The further one gets from department life, moreover, the greater the risk of misjudgment when power is exercised outside systems for peer review. When arbitrary upper-level administrative power is exercised widely against the grain of shared governance and many faculty are affected, resistance and protest often follow, and the administrator may be forced to reverse course or resign. Of course a rogue administrator who is supported by a rogue board of trustees or regents may be able to prevail, despite organized faculty resistance. That is partly what happened in the notorious case of Bennington College, where the president unilaterally eliminated what amounted to a tenure system and fired tenured faculty.

It is also true, however, that few administrators can prevail against a faculty body that acts in concert. Sufficient faculty solidarity is a nearly irresistible force and can be used to guarantee proper forms of shared governance. A president who, say, dissolves a faculty senate, or refuses to form one in the first place, can be compelled to change his or her mind. In the end, a strong vote of no confidence, followed by a strike if necessary, makes it clear how much power resides in a faculty that reaches consensus. Dissolving a faculty senate is a clear example of a governance violation that will produce academic freedom consequences, since senates typically review proposals for program termination and creation.

Such broad assaults on shared governance typically abolish major elements of academic freedom. As Larry Gerber put it in a 2001 *Academe* essay, faculty "need affirmative authority to shape the environment in which they carry out their responsibilities" (23). Under AAUP principles, shared governance gives faculty the authority to shape the curriculum, select who will be their colleagues, arrange teaching schedules, and so forth. When such authority is ceded to administrators who lack disciplinary expertise, academic freedom becomes meaningless.

Since there are institutions where these powers have been ceded—or taken away from faculty—it follows that not all faculty have academic freedom. The academy can be a satisfying and mutually supportive, if contentious, community; it can also become a hostile and counterproductive environment in which to work. The collapse of shared governance readily leads to the latter, often with reprisals for the exercise of free speech. These are not petty concerns, which is why Gerber argues that:

> The practice of shared governance deserves to be supported not as a means of serving the particular interests of faculty, but rather because shared governance ultimately serves the needs of society. Without shared governance, our colleges and universities would be less likely to foster the unimpeded pursuit and dissemination of knowledge that are necessary for the healthy development of society; they would also be less likely to provide students with the broad liberal education they need to become informed citizens who can participate fully in our democracy (22).

Of course the aim of preparing students to be critical participants in a democracy—a somewhat edgier construction than Gerber offers—is exactly what the corporate university typically seeks to undermine. Faculty members' academic freedom gives them the right to shape instruction so as to enhance students' ability to be critical citizens, an increasingly central value in the post-9/11 world, but one already under assault before then. For corporatized universities oriented toward income generation and job training had already begun opting instead for strictly instrumental instructional aims. In the end, therefore, unless shared governance includes a faculty role in defining institutional mission, everything else about the educational environment is at risk. Yet as boards of trustees become increasingly aggressive and assertive, they often become less and less tolerant of faculty input.

The flow of interchange—and the institution's shared governance traditions—needs to move in both directions, from departmental decisions upward and from trustee deliberations downward, if faculty are actually to have a hand in shaping the educational environment and its goals. When any major area of academic life is severed from shared governance, it infects and endangers everything else.

Shared governance can also be slowly undermined both by weak governance structures that are not regularly revived and tested and by an accumulation of decisions by administrative fiat that sidestep multiple forms of due process. Many recent AAUP Committee A reports deal with institutions where academic freedom and shared governance have been pervasively undermined. In its 2007 reports on the aftermath of Hurricane Katrina in New Orleans, universities recounted their wholesale abandonment. But a gradual accumulation of small betrayals of due process can be equally damaging, in part because it is less likely to draw requisite faculty attention and response.

When the University of Illinois' Institutional Review Board (IRB) decided a few years ago to penalize a faculty member—without even telling him he had a case before them—ingrained awareness of due process should have made them aware it was improper. When they threatened him with prior restraint on publication, ingrained awareness of principles of academic freedom should have alerted them to the fact they were in violation of long-established standards. Good governance would have provided checks and balances to build more reflection into the process.

When my provost's office decided to threaten a faculty member with reprisals unless he removed his careful research on diploma mills from a university web site, they should have thought twice before doing so. They should have been willing to defend him, not chastise him, for contributing to the public good. Shared governance and due process should both have produced a different result.

When the U of I president's office in 2004 decided to announce in the newspaper that henceforth all discussion of public policy issues was prohibited on university email, they ought to have realized this flew squarely in the face of the most fundamental notion of academic freedom. Shared governance should have prevented the announcement being issued before being vetted by faculty committees. The initial story appeared in a banner headline above the fold on page one of *The News Gazette* (September 17, 2004). The university spokesperson later retracted her statement in a rather less visible letter to the editor. Shared governance would likely instead have generated a visible repudiation.

In two of these cases, notably, faculty members were bullied and terrorized. They certainly feel shared governance and academic freedom are endangered species in Champaign-Urbana. Most faculty, however, took no notice of these events, despite all being recognized in either news reports or scholarly journals. Focused on their own affairs, faculty stepped nimbly around their colleagues' bodies—as on a battlefield—

and got on with their own business. Shared governance should have produced a public discussion of these cases, so that the structural failures that helped produce them
might have been corrected. The local and national AAUP played a role, but the Faculty
Senate, long controlled by administration allies, said nothing. We recently watched a
highly-ranked graduate program on campus nearly be destroyed without input from
the faculty affected and without Senate oversight. Shared governance was nowhere in
evidence. My own preference is to work collaboratively with upper-level administrators whenever possible. Yet "My Provost right or wrong" does not seem a sufficient
model of professional independence.

The pattern of faculty generally not being aware of individual cases where
academic freedom is violated remains at many large institutions. On a 2008 visit to
the University of California at Irvine I found not one faculty member in the audience
aware of their own administration's legal stance in a potentially critical case involving
one of their colleagues. At stake is whether faculty speech about governance issues in
public institutions is protected. The Irvine administration was on the wrong side, advocating a major abrogation of academic freedom. The national AAUP had submitted an
amicus brief in the case. Selected members of the faculty senate at Irvine had discussed
the matter, but had done so in a closed session without subsequently informing the
faculty as a whole.

Where shared governance and academic freedom are most frequently imperiled—and sometimes largely absent—of course is at religiously-affiliated institutions, including a number of Historically Black Colleges and Universities (HBCU),
and at campuses relying heavily on contingent faculty. Practices at religiously affiliated
schools vary widely by denomination, and they change over time. Faculty at those institutions may often not only willingly but joyfully cede some of the freedoms secular
faculty expect. But the limits on speech need to be arrived at consensually, through
shared governance, not simply imposed.

That need is never more painfully evident than when religiously committed
faculty are punished or silenced against their will. It is a difficult terrain for the AAUP.
We have chosen to keep these schools within the fold and to work with them, when appropriate, to correct practices that cross over the line. So when Brigham Young University (BYU) summarily fired (for "heresy") a devout young faculty member who publicly announced she prayed to god the mother, not god the father, the AAUP eventually
censured them. I have been deeply touched every time faculty members from BYU tell
me how much our intervention mattered to them.

It should be clear to everyone that shared governance is both a structure and
an ongoing process. It only works if it is renewed continually, if good people involve
themselves in it. As my University of Illinois colleague, Ken Anderson, is fond of saying, "Don't expect shared governance to work if you don't do the work of shared gover-

nance." Neglected, shared governance atrophies. Yet the contemporary use of the term is inevitably tinged with a certain institutional sorrow. For shared governance may work best when it is so ingrained in our practices and values that the concept almost never needs to be mentioned. Looking back to a past we have left behind, we foreground the concept because it is often not honored. The term identifies what many institutions have lost and must try to restore. But the lesson now is that we can still lose more.

So how do we preserve all the legs of the stool, once we realize it will topple without them? The UC Irvine story suggests one problem with relying on a faculty senate as the sole agent charged with guarding shared governance. Senates too often develop a cozy relationship with administrators, one that leaves the majority of the faculty out of the loop. My own senate recently charged a small ad hoc committee with renegotiating a major structural violation of shared governance and academic freedom—a campus institute dedicated to funding faculty appointments and research to be controlled by outside donors—while keeping the original, unacceptable "Memorandum of Agreement" secret. The deal was cut to provide cover for the chancellor who negotiated the original plan.

Senates too often make their peace with power, when part of what is needed is an independent voice that will speak truth to power. As Greg Scholtz, now head of the AAUP's Committee A on Academic Freedom and Tenure, points out in workshops he conducts, "the Senate won't be in front of the administration building handing out fliers, but the AAUP can be." An AAUP chapter can play that role and more—it can communicate with the Board of Trustees as an independent organization; it can be an informational and activist resource for work in academic freedom and shared governance; it can, in effect, serve as the Senate's political whip—in order to make good policy options public and press for their adoption, which is one of the reasons why all campuses need to strengthen their chapters or create one. Faculty Senates and AAUP chapters are ideally allies, not opposing forces, but with the AAUP chapter possessing more flexibility and freedom of action. In the absence of strong, unionized grievance procedures, an AAUP chapter can also investigate violations of academic freedom and partner with the national office to gain relief for affected faculty. An AAUP chapter with majority membership can wield considerable power, but even a chapter with 10percent faculty membership can be very effective in addressing academic freedom cases.

But university presidents have been known to close down faculty senates. And the presidents at Bacone and Antioch McGregor fired all their AAUP activists. A faculty handbook that sets out shared governance procedures and academic freedom guarantees may often be unenforceable, though the legal status of handbooks varies from state to state. In right-to-work states and on private university campuses genuine faculty solidarity is the only meaningful alternative. Elsewhere, at least for public higher education, the answer is unequivocal: mirror all your handbook shared governance structures, tenure regulations, and academic freedom guarantees in a legally enforceable union contract. Perhaps it is not too surprising that the one realistic way to do battle with a corporation is to organize. It is not too late for many campuses to preserve the critical features of higher education as we have known it.

Contingent Faculty and the Problem of Structural Repression

Gregory Tropea

The Endangered University

SOMETIMES IT SEEMS THAT ONLY TENDENTIOUS GENERALIZATIONS are available to describe the state of teaching and research across the disciplines in the modern American university. Still, in the face of unprecedented pressures to monetize or politicize virtually every aspect of higher education, we cannot let the difficulties of characterizing our situation force us into modest silence. It is especially helpful to consult indicators that help develop a sense of the issues that form around the rubric of academic freedom, such as the agendas of the professional associations that express prevailing understandings in their fields or the patterns of faculty union activity. Thus we find that the more closely one follows the history and operation of the widely-acknowledged voice of the professoriate in the United States, the American Association of University Professors (AAUP), the more clearly one sees the fragility of the premier values of the American academy, namely, the ideals of free inquiry and critical discussion. Not that the idea of academic freedom itself is fragile—on the contrary, it can claim a level of nominal devotion that suggests it will enjoy a permanent place of honor among academics. But that high level of apparent allegiance is deceptive; it conceals a pernicious problem of constricted teaching and research that is all the more dangerous because of its diffuse nature and diverse modes of appearance.

Academic freedom, for all its conceptual tenacity, exists in an environment that is demonstrably unstable, as one sees by sudden appearance and disappearance of academic trends and fads in responses to vagaries of funding and government policy. This prevailing instability acts upon higher education with an effective systemic repression whose specific manifestations vary by context, but which operates across all disciplines. So pervasive is this repression that some readers may at first question whether we are indulging in hyperbole, but as our analysis will show, indisputable facts about academic life allow one to come to no other conclusion than that repression of ideas and actions is ironically and increasingly built into higher education, despite conflicting with the most cherished ideals of educational institutions dedicated to the pursuit of knowledge and the common good. Moreover, guardians of academic traditions are pressured to answer the persistent and misguided call from some quarters—not only administrators, but well-meaning contributors and even some faculty—that universities be run more like businesses. Leaving aside that these recommendations traffic in vaguely-defined terms, often fly in the face of documented quality-assurance practice,[1] and have nowhere met the burden of proof to establish that universities would do better if they were run as businesses, hearkening to such calls would only serve to make higher education more dependent on a mode of dispensing of contractual/grant support for R&D that narrowly benefits a relatively small number of businesses. This would have the effect of weakening the academic independence that is the historical ground from which the benefits of university research have sprung. As Lesser et.al. significantly, though not surprisingly, report of one discipline from their survey of 111 variously supported studies, "Industry funding of nutrition-related scientific articles may bias conclusions in favor of sponsors' products, with potentially significant implications for public health."[2]

Rather than citing multiple examples of egregious behavior and suggestive studies to build the case that there is a nefarious line of development toward what has been called an academic-industrial complex, we will adopt a theory-and-practice approach. So, first we will examine the notion of *mediating structure* to highlight an important institutional condition in the academy that engenders destructive forms of economic dependence and creates a repressive environment. With that background, we will then look at some strategic decisions of the California Faculty Association to see how one organization's practical responses to these structurally exacerbated problems have mitigated at least some of the danger factors we identify and can serve as a practical example to others facing similar challenges.

In turning our attention to repressive conditions in higher education, we are looking at a problem that is national, even international, in its scope. As such, it will necessarily have diverse expressions in its historical development. One of the key indicators of academic conditions in the United States, the AAUP, provides our point of departure. While the history of the AAUP shows it dedicating itself with increasing awareness to the defense of academic freedom since its 1940 "Statement on Principles of Academic Freedom and Tenure," it was not until 2003 that the AAUP, reacting to demographic changes in the profession in its statement "Contingent Appointments and the Academic Profession," reached a level of radicality that would actually allow it to address the power relations that motivated the 1940 statement. Through attention to the rise of the contingent (non-tenure track) faculty in the United States, the AAUP took itself decisively (and with much debate) beyond issues that could be traced in the traditional way to the actions of administrators and committees. This deeper reflection revealed the worsening structural threat to academic freedom that came with the dramatic increase in part-time and full-time contingent appointments in the second half of the twentieth century, as contingent faculty moved from being a tiny minority in the profession to become a decisive and largely underpaid majority, estimated in a recent American Federation of Teachers report to be about 70 percent of the professoriate.[3] The issue of repression in higher education cannot be discussed apart from the use and abuse of contingent faculty.

To understand the structural problem of repression in the academy, it is necessary to look beyond the often tragic stories of individuals to depersonalize it. Recounting a history of unattractive and even reprehensible actions would surely help document that some kind of problem exists, but no one with any experience in modern higher education needs more convincing that people do nasty things to each other, that good ideas can get beaten down by politics or mere caprice, that institutional policies can come down hard on well-meaning individuals, that the introduction of critical innovations and radical perspectives into teaching and research carries special dangers for all faculty, and that whole careers are distorted or brought to an untimely end by the prerogatives of the powerful. Outrageous stories have a definite role to play in structuring the ways in which we pay attention to the problems they document, but they are not so useful at helping us get at the structural relations and strategic possibilities we need to grasp if there is to be any hope of breaking the cycle of coercion and cynicism that infects higher education today.

Mediating Structures as Defenses Against Repression

Consider the individual in relation to an organization as large as a modern university. In terms of endurance and power, the university operates on a scale that the individual faculty member cannot hope to match. This is true regardless of where in the hierarchy of the professoriate one might be situated. In their small but influential monograph, *To Empower People: The Role of Mediating Structures in Public Policy*,[4] Peter Berger and Richard Neuhaus make it clear that an individual operating alone has little hope of prevailing against a large institution when conflicts arise. Against the frequently-encountered backdrop of such unequal distribution of power, they propose the broad utility of "mediating structures." Such structures are organizations whose purpose is to protect the individual from the unrestrained power of large corporate or governmental entities. They may have a legally-defined role, as in the case of a union that functions as an exclusive bargaining agent, or they may be self-appointed, as with privately-supported environmental advocacy groups that insert themselves into regulatory and legislative processes. Of course, individuals can on occasion exercise powerful influences on institutions, but when that occurs, the individual typically has—in the manner classically described by E.E. Schattschneider in *The Semisovereign People: A Realist's View of Democracy in America*[5]—expanded the conflict to include sufficiently powerful allies that the conflict is no longer truly between an individual and an institution. Berger and Neuhaus were especially interested in the odd task of portraying the corporation as an economic mediating structure that protected the individual from totalitarian government, but any way one looks at it, the lone individual has scant chance of determining the course of a large organization unaided.

In contrast to the virtual powerlessness of the individual, organizations can assemble resources that enable them to affect the behavior of other organizations; on that larger scale of both size and endurance, the power dynamics are importantly different from a contest between an individual and a corporate entity. There is no single template for how mediating structures come into being or develop the ability to exercise power. After a long and often bloody history of building numbers, wealth, and legal status, labor unions eventually became effective mediating structures that were able to win grievances and bend corporate organizations in at least some measure to the will of the working class. While the legal environment has been anything but perfect for labor, the record of unions stands in stark contrast to the history of unrepresented individuals, who rarely prevail against unfair labor practices without government intervention on their behalf. This is important and demonstrates that in a conflict, the individual typically needs the protection of some entity, the mediating structure, in order to maintain some semblance of integrity in the face of overwhelming institutional power.

For purposes of understanding the power dynamics of the modern academic-industrial complex, the labor union is perhaps the most significant mediating structure. In classic fashion, the labor union gives the individual academic worker some measure of protection from the capricious action of the corporate employer. And, as the example of the labor union shows in larger context, however, this is not an unambiguous situation, since individuals have sometimes needed the government or an ad hoc advocacy group to act as a mediating structure between themselves and powerful unions. The fact that mediating structures have an important role to play in achieving fair outcomes certainly does not render them immune to corruption, much less guarantee ideal results for all constituents. Their human character notwithstanding, imperfect mediating structures are still irreplaceable if there is to be anything like a balance of power in a corporate environment.

While achieving fair outcomes is a goal of mediating structures such as labor unions, it is unusual for fair outcomes to be achieved just because they are fair. As our quick discussion above suggests, fair outcomes happen because power relations have been constructed that make some outcomes reality that would otherwise be improbable. For this to occur, there must be associations of sufficient influence and durability to match the corporate entity (of which, we reiterate, the modern university is an example) when wills are tested. This has been a sticky issue for many professors. The elevated ideals of research and inspired teaching are so attractive that unless there is a truly forceful intrusion, many faculty will prefer to let a certain number of compromises with their institutions occur before they are motivated to oppositional action. The AAUP and even what is arguably America's most successful local faculty union, the California Faculty Association, regularly encounter reluctance of faculty to improve their own working conditions. Relying in large measure on its moral authority, though occasionally on more traditional union techniques, the AAUP often mediates outcomes that would be difficult or impossible for faculty members to achieve working individually. But as the AAUP and local faculty unions are realizing, this ability is increasingly under threat by changes in the structures of institutions of higher education.

For purposes of achieving outcomes that depend on the power of mediating structures, in this case faculty unions and professional associations, the key effect of the shift from a predominantly tenured professoriate to a temporary workforce is the subversion of the relatively durable human associations that give mediating structures their cohesiveness, institutional memory, and sheer numbers, both absolutely and as a percentage of their constituency, the faculty broadly defined. The constitution of the faculty itself has been made an issue in this environment, of course, with some tenured and tenure track faculty maintaining the position that adjuncts, who often do the bulk of the teaching in an institution, are not even part of the faculty. In some cases, this position is engraved in the official documents of a university, an academic senate, or a union. The destructiveness of this understanding to faculty power can scarcely be overstated. And when that position is maintained for social status reasons, as it often is, that damage is compounded by a moral deficiency that would almost make the collapse of tenure a deserved consequence, except that the effects will fall upon later generations and not upon those negligent and degenerate members of the profession who see no further than the current state of their own privilege. The point here is not to exercise our options to outrage, remember, but to see the larger structural picture. As we have already observed, there are more than enough outrageous vignettes to occupy us for many lifetimes, but once we have been mobilized to attend to the big picture, these can become red herrings that threaten to substitute outrage for critical analysis of the structural danger.

A Faculty at Odds with Itself

As Joe Berry and Elizabeth Hoffman remind us, speaking for a host of commentators aware of Department of Education statistics, there are at this point at least twice as many people teaching at the post-secondary level on temporary contracts than on the tenure track.[6] This is in stunning contrast to the stereotype of the college professor as a tenured researcher with the time and institutional resources to pursue all manner of ideas. Also, while reliable national surveys are not available to show that a majority of those on contingent contracts consider themselves to be underemployed, anecdotal and other fragmentary evidence flows uniformly in that direction. Attitudinal data are interesting, but like the moral issues on virtually every campus, do not affect the structural reality; we must return to the demographics of which the most minimal interpretation of the cold, hard numbers shows the tenured faculty to be *prima facie* in a disadvantageous position. Over the past half century, a studiously apolitical majority of tenured faculty have allowed their cohort to become a progressively smaller presence on campus at their great collective peril. It is important to realize that while the numbers themselves look bad, the story behind the numbers reveals a more deeply intractable problem than most discussions of the decline of tenure suggest in their emphasis on the undeniably serious classroom quality issues.

Behind the numbers we find a compelling story of an emerging need of the professoriate for more effective mediating structures at precisely the time when the factors contributing to the strength of the needed organizations are running in the opposite direction. As the contingent workforce has grown, so too has a set of attitudes among administrators and tenured faculty that the contingent faculty are disposable laborers who have no entitlement to fair pay, office space, access to instructional technology and supplies, class preparation time, professional development opportunities, and shared governance. One often hears that contingent faculty are hired "only to teach," as if excellence in teaching were simply a matter of showing up when class begins, running out the clock, and leaving before the next instructor needs the room. One cannot imagine a tenured faculty member describing what counts as the total performance of excellent teaching in those terms, but somehow that is often supposed to be appropriate for the contingent faculty. It is obvious that today's students and contingent faculty both pay a heavy price for this double standard; it is less clear, but no less true, that future generations of the professoriate, tenured and not, as well as the students who depend on them, will also be great losers.

The first reason why faculty mediating structures are in trouble is that the disenfranchisement of contingent faculty from the academic community simply splits the professoriate into two competing groups. This creates an artificial weakness when there could be a single, much larger, more cohesive, and more critically aware alliance defending the well-being of the teaching profession. This split, which plays into the hands of any adversary who would divide and conquer, inevitably weakens the voice of each side by the influence of the missing element. For the tenured faculty to abandon the power of numbers that the contingent faculty now possess deprives them of crucial intellectual and political resources. It is hard to imagine a conflict in which the leaders of one side simply decide that it would be better to face the adversary with one third the number of supporters, but this is essentially what occurs every time the tenured faculty willingly sets itself apart from the contingent faculty. Moreover and crucially, this is a long-lasting damage because faithful allies are not often created at a moment's notice. Today's split in the professoriate will take time to heal even if the healing begins tomorrow.

Let us say for a moment that such healing did begin immediately. Let us say further that the healing proceeded much faster than anyone expected. Granting all of that, we would still have a major problem with the health of our mediating structures because the contingent faculty are such a volatile population. Certainly there are some, especially in the humanities, who remain on the job year in and year out, but when there are better options, people exercise them and leave the profession. As one grievant told me before abandoning his case, "I'm not sure why I am taking this shit. I could be earning twice as much outside." Within a month he contacted me with a report that as soon as the semester ended, he would be moving into an admittedly higher-pressure, but also higher-prestige position in private industry paying a respectable six-figure salary that shamed what he was earning as a comparatively well-paid contingent faculty member. The salary numbers may not be typical of contingent faculty who find other work, but the story of contingent faculty leaving teaching because they cannot afford to stay or cannot stand the disrespect is repeated again and again.

This widespread volatility militates against professional mediating structures in higher education especially at the level of the base. There will almost always be a stable cadre of contingent survivors to lead their cohort, but without a rank-and-file constituency that both understands the issues and how to mobilize, the power of the mediating structure is a fraction of what it could be. A few leaders with no followers is a recipe for marginalization. It is the fact of contingency itself that undercuts the mediating structures that would defend academic freedom from the encroachments that are endemic to the academic-industrial complex. The caricature of the disposable assembly-line worker transferred to the classroom makes for a much weaker professoriate both academically (because of reduced professional development opportunities) and organizationally (because of less stable mediating structures) than does the widespread institution of tenure. This is why the attack on tenure is so vicious and sustained; the enemies of liberal education seem to realize better than its classroom purveyors that tenure is the great obstacle to the thorough commercialization of the academy.

Job security, even more than compensation, is the single greatest issue for contingent faculty. Thus, when tenured faculty are complicit in creating working conditions in which contingent faculty are made to feel like outsiders who can be "disappeared" at the slightest whim of supervisors, the seeds of conflicting interests are sown. Not only do the tenured faculty and their organizations lose in numbers when they are split, they lose focus. Contingent faculty must concentrate on two basic survival issues: job security and compensation, including benefits. In most cases, the compensation piece is cast in terms of equity with the regular faculty. This dangerously leaves the tenured faculty to fight the battle for academic integrity on its own. In most cases, the broader problems of soft money, narrowed professional development opportunities, compromised curriculum integrity, and so on are barely on the radar for contingent faculty.

This is not just a problem of two groups with different interests. Those issues that are not generally on the radar for contingent faculty are in fact crucial matters for higher education. They define the parameters according to which the success or failure of institutions in carrying out the historic mission of higher education will be decided. For two thirds of the faculty to be minimally involved in such core issues means that there will be that many fewer who understand what is at stake to address the inevitable tendencies to entropic degeneration of the system. Bearing in mind that politics is more often than not a numbers game, the unfavorable numbers that eventuate when massive numbers of natural allies are excluded from participation in the struggles of the tenured faculty to maintain what is of value in higher education must be reckoned a strategic disaster.

Thoughtful faculty will realize that as individuals without the protections of effective mediating structures they are nearly powerless to address the encroachments of commercial values, including such deteriorations as the increased numbers of contingent faculty and the constant assertion of financial pressures in place of institutional support. In divided camps of separate organizations of regular and contingent faculty, the situation is not much better. There is no substitute for sustained effort at unity. If conflicting initiatives there must be—and let us agree realistically that this will not be a rapidly passing phase no matter how hard we work to make it so—the optimal arrangement for faculty is for regular and contingent faculty to cooperate in mediating structures whose overarching purpose is the well-being of higher education. There are numerous ways for this occur, notably among them plans of action that seek to roll back the reliance on contingent faculty that has become the multi-dimensional problem documented here and elsewhere.

An Example of Strategic Remedial Action

The case of the California Faculty Association is instructive for faculty who are serious about meeting the challenges of the changing academic-industrial complex. The CFA represents the 20,000-plus regular and contingent (lecturer) faculty in the twenty-three-campus California State University (CSU) system. CFA has been representing the CSU faculty since 1983, after being chosen over a more militant rival union by a

very narrow margin. The majority of CFA members in the early days saw their organization more as a collegial professional association than a union, which led to some
stunning defeats in bargaining in the early history of the union. At the beginning of
CFA's exclusive representation, a Public Employee Relations Board decision decreed
that the CFA would include both regular and contingent faculty. The two groups were
compensated on a common salary schedule (though at quite different levels in most
cases), something the more conservative faculty resented. Except for the largely symbolic common salary schedule, statewide contracts severely disadvantaged contingent
faculty and left them without even the basic rights of state labor law.

About fifteen years into its existence, a number of tenured and lecturer faculty
close to contract bargaining realized that CFA needed to transform itself into a more
traditional labor union if the string of bargaining defeats was to be halted. The urgency
of the need to change course was sufficiently recognized that the union elected a slate
of officers who represented a decisive break with the past in a hard fought contest. Interestingly, only among lecturers was there nearly unanimous support for the change.
A former lecturer was elected president of the union and a current lecturer was elected
vice-president. From that time forward, the inclusion of lecturers (then numerically
more than half of the faculty in the CSU but not half of the union's membership) in the
life of the union and support for lecturer organizing increased dramatically.

The first order of business for the newly more inclusive union was to develop
a more successful political program. The first item on that agenda was securing a legis-
lated agency fee arrangement in which all faculty represented by the union paid a fair
share of the costs of representation. Since becoming the exclusive bargaining agent,
the union had been saddled with the expense of defending "free riders" who used services but paid no dues, so the implementation of agency fee resulted in an immediate
enhancement of the union's ability to organize and defend its contract. Political representation was included in membership dues, but not the agency fee. There was some
negative impact on organizing because a number of faculty misunderstood the agency
fee to be union membership dues and believed themselves to have been automatically
enrolled as union members. Agency fee income allowed CFA to build its organization
so that when mobilization was needed, it could transform itself on short notice into a
vital political presence as budget and policy decisions were being made in Sacramento.
The salutary effects of campaign contributions in key state races were bolstered by the
union's success in contests where it was the prime mover. The belief that political organizing would further the faculty agenda for the CSU, which receives about two thirds
of its funding from the state, turned out to be correct. That does not mean, however,
that the union was thereby freed from constant vigilance, lobbying, and participation.
Political influence, once it is won, demands constant refreshing. As it turns out, in the
realm of becoming a legislative player in the battle of the corporatization of the uni-

versity and its pervasive monetizing of university life, there is no substitute for large amounts of money. This has been among the most difficult lessons to absorb for a faculty habituated to the triumph of ideas on their merits.

A second item on the legislative agenda, one that took a patience-testing ten years from conceptualization to full implementation, was restoring state labor law rights to contingent faculty. That it took a decade for lecturers in the CSU to receive basic labor law protections may seem almost impossible in a relatively progressive state like California in the twenty-first century, but by the time CFA decided that lecturer inclusion was a priority, the only right that lecturers had under their contract was "careful consideration" for reappointment. Until a key arbitration, this phrase had often been interpreted to require only a signature on the individual's personnel file attesting to the possibility that the file had been consulted in the making of hiring decisions. CFA had some success at the administrative law level in strengthening careful consideration to include having some kind of rationale for employment decisions, but that was about the extent of lecturer accommodation. After a particularly frustrating bargaining session in the late nineties in which one of the lecturers on the bargaining team had advanced the idea of stronger due process rights, only to receive a flat-out refusal to even consider the idea from the administration, the plan was developed to seek a legislative solution to administration intransigence. Lecturers were the great beneficiaries of the resulting bill, known as SB 1212, which made state labor law a floor for all future contracts. Future unequal balances of power, should they occur, will never again result in the trading away of fundamental legal protections. This bill made a great difference in lecturer job security, which we have analyzed as one of the key factors in building a stable mediating structure.

At the same time, another of our factors for a strong mediating structure, the reduction in the number of contingent faculty also became a priority. To this end, Assembly Concurrent Resolution 73, calling for a ratio of 75 percent regular faculty to 25 percent contingent, was introduced in 2001 and passed. It was not easy for lecturers to get behind the counter-intuitive ACR 73, but because it contained protections for currently-employed lecturers, the union was able to present a united front in lobbying. Legislators appreciate it when organizations speak clearly and unambiguously, which sooner or later can make a valuable contribution to good will. ACR 73 funding was a casualty of California's difficult economic times following the dot com bust, but the united consciousness that it represents is explicitly on the record, ready for implementation at first opportunity.

In subsequent contracts, the union was able to bargain much stronger job security provisions for lecturers, yielding virtually automatic multi-year contracts at the previous year's time base after six years of continuous service. This was a tremendous morale builder to lecturers who were fatigued by endless capricious reviews and financial uncertainty. The multi-year contract provision is important to job stability and thus crucial to the stability and strength of the mediating structure that represents the faculty. Recall that fixation on job security issues takes contingent faculty focus away from other important issues in higher education that the regular faculty cannot safely ignore.

Combining all of these advances in organizational stability gave the CFA power in the legislature and at the bargaining table that was beyond imagination just ten years previously. The changes came fairly quickly and the organization was consistently resourceful in pressing its advantages wherever it could. Even though building contingent faculty participation is difficult because of economics and still-reasonable fears of crossing unscrupulous administrators who might seek revenge, it is unlikely that the CFA would have accumulated its record of successes without the energetic participation of contingent faculty.

Extending this analysis also moves us toward an answer to one of the thorniest questions attending the inclusion of contingent faculty in the same mediating structures as the regular faculty: whether improving working conditions for contingent faculty is a good or bad thing. Of course, the humanitarian position would be that any improvement in working conditions is a good thing and on the face of it, that would seem to settle the question. This has not been the case, however. The counter-argument has been that if contingent work becomes less onerous, the motivation to move in the direction of greater tenure track hiring will be sapped. In other words, the worse the conditions of adjunct work, the more energy will be poured into eliminating the problem of over-reliance on contingent faculty. We can now say that failure to improve working conditions of contingent faculty is more likely to lead to a further deterioration of higher education, rather than the decisive improvement that the status-quo argument asserts. The weaker and more insecure the contingent faculty are, we have seen, the more divergent will be contingent and regular faculty interests and the less energy will be available for unified faculty action. On the basis of our analysis, there should be little question that aggressive action to improve working conditions of the contingent faculty will favor stronger unions and associations, thus strengthening the faculty as a whole.

Addressing the structurally-based repressions of a commercialized academy driven by a simplistic implementation of entrepreneurship is not a single-issue task. It requires among other things strong mediating structures to buffer the power of the institution from acting directly and unconditionally on the individual. One key factor in the strength of mediating structures, the stability of the constituency, has been under sustained pressure over the last half century as a consequence of the dramatically increased use of contingent faculty in higher education. In the legislative and organizational programs of one of the country's most successful faculty unions, the

California Faculty Association, we see how realistic inclusion of contingent faculty has added critical strength as the union has sought to build its effectiveness as a defender of academic values against the onslaught of perpetual cost-cutting and the intrusion of commercial values in the life of the academy.

Because of its success, the CFA has become one of the leading inspirations for faculty unionization in North America. By committing to the strength and effectiveness of their unions, often at great personal risk, contingent academic laborers themselves have progressively developed the critical consciousness to see a way beyond the structural repression they face regularly. Thus it is that by building mediating structures that inhibit institutions from compromising the integrity of the individual, the institutionally weakest members of the faculty are key to countering the forces that insidiously undercut the vitality of higher education.

The Right to Think

Bill Ayers

IN MID-NOVEMBER 2008, I was invited to give three talks at the University of Nebraska College of Education. The college was celebrating its centennial, and a faculty committee determined that I could contribute in some way to the intellectual dialogue that marks these kinds of occasions. I was scheduled to speak on narrative research in schools and communities as part of a student research conference, and then to engage graduate students informally in a "fire-side chat" about qualitative inquiry and their own research agendas, challenges, and demands. Finally, they requested a Keynote Address at the centennial, which I had tentatively called, "We Are Each Other's Keepers: Research and Teaching to Change the World."

On October 17, however, university officials cancelled all proposed talks. This annulment was not unprecedented. After 9/11 I'd been uninvited to speak at the Illinois Humanity Festival and the Chicago Public Library Distinguished Authors Series. An invitation to participate in a conference at the University of Colorado was rescinded and then re-instated in 2006. I was rebuffed at Northwestern University in 2008 "for safety concerns." Moreover, in 2008, an orchestral event at the University of Illinois at Chicago, at which I was to read the words of Abraham Lincoln, was cancelled because of threats of disruption.

The day before the Nebraska cancellation, and at the height of the 2008 presidential campaign, in which right-wing interests exploited my controversial past and tried to link me as a close associate of Democratic president nominee Barack Obama, a "terribly embarrassed" administrator called to say that my pending visit was causing a "firestorm." She related that the governor, a US senator, and the Chairman of the Board of Regents had all weighed in, each belatedly condemning the decision to invite me to the campus.

The university president said, "While I believe that the open exchange of ideas and the principles of academic freedom are fundamental to a university, I also believe the decision to have Ayers on a program to celebrate the College's Centennial represents remarkably poor judgment." The Regents Chairman added that while he welcomed controversial viewpoints, "The authority we grant to the faculty to decide what to teach and who to invite comes with a responsibility to use that authority and that freedom with sound judgment. In this case, I think, that was violated." That last statement struck me as worthy of the disciplinarian of a middle school commenting on a decision about homecoming made by the student council, rather than serious intellectual matters of interest to a broad community.

The administrator told me further that the university was receiving vicious emails and threatening letters, as well as promises of physical disruption from anonymous sources were I to show up. She said that the school's threat assessment group had identified "serious safety concerns."

I sympathized and told her I was terribly sorry that all this was happening to them. I also said that I thought the manufactured media buzz surrounding me was a bit of a tempest in a tea pot, and would soon surely pass. Certainly no matter what a group of extremists claimed they might do, I said, I thought that the Nebraska state police could surely get me to the podium, and I would handle things from there.

She wasn't so sure, and, who knows? I'm not from Nebraska.

Still, I held, we should stand together and refuse to accede to these kinds of pressures on free speech. Is a public university the personal fiefdom or the political clubhouse of the governor? Are there things we dare not name if they happen to offend a donor? Do we institute a political litmus test or a background check on every guest lecturer? Do we collapse in fear if a mob gathers with torches at the gates? I wouldn't force myself on the college, of course, but I argued that canceling my talks would send a terrible message to students, bring shame to the university, and be a perilous step down the slippery slope of abandoning the crucial ideal of a free university in a free society.

It's hard to think what consistently rational argument could have been advanced in the halls of power for canceling my scheduled visit to Lincoln, Nebraska. That I'm not a patriot? I love the country, period, but loving our country mindlessly and thoughtlessly, closing our eyes to those dreadful things that our government has done—and continues to do—cannot be a criterion for intellectual expression, especially in university settings that thrive on argument, stimulating debate, and the free exchange of ideas. In fact, speaking up—engaging significant issues in the public square and resisting injustice—is every citizen's responsibility; it is in fact the essence of democracy. Future generations will decide who the true patriots were: those veterans, for example, who threw their medals at the White House forty years ago, those who had the courage to refuse to fight an illegal and murderous war, those who suffer in silence at home today? Or those who claim to know, as Governor Sarah Palin exuded throughout the campaign, which parts of our country are "the real America."

THE RIGHT TO THINK

So, in Palin's words, I'm an "unrepentant terrorist with no regrets"? I am not and never was a terrorist. Terrorists kidnap and assassinate, employ massive indiscriminate violence against innocent people, and seek to kill and engender fear among as many victims as possible. Nothing I did forty years ago with the Weather Underground was terrorism; the fact is that no one was killed or even injured by any actions of the group. We were militant to be sure, we crossed lines of legality and perhaps even common sense, but we were not terrorists. By contrast, the US invasion and occupation of Viet Nam, at the cost of thousands of civilians killed every month for a decade, was indeed an instance of unspeakable terror.

I make no claim that violence should be part of any progressive movement; indeed, I believe that nonviolent direct action against injustice is the most powerful tool for social change. But I must note here that our government has been the greatest purveyor of violence on earth, as the Rev. Martin Luther King Jr. said in 1967. We live in fact in an absolute sewer of violence, often exported, always rationalized, and hidden through mystification and the frenzied use of bread—material privileges and consumer goods—and circuses—the vast array of spectacles, distractions, and forms of entertainment available to contemporary pseudo-citizens..

If you can't see the violence, you're not opening your eyes and you're in denial, and if opposing all violence is the oath that must be spoken in order to come to the University of Nebraska, consider who will then be excluded: both US Senators and the governor of Nebraska; President Bush and his entire cabinet, all of whom choose violent solutions to social problems virtually every day; the liberal head of the New School and the reactionary president of Liberty University; the leaders of both major political parties; military recruiters; and don't forget Nelson Mandela—he wasn't in prison all those years for committing acts of non-violent civil disobedience. In fact, anyone not a pure, practicing pacifist would have to be turned away.

I am a political radical, a lifelong educator, and a skeptic. But I'm not the least bit radioactive. It's true that I was made unwillingly into an issue in the 2008 presidential campaign, and that unwanted celebrity is the only reason I was not allowed to speak at the University of Nebraska. But the fallout affects me only marginally. The university system as a whole will suffer: after all, the primary job of intellectuals and scholars is to challenge orthodoxy, dogma, and mindless complacency; to be skeptical of all authoritative claims and received truths; to interrogate and trouble the given and the taken-for-granted. The growth of knowledge, insight, and understanding depends on that kind of effort, and the inevitable clash of ideas that follows must be nourished and not crushed. In this case, the University of Nebraska shunned its core responsibility.

Other victims include the high school history teacher on the west side of Chicago or in central Omaha, the English literature teacher in Detroit, or the math teacher in an Oakland middle school. They and countless others immediately get the message:

be careful what you say, stay close to the official story, stick to the authorized text, keep quiet with your head down.

Had I spoken at the University of Nebraska-Lincoln on March 15—ahhh, the Ides of March—I would have focused on the unique characteristics of education in a democracy, an enterprise that rests on the twin pillars of enlightenment and liberation, knowledge and freedom. We as citizens want to know more, to see more, to experience more in order to do more. We want to be more competent, powerful, and capable in our projects and our pursuits, to be more astute and aware; more fully engaged in the world that we inherit, the world we are simultaneously destined to change.

I would have argued that to deny students the right to question the circumstances of their lives, and to wonder how those conditions might be altered or changed, is to deny democracy itself. Banning me from campus was an act of denying democracy itself.

It's reasonable to assume that education in a democracy is distinct from education under a dictatorship or a monarchy, but how? Surely school leaders in fascist Germany, communist Albania, or medieval Saudi Arabia all agreed, for example, that students should behave well, stay away from drugs and crime, do their homework, study hard, and master the subject matters, so those things don't differentiate a democratic education from any other.

What makes education in a democracy distinct is a commitment to a particularly precious and fragile ideal, and that is a belief that the fullest development of all is the necessary condition for the full development of each; conversely, the fullest development of each is necessary for the full development of all. Further, education in a democracy depends on free and full access to information, argument, evidence, and opinion. This axiom too was contradicted by the censoring and repressive events at Lincoln.

Democracy, after all, is geared toward participation and engagement, and it's based on a common faith, every human being is of infinite and incalculable value; each person is a unique intellectual, emotional, physical, spiritual, and creative force. Every human being is born free and equal in dignity and rights; each is endowed with reason and conscience, and deserves a sense of solidarity, brotherhood and sisterhood, recognition and respect.

We want our students to be able to think for themselves, to make judgments based on evidence and argument, to develop minds of their own. We want them to ask fundamental questions—Who in the world am I? How did I get here and where am I going? What are my choices? How shall I proceed? What are my obligations to others?—and to pursue answers wherever they might take them. Democratic educators focus their efforts on the production of fully developed human beings who are capable of controlling and transforming their own lives, becoming citizens who can participate fully in progressing civic life.

Democratic teaching encourages students to develop initiative and imagination, the capacity to name the world, to identify the obstacles to their full humanity, and the courage to act upon reasoned moral imperatives and responsibilities of citizenship. Education in a democracy should be characteristically eye-popping and mind-blowing—always about opening doors and opening minds as students forge their own pathways into a wider world.

How do our schools here and now measure up to the democratic ideal? The University of Nebraska…surely not so much.

Much of what we call schooling forecloses or shuts down or walls off meaningful choice-making. Much of it is based on obedience and conformity, the hallmarks of every authoritarian regime. Much of it banishes the unpopular, squirms in the presence of the unorthodox, hides the unpleasant. There's no space for skepticism, irreverence, or even doubt. While many of us long for teaching as something transcendent and powerful, we find ourselves too-often locked in situations that reduce teaching to a kind of glorified clerking, passing along a curriculum of received wisdom and predigested and often false bits of information. This is a recipe for disaster in the long run.

Educators, students, and citizens must press for an education worthy of a democracy, including an end to sorting people into winners and losers through expensive standardized tests that act as pseudo-scientific forms of surveillance; an end to starving schools of needed resources, and then blaming teachers and their unions for dismal outcomes; and an end to the rapidly accumulating "educational debt" by denying the resources due to communities historically segregated, under-funded and under-served. All children and youth in a democracy, regardless of economic circumstance, deserve full access to richly-resourced classrooms led by caring, qualified, and generously-compensated teachers.

In Bertolt Brecht's play, *Galileo*, the great astronomer set forth into a world dominated by a mighty church and an authoritarian power: "The cities are narrow and so are the brains," he declared recklessly. Intoxicated with insights, Galileo found himself propelled toward revolution. Not only did his radical discoveries about the movement of the stars free them from the "crystal vault" that Church doctrine claimed fastened those luminous spheres to the sky, but his insights suggested something even more dangerous: that we, too, are embarked on a great voyage, that we are free and without the easy support that dogma provides.

Here, Galileo raised the stakes and risked taking on the establishment in the realm of its own authority, and the Church struck back fiercely. Forced to recant his life's work under the exquisite pressure of the Inquisition, he denounced what he knew to be true. He was thereby welcomed back into the Church and the ranks of the faithful, but exiled from humanity—by his own word. A former student—disillusioned and angry—upbraided him in the street, declaring: "Many on all sides followed you…believing that you stood, not only for a particular view of the movement of the stars, but even more for the liberty of teaching—in all fields. Not then for any particular thoughts, but for the right to think at all. Which is in dispute."

While there was no Galileo in the University of Nebraska dispute, this is surely what all the nonsense of demonizing dissident or challenging figures and excluding alternative points of view finally came down to: the right to a mind of one's own, the right to pursue an argument into uncharted spaces, the right to challenge the state or the church and its orthodoxy in the public square. The right to think at all, which is surely in dispute.

Educating for Social Justice
and Liberation

An interview with Peter McLaren

What do you feel about the current state of educational criticism across the world? We hear terms such as democratic schooling and progressive schooling… Are they for real? What would these look like?

Well, in order to answer your question adequately, I will have to specify the context in which such "democratic" and "progressive" education takes place. The educational left is finding itself without a viable critical agenda for challenging in the classrooms and schools across the world, the effects and consequences of the new capitalism. For years now we have been helplessly witnessing the progressive and unchecked merging of pedagogy to the productive processes within advanced capitalism. Capitalism has been naturalized as commonsense reality—even as a part of nature itself—while the term "democratic education" has, in my mind, come to mean adjusting students to the logic of the capitalist marketplace. Critical educators recognize the dangers of capital and the exponential rate of capital's expansion into all spheres of the lifeworld, but they have, for the most part, failed to challenge its power and pervasiveness.

Today capital is in command of the world order as never before, as new commodity circuits and the increased speed of capital circulation works to extend and globally secure capital's reign of terror. The site where the concrete determinations of industrialization, corporations, markets, greed, patriarchy, technology, all come together—the center where exploitation and domination is fundamentally articulated—is occupied by capital. The insinuation of the coherence and logic of capital into everyday life—and the elevation of the market to sacerdotal status, as the paragon of all social relationships—is something that underwrites the progressive educational tradition. What we are facing is educational neoliberalism.

What does this term mean in the context of the critical educational tradition?

As my British colleagues, Dave Hill and Mike Cole, have noted, neoliberalism advocates a number of pro-capitalist positions: that the state privatize ownership of the means of production, including private sector involvement in welfare, social, educational, and other state services (such as the prison industry); sell labor-power for the purposes of creating a "flexible" and poorly regulated labor market; advance a corporate managerial model for state services; allow the needs of the economy to dictate the principal aims of school education; suppress the teaching of oppositional and critical thought that would challenge the rule of capital; support a curriculum and pedagogy that produces compliant, pro-capitalist workers; and make sure that schooling and education ensure the ideological and economic reproduction that benefits the ruling class.

Of course, the business agenda for schools can be seen in growing public-private partnerships, the burgeoning business sponsorships for schools, business "mentoring" and corporatization of the curriculum, and calls for national standards, regular national tests, voucher systems, accountability schemes, financial incentives for high performance schools, and "quality control" of teaching. Schools are encouraged to provide better "value for money" and must seek to learn from the entrepreneurial world of business or risk going into receivership. In short, neoliberal educational policy operates from the premise that education is primarily a sub-sector of the economy.

Can you be more specific in terms of what distinguishes progressive educators from more conservative ones?

The challenge of progressive educators is vigorous and varied and difficult to itemize. Most liberals, of course, unhesitatingly embraced a concern to bring about social justice. This is certainly to be applauded. However, too often such a struggle is antiseptically cleaved from the project of transforming capitalist social relations.

Mainly I would say that liberal or progressive education has attempted, with varying degrees of success, to create "communities of learners" in classrooms, to bridge the gap between student culture and the culture of the school, to engage in cross-cultural understandings, to integrate multicultural content and teaching across the curriculum, to develop techniques for reducing racial prejudice and conflict resolution strategies, to challenge Eurocentric teaching and learning as well as the "ideological formations" of European immigration history by which many white teachers judge African-American, Latino/a, and Asian students, to challenge the meritocratic foundation of public policy that purportedly is politically neutral and racially color-blind, to create teacher-generated narratives as a way of analyzing teaching from a "transformative" perspective, to improve academic achievement in culturally diverse schools, to affirm and utilize multiple perspectives and ways of teaching and learning, to de-reify the curriculum and to expose "metanarratives of exclusion."

These sound like worthwhile goals, do they not?

I am not saying these initiatives are wrong. Far from it. They are, undeniably, very important. I am arguing that they do not go far enough, and, in the end, support the existing status quo social order. And for all the sincere attempts to create a social justice agenda by attacking asymmetries of power and privilege and dominant power arrangements in society, progressive teachers—many who claim that they are practicing a vintage form of Freirean pedagogy—have, unwittingly, taken critical pedagogy out of the business of class struggle and focused instead on reform efforts within the boundaries of capitalist society.

Your own work has been identified with the tradition of critical pedagogy. What is critical pedagogy?

Well, there is no unitary conception of critical pedagogy. There are as many critical pedagogies as there are critical educators, although there are certainly major points of intersection and commonality. There are the writings about critical pedagogy that occur in the academy, which are many and varied. And there is the dimension of critical pedagogy that is most important—that which emerges organically from the daily interactions between teachers and students. Some educators prefer the term "postcolonial pedagogy" or "feminist pedagogy," for instance. Some reject critical pedagogy for focusing mostly on class struggle, and embrace "critical race theory" or "critical multiculturalism" because they feel it focuses more on race. Some would say that critical pedagogy and multicultural education have melded together so much these days that they are virtually indistinguishable. Some might want to use the term, "postmodern pedagogy."

As I recall, the term "critical pedagogy" evolved from the term "radical pedagogy," and I came to associate both terms with the work of my dear friend, Henry Giroux, whose efforts brought me from Canada to the United States in 1985. I have attempted in recent years (with varying degrees of success) to introduce the term "revolutionary pedagogy" or "revolutionary critical pedagogy" (after Paula Allman) as a means of redressing recent attempts to domesticate its practice in teacher education programs throughout and in school classrooms. I would be remiss if I did not include the works of Michel Foucault, Pierre Bourdieu, Gilles Deleuze, Felix Guattari, Antonio Negri, and many other European thinkers who have been lumped under the label of "postmodernist and/or post-Marxist theorists." Also, feminist theory, postcolonial theory, and literary theory have made important contributions to critical pedagogy.

We can also connect critical pedagogy to the Latin American tradition of popular education, to Latin American pastoral traditions of liberation theology and to

European currents of political theology. We need to recognize that political struggles of African-Americans, Latinos, and other minority groups have greatly enhanced the development of critical pedagogy, as have liberation struggles of oppressed groups worldwide. We need to make a distinction here between academic critical pedagogy, and the critical pedagogy engaged by oppressed groups working under oppressive conditions in the urban settings and in rural areas throughout the world.

Is critical pedagogy the same as radical education or does a significant difference exist?

Radical education is wide net term that refers to everything from liberal progressive approaches to curriculum design, policy analysis, educational leadership, and classroom pedagogical approaches to more radical approaches. You will find many approaches to critical education that are anti-corporate, anti-privatization, but you won't find many people positioning their work as anti-capitalist or anti-imperialist. It is incoherent to conceptualize critical pedagogy, as do many of its current exponents, without an enmeshment with the political and anti-capitalist struggle.

Can you share your thoughts on your idea of teachers as transformative intellectuals? How and what is needed to be done in this regard?

This is an important question. I admire Giroux's important call for teachers to develop themselves into transformative intellectuals. To the question of what is to be done, I follow Antonio Gramsci in his concept of developing organic intellectuals. But it is glaringly evident to me that most educationalists offer a perniciously narrow reading of Gramsci that situates the body of his work within the narrow precinct of reform-oriented, counter-hegemonic practice, largely in its forced separation of civil society from the state. It should be remembered that Gramsci's conception of the long struggle for proletarian power is one that mandates organically devised ideological and political education and preparation, including the creation of a system of class alliances for the ultimate establishment of proletarian hegemony as well as the development of workers councils.

      Now, I am not saying that the struggle to build organic intellectuals today is identical to the struggle that Gramsci articulated in his day. I see the challenge of transformative (organic) intellectuals today as developing strategic international alliances with anti-capitalist and working-class movements worldwide, as well as with national liberation struggles against imperialism (and I don't mean here homogeneous nationalisms but rather those that uphold the principles of what Aijaz Ahmad calls multilingual, multidenominational, multiracial political solidarities). Transformative intellectuals should be opposed to policies imposed by the International Monetary

Fund and the World Bank on "undeveloped" countries because such measures are the actual cause of economic underdevelopment.

Transformative intellectuals should set themselves against imperialism. In discussing responses to the imperial barbarism and corruption brought about by capitalist globalization, critical intellectuals frequently gain notoriety among the educated classes. Professing indignation at the ravages of empire and neo-liberalism and attempting to expose their lies, critical intellectuals appeal to the elite to reform the power structures so that the poor will no longer suffer.

Can the existing form of schooling system lead us to a struggle for social justice?

In so far as our goal is to create a society where real equality exists on an everyday basis, it is impossible to achieve this within existing capitalist social relations. To challenge the causes of racism, class oppression, and sexism and their association with the exploitation of living labor, demands that critical teachers and cultural workers re-examine capitalist schooling in the context of global capitalist relations. Here the development of a critical consciousness should enable students to theorize and critically reflect upon their social experiences, and also to translate critical knowledge into political activism.

A revolutionary critical pedagogy actively involves students in the construction of working-class social movements. Because we acknowledge that building cross-ethnic/racial alliances among the working-class has not been an easy task to undertake in recent years, critical educators encourage the practice of community activism and grassroots organization among students, teachers, and workers. They are committed to the idea that the task of overcoming existing social antagonisms can only be accomplished through class struggle, the road map out of the messy gridlock of historical amnesia.

Another challenge that I have been faced with is the immediate dismissal from the teachers that these concepts look good and work well only on paper or these only work in theory, but in real life situations there is no classroom application for such intellectual jargon? What would you say to that?

Well, that is a fair question. In most public schools, and in most private schools for that matter, there are no provisions for classroom applications of these concepts. There are some courageous alternative schools that are trying to employ revolutionary critical pedagogical imperatives into the curriculum, to be sure. But the public schools could not function within capitalism if revolutionary critical educators were to challenge the very foundations upon which they rest. Of course, revolutionary critical pedagogy is a dialectical approach that works with both the concepts of reform and transformation.

Reform efforts are important so that resources are distributed equally among schools in every neighborhood, so that curricula include the voices of ethnic minorities, so that there is equality of access and outcome in education. But we also look towards the transformation of capitalist social relations, at least keep that goal in sight, and work in whatever capacity we can towards its realization. While such a transformation is unlikely in our lifetime, or even in our children's lifetime, it is important to keep the dream of another world—a better world. And we need to believe that a better world is possible.

Can you expand on this?

The problem is that while schools should serve as the moral witness for the social world in which they are housed, they are today little more than functional sites for business-higher education partnerships. The corporate world basically controls the range and scope of the programs, and, of course, military research is being conducted on campuses. As Ramin Farahmandpur and I have argued, universities are now becoming corporations. They embrace the corporate model. We talk in our classrooms about the values of openness, fairness, social justice, compassion, respect for otherness, critical reasoning, political activism, and look at how the university treats it employees, the service workers, and the graduate students who are exploited as assistants to the professors. Many of the campus workers in the cafeterias and in the warehouses and in the offices are paid wages with which they can barely subsist, and they have few, if any, health benefits and little job security. Graduate student-assistants often teach most of the classes, but are paid very small wages, while the professors earn robust salaries. We need to make the university mirror the social justice that many professors talk about in their classrooms.

Recently, in a talk I gave at a university in the Midwest, I spoke about trying to establish more links between the university and social movements for justice that operate outside of the university; there was a lot of opposition from the professors in the audience. When I called for socialist principles and practices to resist corporate principles and practices, I was called "totalitarian" by one well-known professor. When I talked about the problems with capitalism, and the relationship between the university and the corporate state, many professors became very offended. They did not like me using the word "state" because, to them, it sounded too "oppressive." They told me that they preferred to think of universities as places of hope. I replied that "hope does not retreat from the world, but radiates outwards into the world" and gives us the strength for a principled opposition to the imperialist practices that surround us, which prompted some very angry statements from the professors.

Under these circumstances, I see the role of teachers as that of transforming the world, not just describing or interpreting the world and this means understanding the ideological dimension of teacher work and the class-based nature of exploitation within the capitalist economy and its educational and legal apparatuses. For me, the most immediate challenge is to discover ways of feeding the hungry, providing shelter to the homeless, and bringing literacy to those who can't read or write. We need to educate political workers to create sites for critical consciousness, both within the schools and outside of them, in urban and rural spaces where people are suffering and struggling to survive, and we need to discover ways of creating a sustainable environment. My work in critical pedagogy sets as its goal the decolonization of subjectivity as well as its material basis in capitalist social relations. It seeks to reclaim public life under the relentless assault of the corporatization, privatization and commodification of the lifeworld (which includes the corporate-academic complex).

What final message would you want to convey to your readers?

The challenge is to create an authentic socialist movement that is egalitarian and participatory—not merely a different form of class rule. This means struggling against the forces of imperial-induced privatization, not just in education, but in all of social life. In this imperially dominated world, I can say that I live in the "belly of the beast." To support collective struggles for social change, to support a dismantling of civil society dominated by economic superpowers, and to support a positive role for the national state to play—all of this requires steadfastness and focus. The struggle for cooperation, sustainable development, and social justice—which includes efforts to transform gender, political, race, ecological, and international relations—is a struggle that we should not leave solely to social movements outside the sphere of education.

Educators need to be at the heart of this struggle. This is a very difficult proposition to make here in the United States. In my travels around the country, professors in schools are inclined to support the status quo because of the benefits that it has provided for them. Yet, currently, the top one-half of one percent of the population of the United States hold about one-third of the nation's wealth. We have 31 million poor people—approximately the population of Canada. We have 3 million people who live on the streets. And I live in the richest country in the world. This is the belly of the beast, a beast that, in the process of maintaining its great wealth for a few and misery for the vast majority, is destroying the globe.

As I have argued with Noah de Lissovoy and Ramin Farahmandpur, struggling against imperialist exploitation means taking apart the Eurocentric system of cultural valuations that rationalizes globalization as "development" and "progress," and portrays those who suffer its violence—especially the masses of the South—as beneficiaries of the magnanimous and "advanced." We know this to be a lie. From the belly of this lie, the effects of imperialism worldwide are recycled and represented as proof of the need for intervention by transnational corporate elites. Dismantling imperialism means destroying this unholy marriage of capitalist accumulation and neocolonial violence, and creating the possibility of anti-colonial reconfigurations of politico-cultural space at the same time as systems of socialist production are initiated. This is only a vision at this particular historical moment, but it is one that we must continue to defend.

In this regard, no impatient ultimatums can be delivered to the masses from the sidelines. Critique is essential, but it must arise from the popular "common sense." In the terminology of Paulo Freire, the productive ground for the operation of liberatory praxis will be found in the "generative themes" that are truly lived in the "limit-situations" of the people. In the face of such an intensification of global capitalist relations, rather than a shift in the nature of capital itself, we need to develop a critical pedagogy capable of engaging everyday life as lived in the midst of global capital's tendency towards empire. The idea here is not to adapt students to globalization, but make them critically maladaptive, so that they can become agents of change in anti-capitalist struggles.

This interview was originally published on Z Net (http://www.zcommunications.org/znet/viewArticle/11777) on August, 19, 2002.

The Role of Free Universities in Creating Free Societies

John Asimakopoulos

FRIDAY AT NOON, A THREE HOUR CLASS, and I'm reviewing with my students for their exam. The door is open and I see the messenger from the President's office waving me out to the hall. I go, she hands me an envelope, asks me to sign a confirmation of delivery, and leaves. I open it to read that I have not been reappointed. Although I have Rosacea, a reddening of the skin, I turn pale, the students ask what happened, I utter, "They just fired me." According to the union contract, my reappointment would have been automatic after that date. They waited till the last minute to do the deed.

Long story short, I had committed two cardinal academic sins on the tenure-track journey. First, I published and presented at conferences on the topics of Anarchism and Marxism, and thereby swam far from the shore of acceptable discourse. Second, I challenged authority by requesting research funds if my "teaching college" required publications as a condition of employment; I then criticized the reappointment process in an open forum of big-wigs as being subjective and lacking transparency (which is common knowledge).

That was it for me, and no sooner did I close my mouth than did the plot to fire me begin. But since my publication record was sound, my peer and student evaluations were the best in the department, and I provided ample service on academic committees, they could only get me on a ludicrous and absurd charge—lack of collegiality. Never mind that my own Chair declared, in my annual evaluation, that I was extremely collegial and this fact could be corroborated by any number of colleagues!

That's when I met my soon-to-be good friend and colleague, Ali Zaidi, who was also targeted with political firing. When I introduced myself he said, "Oh, you're that Anarchist from your department, great to meet you!" I didn't know that I had a reputation for being a "radical," at which point I realized my problems where just as much ideological as well as political for questioning authority. Fortunately, I could afford an outstanding attorney, Jeffrey Duban Esq., who was fired himself as a professor, his case leading him to become an attorney. I was also fortunate that there was a union, and thus an arbitration process through which I had a much better chance of winning my case than with the court. I was lucky again in getting a fair arbitrator rather than a conservative ideologue.

Ali was unfortunate to be poor. He had to accept the union lawyer who collaborated with management to collectively ram a settlement (read: buy off with petty cash) down his throat, rather than fight his case. Unions are great for negotiating contracts, but good luck if you need their representation in court or arbitration. They always sing about setting bad precedents with so-called weak cases (read: we have better things to spend our resources on), even though his was also self-evident based on the facts, and a tenure case at that, unlike my simple reappointment. They even refused to defend a top historian, KC Johnson of Brooklyn College, when he was attacked for resisting corrupt hiring practices. Fortunately, he too hired a private attorney and won tenure.

At my arbitration, the college's attorney could not even provide a formal definition of "collegiality" let alone a document supporting it as an evaluation category for reappointment when asked by the arbitrator, and instead wrote down the one offered by my own attorney! The whole thing was a joke and even the President was forced to testify at the arbitrator's request, which only sealed my victory. The administration tried to force a settlement on me, but my attorney rejected the offer and successfully tried my case in court. Now I have two years left to my tenure review and I live in constant fear of retaliation and renewed trumped-up charges. I am, however, ready to fight through any obstacles they place in my way.

What came of all this? For one, I was unemployed for a year awaiting arbitration without the compensation due to me, thanks to a horrible union contract. I also expended significant amounts of money since the union does not pay for private representation or related arbitration fees when you do not go with their services. I suppose most people in my shoes would melt into depression, but I put into practice that old bromide about lemons. My academic employer had deluged me with lemons and I produced enough lemonade to supply Lipton. Once I gathered myself I decided to fight back in a meaningful way. As I explained to my poor parents, the problem was not this or some other employer, but the system itself, which permitted and encouraged these unethical preindustrial labor practices to occur. Academe was the guilty one, not CUNY, which was a specific instance of a general institution flawed to its core.

The moment the structural problems with the university system in capitalist society became clear is when my new brother-in-arms, Ali, my former graduate student and great friend Sviatoslav Voloshin, and I decided to establish a true institution of higher learning versus just another corporate knowledge factory. This was the birth of the Transformative Studies Institute (TSI), a policy research and social justice think-tank and graduate school. We decided to recruit all the downtrodden, abused and forgotten, and *most dangerous professors* alive and put them all under one academic roof to see what would happen. We thought a college by definition must be a social movement, and these educators had the credentials and scars to show their relevance to our vision. Book knowledge means nothing if not put into practice to improve the human condition, other species, and the environment. Furthermore, education without free and critical thought is just another form of brainwashing propaganda perpetuated by the educational industrial complex to reproduce future foot-soldier drones in defense of the capitalist status quo.

As a think-tank we will conduct critical research, engagement, and establish a space and place for social justice scholarship. We have already begun this process with an annual conference, panel presentations, a peer-reviewed scholarly journal, policy papers, fellowships and associations, affiliations with fellow critical social justice institutions, a speaker's bureau, and most importantly, so we guarantee our freedom of speech, a peer-reviewed press.

Our graduate school will encourage free thought without retaliation. We will encourage progressive scholarly activism rather than dismiss it as "non-academic." We will only recruit faculty that have earned their wings by being fired from at least one college or banned by a country, as our friend Steve Best earned a lifelong ban from the entire United Kingdom for the crime of exercising his free speech on behalf of animal liberation. We are interested in those who are marginalized, exploited, have been fired, or simply never hired. We will establish a new educational structure complimenting classroom learning with an apprenticeship model where students learn by doing alongside their professors, who act as mentors. We are serious and have thought through the details of this new institution with a great deal of strategic planning, including budgets, goals, and principles. The academic position for our graduate school is as follows:

- The pursuit of social justice, respect of diversity of all, respect for all species, and human and labor rights are the founding principles of TSI and, as such, are part of the curriculum.

- Unlike the meager and tenuous academic freedom at educational institutions in the United States, TSI guarantees substantive rights of free speech for all individuals.

- As education is essential for a good standard of living, global citizenship, and human rights, we are committed to providing free learning to the extent that our resources permit.

- All faculty members have equal rank and salary. As an egalitarian institution, there is no faculty hierarchy at TSI. Tenure can be attained after six years and is based on equally-weighted effectiveness in teaching, research, *and* activism.

- Graduate students are graded based on a tutorial model that allows one to demonstrate mastery of a subject in various ways, rather than submitting to standardized tests. Each student is graded on a personal basis, rather than in comparison to peers.

- Because students work at different paces, all students are considered full-time regardless of their credit load. This assists students with medical insurance and other financial benefits.

- Faculty are the sole instructors, thereby eliminating the exploitative use of graduate students. If a graduate student wants and is competent to teach a course they are paid equal to a faculty member and are listed as such.

- We are committed to eliminating the abusive labor practice of employing adjuncts. To this end, graduate courses are taught only by full-time faculty members.

- Each course is designed by the professor and is not based on a standard text or syllabus set by any other body or individual.

- Academic programs and courses have a theory-to-practice component stressing community service and global responsibility.

- With critical thinking central to our mission, we encourage faculty, staff members, and students to express themselves while remaining respectful to others.

- Members of this college shall not cheat or plagiarize, and shall not engage in dishonest, unethical, destructive, or malicious behavior.

We strategically developed with our board and a financial planner a humble goal of purchasing a large three-story house in New Jersey in the next three years. The Institute will consist of profiting ventures to keep us afloat, as well as volunteer-based projects. The Institute will, at first, consist of a progressive bookstore and café, inclusive classrooms, offices, and bedrooms for visiting fellows and faculty. Our income will be based in three ways: donations, ethical grants, and the bookstore and café (which includes the books from our press).

In retrospect, firing me was probably the best thing my college ever did for me, as it ignited within me a passion I never knew existed. I learned new skills, launched a scholar-activist peer-reviewed journal, made a social contribution, offered a way for others to resist as well, and started a new institution of true learning that prefigures a new society rooted in radical democracy, genuine community, and individual autonomy. Best of all, I met amazing people who have joined TSI such as the editors of this book—Anthony J. Nocella, II, Steve Best, and Peter McLaren—in addition to many other phenomenal people like Deric Shannon, Henry Giroux, Stanley Aronowitz, Marc

Bousquet, Dave Hill, Richard Kahn, Michael Parenti, Emma Pérez, Carl Boggs, Liat Ben-Moshe, Abraham DeLeon, Richard White, and many more amazing people and scholar-activists—all with war stories and battle scars! This book is the first major project involving TSI members that articulates the many problems of corporatized higher education, but it will certainly not be the last.

So this is my message of hope for you the reader: You too can resist repression, reject resignation, and construct viable alternatives to the dehumanizing institutions of capitalist society. TSI invites all professors, scholars, activists, students, and citizens to join us. Join us in our efforts to establish a new graduate school for the twenty-first century that will be the center of a counter-ideology to the academic-industrial complex. We hope this institution will help to launch a new social movement from coast to coast and globally, as well to create free people not free markets. To accomplish our goals, we need volunteers, donations, and of course scholars, artists, activists, and learners. In the end we need not only learn how to dream again but, to dream big and to transform our visions into reality. The ultimate message of the Transformative Studies Institute is that we can transform ourselves and our society, that academic freedom is central to social freedom, and that, in building a new educational institution, we are building a new world altogether.

Afterword

Management's *Kulturkampf*

Marc Bousquet

THIS VOLUME COULD NOT BE TIMELIER. The editors have brought together an exceptionally diverse collection of desperately-needed perspectives on two generations of backlash and reactionary struggle by university management, in close alliance with state and corporate actors. Rather than a feature of a distant era of McCarthyism, or an immediate reaction to 60s radicalism, the assault on academic freedom has accelerated and intensified in the long, grinding era that began in 1980. In July 2007, the American Sociological Association reported that one-third of its members felt that their academic freedoms were threatened, a significantly higher figure than the one-fifth ratio recorded during the McCarthy years. How are we to understand this regression and current moment? How did we get here?

Most people feel that the answer lies, at least in part, in something called the "corporatization" of the university. This is at best an awkward term, because it can and does mean so many things. For one group of observers, it especially signifies the myriad direct relationships between nonprofit campuses and profit-seeking organizations. The consequences of these intimacies between educational and capitalist institutions are of course enormous, ranging from the corporate corruption of research (Washburn 2006) and the militarization of the curriculum (Saltman 2003) to the rampant commercialization of campus life (food, housing, clothing, leisure, culture, and so on). Ali Zaidi's pathbreaking reporting of the relationships between corporate entities and institutions as diverse as Adelphi and the University of Rochester, some of it printed here, has been widely influential in this vein. As one commenter noted, comparing the ethics of university management of campuses like Adelphi to Enron (analogies involving sweetheart deals, corruption, off-balance-sheet transactions, and the like): "It is not the extremity of Adelphi that was the problem, but its very commonality. Adelphi was something of an extreme to be sure, but only in carrying certain widespread assumptions and practices of institutional executives—union busting, program cutbacks, privatization of costs, heavy capitalization, insider enrichment, a logical free-market sequence—beyond the realm of what even New York's conservative attorney general saw as legitimate" (Lauter 2003, 75).

As the experiences of Carl Boggs, Michael Parenti, Ward Churchill, Norman Finkelstein, Sami Al-Arian, Victoria Fontan, and countless others demonstrate, the close relationships with commercial and industrial interests are also intimate dealings with military interests and the state itself. Rather than enjoying special freedom from retaliation under the rubric of academic freedom, taking on the state from a position within the university can mean special vulnerability, as the experience of these five scholars and so many others strongly suggests. And as Stephen Sheehi and numerous other contributors to this volume point out, the vulnerability of some produces a climate of fear for all. One major component of the climate of fear, as so evident in the Ward Churchill case, is the ease with which state power, corporate media, and administrators can highjack the system of peer accountability. Even to those who don't trouble to inform themselves, the lurking suspicion that the victim of the show trial wasn't guilty only adds to the power and terror of the corporate-state complex.

A second usage of the term "corporatization" refers to the rise of for-profit education corporations themselves. With the active support of reactionary government policy, the education industry has taken market shares from traditional campuses, especially the community colleges, and, between 2001 and 2003, publicly-traded education corporations averaged annual returns on investment between 63 and 75 percent.

With these large profits in mind, it is sometimes argued that the rapid growth of for-profit education vendors has "influenced" other campuses (e.g., see Cox 2003). This is an appealing fantasy. However, the reality is that non-profits adopted corporate-managerial techniques long before the for-profit competitors shot to prominence. In fact, as I've observed elsewhere (2008, 8–10), it is the techniques and culture of super-exploitation developed by the not-for-profits (to enable their own accumulation strategies) that made the huge profits of the for-profits possible, not the other way around.

Without any pressure from for-profit competitors, the nonprofits eagerly and voluntarily reduced the tenured stratum to a thin veneer at a broad swath of institutions—receiving accreditation for a curriculum largely delivered by doctoral candidates, masters students, and even undergraduates. Egged on by deregulation, privatization, and lax enforcement, for-profit educational institutions emerged to use the same staffing methods of the nonprofits in the service of maximizing revenue, and the nonprofits, having established contingent appointment as the norm, could hardly cry foul on the basis of the for-profit's nontenurable faculty.

The fact that the nonprofit campuses showed the for-profit schools how to accumulate record returns on capital is, in my view, a key insight for further analysis.

Plainly put, the leading edge of contemporary capitalism is the kind of super-exploitation practiced by campus employers. All other employers want to be like Higher Ed.

As of 2005, at least 70 percent of US faculty were teaching on contingent appointments. Counting the graduate students who do the bulk of teaching on many campuses, and factoring in the tendency of administrations to under-report the non-tenurable, the real number may be 80 percent or more, and the trend line continues sharply upward. At nonprofit institutions, the scant fraction of the tenurable comprise little more than a small group of grant-writers—more and more of them funded by profit-seeking corporations—and the candidate pool for administration posts. At many institutions, the tenurable group amount to little more than the individuals who have served, are serving, or soon enough will serve as deans, department chairs, program heads, and other functionaries.

For decades now it has been the case that the norm of faculty appointment is not tenure or the prospect of tenure, but extreme tenuousness: faculty serving contingently are dismissed at will, enjoy few to no due process protections, often lack basic academic freedoms such as the choice of syllabus or course texts, and many have no future in the profession except on the basis of pleasing management.

We must ask: what does it mean that extreme precariousness is the normal, unexceptional experience of academic employment in the twenty-first century?

The current president of the American Association of University Professors (AAUP), Cary Nelson, told me bluntly in a 2007 interview that faculty serving contingently at most institutions simply don't have academic freedom at all, echoing the conclusions of the organization's ground-breaking 2003 report on contingent appointment. If that's true, "academic freedom" has not been an academic norm for decades, and likely will not be for decades to come.

As Douglas Kellner, Robert Jensen, Emma Perez, Takis Fotopolous, Bill Martin, Mark Rupert, Peter Castro, and Dana Cloud document, individuals and organizations outside the academy have long assaulted academic freedom directly, often with the collaboration of institutional executives. More typically, administrations have curtailed academic freedom by the simple expedient of reserving it—in limited, degraded forms—to the privileged few. The fact is that it is far more typical for police officers, civil servants, and kindergarten teachers to enjoy the basic workplace protections of due process normally associated with tenure than rank-and-file college faculty. As Caroline Kaltefleiter and Mechthild Nagel point out, one does not need to be an enemy of the state, or even a radical philosopher or critical pedagogue, to be dismissed without cause. Any group of five faculty serving on term contracts will have a dozen stories of being terminated for grading too harshly, questioning student assumptions, assigning too much reading, or the like.

In a recent essay, "White Collar Proletariat: The Case of Becky Meadows" (2007), I reported on one of my former grad students whose working-class experience of schooling echoes that of Deric Shannon and William Armaline. Like them, she struggled to pay for books and navigate the institution, but, with the majority of "successful" working class students, she absorbed the lessons of compliance. The chief goal in her academic career was literally to join the administration (sincerely, if naively, believing that as dean she could do some good). Despite her entirely pro-administrative orientation, she was fired from her first full-time faculty job, department chair at an Ivy Tech campus, for proposing a country-music concert to help raise funds for the health insurance of campus adjunct faculty.

Even for the privileged minority, precariousness strongly conditions—and I would say acculturates—the few who succeed in entering the tenurable track: precariousness as a graduate student and graduate employee; temporary hiring as the typical funding option after graduate assistantship expires; contingent appointment during years of failed searches for a tenurable position; and the insecurity of probationary employment (as Maria Cotera's report makes clear: if Andrea Smith can't feel secure, who can?). Moreover, there is the burden of living with education loan debt on bartenders' wages after securing tenure; and the belated discovery that promotion and/or a securing a decent living can depend on pleasing or becoming management. Let's not forget; the fragility of many tenured appointments themselves, which are predicated on the continuation of departments—easily shut down on administrative whim—or on due process protections that have grown gossamer-thin at all but a few institutions with a vigilant or militant faculty. While the minority of faculty serving in the tenure stream are heavily-unionized by US standards, it has generally been the weakest sort of trade-unionism, one that is profoundly complicit in the permatemping and management dominion of campuses and that is all-too happy to sell future faculty into contingent appointment in exchange for 4percent salary increases.

In short, the tenured—as individuals in myriad ways and collectively in faculty senates, committees, and unions—have been actively complicit in disassembling the tenure system and the academic freedoms associated with it.

To a very real extent: we did this to ourselves.

Explaining how we got to this sad impasse is the goal of a third line of thought that approaches "corporatization" as the active, intentional, aggressive transformation of academic culture by university management.

In the 1960s and 1970s, scholars and journalists documented a vigorous, rising "student culture" associated with political activism and lifestyle experimentation, which co-existed with a liberal faculty culture, with strong left-labor contact points that fostered free speech as well as certain civil rights, including collective bargaining. Christian Davenport is correct to point out that the notion of a fundamental relationship between academic life and certain freedoms emerged in recent history, in close relationship to continual, watchful maintenance and activist struggle by determined, diverse actors. With strong faculty and student culture in support of basic academic and social freedoms, those liberties have traditionally existed in the limited form of protections for those who practice what Michael Parenti accurately describes as "politically safe brands of teaching and research." In bold contrast, Parenti notes, "It is a rare radical scholar who has not encountered difficulties when seeking employment or tenure, regardless of his or her qualifications." Many readers of this volume will already understand from experience the vulnerable relationship of the Left to the institutions of liberalism and the dynamics of "repressive tolerance" chronicled by Mark LeVine, even in the best of times. With weak, quietist faculty and student cultures, such as at present, academic freedoms have largely melted away, even for the most compliant.

With the era of reaction that emerged in 1980, a new culture appeared on campus, the culture of administration, which swiftly rose to dominance over students and faculty. This administrative regime emerged in connection with Toyota-inspired organizational-culture theorists who promoted a managerial paradigm for corporations. The purpose of nurturing an administrative culture—one of, by, and for administrators, a bureaucratic solidarity founded in administrator identity, ritual, language, practice, and daily being-together—was itself, literally, reactionary, a response to the perceived strength of existing faculty and student cultures. Administrators now envisioned themselves, in cultural-materialist terms, as "change agents" whose goal was to shape faculty beliefs and values so that they conformed to, rather than contradicted, the instrumental, economic, and hierarchical values of managerial dominance.

Critical contributions by Gaile Cannella and Henry Giroux in this book (and elsewhere) join with the single most significant and sustained analysis of administration's effort to transform campus culture. I am speaking here of the seminal work of Sheila Slaughter, Larry Leslie, and Gary Rhoades (1997, 2004), who coined the term "academic capitalism" to describe how university administrations, in cooperation with state and capitalist actors, entice and compel faculty to engage in market behavior. The full range of these activities is by now enormous and familiar, and include entrepreneurship, competition for resources, incentivized research mission, return-on-investment valuation of activities, and assertion of intellectual property rights. Michael Yates (1998) has closely related these cultural strategies to the critical union literature of speed-up and "management by stress."

An essential companion to the critical, left-labor literature on management's *kulturkampf*, however, is management's own vast literature. Far from concealing its purpose, management is overt in its intention to control the campus by spinning tales (Burton Clark's "organizational saga" [1972]) that bind individuals together, and offering incentives to conform to the organizational mission, while starving out the opposition. In a key essay paralleling the management of HMOs to higher education, "Lessons from Health Care," one of the architects of responsibility-center-management, William Massy (1996), actually celebrates the contemptible, murderous practices of insurers that refuse payment for procedures that health professionals dub necessary to save lives. With denial of payment, Massy cheerfully observes, insurers trigger "organizational learning" so that hospitals, clinics, and individual practitioners "will be less likely to perform the procedure again" (191). Like doctors and their practices, tenure-stream faculty and their organizations (e.g., disciplinary associations, unions, senates, and departments) learn to take the extra ration of gravy and shut up.

Amory Starr's experience underscores the utility and manageability of institutional culture, incorporating non-threatening "dissent," but swiftly moving to isolate and subordinate those who challenge or unintentionally undermine administrative control. One of the essential insights that Slaughter and Rhoades draw out in *Academic Capitalism in the New Economy* is that "the university" is not an innocent victim "subverted by external actors," but rather is a location situating myriad complicit actors—administrators, faculty, students, staff, and workers—in intimate collaboration with corporate and state interests. What this moment of near total administrative-cum-capitalist/state dominance of campus culture means is that any insubordination—for instance, agitation with respect to ability status, racial or gender discrimination, or in-house environmental policies—can mean swift retaliation. Short of severe penalties such as termination, this reprisal often represents dissent or criticism as uncollegial and unprofessional, as if the subordinated were, without administrative intervention, a risk to the freedoms of the compliant and privileged, and to a safe, peaceful, and secure "learning environment" (see the essays by Joy James, Liat Ben-Moshe and Sumi Colligan, Micere Mugo, and Richard Kahn). As Howard Zinn urges, those who can't leave the campus must at least find ways to build counterpower from outside.

With *Academic Repression: Reflections from the Academic-Industrial Complex,* Anthony J. Nocella II, Steven Best, and Peter McLaren have compiled an amazing volume that throws a blinding light on the causes, nature, and effects of the dramatic transformations shaking up universities and colleges, while it shatters quite a few myths regarding the much-fabled "free speech" environment of academia.

Academic repression is, in most cases, inextricable from management's efforts—conditioned by larger social, economic, and political forces—to maximize the extraction of value from its own workforce, and to groom professionals, managers, and trained workers for the production and reproduction of capital. Separating the compliant wheat from the dissident chaff, administrators label those who don't get in or don't persist as failures—market losers bearing a well-deserved fate.

This means we face the oppressor daily, in the workplace, as workers. From Rhoades' early formulation for the degraded posture of tenure-stream faculty (the "managed professional"), I think we have moved to a position where we have to acknowledge that "normal" faculty—serving contingently or living on food-service wages after decades of work and service—are proletarians. Correspondingly, we need to concede that the more fortunate, in the steadily shrinking minority represented by the tenure stream, are, at best, a modest labor aristocracy.

But this begs a question: is the de-professionalization of university and college faculty to be mourned? Certainly the impunity with which management violates our nostalgic sense of professional privilege and pride is hurtful to us psychologically as well as materially, as we see our labor increasingly without illusion, as steadily directed by an administrative hierarchy working in the direct service of capital accumulation.

Management's campaign against the professoriate's professional culture has been too successful for its own good. In our dawning sense of ourselves as workers, there are prospects to celebrate. Once more, there is an academic labor movement, now led by those in the most precarious, always-already repressed positions—graduate students and term faculty. Discovering that we are repressed and exploited in the workplace—therefore that we are in fact workers—is itself a major victory. The step that remains is to seize the understanding that as workers we, not management, are the ultimate "change agents." In accepting the unpleasant truth that we allowed this to happen, we learn that we could have done otherwise. Perhaps we still can.

About the Authors

John Asimakopoulos, Ph.D. is Director of the scholar-activist Transformative Studies Institute (TSI) and Assistant Professor of Sociology at the City University of New York-Bronx. He also edits the interdisciplinary peer-reviewed journal *Theory in Action*. His work focuses on labor, globalization, and sociological theory. He has taught Economics, Sociology, and Political Science at many New York and New Jersey universities. His publications include a number of articles and books focusing on the history of social movements and how they can inform a new working class global movement for the ushering of epochal change toward a just society. His works champion the formation of a counter-ideology, independent working-class media and educational institutions, and direct action toward this end. As the child of immigrant Greek factory workers, formerly landless farmers, he has dedicated his life to promoting equality and social justice for the working people of the world. He is currently working with his colleagues at TSI to establish a new free and progressive university, operated by scholars. The vision is to create a new academe focusing on social justice and activist scholarship that will transform individuals and society.

William Armaline is a multi-disciplinary scholar, activist, and teacher in "Justice Studies" at San Jose State University. His recent research is on systemic racism and human rights abuses through the institutionalization and incarceration of youth. Generally, his areas of interest are social justice, inequality and youth, the philosophy and practice of human rights, and Participatory Action Research.

William Ayers is Distinguished Professor of Education and Senior University Scholar at the University of Illinois at Chicago, and author of several books including *Teaching Toward Freedom*, *A Kind and Just Parent*, *To Teach*, *Fugitive Days*, and (with Bernardine Dohrn) *Race Course*. In 2008, he was the target of a right-wing McCarthy-style attack engineered by the McCain/Palin campaign—Ayers was the "domestic terrorist" Governor Sarah Palin tirelessly accused Barack Obama of "pallin' around with." The attempt to demonize Ayers because of his activities during the Viet Nam war, and at the same time to tar Senator Obama through a guilt-by-association tactic backfired as every mention of Ayers was accompanied by a drop in the polls for the Republican team.

Liat Ben-Moshe is a finishing up her doctoral studies in Sociology, Disability Studies, and Women's Studies at Syracuse University. She is a core member of Beyond Compliance Coordinating Committee (BCCC), active in anti-occupation, anti-war, and disability struggles in Israel and the US, and is trying to nibble at global capital in the process. She is committed to making all struggles inclusive and has written and presented on in/exclusivity in activism and pedagogy. She is co-editor of *Building Pedagogical Curb Cuts: Incorporating Disability in the University Classroom and Curriculum* (SU Press); author of "Infusing Disability in the Curriculum: The Case of Saramago's Blindness," in *Disability Studies Quarterly*, 26 (2); and co-editor (with Sumi Colligan) of a special issue of *Disability Studies Quarterly*, entitled "The State of Disability in Israel/Palestine."

Michael Bérubé is the Paterno Family Professor in Literature at Pennsylvania State University. He is the author of six books: *Marginal Forces / Cultural Centers: Tolson, Pynchon, and the Politics of the Canon* (Cornell UP, 1992); *Public Access: Literary Theory and American Cultural Politics* (Verso, 1994); *Life As We Know It: A Father, A Family, and an Exceptional Child* (Pantheon, 1996; paper, Vintage, 1998); *The Employment of English: Theory, Jobs, and the Future of Literary Studies* (NYU Press, 1998); *What's Liberal About the Liberal Arts? Classroom Politics and "Bias" in Higher Education* (W. W. Norton, 2006) and *Rhetorical Occasions: Essays on Humans and the Humanities* (UNC Press, 2006). He is also the editor of *The Aesthetics of Cultural Studies* (Blackwell, 2004), and, with Cary Nelson, of *Higher Education Under Fire: Politics, Economics, and the Crisis of the Humanities* (Routledge, 1995). Bérubé has written numerous essays for a wide variety of academic journals such as *American Quarterly*, the *Yale Journal of Criticism*, and *Modern Fiction Studies*, as well as for more popular venues such as *Harper's*, the *New Yorker*, *The New York Times Magazine*, the *Washington Post*, and *The Nation*. His most recent book, *The Left at War: Cultural Studies and Democratic Internationalism After 9/11*, will be published in 2009 by NYU Press. *Life As We Know It* was a *"New York Times* Notable Book of the Year" for 1996 and was chosen as one of the best books of the year (on a list of seven) by Maureen Corrigan of National Public Radio.

Steven Best is Associate Professor of Humanities and Philosophy at University of Texas, El Paso. Author and editor of 8 books and over 100 articles and reviews, Best works in the areas of philosophy, cultural criticism, mass media, social theory, postmodern theory, animal rights, bioethics, and environmental theory. Two of his books, *The Postmodern Turn* and *The Postmodern Adventure* (both co-authored with Douglas Kellner) won awards for philosophy books of the year. With Anthony J. Nocella, II, he is co-editor of the acclaimed volumes *Terrorists or Freedom Fighters? Reflections on the Liberation of Animals* (Lantern Books, 2004) and *Igniting a Revolution: Voice in Defense of the Earth* (AK Press, 2006). His newest book is *Animal Rights and Moral Progress: The Struggle for Human Evolution* (Rowman and Littlefield, 2007). Many of his writings can be found at http://www.drstevebest.com.

Carl Boggs is the author of numerous books in the fields of contemporary social and political theory, European politics, American politics, US foreign and military policy, and film studies, including *The Impasse of European Communism*(1982), *The Two Revolutions: Gramsci and the Dilemmas of Western Marxism* (1984), *Social Movements and Political Power* (1986), *Intellectuals and the Crisis of Modernity* (1993), *The Socialist Tradition* (1996), and *The End of Politics: Corporate Power and the Decline of the Public Sphere* (Guilford, 2000). With Tom Pollard, he authored a book titled *A World in Chaos: Social Crisis and the Rise of Postmodern Cinema*, published by Rowman and Littlefield in 2003. He edited an anthology, *Masters of War: Militarism and Blowback in an Era of American Empire* (Routledge, 2003). He is the author of *Imperial Delusions: American Militarism and Endless War* (Rowman and Littlefield, 2005). A new book, *The Hollywood War Machine: Militarism and American Popular Culture* (co-authored with Tom Pollard), was released by Paradigm Publishers in 2006. He is currently finishing a book titled *Crimes of Empire: How US Outlawry is Destroying the World*. He is on the editorial board of several journals, including *Theory and Society* (where he is book-review editor) and *New Political Science*. For two years (1999–2000) he was Chair of the Caucus for a New Political Science, a section within the American Political Science Association. In 2007 he was recipient of the Charles McCoy Career Achievement Award from the American Political Science Association. He has written more than two hundred articles along with scores of book and film reviews, and has had three radio programs at KPFK in Los Angeles and was a political columnist for the *L.A. Village View* during the 1990s. After receiving his Ph.D. in political science at U.C., Berkeley, he taught at Washington University in St. Louis, UCLA, USC, UC, Irvine, and Carleton University in Ottawa. For the past 20 years he has been professor of social sciences at National University in Los Angeles, and more recently has been an adjunct professor at Antioch University in Los Angeles.

Marc Bousquet is a tenured associate professor at Santa Clara University, where he teaches courses in radical US culture, internet studies, and writing with new media. His most recent book is *How the University Works: Higher Education and the Low-Wage Nation* (NYU, 2008). He is at work on a project on the topic of undergraduate labor, as well as a book about participatory culture in the United States. He serves on the national council of the American Association of University Professors (AAUP) and was the founding editor of *Workplace: A Journal for Academic Labor.*

A. Peter Castro is an applied cultural anthropologist specializing in natural resource management, participatory development, and conflict management. His books include the co-edited volumes, *Negotiation and Mediation Techniques for Natural Resource Management: Case Studies and Lessons Learned* (Rome: Food and Agriculture Organization, 2007); *Natural Resource Conflict Management Case Studies: An Analysis of Power, Participation and Protected Areas* (Rome: Food and Agriculture Organization, 2003); and the single-authored study, *Facing Kirinyaga: A Social History of Forest Commons in Southern Mount Kenya* (London: Intermediate Technology Publications/Practical Action, 1995). Dr. Castro's other publications have appeared in *World Development, Environmental Science and Policy, Journal of Development Studies, Human Ecology, American Anthropologist, American Ethnologist,* along with other journals and several edited volumes. He has been a consultant for the Food and Agriculture Organization of the United Nations, the United States Agency for International Development, the United Nations Development Programme, and other organizations, and he served as a member of the BASIS-Collaborative Research Program's Greater Horn of Africa research team from 1999 to 2007. He is currently an Associate Professor of Anthropology in the Maxwell School of Citizenship and Public Affairs at Syracuse University, where he served as department chair from 2000 to 2005. His Ph.D. is from the University of California at Santa Barbara.

Ward Churchill is a Creek and enrolled Keetoowah Band Cherokee, professor, longtime Native rights activist, acclaimed public speaker, and award-winning writer. A member of the Governing Council of the American Indian Movement of the Colorado chapter of the American Indian Movement, he also serves as Professor of Ethnic Studies and Coordinator of American Indian Studies for the University of Colorado. He is a past national spokesperson for the Leonard Peltier Defense Committee and has served as a delegate to the United Nations Working Group on Indigenous Populations (as a Justice/Raporteur for the 1993 International People's Tribunal on the Rights of Indigenous Hawaiians), and is an advocate/prosecutor of the First Nations International Tribunal for the Chiefs of Ontario.

Dana L. Cloud received her Ph.D. in rhetorical studies from the University of Iowa in 1992. Since that time, she has been on the faculty of the Department of Communication Studies at the University of Texas, where she teaches in the areas of social movements, gender and communication, rhetorical criticism, public sphere theory, Marxist theory, and feminist theory. Professor Cloud's research interests lie in the areas of rhetoric and social movements, critique of representations of race and gender in the mass media, and the defense of historical materialist theory and method in communication studies. Currently she is working on a book about dissident union activists and a project on rhetoric and violence. Her work has appeared in the scholarly journals *Communication and Critical/Cultural Studies*, *Quarterly Journal of Speech*, *Critical Studies in Media Communication*, *Rhetoric and Public Affairs*, and the *Western Journal of Communication*. In addition, she has one published book, *Control and Consolation in American Culture and Politics: Rhetorics of Therapy* (Sage, 1998) and numerous book chapters. With Lee Artz and Steve Macek, she co-edited the volume *Marxism and Communication Studies: The Point Is To Change It* (Peter Lang, 2006). Professor Cloud was recently identified by the right-wing pundit David Horowitz as one of the most dangerous 101 professors in the United States, and he has targeted her again in his new book *Indoctrination U*, prompting her to do a lot of writing about academic freedom. A longtime activist and socialist, Professor Cloud lives in Austin, Texas with her partner Katie Feyh and her daughter Samantha.

Sumi E. Colligan is a professor in the Department of Sociology, Anthropology, and Social Work at Massachusetts College of Liberal Arts, a four-year public institution in the Berkshires. She received her undergraduate degree from the University of California, Berkeley and her doctorate from Princeton University, both in cultural anthropology. She also holds a Masters in Public Health from UC Berkeley. She served on the Board of the Society for Disability Studies from 2002–05 and remains an active member. She has published several articles on disability, including "Global Inequities and Disability" in *The Encyclopedia of Disability*, "Why the Intersexed Shouldn't Be Fixed: Insights from Queer Theory and Disability Studies" in *Gendering Disability*, and "The Ethnographer's Body as Text and Context: Revisiting and Revisioning the Body through Anthropology and Disability Studies" in the *Disability Studies Quarterly*. She has just completed co-editing a special issue entitled "The State of Disability in Israel/Palestine" with Liat Ben-Moshe for the *Disability Studies Quarterly*. She is presently engaged in interviewing disability rights activists in Israel in order to explore their understandings of social justice.

Maria Eugenia Cotera holds a B.A. in Liberal Arts from the University of Texas at Austin (1986), an M.A. in English from U.T.-Austin (1994), and a Ph.D. in Modern Thought and Literature from Stanford University (2001). From 1992 to 1994 Cotera worked with Dr. Jose Limon of the English Department at the University of Texas on a recovery project that uncovered a lost manuscript by Texas folklorist Jovita Gonzalez. Published in 1996 by Texas A&M Press, the manuscript, entitled *Caballero: An Historical Novel* includes a critical epilogue written by Cotera. She is the recipient of a 1999–2000 Ford Foundation Dissertation Fellowship and a 2003–2004 Ford Foundation Post-Doctoral Fellowship. Cotera has published numerous essays on Jovita Gonzalez, and Sioux ethnographer Ella Deloria and has recently completed editing and writing an Introduction for Jovita González's masters thesis, published as *Life Along the Border* by Texas A&M Press. Ms. Cotera currently holds a joint appointment as an assistant professor in the Program in American Culture/Latino Studies and the Women's Studies Department at the University of Michigan, Ann Arbor. Her forthcoming book, *Native Speakers: Ella Deloria, Zora Neale Hurston, Jovita González and the Poetics of Culture,* will be published by University of Texas Press in Fall 2008.

Christian Davenport is a Professor of Peace Studies and Political Science at the Kroc Institute for International Peace Studies (University of Notre Dame) as well as Director of the Radical Information Project (RIP) and Stop Our States (SOS). His primary research interests include political conflict, measurement, and racism. Professor Davenport is the author of numerous articles appearing in the *American Political Science Review*, the *American Journal of Political Science*, the *Journal of Conflict Resolution*, and *Monthly Review* (among others). He is the recipient of numerous grants (including 6 from the National Science Foundation) and awards (e.g., the Residential Fellowship at the Center for Advanced Study in the Behavioral Sciences). He is the author of *State Repression and the Promise of Democratic Peace* (Cambridge University Press, 2008) and *Media Bias and State Repression: The Black Panther Party* (Cambridge University Press, Forthcoming), the editor of two books and he is currently working on another book entitled *(N)ever Again, Until Tomorrow: Ending Genocide and Large-Scale State Repression*. For more see: www.christiandavenport.com.

Victoria Fontan is the Director of Academic Development and Assistant Professor of Peace and Conflict Studies at the United Nations-mandated University for Peace in San Jose, Costa Rica, since 2005. Prior to her appointment to University of Peace, United Nations Victoria was a consultant in Peace and Conflict Studies at Salahaddin University, Erbil, Iraq, where she was in charge of developing a permanent conflict resolution curriculum in Northern Iraqi universities. Other former academic positions include a Visiting Assistant Professorship of Peace Studies at Colgate University, NY, a Post-Doctoral Research Fellowship at Sabanci University, in Turkey. Victoria holds a Ph.D. in Peace and Development Studies form the University of Limerick, Ireland. Central to her work has been a conceptualization of terrorism and political violence through the study of humiliation. She conducted field research in Lebanon with the Hezbollah, in Bosnia-Herzegovina on human trafficking and organized crime, and in Fallujah and Doloya (post-Saddam Iraq) on various armed groups. Former consultancy projects include organizations such as UNHCR and USAID-Irak. Her interdisciplinary approach had brought her to brief an eclectic body of government and political agencies such as members of the US Congress, the US Military Academy at West Point, and various UN agencies.

Takis Fotopoulos is a political writer, editor of Democracy and Nature/The International Journal of Inclusive Democracy; he is also a columnist for the Athens Daily Eleftherotypia. He was previously (1969–1989) Senior Lecturer in Economics at the University of North London. He is the author of Towards An Inclusive Democracy (London & New York: Cassell, 1997) which has been translated into French, German, Spanish, Italian and Greek. He is also the author of numerous books in Greek on development, the Gulf war, the neo-liberal consensus, the New World Order, the drug culture, the New Order in the Balkans, the new irrationalism, globalization and the left, the "war against terrorism," Noam Chomsky and Michael Albert, and the present multi-dimensional crisis. He is also the author of over 600 articles in English, American and Greek theoretical journals, magazines and newspapers, several of which have been translated into French, German, Spanish, Dutch, Norwegian, Chinese, Turkish and Arab (see www.inclusivedemocracy.org/fotopoulos).His latest book is The Multidimensional Crisis and Inclusive Democracy, an International Journal of Inclusive Democracy (2005), which is an English translation of the book with the same title published in Athens in 2005: www.inclusivedemocracy.org/journal/ss/ss.htm.

Henry A. Giroux currently holds the Global TV Network Chair Professorship at McMaster University in the English and Cultural Studies Department. His most recent books include:

Take Back Higher Education (co-authored with Susan Giroux–2006), The Giroux Reader (2006); Beyond the Spectacle of Terrorism (2006), Stormy Weather: Katrina and the Politics of Disposability (2006), and The University in Chains: Confronting the Military-Industrial-Academic Complex (2007).

Adam Habib graduated as a political scientist having received his Bachelor and Master of Arts degrees from the University of Kwazulu Natal, Bachelor of Arts (Honours) from the University of Witwatersrand, and his MPhil and PhD from the Graduate School of the City University of New York. He has held academic appointments over the last decade at the Universities of Durban-Westville and Kwazulu-Natal and the Human Science Research Council. Prior to being appointed Deputy Vice-Chancellor Research, Innovation and Advancement at the University of Johannesburg, he served as the Executive Director of the Democracy and Governance Programme of the Human Science Research Council. Before that, he was the founding director of the Centre for Civil Society and a research professor in the School of Development Studies at the University of Kwazulu-Natal. Habib has served as co-editor of both the social science academic journal Transformation and the official disciplinary journal of the South African Association of Political Science, Politikon. He also sits on the editorial boards of Voluntas and the South African Labour Bulletin. He has served as an external examiner and examined Masters and Doctoral dissertations for a number of South African Universities including Durban-Westville, Kwazulu-Natal, Witwatersrand, Cape Town, and Rhodes. He has also served on a number of boards and councils including those of the University of Durban-Westville, the Durban University of Technology, the International Society for Third Sector Research, Sangonet, the Centre for Public Participation, and the Centre for Policy Studies. Habib has published numerous edited books, book chapters and journal articles over the last two decades in the thematic areas of democratization and its consolidation in South Africa, contemporary social movements, philanthropy, giving and its impact on poverty alleviation and development, institutional reform, changing identities and their evolution in the post-apartheid era, and South Africa's role in Africa and beyond. He is a well-known public figure in South Africa whose opinions are often sought by both the print and broadcasting media.

Joy James, is the John B. and John T. McCoy Presidential Professor of the Humanities & College Professor in Political Science at Williams College, and senior research fellow in the Center for African and African American Studies at UT-Austin. James holds a Ph.D. in Political Philosophy from Fordham University and a postdoctorate degree in religious ethics from Union Theological Seminary. Her work focuses on political and feminist theory, critical race theory, and incarceration. Her publications include: *Resisting State Violence: Gender, Race, and Radicalism in US Culture* (University of Minnesota Press, 1996); *Transcending the Talented Tenth: Black Leaders and American Intellectuals* (Routledge, 1997); *Shadowboxing: Representations of Black Feminist Politics* (St. Martin's, 1999), and the forthcoming, *Memory, Shame and Rage: The Central Park Case, 1989–2002* (University of North Carolina Press). She is editor of *The Angela Y. Davis Reader* (Blackwell, 1998). Co-edited works include: *Spirit, Space and Survival: African American Women in (White) Academe* (Routledge, 1993), which received the 1994 Gustavus Myers Outstanding Book on Human Rights Award; *The Black Feminist Reader* (Blackwell, 2000); and *The Problems of Resistance: Studies in Alternate Political Cultures* (New York: Humanity Books, 2001). Her edited collections on radical politics and incarceration include: *States of Confinement: Policing, Detention and Prisons* (St. Martin's,2000, revised edition 2002); *Imprisoned Intellectuals: America's Political Prisoners Write on Life, Liberation, and Rebellion* (Rowman& Littlefield, 2003); *The*

New Abolitionists: (Neo)Slave Narratives and Contemporary Prison Writings (SUNY Press, 2005); and Warfare *in the American Homeland: Policing and Prison in a Penal Democracy* (Duke, 2007).

Robert Jensen is a journalism professor at the University of Texas at Austin and board member of the Third Coast Activist Resource Center http://thirdcoastactivist.org. His latest book is *Getting Off: Pornography and the End of Masculinity* (South End Press, 2007). Jensen is also the author of *The Heart of Whiteness: Race, Racism, and White Privilege* and *Citizens of the Empire: The Struggle to Claim Our Humanity* (both from City Lights Books); and *Writing Dissent: Ta king Radical Ideas from the Margins to the Mainstream* (Peter Lang). He can be reached at rjensen@uts.cc.utexas.edu, and his articles can be found online at http://uts.cc.utexas.edu/~rjensen/index.html.

Richard Kahn is an Assistant Professor of Educational Foundations & Research at the University of North Dakota. He has published regularly on topics related to the intersection of ecology, technology, politics, culture, and education. Further information about him, including many of his articles, can be obtained at his website: http://richardkahn.org

Caroline Kaltefleiter is Coordinator of Women's Studies and Associate Professor of Communication Studies at the State University of New York College at Cortland. She has over twenty years of broadcast activism experience as a news anchor and producer for public and community radio stations in Texas, Georgia, Ohio and New York. She served as producer and director of the documentary *Burn Out in the Heartland* a sixty-minute that investigates the crystal methamphetamine culture among teens in Iowa and Nebraska. She continues to work on radio documentaries for National Public Radio and anchors a radio program titled, *The Digital Divide on Public Radio station WSUC-FM*. She received her PhD from Ohio University in Communication and Women's Studies. She holds an MA from Miami University and participated in the Center for Cultural Studies where she began her research on youth subcultures and activism including work on Youth Culture Capitalism, Post-Feminism, and Popular Culture. Her forthcoming text (Garland Press) *Revolution Girl Style Now: Trebled Reflexivity and the Riot Grrrl Network*, examines the Girl feminist movement and its use of alternative media forums such as 'zines, websites, and mp3 musical recordings. Her current research project articulates cyberfeminism within a discourse of new media studies. The project examines the construction, manipulation and re-definition of women's lives within contemporary technoscientific cultures.

Douglas Kellner is George Kneller Chair in the Philosophy of Education at UCLA and is author of many books on social theory, politics, history, and culture, including *Camera Politica: The Politics and Ideology of Contemporary Hollywood Film*, co-authored with Michael Ryan; *Critical Theory, Marxism, and Modernity*; *Jean Baudrillard: From Marxism to Postmodernism and Beyond*; works in cultural studies such as *Media Culture and Media Spectacle*; a trilogy of books on postmodern theory with Steven Best; and a trilogy of books on the media and the Bush administration, encompassing *Grand Theft 2000, From 9/11 to Terror War*, and *Media Spectacle and the Crisis of Democracy*. Author of *Herbert Marcuse and the Crisis of Marxism*, Kellner is editing collected papers of Herbert Marcuse, four volumes of which have appeared with Routledge. Kellner's latest book is *Guys and Guns Amok: Domestic Terrorism and School Shootings from the Oklahoma City Bombings to the Virginia Tech Massacre*. His website is at http://www.gseis.ucla.edu/faculty/kellner/kellner.

Mark LeVine, Ph.D. from New York University in Middle Eastern Studies teaches at the University of California, Irvine. His publications have appeared in leading newspapers and journals around the world such as the *Los Angeles Times*, *Le Monde* and the *Christian Science Monitor* he also has appeared on many television news programs such as The News Hour with Jim Lehrer, CNN, The O'Reilly Factor, KCAL 9/Channel 2 News, KCET's "Life and Times," and the Dennis Prager Show. He has published numerous books including, *Overthrowing Geography: Jaffa, Tel Aviv and the Struggle for Palestine* (University of California Press), *Why They Don't Hate Us: Lifting the Veil on the Axis of Evil* (Oxford-based Oneworld Publications), with Viggo Mortensen and Pilar Perez, *Twilight of Empire: Responses to Occupation*, and *Religion, Social Practices and Contested Hegemonies: Reconstructing the Public Sphere in Muslim Majority Societies*, co-edited with Armando Salvatore. Besides his academic, journalistic and consulting activities, LeVine has a long history of blending art, scholarship and activism. As a musician he has recorded, performed and toured all over the world with artists including Mick Jagger, Chuck D, Michael Franti, Dr. John, Ozomatli, Hassan Hakmoun, Arab/Muslim heavy metal and hiphop artists The Kordz (Lebanon), MC Rai (Tunisia), Salman Ahmed (Junoon—Pakistan), Reda Zine (Morocco), Ghidian Qaymari (Palestine), blues greats Johnny Copeland and Albert Collins, world music artists Sara Alexander and al-Andalus, and numerous R&B and hiphop acts.

Bill Martin is Professor of Philosophy at DePaul University in Chicago. He is the author of numerous books, including *Humanism and its aftermath*, *Listening to the Future*, and, most recently, *Ethical Marxism: the categorical imperative of liberation* (Open Court, 2008). He is also a musician by vocation, and by avocation an avid bicyclist and chess player. At present he is completing a book under the title, *People, We Need a New Society: Home Truth, Bullshit, and the Social Future*.

Peter McLaren is Professor of Education, Graduate School of Education and Information Studies, University of California, Los Angeles. He is the author, co-author, editor and co-editor of approximately forty books. Professor McLaren's writings have been translated into twenty languages. Four of his books have received the American Education Studies Association Critics Choice Award for outstanding books in education. His book, *Life in Schools*, was named one of the 12 most important educational books ever published by an international panel of educators (other authors on the list included Paulo Freire, Pierre Bourdieu and Ivan Illich). La Fundacion McLaren has been created in his name by scholars and activists in Northern Mexico, and La Catedra Peter McLaren has been created at the Bolivarian University of Venezuela in Caracas. Several edited volumes about Professor McLaren's work have been published: Teaching Peter McLaren (Peter Lang Publishers) and Peter McLaren, Education and the Struggle for Liberation (in press, Hampton Press). Professor McLaren holds a Ph.D. from the University of Toronto, Canada and an honorary doctorate from the University of Lapland.

Mĩcere Gĩthae Mũgo, Meredith Professor for Teaching Excellence and Chair of the Department of African American Studies at SU is a poet, playwright and literary critic who has published 6 books, 8 co-edited supplementary school readers, 3 monographs and edited the journal, *Third World in Perspective*. Her works include: *Daughter of My People, Sing!* (Poetry); *My Mother's Poem and Other Songs* (Poetry); *The Long Illness of Ex-Chief Kiti* (Play); *Visions of Africa* (Literary Criticism), *African Orature and Human Rights* (Monograph) and *The Trial of Dedan Kimathi* (Play, co-authored with Ngũgĩ wa Thiong'o). Recently Mĩcere received the Distinguished Africanist Award from the New York African Studies Association for her scholarly contribution while in November 2002, "The East African Standard Century" listed her among "The Top 100: They Influenced Kenya Most During the 20th Century." Mĩcere is a member of numerous organizations and serves on many committees, advisory/executive boards and directorships—locally as well as internationally. A committed community activist, Mĩcere is a passionate advocate for human rights especially as they have been historically denied to marginalized groups. She describes her daughters, Mũmbi and Njeri, as her best friends and indispensable comrades in the struggle for social justice. This special relationship developed during Mĩcere's years of exile from Kenya with her daughters, 1982–1993, at the height of President Daniel arap Moi's dictatorship which targeted activists, progressive writers, artists, cultural workers, journalists, community leaders, academicians and other champions of human rights.

Mechthild Nagel is professor of philosophy at the State University of New York, College at Cortland and a Senior Visiting Fellow at the Institute for African Development at Cornell University. She is author of *Masking the Abject: A Genealogy of Play* (Lexington, 2002), co-editor of *Race, Class, and Community Identity* (Humanities, 2000), *The Hydropolitics of Africa: A Contemporary Challenge* (Cambridge Scholars Press, 2007) and *Prisons and Punishment: Reconsidering Global Penality* (Africa World Press, 2007). Nagel is editor-in-chief of the online journal *Wagadu: A Journal of Transnational Women's and Gender Studies* (wagadu.org). As a graduate student at Umass Amherst, she was blacklisted for a while from teaching philosophy after leading a strike for union recognition. She can be reached at nagelm@cortland.edu.

Cary Nelson is Jubilee Professor of Liberal Arts and Sciences and Professor of English at the University of Illinois at Urbana-Champaign, where he teaches modern poetry and critical theory. He was elected as the 49th President of the American Association of University Professors (AAUP) in 2006 and reelected in 2008. Among his books are *Repression and Recovery: Modern American Poetry and the Politics of Cultural Memory—1910–1945*; *Revolutionary Memory: Recovering the Poetry of the American Left*; *Manifesto of a Tenured Radical*; *Academic Keywords: A Devil's Dictionary for Higher Education*;, and *Office Hours: Activism and Change in the Academy*.

Anthony J. Nocella, II, while working on his Ph.D. in Social Science at Syracuse University, he is a Visiting Scholar of SUNY Cortland's Center for Ethics, Peace and Social Justice (CEPS), a professor at Le Moyne College in Criminology, and a Life Skills teacher at a youth detention facility in New York. He is also an associate of a number of scholarly institutes including the Program on the Analysis and Resolution of Conflicts (PARC) along with being on the board of the Noble Peace Prize winning American Friends Service Committee (AFSC). He has provided conflict transformation workshops and classes to NGOs, ROTC, US military, law enforcement, public safety, also in prisons, juvenile halls, and middle and high schools with Alternative to Violence Program and AFSC. He is co-founder of more than ten active political organizations and four scholarly journals. He has written in more than two dozen publications and is working on his tenth book (co-edited with Richard Kahn) *Greening the Academy* being published by Syracuse University Press.

Michael Parenti received his Ph.D. in political science from Yale University and has taught at a number of colleges and universities. His twenty-one books include *The Culture Struggle*; *Superpatriotism*; and *The Assassination of Julius Caesar* (which was selected as Book of the

Year, 2004 by Online Review of Books). Portions of his writings have been translated into some twenty languages, and have been used extensively in college courses. He lectures frequently across North America and abroad, has lectured Tapes of his various talks and interviews have played widely on community radio stations and public access television. More than 280 articles of his have been published in scholarly journals, magazines and newspapers, books of collected readings, and online publications. He has won awards from various academic and social activists organizations, and serves on advisory boards for Project Censored, Education Without Borders, the Jasenovic Foundation, and several publications. For further information, visit his website: http://wwwmichaelparenti.org.

Emma Pérez has published essays in history and feminist theory as well as a book of history and theory titled, *The Decolonial Imaginary: Writing Chicanas into History*. Her novel, *Gulf Dreams*, was one of the first Chicana lesbian novels published by a Chicana lesbian. In fall 2003, she joined the Department of Ethnic Studies at University of Colorado, Boulder where she is an Associate Professor.

Mark Rupert is professor of political science at Syracuse University's Maxwell School of Citizenship and Public Affairs, and teaches in the areas of international relations, political economy, and the political theories of Karl Marx and Antonio Gramsci. Mark's research focuses on the intersection of the US political economy with global structures and processes. He is the author of *Producing Hegemony: the politics of mass production and American global power* (Cambridge, 1995); and *Ideologies of Globalization: Contending Visions of a New World Order* (Routledge, 2000); and co-author (with Scott Solomon) of *Globalization and International Political Economy* (Rowman and Littlefield, 2006). Mark's home page can be found at http://faculty.maxwell.syr.edu/merupert/merindex.htm.

Rik Scarce joined the Skidmore College faculty in 2003. His specialty courses include Environmental Sociology, Collective Behavior and Social Movements, Classical and Contemporary Social Theory, Political Sociology, and others. His current research is a social and ecological history of the Hudson region's landscape, which will take both book and documentary form. Rik's previous books include *Contempt of Court: A Scholar's Battle for Free Speech from Behind Bars* (Alta Mira Press, 2005); *Fishy Business: Salmon, Biology, and the Social Construction of Nature* (Temple University Press, 2000); and, most recently, an updated edition of his 1990 book *Eco-Warriors: Understanding the Radical Environmental Movement* (Left Coast Press, 2006). His scholarly articles have appeared in *Symbolic Interaction, Society and Natural Resources, Law and Social Inquiry, Journal of Contemporary Ethnography, The American Sociologist,* and elsewhere, as well as chapters in several books. Rik's Ph.D. is from Washington State University (1995). His M.A. is from the University of Hawaii (1984), and his B.A. is from Stetson University in Florida (1981); both are in political science. He enjoys hiking, photography, and serious recreational bicycle riding.

Gabriel Matthew Schivone is an editor of *Days Beyond Recall Alternative Media* and *Literary Journal*. His articles, having been translated into multiple languages, have appeared in numerous journals such as *Z Magazine, Counterpunch* and the *Monthly Review*, as well as *Contre Info* (France), and *Caminos* (Cuba). He is most recently the recipient of the 2007 Frederica Hearst Prize for Lyrical Poetry. He is also an active member of the University of Arizona chapter of Amnesty International, Voices of Opposition (to War, Racism and Oppression), Students Organized for Animal Rights, Sweatshop-Free Coalition, and Dry River

Radical Resource Center. He can be reached at gabrielm@email.arizona.edu and gabrielm@ mit.edu.

Deric Shannon is a PhD. candidate in sociology at the University of Connecticut, where he studies prefigurative politics in the context of Food Not Bombs activism. He is a long time anarchist militant with roots in groups like Anti-Racist Action and Food Not Bombs. He is a co-editor of the forthcoming book *Contemporary Anarchist Studies: An Introductory Reader of Anarchy in the Academy* and co-hosts the feminist radio show, The F-Files (http://www. ffiles.net), where he has had the honor of talking with fellow radicals like Noam Chomsky, Catharine MacKinnon, and Martha Ackelsberg. He is a proud member of ARRGH! (the Area Radical Reading Group of Hartford) and Hartford Food Not Bombs and runs the independent record label, Wooden Man Records.

Stephen Sheehi is Associate Professor of Arabic and Arab Culture and Director of the Arabic Program at the University of South Carolina. His Foundations *of Modern Arab Identity* (Florida, 2004) examines how 19th century Arab intellectuals, reformers and literati disseminated new paradigms of self and culture that internalized Western authority and inscribed Eastern "inferiority". His research on Arab culture, thought and literature have appeared in journals such as *The International Journal for Middle Eastern Studies, The British Journal of Middle East Studies, Critique, The Journal of Arabic Literature, Jouvert: Journal for Postcolonial Studies,* and *The Journal of Comparative South Asian, African, and Middle Eastern Studies.* Currently, Prof. Sheehi is working on two manuscripts: *Why We Should Hate You: American Origins of Arab Rage* and *The Arab Imago: Consumerism, Capital and the Social History of Arab Photography.* Prof. Sheehi is an anti-authoritarian activist involved in the movements for Palestinian self-determinion, anti-globalization, and social and economic justice in the Middle East.

Amory Starr's manuscript of *Naming the Enemy: Anti-Corporate Movements Confront Globalization* was completed in 1998, more than a year before the Seattle WTO protests. Later published by Zed Books, it is the first systematic survey of the movements which would shortly converge into the anti-globalization movement. Her second book, *Global Revolt: A Guide to Alterglobalization,* is an introductory text, reviewing points of consensus, disagreements, and some of the tactics from the global struggle. She also wrote and directed *This is What Free Trade Looks Like,* a 2004 documentary which examines México's experience with NAFTA as a basis for understanding the WTO. Work in progress includes a comparison of forms of participatory democracy in use by Latin American social movements and an analysis of the social control of dissent in the Global North in the post-Seattle era. Her current community-organizing focuses on the political economy of food.

Gregory Tropea began his involvement with community-benefit organizing during the Vietnam war and since then has helped organize or manage a number of community nonprofits, has chaired the City of Chico Arts Commission, has served on and chaired several city task forces, and has served the California Faculty Association since the early nineties at both the local level and as a statewide officer and member of the contract bargaining team. He holds a BA in German from Moravian College, an MA in Linguistic Theory from Syracuse University, and a PhD in Cultural Symbol Systems, also from Syracuse University. He has taught at Syracuse University and Chinese Culture University in Taipei. He is currently a lecturer in Philosophy at California State University, Chico, where he coordinates Critical

Thinking courses and the Certificate in Teaching Critical Thinking. Dr. Tropea is the author of numerous papers on philosophical counseling, Eastern thought, and postmodern philosophy. His book is *Religion, Ideology, and Heidegger's Concept of Falling*. At this writing, he is at work on a second book under the title *Religion, Ideology, and the Logic of Revelation*.

Ali Shehzad Zaidi teaches Spanish at the State University of New York at Canton. His degrees in literature include a masters in English from the University of Peshawar (Pakistan), a masters in Spanish from Queens College (City University of New York) and a doctorate in comparative literature from the University of Rochester. Zaidi has published comparative studies on Shakespeare and Calderón in *Studies in Philology, Hispanófila, Bulletin of the Comediantes*, and *The Grove*. His essays on the fantastic fiction of Mircea Eliade have been published in *Balkanistica* and *International Journal on Humanistic Ideology*. His essays on higher education have appeared in *Against The Current, Z, Monthly Review, Covert Action Quarterly*, and *New Politics*. He is the Director of Publications at the Transformative Studies Institute: transformativestudies.org.

Howard Zinn was a shipyard worker and an Air Force bombardier in World War II before taking advantage of the G.I. Bill of Rights to further his education. He received his B.A. from New York University 1951, his M.A. from Columbia University in 1952, his Ph.D. from Columbia University in 1958. His doctoral dissertation "LaGuardia in Congress" was an Albert Beveridge Prize publication of the American Historical Association. His first full time teaching position was at Spelman College in Atlanta, where he was chair of the department of history and social science from 1956–1963. While in the South he became active in the civil rights movement as a writer-participant, in Albany, Georgia, Selma, Alabama, and various towns in Mississippi. At this time he began publishing articles in *Harper's, The Nation*, and *The New Republic*. In 1964 he joined the faculty of Boston University, and that year he published two books on the South: *The Southern Mystique* (Knopf), and *SNCC: The New Abolitionists* (Beacon Press). Since that time he has published roughly twenty books, his best known being *A People's History of the United States*, which has gone through a number of editions, sold over a million copies, and been translated into a dozen languages. With Anthony Arnove he has edited the collection, *Voices of A People's History*. He has taught abroad as a visiting professor in Paris and Bologna, and has lectured in South Africa and Japan. He retired from Boston University in 1988 and is now Professor Emeritus there. He has received a number of awards, including the Lannan Foundation Literary Award. One of his recent publications is an Introduction to the new Princeton University Press edition of Henry David Thoreau's political writings. Many of his essays are collected in *The Zinn Reader* (Seven Stories Press). He spends much of his time these days speaking and writing on behalf of the abolition of war.

Notes

The Company We Keep (Berube, 1)

1 See Marc Bousquet, "AP Profile of Cary Nelson," *Brainstorm: Lives of the Mind*, 16 July 2008, http://chronicle.com/review/brainstorm/bousquet/associated-press-profiles-cary-nelson

2 American Council of Trustees and Alumni, "How Many Ward Churchills?" (Washington, D.C.: ACTA), 8, https://www.goacta.org/publications/downloads/ChurchillFinal.pdf.

3 Stuart Hall, "Authoritarian Populism: A Reply to Jessop et al.," in *The Hard Road to Renewal: Thatcherism and the Crisis of the Left*. (London: Verso, 1988), 151.

Introduction (Best, Nocella & McLaren, 13)

1 Through signing statements, a President can publically approve a legal act but then privately revise it to support Executive prerogative, rather than the wishes of Congress or intent of the law, such as demonstrated in January 2008 when Bush overrode Congress's prohibition on building permanent military bases in Iraq. Although there is a long history of Presidential use of signing statements dating back to James Monroe in 1822, Bush is unprecedented in the degree to which he deployed this problematic authority to enforce unitary executive power and undermine the separation of powers. On Bush's appalling use and abuse of over 800 signing statements, see Charlie Savage's superb exposé, "Bush challenges hundreds of laws," *The Boston Globe*, April 30, 2006, http://www.boston.com/news/nation/articles/2006/04/30/bush_challenges_hundreds_of_laws/. A full list of Bush's signing statements can be found at: http://www.coherentbabble.com/signingstatements/TOCindex.htm.

2 On the nature of free speech rights and the turbulent history of the First Amendment, see Anthony Lewis, *Freedom for the Thought That We Hate: A Biography of the First Amendment*. (New York: Basic Books, 2007). In the landmark 1969 case, Brandenburg v. Ohio, the Supreme Court ruled that one has the right to defend violence up to the point where "such advocacy is directed to inciting or producing imminent lawless action and is likely to incite or produce such action." See Brandenburg v. Ohio, 395 U.S. 444 (1969), at: http://caselaw.lp.findlaw.com/scripts/getcase.pl?court=US&vol=395&invol=444.

3 See Paul Wright (ed.), *Prison Nation: The Warehousing of America's Poor* (New York: Routledge, 2003); Ken McGrew, *Education's Prisoners: Schooling, The Political Economy, and the Prison Industrial Complex* (New York: Peter Lang, 2007); and Joel Dyer, *Perpetual Prisoner Machine: How America Profits From Crime* (New York: Basic Books, 2000).

4 Anti-communist loyalty oaths were imposed on University of California employees throughout the McCarthy era, and a few principled resisters were fired, but reinstated with back pay a decade later. It is still a requirement for all UC employees to swear allegiance to the US system "against all enemies, foreign and domestic" (see California Constitution, "Article 20, Miscellaneous Subjects," http://www.leginfo.ca.gov/.const/.article_20). In two separate incidents during the 2007–2008 academic year, two Quaker women—Wendy Gonaver at Cal State Fullerton and Marianne Kearney-Brown at Cal State East Bay—refused to sign the oath without qualification that their patriotism would not require engaging in any kind of violence. Both were fired, but reinstated upon signing a revised contract that included a non-violent stipulation. See "Loyalty Oaths Threaten Faculty Rights," the American Association of University Professors (AAUP), http://www.aaup.org/AAUP/issues/AF/oaths.htm.

5 On the history of political repression in the US, see Bud Schultz and Ruth Schultz, *It Did Happen Here: Recollections of Political Repression in America* (Los Angeles, CA: University of California Press, 1990); Robert Justin Goldstein, *Political Repression in Modern America: From 1870 to 1976* (Urbana and Chicago: University of Illinois Press, 2001); and Bud Schultz, *The Price of Dissent: Testimonies to Political Repression in America* (Berkeley, CA: University of California Press, 2001); and Chris Finan, *From the Palmer Raids to the Patriot Act: A History of the Fight for Free Speech in America* (Boston: Beacon Press, 2008).

6 For the early history of academic freedom and repression, see Richard Hofstadter and Walter P. Metzger, *The Development of Academic Freedom in the United States* (New York: Columbia University Press, 1957); Walter P. Metzger, *Academic Freedom in the Age of the University* (New York: Columbia University Press, 1961). Two early philosophical analyses of academic freedom are: Russell Kirk, *Academic Freedom: An Essay in Definition* (Chicago: Henry Regnery Company, 1955); and Robert M. MacIver, *Academic Freedom in Our Time* (New York, Columbia University Press, 1955).

7 On the Bemis case, see Bertell Ollman, "The Ideal of Academic Freedom as the Ideology of Academic Repression, American Style," August 2006, http://www.nyu.edu/projects/ollman/docs/academic_freedom.php. Also see Harold E. Bergquist, Jr., "The Edward Bemis Controversy at the University of Chicago," *American Association of University Professors Bulletin*, 58 (1972), 383–393.

8 Our emphasis. Cited in Theodore Herfurth's vivid account of the Ely affair in "Sifting and Winnowing," http://www.library.wisc.edu/etext/WIReader/WER1035-Chpt1.html.

9 According to the *NationMaster Encyclopedia* entry on Jane Stanford, "This resulted in the American Association of University Professors' 'Report on Academic Freedom and Tenure' (1915), by Arthur Oncken Lovejoy and Edwin R. A. Seligman, and in the writing of the AAUP 1915 Declaration of Principles." http://74.125.45.132/search?q=cache:6QfwihQLpwsJ:www.nationmaster.com/encyclopedia/Jane-Stanford+Edward+Ross+fired+from+stanford&hl=en&ct=clnk&cd=2&gl=us

10 Walter Metzger, *Academic Freedom in the Age of the University*.

11 On the Nearing case, see Bertell Ollman, "The Ideal of Academic Freedom as the Ideology of Academic Repression, American Style," op.cit.

12 Dewey cited in Robert B. Westbrook, *John Dewey and American Democracy* (Ithaca, NY: Cornell University Press, 1993), 91.

13 Ibid.

14 William Tierney and Vicente Lechuga, "Academic Freedom in the 21st Century," *Thought and Action*, Fall 2005, 2.

15 Tierney and Lechuga, Ibid. On the origins and development of the AAUP, see Walter P. Metzger, "Origins of the Association," *AAUP Bulletin*, Volume 51, Number 3 (Summer 1965): 229–237, http://www.aaup.org/NR/rdonlyres/165DDCF2-6391-488F-824E-9E57BF919046/0/OriginsoftheAssociation.pdf. On the nature, emergence, development, and current imperiled state of the university tenure system, see James T. Richardson, "Tenure in the New Millennium: Still a Valuable Concept," http://wolfweb.unr.edu/homepage/jtr/tenure.html. Among other things, the 1915 AAUP "Declaration of Principles on Academic Freedom and Academic Tenure" averred that faculty appointments be made within a tenure system, through employment contracts, and with clearly stated grounds for dismissal. The 1940 statement recommended that the tenure probationary period be seven years, which became the norm. In 1930, the AAUP also developed a system for censuring universities and colleges for violating recognized principles of tenure and academic freedom; see: "What Is Censure?" http://www.aaup.org/AAUP/issues/AF/censure.htm.

16 Certainly, for all the AAUP has accomplished, not everyone is happy with the organization's representation, particular many contemporary radical scholars. The "Ward Churchill Solidarity Network" site, for example, claims: "Academic freedom is supposed to be protected by the American Association of University Professors, which was created to counter pressure from trustees and corporate interests, but the AAUP is known for its thundering silence in the face of McCarthyism as well as the current attacks on scholars like Ward Churchill," http://www.uncutconscience.com/index.html.

17 For documents on the history of the origins and evolution of the AAUP, see "History of the AAUP," http://www.aaup.org/AAUP/about/history/default.htm. See the "1915 Declaration of Principles on Academic Freedom and Academic Tenure," http://www.aaup.org/AAUP/pubsres/policydocs/contents/1915.htm; and the "1940 Statement of Principles on Academic Freedom and Tenure"; and the "1970 Interpretive Comments," http://www.aaup.org/AAUP/pubsres/policydocs/contents/1940statement.htm. Importantly, one of the reports entitled, "The McCarthy Era," is a self-criticism of the organization's failures to confront the systematic repression, mire firings, and blacklisting from 1949–1954, whereupon the article clams a new general secretary, Ralph Fuchs, took much firmer stands in favor of academic freedom." See *Academe*, May–June, 1989, p. 29–30, http://www.aaup.org/NR/rdonlyres/31BF8601-1107-4CD6-BF74-058E04454C5B/0/ARestrospective.pdf.   The thirty-fifth annual meeting of the AAUP reaffirmed its belief that "institutions of higher education, both public and private, should be free form all political interference, and that the administrative and education policies of these institutions should be determined and controlled only by their duty constituted governing boards, their administrative officers, and their faculty" (Ibid.).

18 For a contemporary critique of these very ideas criticized by Dewey a century ago, see Jennifer Washburn, *University, Inc.: The Corporate Corruption of Higher Education* (New York: Basic Books, 2005).

19 For the argument that education promotes democratic character and contributes to the common good and a just society, see Dewey's classic analysis, *Democracy and Education* (New York: Free Press, 1997). Two decades after this book, Dewey reformulated his ideas by grounding education in a philosophy of experience, resulting in his book, *Experience and Education* (New York: Free Press, 1997).

20 Indeed, because of his defense of free speech and substantive democracy, his criticism of corporate-state domination, and his association with reformers and radicals of all stripes, Dewey was himself under FBI surveillance.

21 On HUAC's war against liberal Hollywood, see John Joseph Gladchuk, *Hollywood and Anticommunism: HUAC and the Evolution of the Red Menace, 1935–1950* (New York: Routledge, 2006).

22 On the Rapp-Coudert Committee and CCNY faculty and student political actions, see "The Struggle for Free Speech at CCNY," http://www.virtualny.cuny.edu/gutter/panels/panel16.html.

23 Bertrand Russell, *The Autobiography of Bertrand Russell: The Middle Years: 1914–1944* (New York: Bantam, 1969), 320. On the fascinating details and implications of the Russell controversy, see Thom Weidlich, *Appointment Denied: The Inquisition of Bertrand Russell* (New York: Prometheus Books, 1999). Also see John Dewey and Horace M. Kallen (eds.) *The Bertrand Russell Case* (New York: The Viking Press, 1941). This was neither the first nor the last time Russell had been denied a teaching appointment because of his politics. In 1916, due to the row over his anti-war protests, he was dismissed from Trinity College, and two years later, persistent in his pacifist demonstrations, he was charged with violating the Defence of the Realm Act and sentenced to six months in Brixton prison, beginning in September 1918. In 1961, three years after founding the Campaign for Nuclear Disarmament, Russell spent a week in jail for involvement in anti-nuclear protests. Contemptuous of wars, Russell quipped that "patriotism is the willingness to kill and be killed for trivial reasons."

24 Among the victims was labor historian Jack D. Foner, who was accused of giving excessive attention to the role of Blacks in American history. Foner refused to testify before the committee, was subsequently fired and blacklisted, and unable to secure academic employment for nearly three decades. Better late than never, in 1979 the New York State Board of Higher Education apologized for the committee's inquisition and mass firing as "an egregious violation of academic freedom" (cited in the memorial for Jack D. Foner, American Historical Association, April 2000, http://www.historians.org/perspectives/issues/2000/0004/0004mem2.cfm).

25 For a compelling account of how McCarthyism spread throughout higher education and placed an onerous burden on individuals called to testify before committee hearings, see Ellen Schrecker, *No Ivory Tower: McCarthyism and the Universities* (New York: Oxford University Press, 1986). Also see her more general critique of the many broad strands of "McCarthyism" operating in *Many Are the Crimes: McCarthyism in America* (New York: Little, Brown, and Company, 1998), as well as her

brief history and valuable collection of historical documents in *The Age of McCarthyism: A Brief History with Documents*, 2nd Edition (New York: Palgrave Macmillan, 2002). For a fascinating attempt to apply materialist sociology to the shifts in philosophy after the war, to show how McCarthyism dramatically affected philosophy by driving it toward an analytic, detached, and apolitical attitude, see John McCumber, *Time in the Ditch: American Philosophy and the McCarthy Era* (Evanston, Ill.: Northwestern University Press, 2001).

26 See David Cole, "The New McCarthyism: Repeating History in the War on Terrorism," *Harvard Civil Rights Civil Liberties Law Review* 1 (2003), 38. http://www.law.harvard.edu/students/orgs/crcl/vol38_1/cole.pdf.

27 For critical perspectives on the FBI, COINTELPRO, and the government's ruthless war against its own citizens throughout the entire spectrum of dissent in the 1960s, the 1970s, and beyond, see Nelson Blackstock, *Cointelpro: The FBI's Secret War on Political Freedom* (New York: Pathfinder Press, 1988); Brian Glick, *War at Home: Covert Action against U.S. Activists and What We Can About It* (Boston: South End Press, 1999); Ward Churchill and Jim Vander Wall, *The COINTELPRO Papers: Documents from the FBI's Secret Wars Against Dissent in the United States* (Boston: South End Press, 2001); Ward Churchill and Jim Vander Wall, *Agents of Repression: The FBI's Secret Wars Against the Black Panther Party and the American Indian Movement* (Boston: South End Press, 2001); Athan Theoharis, *The FBI & American Democracy: A Brief Critical History* (Lawrence, Kansas: University of Kansas Press, 2004); and David Cunningham, *There's Something Happening Here: The New Left, the Klan, and FBI Counterintelligence* (Berkeley: University of California Press, 2005). There is also a good collection of resources at: http://en.wikipedia.org/wiki/COINTELPRO.

28 Ollman describes the saga of his rejection and subsequent court trial in his book, *Ballbuster? True Confessions of a Marxist Businessman* (New York: Skull Press, 2002).

29 Cited in *Angela Davis: An Autobiography* (New York: International Publishers, 1989), 379.

30 The CIA was also involved in domestic surveillance and repression. Astonishingly, in June 2007, the CIA released its "family jewel" internal reports that secretly documented their surveillance tactics on social movements and progressives, available at: https://www.cia.gov/.

31 On the FBI war against CISPES, see Ross Gelbspan, *Break-Ins, Death Threats and the FBI: The Covert War Against the Central America Movement* (Boston, MA: South End Press, 1999). See David Fellman, "Academic Freedom," *Dictionary of the History of Ideas*, http://etext.lib.virginia.edu/cgi-local/DHI/dhiana.cgi?id=dv1-02.

32 See David Fellman, "Academic Freedom," *Dictionary of the History of Ideas*, http://etext.lib.virginia.edu/cgi-local/DHI/dhiana.cgi?id=dv1-02.

33 For a wide-ranging anthology on the concept of academic freedom, exploring topics from campus speech codes and the limits of academic freedom to the ethical issues involved in being an academic, see Louis Menand (ed.), *The Future of Academic Freedom* (Chicago: University of Chicago Press, 1998). An excellent resource of materials on academic freedom can be found in Stephen H. Aby and James C. Kuhn (compilers), *Academic Freedom: A Guide to the Literature* (New York: Greenwood Press 2000). Also, see Conrad Russell, *Academic Freedom* (New York: Routledge, 1993); Beshara Doumani, "Between Coercion and Privatization: Academic Freedom in the Twenty-First Century," in *Academic Freedom After September 11*, edited by Beshara Doumani (Cambridge, MA: Zone Books, 2006), 11–57; and Evan Gerstmann and Matthew J. Streb, *Academic Freedom at the Dawn of a New Century: How Terrorism, Governments, and Culture Wars Impact Free Speech* (Stanford: Stanford University Press, 2006). A sustained and informative discussion of academic freedom after 9/11 can be found in Tom Abowd, et. al., *Academic Freedom and Professional Responsibility After 9/11: A Handbook for Scholars and Teachers* (New York: Task Force on Middle East Anthropology, 2006), available online at http://www.meanthro.org/Handbook-1.pdf). See also the AAUP, "Academic Freedom and National Security in a Time of Crisis," *Academe* 89:6 (2003), www.aaup.org/AAUP/About/committees/committee+repts/cristime.htm; Jonathan R. Cole, "Academic Freedom Under Fire," *Daedalus* 134:2 (2005), pp. 1–23; and American Federation of Teachers, *Academic Freedom in the 21st-Century College and University* (2007), http://www.aft.org/higher_ed/pubs-reports/AcademicFreedomStatement.pdf.

There is a rich collection of documents and links on the Middle East Studies Association site, http://www.mesa.arizona.edu/aff/af_other_readings.htm. For a good discussion of the medieval origins of academic freedom, see William J. Hoye, "The religious roots of academic freedom." *Theological Studies* 58 (1997) 3:409–428.

34 See Rachel Levinson, "Academic Freedom and the First Amendment (2007)," AAUP, July 2007, http://www.aaup.org/AAUP/protect/legal/topics/firstamendment.htm. For an argument against the notion that academic freedom is a strong legal or political right, valid by virtue of being a "subset of freedom in general," see Stanley Fish, "Academic Freedom is Not a Divine Right," *The Chronicle of Higher Education*, September 5, 2008, http://chronicle.com/free/v55/i02/02b01001.htm.

35 See Louis Manand, "The Future of Academic Freedom," in *The Future of Academic Freedom*, 3–20.

36 This was acknowledged early on by the AAUP, in their "1940 Statement of Principles on Academic Freedom and Tenure," which reads: "Teachers are entitled to full freedom in research and in the publication of the results, subject to the adequate performance of their other academic duties… Teachers are entitled to freedom in the classroom in discussing their subject, but they should be careful not to introduce into their teaching controversial matter that has no relation to their subject… College and university teachers are citizens, members of a learned profession, and officers of an educational institution. When they speak or write as citizens, they should be free from institutional censorship or discipline, but their special position in the community imposes special obligations. As scholars and educational officers, they should remember that the public may judge their profession and their institution by their utterances. Hence they should at all times be accurate, should exercise appropriate restraint, should show respect for the opinions of others, and should make every effort to indicate that they are not speaking for the institution." http://www.aaup.org/AAUP/pubsres/policydocs/contents/1940statement.htm.

37 For a sharp rebuttal of the charges that liberal/left academics indoctrinate rather than educate their students, see "Freedom in the Classroom," the AAUP (2007), http://www.aaup.org/AAUP/comm/rep/A/class.htm. Also see their "Statement on Professional Ethics" (1966), http://www.aaup.org/AAUP/pubsres/policydocs/contents/statementonprofessionalethics.htm.

38 On student rights, see Gary Pavela, "Academic Freedom for Students Has Ancient Roots," *The Chronicle of Higher Education,* May 27, 2005, Volume 51, Issue 38, page B8. "Although the idea of student academic freedom may seem surprising to many faculty members," Pavela writes, the Supreme Court recognized the concept almost fifty years ago in Sweezy v. New Hampshire (1957). The court observed that "teachers and students must always remain free to inquire, to study, and to evaluate, to gain new maturity and understanding; otherwise our civilization will stagnate and die." Pavela claims that since the earliest roots of the academy, in Plato's circles, teachers were to stimulate the minds of students in a lively and relatively equal context, and not dogmatically dictate to them. Moreover, the "Socratic conception of teaching is also ingrained in the earliest formulations of academic freedom by the American Association of University Professors," which emphasized both the freedom to teach and the freedom to learn. Pavela also observes that "The idea that students should be seen as partners in academic inquiry was also embraced in the "Joint Statement on Rights and Freedoms of Students," endorsed by ten higher-education associations, and codified by the AAUP in 1967."

39 See Louis Althusser, *For Marx* (London: Verso, 2006); and Louis Althusser and Etienne Balibar, *Reading Capital* (London: Verso, 2009). By linking education to the functional role of reproducing capitalist social relations and granting important to the revolutionary project of demystifying ideology, Althusser was akin to Gramsci, although his structuralist Marxist led him down a path of economic determinism Gramsci avoided in order to theorize conditions of consciousness subject to change. For a classic argument that schools are crucial instruments of capitalist socialization and reproducing class hierarchies, see Paul Willis, *Learning to Labor: How Working Class Kids Get Working Class Jobs* (New York: Columbia University Press, 1981). The writings of Henry Giroux, Peter McLaren, and other contemporary critical pedagogues are rich with insights into the role schools play in capitalist oppression and human liberation as well.

40 For a remarkably astute and prescient critique of the instrumentalization of university education, whereby the rich pursuit of knowledge for personal enrichment and development of one's humanity rather than for capital enrichment and training for a career, see W. E. Du Bois' critique of his contemporary, Booker T. Washington. Whereas Washington advocated an industrial model of education that taught practical skills for the independence and survival of Blacks, Du Bois assailed the uncritical and obeisant attitude toward capitalism and the vulgar utilitarianism of this model quite influential in its day. This model capitulated to practical realities and social hierarchy and injustice, and catered more to the body than to the mind; hence, Du Bois asked, "Is not life more than meat, and the body more than raiment?.., We shall hardly induce black men to believe that if their stomachs be full, it matters little about their brains." (citations from *Three African American Classics* [Mineola, New York, 2007], 224, 232). This was a theory, Du Bois argued, that kept blacks "in their place" and acquiesced to racist dehumanization of blacks born to labor not think. Against this, Du Bois argued for a far richer notion of education that "must develop [all] men" in their whole being and potentials (232), that tried to "evolve that higher individualism which the centres of culture protect," such as would bring about "a loftier respect for the sovereignty of the human soul," that promoted freedom, self-development, and a "permanent uplifting and civilization of black men in America" (232, 224).

41 Bertell Ollman, "The Ideal of Academic Freedom as the Ideology of Academic Repression, American Style," http://www.nyu.edu/projects/ollman/docs/academic_freedom.php.

42 On the incredible campaign of censorship led by the Bush-Cheney administration and global oil giants like Exxon-Mobil, see Mark Bowen, *Censoring Science: Inside the Political Attack on Dr. James Hansen and the Truth of Global Warming* (New York: Dutton Adult, 2007). For analysis of the general aspects of Bush's war against science, see Seth Shulman, *Undermining Science: Suppression and Distortion in the Bush Administration* (University of California Press, 2008), and Chris Mooney, *The Republican War on Science* (New York: Basic Books, 2006).

43 Marc Bousquet offers a good discussion of the hyper-exploitation of teaching labor in his book *How the University Works: Higher Education and the Low-Wage Nation* (New York: NYU Press, 2008). For the numbers on how much profit a college or university can make by substituting part time instructors or even graduate students for tenured professors, see Cary Nelson, "The Corporate University," in Cary Nelson and Stephen Watt, *Academic Keywords: A Devil's Dictionary for Higher Education* (New York: Routledge, 1999) and online at: http://www.cary-nelson.org/nelson/corpuniv.html.

44 Foucault's genealogical analysis of power as a subtle force enacted through discipline, (which targets the body and behaviors through "techniques for assuring the ordering of human multiplicities" (1979: 218)) and normalization (which seeks the elimination of psychological and social irregularities to facilitate the production of homogeneously useful and docile subjects) is laid out in two key later works: *Discipline and Punish* (New York: Vintage Books, 1979) and *The History of Sexuality (Vol. 1)* (New York: Vintage Books, 1980).

45 For recent works on the militarization of the university, see: Jonathan Feldman, *Universities in the Business of Repression: The Academic-Military Industrial Complex in Central America* (Boston MA: South End Press, 1989); Sigmund Diamond, *Compromised Campus: The Collaboration of Universities with the Intelligence Community, 1945–1955* (New York: Oxford University Press, 1992); Richard C. Lewontin, *The Cold War & the University: Toward an Intellectual History of the Postwar Years* (New York: The New Press, 1997); Rebecca S. Lowen, *Creating the Cold War University: The Transformation of Stanford* (Berkeley: University of California Press, 1997); Christopher Simpson, *Universities and Empire: Money and Politics in the Social Sciences During the Cold War* (New York: New Press, 1999); Kenneth J. Saltman, *Education as Enforcement: The Militarization and Corporatization of Schools* (New York: RoutledgeFalmer, 2003); Henry Giroux, *The University in Chains: Confronting the Military-Industrial-Academic Complex* (New York: Paradigm Publishers, 2007); and Nick Turse, *The Complex: How the Military Invades Our Everyday Lives* (New York: Metropolitan Books. 2008).

46 Henry Giroux, *The University in Chains*; op. cit.

47 On the decline in state funding and the rise in private funding, see Cary Nelson, "The Corporate University," and Christopher Newfield, *Unmaking the Public University: The Forty-Year Assault on the*

Middle Class (Cambridge MA: Harvard University Press, 2008); and Christopher Newfield, *Ivy and Industry: Business and the Making of the American University* (Duke University Press 2003). For recent works on the corporatization of the university, see Bill Readings, *The University in Ruins* (Cambridge, MA: Harvard University Press, 1997): Lawrence C. Sole, *Leasing the Ivory Tower: The Corporate Take-over of Academia* (Boston: South End Press, 1999); Geoffry D. White and Flannery C. Hauck, *Campus, Inc.: Corporate Power in the Ivory Tower* (New York: Prometheus Books, 2000); Stanley Aronowitz, *The Knowledge Factory: Dismantling the Corporate University and Creating True Higher Learning* (Boston: Beacon Press, 2001); Derek Bok, *Universities in the Marketplace: The Commercialization of Higher Education* (Princeton: Princeton UP, 2003); Jennifer Washburn, *University, Inc.: The Corporate Corruption of Higher Education* (New York: Basic Books, 2006); and Frank Donoghue, *The Last Professors: The Corporate University and the Fate of the Humanities* (New York: Fordham University Press, 2008).

48 As President John F. Kennedy said in a television address on June 7, 1963: "The Negro baby born in America today, regardless of the section of the nation in which he is born, has about one-half as much chance of completing high school as a white baby born in the same place on the same day; one third as much chance of completing college; one third as much chance of becoming a professional man; twice as much chance of becoming unemployed; about one-seventh as much chance of earning $10,000 a year; a life expectancy which is seven years shorter; and the prospects of earning only half as much." Education is the key to overcoming such diminished expectations, and unequal access to higher learning erects steel barriers in the development of a culture, thwarting human potential and provoking a sense of desperation that leads to drugs, crime, violence, and other social scourges.

49 SDS and Davidson quotes are cited in George Keller, "Six Weeks That Shook Morningside," p. 7, http://www.thestickingplace.com/pdf/film/cct_spring_1968.pdf.

50 Ibid.

51 On the Columbia protests, see Joanne Grant, *Confrontation On Campus: The Columbia Pattern for the New Protest* (New York: Signet, 1969).

52 George Keller, "Six Weeks That Shook Morningside."

53 Interestingly, once members of the Student Afro Society (SAS) joined the Hamilton Hall take over, they debated SDS members over the real significant of the proposed construction; whereas SDS framed it as an environment issue, SAS members saw it in racial terms, believing that Columbia wanted literally to segregate the residents of Harlem from the predominantly white university population.

54 As René Viénet phrased the importance of this incipient movement from the outskirts of Paris, "The agitation launched at Nanterre by four or five revolutionaries, who would later constitute the Enragés, was to lead in less than five months to the near liquidation of the state." See Viénet's book, *Enragés and Situationists in the Occupations Movement* (1968), http://www.cddc.vt.edu/sionline/si/enrages.html.

55 On the background and controversy surrounding affirmative action policies, see Nicolaus Mills (ed.) *Debating Affirmative Action: Race, Gender, Ethnicity, and the Politics of Inclusion* (New York: Dell Publishing, 1994).

56 See Antonio Gramsci, *Selections from the Prison Notebooks* (New York: International Publishers, 2008).

57 On the complexities of identity politics, see Steven Best and Douglas Kellner, *Postmodern Theory: Critical Interrogations* (New York: Guilford Press, 1991).

58 We are aware of the problematic nature of the oppositions between right/left and conservative/liberal as if they were two polar opposites. The meaning of these terms have changed since first introduced in the eighteenth century and continue to change, but we follow the conservative convention of positing a sharp break and dichotomy between the conservative and liberal traditions, while also at times dismantling the dichotomy. See, for instance, Horowitz's numerous efforts to stabilize and separate the meanings of these terms on his site, *FrontPageMagazine.com*.

59 And yet, as we write, the class divide can never be sharper—due to unregulated credit schemes, massive government bailouts of corporations (which under Bush at least amounted to nothing less that legalized theft for exorbitant CEO bonuses), dramatic drops in home ownership rates and val-

ues, spikes in unemployment, and overall the gravest economic decline since the Great Depression. Obama's electoral win of republican state strongholds such as Iowa demonstrate his crossover and unifying appeal, but his rhetoric of "one America" simply obfuscates class issues. Palin and the far right were able to build support among poor and working class by portraying liberals as upper-class elites, and so the oppressed bond with the oppressor through ideology and morality, with economic contradictions rendered illusory.

60 This right-wing conflation was blatantly manifest in the 2008 presidential campaign, in which John McCain demonized Barack Obama as a "socialist" for proposing even modest measures of reform in a society so tilted toward the financial elite on Wall Street and elsewhere it is slipping into an abyss—as the state and Federal Reserve, in grand socialist style, doled out hundreds of billion dollars to prop up failing banking and insurance giants.

61 Daniel Pipes, "Why Do So Many Professors Hate America?" *History News Network*, November 18, 2002, online at: http://hnn.us/articles/1013.html.

62 Friedrich Nietzsche, *The Twilight of the Idols and The Anti-Christ: or How to Philosophize with a Hammer* (New York: Penguin Classics, 1990).

63 The "Marxism 101" reference was made in a 1988 Austin cable television interview by University of Texas at Austin philosophy department professor, Daniel Bonevac (who later reigned in quintessential McCarthyesque form as department chair and, sensing a good thing, cashed in on multiculturalism through a series of textbooks!). The later remark is from the John William Pope Center for Higher Education Policy scholar, Jay Schalin, in his article, "Teaching Marxist Subversion at UNC [University of North Carolina]," online at: http://www.popecenter.org/clarion_call/article.html?id=2086.

64 Roger Kimball, *Tenured Radicals, How Politics Has Corrupted Our Higher Education* (Chicago: Ivan R. Dee, 2008).

65 Michel Foucault, *Power/Knowledge: Selected Interviews and Other Writings, 1972–1977* (New York: Pantheon, 1980).

66 Paul Gross and Norman Levitt's *Higher Superstition: The Academic Left and Its Quarrels with Science* (Baltimore, MD: Johns Hopkins University Press, 1994).

67 In 2004, Bill O'Reilly of FOX News took the culture wars to an absurd extreme by joining the John Birch Society and other right-wing ideologues in polemicizing against secular culture's alleged "war on Christmas." This mother-of-all wars is being waged apparently through tactics such as denying religious floats in holiday parades and a vast conspiracy to replace the traditional greeting "Merry Christmas" with the corrupt secular phrase, "Happy Holidays." See "FOX hypes stories to claim 'Christmas Under Siege.'" *Media Matters For America*, December 10, 2004. http://mediamatters.org/items/200412100006.

68 For a history of the origin and use of "PC," see Ruth Perry, "A short history of the term 'politically correct'" in Patricia Aufderheide (ed.), *Beyond PC: Toward a Politics of Understanding* (Saint Paul, MN: Graywolf Press, 1992). A good overview of the debates over political correctness is Paul Berman, *Debating P.C.: The Controversy over Political Correctness on College Campuses* (New York: Laurel, 1992). For typically shrill right-wing critiques of the alleged politically correct outlook, see David Thibodaux, *Beyond Political Correctness: Are There Limits to This Lunacy?* (Lafayette, LA: Huntington House Publishers, 1994). Also see Dinesh D'Souza, *Illiberal Education: The Politics of Race and Sex on Campus*. (New York: Macmillan, 1991). From another far-right perspective, Bill Lind's essay, "The Origins of Political Correctness," tries to root PC in Marxist totalitarianism, cultural Marxism, and the Frankfurt School (http://www.academia.org/lectures/lind1.html). A good left-wing defense of the positions stigmatized as "PC," and discussion of how the term "politically correct" originated with in a humorous, self-effacing way, see John K. Wilson, *The Myth of Political Correctness: The Conservative Attack on Higher Education* (Durham NC: Duke University Press 1995). For significant works on culture wars and debates on multiculturalism, see: Thomas J. La Belle and Christopher R. Ward, *Multiculturalism and Education: Diversity and Its Impact on Schools and Society* (Albany: SUNY Press, 1994); David Theo Goldberg, *Multiculturalism: A Critical Reader* (Cambridge, MA: Blackwell Publishers, 1994); Russell Jacoby, *Dogmatic Wisdom: How the Culture Wars Divert Education and Distract America* (New

York: Doubleday, 1994); Liza Fiol-Matta and Mariam K. Chamberlain, *Women of Color and the Multicultural Curriculum: Transforming the College Classroom* (New York: The Feminist Press, 1994); and Todd Gitlin, *The Twilight of Common Dreams: Why America Is Wracked by Culture Wars* (New York: Henry Holt, 1995).

69 John K. Wilson, *The Myth of Political Correctness: The Conservative Attack on Higher Education.* Op. cit.

70 The University of the Pacific, for example, composed a policy on "Harassment, Coercion, and Discrimination," which prohibits any conduct "that undermines the emotional, physical, or ethical integrity of any community member," such as includes any expression, "intentional or unintentional," that "has the effect of demeaning, ridiculing, defaming, stigmatizing, intimidating, slandering or impeding the work or movement of a person or persons or conduct that supports or parodies the oppression of others." Cosmic in vagueness, this policy explicitly forbade any expression including "insults," "jokes," "teasing," and "derogatory comments," and seemed to virtually ensures the muzzling of free expression in campus dramas, paintings, literature classes, and protest actions, and thus it should be no surprise that many campus free speech codes were challenged in court. One group has come to specialize in challenging speech codes as violations of students' academic freedom, namely, the Foundation for Individual Rights in Education (FIRE), founded in 1999 by professors Alan Charles Kors and Harvey A. Silverglate, and has catalogued a huge number of cases at its website, http://www.thefire.org/. For an excellent history, critical analysis, and case study approach of how speech codes were used at numerous universities, see Donald Alexander Downs, *Restoring Free Speech and Liberty on Campus* (Cambridge: Cambridge University Press, 2006).

71 Cathy Young, "On campus, an absurd overregulation of sexual conduct," May 22, 2006, *The Boston Globe*, http://www.boston.com/news/globe/editorial_opinion/oped/articles/2006.

72 Quite consistently, the AAUP has criticized censorship of controversial viewpoints simpliciter, whether coming from the right or the left, and describes numerous cases of progressives blocking conservatives from speaking on their campuses; see a useful short history from the Cold War to post-9/11 of banning speakers by Jordan E. Kurland, "Ban Outside Speakers? Not on Our Watch," *Academe Online*, http://www.aaup.org/AAUP/pubsres/academe/2007/SO/Feat/Kurl.htm

73 John K. Wilson, *Patriotic Correctness: Academic Freedom and its Enemies* (Durham NC: Duke University Press: 1995).

74 On the student alterglobalization movement, see Liza Featherstone, "The New Student Movement," *The Nation*, May 15, 2000, pp. 11–18; and Jeremy Brecher, Tim Costello, and Brendan Smith, *Globalization from Below: The Power of Solidarity* (Boston MA: South End Press, 2000).

75 On the long and deplorable anti-union record of Yale University, see Kim Phillips Fein, "Yale Bites Unions: God, Country, and the Ruling Class," *The Nation*, July 2, 2001, 11–18.

76 On the global ambitions that motivated Bush's "war on terror," see Michel Chossudovsky, "America's War for Global Domination," Information Clearing House, December 15 2003, http://www.informationclearinghouse.info/article5428.htm. See also Amnesty International's monitoring of how nation states throughout the world—following the US example—began using the "war on terror" as a cover to suppress rights, in "The War on Terrorism," Amnesty International USA, Summer 2002, http://www.amnestyusa.org/Summer_/Charting_the_War_on_Terrorism/page.do?id=1105423&n1=2&n2=19&n3=405.

77 Blair cited in Christopher Caldwell, "The Post-8/10 World," *The New York Times*, August 20, 2006, http://www.nytimes.com/2006/08/20/magazine/20wwln_essay.html?_r=2&oref=slogin.

78 On the tenuous status of rights in the post-9/11 world, see Aryah Neier, "Did the Era of Rights End on September 11?," Crimes of War Project, http://www.crimesofwar.org/sept-mag/sept-neier-printer.html. For examples of how the USA PATRIOT Act has been used against law-abiding citizens, see Steve Watson, "Patriot Act Use Against US Citizens Extended," *Infowars.net*, September 9, 2005, http://infowars.net/articles/december2005/091205Patriot_act.htm. A profound case in point of the current assault on civil liberties is how the corporate-state complex pushed through new laws to criminalize a

broad range of animal rights protest activities, such as resulted in the imprisonment of the "SHAC 7" animal rights activists; see Steven Best, "The Animal Enterprise Terrorism Act: New, Improved, and ACLU Approved," *The International Journal of Inclusive Democracy*, Vol. 3, #3, July 2007, http://www.inclusivedemocracy.org/journal/vol3/vol3_no3_best.htm.

79 On the US government's treatment of non-citizens, see David Cole, *Enemy Aliens: Double Standards and Constitutional Freedoms in the War on Terrorism* (New York: New Press, 2005). On the long prehistory of using terrorism as a propaganda cover for crackdowns on human rights and civil liberties, see Sheldon Rampton, "Terrorism to End Terrorism," *PR Watch Newsletter*, Volume 8, No. 4, 2001, http://www.prwatch.org/prwissues/2001Q4/end_terror.html.

80 For critical analysis of the USA PATRIOT Act (a surreal acronym for "Uniting & Strengthening America Providing Appropriate Tools Required to Intercept and Obstruct Terrorism Act") in terms of its violation of the Constitution and threats to civil liberties, see Nancy Chang, *Silencing Political Dissent: How Post-September 11 Anti-Terrorism Measures Threaten Our Civil Liberties* (New York: Seven Stories Press, 2002); David Cole and James Dempsey, *Terrorism and the Constitution: Sacrificing Liberties in the Name of National Security* (New York: W. W. Norton & Company, 2002); and Nat Hentoff, *The War on the Bill of Rights and the Gathering Resistance* (New York: Seven Stories Press, 2003) For online resources, see the Electronic Freedom Foundation (http://www.eff.org/), the Center for Constitutional Rights (http://www.ccr-ny.org/v2/home.asp), and the Bill of Rights Defense Committee (http://www.bordc.org/).

81 On the cooperation of major phone and internet companies with the government's surveillance program, see Eric Lichtblau and James Risen, "Spy Agency Mined Vast Data Trove, Officials Report," *The New York Times*, December 24, 2005, at: http://www.nytimes.com/2005/12/24/politics/24spy.html?ei=5090&en=016edb46b79bde83&ex=1293080400&pagewanted=print. The state also worked with airlines to compile passenger information and placing many citizens on a "no fly" list. On the government's creation of a Terrorist Identity List with the cooperation of the major airlines, see William J. Krouse, "Terrorist Identification, Screening, and Tracking Under Homeland Security Presidential Directive," http://www.fas.org/irp/crs/RL32366.pdf.

82 In December 2005, NBC News revealed details from a 400-page Department of Defense database document on domestic "threats" to its installations, detailing 1,500 "suspicious incidents" from a 10-month period (see Lisa Myers et. al, "Is the Pentagon Spying on Americans?," MSNBC.com, December 14, 2005, http://www.msnbc.msn.com/id/10454316/). Dozens of peace groups were on the list, with a special focus on military counter-recruitment activities. According to NBC News, the database "includes nearly four dozen antiwar meetings or protests, including some that have taken place far from any military installation, post or recruitment center." Though hundreds of incidents were discounted as a threat, their names and details remained in the database. Similarly, the ACLU has obtained numerous documents showing government surveillance of innocent Americans (http://www.aclu.org/spyfiles). The Pentagon documents obtained by the ACLU reveal that "counterterrorism resources were used to monitor American groups opposed to the war in Iraq and military recruitment." The Pentagon's Threat and Local Observation Notice (TALON) database describe as "threats" planned demonstrations at military recruitment stations (http://www.aclu.org/safefree/spying/27459lgl20061121.html). For additional information on government surveillance of citizens, see: "Documents Reveal Widespread Domestic Surveillance of Political Groups," and The Bill of Rights Defense Committee reports at http://www.bordc.org/threats/spying-protesters.php.

83 On the Green Scare and general documentation of state repression, see Steven Best, "It's War! The Escalating Battle Between Activists and the Corporate State-Complex," in Steven Best and Anthony J. Nocella III (eds.), *Terrorists or Freedom Fighters? Reflections on the Liberation of Animals* (New York: Lantern Books, 2001), 300–339. Also see Will Potter's blog at: Greenisthenewred.com, and the "Greenscare" site at: http://www.greenscare.org/.

84 See Tariq Ramadan, "Why I'm Banned in the USA," *The Washington Post*, October 1, 2006, p. B01; Burton Bollag, "Politics Keeps Scholars Out of the U.S., Critics Say," *The Chronicle of Higher Education*, June 15, 2007; http://chronicle.com/free/v53/i41/41a00101.htm; Bruce Craig, "Scholars Become Targets of the Patriot Act," American Historical Association, December 29, 2008, http://www.historians.

org/perspectives/issues/2006/0604/0604new1.cfm; and Nina Bernstein, "A Music Scholar is Barred from the U.S., but No One Will Tell Her Why," *The New York Times*, September 17, 2007, A19.

85 In 2008, Congress wisely repealed the changes to revert the Insurrection Act to its prior state, but the US Army then announced plans to use soldiers battle-hardened in the Iraq war as part of the US Army Northern Command (NORTHCOM), created after 9/11 to respond to terrorist attacks, natural disasters, and "civil unrest and crowd control" in domestic conflicts—a clear move toward a fascist state that declares martial law and uses military forces to subdue civil unrest. For the text of the 2007 Defense Authorization Act, see: http://www.govtrack.us/congress/bill.xpd?bill=h109-5122.

86 The text of H.R. 1955 is online at: http://thomas.loc.gov/home/gpoxmlc110/h1955_rfs.xml. The bill was passed by the House but as of this writing has not yet cleared the Senate.

87 On the impact of neo-McCarthyism and the "war on terror" on academic culture, see Ellen Schrecker, "The New McCarthyism in Academe"; John K. Wilson, "Academic Freedom in America after 9/11"; and William G Tierney and Vicente M. Lechuga, "Academic Freedom in the 21st Century," in *Special Focus: Higher Education and the National Security State*, http://wwwZ.nea.org/he/ heta05/images/2005pg91.pdf. For a full treatment of the conservative assault on liberal politics and free speech in the post-9/11 context, see Beshara Doumani (ed.), *Academic Freedom after September 11* (op. cit.); John K. Wilson, *Patriotic Correctness: Academic Freedom and its Enemies* (op.cit.); and Evan Gerstmann and Matthew Streb (eds), *Academic Freedom at the Dawn of a New Century: How Terrorism, Governments, and Culture Wars Impact Free Speech* (Palo Alto, CA: Stanford University Press, 2008).

88 Robin Wilson, "Professors Found to Keep Political Views Quiet, but Students Detect Them," *The Chronicle of Higher Education*, October 17, 2008, http://chronicle.com/daily/2008/10/5176n.htm.

89 See their website at: http://www.goacta.org/.

90 Cited at http://www.uncutconscience.com/academic.html.

91 On the lavish funding of right-wing culture wars are lavish funded; see Steven Selden, "Who's Paying for the Culture Wars? Conservative critiques of higher education rely on liberal doses of cash," *Academe*, September 2005.

92 Joe Lieberman, "Letter to ACTA," *The Nation*, January 17, 2002, http://www.thenation.com/ doc/20020128/lieberman20020117.

93 Joel Benin, "The New American McCarthyism: Policing Thought about the Middle East," http:// www.stanford.edu/~beinin/New_McCarthyism.html.

94 Jerry L. Martin and Anne D. Neal, "Defending Civilization: How Our Universities Are Failing America and What Can be Done About It," *ACTA Report*, November 2001, http://www.la.utexas.edu /~chenry/2001LynnCheneyjsg01ax1.pdf. This statement was deleted from the revised February 2002 version of the report available on the ACTA website at: http://www.goacta.org/publications/Reports/ defciv.pdf.

95 Carolyn Baker, "Ward Churchill and the Imminent Destruction of American Higher Education." February 7, 2005, *Dissident Voice*, http://www.dissidentvoice.org/Feb05/Baker0207.htm.

96 For an excellent critique of the sheer absurdity of the report, see Paul Street, "Defending Civilization and The Myth of Radical Academia," *Znet*, July 15, 2002, http://www.zmag.org/znet/viewArticle/11888.

97 Anne D. Neal, ACTA Vice President, http://www.hartford-hwp.com/archives/45/196.html.

98 Anne D. Neal et. al., *How Many Ward Churchills?: A Study by the American Council of Trustees and Alumni* (Washington, DC: American Council of Trustees and Alumni, May 2006), 22, https://www. goacta.org/publications/downloads/ChurchillFinal.pdf.

99 See Leslie Rose, "David Horowitz: Battering Ram for Bush Regime," *Revolution Online* (August 28, 2005), http://rwor.org/a/013/horowitz-battering-ram.htm. For evidence of Hurwitz's paranoia, see

"Horowitz: 'There are 50,000 professors…[who] identify with the terrorists,'" http://mediamatters.org/items/200603030013.

100 On his conversion, demonization of the 1960s, see *Radical Son: A Generational Odyssey* (1998), (with Peter Collier) *Destructive Generation: Second Thoughts About the '60s* (1996), and *Left Illusions: An Intellectual Odyssey* (2003). A vivid summary and psychological interpretation of his political journey is provided by Scott Sherman's article, "David Horowitz's Long March," *The Nation,* June 15, 2009, http://www.thenation.com/doc/20000703/sherman/.

101 On Horowitz's funding, see the Media Transparency portrait, at: http://www.mediatransparency.org/personprofile.php?personID=15. This is an excellent resource site on Horowitz's mercenary work, agenda, and misadventures. On right-wing funding sources in general, see Dave Johnson, "Who's Behind the Attack on Liberal Professors?" *History News Network* (February 10, 2005), http://hnn.us/articles/1244.html.

102 See Rosa Brooks, *The Los Angeles Times,* September 15, 2006, http://www.latimes.com/news/opinion/la-oe-brooks15sep15,0,5829330.column?coll=la-opinion-center. Also see David Horowitz and Ben Johnson, "Campus Support for Terrorism," *DiscovertheNewtworks.org,* http://www.discoverthenetworks.org/Articles/CSPC_CampusTerrorism_EDr.pdf.

103 Thus, the Braun Alumni site asked students: "Do you have a professor who just can't stop talking about President Bush, about the war in Iraq, about the Republican Party, or any other ideological issue that has nothing to do with the class subject matter? It doesn't matter whether this is a past class, or your class for this coming winter quarter. If you help…expose the professor, we'll pay you for your work" (www.uclaprofs.com/studentshelp.html). M. Junaid Alam pens a forceful critique of the nefarious tactics used by Jones, so unscrupulous that even Horowitz complained; see "A Snapshot of the Right Wing Tactics," *AlterNet,* January 30, 2006, http://www.wiretapmag.org/stories/31536.

104 See the Bruin Alumni Association site at: www.bruinalumni.com/aboutus.html, and UCLAProfs.com at: http://www.uclaprofs.com/.

105 For a vivid description of the real impact of these smear tactics on professors, and the neo-McCarthyism spreading into school systems in general, see Gary Younge, "Silence in class," *The Guardian,* April 4, 2006, http://www.guardian.co.uk/education/2006/apr/04/internationaleducationnews.highereducation.

106 Horowitz, *How to Beat the Democrats and Other Subversive Ideas.* (Spence Publishing, 2002).

107 For the basic text of the Academic Bill of Rights, see the Students for Academic Freedom website, at: http://www.studentsforacademicfreedom.org/documents/1925/abor.html. Also, see David Horowitz, "In Defense of Intellectual Diversity," *The Chronicle of Higher Education,* February 13, 2004, http://chronicle.com/free/v50/i23/23b01201.htm.

108 For a critical dissection of studies used by Horowitz and the right to support their fallacious claim of a hegemonic "academic left," see Yoshie Furuhashi, "Conservatives: Underrepresented in Academia?" *Critical Montages Blog,* April 2, 2005, http://montages.blogspot.com/2005/04/conservatives-underrepresented-in.html. Also, see John F. Zipp and Ruddy Fenwick, "Is the Academy a Liberal Hegemony? The Political Orientation and Educational Values of Professors," *Public Opinion Quarterly* 70:3 (2006), http://poq.oxfordjournals.org/cgi/content/full/70/3/304?ijkey=dVt13UcYfsj5AyF&keytype=ref#SEC5; and the Free Exchange Coalition critique, http://www.freeexchangeoncampus.org/index.php?option=com_content&task=view&id=4&Itemid=5.

109 For a damning list of instances in which Horowitz and Co. get their facts wrong about professors, their teaching methods, and alleged student victimization, see the *Wikipedia* entry on Horowitz at: http://en.wikipedia.org/wiki/David_Horowitz.

110 For the AAUP critique of "balanced" teaching, see "Freedom in the Classroom" (2007), http://www.aaup.org/AAUP/comm/rep/A/class.htm. Also see the critique of the Free Exchange on Campus Coalition, http://www.freeexchangeoncampus.org/index.php?option=com_content&task=view&id=4&Itemid=5; and Stanley Fish's essay, "On Balance," *The Chronicle of Higher Education,* April 1, 2005, http://chronicle.com/jobs/2005/04/2005040101c.htm.

111 See Russell Jacoby, "The New PC: Crybaby Conservatives," *The Nation*, March 16, 2005, http://www.thenation.com/doc/20050404/jacoby.

112 "Intellectual Diversity and the So-Called Academic Bill of Rights: FAQs," Free Exchange on Campus Coalition, online at: http://www.freeexchangeoncampus.org/index.php?option=com_content&task=view&id=4&Itemid=5.

113 Craig Smith, "Crib Sheet: The American Council of Trustees and Alumni: How their 'Intellectual Diversity' agenda is advocating censorship," *CampusProgress.org*, March 27, 2007, http://www.campusprogress.org/tools/1489/crib-sheet-the-american-council-of-trustees-and-alumni.

114 Saree Makdisi, "Neocons Lay Siege to the Ivory Towers," *The Los Angeles Times*, May 4, 2005, http://www.latimes.com/news/opinion/commentary/la-oe-makdisi4may04,0,1186970.story?coll=la-news-comment-opinions.

115 David Beito, Ralph E. Luker, and Robert K. C. Johnson, "The AHA's Double Standard on Academic Freedom," *American Historical Association*, March 2006, http://www.historians.org/Perspectives/issues/2006/0603/0603vie2.cfm.

116 One can imagine these professors screaming out, similar to the authors in Bertolt Brecht's poem, "The Burning of the Books," in relation to the Nazi's book burnings:

> "One of the best, discovered with fury, when he studied the list
> Of the burned, that his books
> Had been forgotten. He rushed to his writing table
> Burn me, he wrote with hurrying pen, burn me!
> Do not treat me in this fashion. Don't leave me out."

Bertolt Brecht, *The Burning of the Books* (trans. H.R. Hays) (New York: NY: Grove Press, 1959).

117 See M. Junaid Alam, "A Snapshot of the Right Wing Tactics."

118 For a site that tracks the ever permutating fortunes of Horowitz's bill, see: http://www.freeexchangeoncampus.org/. For the AAUP's critical response to Horowitz's charges and his proposed Academic Bill of Rights, see "Academic Bill of Rights" (2003), http://www.aaup.org/AAUP/comm/rep/A/abor.htm, and their follow-up response, "The Academic Bill of Rights: Government Oversight of Teaching and Learning" (2008), http://www.aaup.org/AAUP/issues/ABOR/. The AAUP takes faculty abuse of power seriously, but insists on the importance of internal faculty self-review: "academic freedom can only be maintained so long as faculty remain autonomous and self-governing. We do not mean to imply, of course, that academic professionals never make mistakes or act in improper or unethical ways. But the AAUP has long stood for the proposition that violations of professional standards, like the principles of neutrality or nonindoctrination, are best remedied by the supervision of faculty peers" (http://www.aaup.org/AAUP/comm/rep/A/abor.htm).

119 The bill is online at: http://www.azleg.gov/FormatDocument.asp?inDoc=/legtext/48leg/2R/proposed/H.1108RP2.DOC.htm. Also, see James Vanlandingham, "Capitol Bill Aims to Control Leftist Profs," *Independent Florida Alligator*, March 23, 2005, http://www.alligator.org/pt2/050323freedom.php; and Scott Jaschik, "$500 Fines for Political Profs," Inside Higher Ed, February 19, 2007,http://insidehighered.com/layout/set/print/news/2007/02/19/ariz.

120 "Intellectual Diversity and the So-Called Academic Bill of Rights: FAQs," *Free Exchange on Campus Coalition*, http://www.freeexchangeoncampus.org/index.php?option=com_content&task=view&id=4&Itemid=5.

121 See Rosa Brooks, "Fear-Mongering Conservatives Are on Their Perennial Crusade To Purge Universities of Liberal Professors" (op.cit.).

122 See Christopher Newfield, *Unmaking the Public University: The Forty-Year Assault on the Middle Class* (Cambridge, MA: Harvard University Press, 2008).

123 For a video clip of Coulter's remark, see: http://www.greenisthenewred.com/blog/ann-coulter-joseph-mccarthy/977/

124 In his *Wall Street Journal* editorial entitled, "Why I fired Professor Churchill," (July 26, 2007), Brown actually acknowledged that the right-wing outcry surrounding Churchill's article prompted the investigation that led to his termination. Not satisfied with eliminating one tenured professor, Brown stated that UC would use Churchill's case as the basis for a broader "reform" of the university's tenure system, suggesting that administrators intended to undermine the tenure institution or that tenure would no longer guarantee free speech rights.

125 ACLU letter cited at: http://www.wsws.org/articles/2007/aug2007/chur-a28.shtml. On April 2, 2009, a jury of four men and two women ruled that the University of Colorado-Boulder unlawfully fired Churchill for expressing his political beliefs. Churchill has been lobbying to get his former position back, but UCB remains intransigently hostile to him.

126 The dragnet of academic repression is not limited to the US, of course, as a Nottingham student and staff member were detained for a week under British terrorism laws for attempting to print an al-Qaeda handbook for research purposes, and UK academics teaching or research subjects related to terrorism have to be extremely cautious lest they meet the same fate. The situation for academics is considerably worse in countries like Iraq, where kidnappings and murder of academics is common. For a good source of news on academic freedom issues worldwide, see: http://www.universityworld-news.com/.

127 See Juan Cole, "The New McCarthyism," *Salon.com*, March 22, 2005, http://dir.salon.com/story/opinion/feature/2005/04/22/mccarthy.

128 For a useful analysis of the commonalities as well as the differences underlying these recent Zionist attacks on academic freedom, see George Salzman, "Zionist censorship at colleges and universities: U of Ottawa, Canada; U of Cal at Santa Barbara; De Paul Univ, Chicago; Bard College, NY State; Clark U, Worcester, Mass.," May 12, 2009, http://site.www.umb.edu/faculty/salzman_g/t/2009-05-12.htm.

129 On neo-McCarthyism, see David Cole, "The New McCarthyism: Repeating History in the War on Terrorism," op. cit. Also see Ellen Schrecker, "The New McCarthyism in Academe," Fall 2005, Thought and Action, pp.103–119, http://www2.nea.org/he/heta05/images/2005pg103.pdf; Matthew Rothschild, "The New McCarthyism," *The Progressive*, January 2002, http://www.progressive.org/0901/roth0102.html; Juan Cole, "The New McCarthyism"; Joel Beinin, "The New McCarthyism: Policing Thought about the Middle East," in *Academic Freedom after September 11* (op. cit.).

130 See, for instance, the report on *Campus Watch*, stating, "One of Obama's close friends is PLO operative and anti-Israel professor from Columbia, Rashid Khalidi"—a patient fabrication (http://www.campus-watch.org/article/id/6080).

131 One firing of note, however, involves not a college professor but a high school teacher, Dave Warwak, who was terminated by the Fox Grove, Illinois school board in 2008 for the crime of teaching veganism to his students!

132 Churchill cited in Justin M. Park, "Under Attack: Free Speech on Campus," *Clamor Magazine*, Issue 34, September/October, http://clamormagazine.org/issues/34/culture.php.

133 Schrecker cited in Justin M. Park, "Under Attack: Free Speech on Campus."

134 As clear from the many examples given here and throughout the book, the most controversial territory and treacherous waters to wade is Middle Eastern Studies, given the intensity of the Israel-Palestine conflict and the massive influence of the Israeli lobby and Zionist ideologues in the US. See Joel Beinin, "The New McCarthyism: Policing Thought about the Middle East" (op. cit.).

135 Danile Pipes, founder of Campus Watch, is quite explicit about overriding faculty autonomy. Railing against professors who voice "relentless opposition to their own government," Pipes calls for "outsiders (alumni, state legislators, nonuniversity specialists, parents of students and others)" to "take steps to…establish standards for media statements by faculty." Cited in Eric Foner and Glenda Gilmore, "Rejoinder to Daniel Pipes: Fighting for Freedom of Speech," History News Network, December 30, 2002, http://hnn.us/articles/1186.html.

136 On the accountability of academics to a rigorous set of norms, such as best evaluated within faculty review committees, see AAUP documents, "Freedom in the Classroom" (2007), http://www.aaup.org/AAUP/comm/rep/A/class.htm.

137 Cited from the Ad Hoc Committee to Defend the University website, http://defend.university.googlepages.com/home. //ref?: http://www.insidehighered.com/news/2007/10/23/freedom

138 David N. Gibbs, "Spying, Secrecy and the University: The CIA is Back on Campus," April 7, 2003, *CounterPunch*, http://www.counterpunch.org/gibbs04072003.html.

139 Henry Giroux, *The University in Chains* (op. cit.). Also see Nicholas Turse, "The Military-Academic Complex," *TomDispatch.com*, April 29, 2004, http://www.countercurrents.org/us-turse290404.htm.

140 On the impact of computer technologies and "deskilling" of the labor force, see Harry Braverman, *Labor and Monopoly Capital: The Degradation of Work in the Twentieth Century* (New York: Monthly Review Press, 1998).

141 See David F. Noble, *Digital Diploma Mills: The Automation of Higher Education* (New York: Monthly Review Press, 2001).

142 http://www.nyu.edu/projects/ollman/docs/academic_freedom_content.php.

143 On the decline of the tenure system, see Alan Finder, "Decline of the Tenure Track Raises Concerns," *The New York Times*, November 20, 2007, http://www.nytimes.com/2007/11/20/education/20adjunct.html.

144 On the increasing use and abuse of adjunct instructors, see "Breadth of Adjunct Use and Abuse," *Inside Higher Education*, December 3, 2008, http://www.insidehighered.com/news/2008/12/03/adjunct. For statistics on the growth of the contingent workforce, see http://www.aftface.org/storage/face/documents/national_data_sheet.pdf. A critical response is given in Joe Berry's book, *Reclaiming the Ivory Tower: Organizing Adjuncts to Change Higher Education* (New York: Monthly Review Press, 2005). For recent alarming statistics, see Audrey Williams June, "Who's Teaching at American Colleges? Increasingly, Instructors Off the Tenure Track," *The Chronicle of Higher Education*, May 12, 2009, http://chronicle.com/daily/2009/05/17970n.htm.

145 Roger Bowen, "A Faustian Bargain for Academic Freedom," *The Chronicle of Higher Education*, October 3, 2008, Volume 55, Issue 6, A36, http://chronicle.com/weekly/v55/i06/06a03601.htm.

146 http://www2.nea.org/he/freedom/images/WVCC06cm.ppt#284.26.ContingentFaculty.

147 Faculty must also know their rights, and how to respond if their academic freedom is attack by a hostile force, to this end, see the excellent resource created by the Taskforce on Middle East Anthropology, "Academic Freedom and Professional Responsibility after 9/11: A Handbook for Scholars and Teachers," http://www.meanthro.org/handbook.htm.

148 See the Ad Hoc Committee to Defend the University (http://defend.university.googlepages.com/home); Scholars at Risk (http://scholarsatrisk.nyu.edu/); the American Federation of Teachers' report, "Academic Freedom in Higher Education" (http://www.aft.org/topics/academic-freedom/index.htm); the National Project to Defend Dissent & Critical Thinking in Academia (http://www.defendcritical-thinking.info/); Uncut Conscience: Official Site of Ward Churchill Solidarity Network (http://uncut-conscience.com/video_wardspeaks.html); and Support Bill Ayers (http://www.supportbillayers.org/).

Higher Education after September 11th (Giroux, 92)

1 Anthony Lewis reinforces this idea with his characterization of George W. Bush as "the Terror President." See Anthony Lewis, *New York Review of Books* (May 1, 2008), 43. The punishing state suspends important civil liberties in the name of liberty, reinforced through a culture of fear and the criminalization of social problems. See Randy Martin, "War, by All Means," *Social Text* 91 (Summer 2007), 13–22.

2 Michael Hardt and Antonio Negri, *Multitude: War and Democracy in the Age of Empire* (New York: Penguin Press, 2004).

3 Michel Foucault, *Society Must be Defended: Lectures at the College de France 1975–1976* (New York: Palgrave, 2003), 50–51.

4 Hardt and Negri, *Multitude*, 341.

5 I take these issues up in great detail in Henry A. Giroux, *The University in Chains: Confronting the Military-Industrial-Academic Complex* (Boulder: Paradigm, 2007).

6 Ian Angus, "Academic Freedom in the Corporate University," in Mark Cote, Richard J. F. Day, and Greig de Peuter, eds., *Utopian Pedagogy: Radical Experiments Against Neoliberal Globalization* (Toronto: University of Toronto Press, 2007), 69.

7 Philip Leopold, "The Professorial Entrepreneur," *Chronicle of Higher Education* (August 30, 2007). Online at: http://chronicle.com/jobs/news/2007/08/2007083001c/careers.html.

8 Jeffrey Brainard, "U.S. Defense Secretary Asks Universities for New Cooperation," *The Chronicle of Higher Education* (April 16, 2008). Online at: http://chronicle.com/news/article/4316/us-defense-secretary-asks-universities-for-new-cooperation.

9 I take this issue up in great detail in Henry A. Giroux and Susan Searls Giroux, *Take Back Higher Education* (New York: Palgrave Macmillan, 2004) and Henry A. Giroux, *Against the Terror of Neoliberalism* (Boulder: Paradigm Publishers, 2008).

10 John Dewey cited in E.L. Hollander, "The Engaged University," *Academe* (July–August, 2000). Online at: http://www.aaup.org/publications/Academe/2000/00ja/JA00Holl.htm.

11 John Dewey, *Individualism: Old and New* (New York: Minton, Balch, 1930), 41.

12 Richard J. Bernstein, *The Abuse of Evil: The Corruption of Politics and Religion since 9/11* (Cambridge: Polity Press, 2005), 45.

13 For an excellent analysis of this attack, see Beshara Doumani, "Between Coercion and Privatization: Academic Freedom in the Twenty-First Century," in *Academic Freedom After September 11*, ed. Beshara Doumani (Cambridge, MA: Zone Books, 2006), pp. 11–57; and Evan Gerstmann and Matthew J. Streb, *Academic Freedom at the Dawn of a New Century: How Terrorism, Governments, and Culture Wars Impact Free Speech* (Stanford: Stanford University Press, 2006). A sustained and informative discussion of academic freedom after 9/11 can be found in Tom Abowd, Fida Adely, Lori Allen, Laura Bier, and Amahl Bishara et al., *Academic Freedom and Professional Responsibility After 9/11: A Handbook for Scholars and Teachers* (New York: Task Force on Middle East Anthropology, 2006), available online at: http://www.meanthro.org/Handbook-1.pdf. See also AAUP, "Academic Freedom and National Security in a Time of Crisis," *Academe* 89:6 (2003), online at: www.aaup.org/AAUP/About/committees/committee+repts/cristime.htm; Jonathan R. Cole, "Academic Freedom Under Fire," *Daedalus* 134:2 (2005), pp. 1–23; and American Federation of Teachers, *Academic Freedom in the 21st-Century College and University* (2007), online at: http://www.aft.org/higher_ed/pubs-reports/AcademicFreedomStatement.pdf. For a diverse discussion of academic freedom in America, see Louis Menand, ed., *The Future of Academic Freedom* (Chicago: University of Chicago Press, 1996).

14 Editorial, "Targeting the Academy" *Media Transparency* (March 2003). Online at: http://www.mediatransparency.org/conservativephilanthropy.php?conservativePhilanthropyPageID=11

15 Ibid.

16 Max Blumenthal, "Princeton Tilts Right," *The Nation* (March 13, 2006), 14.

17 Kelly Field, "Recruiting for the Right," *The Chronicle of Higher Education* (January 12, 2007), A35.

18 Lewis F. Powell, Jr., "The Powell Memo," *ReclaimDemocracy.org* (August 23, 1971), available online at: http://reclaimdemocracy.org/corporate_accountability/powell_memo_lewis.html.

19 Ibid.

20 Lewis H. Lapham, "Tentacles of Rage—The Republican Propaganda Mill, a Brief History," *Harper's* (September 2004), 32.

21 Dave Johnson, "Who's Behind the Attack on Liberal Professors?" *History News Network* (February 10, 2005), available online at: http://hnn.us/articles/printfriendly/1244.html.

22 Alan Jones, "Connecting the Dots," *Inside Higher Ed* (June 16, 2006), available online at: http://insidehighered.com/views/2006/06/16/jones.

23 Ellen Schrecker, "Worse Than McCarthy," *Chronicle of Higher Education* 52:23 (February 10, 2006), B20.

24 Joel Beinin, "The New McCarthyism: Policing Thought about the Middle East," in *Academic Freedom after September 11*, ed. Beshara Doumani (New York: Zone Books, 2006), 242.

25 Jerry L. Martin and Anne D. Neal, "Defending Civilization: How Our Universities Are Failing America and What Can be Done About It," ACTA Report, November 2001; available online at: http://www.la.utexas.edu/~chenry/2001LynnCheneyjsg01ax1.pdf. This statement was deleted from the revised February 2002 version of the report available on the ACTA website at: http://www.goacta.org/publications/Reports/defciv.pdf.

26 I have taken this term, at least part of it, from a quote by Sheila Slaughter. Cited in Richard Byrne, "Scholars See need to Redefine and Protect Academic Freedom," *The Chronicle of Higher Education* (April 7, 2008). Online at: http://chronicle.com/daily/2008/04/2384n.htm.

27 See http://www.targetofopportunity.com/enemy_targets.htm.

28 Nicholas Turse, "The Military-Academic Complex," *TomDispatch.com* (April 29, 2004), http://www.countercurrents.org/us-turse290404.htm

29 Jonathan R. Cole, "The New McCarthyism," *Chronicle of Higher Education* 52:3 (September 9, 2005), B7.

30 Nina Bernstein, "A Music Scholar is Barred from the U.S., but No One Will Tell Her Why," *New York Times* (September 17, 2007), A19.

31 Ibid.

32 Burton Bollag, "Politics Keeps Scholars Out of the U.S., Critics Say," *The Chronicle of Higher Education* (June 15, 2007). Available online at: http://chronicle.com/free/v53/i41/41a00101.htm.

33 Annie Shuppy, "U.S. Denies a Visa to Swiss Muslim Scholar Who Was Barred in 2004," *Chronicle of Higher Education* (September 26, 2006). Available online at: http://chronicle.com/daily/2006/09/2006092603n.htm.

34 Tariq Ramadan, "Why I'm Banned in the USA," *Washington Post* (October 1, 2006), B01.

35 Herbert Marcuse, *Negations: Essays in Critical Theory*, trans. Jeremy J. Shapiro (New York: Penguin Press, 1969), 26.

36 I take these cases up in great detail in Henry A. Giroux, *The University in Chains* (Boulder: Paradigm Publishers, 2007).

37 Cited in Scott Smallwood, "Ward Churchill Gets a Warm Welcome in Speech in U. of Hawaii," *Chronicle of Higher Education* (February 24, 2005), online at: http://chronicle.com/daily/2005/02/2005022402.

38 Anne D. Neal et al., *How Many Ward Churchills?: A Study by the American Council of Trustees and Alumni* (Washington, DC: American Council of Trustees and Alumni, May 2006), 22.

39 Ibid., 2.

40 Ellen Schrecker, cited in Justin M. Park, "Under Attack: Free Speech on Campus," *Clamor* 34 (September/October, 2005), available online at: http://www.refuseandresist.org/culture/art.php?aid=2207.

41 Anne D. Neal et al., *How Many Ward Churchills?* 12.

42 James Pierson, "The Left University," *The Weekly Standard* 11:3 (October 3, 2005), available online at: http://www.weeklystandard.com/Content/Public/Articles/000/000/006/120xbklj.asp.

43 Roger Kimball, "Rethinking the University: A Battle Plan," *The New Criterion* 23 (May 2005), available online at: http://www.newcriterion.com/archive/23/may05/universe.htm.

44 CBN News, transcript of an interview with David Horowitz, "The 101 Most Dangerous Professors in America", *CBN News.com* (March 22, 2006), available online at: http://cbn.com/cbnnews/commentary/060322a.aspx.

45 Jonathan Cole, "Academic Freedom Under Fire."

46 Cited in Jennifer Jacobson, "What Makes David Run," *Chronicle of Higher Education* (May 6, 2005), A9.

47 The Academic Bill of Rights is available online at: http://www.studentsforacademicfreedom.org/abor.html.

48 David Horowitz, "In Defense of Intellectual Diversity," *Chronicle of Higher Education* 50:23 (February 13, 2004), B12.

49 See, for instance, John K. Wilson, *Patriotic Correctness: Academic Freedom and Its Enemies* (Boulder, CO: Paradigm Publishers, 2006); Russell Jacoby, "The New PC: Crybaby Conservatives," *The Nation* (April 4, 2006), pp. 11–15; Plissner, "Flunking Statistics"; and Yoshie, "Conservatives: Underrepresented in Academia?" *Critical Montages* blog (April 2, 2005), available online at: http://montages.blogspot.com/2005/04/conservatives-underrepresented-in.html.

50 See Lionel Lewis' response to Anne D. Neal in "Political Bias on Campus," *Academe* (May 5, 2005), available online at: http://www.aaup.org/publications/Academe/2005/05/mj/05mjlte.htm.

51 Gary Younge, "Silence in Class," *The Guardian* (April 3, 2006), available online at: http://www.guardian.co.uk/usa/story/0,1746227,00.html.

52 Jennifer Jacobson, "Conservatives in a Liberal Landscape," *Chronicle of Higher Education* 51:5 (September 24, 2004), A8–A11.

53 John F. Zipp and Ruddy Fenwick, "Is the Academy a Liberal Hegemony? The Political Orientation and Educational Values of Professors," *Public Opinion Quarterly* 70:3 (2006), available online at: http://poq.oxfordjournals.org/cgi/content/full/70/3/304?ijkey=dVt13UcYfsj5AyF&keytype=ref#SEC5.

54 Stanley Fish, "On Balance," *Chronicle of Higher Education* (April 1, 2005), available online at: http://chronicle.com/jobs/2005/04/2005040101c.htm.

55 Jacoby, "The New PC," 13.

56 The Students for Academic Freedom website address is: http://www.studentsforacademicfreedom.org.

57 Fulvia Carnevale and John Kelsey, "Art of the Possible: An Interview with Jacques Rancière," *Artform* (March 2007), 259.

58 David Horowitz, *The Professors: The 101 Most Dangerous Academics in America* (Washington, D.C.: Regnery Publishing, 2006).

59 Free Exchange on Campus, "Facts Count: An Analysis of David Horowitz's The Professors: The 101 Most Dangerous Academics in America," May 2006, 1. This report is available online: http://www.freeexchangeoncampus.org/index.php?option=com_docman&Itemid=25&task=view_category&catid=12&order=dmdate_published&ascdesc=DESC.

60 David Horowitz, *The Professors*, 200.

61 Cited in Bill Berkowitz, "Horowitz's Campus Jihads," *Dissident Voice* (October 9–19, 2004), pp. 1–6. Available online at: http://www.dissidentvoice.org/Oct04/Berkowitz1009.htm.

62 Cited in Leslie Rose, "David Horowitz: Battering Ram for Bush Regime," *Revolution Online* (August 28, 2005), available online at: http://rwor.org/a/013/horowitz-battering-ram.htm.

63 Larissa MacFarquhar, "The Devil's Accountant," *New Yorker* (March 31, 2003), available online at: http://www.analphilosopher.com/files/MacFarquhar,_The_Devil's_Accountant_(2003).pdf.

64 David Horowitz, *Unholy Alliance: Radical Islam and the American Left* (New York: National Book Network, 2004), 56.

65 This silly shame and smear list can be found online at: http://www.discoverthenetworks.com/individual.asp.

66 James Vanlandingham, "Capitol Bill Aims to Control Leftist Profs," *Independent Florida Alligator* (March 23, 2005), available online at: http://www.alligator.org/pt2/050323freedom.php.

67 In the House of Representatives, ABOR was taken up as HR 3077, which was part of HR 609. It is Title VI of the Higher Education Act. This is why it also called Title VI in some discussions. This house version is also called the College Access and Opportunity Act and passed the House. It has been recommended with some significant revisions to the Senate as S 1614. For a summary of the differences, see the AAUP analysis, online at: http://aaup.org/govrel/hea/index.htm.

68 Scott Jaschik, "$500 Fines for Political Profs," *Inside Higher Ed* (February 19, 2007), available online at: http://insidehighered.com/layout/set/print/news/2007/02/19/ariz.

69 Fish, "On Balance."

70 See Beinin, "The New McCarthyism."

71 I have taken up the issues of critical pedagogy, democracy, and schooling in a number of books. See Henry A. Giroux, *Border Crossings* (New York: Routledge, 2005); *Democracy on the Edge* (New York: Palgrave, 2006); *The Giroux Reader*, ed. Christopher Robbins (Boulder, CO: Paradigm Publishers, 2006); Henry A. Giroux and Susan Searls Giroux, *Take Back Higher Education* (New York: Palgrave, 2006); and Henry A. Giroux, *The University in Chains* (Boulder: Paradigm Publishers, 2007).

72 For an excellent analysis of contingent academic labor as part of the process of the subordination of higher education to the demands of capital and corporate power, see Marc Bousquet, *How the University Works: Higher Education and the Low-Wage Nation* (New York: New York University Press, 2008).

73 Ian Angus, "Academic Freedom in the Corporate University," 67–68.

74 These themes in Arendt's work are explored in detail in Elizabeth Young-Bruehl, *Why Arendt Matters* (New Haven: Yale University Press, 2006).

75 Jacques Rancière, cited in Fulvia Carnevale and John Kelsey, "Art of the Possible: An Interview with Jacques Rancière," *Artform* (March 2007), 263.

76 Hannah Arendt, *Origins of Totalitarianism* (New York: Harcourt Trade Publishers, New Edition, 2001).

77 Ian Angus, "Academic Freedom in the Corporate University," 64–65.

78 Greig de Peuter, "Universities, Intellectuals, and Multitudes: An Interview with Stuart Hall," ed. Mark Cote, Richard J. F. Day, and Greig de Peuter, *Utopian Pedagogy: Radical Experiments Against Neoliberal Globalization* (Toronto: University of Toronto Press, 2007), 113–114.

79 Zygmunt Bauman, cited in Zygmunt Bauman and Keith Tester, *Conversations with Zygmunt Bauman* (London: Polity Press, 2001), 4.

80 Hannah Arendt, *Men in Dark Times* (New York: Harcourt Brace, 1983), 4–5.

81 Zygmunt Bauman, *Liquid Life* (London: Polity Press, 2005), 151.

Academic Repression Past and Present (Parenti, 112)

1 For a fuller discussion of this point, see herein selection 24, "Monopoly Culture and Social Legitimacy."

2 For an early critique, see Thorstein Veblen's classic: *The Higher Learning in America, A Memorandum on the Conduct of Universities by Business Men* (B.W. Huebsch, 1918). On who dominates the university and who is served by it, see David N. Smith, *Who Rules the Universities?* (Monthly Review Press, 1974), John Trumpbour (ed.), *How Harvard Rules: Reason in the Service of Empire* (South End Press, 1989); and Geoffry D. White and Flannery Hauck, *Campus Inc.*(Prometheus, 2000). That the university is an extension of the ideological conformity found in primary and secondary schools is suggested by such works as Joel Spring, *Education and the Rise of the Corporate State* (Beacon Press, 1972).

3 Donald Tewksbury, *The Founding of American Colleges and Universities Before the Civil War* (Archon Press, 1965).

4 Richard Hofstadter and Walter Metzger, *The Development of Academic Freedom in the United States* (Columbia University Press, 1955).

5 The White and Elliot quotations are from Smith, *Who Rules the Universities?*, 85–86, 88.

6 Richard Hofstadter and Wilson Smith, *American Higher Education*, vol. 2 (University of Chicago Press, 1961), 883–892. See also Scott Nearing, *The Making of an American Radical: A Political Autobiography* (Harper & Row, 1972).

7 See the discussion in Ellen Schrecker, *No Ivory Tower* (Oxford University Press, 1986); and in regard to a specific discipline, see David Price, *Threatening Anthropology: McCarthyism and the FBI's Surveillance of Activist Anthropologists* (Duke University Press, 2004).

8 Paul Lasersfeld and Wagner Thielens Jr., *The Academic Mind* (Free Press, 1958), 52–53 and passim; also Robert MacIver, *Academic Freedom in Our Time* (Columbia University Press, 1955).

9 For details, see my "Struggles in Academe, A Personal Account," in Michael Parenti, *Dirty Truths* (City Lights Books, 1996), 235–252.

10 Angela Davis, *If They Come in the Morning* (New American Library, 1971); Marlene Dixon, *Things Which Are Done in Secret* (Black Rose Books, 1976); Philip Meranto and Matthew Lippman, *Guarding the Ivory Tower: Repression and Rebellion in Higher Education* (Lucha Publications, 1985), chapter 5.

11 *San Francisco Chronicle*, 8 December 1996.

12 Meranto and Lippman, *Guarding the Ivory Tower*, chapter 4.

13 This exchange was reported to me by Lombardi.

14 Ellen Schrecker, "Academic Freedom," in Cariag Kaplan and Ellen Schrecker (eds.), *Regulating the Intellectuals* (Praeger, 1983).

15 Florence Howe and Paul Lanter, *The Impact of Women's Studies on the Campus and the Disciplines* (National Institute of Education, 1980); Alan Colon, "Critical Issues in Black Studies: A Selective Analysis," *Journal of Negro Education* 53 (December 1984), 274–281; Carols Brossard, "Classifying Black Studies Programs," *Journal of Negro Education* 53 (November 1984), 282–290.

16 Bertell Ollman and Edward Vernoff (eds.), *The Left Academy: Marxist Scholarship on American Campuses* (McGraw Hill, 1982); and my article "Political Science Fiction," in Parenti, *Dirty Truths*, 221–233.

17 Ted Hayes, conversation with me, July 1979.

18 John Gerassi, correspondence to his department, 15 May 1994, made available to me by Gerassi.

19 Willard Miller interviewed by me, 11 July 1994.

20 *San Francisco Chronicle*, 2 June 2006.

21 *San Francisco Chronicle*, 2 December 2004.

22 Oneida Meranto, "The Third Wave of McCarthyism: Co-opting the Language of Inclusivity." *New Political Science* (27 June 2005), 221.

The War Against the "Academic Left" From Gross and Levitt to Gitlin (Best & Kellner, 122)

This study draws on an unpublished paper on Gross and Levitt by Steven Best and Douglas Kellner written during the time of their collaboration on *The Postmodern Turn* (New York: Guilford Press, 1997) and on a critique of the work of Todd Gitlin by Douglas Kellner published as "Education and the Academic Left: Critical Reflections on Todd Gitlin," *College Literature* 33/4 (Fall 2006): 137–154.

1 For an excellent critique of so-called "PC," see John Wilson, *The Myth of Political Correctness: The Conservative Attack on Higher Education* (Durham: Duke University Press, 1995).

2 Alan Sokal, "Transgressing the Boundaries: Toward a Transformative Hermeneutics of Quantum Gravity," *Social Text* 14 (1,2), 1996: 217–252.

3 It is clear that Sokal got many of his examples from Gross and Levitt and he is dishonest in utilizing their sources and arguments without properly attributing their contribution to his hoax. In his "satire," he describes their critiques as "right-wing" and "a vicious right-wing attack" ("Transgressing the Boundaries," notes 41 and 52). But in a May 15, 1996, National Public Radio interview and a *New York Times* interview (May 18, 1996: A11), Sokal admits that Gross and Levitt's jeremiad was the source of his inspiration. Further, there is evidence that others collaborated with Sokal who he has also failed to credit in his published accounts of the fraud. Ruth Rosen, in a *Los Angeles Times* article (May 23, 1996), indicates that she contributed to the article, Barbara Epstein was identified in an *In These Times* article as a "contributor" (May 27, 1996: 23), and we have talked to others who claim that they too contributed, indicating that Sokal had circulated his satire to a circle of friends and colleagues who helped him produce it. Indeed, it appears that Sokal was really not adroit or conversant enough with the sources he quotes to write the satire himself. For his post-*Social Text* foray into the science wars, see Alan Sokal and Jean Bricmont, *Fashionable Nonsense: Postmodern Intellectuals' Abuse of Science*. New York: Picador, 1999.

4 It becomes clear by page 38 of their book, that Gross and Levitt's real enemy is not the "academic left," but academic postmodernists, or radical social constructionists of various stripes. Indeed, they often substitute the term "academic postmodernism" for "academic left" or use the term "the postmodern academic left" (e.g., 104). The concept of "academic left" by contrast confuses the issue that their real target is Nietzsche, not Marx (indeed, Marx began the radical tradition of dialectical critique and support of the sciences and, if anything, was too uncritical). They see Nietzsche's doctrine of perspectivism to be "the central tenet of…the academic left" (38), but this is not a widely accepted position of traditional Marxists or others like radical environmentalists and animal rights activists who are also blended into the "academic left" soup. One of the great "howlers" of their book (to use one of their favorite terms as they point out factual errors in the "left" critique of science) is their equation of postmodern theory with the "critical theory" of the Frankfurt School (39), which otherwise they never mention (see below), failing to understand the significant tensions and contradictions between postmodern theory and the Frankfurt school (see Steven Best and Douglas Kellner, *Postmodern Theory: Critical Interrogations*. New York: Guilford Press, 1991; and Steven Best, *The Politics of Historical Vision: Marx, Foucault, and Habermas*. New York: Guilford Press, 1995).

5 Attacking an earlier study of postmodern science written by Best, "Postmodern Science and Social Theory," *Science-as-Culture* #11 (1991), Gross and Levitt attempt to smear him as a blind champion of postmodernism, despite his explicit criticisms and distance from many postmodern positions. And while they cited Best's collaboration with Kellner in *Postmodern Theory*, they obviously never read the book, or they would have discovered a defense of the project of the Enlightenment—also found in Best's *The Politics of Historical Vision*. While they feel they need to correct Best for an error in interpreting Newton's mathematics, they reveal themselves to be incapable of even correctly citing the works and authors they list in their bibliography, misreferencing Kellner in their bibliography as "David" rather than "Douglas," and referring the journal in which Best's article appeared as *Science and Culture* rather than Science-as-Culture (1994: 95). These blunders clearly disclose Gross and Levitt's haphazard "scholarship." Consequently, anyone in the scientific world or elsewhere seeking a reliable

reading of postmodern theories and contemporary analyses of science should definitely not consult Gross and Levitt.

6 See Steven Best, *The Politics of Historical Vision*.

7 We should also note that although the right had a predictable field day using the Sokal Affair to attack the so-called "academic left" in publications like *The Wall Street Journal*, *Fortune*, and *The Washington Times*, in which they called upon state legislators to monitor the "nonsense" going on in the universities, and to denigrate the humanities and cultural studies per se. Sokal also received positive publicity in progressive publications like *The Nation*, *In These Times*, and *Z Magazine*. The latter critiques point to a split within the Left between its more theoretically-inclined and university-based cadres and those outside the university and/or opposed to the new developments in critical theory.

8 Todd Gitlin, *The Whole World is Watching*. Berkeley: University of California Press, 1980; *Inside Prime Time*. New York: Pantheon, 1983; *The Sixties: Years of Hope, Days of Rage*. New York: Bantam Books, 1987; *The Twilight of Common Dreams: Why America is Wracked by Culture Wars*. New York: Metropolitan Books, 1995; and *The Intellectuals and the Flag*. New York: Columbia University Press, 2006.

9 Allan Bloom, *The Closing of the American Mind*. New York: Simon and Schuster, 1987.

10 On Marcuse, the great refusal, and the New Left, see Douglas Kellner, *Herbert Marcuse and the Crisis of Marxism*. Berkeley and London: University of California Press and Macmillan Press, 1984; and *Herbert Marcuse and the New Left*, edited with Introduction by Douglas Kellner. London and New York: Routledge, 2004.

11 On Marcuse's contributions to developing a critique of education and alternative pedagogies, see the essays collected from a UCLA AERA panel and graduate seminar on "The Origins of Critical Pedagogy" in *Policy Futures in Education*, Volume 4 Number 1 (2006) at http://www.wwwords.co.uk/pfie/content/pdfs/4/issue4_1.asp; this project has been developed in a greatly expanded version in a book on Marcuse's *Challenges to Education* published by Rowman and Littlefield in 2009.

12 On Foucault, see Steven Best and Douglas Kellner, *Postmodern Theory: Critical Interrogations*, and Steven Best, *The Politics of Historical Vision: Marx, Foucault, and Habermas*.

13 On varieties of postmodern theory, see Best and Kellner, *Postmodern Theory*.

14 See Douglas Kellner, *Media Culture: Cultural Studies, Identity and Politics Between the Modern and the Postmodern*. London and New York: Routledge, 1995.

15 Douglas Kellner, "Cultural Studies and Philosophy: An Intervention," in Toby Miller, editor, *A Companion to Cultural Studies*, Cambridge and Boston: Blackwell, 2001: 139–153. For critique of an early TV anthology that Gitlin helped produce, see Steven Best and Douglas Kellner, "(Re)Watching Television: Notes Toward a Political Criticism," *Diacritics* (Summer 1987), 97–113.

16 See Douglas Kellner, "Technological Transformation, Multiple Literacies, and the Re-visioning of Education," *E-Learning*, Volume 1, Number 1 2004: 9–37; Jeff Share and Douglas Kellner, "Toward Critical Media Literacy: Core concepts, debates, organization, and policy," *Discourse: Studies in the Cultural Politics of Education*, Vol. 26, Nr. 3 (September 2005): 369–386; and Richard Kahn and Douglas Kellner, "Oppositional Politics and the Internet: A Critical/Reconstructive Approach," *Cultural Politics*, Vol. 1, Issue 1, 2005: 75–100.

17 Henry A. Giroux, *Stormy Weather: Katrina and the Politics of Disposability*. Boulder Colorado: Paradigm Press, 2006.

18 On intellectuals, see Douglas Kellner, "Intellectuals, the Public Sphere, and New Technologies," in *Research in Philosophy and Technology*, Vol. 16 (1997): 15–32. On teachers as intellectuals, see Henry A. Giroux, *Teachers as Intellectuals*. Westport Ct.: Greenwood Press, 1988.

19 Stanley Aronowitz and Henry Giroux, *Education Still Under Siege*. Bergin & Garvey, 1993; and Henry Giroux and Susan Searls Giroux, *Take Back Higher Education: Race, Youth, and the Crisis of Democracy in the Post-Civil Rights Era*. London: Palgrave MacMillan, 2004.

20 See Douglas Kellner, *From September 11 to Terror War: The Dangers of the Bush Legacy*. Lanham, Md.: Rowman and Littlefield, 2003, and *Media Spectacle and the Crisis of Democracy*. Boulder, Col.: Paradigm Press, 2005; Henry A. Giroux, *Beyond the Spectacle of Terrorism: Global Uncertainty and the Challenge of the New Media*. Boulder, Col.: Paradigm Press, 2005; Stephen Eric Bronner, *Blood in the Sand*. Lexington, Ky.: University of Kentucky Press, 2005; Carl Boggs, *Imperial Delusions: American Militarism and Endless War*. Lanham, Md.: Rowman and Littlefield, 2005. Gitlin rarely refers to literature from solid radical scholars who he rather tars with broadside polemics and clichés, raising questions whether he really knows much about the "academic left" that has become the target of his rage and polemical assaults over the past decade.

21 See http://www.uclaprofs.com/articles/dirtythirty.html. The blacklist was compiled by a former UCLA Graduate student, Andrew Jones, who had previously been fired by his mentor David Horowitz for pressuring "students to file false reports about leftists" and for stealing Horowitz's mailing list of potential contributors to fund research for attacks on left-wing professors that he could make use of and profit from himself; see Stuart Silverstein, "Campus Activist Goes Right at 'Em," *The Los Angeles Times*, January 22, 2006: B1 and B16. This article also documents Jones' failure to hold down a job and resentment against left academics. Ultimately, Jones' offer to pay students $100 to spy on their teachers and record subversive comments aroused media critique and legal issues that distanced other conservatives from his witch-hunt.

22 Todd Gitlin, "The Self-Inflicted Wounds of the Academic Left" in *The Chronicle for Higher Education*, Vol. 52, Issue 35 (May 5, 2006): B6.

23 In the article cited in the previous note, Gitlin reviews Timothy Brennan, *Wars of Position: The Cultural Politics of Left and Right*. New York: Columbia University Press, 2006; Eric Lott, *The Disappearing Liberal Intellectual*. New York: Basic Books, 2006; and David Horowitz, *The Professors: The 101 Most Dangerous Academics in America*. New York: Regnery Publishing, 2006.

24 Daniel Lazare, "Review of Todd Gitlin's *The Intellectuals and the Flag*," *The Nation*, March 20, 2006 and Todd Gitlin, "Hatchet Man's Heresy Hunt," *The Nation*, April 3, 2006: 2.

25 For historical background on patriotism in the US, analysis of how it functions in everyday life and US culture and society, and a sharp critique of the connections between patriotism and militarism, see Boggs, *Imperial Delusions*.

Systemic Aspects of Academic Repression in the New World Order (Fotopolous, 143)

1 See Takis Fotopoulos, "Mass media, Culture and Democracy," *Democracy & Nature* (Volume 5 Number 1, March 1999).

2 See Takis Fotopoulos, *Towards An Inclusive Democracy* (London/N.Y.: Cassell/Continuum, 1997), Chapter 2

3 See Takis Fotopoulos, "The Myth of postmodernity," *Democracy & Nature*, vol 7 no 1 (March 2001), 27–76

4 Isaiah Berlin, "Two Concepts of Liberty" in Isaiah Berlin, *Four Essays on Liberty* (Oxford: Oxford University Press, 1969).

5 Karl Marx, *Critique of the Gotha Programme* (Moscow: Progress Publishers, 1966), 16.

6 See Takis Fotopoulos, *Towards An Inclusive Democracy*, Chapter 5; see also, for a brief description, the entry "Inclusive Democracy" in *Routledge Encyclopaedia of International Political Economy*, vol 2, 732–740 (London: Routledge, 2001).

7 See Takis Fotopoulos, "From (mis)education to Paideia," *Democracy & Nature*, vol. 9, no.1, (March 2003)

8 Ibid.

9 Karl Hess, "Rights and Reality" in *Renewing the Earth: The Promise of Social Ecology*, John Clark, ed. (London: Greenprint, 1990), 130–33.

Academic Freedom on the Rock(s) (Jensen, 164)

1 *Dennis v. United States*, 341 U.S. 494 (1951).

2 *Yates v. United States*, 354 U.S. 298 (1957).

3 See Noam Chomsky, et. al., *The Cold War and the University* (New York: New Press, 1997).

4 See http://w3.usf.edu/~uff/AlArian/. Al-Arian was indicted in 2003 by the US government on charges that he used an academic think-tank at USF and an Islamic charity as fronts to raise money for the Palestinian Islamic Jihad. A jury in December 2005 acquitted Al-Arian on eight counts, but deadlocked on nine others. To avoid another trial, Al-Arian in April 2006 pleaded guilty to one count of providing services to the group's members and was sentenced to four years and nine months, with credit for the three years and three months already served. See http://www.sptimes.com/2005/web-specials05/al-arian/.

5 http://www.commondreams.org/views01/0912-08.htm

6 Robert Jensen, "US just as guilty of committing own violent acts." *Houston Chronicle*, September 14, 2001, p. A-33. http://www.chron.com/cs/CDA/story.hts/editorial/1047072

7 Larry R. Faulkner, "Jensen's words his own," *Houston Chronicle*, September 19, 2001, p. A-39. http://www.chron.com/cs/CDA/story.hts/editorial/1053207#jensen

8 http://studentorgs.utexas.edu/yct/events/watchlist/

9 At one point I did publicly identify myself as gay. Presently, I am most accurately categorized as bisexual. For details, see Robert Jensen, "Homecoming: The Relevance of Radical Feminism for Gay Men," *Journal of Homosexuality*, 47:3/4 (2004): 75–81. Reprinted in Todd G. Morrison, ed., *Eclectic Views on Gay Male Pornography: Pornucopia* (Binghamton, NY: Harrington Park Press, 2004).

10 http://studentorgs.utexas.edu/yct/events/watchlist/

11 http://www.studentsforacademicfreedom.org/

12 For details on Horowitz, see http://www.frontpagemag.com/. Horowitz also has pursued this strategy in his book *The Professors: The 101 Most Dangerous Academics in America* (Washington, DC: Regnery, 2006). The description of me in that book borrows from the YCT list.

13 For an analysis of the limits of diversity talk, see "Against Diversity, For Politics" in Robert Jensen, *The Heart of Whiteness: Confronting Race, Racism, and White Privilege* (San Francisco: City Lights, 2005), 77–87.

14 For an assessment of Horowitz's and SAF's tactics and honesty, see Molly Riordan, "Academic Freedom Takes a Step to the Right," *PR Watch*, 2005. http://www.prwatch.org/prwissues/2005Q3/saf.html The group Free Exchange on Campus has also scrutinized Horowitz's book and found numerous errors and distortions. See http://www.freeexchangeoncampus.org/.

15 To be fair, this is perhaps not completely accurate. When I made this point in a committee meeting, a faculty member objected, saying he had been on the Parking Committee, which had the ability to set policy. To date, I have not taken the time to find out if this is true.

16 http://www.utexas.edu/faculty/council/2001-2002/legislation/ccafr.htm

17 Robert Jensen, "Abe Osheroff: On the joys and risks of living authentically in the empire," October 2005. http://thirdcoastactivist.org/abe-osheroff.pdf

The Myth of Academic Freedom (Churchill, 179)

These notes have been highly abbreviated due to space limitations. For full annotation, see the longer version of the essay forthcoming in *Works and Days* 51/51, Vol. 26 (2008). I would like to thank Akilah Jenga Kinnison for her exemplary editorial assistance in condensing it to the length appearing herein.

1 The language is quoted from the Laws of the Regents of the University of Colorado as amended on 10/10/02, at 5.D.1.

2 See Mary O'Melveny, "Portrait of a U.S. Political Prison: The Lexington High Security Unit for Women," in *Cages of Steel: The Politics of Imprisonment in the United States*, ed. Ward Churchill and J.J. Vander Wall (Washington, D.C.: Maisonneuve Press, 1992), 112–22.

3 On the Horowitz operation, see Scott Sherman, "David Horowitz's Long March," *The Nation*, July 2000; Media Transparency, "Center for the Study of Popular Culture" (available at http://www.media-transparency.org/recipientgrants.php). On Cheney and ACTA, see Annette Fuentes, "Trustees of the Right's Agenda: Conservative Appointees Holding Increasing Sway Over Public Higher Education," *The Nation*, Oct. 5, 1998.

4 Cecilia Le, "Ex-Radical Declines Position: Rosenberg Won't Teach at Hamilton," *Utica Observer-Dispatch*, Dec. 9, 2004; Sapna Kollali, "'60s Radical Won't Teach Course at Hamilton: College Worried About Bad Publicity," *Syracuse Post-Standard*, Dec. 9, 2004.

5 My op-ed, "Some People Push Back: On the Justice of Roosting Chickens," was written on 9/11 and posted on the *Dark Night* website on Sept. 12, 2001.

6 Ian Mandel, "Controversial speaker to visit Hill," *The Spectator* (Hamilton College), Jan. 21, 2005; Alaina Potrikus, "Controversy Festers on Hamilton Campus Again," *Syracuse Post-Standard*, Jan. 26, 2005.

7 "Review and Outlook: There They Go Again," *Wall Street Journal*, Jan. 28, 2005.

8 Brian Montopoli, "Spin Buster: Of Agendas, Fetishes and Crusades," *CJR Daily*, May 23, 2005; Scott Smallwood, "Inside a Free-Speech Firestorm: How a Professor's 3-year-old essay sparked a national controversy," *Chronicle of Higher Education*, Feb. 18, 2005.

9 Valerie Richardson, "Professor is disinvited to speak: College cites death threats," *Washington Times*, Feb. 2, 2005; Errol A. Cockfield, Jr., "Controversial speaker raises Pataki's wrath," *New York Newsday*, Feb. 1, 2005.

10 Alaina Potrikus, "Speaker Added to Panel at Hamilton: Angry Reaction to Scheduling of Activist Ward Churchill Prompts College's Decision," *Syracuse Post-Standard*, Jan. 31, 2005.

11 Richardson, "Professor disinvited"; Elizabeth Mattern Clark, "Churchill's N.Y. talk canceled: Death threats made against professor, Hamilton president," *Daily Camera*, Feb. 2, 2005.

12 On Rabinowitz's "resignation under duress," see the story from *New York Newsday*, Feb. 11, 2005, reprinted in the "Censorship Update" of *Newsletter on Intellectual Freedom*, Vol. LIV, No. 3 (May 2005) (available at http://members.ala.org/nif/v54n3/dateline.html). For the hard-right view, see David Horowitz, "Reforming Hamilton U. in the Wake of Ward Churchill," *FrontPageMagazine*, Feb. 14, 2005 (available at http://www.frontpagemag.com).

13 O'Reilly Factor Flash, Feb. 1, 2005 (transcript available at http://www.FoxNews.com).

14 O'Reilly made the claim on at least seven occasions, Hannity twice, Scarborough twice, and Limbaugh numerous times. The same was stated repeatedly in both of Colorado's major newspapers, the *Denver Post* and the *Rocky Mountain News*.

15 Talks were cancelled at the ostensibly First Amendment-oriented Wayne Morse Center for Law and Politics at the University of Oregon and the archetypal liberal Antioch College. At Eastern Washington University (EWU), students and faculty brought me to campus, rejecting President Stephen Jordan's attempt to cancel my visit.

16 Charlie Brennan, "CU postpones prof's talk: Security concerns cited as reason for sudden decision," *Rocky Mountain News*, Feb. 8, 2005; Charlie Brennan, "'I do not work for taxpayers,' prof says: Professor's supporters use speech as rally point," *Rocky Mountain News*, Feb. 9, 2005.

17 Joseph Thomas, "Safety vs. Free Speech: Churchill supporters take cancellation order to court," *Colorado Daily* (Boulder), Feb. 8, 2005.

18 Brennan, "'I do not work for taxpayers'"; Howard Pankratz and George Merritt, "Prof: Never back down," *Denver Post*, Feb. 9, 2005; Elizabeth Mattern Clark, "Churchill defends essay: Cheers, jeers from crowd for professor," *Daily Camera* (Boulder). Feb. 9, 2005; Joseph Thomas, Erin Wiggins and Katherine Crowell, "Churchill's side: Professor speaks out on campus; few or no problems in packed house," *Colorado Daily*, Feb. 9, 2005; Pierrette J. Shields, "Churchill fires back: CU professor says 9/11 words weren't referring to bystanders, firefighters," *Longmont Times-Call* (Colo.), Feb. 9, 2005.

19 AP, "Lawmakers urge cancellation of talk," *Rocky Mountain News*, Feb. 23, 2005.

20 Nass appeared on *The O'Reilly Factor* on Feb. 11, Horowitz on Feb. 16, and McCallum on Feb.18. Owens had appeared on Feb. 8 *Factor*; Montopoli, "Spin Buster." On Pataki, see note 9.

21 Aaron Nathans, "Chancellor Reviews Lecture Controversy," *Capital Times*, Mar. 26, 2005. The university had credentialed a total of 112 journalists and other media personnel; Samara Kalk Derby, "450 Grab Tickets: 200 Put on 'Free Speech Festival,'" *Capital Times*, Mar. 2, 2005.

22 Jeanette J. Lee (AP), "Prof draws crowd for Hawaiian speech: Dozens couldn't get seats at Ward Churchill's appearance; About 20 students protested it," *Denver Post*, Feb. 23, 2005.

23 By mid-2007, the "number of episodes of *The O'Reilly Factor* in which [my] name had been mentioned at least four times" had risen to seventy-nine; John Gravois, "Ward Churchill, by the Numbers," *Chronicle of Higher Education* News Blog, July 26, 2007 (available at http://chronicle.com/news/article/2753/ward-churchill-by-the-numbers).

24 Bill O'Reilly, "Talking Points," Feb. 2, 2005; quoted in Montopoli, "Spin Buster."

25 Barry Poulson, "From George Norlin to Ward Churchill: The University of Colorado, then and now," *Daily Camera*, Mar. 13, 2005.

26 Clint Talbot, "Target: tenure; During the Red Scare, an ambitious governor helped a renegade FBI director persecute suspected 'subversive' teachers and professors," *Daily Camera*, Feb. 13, 2005; Diane Carmen, "Churchill brouhaha echoes previous dissent at CU," *Denver Post*, Feb. 3, 2005.

27 Talbot, "Target: tenure."

28 Bronson Hilliard, "Trumbo's son to speak today: Fountain namesake Dalton Trumbo's son Chris to talk free speech, blacklist," *Colorado Daily*, Apr. 15, 2005.

29 T.R. Reid, "Professor Under Fire for 9/11 Comments: Free Speech Furor Roils Over Remarks," *The Washington Post*, Feb. 5, 2005. Also see Julie Greene, "Is Colorado in America?" *OAH Newsletter*, May 2005.

30 Both quoted in Carmen, "Churchill brouhaha."

31 "Churchill's 9/11 views not CU's, officials say: Professor's comments draw fire from congressmen," *Daily Camera*, Jan. 28, 2005.

32 Todd Neff, "Churchill raises some regents' ire: Regents will likely discuss professor at upcoming meeting," *Daily Camera*, Jan. 29, 2005.

33 "Churchill's 9/11 views not CU's."

34 See the banner headline on the front page of the *Rocky Mountain News* on Feb. 2: "Gov. to Prof: Quit." Also see Ryan Morgan, "Lawmakers condemn professor's remarks," *Boulder Daily Camera*, Feb. 1, 2005; "Regents should show Churchill the door," *Rocky Mountain News*, Feb. 2, 2005; Lynn Bartels, "Lawmakers urge firing of professor," *Rocky Mountain News*, Feb. 10, 2005.

35 See Julia C. Martinez, "Owens, wife of 28 years separate," *Denver Post*, Sept. 6, 2003; Michael Roberts, "Fooling Around," *Westword* (Denver), Apr. 1, 2005.

36 Charlie Brennan, "Owens: Prof must go: Governor weighs in on controversy over tenured professor," *Rocky Mountain News*, Feb. 2, 2005; Peggy Lowe, "Uproar at state Capitol: Legislators, Owens denounce professor; pass 9/11 resolution," *Rocky Mountain News*, February 3, 2005; "Prof denounced as 'inflammatory': State Senate condemns professor's 9/11 remarks," *Colorado Daily*, Feb. 4, 2005; Dave Curtin and Howard Pankratz, "Governor renews call for CU regents to dismiss Churchill," *Denver Post*, Feb. 10, 2005; Elizabeth Mattern Clark, "Owens renews call to fire Churchill: CU professor's scholarly work under scrutiny," *Boulder Daily Camera*, Feb. 10, 2005.

37 Jim Hughes, "Effort to oust CU prof rejected: Lawmaker tries to alter funding," *Denver Post*, March 10, 2005; Marianne Goodland, "House debates Long Bill amendment: Staff pay raises, Churchill issue targeted again," *Silver & Gold Record* (UCB), Apr. 14, 2005.

38 Jefferson Dodge, "Faculty defend free-speech rights of UCB prof amid public outcry: Regents to respond to Churchill's essay at meeting today," *Silver & Gold Record*, Feb. 3, 2005.

39 Elizabeth Mattern Clark, "CU to study professor's work, consider firing," *Daily Camera*, Feb. 4, 2005; Ryan Morgan, "GOP applauds CU actions on Churchill: One lawmaker calls for broader look at tenure system," *Daily Camera*, Feb. 4, 2005; Elizabeth Mattern Clark, "Churchill fires back at critics: 'No line' speech can't cross," *Daily Camera*, Mar. 4, 2005.

40 Arthur Kane, "Prof faces CU review: Regents apologize to nation," *Denver Post*, Feb. 4, 2005; Jefferson Dodge, "Regents endorse review of Churchill's scholarly record, issue apology to the U.S.," *Silver & Gold Record*, Feb. 10, 2005; Jefferson Dodge, "Churchill calls CU's review 'a hunting expedition," *Silver & Gold Record*, Feb. 10, 2005.

41 Dave Curtin and Arthur Kane, "CU weighs buyout for firebrand prof," *Denver Post*, Feb. 27, 2005.

42 Matthew Beaudin, "Churchill quits chairmanship: CU professor will continue tenured teaching position," *Daily Camera*, Feb. 1, 2005.

43 Charlie Brennan, "CU, Churchill near agreement: Settlement would end professor's tenure, lawyer says," *Rocky Mountain News*, Mar. 11, 2005.

44 Elizabeth Mattern Clark, "CU tenure attacked after spat: Professor's essay sparks calls to end protective system," *Daily Camera*, Feb. 6, 2005; AP, "Hoffman hints at changes in university's tenure policy: CU to announce decision on status of Churchill Monday," *Daily Camera*, Mar. 23, 2005.

45 Arthur Kane and Dave Curtin, "Regents balk at Churchill deal: Plagiarism allegation stalls buyout proposal," *Denver Post*, March 13, 2005; Laura Frank, "Churchill denies sole authorship: 'It won't be pretty' wasn't threat, lawyer says," *Rocky Mountain News*, Mar. 14, 2005.

46 Charlie Brennan, "No ruling on professor: CU interim chancellor still leading investigation of controversial figure," *Rocky Mountain News*, Mar. 9, 2005.

47 Quoted in John C. Ensslin, "Hoffman warns CU faculty of 'new McCarthyism': But president notes obligation to probe Churchill's record," *Rocky Mountain News*, Mar. 4, 2005.

48 Elizabeth Mattern Clark, "Ad demands halt to review: 200 faculty members call for halt to investigation," *Daily Camera*, Feb. 26, 2005.

49 Desiree Belmarez, "Activist empathizes with Churchill: Former Black Panther Angela Davis speaks at CU," *Daily Camera*, Mar. 2, 2005.

50 "Defend Dissent and Critical Thinking on Campus: An Open Letter from 400 Concerned Academics," *Daily Camera*, Mar. 22, 2005. Also see Brittany Anas, "375 Churchill supporters sign letter: Academics say investigation threatens freedom," *Daily Camera*, Mar. 19, 2005.

51 "Some Questions We Should Be Asking About the Attacks on Ward Churchill," *Daily Camera*, Mar. 25, 2005.

52 Elizabeth Mattern Clark, "Hoffman called on to resign: Regents Steinhauer and Bosley voice support for CU president," *Daily Camera*, Mar. 5, 2005; for editorials, see, e.g., "The sky-is-falling rhetoric at CU," *Denver Post*, Mar. 1, 2005; "Phony fears of McCarthyism," *Rocky Mountain News*, Mar. 5, 2005; Mike Rosen, "The McCarthy Gambit," *Rocky Mountain News*, Mar. 11, 2005.

53 Kirk Johnson, "University President Resigns at Colorado Amid Turmoil: Football and Professor's 9/11 Essay Cited," *The New York Times*, Mar. 8, 2005.

54 Hoffman had already been rendered vulnerable by scandals in both the athletic department and the university foundation, both of which were subjects of grand jury investigations; "Grand jury looking into Colo. Foundation, football camp," *USA Today*, Aug. 5, 2004.

55 David Curtin, Howard Pankratz, and Arthur Kane, "Questions stoke Churchill's firebrand past: Since Vietnam, a radical voice that inspires some, repels others and raises many questions," *Denver Post*, Feb. 13–14, 2005; Charlie Brennan, "Ward Churchill: A contentious life," *Rocky Mountain News*, Mar. 26, 2005.

56 See, e.g., Brittany Anas, "American Indian activist criticized CU's Churchill: Tape from 1992 sent to panel that is investigating tenured professor," *Daily Camera*, Mar. 17, 2005.

57 Matt Williams, "Road to professorship: Churchill path unusual, but not remarkable, CU insiders say," *Colorado Daily*, Feb. 18, 2005.

58 Larson, "Churchill's resume"; Curtin, Pankratz, and Kane, "Churchill's firebrand past"; Brennan, "Contentious life"; Steers, "Churchill…enigma"; Evans, "Churchill's real sin"; Amy Herdy, "Tribe shifts stand, acknowledges Churchill's alleged Cherokee ancestry," *Denver Post*, May 20, 2005.

59 Paul Campos, "Truth tricky for Churchill," *Rocky Mountain News*, Feb. 8, 2005. In fact, LaVelle does not accuse me of plagiarism. Rather, he suggests that I wrote material for which others have taken credit; John LaVelle, "The General Allotment Act 'Eligibility' Hoax: Distortions of Law, Policy, and the Derogation of American Indian Tribes," *Wicazo Sa Review* (Spring 1999), 251–52.

60 Philip DiStefano, "Report on Conclusion of Preliminary Review in the Matter of Professor Ward Churchill" (available at http://www.colorado.edu/news/reports/churchill/report.html).

61 See the entry on "Trial by news media" in *Black's Law Dictionary*, 6th ed. (St. Paul: West, 1990), 1505. Also see "Churchill tried in the media," *Critical Mass*, June 4, 2005.

62 Philip DiStefano to Prof. Joe Rosse, "Referral to the Standing Committee on Research Misconduct, University of Colorado at Boulder; Professor Ward Churchill," Mar. 29, 2005, 3 (copy on file; hereinafter cited as DiStefano Referral). The references are to "Bringing the Law Back Home: Application of the Genocide Convention to the United States," in my *Indians Are Us? Culture and Genocide in Native North America* (Monroe, ME: Common Courage Press, 1993), 11, 35; and *A Little Matter of Genocide: Holocaust and Denial in the Americas, 1492 through the Present* (San Francisco: City Lights, 1997), 155–56.

63 DiStefano "Referral," 1–2. The references are to the essay "Perversions of Justice: Examining the Doctrine of U.S. Rights to Occupancy in North America," in my *Struggle for the Land: Indigenous Resistance to Genocide, Ecocide and Expropriation in Contemporary North America* (Monroe, ME: Common Courage Press, 1993), 49; and "Like Sand in the Wind: The Making of an American Indian Diaspora in the United States," in the revised and expanded 2nd ed. of the same book, *Struggle for the Land: Native North American Resistance to Genocide, Ecocide and Colonization* (San Francisco: City Lights, 2002), 341.

64 DiStefano "Referral," 2. The reference is to the essay "Nobody's Pet Poodle: Jimmie Durham, An Artist for Native North America," in my *Indians Are Us?*, 89, 92.

65 DiStefano "Referral," 4. The first reference is to language from an article published under the by-line of Rebecca L. Robbins incorporated verbatim and without attribution into my essay "Perversions of Justice" (see note 81) at 93; and again in the same essay as it appears in my *Perversions of Justice: Indigenous Peoples and Angloamerican Law* (San Francisco: City Lights, 2003), 14. The last concerns language duplicating with insufficient attribution material in an article by Fay G. Cohen included in one of my anthologies. Curiously, the apparent plagiarism occurs in an essay that was not authored by me; see Institute for Natural Progress, "In Usual and Accustomed Places: Contemporary American Indian Fishing Rights Struggles," in M. Annette Jaimes, ed., *The State of Native America: Genocide, Colonization, and Resistance* (Boston: South End Press, 1992), 217–40.

66 "The question of Professor Churchill's Indian status with respect to research misconduct is whether he attempted to gain a scholarly voice, credibility, and an audience for his scholarship by wrongfully asserting that he is an American Indian... The committee should inquire as to whether Professor Churchill can assert a reasonable basis for clarifying such identity"; DiStefano "Referral," 5.

67 "A news story, in and of itself, does not constitute a new complaint"; UCB spokesperson Pauline Hale, quoted in Charlie Brennan and Kevin Vaughan, "For now, focus of Churchill probe set: At this stage, panel isn't allowed to consider new questions about professor," *Rocky Mountain News*, June 10, 2005.

68 Charlie Brennan, "CU expanding inquiry: Evidence uncovered by News to be included," *Rocky Mountain News*, June 16, 2005.

69 Kevin Vaughan, "Shifting facts amid a tide of contention: Sources cited don't back other smallpox claims by Churchill," *Rocky Mountain News*, June 6, 2005.

70 Laura Frank, "'The Water Plot' thickens: Essays listing professor as author mirror 1972 work by Canadian dams group," *Rocky Mountain News*, June 3, 2005.

71 Laura Frank, "Experts: Professor broke copyright law," *Rocky Mountain News*, June 3, 2005.

72 Charlie Brennan, "Family urges probe on Churchill book," *Rocky Mountain News*, June 18, 2005. On DiStefano's reversal of position, see Charlie Brennan, "Complaints by family sent to Churchill panel," *Rocky Mountain News*, Aug. 27, 2005.

73 See my biographical preface, "Kizhiibaabinesik: A Bright Star Burning Briefly," in Leah Renae Kelly, *In My Own Voice: Explorations in the Sociopolitical Context of Art and Cinema* (Winnipeg: Arbiter Ring, 2001), 9–58.

74 Letter, Rosse to DiStefano, Aug. 30, 2005 (copy on file). Also see AP, "3 allegations about Churchill not misconduct: CU panel tells DiStefano it is not committee's job to judge inaccuracies," *Daily Camera*, Sept. 8, 2005.

75 "Report to the Standing Committee on Research Misconduct from the Inquiry Subcommittee Appointed to Consider Allegations of Research Misconduct Against Professor Ward Churchill," Aug. 19, 2005 (copy on file; hereinafter referenced as Inquiry Report). Also see Amy Herdy, "CU panel drops three allegations against Churchill," *Denver Post*, Sept. 7, 2005.

76 These consisted of (1) my alleged misrepresentation of the 1887 Act, (2) similar misrepresentation of the 1990 Act, (3) my supposed fabrication of the John Smith/smallpox connection, circa 1614, (4) a similar fabrication of the U.S. Army/smallpox connection in 1837, (5) plagiarizing Dam the Dams, (6) plagiarizing Fay Cohen, and (7) plagiarizing Rebecca Robbins, an independent scholar; Inquiry Report (passim).

77 Charlie Brennan, "Churchill faces full CU inquiry: Panel zeroes in on seven allegations against professor," *Rocky Mountain News*, Sept. 10, 2005.

78 University of Colorado at Boulder, Operating Rules and Procedures of the Standing Committee on Research Misconduct, Sec. VI(A): Appointment of Investigative Committee (hereinafter cited as SCRM Rules; available at http://www.colorado.edu/Academics/research_misconduct_rules.html).

79 Email, Churchill to Rosse, Oct. 12, 2005. Also see email, Churchill to Rosse, Oct. 8, 2005, Subject: Re: Possible members of the SCRM Investigative Committee (copy on file).

80 Testimony of Joseph G. Rosse; Transcript, IN RE: Dismissal for Cause Hearing for Professor Ward Churchill (Jan. 20, 2007), 1886–87. This document is hereinafter cited as P&T Transcript.

81 Email, Churchill to Rosse, Oct. 8, 2005.

82 Email, Marianne (Mimi) Wesson to [name withheld at the request of the recipient], Feb. 28, 2005, Subject: SUSPECT: Re: [SALT] Letter Supporting Ward Churchill (copy on file). The acronym "SALT" refers to the Society of American Law Teachers.

83 P&T Transcript (Jan. 20, 2007), 1899–1900, 1937–42, 1962.

ACADEMIC REPRESSION

84 Wesson testified that she turned copies of all offending emails over to Rosse, in his capacity as chair of the SCRM, with the expectation that he, in turn, would provide copies to me, and professed "surprise" that he'd not done so; P&T Transcript (Jan. 8, 2007), 147–48, 154–55. Rosse, for his part, stated repeatedly that he did not recall her doing so; P&T Transcript (Jan. 20, 2007), 1938–40. In any case, copies have never been divulged by the university, despite its obligation under the Colorado Open Records Act to do so.

85 "The investigation is an information-seeking, non-adversarial proceeding"; SCRM Rules, Sec. IV.

86 P&T Transcript (Jan. 20, 2007) 1997.

87 While McIntosh also professed competence in both oral history and African history, her CV indicates her last training in African history was in 1963, and that she has no training at all in oral historiography (McIntosh CV [2006], on file). On McIntosh's claims, see Marianne Wesson, Robert N. Clinton, José E. Limón, Marjorie K. McIntosh, and Michael L. Radelet, "Report of the Investigative Committee of the Standing Committee on Research Misconduct at the University of Colorado at Boulder concerning Allegations of Academic Misconduct against Professor Ward Churchill" (May 9, 2006), 104–5 (hereinafter cited as Investigative Report; available at http://www.wardchurchill.net).

88 Radelet's CV is available at http://ibs.colorado.edu/directory/profiles/?people=radeletm.

89 Williams holds a joint appointment in the law school and the American Indian Studies program at Arizona. He also serves as a tribal judge for both the Pascua Yaqui and Tohono O'odam, as well as a legal consultant for the Navajo Nation; P&T Transcript (Jan. 11, 2007), 1298–99.

90 When asked at a subsequent hearing whether he'd perceived that the UCB administrators involved "had an agenda to get Churchill," Williams replied, "I was not comfortable with my conversations with Professor Wesson... I got the sense that she would be perfectly happy to see me go away; that I was a loose cannon, and that she didn't know quite what to do with me"; P&T Transcript (Jan. 11, 2007) 1393.

91 Testimony of Robert A. Williams, Jr., P&T Transcript (Jan. 11, 2007), 1309–10.

92 AP, "Churchill panel members named: CU identifies committee members," *Colorado Daily*, Nov. 3, 2005. The press release itself is dated Nov. 1, 2005.

93 See, e.g., Caplis and Silverman, "Is the Churchill review committee compromised?" (audio archive available at http://www.khow.com/hosts/caplis-silverman.html).

94 "Churchill inquiry hits another wall," *Rocky Mountain News*, Nov. 5, 2005.

95 Johansen recounts his experience with Paine and the Denver media in his *Silenced: Academic Freedom, Scientific Inquiry, and the First Amendment Under Siege in America* (Westport, CT: Praeger, 2007), xi–xiii; for Williams' recollections, see P&T Transcript (Jan. 11, 2007), 1304–9.

96 As Williams later testified, "I have never seen a process so mismanaged. It was becoming an absolute fiasco...so I said, you know, you've already destroyed Ward's reputation by the sloppy way you've run this. I'm not going to let you destroy [mine]"; P&T Transcript (Jan. 11, 2007), 1306–8.

97 Michael Yellow Bird, an associate professor of Indigenous Nations Studies at the University of Kansas, and probably the most knowledgeable scholar in the country with regard to indigenous understandings of the 1837 events at Fort Clark, was passed over because he was "too junior" in rank. Former UCB law professor Richard Delgado, acknowledged founder of an analytic method known as Critical Race Theory, was not selected because Rosse and Wesson decided his schedule might make it difficult for him to attend all of the meetings. Limón, who was selected instead of Delgado, was unable to attend all but the last meeting. On Yellow Bird's expertise, see P&T Transcript (Jan. 11, 2007), 1257–60; on his being passed over for selection, see Rosse testimony, P&T Transcript (Jan. 20, 2007), 1893. On Delgado's scholarly background, see P&T Transcript (Jan. 12, 2007), 1722–25; on his being passed over for selection, see P&T Transcript (Jan. 12, 2007), 1727.

98 Limón claims proficiency in "oral history" although his training is in English and anthropology, and his research/publications have been devoted entirely to literary analysis and "folklore." Similarly, although he bills himself as a "Chicano Studies scholar," his only experience in the discipline appears

to have been an appointment by the University of Texas administration to preside over the dismantlement of the previously vibrant Chicano Studies program on the Austin campus; Jordan Smith, "Closing the Books: UT editor says Mexican-American imprint was shuttered as whistle-blower retaliation," *Austin Chronicle*, Sept. 12, 2003.

99 See, e.g., testimony of Robert A. Williams, Jr., P&T Transcript (Jan. 11, 2007), 1321.

100 Email, Churchill to Rosse, Dec. 21, 2005, Subject: RE: committee (copy on file).

101 Transcript, Standing Committee on Research Misconduct Investigative Committee, Ward Churchill Case, Feb. 18, 2006 (copy on file; hereinafter cited as Investigative Transcript), 241. Also see Matt Williams, "Breaking silence: Committee investigating Churchill sets May 9 due date," *Colorado Daily*, Feb. 24, 2006.

102 Letter, Eric Elliff to Lane, Mar. 22, 2006 (copy on file). Elliff served as the panel's legal counsel.

103 The rules provide that the investigative panel will submit its report "upon its completion, no later than 120 days from initiation of the investigation. If unable to meet this time requirement, [it can] submit to the Office of Research Integrity [i.e., Rosse] a request for extension. The request must include an explanation for the delay, an interim report on progress to date, and an estimated date of completion"; SCRM Rules, Sec. IV D(10).

104 Investigative Report, 113–14.

105 Letter, Lane to Wesson, Jan. 25, 2006 (copy on file).

106 Investigative Report, 10.

107 Ibid.

108 University of Colorado, Faculty Senate Committee on Privilege and Tenure, Panel Report Regarding Dismissal for Cause of Ward Churchill and the Issue of Selective Enforcement, April 11, 2007, 13. This document is hereinafter cited as P&T Report (available at http://www.wardchurchill.net).

109 McCabe underwent neither particularized training in academic ethics nor the broader domain of philosophical ethics from which the subset ostensibly arose. He testified for UCB as a paid consultant; P&T Transcript (Jan. 8, 2007), 338–40.

110 P&T Transcript (Jan. 8, 2007), 351.

111 See the cross-examination of McCabe by Lane and myself; P&T Transcript (Jan. 8, 2007), 357–95.

112 Sara Burnett and Kevin Vaughan, "CU committee blasts Churchill: Panel alleges prof plagiarized, violate research standards," *Rocky Mountain News*, May 17, 2006; Jennifer Brown, "Panel on Churchill: Fire or Suspend Him," *Denver Post*, May 17, 2006.

113 Investigative Report, 99–102.

114 Pamela White, "A dangerous precedent: The investigation into Professor Ward Churchill draws fire from faculty and activists," *Boulder Weekly*, May 18, 2007.

115 University of Colorado at Boulder, Office of Research Integrity, Report and Recommendations of the Standing Committee on Research Misconduct Concerning Allegations of Research Misconduct by Professor Ward Churchill, June 13, 2006 (copy on file; hereinafter cited as SCRM Report). Also see Sara Burnett, "Faculty panel: Fire Churchill," *Rocky Mountain News*, June 14, 2006.

116 Letter, DiStefano to Churchill, Re: Notice of Intent to Dismiss, June 26, 2006 (copy on file). For press coverage, see, e.g., Brittany Anas, "Chancellor: Fire Churchill," *Daily Camera*, June 27, 2006.

117 The P&T hearings encumbered seven full days—extended from the five originally scheduled—ending on Jan. 21, 2007. The panel's report was submitted on April 11.

118 Interestingly, the SCRM Rules provide that a "preponderance of the evidence" is sufficient to establish "guilt," while the P&T requires that evidence be "clear and convincing." It is the latter standard that the investigative panel failed to meet.

119 See the longer version of this essay in *Works and Days* 51/51, Vol. 26 (2008).

120 P&T Report, 38, 42.

121 Ibid., 42.

122 Ibid., 48, 52

123 Ibid., 52, 53.

124 Ibid., 49.

125 Ibid., 51.

126 Ibid., 54.

127 Bernard Pratte, Jr., captain of the St. Peter's—the boat on which the infected items were transported upriver—stated in interview some thirty years after the fact that they were brought to St. Louis from Baltimore by an unnamed fur company employee who I've been able to identify as William May. Pratte says May placed the items aboard the St. Peter's itself. An independent source both identifies the infected items as having been blankets, and says that they were towed upriver in a pair of Mackinaw boats. It is confirmed that the St. Peter's was towing such boats. I have also been able to confirm that smallpox was present in Baltimore in late 1836, reaching epidemic proportions in 1837. Citations regarding these matters are being withheld, pending publication of an essay fully-devoted to the topic.

128 Investigative Transcript (Feb. 18, 2006), 107, 109.

129 In my initial 3-sentence depiction of the events at Ft. Clark in a 1991 legal brief later collected in slightly revised form in my *Indians Are Us?* (1993), I erroneously referred to "army doctors" being present. The error—which I've acknowledged—was not repeated in my subsequent publications and *Indians Are Us?* was never reprinted (thus precluding my correcting it therein).

130 Investigative Report, 73.

131 For the paragraphs in question, see my *Little Matter of Genocide*, 155–56. A pair of amplification notes are also included at the bottom of 155. On the sources cited by and contradicting McIntosh, see Charles Larpenteur, *Forty Years a Fur Trader on the Upper Missouri: The Personal Narrative of Charles Larpenteur*, 1833–1872 (Lincoln: University of Nebraska Press, 1989), 102, 369; R.G. Robertson, *Rotting Face: Smallpox and the American Indian* (Caldwell, ID: Caxton Press, 2001), 145.

132 See Barton H. Barbour, *Fort Union and the Upper Missouri Fur Trade* (Norman: University of Oklahoma Press, 2001) 136; Robertson, Rotting Face, 175–76; testimony of Michael J. Timbrook, Investigative Transcript (Feb. 18, 2006), 116.

133 Larpenteur, Forty Years, pp. 110–1. Also see Hiram Martin Chittendon, *A History of the American Fur Trade in the Far West*, 2 vols. (Stanford, CA: Academic Reprints, 1954) Vol. II, 625.

134 Annie Louise Able, ed., *Chardon's Journal at Fort Clark, 1834–1839* (Freeport, NY: Books for Libraries Press, 1932), 132.

135 Robertson, *Rotting Face*, 182. On the state of knowledge of contagion during the relevant period, see the Timbrook testimony, Investigative Transcript (Feb. 18, 2006), 115–16.

136 The Hidatsas were referred to by whites as "Minnetarees" and "Gros Ventres" in 1837. Two reputable analysts have indicated that the Minnetarees were reduced from 1,500 to 500, while the Gros Ventres, which had numbered 3000 in 1836, were "almost exterminated." They also state that of an estimated 1,600 Mandans in 1836, only 31 survived; E. Wagner Stearn and Allen E. Stearn, The Effect of Smallpox on the Destiny of the Amerindian (Boston: Bruce Humphries, 1945), 94.

137 Russell Thornton, *American Indian Holocaust and Survival: A Population History Since 1492* (Norman: University of Oklahoma Press, 1987), 94–5; cite on 95.

138 On pp. 62–63 of the Investigative Report, McIntosh discusses my citation, in "An American Holocaust?"—wherein I made my sole attribution of a number "as high as 400,000" to Thornton—of Stearn and Stearn, pp. 89–94. Since she describes what is said on pp. 89–90 of the latter, one assumes that McIntosh reviewed 94 as well. The book in question is Stearn and Stearn, *Effect of Smallpox*.

139 Stearn and Stern, *The Effect of Smallpox*, 94; see also Robert Boyd, *The Coming of the Spirit of Pestilence: Introduced Infectious Diseases and Population Decline Among Northwest Coast Indians* (Vancouver: University of British Columbia Press, 2000), 136.

140 See my "Closing Argument to the P&T Appeal Panel," Feb. 9, 2007 (available at http://www.wardchurchill.net).

141 P&T Report, 54.

142 P&T Transcript (Jan. 8, 2007), 365; also see 243, 249, 370.

143 Ibid., 365.

144 Ibid., 389–91.

145 Ibid. (Jan. 21, 2007), 2290–91.

146 Ibid. (Jan. 8, 2007), 387–93; Langer's rulings at pp. 390, 392. On ghostwriting, see Lois Einhorn, "Ghostwriting: Two Famous Ghosts Speak on Its Nature and Its Ethical Implications," in *Ethical Dimensions of Political Communication*, ed. Robert E. Denton, Jr., (Westport, CT: Praeger, 1991), 127, 133.

147 Investigative Report, 90. McCabe, also offering no supporting evidence, made an all but identical assertion; P&T Transcript (Jan. 8, 2007), 394. For their part, the P&T reviewers, "acknowledg[ing] the difficulty in finding specific guidelines related to ghostwriting"—in other words, they'd found none at all—nonetheless went on to speak of "what we take to be accepted standards by large components of the academic world [emphasis added]"; P&T Report, 66.

148 P&T Report, 66.

149 Ibid., 57.

150 The volume was Critical Issues in Native North America.

151 "Native America: The Water Plot," Z Magazine 4, no. 4 (Apr. 1991), 88–92.

152 Investigative Report, pp. 84, 87; P&T Report, 55, 56, 59.

153 Investigative Transcript (Apr. 1, 2006), 186–9; Investigative Report, 86–7; P&T Transcript (Jan. 8, 2007), 265; P&T Report, 56.

154 P&T Report, 59.

155 Dam the Dams is credited as first author, and "23 members of the original Dam the Dams team creating the pamphlet are listed by name" in the 1988 book chapter; P&T Report, 55.

156 Wesson testimony, P&T Transcript (Jan. 8, 2007) 263; quoted approvingly in the P&T Report, 59.

157 Quoted in Berny Morson, "1993 essay also raises questions: Churchill says pieces credited to others are actually his work," *Rocky Mountain News*, June 7, 2005.

158 Prof. Stephen Cahn, a specialist in academic ethics at the CUNY Graduate Center, quoted in Morson, "1993 essay also raises questions."

159 "There is no refutation of Professor Churchill's claim that others were responsible for the alleged plagiarism"; Investigative Report, 92, as paraphrased in P&T Report, 68.

160 P&T Report, 67; citing "Investigative Report, 91, as well as Dalhousie document itself.

161 The document at issue assumes the form of a letter: Brian C. Crocker, Q.C., University Secretary and Legal Counsel, Dalhousie University, to Social Sciences and Humanities Research Council of Canada, Re: Plagiarism, Feb. 9, 1997 (copy on file).

162 Investigative Report, 93; Investigative Transcript (Apr. 1, 2006), 119–28.

163 Cohen to Elliff (Apr. 11, 2006), 3.

164 See note 68 and attendant text.

165 At 6 of the P&T Report, the reviewers refer to "the allegations submitted by Professor LaVelle." At pp. 13–14 of the SCRM Report, however, it is observed that Rosse "posed this question directly to

Professor LaVelle, who responded by saying that he had not filed any complaint with the University [emphasis added]." On the same pages, Getches is paraphrased as saying that he had been in possession of the LaVelle article upon which the legal portions of DiStefano's complaint were based for roughly three years.

166 P&T Transcript (Jan. 20, 2007), 1784–91, 1823; SCRM Report, 14. For DiStefano's dating of the Getches/LaVelle call, see P&T Transcript (Jan. 10, 2007), 1110.

167 P&T Transcript (Jan. 20, 2007), 1823.

168 DiStefano testimony, P&T Transcript (Jan. 10, 2007), 1107.

169 P&T Report, 70; Investigative Report, 93.

170 P&T Report, 61; Investigative Report, 88.

171 P&T Report, 64, 66.

172 Ibid., 66.

173 Investigative Report, 89.

174 P&T Report, 66, 65; Investigative Report, 89.

175 All three are quoted in Morson, "1993 essay also raises questions."

176 McCabe testimony, P&T Transcript (Jan. 8, 2007), 337–97.

177 P&T Report, 64.

178 As is clearly stated on the first page of the P&T Report, it is the university's responsibility "to show by clear and convincing evidence" that I had in fact "engaged in 'conduct which falls below the minimum standards of professional integrity.'"

179 Investigative Report, 23, 24, 31.

180 Ibid., 23, 24, 31, 90.

181 In addition to the Williams testimony and testimony by Cornell professor and AIS scholar Eric Cheyfitz, I provided the reviewers with quotes and/or xeroxed excerpts from more than a dozen sources.

182 P&T Report, 66.

183 On Brown's background and appointment at CU, see Rachel Burns, "Don't dismiss him: Scholars publish letter requesting reversal," *Colorado Daily*, Apr. 12, 2007. The reference in her subtitle is to a full-page letter signed by Derrick Bell, Noam Chomsky, Juan Cole, Drucilla Cornell, Richard Delgado, Richard Falk, Irene Gendzier, Rasid Knaladi, Mahmood Mamdani, Immanuel Wallerstein, and Howard Zinn, which appeared in the *New York Review of Books* on Apr. 12, 2007.

184 Brown to Patricia "Pat" Hayes, Chair, Board of Regents of the University of Colorado, May 25, 2007 (copy on file). For press reaction, see, e.g., Jeff Kass and Lynn Bartles, "CU president recommends firing of Churchill," *Rocky Mountain News*, May 29, 2007.

185 Allison Sherry and Tom McGee, "Regents ax prof; battle not yet settled," *Denver Post*, July 25, 2007.

186 Jefferson Dodge, "Regents dismiss Churchill: Carlisle is sole Board member to vote against firing," *Silver & Gold Record*, July 26, 2007; Paula Plant, "Churchill sues CU: Carlisle explains her lone dissenting vote," *Colorado Daily*, July 26, 2007.

187 Cheyfitz is quoted extensively in Jefferson Dodge, "Debate over Churchill case persists: P&T report to go to President Brown next week," *Silver & Gold Record*, Mar. 29, 2007.

188 Brittany Anas and Vincent Bradshaw, "Students rally for prof: Group organizes talk about disputed professor," *Daily Camera*, Apr. 12, 2007. For backdrop, see "Statement of the AAUP Chapter at the University of Colorado at Boulder Regarding the Investigation and Recommended Termination of Professor Ward Churchill," Jan. 25, 2007 (available at http://www.aaup-cu.org/publications/chapter-statements.html).

189 Mimi Wesson, "An Error in report on Churchill needs correction," *Silver & Gold Record*, Apr. 12, 2007. Although "writing in [her] capacity as chair of the investigative committee," Wesson purported speak only for herself ("It is not possible at this juncture for me to speak in behalf of the entire committee…").

190 Professors Eric Cheyfitz, Elisa Facio, Vijay Gupta, Margaret LeCompte, Paul Levitt, Tom Mayer, Emma Perez, Martin Walter, and Michael Yellow Bird, "Open Letter from Faculty Calling for Churchill Report Retraction," *Silver & Gold Record*, Apr. 23, 2007.

191 Professors Vijay Gupta, Margaret LeCompte, Paul Levitt, Thomas Mayer, Emma Perez, Michael Yellow Bird, Eric Cheyfitz, Elisa Facio, Martin Walter, Leonard Baca, and Brenda Romero, "A Filing of Research Misconduct Charges Against the Churchill Investigating Committee," submitted to the SCRM on May 10, 2007 (available at http://wardchurchill.net). For background, see Jefferson Dodge, "Group: Look into Churchill committee," *Silver & Gold Record*, May 17, 2007.

192 Jennifer Harbury and Sharon H. Venne, attorneys, and Professors James M. Craven (Clark College), Ruth Hsu (University of Hawaii), David E. Stannard (University if Hawaii), and Haunani-Kay Trask (University of Hawaii), "Research Misconduct Complaint Concerning Investigative Committee Report of May 9, 2006," submitted to the SCRM on May 28, 2007 (available at http://www.wardchurchill.net).

193 Brittany Anas, "Professor fires back at CU: Churchill accuses investigators of serial plagiarism," *Daily Camera*, July 21, 2007.

194 Joseph H. Wenzel, "Comments regarding the May 9, 2006, Report of the Standing Committee on Research Misconduct at the University of Colorado, Boulder, against Professor Ward Churchill and an included Complaint of Research Misconduct against Professor Marjorie K. McIntosh, in particular, and the Committee Members, by their endorsement of the report," submitted to Joseph Rosse on Dec. 3, 2007 (copy on file). In a separate communication to me, dated Nov. 9, 2007, Wenzel also recommended the filing ethics charges against Wesson and Clinton with the relevant bar associations (copy on file).

195 My original grievance concerning the administration's continuous breaches of confidentiality was filed in June 2005.

196 Professors Lynda Dickson (chair), Jana Everett, Laurie Gaspar, and Joe Juhasz, "Level 2 Panel Report: Grievance on Breaches of Confidentiality against Professor Ward Churchill," July 10, 2007 (copy on file), 2–3.

197 Ibid., 3.

198 Ibid., 4.

199 Peterson to Weldon A. Lodwick, Privilege and Tenure Chair, Sept. 18, 2007 (copy on file).

200 DiStefano—who undoubtedly thought his services in my case would be more suitably rewarded—was thereupon forced to reclaim his permanent position as provost, displacing Susan Avery, who then returned to the faculty. Such is often the lot of liberals who collaborate in the fulfillment of reactionary agendas.

201 Letter, Rosse to Churchill, Re: Allegations of Research Misconduct, July 18, 2007 (copy on file).

202 Jefferson Dodge, "Churchill, others had filed claims against committee," *Silver & Gold Record*, July 26, 2007.

203 For one of many such statements by university officials, see DiStefano, as quoted in Dodge, "Debate over Churchill case persists."

204 Investigative Report, 12, 35. Also see Clinton testimony, P&T Transcript (Jan. 9, 2007), 622.; and McIntosh's claims of having engaged in primary research; Investigative Report, 41n82 and attendant text, 43n87, 44n89.

205 The Investigative Report includes such scholarly accoutrements as a review of the literature pertaining to the 1837 outbreak of smallpox on the upper Missouri (58–60), McIntosh's claim to have

engaged in primary research (see note 236), the "tracing of citation trials" (e.g., 76n199), and some 254 footnotes. As Clinton explained during his appearance before the P&T reviewers, "When you essentially attempt to present works as scholarship with footnotes, then presumably, you're saying, This is the result of research"; P&T Transcript (Jan. 9, 2007), 685.

206 In her P&T testimony, Wesson went further still, concurring in the assessment that McIntosh's section of the report—complete with "maps, charts, documents about the [1837] smallpox epidemic"— was "ready for publication right now"; P&T Transcript (Jan. 8, 2007), 254.

207 Clinton testimony, P&T Hearing Report (Jan. 9, 2007) 619; also see McIntosh testimony, P&T Transcript (Jan. 10, 2007), 919.

208 Quoted in Dodge, "Churchill, others had filed claims against committee."

209 "Submission of Professor Ward Churchill to the Board of Regents of the University of Colorado," July 12, 2007 (copy on file).

210 "An important letter from CU President Brown forwarded to CU alumni," July 24, 2007 (distributed by CU Boulder Alumni Association [cobadmin@coloradoalum.org] under the heading "Breaking news re: CU professor Churchill"). For background and analysis, see, e.g., Allison Sherry, "Donors applaud Churchill decision: A CU spokesman says money wasn't a factor in firing the prof, but there's no denying higher ed is in a squeeze," *Denver Post*, July 26, 2007.

211 See, e.g., Hank Brown, "Why I Fired Professor Churchill," *The Wall Street Journal*, July 26, 2007.

212 Berny Morson, "Fundraising record of $125 million in CU's sights," *Rocky Mountain News*, June 7, 2007. Brown attributed such largesse on the part of right-wing donors to "renewed confidence" in the university's leadership.

213 There were other candidates, but their names—and credentials—were withheld even from the regents on grounds of "confidentiality." On Benson's background, see "Bruce Benson Biography," *Daily Camera*, Feb. 21, 2008.

214 Stanley Fish, "Wanted: Someone Who Knows Nothing About the Job," *The New York Times*, Feb. 24, 2008.

215 Allison Sherry, "Benson barrels by foes: CU regents pledge support to new president after partisan 6-3 vote," *Denver Post*, Feb. 21, 2008.

216 See, e.g., Stephanie Simon, "Help Wanted: Lefty College Seeks Right-Wing Prof; CU-Boulder Bid to Endow a 'Conservative' Chair Leaves Both Sides Uneasy," *The Wall Street Journal*, May 13, 2008.

217 "University seeks suit dismissal: Fired professor alleges regents violated his First Amendment rights," Colorado Daily, Sept. 6, 2007.

218 Matt Labash, "The Ward Churchill Notoriety Tour: The worst professor in America meets his adoring public," *Weekly Standard*, Apr. 25, 2005.

219 David Horowitz, *The Professors: The 101 Most Dangerous Academics in America* (Washington, D.C. Regnery, 2006), ix–xxxvii.

220 ACTA, How Many Ward Churchills? May 2006 (promo available at http://www.goacta.org/press/ Press Releases/5-12-06/PR.pdf).

221 Although technically retired after thirty years in the Colorado state personnel system, I continue to write and publish at a steady rate, have delivered more than fifty invited lectures since 2005, and, at the request of a group of politically-motivated students, even taught a two-semester, non-credit course on the UCB campus during academic year 2007–08. See generally, Jefferson Dodge, "The firing of Ward Churchill: One year later; Former UCB prof taught, published, gets PERA checks," *Silver & Gold Record*, July 24, 2008; Ashleigh Oldland, "Firing hasn't pushed Churchill off stage: Facebook, scuffle with reporter keep ex-prof in sight," *Rocky Mountain News*, Aug. 31, 2008.

Operation Get Fired (Kahn, 200)

1 See http://www.caedefensefund.org/faq.html.

2 See http://thinkprogress.org/2006/07/24/inhofe-third-reich/.

3 See http://epw.senate.gov/109th/MARTOSKO_TESTIMONY.pdf.

4 See http://www.academia.org/campus_reports/2003/mar_2003_3.html.

5 See http://www.gourmetcruelty.com/news20041202.php.

6 See http://www.fbi.gov/pressrel/pressrel07/nsheab100307.htm.

7 See http://www.aaup-cu.org/whatwedo/anderson.html.

8 See http://www.thefire.org/index.php/article/8531.html.

9 See http://www.thefire.org/index.php/article/9440.html.

References

Altbach, 2007. *Academic Freedom in a Global Context: 21st Century Challenges.* The NEA 2007 Almanac of Higher Education. Washington, DC: National Education Association: 49–56.

Best, S. 2003. "The Fresno Frenzy: Invasion of the ELF and ALF." *Impact Press* (Apr/May). Online at: http://www.impactpress.com/articles/aprmay03/best4503.html.

———. 2004. "Banned in the UK!: The Home Office says 'Stay Home!' to U.S. Animal Rights Activists." *Impact Press* (Dec/Jan). Online at: http://www.impactpress.com/articles/decjan05/best120105.html.

———. 2006. "Senator James Inhofe: Top Terrorist Threat to the Planet Earth". *Impact Press* (Dec/Jan). Online at: http://www.impactpress.com/articles/winter06/bestwinter06.html.

Connelly, 2008. "ADL Condemns BIAW." *Seattle Post Intelligencer.* Online at: http://blog.seattlepi.nwsource.com/seattlepolitics/archives/141678.asp.

Cunningham, D. 2004. *There's Something Happening Here: The New Left, the Klan, and FBI Counterintelligence.* Berkeley, CA: University of California Press.

Giroux, H. 2007. *The University in Chains: Confronting the Military-Industrial-Academic Complex.* Boulder, CO: Paradigm Publishers.

Krupnik, M. 2008. "UC Seeks Law to Crack Down on Animal-Rights Protests." *Contra Costa Times* (April 14).

Marcuse, H. 1969. "Repressive Tolerance." In R. Wolff, B. Moore, Jr. and H. Marcuse (eds.), *A Critique of Pure Tolerance.* Boston: Beacon Press: 95–137.

Murr, A. 2008. "Targeting Researchers: A Court-Order says Animal Rights Activists Have Gone Too Far." *Newsweek* (Feb. 27). Online at: http://www.newsweek.com/id/116644/page/1.

Popper, K. 1971. *The Open Society and its Enemies* (Vol. 1). Princeton University: Princeton University Press.

Shor, I. & Freire. 1987. *A Pedagogy of Liberation: Dialogues on Transforming Education.* South Hadley, MA: Bergin and Garvey.

Scarce, R. 2005. *Contempt of Court: A Scholar's Battle for Free Speech from Behind Bars.* Lanham, MD: AltaMira Press.

Smallwood, S. 2005. "Speaking for the Animals, or the Terrorists?" *The Chronicle of Higher Education.* Vol. 51(48): A8.

Spanier, G. B. 2008. "National Security Intersects Higher Education." Online at: http://president.psu.edu/editorials/articles/NationalSecurity.html.

Radical Is as Radical Does (Martin, 226)

References

King, Mel. 1981. *Chain of Change: Struggles for Black Community Development*. South End Press.

Schmidt, Jeff. 2000. *Disciplined Minds: A Critical Look at Salaried Professionals and the Soul*. Rowman & Littlefield.

Scholarship Under the Gun, Lawsuit, and Innuendo (Davenort, 223)

1 http://www.aaup.org/AAUP/pubsres/policydocs/contents/1940statement.htm

2 Obviously there might be some overlap here, as private corporations might have some connection to the mass media, owning one or several different types or some within a particular category (e.g., radio, television, and newspapers).

3 The interested reader can find all of the relevant information at: http://web.mac.com/christiandavenport/iWeb/Sitepercent207/GenoDynamics.html

References

Cunningham, David. 2004. *There's Something Happening Here: the New Left, the Klan, and FBI Counterintelligence*. Berkeley: University of California Press.

Dahlerus, Claudia and Christian Davenport. 2000. "Tracking Down the Empirical Legacy of the Black Panther Party (or Notes on the Perils of Pursuing the Panthers)." In *Liberation, Imagination and the Black Panther Party*, Kathleen Cleaver and George Katsiaficas, eds. Boulder: Routledge. 2000.

Davenport, Christian. 1995. "Multi-Dimensional Threat Perception and State Repression: An Inquiry into Why States Apply Negative Sanctions." *American Journal of Political Science* 39(3):683–713

———. 1999. "Human Rights and the Democratic Proposition." *Journal of Conflict Resolution* 43(1): 92–116.

———. 2007a. *State Repression and the Domestic Democratic Peace*. New York/Cambridge, UK: Cambridge University Press.

———. 2007b. "State Repression and Political Order." *Annual Review of Political Science* 10: 1–25.

Davenport, Christian, Carol Mueller, and Hank Johnston, eds. 2004. *Repression and Mobilization*. Minneapolis, MN: University of Minnesota Press.

Davenport, Christian and Allan Stam. 2003. "Mass Killing and the Oases of Humanity: Understanding Rwandan Genocide and Resistance." National Science Foundation (SES-0321518).

Earl, Jennifer. 2003. "Tanks, Tear gas and Taxes: Toward a Theory of Movement Repression." *Sociological Theory* 21(1): 44–68.

Fein, Helen. 1995. "More Murder in the Middle—Life-Integrity Violations and Democracy in the World, 1987." *Human Rights Quarterly* 17(1): 170–91.

Gamson, William. 1975. *The Strategy of Social Protest*. Homewood, IL: Dorsey.

Goldstein, Robert. 1978. *Political Repression in Modern America: from 1870 to the Present*. Cambridge, MA: Schenkman.

Gross, Neil and Solon Simmons. 2007. "The Social and Political Views of American Professors." Working Paper.

Hafner-Burton, Emilie. 2005. "Right or Robust? The Sensitive Nature of Repression to Globalization." *Journal of Peace Research* 42(6):679–98.

Harff, Barbara. 2003. "No Lessons Learned from the Holocaust: Assessing Risks of Genocide and Political Mass Murder Since 1955." *American Political Science Review* 97(1): 57–74.

Poe Steve and C. Neal Tate. 1994. "Repression of Human Rights to Personal Integrity in the 1980s—a Global Analysis. *American Political Science Review* 88(4): 853–72.

Soule, Sarah A. 1997. "The Student Divestment Movement in the United States and Tactical Diffusion: The Shantytown Protest." *Social Forces* 75(3): 855–82.

Tilly, Charles. 1978. *From Mobilization to Revolution*. Reading, MA: Addison-Wesley.

Walter, Eugene. 1969. *Terror and Resistance; a Study of Political Violence, with Case Studies of Some Primitive African Communities*. New York: Oxford University Press.

Academic Repression and Academic Responsibility (Castro, 247)

Doctorow, E.L. "The White Whale." *The Nation*, July 14, 2008, 28–32.

Goldenweiser, A. 1936. "Loose Ends of a Theory on the Individual, Pattern, and Involution in Primitive Society," 99–104 in R.H. Lowie (ed.), *Essays in Anthropology Presented to A.L. Kroeber in Celebration of His 60th Birthday, June 11, 1936*. Berkeley: University of California Press.

Hentoff, Nate. 1997. *Speaking Freely*. New York: Alfred A. Knopf.

Malik, Kenan. 2001. *Man, Beast and Zombie: What Science Can and Cannot Tell Us About Human Nature*. London: Phoenix.

Mencken, H. L. 1922. *Prejudices: Third Series*. New York: Alfred A. Knopf.

Price, David. 2004. *Threatening Anthropology: McCarthyism and the FBI's Surveillance of Activist Anthropologist*. Durham: Duke University Press.

Seldes, George. 1943. *Facts and Fascism*. New York: In Fact.

Seldes, George. 1968. *Never Tire of Protesting*. New York: Lyle Stewart.

Seldes, George, 1997. *Witness to a Century*. New York: Ballantine Books.

Seldes, George, various dates. *In Fact*.

Stone, Geoffrey R. 2004. *Perilous Times*. New York: Norton.

United States, Department of Homeland Security, Traveler Redress Inquiry Program. 2008. http://www.dhs.gov/trip.

Wax, Dustin M. (editor). 2008. *Anthropology at the Dawn of the Cold War*. London: Pluto Press.

Teaching in a State of Fear* (Sheehi, 248)

* This essay is dedicated to Sami al-Arian, Mumia Abu Jamal, Leonard Peltier, Jalil Abdul Muntaqim, David Gilbert, Herman Bell and their six comrades in San Francisco, and the many other political prisoners in US jail for daring to speak, organize, and act for true equality and freedom.

1 Alexander Cockburn, "A Federal Witch Hunt: The Prosecution of Sami al-Arian" in *CounterPunch*, March 3–4, 2007, at: http://www.counterpunch.org/cockburn03032007.html. Information regarding al-Arian's plight is found in the archives at http://www.freesamialarian.com. I would like also to thank Laila al-Arian for providing me with other details about the case and the professor's incarceration.

2 See Corporate Crime Reporter, "'No Fingernails, No Good': Al-Arian Prosecutor Has Bias Against Muslims" in *CounterPunch*, March 3–4, 2007, at http://www.counterpunch.org/ccr03032007.html.

3 See John Turley's entry in his website, "Justice Department Calls Dr. Sami Al-Arian Before Third Grand Jury," March 3, 2007, at: http://jonathanturley.org/2008/03/03/the-justice-department-calls-dr-sami-al-arian-before-third-grand-jury.

4 For a letter of protestation regarding al-Arian's right to due process, see the United Faculty of Florida letter at: http://w3.usf.edu/~uff/AlArian.

5 See Rob Brannon, "Al-Arian: Throw Out Suit," in the university's paper, *The Oracle*, September 18, 2002, at: http://media.www.usforacle.com/media/storage/paper880/news/2002/09/18/News/AlArian.Throw.Out.Suit-1680560.shtml.

6. The Department of Justice led this misrepresentation in its press release, "Sami Al-Arian Pleads Guilty to Conspiracy to Provide Services to Palestinian Islamic Jihad," April 17, 2006, at: http://www.usdoj.gov/opa/pr/2006/April/06_crm_221.html.

7 One of the most notable examples is the story of Palestinian-Americans Michel Shehadeh and Khader Hamide. They were arrested with five other Palestinian and Sudanese immigrants in 1987, tried and acquitted on charges accusing USA PATRIOT Act and John Ashcroft's malevolently watchful eye. Shehadeh was key in building the Arab American Anti-Defamation Committee (ADC) in the 1990s. Despite major protests within the organization, the cowardly ADC fired Shehadeh as Regional Director in 2002 due to its spineless capitulation to the State's paranoid vision of the Arab Fifth Column after 9/11. The government's attempt to deport Shehadeh and Hamide was dismissed by the heroic Judge Bruce Einhorn, who wrote a thorough and blistering opinion of the case and proceedings as represented by the counsel for Homeland Security. See, Will Youmans, "A Palestinian Zionist and the End of the World," in *CounterPunch*, May 5 2006, at: http://www.counterpunch.org/youmans05052004.html. On Shehadeh and the ADL, see Camille Taiara, "The Struggle Within: An Internal Battle over Tactics and Control in the Arab Anti-Discrimination Committee," in *San Francisco Bay Guardian* Online, Sept. 11 2002, at: http://www.sfbg.com/36/50/cover_adc.html. Also, see the judge's eleven page opinion, "United States Department of Justice, Executive Office for Immigration Office: *US Department of Homeland Security v. Hamide and Shehadeh*," pdf file available at the ACLU of Southern California, http://www.aclu-sc.org/News/Releases/2007/102313.

8 See the Anti-Defamation League's website, "Backgrounder: Jewish Defense League" at: http://www.adl.org/extremism/jdl_chron.asp.

9 See the forty-two page Human Right Watch report, "We Are Not the Enemy: Hate Crimes Against Arabs, Muslims, and Those Perceived to be Arab or Muslim after September 11," *Human Rights Watch*, Vol. 15, No.6 (G), November 2002; at: http://www.hrw.org/reports/2002/usahate. Also, see the summary "U.S. Officials Should Have Been Better Prepared for Hate Crime Wave," *Human Rights Watch*, November 12, 2002, at: http://www.hrw.org/press/2002/11/usahate.htm

10 See "Savage: Arabs are 'non-humans' and 'racist, fascist bigots,'" at *Media Matters*, May 14, 2004, at: http://mediamatters.org/items/200405140003.

11 According to the testimony of Georgetown University Professor of Law, David Cole, in front of a Senate Judiciary Committee, May 10, 2005: "Men were locked up and designated 'of interest' on the basis of such information as a tip that 'too many Middle Eastern men' were working at a convenience store…Not one defendant out of 8,000 was found guilty of any criminal intent or wrong-going." The transcript can be found at: http://judiciary.senate.gov/testimony.cfm?id=1493&wit_id=4257. Also, see Cole's important book on abuse of aliens by military and criminal justice officials, *Enemy Aliens: Double Standards and Constitutional Freedoms in the War on Terrorism* (NY: The New Press, 2003)

12 Despite a tepid protest from the Arab-American Anti-Defamation Committee, these comments made few ripples in the mainstream media. For a rare example, see Emil Guillermo, "Dangerous Talk," in *SFGate.com*, July 2002, at: http://www.sfgate.com/cgi-bin/article.cgi?file=/gate/archive/2002/07/30/eguillermo.DTL

13 See Michelle Malkin, *In Defense of Internment: The Case for Racial Profiling During WWI and the War on Terror* (New York: Regnery Publishing, 2004); and Daniel Pipes, "Why the Japanese In-

ternment Still Matters," in *The New York Sun*, Dec. 28 2004, reprinted at: http://www.danielpipes.org/article/2309

14 For one announcement of the contract see, Katherine Hunt, "KBR Awarded Homeland Security Contract Worth Up to $385M," *Market Watch*, Jan. 24 2006, at: http://www.marketwatch.com. For an excellent analysis see, Maurin Farrell, "Detention Camp Jitters," in *Buzzflash*, Feb. 13 2006, at: http://www.buzzflash.com/farrell/06/02/far06003.html; also see Ronald Takaki, "Will Bush's War on Terror Bring Back Detention Camps?" in *New America Media*, Feb 06, 2006, at: http://news.ncmonline.com/news/view_article.html?article_id=de9dd9fbbbbd59388d802c3f4e0e1288. The announcement garnished attention in Muslim and Arab-American communities and elicited concern. For example, see Sheila Musaji's short but informative essay, "Why is Halliburton Building Internment Camps?" in *The American Muslim*, Feb. 25 2006. at: http://theamericanmuslim.org/tam.php/features/articles/why_is_halliburton_building_internment_camps.

15 Congressman Howard Coble stated "there were Japanese-Americans who wanted to do us harm then, just as there are Arab-Americans who wish to do us harm now." Michael Betsch, "Free Speech No Excuse for Republican's 'Racist' Remarks, Critics Say" in *CNS News*, February 07, 2003, at: http://www.cnsnews.com/ViewPolitics.asp?Page=%5CPolitics%5Carchive%5C200302%5CPOL20030207d.html. Representative Sue Myrick insinuated that "a potential link" between Arab-Americans and global terrorism exists: "Look who runs all the convenience stories across the country" because of "the illegal trafficking of food stamps through convenience stores for the purpose of laundering money to countries known to harbor terrorists" See Pat Morrison, "Two NC Republicans Draw Fire from 'Outrageous' Ethnic Comments," in *National Catholic Reporter*, Feb 28, 2003, at: http://ncronline.org/NCR_Online/archives/022803/022803k.htm.

16 From ACTA's website, "Academic Freedom," at: http://www.goacta.org/issues/academic_freedom.html

17 See http://thomas.loc.gov/cgi-bin/bdquery/z?d109:h.r.00509, http://www.govtrack.us/congress/bill.xpd?bill=h109-509, and substitute amendments passed on voice vote on June 16 2005. Amendment contents can be found at: http://republicans.edlabor.house.gov/archive/markups/109th/sed/hr509/616main.htm.

18 "Opening Statements by Congressman Patrick J. Tiberi," Subcommittee on Select Education, Committee on Education and Workforce, 109th Congress; http://republicans.edlabor.house.gov/archive/markups/109th/sed/hr509/616st.htm.

19 H.R. Bill 506, "To amend and extend title VI of the Higher Education Act of 1965," Sec. 633, 2.B and 2.C: 7.

20 H.R. Bill 506,. Sec. 633, (c.) Membership, 1. Appointment and 2. Representation: 18–19.

21 H.R. Bill 506,. Sec. 633, (b), Independence of International Advisory Board; 18).

22 H.R. Bill 506,. Sec. 634, Recruiter Access to Students and Student Recruiting Information: 27.

23 Robert Scholes, "An Advisory Board to Be Wary Of," in *The Chronicle for Higher Education*, vol. 50, 36: B13, at: http://chronicle.com/weekly/v50/i36/36b01301.htm. For the AAUP's position on H.R. 3077, see the article by its director of Government Relations, Mark F. Smith, "Government Relations: Will Wisdom Survive" in *Academe* (Jan-Feb) 2004, at: http://www.aaup.org/AAUP/pubsres/academe/2004/JF/Col/gr.htm. Several other academic organizations have denounced HR 3077 and 506, including the Latin American Studies Association, the American Folklore Society and the American Anthropology Association's Taskforce on Middle East Anthropology, which wrote a handbook for scholars, entitled "Academic Freedom and Professional Responsibility after 9/11" (2006).

24 Tariq Ramadan, "Why I'm Banned in the USA," in *Washington Post*, October 1, 2006, at: http://www.washingtonpost.com/wp-dyn/content/article/2006/09/29/AR2006092901334.html.

25 See Timothy Egan, "Computer Student on Trial Over Muslim Web Site Work," in *The New York Times*, April 27, 2004, at: http://query.nytimes.com/gst/fullpage.html?res=9B06E4D9113AF934A15757C0A9629C8B63. Also see, "Jury Acquits Idaho Webmaster Charged With Terrorism For Hosting Anti-American Websites," at: http://www.democracynow.org/2004/6/16/jury_acquits_idaho_web-

master_charged_with. Also of interest is *US v. Sami Omar al-Hussayen* court docket, at: news.findlaw. com/hdocs/docs/ terrorism/usalhussyn304sind2.pdf. Numerous Arab students have been detained and/or denied entry upon arrival to the US despite having valid visas issued from American embassies in their respective countries. For one absurd example, see the story of doctoral student Saif Khalifa Al Sha'al, his wife and three young children, who were detained for two days then deported upon his return to Claremont University from the United Arab Emirates. See Bassma Al Jandaly, "Al Sha'ali Lands in a Quandary," *Gulf News*, Aug.25 2006, at: http://www.gulf-news.com/nation/Society/10062584.html; and "Back from Hell" in Khaleej Times Online, Sept. 1 2006, at: http://www. khaleejtimes.ae/DisplayArticleNew.asp?xfile=data/weekend/2006/September/weekend_September8. xml&section=weekend&col=.

26 See Amnesty International USA, "Issue Brief: The REAL ID Act of 2005 and its Negative Impact on Asylum Seekers," March 2005: 3.

27 See Ralph E. Shaffer and R. William Robinson, "Here Comes the Thought Police," at: *Common Dreams*, http://www.commondreams.org/archive/2007/11/19/5320/. Also, see Amy Goodman's interview with independent journalist Jessica Lee and civil rights attorney Kamau Karl Franklin, "Homegrown Terrorism Prevention Act Raises Fears of New Government Crackdown on Dissent," November 20, 2007, at: http://www.democracynow.org/2007/11/20/homegrown_terrorism_prevention_act_raises_fears.

28 See Dinitia Smith, "Arafat's Man in New York," in *New York Magazine*, Vol. 22, No. 4, January 25, 1989, pp. 40–6. Or the notorious polemic, see Edward Alexander, "Professor of Terror" in *Commentary* 88 (2): 1989: 49–50.

29 For one example of parroting Horowitz's assertions, see Leslie Carbone, "Terror's Faculty Sympathizers," in *Campus Support for Terrorism*, David Horowitz and Ben Johnson eds. (Los Angeles: Center for the Study of Popular Culture, 2004): 71–5.

30 See Zackary Lockman, *Contending Visions of the Middle East: The History and Politics of Orientalism* (Cambridge: Cambridge University Press, 2004): 215–67; and Joel Beinin, "New American McCarthyism: Policing Thought about the Middle East," in *Race and Class*, 46 (1), 2004: 101–15. For an intelligent analysis and a handful of lesser known examples of harassment, see Joan Scott, "Middle East Studies Under Attack," in *The Link*, published by the Americans for Middle East Understanding, Vol. 39, issue 1, (January–March), 2005: 2–12, and available online at: www.ameu.org/uploads/vol39_issue1_2006.pdf. Also, see Sophia McClennen, "The Geopolitical War on U.S. Higher Education," *College Literature*, 33.4 (Fall) 2006: 43–75. For a succinct overview of the attack on academic freedom since 9/11, see William G. Tierney and Vicente M. Lechuga, "Academic Freedom in the 21st Century," in *Thought and Action Journal*, vol. XXI (Fall) 2005: 7–21; and Sara Roy, "Strategizing Control of the Academy" in *Thought and Action*, vol. XXI (Fall) 2005: 147–162. For an examination of the attacks on Middle East studies faculty at Columbia, see Ashley Dawson, "The Crisis at Columbia: Academic Freedom, Area Studies, and Contingent Labor in the Contemporary Academy," in *Social Text*, 90. vol. 25, no. 1 (Spring), 2007: 63–84.

31 For MESA's position on academic freedom, see "In Defense of Academic Freedom" at: http://mesa. arizona.edu/aff/academic_freedom.htm.

32 In 2003, the AAUP issued a report on academic freedom after 9/11, see "Academic Freedom and National Security in the Time of Crisis," available at: http://www.aaup.org/AAUP/comm/rep/crisistime.htm

33 Campus Watch accuses Islamic studies scholar, Natana Delong-Bas, of being an apologist for Arab "jihad." Ironically, MESA, which is accused of suppressing "academic freedom," had protested to the Egyptian government for the banning Delong-Bas' book. See their letter of protest to Pres. Husni Mubarak, at: http://www.mesa.arizona.edu/about/cafmenaletters.htm#113005.

34 For a truncated version of their paper, see John Mearsheimer and Stephen Walt's now well-known article, "The Israel Lobby and U.S. Foreign Policy," in *London Review of Books*, Vol. 28, No. 6 (March 23, 2006).

35 Tony Judt, "Israel: The Alternative," in *The New York Review of Books*, vol.50. no.16 (October 23), 2003, also available at: http://www.nybooks.com/articles/16671.

36 For an account see, Stu Woo, "Arabic Professor at San Francisco State U. Waits in Canadian Limbo for US Visa," in *The Chronicle of Higher Education*, September 11 2006, at: http://chronicle.com/daily/2006/09/2006091106n.htm. On the resolution of the issue, see Ian Thompson and Jeffrey Shuffle, "Professor Returns to Class after Long Visa Ordeal," *SFGate*, September 20, 2006, at: http://xpress.sfsu.edu/archives/news/006906.html.

37 See Scott Baldaulf, "South African Fights Denial of U.S. Visa," in the *Christian Science Monitor*, November 16, 2007, at http://www.csmonitor.com/2007/1116/p07s01-woaf.html.

38 Brad Wong, "Iraqi Doctor Who Disputes Official Death Toll is Denied Visa to UW," *Seattlepi*, April 20 2007, at: http://seattlepi.nwsource.com/local/312411_iraqvisa20.html.

39 See Massad's own statement at the University's investigation, at: http://www.columbia.edu/cu/mealac/faculty/massad/#adhoc.

40 Joan W. Scott notes the relationship between these student groups and the "pro-Israel lobby" in "Middle East Studies Under Siege," op. cit. 3. For one frightening example of a manual on how to manage the Palestine-Zionist debate on campus, see Mitchell G. Bard, "Myths and Facts: A Guide to the Arab-Israeli Conflict," (Chevy Chase; 2000), published by the American Israeli Cooperative Enterprise.

41 See: http://www.aipac.org/For_Students/index_1732.asp#343; also for a series of "training" workshops see: http://www.aipac.org/For_Students/Training_Opportunities/default_689.asp.

42 Lisa Eisen and Wayne Fireston, "Opening Remarks" in *Tenured or Tenuous: Defining the Role of Faculty in Supporting Israel on Campus*, prepared by Mitchell Bard (Washington D.C: Israel on Campus Coalition, s.d): 3.

43 Mitchell Bard, "Proposals for Reclaiming Middle Eastern Scholarship," in *Tenured or Tenuous*; 34.

44 Ibid., 36.

45 Ellen Shrecker, "The New McCarthyism in Academe," *Thought and Action*, Fall 2005: 103–18.

46 See John Tierney *The Politics of Peace: What's Behind the Anti-War Movement* (Washington DC: Capital Research Center, 2005). The quote is from Capital Research Center's newsletter discussing Tierney's book, http://www.capitalresearch.org/pubs/pdf/OT0305.pdf: 3.

47 Gary A. Tobin and Aryeh K. Weinberg, *A Profile of American College Faculty: Political Beliefs and Behavior* Vol. 1 (San Francisco: Institute for Jewish and Community Research, 2006): ii–iii.

48 Ibid., 67.

49 Ibid., 8.

50. See Kenneth Stern's biography at: http://www.ajc.org/site/c.ijITI2PHKoG/b.835879/k.2F9B/AJC_Experts.htm. Also, see Kenneth Stern, *Bigotry on Campus: A Planned Response* (New York: American Jewish Committee, 1990): 9.

51 Kenneth Stern, *Why Campus Anti-Israel Activity Flunks Bigotry 101* (New York: American Jewish Committee, 2002): 13.

52 Ibid., 10–11, 20.

53 See the CAMERA website at: http://www.camera.org/index.asp?x_context=4&x_outlet=28&x_article=384.

54 *Fighting Back*: 10.

55 Ibid., 10.

56. Anti-Defamation League, *Fighting Back: A Handbook for Responding to Anti-Israel Rallies on College and University Campuses* (s.p: s.n., 2003), 3.

57 *Fighting Back*, 4–6 (my italics).

58 Ibid., 19.

59. For the US Civil Rights Commission Report on campus activities, see: http://www.usccr.gov/pubs/081506campusantibrief07.pdf. For MESA's letter of concern to the Commission, see: http://www.mesa.arizona.edu/about/cafmenaletters.htm#USCCRJune11.

60. The bi-partisan US Commission remains very close with these organizations. For example, Commission Kenneth Marcus co-organizes events with the Institute for Jewish and Community Research (IJCR). Most of these organizations maintain "campus programs" that, in the words of the Zionist Organization of America, "combat Arab propaganda." The IJCR's report, A Profile of American College Faculty (2006), asserts that the majority of American college-faculty are "liberal," and hostile to Israel, the US, and capitalism. See: http://www.jewishresearch.org/Book-College.htm. The IJCR's study, *The UnCivil University*, targets universities and faculty who are critical of Israel or the US; see *The UnCivil University: Politics and Propaganda in American Education* ([San Francisco]: Institute for Jewish & Community Research, 2005). At Wayne State University, Anti-Racist Action (ARA) has been targeted as anti-Semitic because of its anti-war and anti-Zionist activism. Despite explicitly denouncing anti-Semitism, Marcus states that "anti-Zionist, and even anti-war, ideologies can lead to anti-Semitism." See Brandi Trapp, "Student groups ready for debate after anti-Semitism lecture," *The South End*, March 28, 2007, at: http://thesouthend.typepad.com/tsenews/2007/03/student_groups_.html.

61 See the AJC website at: http://www.ajcongress.org/site/PageServer?pagename=about.

62 See the ZOA website, at: http://www.zoa.org/about.htm.

63 See Joe Kaufman's shameless innuendo, which slanders and black-jackets the MSA and its student members, "Tar Heel Terror," *FrontPageMagazine.com*, March 2006, at: http://www.frontpagemag.com/Articles/ReadArticle.asp?ID=21541.

64 Erick Stakelbeck, "Islamic Radicals on Campus," in *Campus Support for Terrorism*, David Horowitz and Ben Johnson eds. (Los Angeles: Center for the Study of Popular Culture, 2004), 57.

65 See interview between Aaron Hanscom and Walid Shoebat on the UCI campus, posted online June 4, 2007 at: http://pajamasmedia.com/2007/06/islamism_on_campus.php.

66 Candace de Russy, "Thin Red Line: Terrorism in the Ivory Tower," on Hudson Institute website, Publications and Op-Eds, Oct. 12 2006; at: http://www.hudson.org/index.cfm?fuseaction=publication_details&id=4242.

67 Maria Jo Fisher, "FBI Actions at UCI Questioned," in *Orange County Register*, May 18, 2007, at: http://www.ocregister.com/ocregister/news/local/irvine/article_1699052.php.

68 "Report" by the Task Force on Anti-Semitism at the University of California, Irvine, Feb. 8, 2008; 26, at: http://octaskforce.wordpress.com/2008/02/13/oc-task-force-investigation-finds-anti-semitism-at-university-of-california-irvine-and-reviews-findings-of-doe's-office-for-civil-rights.

69 For example, a federal judge agreed to the request by the FBI and US Attorney General to subpoena files pertaining to an anti-war student group at Drake University as well as all documents related to the National Lawyers Guild who had sponsored an anti-war forum at the university. After a maelstrom of protest, the subpoenas were withdrawn three months later. For a summary, see: Ryan Foley, "University Ordered to Turn Over Records on Anti-War Activists," at: http://www.commondreams.org/headlines04/0207-07.htm; or see Sharon Walsh, "The Drake Affair," *The Chronicle for Higher Education*, March 5, 2004, at: http://chronicle.com/weekly/v50/i26/26a00801.htm. In the meantime, US Army Intelligence spied on invited participants and attendees at a conference on Human Rights and Islam at the University of Texas at Austin. See Janet Elliot, "Presence of Army agents stirs furor: Roster sought of attendees at UT meeting on Islam," at: http://www.texascivilrightsproject.org/newspub/pressclippings2004spring.html. Also, see the National Lawyers Guild protest to this spying at: http://www.nlg.org/news/statements/UTexasLaw_pressrelease.htm.

70 Al-Awdah is a coalition of several student and activist groups at UCSD, UCLA, and UC Riverside that supports the right of return of Palestinian refugees. See al-Awdah convention invitation at: http://www.al-awda.org/convention5/signup2.html. See Lee Kaplan's "A Victory Against Campus Ex-

tremism," in *Frontpage Magazine*, May 24 2007, at: http://www.frontpagemag.com/articles/Printable.aspx?GUID={7D383BC4-3DB6-416B-8607-8E51053EF633}

71 For the national move to suppress anti-war activism, see Michael Gould-Wartofsky, "Repress U," in *The Nation*, January 28, 2008, at: http://www.thenation.com/doc/20080128/gould-wartofsky.

72 Daniel Pipes, "Redeeming the Wayward University System" in *The New York Sun*, November 28 2006; found at http://www.nysun.com/article/44184. My italics.

73 This phrase is taken from Ward Churchill's, *Speaking Truth in the Teeth of Power: Lectures on Globalization, Colonialism, And Native North America* (Oakland: AK Press, forthcoming).

From Colgate to Costa Rica (Fontan, 280)

1 Cockburn (2008). "If there is no change in three months, there will be war again," *The Independent*. London.

2 HRW (2003). *Violent Response: The U.S. Army in al-Falluja*. New York: Human Rights Watch.

3 Fontan, V. (2006). "Polarization between occupier and occupied in Post-Saddam Iraq: humiliation and the formation of political violence." *Terrorism and Political Violence* 18(2): 217–238.

4 Bremer, L. (2006). *My Year in Iraq: The Struggle to Build a Future of Hope*. New York: Simon and Schuster.

5 Fisk, R. (2005). *The Great War for Civilization: The Conquest of the Middle East*. London: Fourth Estate Publishers.

6 I subsequently withdrew this article from *Peace and Change* and incorporated it in my *Voices from Post-Saddam Iraq* book as Chapter 4.

7 http://www.colgate.edu/DesktopDefault1.aspx?tabid=730&pgID=6013&nwID=3484

8 http://www.littlegreenfootballs.com/weblog/?entry=14483&only

9 http://www.littlegreenfootballs.com/weblog/?entry=14483&only

10 http://wizbangblog.com/content/2005/01/27/university-prof.php

11 http://www.groupsrv.com/hobby/about135661.html

12 http://pierrelegrand.net/2005/01/27/the-email-i-sent-to-colgate-protesting-this-shameful-behavior.htm

13 http://media.www.maroon-news.com/media/storage/paper742/news/2005/03/04/News/Peace.Studies.Professors.Research.Causes.Conflict-886076.shtml; http://www.colgate.edu/DesktopDefault1.aspx?tabid=730&pgID=6013&nwID=3484

14 http://media.www.maroon-news.com/media/storage/paper742/news/2005/03/04/News/Peace.Studies.Professors.Research.Causes.Conflict-886076.shtml

15 http://media.www.maroon-news.com/media/storage/paper742/news/2005/03/04/News/Peace.Studies.Professors.Research.Causes.Conflict-886076.shtml

16 http://www.sa4c.com/documents/fontan_interview.htm

17 http://www.sa4c.com/documents/fontan_interview.htm

18 See http://meetingresistance.com.

19 Cockburn (2008). "If there is no change in three months, there will be war again." *The Independent*. London.

20 http://www.upsam.upeace.org

21 Fontan, V. (forthcoming). *Voices from Post-Saddam Iraq: Living with Terrorism, Insurgency, and New Forms of Tyranny*. Westport, CT: Praeger Security International.

When Knowledge Kills (Levine, 292)

1 The chair of the AAUP's Committee on Academic Freedom and Tenure, David Rabban, argues that, despite some high profile cases, such as those of Joseph Massad, Ward Churchill, and Norman Finkelstein, and the palpable sense of attack felt by many, especially younger and untenured members of the profession, the majority of colleges and universities are adequately protecting the free speech rights and academic freedom of their professors. I would argue that he is missing the disciplining function of these few well-publicized cases, as they serve as a warning to other young or untenured academics as to the fight they will have if they pursue lines of research or public writing and speaking that critique Israel or US foreign policy too harshly or regularly or, indeed, take any dissenting or political position. See Rabban's review of Beshara Doumani, ed., "Academic Freedom After September 11," in *Academe* Online, January–February 2007.

2 Joel Beinin, "The New American McCarthyism: Policing Thought about the Middle East," *Race & Class*, Vol. 46, No. 1, 101–115 (2004). For discussion of a similar dynamic in the UK, see the blog of Gabriele Maranci, at http://marranci.wordpress.com/2007/12/19/a-lesson-to-learn/#more-63.

3 For a report on the controversy surrounding the Ford Foundation's decision to insert so-called "anti-terrorism" language into their funding contracts, Daniel Golden, "Colleges Object To New Wording In Ford Grants: Colleges Object To New Wording In Ford Grants," *Wall Street Journal*, May 4, 2004. Also see William G. Tierney and Vicente M. Lechuga, "Academic Freedom in the 21st Century," *The NEA Higher Education Journal*, Fall 2005.

4 AAUP, 2007 Report on Freedom in the Classroom, available at http://www.aaup.org/AAUP/pubsres/policydocs/contents/1940statement.htm. Instructors are often accused of "indoctrinating," rather than educating students, or being "intolerant" of divergent points of view, and even creating a hostile environment for students. In fact, the conduct of which they are charged more accurately represents the position of conservative attackers, who "dogmatically insist on the truth of such propositions" rather than merely "vigorously assert[ing] a proposition or a viewpoint, however controversial... The essence of higher education does not lie in the passive transmission of knowledge but in the inculcation of a mature independence of mind" (AAUP, "Freedom in the Classroom," 2007, http://www.aaup.org/AAUP/comm/rep/A/class.htm).

5 By "practical political knowledge," I mean knowledge that, regardless of the accuracy of its representation of the realities under discussion, plays a determinative role in the shaping of both US foreign policy and the larger media and public discussions of the MENA and Islam more broadly.

6 David Horowitz, *The Professors: The 101 Most Dangerous Academics in America*, Washington, DC: Regnery Publishing, 2006. The scholars critical of Horowitz include Juan Cole, Joel Beinin, and other well-known academics.

7 Martin Kramer, "MESA jumps in Massad's trench," http://sandbox.blog-city.com/mesa_jumps_in_massad.htm, 23 August 2005.

8 A list of the winners of the Malcolm Kerr Dissertation Award since 1982 is available at http://www.mesa.arizona.edu/excellence/kerr_winners_list.htm.

9 William Tierney and Vincente Lechuga, "Academic Freedom in the 21st Century," *Thought and Action*, Fall 2005, 12.

10 This was to occur through the "International Studies in Higher Education Act, H.R. 3077" passed by the House of Representatives in 2003. A good example of this phenomena is the politicization of anti-Semitism, in which so-called "pro-Israel" groups have expanded the definition to cover critiques of Israel and other forms of speech that are clearly not anti-Jewish, as even the conservative-controlled US Civil Rights Commission concluded after a detailed investigation into charges of anti-Semitism at my own university, UC Irvine. As former MESA President Zachary Lockman noted, such investigations claim that "many university departments of Middle East studies provide one-sided, highly polemical academic presentations and some may repress legitimate debate concerning Israel" (See Zachary Lockman/MESA letter to US Commission on Civil Rights Chair Gerald Raynolds," June 11,

2007. Other critiques of this trend include Juan Cole, "The New McCarthyism," Salon.com, April 22, 2005 and Joan W. Scott, "Middle East Studies Under Siege," The Link, January–March, 2006).

11 Edward Said, *Orientalism*, New York: Vintage Books, 1979, 1–5.

12 A good example is Ziad Abdelnour, an asset manager listed as an expert under Lebanon and Hezbollah for the Middle East Forum.

13 The Association's website is http://www.asmeascholars.org/Home/tabid/592/Default.aspx.

14 Annie Karni, "Group Formed To Improve Middle East Scholarship," *New York Sun*, November 8, 2007

15 Ibid.

16 Personal interview with former Israel-based *New Yorker* correspondent, Spring 2007.

17 Rodney Fopp, "Herbert Marcuse's 'Repressive Tolerance' and its Critics," *Borderlands*, Vol. 6, 1, 2007.

18 Peter Novick, *That Noble Dream: The "Objectivity Question" and the American Historical Profession*, Cambridge: Cambridge University Press, 1988, 28, 34, 38, 64, 241, 251, 294–309.

19 Ibid, 38.

20 Ibid, 64.

21 Ibid, 294–309.

22 Herbert Marcuse, "Repressive Tolerance," available online at http://www.marcuse.org/herbert/pubs/60spubs/65repressivetolerance.htm.

23 Ibid.

24 Montgomery McFate, "Anthropology and Counterinsurgency: The Strange Story of their Curious Relationship," *Military Review*, March–April, 2005, available at http://www.army.mil/professionalwriting/volumes/volume3/august_2005/7_05_2.html.

25 One of the first examples of this NSF-DoD cooperation was a program titled, "Social and Behavioral Dimensions of National Security, Conflict, and Cooperation (NSCC), Program Solicitation NSF 08-594," published on the NSF website in the mid-summer of 2008. http://www.nsf.gov/pubs/2008/nsf08594.htm?govDel=USNSF_25.

26 For Gates' remarks, see his speech to the Association of American Universities, April 14, 2008, available at http://www.defenselink.mil/speeches/speech.aspx?speechid=1228. For a critique, see David Price, "Social Science in the Harness," *CounterPunch*, June 24, 2008, http://www.counterpunch.org/price06252008.html.

27 Laurie King-Irani, note 22 to discussion forum, "Anthropologists of the World, Unite!" *SavageMinds.org*, September 20, 2007. http://savageminds.org/2007/09/18/anthropologists-of-the-world-unite/#comment-119581.

28 The two fatalities were Michael Bhatia, a PhD student at Oxford specializing in the combat motivations of Afghan mujahidin, who was killed while on patrol with US soldiers in a remote region of Afghanistan in May 2008, and Nicole Suvegas, a political science PhD candidate at Johns Hopkins focusing on markets and religion in the Muslim world, killed in Sadr City the following month. Suvegas was also an Army Reservist, although at the time of her death she was in Iraq as a civilian employee of the defense firm BAE Systems' Technology Solutions & Services, working on a HTS contract.

29 The Executive Board of the AAA "expresses its disapproval of the HTS program," although the Association's Ad Hoc Commission on the Engagement of Anthropology with Security and Intelligence Communities issued a watered down report a month later that "did not recommend nonengagement" more broadly. Specifically, the report on HTS argued that "the HTS program creates conditions which are likely to place anthropologists in positions in which their work will be in violation of the AAA Code of Ethics and that its use of anthropologists poses a danger to both other anthropologists and

persons other anthropologists study" (AAA, Executive Board statement on HTS project, October 31, 2007).

30 L. King-Irani, PhD, Georgetown University, message to AAA blog.

31 Montgomery McFAte, "The Cultural Knowledge Gap and Its Consequences for National Security," Project Report Summary, US Institute of Peace, May 10, 2007, http://www.usip.org/fellows/reports/2007/0510_mcfate.html#resources.

32 David Price, "Pilfered Scholarship Devastates General Patraues' Counterinsurgency Manual," www.counterpunch.org, October 30, 2007.

33 See David Vine, "Enabling the Kill Chain," *The Chronicle of Higher Education*, November 30, 2007; Cohen, op cit. This is clear from the defense of participation by several scholars cited in this article, who, without comment, move from justifying general cooperation to participation in specific actions. As explained in the periodical *Military Review* (September–October 2006), Human Terrain Teams are to input data about local populations into what is called "Mapping Human Terrain software." That "data will cover such subjects as key regional personalities, social structures, links between family and clans, economic issues, agricultural production, and the like" (p. 13). That information is to be sent back to the HTS Reachback Research Center in Fort Leavenworth, Kansas. There, cultural and ethnographic experts further analyze, collate, and process that data. They then return it to the local Human Terrain Team and share it with other US military and intelligence organizations (p. 14). In the end, as John Wilcox—Assistant Deputy under Secretary of Defense—explained, mapping the human terrain, "Enables the entire kill chain for the GWOT" (i.e. Global War on Terror). (For the PDF version of Wilcox's presentation, see: http://concerned.anthropologists.googlepages.com/WilcoxKillChain.pdf). Also, see the remarks by John Hawkins (Department of Anthropology, Brigham Young University, recent visiting faculty, US Army War College) on the AAA blog established to comment on the Executive Board report on Human Terrain systems.

34 Jeff Cohen and Norman Solomon, "30-year Anniversary: Tonkin Gulf Lie Launched Vietnam War," *Media Beat*, July 27, 1994.

35 According to Nobel Laureate economist, Joseph Stiglitz, the economic costs could well exceed $3 trillion (Joseph Stiglitz and Linda Blimes, *The Three Trillion Dollar War: The True Cost of the Iraq Conflict*, New York: WW Norton & Co, 2008). As a former President of MESA explains, "The question isn't who's right or more accurate. It's about whose books are featured in airport bookstores and whose books are on the bedside tables of the powerful. Even if the work [of those associated with the CMESE] isn't taken seriously by scholars, their language of imperial power still remains the common idiom" (Interview with former MESA President, December 2007, email communication).

36 See Doumani's argument in the introduction to his edited volume, *Academic Freedom After September 11*, Cambridge: MIT Press, 2006.

37 Interviews with three presidents of MESA, 2005–2008. For a discussion of the problems associated with the uncritical positions of the dominant groups in the global peace and justice movement, see chapters 7–9 of my *Why They Don't Hate Us*.

38 See Beshara Doumani, "Academic Freedom Post-9/11," *ISIM Review*, No. 15, Spring 2005; Manuel Castells, *The Power of Identity*, London: Blackwell, 1996.

39 Immanuel Kant, *Was ist Aufklarung?* (*What is Enlightenment?*), Internet edition.

40 There would seem to be no more urgent task for scholars today than to help their fellow citizens achieve such a level of maturity. And yet the very idea of doing so would surely elicit the cries of elitism and being "out of touch" with the "real concerns of Americans" that have been deployed so brilliantly by conservatives since Nixon to marginalize any force that seeks to challenge the status quo. As Kant predicted, it will take a "self-imposed" emergence by the American people at large, and with them, a good share of the world's population, out of their political, cultural, and moral "immaturity" before the kinds of transformation in political culture could be achieved that would allow a full flowering of academic and, indeed, social freedom, both in the United States and globally as well.

The Role of African Intellectuals and Their Relevance to the US (Mugo, 307)

1 Frantz Fanon, *The Wretched of the Earth*, New York: Grove Press [1963], 7.

2 Frantz Fanon, *Black Skin White Masks*, New York: Grove Press, 1967.

3 Frantz, Fanon, *The Wretched of the Earth*, 7.

4 Okot p'Bitek, *Song of Lawino*, Nairobi: East African Publishing House, 1966.

5 Mũgo wa Gatheru, *Child of Two Worlds*, London: Heinemann, 1968.

6 Paulo Freire, *Pedagogy of the Oppressed*, New York: Continuum, 1992 Ed., 150.

7 Frantz Fanon, *The Wretched of the Earth*, op.cit. 152.

8 Chinweizu, *The West and the Rest of Us: White Predators, Black Slaves and the African Elite*, New York: Vintage, 1975, 355–56.

9 Paulo Freire, *Pedagogy of the Oppressed*, op.cit. 126.

10 Ibid., 127.

11 Walter Rodney, *Walter Rodney Speaks: The Making of an African Intellectual*, Trenton, N.J.: Africa World Press, 1990, 111–12.

12 Fanon, op.cit. 148–205.

13 Frantz Fanon, "Pitfalls of nationalism," *The Wretched of the Earth*, Ibid., 171.

14 Kamukunji, the original name of a place where political rallies used to be held during the struggle for Kenya's independence. The name was adopted by the University of Nairobi Students and simply used in reference to any of their political rallies, normally convened preceding a demonstration.

Women of Color, Tenure, and the Neoliberal University (Cotera, 328)

1 Of the four jointly-appointed women of color who came up for tenure in 2007, two—myself and Andrea Smith—were jointly appointed in the Women's Studies Department and the Program in American Culture: one was hired in both Women's Studies and the Sociology Department, and another held a dual appointment in the English Department and the Program in American Culture. It should be noted that the Program in American Culture recommended tenure for all three of its jointly appointed women of color faculty. Unfortunately, the English Department and the Women's Studies Department made negative recommendations on two tenure promotion cases. Although the English Department's vote was eventually overturned by the College Executive Committee, the other negative decisions were upheld.

2 Michael Denning offers a brief account of these historical shifts in his article: "Lineaments and Contradictions of the Neoliberal University System."

References

Cantor N. & Lavine S.D. (2006). "Point of View: Taking Public Scholarship Seriously." *The Chronicle of Higher Education*, June 9, 2006, cited in Introduction, *Arts of Citizenship* website; online at: http://ginsberg.umich.edu/artsofcitizenship/index.html

Ciafone, A. (2005). "Endowing the Neoliberal University." *Work & Culture*, 7, online at: http://www.yale.edu/laborculture/work_culture.html

Denning, M. (2005) "Lineaments and Contradictions of the Neoliberal University System." *Work & Culture*, 2; online at: http://www.yale.edu/laborculture/work_culture.html.

Gilbert, D. A. (2005) "The Corporate University and the Public Intellectual." *Work & Culture*, 8; online at: http://www.yale.edu/laborculture/work_culture.html

Harvey, D. (2005). *A Brief History of Neoliberalism*. New York: Oxford University Press.

Said, E. (1994). *Representations of the Intellectual*. New York: Pantheon Books.

Smith, A. (2006) "Heteropatriarchy and the Three Pillars of White Supremacy: Rethinking Women of Color Organizing." *Color of Violence: The Incite! Anthology*. Cambridge, MA: South End Press.

Teaching Theory, Talking Community (James, 337)

1 This essay was written while I was an assistant professor in women's studies at a large university in New England, and originally published in Joy James and Ruth Farmer, eds., *Spirit, Space, and Survival: African American Women in (White) Academe* (New York: Routledge, 1993). It appears here in edited and abbreviated form.

2 Barbara Christian, "The Race for Theory," reprinted in Gloria Anzaldua, ed. *Making Face, Making Soul; Haciendo Caras* (San Francisco: Aunt Lute Foundation, 1990), 336.

3 Scholar Samir Amin writes: "Eurocentrism is a specifically modern phenomenon, the roots of which go back only to the Renaissance, a phenomenon that did not flourish until the nineteenth century. In this sense, it constitutes one dimension of the cultur̦ and ideology of the modern capitalist world." Samir Amin, *Eurocentrism* (New York: Monthly Review Press, 1989), vii.

4 European American feminist Elizabeth Spelman cites this quote from a journal issue on African Americans and philosophy in her work, *Inessential Woman: Problems of Exclusion in Feminist Thought* (Boston: Beacon Press, 1988).

5 Amin, *Eurocentrism*, Ibid.

6 Cornel West, "A Genealogy of Modern Racism," *Prophesy Deliverance* (Philadelphia: Westminster Press, 1982).

7 Elizabeth Spelman explores "white solipsism" in *Inessential Woman.*

8 Patricia Hill Collins describes the academic worldview in which research methods prescribe "a distancing of the researcher as a 'subject'…the absence of emotions from the research…ethics and values [as] inappropriate in the research process…adversarial debates." See: Patricia Collins, "Learning from the Outsider Within: The Sociological Significance of Black Feminist Thought," *Social Problems* 33:6. Yet, Collins also uncritically argues for "rearticulation" specialists.

9 For a discussion of ash`e, see: Henry and Margaret Drewal, eds., *Gelede: Art and Female Power Among the Yoruba* (Bloomington: Indiana University Press), 74.

10 Theologian Bernard Lonergan discusses in *INSIGHT: An Understanding of Human Knowing* (New York: Harper and Row, 1957) a similar epistemology in which knowledge exists for the sake of communal and individual human liberation (which are not presented as oppositional). For Lonergan, experience, reflection, judgment, and action are part of the four-part process by which people (knowingly or unknowingly) learn. Action is indispensable to the learning process: You know how to ride a bicycle or drive a car not from merely reading books about bicycles or cars, but from riding or driving one as well (building a vehicle deepens your knowledge). We know how to live, learn, and teach without repression by doing actions that confront and diminish repression.

11 Bernice Johnson Reagon argues this point in her discussion of Martin Luther King, Jr. and charges of plagiarism in his dissertation. See Bernice Johnson Reagon, "Nobody Knows the Trouble I See; or By and By I'm Gonna Lay Down My Heavy Load," *The Journal of American History* (vol. 78, no. 1, June 1991).

12 Prior to his assassination by the Federal Bureau of Investigation (FBI) and the Chicago police in 1969, Fred Hampton prophesied: "I'm going to die for the people because I live for the people." See: "A Nation of Law? (1968–71)," *Eyes on the Prize*: Part 11, which documents Hampton's political work, the

FBI's disruption of the black liberation movement and its killings of Fred Hampton and Mark Clark. This segment of *Eyes on the Prize* also covers the Attica prison uprising for human rights and its violent repression by New York State Governor Nelson Rockefeller.

13 Toni Morrison, "Rootedness: The Ancestor as Foundation," in Mari Evans, ed., *Black Women Writers: A Critical Evaluation* (New York: Anchor Press/Doubleday, 1984), 344–345.

"You Are a Scary Woman" (Cloud, 347)

1 Here is an example that, in one paragraph, manages to accomplish all of these objectives: "What I don't understand about misguided people llike you is why you subject yourself to the live in a country like the United States for which ou harbor such an obvious disdain? Why not go live in Iraq or Afghanistan? You don't because most whining liberals like yourself are hypocrites. You don't have the courage to do anything other than whine. You don't even have the guts to go out into the real world and get a job. you feel save in the 'theoretical' academic environment where you can espouse your warped view of the world to easily manipulated young people. I pity your young daughter. That unfortunate young girl is being taught to hate her country much the way young Palenstinian children are taught to hate Jews and Americans. You're pathetic and disgusting." (Bob O'Malley, bobomalley@yahoo.com, July 8, 2002; all errors, sic.)

2 It is beyond the scope of this essay to investigate the full complexity of these connections suggested by any number of examples. For example, Christina Hoff-Summers, Laura Ingraham, and Tammy Bruce are prominent, outspoken, aggressive, conservative women who win univocal praise from their conservative audiences, made up mostly of men. In part, their acceptability is explained by their express loyalty to the nation. (In addition, they seem to occupy a role akin to that of Artemis, forever virginal Greek goddess of the hunt.) Anti-war protesters may in some instances—such as that of Cindy Sheehan, Code Pink, or Women in Black—"get away with" being women protestors because of their enactment of recognizable feminine-maternal roles. There is little doubt that the expectations of men and women in public life diverge along gender-ideological lines, whether this be Hillary Clinton vs. Barack Obama, Helen Gurley Flynn and Mother Jones vs. Eugene Debs or Bill Haywood, Emma Goldman vs. Leon Trotsky, or Susan Sontag vs. Seymour Hirsch. All might face the ire of conservatives on political grounds, but the women are special targets because to be political is itself to be in violation of a set of gendered rules that bind the nation together.

References

AmericanPolitics.com. (2004, January 15). "Knuckledraggers vs. Margaret Cho." Message posted to http://www.americanpolitics.com/20040114CroMag.html.

Brock, D. (2004). *The Republican Noise Machine.* New York: Random House.

Bruce, T. (2002, July 9). "A Scrap of Cloth," *FrontPageMag.com*, at: http://www.frontpagemag.com/Articles/Read.aspx?GUID=9F7B510E-F1E6-4657-878F-3E896C3114A2.

Carr, D. (2005, March 10). "Need Some New Luster? Create it by the Blogful. *The New York Times*, E1. Retrieved April 10, 2008, from Factiva database.

Carroll, D. (1979). *Dear Sir, Drop Dead! Hate Mail through the Ages.* New York: Collier.

Cho, M. (Speaker). (2005). *Assassin* [CD]. Nettwerk American. Hate mail from Bush supporters

Cloud, D. L. (2001, September 22). "Jensen vs. U.T.: Ideas Unwelcome? Letter to the editor, The Houston Chronicle, at: http://www.chron.com/disp/story.mpl/editorial/1057377.html.

———. (2002, June 1). "A Pledge for the Workers." Letter to the editor, *The Daily Texan*.

———. (2004, August). "To Veil the Threat of Terror: Afghan Women and the Clash of Civilizations in the Imagery of the U.S. War on Terrorism." *Quarterly Journal of Speech*, 90(3), 285–306.

De C. (2004, January 15). "The Cho Hate Mail Archive Project. Message posted to: http://www.ameri-canpolitics.com/20040114CroMag.html.

Ehrenreich, B., & English, D. (1978). *For Her Own Good: 150 Years of the Experts' Advice to Women*. New York: Anchor-Doubleday.

Faulkner, L. (2001, September 19). "Jensen's words his own." editorial, *The Houston Chronicle*, A39.

Festinger, L. (1957). *A Theory of Cognitive Dissonance*. Los Angeles: Stanford University Press.

Foucault, M. (1988). *Madness and Civilization*. New York: Vintage. (Original work published 1965)

Friedman, J. (2007, Summer). "Blogging While Female." *Bitch*, (36), 17.

Gould, (1007). "Civil Society and the Public Woman." *Journal of the Early Republic*, 28, 29–46.

Grayzel, S. R., J.D. Keene, K. Schultheiss, S.E. Cooper, E. Jacobs, L. Doan, G.J. Degroot, S. Tegel, a. Kel-sch, J.F. McMillan (1999). *Women's Identities at War: Gender, Motherhood, and Politics in Britain and France During the First World War*. Chapel Hill: University of North Carolina Press.

Hanson, C. (2002, May/June). "Women Warriors: How the Press has Helped and Hurt in the Battle for Equality." *CJR: Columbia Journalism Review*, 46–49.

"Hate Mail for Nurse Insisting on Respect. (2008, January 30). *Nursing Standard*, 22(21), 5.

Hansen, L. (2001). "Gender, Nation, Rape: Bosnia and the Construction of Security." *International Feminist Journal of Politics*, 3, 55–75.

Horowitz, D. (1999). *The Art of Political War: How Republicans Can Fight to Win*. Washington, D.C.: Committee for a Non-Left Majority.

Horowitz, D. (2006). *The Professors: The Most Dangerous Academics in America*. Washington, D.C.: Regnery.

Horowitz, D. (2007). *Indoctrination* U. New York: Encounter Books.

Jaschik, S. (2008, February 19). "Communicating about David Horowitz." *InsideHigherEd.com*, at: http://insidehighered.com/news/2008/02/19/horowitz.

Jensen, R. (2001, September 14). "U.S. as Guilty of its own Violent Acts." editorial, *The Houston Chron-icle*, at: http://www.chron.com/disp/story.mpl/editorial/1047072.html.

Jones, A. (2006, June 16). "Connecting the Dots." *InsideHigherEd.com*, at: http://www.insidehighered.com/views/2006/06/16/jones.

Kaplan, C., N. Alarcon, & M. Moallem (Eds.) (1999). *Between Woman and Nation: Nationalisms, Transnational Feminisms, and the State*. Durham: Duke University Press.

MacKinnon, C. A. (1993). *Only Words*. Cambridge, MA: Harvard University Press.

Ranchod-Nelson, S. and M. Tetreault (Eds.) (2000). *Women, States, and Nationalism: At Home in the Nation?* New York: Routledge.

Richardson, B. K., and McGlynn, J. (2007, May 28). "Gendered Retaliation, Irrationality, and Struc-tured Isolation: Whistle-Blowing in the Collegiate Sports Industry as Gendered Process." *Creat-ing Organizational Resistance*. Symposium conducted at the meeting of the International Com-munication Association, San Francisco, CA. Retrieved April 10, 2008, from Academic Search Premier database.

Stoler-Liss, S. (2003, Fall). "'Mothers Birth the Nation: The Social Construction of Zionist Mother-hood in Wartime in Israeli Parents' Manuals." *Nashim: A Journal of Jewish Women's Studies and Gender Issues*, (6), 104–118.

Valentine, G. (1998). "Sticks and Stones May Break My Bones": A Geography of Personal Harassment." *Antipode*, 30(4), 305–332. Retrieved April 10, 2008, from Academic Search Premier database.

Werbner, and N. Yuval Davis (Eds.) (1999). *Women, Citizenship, and Difference*. London: Zed Books.

Wilkinson, S. (2004, Winter). "Where the girls aren't." *Nieman Reports*, 30.

Wolf, N. (2007 [1991]). *The Beauty Myth* (New edition.). New York: Vintage.

Yuval-Davis, N. (1997). *Gender and Nation*. London: Sage.

Decolonial Critics For Academic Freedom (Pérez, 364)

1 David Horowitz, *The Professors: The 101 Most Dangerous Academics in America* (Washington DC: Regnery Publishing Inc., 2006), see the introduction.

2 Emma Perez, *The Decolonial Imaginary: Writing Chicanas into History* (Indiana University Press, 1999), 5–7.

3 The investigative report by the Standing Committee on Research Misconduct (SCRM) that charged Professor Ward Churchill with "research misconduct" is 120 pages long. Within that report, forty-four pages are devoted to two paragraphs by Churchill on the 1837 smallpox pandemic. While SCRM could not argue with Churchill's synthesis of American Indian history, the Committee combed through over ten books, one-hundred articles, and other published works to determine that his sources in four specific cases were questionable and therefore merited research misconduct. Overall, the Committee disagreed with Churchill's interpretation of American Indian History, and while there were no American Indian scholars on the Committee, SCRM repeatedly dismissed American Indian scholarship and deemed themselves experts on American Indian history. Professor Eric Cheyfitz, a scholar of American Indian studies at Cornell University, pointed out that Churchill's arguments were legitimate from one school of thought in American Indian studies. For a full discussion, a timeline, and an analysis of the controversy, see http://www.wardchurchill.net/. CU Boulder's website also has an online archive of the many reports and documents on the case; see for example: http://www.colorado.edu/news/reports/churchill. This website leads to other links on the case. The plagiarism charges were also disputed; see the discussion by Professor Tom Mayor on the Churchill website, and Churchill in this volume.

Regimes of Normalcy in the Academy (Ben-Moshe & Colligan, 374)

Abram, S. (2003). "The Americans with Disabilities Act in Higher Education: The Plight of Disabled Faculty." *Journal of Law and Education*, 32(1), 1–20.

Anderson, Benedict (1983, 1991). *Imagined Communities*. London and New York: Verso.

Anderson, Robert C. (2006). *Bodies of Knowledge: Faculty Members with Disabilities in Higher Education*. Unpublished dissertation, University of Alabama.

Hemby-Grubb, Virginia (2007). "Traumatic Brain Injury and its Challenges for a College Professor." In Vance, M. J. (ed.) Disabled faculty and staff in a disabling society. *AHEAD: The Association on Higher Education and Disability*.

hooks, bell (1989). *Talking Back: Thinking Feminist, Thinking Black*. Boston: South End Press.

Linton, Simi (1998). *Claiming Disability*. New York: NYU Press.

———. (2006). *My Body Politic: a Memoir*. Ann Arbor: University of Michigan Press.

McIntosh, Peggy (2001) "White Privilege and Male Privilege." Richardson, Laurel, Verta Taylor, and Nancy Whittier, *Feminist Frontiers*, 5th edition. New York, NY: McGraw-Hill Higher Education.

McRuer, Robert (2006). "Compulsory Able-bodiness and Queer/Disabled Existence." Davis, L. (ed.), *The Disability Studies Reader*, 2nd edition, New York: Routledge.

Michalko, Rod (2001) "Blindness Enters the Classroom." *Disability and Society*, 16, 349–360.

Mikochik, S. L. (1991). "Law Schools and Disabled Faculty: Toward a Meaningful Opportunity to Teach." *Journal of Legal Education*, 41 (3,4), 351–54.

Murphy, Robert (1987). *The Body Silent*. New York: Henry Holt and Company.

Slone, Mary Beth (2007). "Navigating the Academy When your Ship is Thrown Off Course: The Effects of Multiple Sclerosis on One College Professor." Vance, M. J. (ed.) Disabled faculty and staff in a disabling society. *AHEAD: The Association on Higher Education and Disability*.

Stapleton, D. C., and Burkhauser, R. V. (Eds.). (2003). *The Decline in Employment of People with Disabilities: A Policy Puzzle*. Kalamazoo, MI: W. E Upjohn Institute.

Thomson, Rosemarie Garland (2002). "Integrating Disability, Transforming Feminist Theory." NWSA Journal. 14:3, 1–31.

Vance, Mary Lee (ed.) (2007). "Taking Risks." Vance, M. J. (ed.) Disabled Faculty and Staff in a Disabling Society. *AHEAD: The Association on Higher Education and Disability*.

Vital Signs: Crip Culture Talks Back (2005). Documentary produced by David Mitchell and Sharon Snyder, Fanlight Productions.

Adelphi Recovers "The Lengthening View" (Zaidi, 388)

1 Doreen Carvajal, "Adelphi University Issues Criticism of State Case." *The New York Times* (2 February 1996): B7.

2 Doreen Carvajal, "President's Pay Rankles Some at Adelphi." *The New York Times* (31 September 1995): 1, 26.

3 Norman Ashcraft, "Adelphi Offers Lessons for Higher Education." *The New York Times* (6 September 1996): A26.

4 G. Bruce Knecht, "William Simon Is Kinder and Gentler, But Investments Lag." *The Wall Street Journal* (15 September 1995): 1.

5 Jack Sirica, "Olin Yanks Plug on Adelphi." *Newsday*. (23 June 1996).

6 William E. Simon, *A Time for Truth*. New York: McGraw-Hill, 1978.

7 Emily Eakin, "Oracle at Adelphi." *New York Magazine* (16 October 1995): 42–47.

8 Diams Tollinchi, "Do You Feel That Adelphi University Is Fulfilling Its 'Commitment to Intellect'?" *Afrika Unbound* (student newspaper) (November 1995): 8.

9 William H. Honan, "A Slow and Steady Revival." *The New York Times* (21 August 1997): B1.

10 Deborah Bazemore, Haendel St. Juste, and Jackie Parker, "An Interview with President Diamandopoulos." *Afrika Unbound* (November 1995): 4.

11 Lionel S. Lewis, *When Power Corrupts*. New Brunswick, New Jersey: Transaction Publishers, 2000: 140–41.

12 Lewis 123.

13 Marie Alzi, "Skepticism in the Phasing Out of HEOP." *Afrika Unbound* (March 1996): 6.

14 Jackie Parker, "The Big Lie: WBAU." *Afrika Unbound* (February 1996): 14–15.

15 John McQuiston, "Adelphi Chief Tells Students His Trouble Is Not Theirs." *The New York Times* (14 March 1996): B7.

16 Miryam Douglass and Mashona Watson, "President Diamandopoulos Speaks To Students in an Open Forum." *Afrika Unbound* (March 1996): 4, 26.

17 Kennedy Fraser, "As Writers Despair, Book Chains Can Only Exult." *The New York Times* (13 October 1997): E2.

18 Daniel Gross, "Under the Volcano," *Lingua Franca* (November/December 1995): 44–53.

19 Saul Cohen, "Regents Panel Report on Adelphi." (10 February 1997).

20 Lewis, 52.

21 Lewis, 52–53.

22 Lewis, 56.

23 Lewis, 114.

24 Lewis, 99–100

25 Lewis, 102–103.

26 Lewis, 154.

27 Robert Atwell, "After Adelphi: Private Colleges and the Public Interest." *The Chronicle of Higher Education* (7 March 1997): B7.

28 John Trumpbour, "Introducing Harvard." *How Harvard Rules*. edited by John Trumpbour. Boston: South End Press, 1989, 8.

29 John Trumpbour, "The Business-University Revisited." *How Harvard Rules*: 145.

30 Michelle C. Siry, "President Norton: Caring for the Future of Adelphi." *The Delphian* (11 Nov. 1997): 1.

31 During the eight years that I taught at CUNY, from 1999 until 2007, I witnessed numerous violations of academic freedom, the most recent instance of which was the non-reappointment of sociology professor John Asimakopoulos at Bronx Community College, despite his eminent qualifications for promotion on all possible criteria. In August 2008, however, a labor arbitrator reinstated Asimakopulos in his teaching position. Goldstein must share responsibility for the brutal atmosphere at CUNY. Adelphi was indeed fortunate that Goldstein moved on.

32 Paul Lauter. "From Adelphi to Enron—and Back." *Tenured Bosses and Disposable Teachers: Writing Instruction in the Managed University*. Carbondale, Illinois: Southern Illinois University Press, 2004.

33 Robert A. Scott, "The University as a Moral Force." *On The Horizon*. 11.2 (2003): 33.

34 Lewis, 127.

35 This is an updated version of an essay that appeared in *Thought and Action* (Spring 1998) and *Against The Current* (November/December 1998).

The Carceral Society (Kaltefleiter & Nagel, 400)

1 By contrast, when we organized a conference on the prison industrial complex at SUNY Cortland, things went quite differently. We invited a major figure from the Attica prison uprising in 1971 as a keynote speaker. When the group "The forgotten victims of Attica" found out about it, they called their state senator who held a press conference to denounce our conference and threatened to not only close down our conference but to defund SUNY Cortland as well. The group represents the families of the guards who lost their lives during the shootout in Governor Rockefeller's violent takeover of the yard where 1,000 prisoners striked for humane prison conditions. Their ire was directed at our keynote speaker because he allegedly killed a guard during the uprising, which he denies. Called into the college's president's office, we had to defend our decision to invite controversial keynote speakers, and luckily for us, the president conveyed to us that "the truth hurts" and encouraged us to hold the conference. Ironically, we had to hire police to protect our audience and speakers, however the protesting group never showed up to make good on their threat to disrupt the conference proceedings. (It was the only time that the president ever had to field a call from the SUNY chancellors' office.)

References

Abercrombie, Nicolas. & John Urry, 1983. *Capital Labor and the Middles Classes*. George Allen and Unwin: London.

Academe. April, 2008. "Background Facts on Contingent Faculty." Online at: http://www.aaup.org/AAUP/issues/contingent/contingentfacts.htm.

Acoli, Sundiata. 1998. *An Updated History of the New Afrikan Prison Struggle.* Harlem, NY: Sundiata Acoli Freedom Campaign.

Arnold, Millard. 1978. *Steve Biko, Black Consciousness in South Africa.* New York: Random House.

Althusser, Louis. 1971. "Ideology and Ideological State Apparatuses (Notes towards an Investigation)," in *Lenin and Philosophy and Other Essays,* trans. Ben Brewster (New York: Monthly Review Press.

Aronowitz, Stanley. 1998. "Introduction" in Paulo Freire, *Pedagogy of Freedom.* Boulder: Roman and Littlefield.

Bourdieu, Pierre. 1970, 1990. *Reproduction in Society, Education, and Culture.* Trans. Richard Nice; reprint 1990. London: Sage.

Blue Triangle Network (BTN). January, 2003. "Stop the Repression Against Muslim, Arab, and South Asian Immigrants." Pamphlet.

Braverman, H. 1974. *Labour and Monopoly Capital.* New York: Monthly Press Review.

Caffentzis, George. 2003. "Why Unions Should Work to Repeal the USA PATRIOT Act." Midnight Notes.

Castoriadis, Carlos. 1997. "Democracy as a Procedure and Democracy as a Regime." *Constellations* 4:1. 5.

Cotera, Maria. 2008. "Faculty of Color in the Academic Industrial Complex." Unpublished Paper presented at the Students of Color of Rackham (SCOR) Conference at the University of Michigan, Feb. 15.

Cox, Aimee. 2008. "Talking Tenure." Campus Lockdown Conference 2008, p.1. Online at: http://www.woclockdown.org/TalkingTenureNewsletter.pdf.

Craven, Matt. 2008. "Student Uses Twitter to Alert Others About his Arrest in Egypt." *Blog Herald.* April 16, 2008.

Forgacs, David. 1971. *An Antonio Gramsci Reader.* New York: Schocken Books.

Freire, Paulo. 2000. *Pedagogy of the Oppressed.* New York: Continuum International Publishing Group.

Horowitz, David. 2006. *The Professors: The 101 Most Dangerous Academics in America.* Regnery.

Hendricks, T. 2008. "Pacifist Teacher Gets Cal State Job back." *San Francisco Chronicle.* March 8, 2008.

Hussain, Zareena. 1998. "Arabs Under 'Siege' in Film." Online at: www-tech.mit.edu/V118/N57/hussain.57c.html.

James, Joy. 1998. Introduction. *The Angela Y. Davis Reader.* Malden, MA: Blackwell.

Keyishian et al v. Board of Regents of the University of the State of York et al. 1967.

No. 105. Supreme Court of the United States. 385 U.S. 589. Argued November 17, 1966. Decided January 23, 1967.

Levasseur, Ray Luc. 2007. "On Trial." *Imprisoned Intellectuals,* Joy James (Ed.), Lanham, MD: Rowman & Littlefield.

Marx, Karl. 1976. *Capital* (Vol. 1). Harmondsworth, Penguin.

McCumber, John. 2001. *Time in the Ditch: American Philosophy and the McCarthy Era.* Evanston, Ill.: Northwestern University Press.

Rabinowitz, Dan & Shamir, Ronen. 2008. "Who Got to Decide on Nadia Abu El Haj's Tenure?" *Academe,* Jan–Feb.: 45–46.

NOTES

McLaren, Peter. 1999. *Schooling as Ritual Performance*. New York: Roman & Littlefield Publi...

Retamar, R. F. 1971. "Caliban: Notes towards a discussion of culture in our America." *Massac Review*, Vol 15. No 1 and 2: 71.

Ray, Daniel & Sarah Sorscher. 2008. "New Law Expands Surveillance Powers." *Jolt Digest*: Harvard Journal of Law and Technology Online. July 12, 2008: 1.

Solomon, Alisa. (June 3, 2003). "The Big Chill." *The Nation*: 17–22.

Shakur, Assata. 1987. *Assata: An Autobiography*. Chicago: Lawrence Hill Books.

Smith, Andrea. 2007. "Social-Justice Activism in the Academic Industrial Complex," *Journal of Feminist Studies in Religion*, 23(2), Fall: 140–145.

Strickland, Ronald. 2002. "Gender, Class and the Humanities in the Corporate University." *Genders*, 35. Online at: http://www.genders.org/g35/g35_strickland.html

Wallach, Evan. November 4, 2007. "Tables Turned: Waterboarding Used to Be a Crime." *Washington Post*: B01, online at: http://www.washingtonpost.com/wp-dyn/content/article/2007/11/02/AR2007110201170_2.html.

Willis, Paul. 1977. *Learning to Labor*. Farnborough: Saxon House.

Zinn, Howard. 2002. *You Can't Be Neutral on a Moving Train*. Boston: Beacon Press.

A Working Class Student is Something to Be (Shannon & Armaline, 415)

1 Despite our class-based focus, we do not argue for the "primacy of class struggle." Systems of oppression and privilege are often closely intertwined (Collins 2000), and many of our arguments here can be extended to other identities beyond "class." For example, largely due to the feminization of poverty (see, for example, Goldberg and Kremen 1990) and the racist distribution of resources in our world (i.e. global manifestations of systemic racism, see: Feagin 2001, 2006; Winant 2001), women and people "of color" are disproportionately represented among those belonging to the working class and those experiencing poverty.

2 See, for a few examples, www.nefac.net, www.workersolidarity.org, www.wsm.ie, www.zabalaza.net.

References

California Faculty Association. (2008). http://www.cfa.org.

Collins, P.H. (2000). *Black Feminist Thought* (2nd Ed.). New York: Routledge.

Dewey, John. (1938). *Experience and Education*. New York: Collier Books.

———. (1944). *Democracy and Education*. New York: Free Press.

Feagin, J. (2001). *Racist America: Roots, Current Realities, and Future Reparations*. New York: Routledge.

_____. (2006). *Systemic Racism: A Theory of Oppression*. New York: Routledge.

Feagin, J. and Hernan Vera. (2001). *Liberation Sociology*. Boulder, CO: Westview Press.

Foucault, Michel. (1980). *Power/Knowledge: Selected Interviews and Other Writings, 1972–1977*. New York: Pantheon.

Freire, Paulo. (1970). *Pedagogy of the Oppressed*. New York: Continuum.

Goldberg, Gertrude S. and Eleanor Kremen, eds. (1990). *The Feminization of Poverty: Only in America?* New York: Praeger.

Harris, Laura A. (2002) "Notes from a Welfare Queen in the Ivory Tower," in Gloria E. Anzaldúa and AnaLouise Keating (eds.) *This Bridge We Call Home: Radical Visions for Transformation*, New York: Routledge.

Kornegger, Peggy. (1996) "Anarchism: The Feminist Connection," in Howard J. Ehrlich (ed.) *Reinventing Anarchy, Again*. Oakland, CA: AK Press.

McLaren, Peter. (1997). *Revolutionary Multiculturalism: Pedagogies of Dissent for the New Millennium*. Boulder, CO: Westview Press.

Spring, Joel. (2000). *The Universal Right to Education: Justification, Definition, and Guidelines*. Mahwah, NJ: LEA Pub.

Vaneigem, Raoul. (2003). *Revolution of Everyday Life*. London: Rebel Press.

Weis, Lois, and Michelle Fine (eds.). (2000). *Construction Sites: Excavating Race, Class, and Gender Among Urban Youth*. New York: Teachers College Press.

Winant, Howard. (2001). *The World Is a Ghetto*. New York: Basic Books.

Academia and the Culture of Militarism (Rupert, 428)

1 David Barstow, "Behind Analysts, the Pentagon's Hidden Hand," *The New York Times*, April 20, 2008.

2 E-mail addressed to me from Community Relations and Public Liaison, Office of the Secretary of Defense, Pentagon, Room 2C546, dated October 23, 2007.

3 *Why We Serve* homepage: http://www.whyweserve.mil/.

4 E-mail addressed to me from Community Relations and Public Liaison, Office of the Secretary of Defense, dated October 24, 2007.

5 Gerry Gilmore, "Outreach Program Puts Human Face on Military Service," American Forces Press Service, October 4, 2007. Available online at: www.defenselink.mil/news/newsarticle.aspx?id=47682&447682=20071011.

6 Gilmore, "Outreach Program."

7 When others on campus organized a Why We Serve event after I declined to do so, critical voices and explicitly political questions were marginalized during the event in precisely the way I had suspected. See Mariam Jukaku, "Soldiers: Why We Serve; Anti-War Talk Takes Back Seat at SU Panel Discussion," *Syracuse Post-Standard*, December 1, 2007.

8 For press coverage, see: Sean Kirst, "Who's Controlling the Information War?" *Syracuse Post-Standard*, November 29, 2007; Jukaku, "Anti-War Talk Takes Back Seat," *Syracuse Post-Standard*, December 1, 2007; and Heather Collura, "Veterans explain on campuses why they serve; servicemembers share experiences abroad, but critics say forums too limited," *USA Today*, December 6, 2007. The story was picked up on the *The Wall Street Journal*'s blog called "Best of the Web Today" (http://www.opinionjournal.com/best/?id=110010940), and spread to other right-wing blogs from which, I infer, much of my hatemail originated.

9 *America Supports You* homepage: http://www.americasupportsyou.mil/americasupportsyou/index.aspx. See also the online dossier at SourceWatch: www.sourcewatch.org/index.php?title=America_Supports_You.

10 Allison Barber quoted by *SourceWatch*: www.sourcewatch.org/index.php?title=America_Supports_You. Ms. Barber is profiled at *SourceWatch*: http://www.sourcewatch.org/index.php?title=Allison_Barber. And her official bio is online: http://www.whitehouse.gov/government/abarber-bio.html.

11 Donna Miles, "America Supports You Summit Helps Groups Build on Momentum," American Forces Press Service, January 25, 2008.

12 ASY blog, My Space, and You Tube pages:http://www.asylive.blogspot.com/; http://www.myspace.com/americasupportsyou.; www.youtube.com/americasupportsyou

13 Allison Barber paraphrased and quoted in Samantha Quigley, "America Supports You: Bush Thanks Troop-Support Groups" American Forces Press Service, February 28, 2007.

44444

14 George Bush quoted in Donna Miles, "America Supports You: Bush Urges Americans to Support Modern-Day Patriots," American Forces Press Service, July 5, 2007.

15 George Bush quoted in Quigley, "Bush Thanks Troop-Support Groups."

16 Andrew Bacevich, *The New American Militarism* (Oxford: Oxford University Press, 2005); Henry Giroux, *The University in Chains: Confronting the Military-Industrial-Academic Complex* (Boulder: Paradigm Publishers, 2007); Nick Turse, *The Complex: How the Military Invades our Everyday Lives* (New York: Metropolitan Books, 2008).

17 Susan Jeffords, *The Remasculinization of America: Gender and the Vietnam War* (Bloomington: Indiana University Press, 1989); James Gibson, *Warrior Dreams: Paramilitary Culture in Post-Vietnam America* (New York: Hill and Wang, 1994); H. Bruce Franklin, *MIA or Mythmaking in America* (New York: Lawrence Hill Books, 1992); Jerry Lembke, *The Spitting Image: Myth, Memory, and the Legacy of Vietnam* (New York: New York University Press, 1998); and Kevin Baker, "Stabbed in the back! The past and future of a right-wing myth," *Harper's* (June 2006), http://www.harpers.org/archive/2006/06/0081080.

18 Bacevich, *New American Militarism*, 2.

19 "Commander in Chief lands on USS Lincoln," *CNN.com*, May 2, 2003, available online: http://www.cnn.com/2003/ALLPOLITICS/05/01/bush.carrier.landing/.

20 For an overview of the military-industrial-academic complex, and an impassioned argument that critical and emancipatory discourses on the nation's campuses continue to contest the militarization of the academy and social life more generally, see Giroux, *University in Chains*.

21 Marc Lindemann, "Storming the Ivory Tower: The Military's Return to America's Campuses" *Parameters* (Winter 2006–07), 52. Of course, one article by a junior officer is not exactly the *Pentagon Papers*. On the other hand, *Parameters* is a leading journal of military thought, and the fact that I was unable to find other articles in that journal either questioning Lindemann's arguments or presenting alternative views of the relationship between the military and academia suggests that the views he expressed may not be far from the mainstream of military thought.

22 Lindemann, *Storming the Ivory Tower*, 53.

23 Susan Peterson, Michael Tierney, and Daniel Maliniak, "Teaching and Research Practices, Views on the Discipline, and Policy Attitudes of International Relations Faculty at U.S. Colleges and Universities," research report, College of William and Mary, Williamsburg, VA, August 2005. The International Relations scholars' statement of opposition to US empire remains online at the Coalition for a Realistic Foreign Policy, http://www.realisticforeignpolicy.org/static/000027.php.

Powerful Compassion (Zaidi, 437)

1 Martin H. Bush, *Ben Shahn: The Passion of Sacco and Vanzetti*. Syracuse University Press, 1968.

2 Stan Pinkwas, "Ben Shahn: Portrait of the Artist," *Daily Orange*. March 4, 1968.

3 Unless otherwise indicated, all quotations in this essay are from interviews conducted with the author in September 1998.

4 Upton Sinclair, *The Goose-Step*. Pasadena, California, Self-Published, 1923: 285.

5 *Unity News* (SEIU Newsletter at SU), April 1998: 1.

6 David H. Stam, "Annual Report. Syracuse University Library. July 1996 to June 1997." June 20, 1998: 7–8.

7 Joy Davia, "SU Moves Into M-Street With Mall Purchase," *Daily Orange*. August 31, 1998: 12.

8 Advertisement. *Daily Orange*. August 31, 1998: 6.

9 *Negotiation News*. "The Myth of the 'Memo,'" September 3, 1998: 1.

10 Sapna Kollali, "SU Faculty Hold Sit-In," *Daily Orange*. September 2, 1998: 1, 3.

11 Dave Levinthal, "Strike Forum Features SU, Local 200A," *Daily Orange*. September 2, 1998: 7.

12 James Roscoe Day, *My Neighbor The Working Man*. New York: The Abingdon Press, 1920, 101, 372.

13 "Memo Underscores SU's Commitment To Fairness, Healing," *Negotiation News*. Sept. 25, 1998: 2.

14 Robert L. Smith, "Cutbacks Target SU Administration Along With Academics," *Post-Standard*. December 17, 1991: A4.

15 Kenneth Shaw, "SU Aims To Cut With Finesse, Not Brutality," *Syracuse Herald American*. February 16, 1992: B7.

16 "Searching for Words," *Syracuse New Times*. February 16–26, 1992.

17 Frank Herron, "Downsizing SU," *Syracuse Herald-Journal*. February 18, 1992.

18 Shaw, "SU Aims To Cut": B7

19 Kenneth Shaw, "Building On Strength: Values For The Future," *Syracuse Record*. November 18, 1991: 9

20 Kenneth Shaw, "What Is Quality?" *Syracuse Record*. September 23, 1996.

21 Bill Readings, *The University In Ruins*. Cambridge: Harvard UP, 1996, 10–11.

22 Adriel Bettelheim, "SU Chancellor Says Private, Public Sectors Must Cooperate," *Syracuse Herald Journal*. June 2, 1988.

23 "Revolutionary Robotics," *Syracuse University Magazine*. Fall 1998: 5.

24 Bruce Wilshire, *The Moral Collapse of the University*. Albany: SUNY Albany Press, 1990, 11–12.

25 Shaw, "Building On Strength: 7.

26 Sapna Kollali, "Faculty Leads Chapel Protest," *Daily Orange*. September 3, 1998, 1, 3

27 An earlier version of this essay was published in the September 1999 issue of *Monthly Review*. A sequel to this story, "'I'm Lost But I'm Making Record Time': A Successful President Transforms Syracuse University," appeared in *New Politics*, Vol. IX, No. 1 (New Series), Summer 2002, pp. 180–192. For a recent view on the militarization of SU, see Linda Ford and Ira Glunts, "Syracuse University Enlists in the Global War on Terror," August 3, 2007, *CounterPunch*, online at: www.counterpunch.org/ford08032007.html.

Intellectuals and Empire (Boggs, 450)

1 For a more elaborate critique of American political science for its failure to study the dynamics of US military and global power, see Carl Boggs, *Imperial Delusions: American Militarism and Endless War* (Lanham, MD.: Rowman and Littlefield, 2004), Chapter. 1.

2 C. Wright Mills, *The Power Elite* (New York: Oxford University Press, 1956), Chapters. 8 and 12.

3 Noam Chomsky, *American Power and the New Mandarins* (New York: Vintage Books, 1969), 72.

4 See G. William Domhoff, *Who Rules America?* (New York: McGraw-Hill, 2002).

5 Michael Hardt and Antonio Negri, *Empire* (Cambridge, MA.: Harvard University Press, 2000).

6 Herbert Marcuse, *One Dimensional Man* (Boston: Beacon Press, 1964).

The Three-Legged Stool (Zinn, 458)

Birnbaum, Robert, "The End of Shared Governance: Looking Forward or Looking Back," unpublished manuscript (2003).

Bok, Derek, "Academic Values and the Lure of Profit," *Chronicle of Higher Education* (April 4, 2003): B7–B9.

Challenges for Governance: A National Report (Los Angeles: Center for Higher Education Policy Analysis, 2003).

"College and University Government: Miami-Dade Community College," *Academe* (May/June 2000): 73–88.

Fish, Stanley, "Shared Governance: Democracy is Not an Educational Idea," *Change Magazine* (March/April 2007).

Gerber, Larry, "Inextricably Linked: Shared Governance and Academic Freedom," *Academe* (May/June 2001): 22–24.

"On the Relationship of Faculty Governance to Academic Freedom," *AAUP Policy Documents & Reports*, tenth edition (Baltimore: AAUP/Johns Hopkins University Press, 2006): 141–44.

"Report—College and University Government: Elmira College," *Academe* (September/October 1993): 42–52.

"Report—College and University Government: Lindenwood College," *Academe* (May/June 1994): 60–68.

"Report—College and University Government: Francis Marion University," *Academe* (May/June 1997): 72–84.

Scholtz, Greg, "What Is Shared Governance Anyway?" unpublished manuscript (2007).

"Statement on Government of Colleges and Universities," *AAUP Policy Documents and Reports*: 135–40.

Contingent Faculty and the Problem of Structural Repression (Tropea, 479)

1 See, for example, W. Edwards Deming's *Out of the Crisis*. Cambridge, MA: The MIT Press, 2000.

2 L.I. Lesser, C.B. Ebbeling, M. Goozner, D. Wypij, D.S. Ludwig, "Relationship between Funding Source and Conclusion among Nutrition-Related Scientific Articles," *PLoS Medicine* Vol. 4, No. 1, e5 doi:10.1371/journal. Pmed.0040005.

3 JBL Associates, Inc., *Reversing Course: The Troubled State of Academic Staffing and a Path Forward*. American Federation of Teachers, 2008.

4 Peter Berger and Richard Neuhaus, *To Empower People: The Role of Mediating Structures in Public Policy*, Washington, D.C.: AEI Press, 1977.

5 E. E. Schattschneider, *The Semisovereign People: A Realist's View of Democracy in America*. New York: Dryden, 1960.

6 Joe Berry and Elizabeth Hoffman, "Including Contingent Faculty in Governance," *Academe*, Nov-Dec 2008: 29–31.

Afterword: Management's *Kulturkampf* (Bousquet, 510)

American Association of University Professors. "Contingent Appointments and the Academic Profession" (2003). Available at: http://www.aaup.org/AAUP/pubsres/policydocs/contents/contingstmt.htm.

Bousquet, Marc. "White Collar Proletariat: The Case of Becky Meadows." *JAC* Vol. 27 Nos 1–2 (2007): 303–328.

————. *How The University Works: Higher Education and the Low-Wage Nation*. New York: New York University Press, 2008.

Clark, Burton R. "The Organizational Saga in Higher Education." *Administrative Science Quarterly*, Vol. 17, No. 2 (June, 1972): 178–184.

Cox, Ana. "None of Your Business." In B. Johnson, Kavanagh, and K. Mattson, eds., *Steal This University: The Rise of the Corporate University and the Academic Labor Movement*. New York: Routledge, 2003, 15–32.

Lauter, Paul. "Content, Culture, Character." *Works and Days* 21:1–2 (2003): 51–56.

Massy, William. "Lessons from Health Care." In William Massy, ed. *Resource Allocation in Higher Education*. Ann Arbor: University of Michigan Press, 1996, 193–222.

Rhoades, Gary. *Managed Professionals: Unionized Faculty and Restructuring Academic Labor*. Albany: SUNY Press, 1998.

Saltman, Kenneth. "Education as Enforcement." *Cultural Logic*, Vol. 6 (2003). Available at: http://clogic.eserver.org/2003/saltman.html

Slaughter, Sheila and Larry Leslie. *Academic Capitalism: Politics, Policies, and the Entrepreneurial University*. Baltimore: Johns Hopkins, 1997.

Slaughter, Sheila, and Gary Rhoades, *Academic Capitalism in the New Economy*. Baltimore: Johns Hopkins, 2004.

Washburn, Jennifer. *University, Inc.: The Corporate Corruption of Higher Education*. New York: Basic Books, 2006.

Yates, Michael. "Lambs to the Slaughter." *Workplace: A Journal for Academic Labor*, 1.2 (December 1998). Available at: www.workplace-gsc.com.

Support AK Press!

AK Press is one of the world's largest and most productive anarchist publishing houses. We're entirely worker-run and demo-cratically managed. We operate without a corporate structure—no boss, no managers, no bullshit. We publish close to twenty books every year, and distribute thousands of other titles published by other like-minded independent presses from around the globe.

The Friends of AK program is a way that you can directly contribute to the continued existence of AK Press, and ensure that we're able to keep publishing great books just like this one! Friends pay a minimum of $25 per month, for a minimum three month period, into our publishing account. In return, Friends automatically receive (for the duration of their membership), as they appear, one free copy of every new AK Press title. They're also entitled to a 20% discount on everything featured in the AK Press Distribution catalog and on the web-site, on any and every order. You or your organization can even sponsor an entire book if you should so choose!

There's great stuff in the works—so sign up now to become a Friend of AK Press, and let the presses roll!

Won't you be our friend? Email friendsofak@akpress.org for more info, or visit the Friends of AK Press website: http://www.akpress.org/programs/friendsofak